Annual Review of
INFORMATION SCIENCE AND TECHNOLOGY

Annual Review of
INFORMATION SCIENCE AND TECHNOLOGY

Volume 42 • 2008
Blaise Cronin, Editor

Published on behalf of the
American Society for Information Science and Technology
by Information Today, Inc.

Information Today, Inc.
Medford, New Jersey

ISBN: 978-1-57387-308-6
ISSN: 0066-4200
CODEN: ARISBC
LC No. 66-25096

Published and distributed by
Information Today, Inc.
143 Old Marlton Pike
Medford, NJ 08055-8750

On behalf of

The American Society for Information Science and Technology
1320 Fenwick Lane, Suite 510
Silver Spring, MD 20910-3602, U.S.A.

Information Today, Inc. Staff
President and CEO: Thomas H. Hogan, Sr.
Editor-in-Chief and Publisher: John B. Bryans
Managing Editor: Amy M. Reeve
Proofreader: Penelope Mathiesen
VP Graphics and Production:
  M. Heide Dengler
Cover Designer: Victoria Stover
Book Designer: Kara Mia Jalkowski

ARIST Staff
Editor: Blaise Cronin
Associate Editor: Debora Shaw
Copy Editors: Dorothy Pike,
  Andrea Falcone
Indexer: Amy Novick

Contents

SECTION I

Information Seeking and Retrieval

SECTION II

The Nature of Academic Disciplines

SECTION III
Information Management and Systems

SECTION IV
Issues in Information Science

Introduction

Blaise Cronin

Volume 42 includes several chapters on topics of longstanding interest to the field. Regular *ARIST* readers will not be surprised to see a section devoted to information seeking and retrieval, or chapters reviewing developments in knowledge management and education for information science. Coverage of syndromic surveillance systems and education informatics takes us in somewhat newer directions, as does the section on academic disciplines, about which I would like to say a little more.

We tend to take academic writing for granted, like wallpaper or muzak. It's as if writing is unrelated to the doing of science: a mere afterthought. But writing in all its manifestations, from jottings in a lab notebook to the polished prose of the peer-reviewed article in the journal of record, cannot be separated from the material practices of scholars and researchers, a point made succinctly by Montgomery (2003, p. 1): "There are no boundaries, no walls, between the doing of science and the communication of it; communication *is* the doing of science."

Texts are not simple reflections or representations of the world-as-is. Rather they are shaped by, and in turn shape, the disciplines and discourse communities of which they are constitutive elements. Different academic disciplines have different conventions when it comes to the formal presentation of research findings and claim staking. We use, more or less consciously, a battery of rhetorical devices (e.g., hedging, the passive voice, copious referencing) to marshal evidence, mobilize support, and, ultimately, persuade the reader of our viewpoint. Styles of writing are as varied as the epistemic cultures with which they are associated. The textual outputs of critical theorists and high-energy physicists, for instance, would not easily be confused; these two tribes inhabit mutually unintelligible discourse domains (Sokal & Bricmont, 1998). But one should be careful not to reify disciplines; disciplines do not exist independently of the congeries of norms, institutional arrangements, social relations, professional values, and language with which they are associated; disciplines *are* these assemblages. In recounting the history of sociology at the University of Chicago, Abbott (1999, p. 87) notes at one point that there "was no discipline of which the *AJS* [*American Journal of Sociology*] was the journal. Quite the reverse. The *AJS*, with a few other institutions and networks, created the discipline."

It is nearly 30 years since Latour and Woolgar (1979, p. 88) provocatively described the scientifically complex activities performed at the Salk Laboratory as "the organization of persuasion through literary inscription." Almost overnight, academic writing ceased to be a straightforward, after-the-fact activity: It had been, to use the vogue term, "problematized." To understand science and scientists, one needs to understand the material and discursive practices of those doing and reporting the science. And these days reporting is more often than not a collective activity. In almost every field of scientific endeavor, co-authorship is commonplace. "The author is dead, long live the contributor!" has become the fashionable cry. Sometimes the numbers involved are modest, sometimes massive. As a result, authorship, too, has been problematized. Who precisely is the author, and what exactly does authorship entail when literally hundreds of names appear on the byline? The issues (e.g., trust, oversight, ownership) are many and varied. One thing is clear: What holds for writing holds for authorship. As Biagioli (2003, p. 274) observes: "Scientific authorship, whatever shapes it might take in the future, will remain tied to specific disciplinary ecologies." There are at least as many kinds of writing and as many conceptions of authorship as there are disciplinary cultures and subcultures.

In recent years, genres of writing and forms of authorship have themselves become the stuff of scholarly investigation, attracting the attention of socio-linguists, information scientists, and others. This year's *ARIST* has for the first time a section on the "Nature of Academic Disciplines," in which these topics, heretofore either ignored or at best treated cursorily, are explored in thoroughgoing fashion. Lest we forget, information science grew out of documentation: Did not *American Documentation* metamorphose into the *Journal of the American Society for Information Science*? Our field's historic focus has been on documents: their production, codification, assembly, and retrieval. In his splendid book, *Deflating Information: From Science Studies to Documentation*, Frohmann (2004, p. 17) refocuses our attention on the nature of *documentary practices*: "If we can obtain a clear understanding of the many things scientists do, we can begin to ask fruitful questions about the place among them of the production and use of documents."

It behooves us as information scientists to familiarize ourselves with the nature of disciplines and the ways in which different material cultures shape knowledge production processes. The texts we handle, physically and virtually, emerge from a rich variety of epistemic cultures; they are imbued with the values and norms of those cultures and both reflect and shape prevailing discursive practices. To understand academic writing it is first necessary to understand the nature of academic disciplines. The doing and the writing of science are not disjoint activities; rather they are tightly coupled. In sum, texts have contexts and documents a "social life" (Seeley Brown & Duguid, 1996). The remit of information science extends to the analysis of those contexts and social lives, as I hope this volume makes clear.

References

Abbott, A. (1999). *Department & discipline: Chicago sociology at one hundred.* Chicago: University of Chicago Press.

Biagioli, M. (2003). Rights or rewards? Changing frameworks of scientific authorship. In M. Biagioli & P. Galison (Eds.), *Scientific authorship: Credit and intellectual property in science* (pp. 255–279). New York: Routledge.

Frohmann, B. (2004). *Deflating information: From science studies to documentation.* Toronto, Canada: University of Toronto Press.

Latour, B., & Woolgar, S. (1979). *Laboratory life: The social construction of scientific facts.* Beverly Hills, CA: Sage.

Montgomery, S. L. (2003). *The Chicago guide to communication science.* Chicago: University of Chicago Press.

Seely Brown, J., & Duguid, P. (1996). The social life of documents. *First Monday, 1*(1). Retrieved March 18, 2007, from www.firstmonday.dk/issues/issue1/documents

Sokal, A., & Bricmont, J. (1998). *Fashionable nonsense: Postmodern intellectuals' abuse of science.* New York: Picador.

Acknowledgments

Many individuals are involved in the production of *ARIST*. I gratefully acknowledge the contributions of our Advisory Board members and outside reviewers. Their names are listed in the pages that follow. Andrea Falcone and Dorothy Pike were enormously helpful with copyediting and bibliographic checking. Amy Novick produced the thorough index. As always, Debora Shaw did what a first rate associate editor is supposed to do.

ARIST Advisory Board

Chapter Reviewers

Judit Bar-Ilan
Nick Belkin
Ann Bishop
Julie Bobay
Christine Borgman
Katy Börner
Kevin Boyack
Terrence Brooks
John Budd
Charles Cole
Elisabeth Davenport
Ron Day
Phil Doty
Carl Drott
Susan Dumais
David Ellis
Sanda Erdelez
Kristin Eschenfelder
Jonathan Furner
Benoît Godin
Noriko Hara

Glynn Harmon
Samantha Hastings
Caroline Haythornthwaite
Tsai-Youn Hung
Andrew Large
Loet Leydesdorff
Katherine McCain
Claire McInerney
Javed Mostafa
Dan O'Connor
Charles Oppenheim
Roy Rada
Alice Robbin
Yvonne Rogers
Ronald Rousseau
Alan Smeaton
Soma Sanyal
Danny Wallace
Julian Warner
Tom Wilson
Alesia Zuccala

Contributors

Jack Andersen is an Associate Professor at the Royal School of Library and Information Science in Copenhagen, Denmark. His main research area is knowledge organization, approached from both a genre and a social theoretical perspective. The primary objective of Dr. Andersen's research is to broaden our understanding of knowledge organization activities and their function and consequences in culture and society: In what areas and spheres of society do knowledge organization activities take place and what do they accomplish on behalf of whom and why?

Hsinchun Chen is the McClelland Professor of Management Information Systems at the University of Arizona and the founding director of the university's Artificial Intelligence Lab. He received the B.S. degree from the National Chiao-Tung University in Taiwan, the M.B.A. degree from SUNY Buffalo, and the Ph.D. degree in Information Systems from New York University. Dr. Chen is a Fellow of IEEE and AAAS; he received an IEEE Computer Society Technical Achievement Award for 2006. He is the author/editor of 13 books, 17 book chapters, and more than 130 scholarly journal articles covering intelligence analysis, biomedical informatics, data/text/Web mining, digital libraries, knowledge management, and Web computing.

Charles Cole is a Research Associate at the Graduate School of Library and Information Studies, McGill University, Montreal, and an information design consultant. His research interest is the design of IR system interface devices for undergraduate social science students researching their course essays. He holds a B.A. (History-Geography) and M.L.I.S from McGill University, and a Ph.D. from the University of Sheffield. He has recently edited (with Amanda Spink) two books in Springer's New Directions series; he has published over 35 refereed articles in journals such as the *Journal of the American Society for Information Science and Technology* and *Information Processing & Management*.

Melissa H. Cragin is a doctoral student in the Graduate School of Library and Information Science (GSLIS) at the University of Illinois at Urbana-Champaign. Her research deals with biomedical information work, with a particular focus on the roles of digital data collections and the relationship of data practices to scholarly communication. Melissa is also the project coordinator for the Data Curation Education Program at GSLIS, a project funded by the Institute for Museum and Library Services to develop a master's degree concentration in data curation.

Peter G. B. Enser is Professor of Information Science in the University of Brighton and Head of Research in the university's School of Computing, Mathematical and Information Sciences. He has extensive teaching and management experience in higher education, together with longstanding research interests in visual image retrieval and asset management. His publications and conference presentations have addressed international communities in library and information science, computer science, and cultural heritage, and he has directed a number of externally funded research projects in this field. One of the founders of the international *Challenge of Image and Video Retrieval* series of conferences, Dr. Enser also has an association with the Department of Information Science at City University as an Honorary Visiting Professor. He is a past President of the Institute of Information Scientists, Chair of the Accreditation Board of the Chartered Institute of Library and Information Professionals (CILIP), and a member of the UK Arts and Humanities Research Council Peer Review College. He also serves on a number of editorial and advisory committees.

Nigel Ford is Professor and Head of the Educational Informatics Research Group at the Department of Information Studies, University of Sheffield, U.K. His research interests in educational technology, adaptive systems, artificial intelligence, and the interaction between information science and learning come together in his current work on educational informatics, which represents the intersection of aspects of these different areas. He has led a number of research projects in related areas, including the role of individual differences in information seeking, information skills to support student-centered learning, and information seeking in schools. He has published widely in educational and information science journals.

Ken Hyland is Professor of Education and director of the Centre for Academic and Professional Literacies at the Institute of Education, University of London. Until arriving in London in 2003, he taught overseas for twenty-six years, mainly in Asia and Australasia. He has published over 120 articles and eleven books on language education and academic writing, most recently *Second Language Writing* (Cambridge University Press, 2003), *Genre and Second Language Writing* (University of Michigan Press, 2004), *Metadiscourse* (Continuum, 2005),

English for Academic Purposes (Routledge, 2006), and *Feedback in Second Language Writing* (edited with Fiona Hyland, Cambridge University Press, 2006). He is co-editor of the *Journal of English for Academic Purposes*.

Michael E. D. Koenig is Professor and former and founding Dean of the College of Information and Computer Science at Long Island University. His career has included senior management positions in the information industry: Manager of Research Information Services at Pfizer Inc., Director of Development at ISI, Vice President–North America at Swets & Zeitlinger, and Vice President Data Management at Tradenet. He has also held academic positions as Associate Professor at Columbia University and Dean and Professor at Dominican University. His Ph.D. in information science is from Drexel University, his M.B.A. in mathematical methods and computers and his M.A. in library and information science are from the University of Chicago, and his undergraduate degree is from Yale University. A Fulbright Scholar in Argentina, he is the author of over 100 professional and scholarly publications and is the co-editor of *Knowledge Management for the Information Professional* (2000) and *Knowledge Management Lessons Learned: What Works and What Doesn't* (2003). A member of the editorial board of more than a dozen journals, he is also the past president of the International Society for Scientometrics and Informetrics. In 2005 he was awarded the Jason Farradane Award "in recognition of outstanding work in the information field."

Nancy Kranich is a past president of the American Library Association and was instrumental in launching the ALA's Information Commons workshops and Membership Initiative Group. While serving as a senior research fellow at the Free Expression Policy Project in 2003–2004, she published *The Information Commons: A Public Policy Report* (New York: Free Expression Policy Project, June 2004). Previously, she was Associate Dean of Libraries at New York University.

Bill Martin is Director of Research at the School of Business IT, RMIT University in Melbourne. He is active nationally and internationally as an author, speaker, and facilitator. In addition to research administration, mentoring staff, and supervising a large cadre of research students, his research interests include knowledge in business models and metrics for knowledge. Professor Martin is currently leading a digital publishing research team funded by the Australian Research Council and partnering with CCH Australia to investigate current developments in the digital publishing space with particular emphasis upon emerging value propositions and business models for the sector.

Elizabeth M. Mezick, CPA, is an Assistant Professor in the Center for Business Research, B. Davis Schwartz Memorial Library on the C. W.

Post Campus of Long Island University. She holds an M.L.S. in library science and an M.S. in accountancy, both from Long Island University. Her career in accountancy included internal audit positions at New York Life Insurance Company and Pan American World Airways. Her publications have appeared in the *Journal of Business & Finance Librarianship* and *Scientometrics*.

Steven A. Morris received degrees in Electrical Engineering from Oklahoma State University (Ph.D., 2005) and Tulsa University (M.S., 1986). He was employed as a research scientist at the Amoco Production Company Tulsa Research Center from 1985 to 1999. From 1999 to 2006 he performed contract research at Oklahoma State University in Stillwater, participating in projects for the development of technology forecasting techniques based on monitoring journal literature and patents. His research interests include information visualization, descriptive bibliometrics, and technology forecasting. He is currently employed by Baker-Hughes/INTEQ in Houston, Texas.

Carole L. Palmer is an Associate Professor in the Graduate School of Library and Information Science at the University of Illinois at Urbana-Champaign. Her research explores how information systems can best support the work practices of scientists and humanities scholars. She is author of *Work at the Boundaries of Science: Information and the Interdisciplinary Research Process* and a series of papers on improving digital information resources for interdisciplinary inquiry, scientific discovery, and digital scholarship. Her current projects focus on the development of federated digital collections and institutional repositories, and related educational initiatives in data curation and biological informatics.

Ian Ruthven is a Senior Lecturer in the Department of Computer and Information Sciences at the University of Strathclyde where he currently heads the i-lab research group. His research centers on the development and evaluation of effective and usable information access systems. This involves active lines of research on the modeling and design of interactive information access systems, investigations of people's use of information access systems, and the development of methodologies for evaluating information access.

Françoise Salager-Meyer holds a B.A. and an M.A. in Russian Language and Literature from the University of Lyons (France) and a Ph.D. in Foreign Language Education from the University of Texas at Austin. She has published over eighty papers relating to the analysis of scientific discourse and was twice awarded the Horowitz Prize: in 1994 for her research on the socio-pragmatic phenomenon of hedging, and in 2004 for her diachronic and cross-linguistic/cultural research on academic conflict. In 1990, she created the Multilingual and Multidisciplinary

Research Group on Scientific Discourse Analysis (Universidad de los Andes) and remains its coordinator. She is a member of the editorial board of several leading journals dedicated to the study of academic discourse.

Jorge Reina Schement is Distinguished Professor and Co-Director of the Institute for Information Policy, in the College of Communications, as well as in the School of Information Sciences and Technology at Pennsylvania State University. He is the author of more than 200 papers and articles and is editor-in-chief of the *Encyclopedia of Communication and Information*.

Amanda Spink is Professor in the Faculty of Information Technology at the Queensland University of Technology. She has a B.A. (Australian National University); Graduate Diploma of Librarianship (University of New South Wales); M.B.A. (Fordham), and a Ph.D. in Information Science (Rutgers University). Dr. Spink researches information behavior, interactive IR, Web use, and information science theory. Her research sponsors include NEC, IBM, AltaVista, Lockheed Martin, Vivisimo, and InfoSpace, Inc. She has published over 260 journal articles, refereed conference papers, and book chapters. Her recent Springer books include *New Directions in Cognitive Information Retrieval, New Directions in Human Information Behavior*, and *Web Search: Interdisciplinary Perspectives* (forthcoming).

Betsy Van der Veer Martens is an assistant professor at the School of Library and Information Studies at the University of Oklahoma. She received her doctorate in information transfer from the Syracuse University School of Information Studies in 2004. Her research interests include the development and diffusion of theories, the sociology of citation systems, and the structuration of epistemic communities.

Mary Waller earned an M.S. in Information Systems from the University of Colorado and a Ph.D. in Organizational Behavior from the University of Texas at Austin. She is currently Professor of Team Dynamics in the School of Economics and Business Administration at Maastricht University, The Netherlands. Her research focuses on team dynamics and multitasking during time-pressured, complex, and unexpected situations, with a particular focus on aviation and nuclear power crews. Her work has appeared in peer-reviewed journals such as the *Academy of Management Journal, Academy of Management Review, Management Science*, and *Journal of Organizational Behavior*.

Professor **T. D. Wilson** has worked in the information sector since 1951, holding positions in the public sector, industry, colleges, and universities. He was Head of the Department of Information Studies, University of Sheffield, for fifteen years and in 2000 he was awarded the

ALISE Professional Contribution Award for his services to education. Following his retirement he was awarded the title of Professor Emeritus and is now a Visiting Professor at Leeds University Business School and at the Swedish School of Library and Information Science, Gothenburg University and Högskolan i Borås, Sweden. He is Publisher and Editor in Chief of the electronic journal, *Information Research*.

Ping Yan is currently pursuing the Ph.D. degree in the Department of Management Information Systems at the Eller College of Management of the University of Arizona. She received her B.S. degree in computer science from the University of Science and Technology of China, Hefei, and her M.S. in computer science from the University of Hong Kong. Yan's research interests include public health informatics, systems architectures for public health systems, and data mining for health-related applications.

Daniel Zeng is an Associate Professor and the Director of the Intelligent Systems and Decisions Laboratory in the Department of Management Information Systems at the University of Arizona's Eller College of Management. He is also an affiliated professor at the Institute of Automation, the Chinese Academy of Sciences. He received his Ph.D. from Carnegie Mellon University. His research interests include software agents and multi-agent systems, spatio-temporal data analysis, security informatics, infectious disease informatics, complex systems analysis, recommender systems, digital economic institutions, and automated negotiation and auction. He is the chair of the INFORMS College on Artificial Intelligence and the Vice President for Technical Activities of the IEEE Intelligent Transportation Systems Society. He is a Senior Member of the IEEE.

About the Editor

Blaise Cronin is the Rudy Professor of Information Science at Indiana University, Bloomington, where he has been Dean of the School of Library and Information Science for sixteen years. From 1985–1991 he held the Chair of Information Science and was Head of the Department of Information Science at the University of Strathclyde Business School in Glasgow. He is concurrently a visiting professor in the School of Computing, Napier University, Edinburgh and for six years was the Talis Information Visiting Professor of Information Science at the Manchester Metropolitan University. Dr. Cronin is the author of numerous research articles, monographs, technical reports, conference papers, and other publications. Much of his research focuses on collaboration in science, scholarly communication, citation analysis, the academic reward system, and cybermetrics—the intersection of information science and social studies of science. His books include *The Citation Process* (1984), *The Scholar's Courtesy* (1995), and *The Hand of Science* (2005). He has also published on topics such as information warfare, information and knowledge management, strategic intelligence, and digital pornography. Professor Cronin sits on a number of editorial boards, including *Journal of the American Society for Information Science and Technology*; *Journal of Informetrics, Scientometrics, Cybermetrics*; and *International Journal of Information Management*. He has extensive international experience, having taught, conducted research, or consulted in more than thirty countries: Clients have included the World Bank, NATO, Asian Development Bank, UNESCO, U.S. Department of Justice, Brazilian Ministry of Science & Technology, European Commission, British Council, Her Majesty's Treasury, Hewlett-Packard Ltd., British Library, Commonwealth Agricultural Bureaux, Chemical Abstracts Service, and Association for Information Management. He has been a keynote or invited speaker at scores of conferences, nationally and internationally. Professor Cronin was a founding director of Crossaig, an electronic publishing start-up in Scotland, which was acquired in 1992 by ISI in Philadelphia. He was educated at Trinity College Dublin (M.A.) and the Queen's University of Belfast (Ph.D., D.S.Sc.). In 1997, he was awarded the degree Doctor of Letters (D.Litt., *honoris causa*) by Queen Margaret University College, Edinburgh for his scholarly contributions to information science. In 2006 he received the Award of Merit from the American Society for Information Science and Technology.

About the Associate Editor

Debora Shaw is a Professor at Indiana University Bloomington and also Associate Dean of the School of Library and Information Science. Her research focuses on information organization and information seeking and use. Her work has been published in the *Journal of the American Society for Information Science and Technology*, the *Journal of Documentation*, *Scientometrics*, and *First Monday*, among others. Dr. Shaw served as President of the American Society for Information Science (1997), and has also served on the Society's Board of Directors. She has been affiliated with *ARIST* as both a chapter author and as indexer since 1986. Dr. Shaw received bachelor's and master's degrees from the University of Michigan and the Ph.D. from Indiana University. She was on the faculty at the University of Illinois before joining Indiana University.

Information Seeking and Retrieval

CHAPTER 1

Visual Image Retrieval

Peter G. B. Enser
University of Brighton

Introduction

A Tale of Two Communities

The significance of visual images as a means of communication was established at the very earliest stages of society. The later privileging of literacy in our communication processes brings added significance to the observation that we appear to be "on the hinge of an important historical swing back towards what may be called the primacy of the image" (Jörgensen, 2003, p. ix). A number of technological advances have fueled this shift in communication praxis, including, most recently, deep penetration into the domestic market of a panoply of portable image-capture devices. That the predicted number of images captured on camera phones will reach 227 billion by 2009 lends support to this observation (Infotrends/CAP Ventures, 2005). The addition of such an enhanced domestic dimension to the curatorial and commercial dimensions of image management, complemented by ever-advancing capabilities in digital image analysis and manipulation, imbue the topic of image retrieval with a particular vibrancy.

Such a major sociotechnological thrust can be perceived as both opportunity and challenge by those involved in the professional practice of visual asset management and by those at the cutting edge of research in image retrieval. Both communities, it is argued here, need a shared perception of the principles and practices that guide their respective endeavors if both opportunity and challenge are to be addressed effectively. Some fifteen years ago, however, the late Tony Cawkell (1992) first drew attention to a communication gap between these two communities. Sadly, it remains the case that professional practitioners have only a minimal engagement with the activities of those occupied in image retrieval research, and the endeavors of the latter community have been little informed by the needs of real users or the logistics of managing large scale image collections (Harper & Eakins, 1999; Jörgensen, 2003).

This communication gap has a number of undesirable properties, significant among which are, first, the development of procedures and products that esteem technological feasibility above utility; second, the leveraging of access to heritage artifacts with diminished regard for the authoratitive curation of their semantic content; and third, the potential failure to optimize Web-enabled access to images, not least with regard to significant new trends in participative indexing. Each of these considerations will be further articulated during the course of this chapter.

Early in 1997 the idea was first mooted in the U.K. of hosting a conference to provide a forum where members of both research and practitioner communities could become better informed about their respective endeavors and environments. The ensuing Challenge of Image Retrieval conference, held in Newcastle-upon-Tyne in February 1998, was the precursor to the Challenge of Image and Video Retrieval (CIVR) International Conference series. The annual CIVR gatherings have become key events in the image retrieval research community's calendar but retain the specific brief of bringing that community together with the practitioner community "to illuminate critical issues and energize both communities for the continuing exploration of novel directions for image and video retrieval" (Sundaram, Naphade, Smith, & Yong, 2006, p. v).

This chapter adopts the same overall aim. The intention is to inform the perspectives of, and help bridge the communication gap between, the practitioner and research communities engaged in that absorbing variant of information retrieval wherein knowledge is recorded in the form of still and moving images. To this end attention is focused on the principles and practice of visual image retrieval, first within the practitioner environment, and second within the research environment.

An Image Taxonomy

Moving imagery is readily understood to be film and video; the variety of physical formats in which still images are cast, however, is less readily recognized in the literature. The simple taxonomy presented in Figure 1.1 seeks to encompass the various forms in which the visual image may be encountered (Enser, Sandom, & Lewis, 2005b).

The *direct picture*, whether captured by photographic process or created by human endeavor as a work of art, is that form of image at which the majority of literature concerned with the indexing and retrieval of still images has been directed. The *indirect picture* is most frequently encountered in the field of medicine, where variants of this form of image include X-rays and ultrasound, magnetic resonance (MR), and computed tomography (CT) scans. Other domains in which indirect pictures may be sought include molecular biology, optical astronomy, archaeology, and picture conservation.

The *hybrid picture* is frequently encountered in the form of posters and cartoons, where the interpretation of the picture is facilitated by a textual component within the image itself. Among the variant forms of *visual surrogate*, architecture and engineering provide commonly

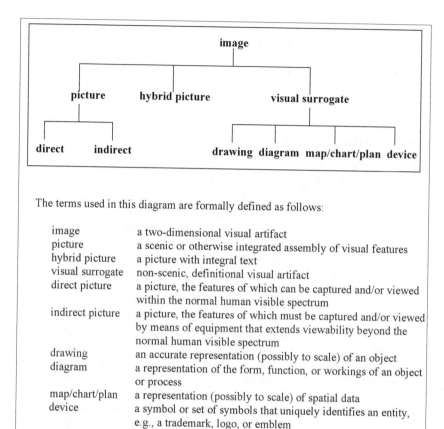

The terms used in this diagram are formally defined as follows:

image	a two-dimensional visual artifact
picture	a scenic or otherwise integrated assembly of visual features
hybrid picture	a picture with integral text
visual surrogate	non-scenic, definitional visual artifact
direct picture	a picture, the features of which can be captured and/or viewed within the normal human visible spectrum
indirect picture	a picture, the features of which must be captured and/or viewed by means of equipment that extends viewability beyond the normal human visible spectrum
drawing	an accurate representation (possibly to scale) of an object
diagram	a representation of the form, function, or workings of an object or process
map/chart/plan	a representation (possibly to scale) of spatial data
device	a symbol or set of symbols that uniquely identifies an entity, e.g., a trademark, logo, or emblem

Figure 1.1   A taxonomy of still images.

encountered application scenarios for the *drawing* (as distinct from the artistic sketch, which is a type of *direct picture*) and the *map, chart,* or *plan* is commonplace in geography, astronomy, and meteorology. Trademarks, logos, emblems, marques, and insignia are oft-encountered forms of the *device*.

Image composites are encountered when any of the types of image depicted in Figure 1.1 are assembled as mosaics of images representing a single physical and semantic unit. The set of frames which comprise a film (or physical subset such as a shot or clip) is an *image composite,* therefore, and a frame might itself take the form of an image composite.

Whereas films and videos, with their complementary visual and audio tracks, are perceived to be innately multimedia documents, still images appear at first sight to be monomodal formulations. In fact, elements within Figure 1.1 provide examples of fused modalities. The *hybrid picture* is one such example; the within-image textual annotations associated with maps, charts, and architectural and engineering drawings are further examples. In the digital era, with, typically, the co-location of textual metadata and image in a digitally encoded, composite document, the multimedia properties of still images have become clearer. Accordingly, image retrieval—both still and moving—is increasingly seen as part of the more general problem of multimedia retrieval.

The Practitioner Environment

Image Collections

Central to the professional practitioner environment is the management of organized collections of images, stewardship of which reflects either a curatorial or commercial imperative. In fact, the distinction between these two imperatives has become somewhat blurred by the impact new technology-powered economic factors have exerted on the curatorial role. The largest collections, encountered in both the private and public sectors, house many millions of still images. Some idea of the diversity and size of professionally managed picture collections is provided by Evans and Evans (2003, p. vii), a key source, regularly updated since its first publication in 1975, one of the aims of which is "to direct the (picture) researcher towards *intelligent* sources—those where the staff are experts in their particular field and can offer the researcher not only a picture but background information and guidance." Details about some 400 collections that are members of the British Association of Picture Libraries and Agencies (2004) may also be found in this directory.

Collections of film and video, although fewer in number, also contribute significantly to the professional practitioner environment in image retrieval. The Moving Image Collections (MIC) initiative, part of the National Science Digital Library, lists over 200 archives worldwide (Moving Image Collections, 2006b). Angelini (2006) provides full details about more than 600 film, television, radio, and related documentation collections in the United Kingdom and Ireland alone. The British Broadcasting Corporation's (2007) Motion Gallery is said to be the largest such archive, currently containing some 500 million feet of film and 600,000 hours of video. In addition to online access to tens of thousands of clips, users may employ the services of expert researchers to tap into the rest of the BBC's "vast motherlode" of content (British Broadcasting Corporation, 2007, online). In a similar vein, CNN reports more than 150 hours ingest per day (Optibase Inc., 2007) and the vaults of University of California at Los Angeles's (2007) Film and Television Archive currently hold more than 220,000 motion picture and television titles and 27 million feet of newsreel footage.

In recent years managers of such image collections have embarked upon programs of digitization, and the majority of image and film libraries and archives now have some form of online presence. Trant's (2004) survey of image databases available wholly or in part on the Web is a useful source of reference; the U.K. Technical Advisory Service for Images (2007) provides valuable case studies in image library digitization projects.

The dominant type of image within the professionally managed still-image collections is the *direct picture*. Figure 1.1 nevertheless includes representatives of all the types of images included among the huge, general-purpose collections maintained by such organizations as Getty Images, Corbis, the British Library, and the Library of Congress. Other types of images within the taxonomy are less frequently encountered in the form of managed collections upon which image retrieval operations can be conducted. For example, *indirect pictures* in the form of medical images and architectural or engineering *drawings* are generated as adjuncts to parent records that uniquely identify a patient or constructed object. Their recovery is a data retrieval, rather than an information retrieval process. However, such images, when disengaged from their parent records and formed into collections as an educational resource, do enter the image retrieval arena.

Interestingly, some of the applications in which images—especially moving images—are being acquired most quickly have no archiving tradition in the formal sense understood by the professional practitioner in image retrieval. The widening range of commercial, industrial, and scientific processes that generate visual records of continuous monitoring operations, using satellite and remote camera technology, are cases in point. Medical imagery, also, is being captured at a phenomenal rate: Müller, Michoux, Bandon, and Geissbuhler (2004) report that the radiology department of University Hospital Geneva alone produced more than 12,000 images per day in 2002; cardiology, notably videos of cardiac catheterization, is especially prolific (generating 1 terabyte in 2002) and endoscopic videos also produce enormous amounts of data.

The primacy of the professionally managed image collections is also called into question by the truly vast resource in the form of still images openly available on the World Wide Web, complemented more recently by developing capabilities in video search and retrieval based on closed-caption transcript text, provided by Google (2007b) and Yahoo! (2007b). To these phenomena must be added collections of personal imagery, of different degrees of formality, the scale of which has been radically affected by new opportunities for digital image capture on both fixed and mobile platforms (Boll, 2005). Most remarkable has been the ascendancy of YouTube (YouTube Inc., 2007), a community Web site launched in February 2005, to which members of the public upload their own video clips. By late 2006 "clip culture" had so far permeated society that some 100 million videos were being viewed every day on the YouTube Web site (British Broadcasting Corporation, 2006, online).

These Web-enabled facilities are not "collections" in the sense in which the term is used in professional practice. They lack some of the key characteristics of professionally managed collections, such as an acquisition or other collection management policy, ownership rights, and comprehensive metadata support. Nevertheless, régimes of opportunistic acquisition of images by spidering, or unsolicited acquisition by gifting, are revolutionizing image asset availability. In the author's view, it is important that the research community, whose attention is heavily engaged with these developments (Kherfi, Ziou, & Bernardi, 2004), work collaboratively with the practitioner community in order to harness, to positive advantage, the impact that these recent phenomena are having on the whole context of image retrieval.

Metadata

Standards

A very important characteristic of the image collections managed by the professional practitioner community is the attention devoted to cataloging the holdings. Four types of attributes that should be recognized in the cataloging of images have been proposed, namely: biographical (creation, location and ownership, value history, and amendment record), subject (classification by object, time, space, and activities/events facets), exemplified (physical form of the image), and relationship (logical linkage with other images/texts, as in preliminary sketch and final painting) (Shatford Layne, 1994).

All four attributes are included in the Visual Resources Association (VRA) Core Categories Version 3.0, which is one of the major cataloging standards for still images (Visual Resources Association, 2002). These are an expansion of the Dublin Core metadata set, tailored to visual resources. A second major cataloging standard, and one from which the VRA Core was adapted, is the Categories for the Description of Works of Art; this is a product of the Getty Standards Program and also encompasses the full set of attributes Shatford Layne (1994) described (Baca & Harpring, 2005).

Other cataloging standards used with still image collections include Dublin Core (Dublin Core Metadata Initiative, 2006), *Anglo-American Cataloguing Rules*, second edition (AACR2R) (Joint Steering Committee for Revision of AACR, 2005), and MARC (MAchine Readable Cataloging) (Library of Congress, 2005); the last two, however, provide only limited support for image material. Jörgensen (2003) presents a detailed consideration of the various standards and their shortcomings for application with images.

In the case of moving images the Fédération Internationale des Archives du Film (FIAF), a collaborative association of the world's leading film archives, specifies *Cataloguing Rules for Film Archives* (Harrison, 1991), and the Library of Congress provides a cataloging manual for *Archival Moving Image Materials* (White-Hensen, 2000). Dublin Core, AACR2, and MARC are more general tools for this type of document.

A relatively recent addition to these well-established standards is MPEG-7 (Moving Picture Experts Group), otherwise formally known as the "Multimedia Content Description Interface." MPEG-7 is a cataloging standard (an ISO [International Organization for Standardization] standard since 2001) with the ability to describe both low-level features and high-level semantics, together with structural aspects of any multimedia file (Graves & Lalmas, 2002). Modalities may include still pictures, video, graphics, 3D models, audio, speech, and composition information about how these elements are combined in a multimedia presentation. Central to these capabilities is Description Definition Language (DDL), which formally expresses the description tools that define the syntax and semantics of the various components and the structure and semantics of the relationships among them. The MPEG-7 DDL is expressed in a suitably expanded version of eXtensible Mark-up Language (XML) (Martinez, 2004). The Moving Image Collections (MIC), to which reference was made earlier, uses MPEG-7 and MARC, with other standards to follow, in its union catalog to provide access to the moving images of 14 (as of October 2006) major U.S. screen archives (Moving Image Collections, 2006a).

Indexing

For the image professional, the representation of subject matter in image material is a critical issue, and there is a significant literature on the topic. In an earlier *ARIST* chapter, Rasmussen (1997) provided a comprehensive account of the principles and practice of image indexing; other contributions include those by Enser (2000), Krause (1998), Enser (1995), Svenonius (1994), and Shatford (1986). They reflect the challenges that confront the indexer in trying to translate visually encoded knowledge into a verbal surrogate. Inherent in these challenges is our limited physiological and intellectual capacity to advance from an initial perceptual response to an image toward cognitive reasoning about its semantic content (Greisdorf & O'Connor, 2002). Central to this reasoning process is the interpretation of semantic layers in an image, founded on collective knowledge, cultural conditioning, personal knowledge, and personal experience. Jörgensen (2003) provides a comprehensive account of the relationship between the physiological processes of visual perception and the cognitive and contextual processes that produce image comprehension and understanding in the human.

The nature of the semantic layering in our interpretation of image material has been articulated by a number of authors. One of the simplest formulations recognizes three levels corresponding with visual primitives (color, texture, shape), logical or "derived" features (objects, activities, events), and inductive interpretation (abstract features) (Eakins & Graham, 1999; Greisdorf & O'Connor, 2002). A more complex formulation is that of the art historian Panofsky (1962) who, in the particular context of Renaissance art images, identified three modes of analysis, these being *pre-iconography*, denoting primary subject matter and embracing factual (the actual entities, attributes, and actions featured) and expressional (the mood of the work) facets;

iconography, signifying secondary subject matter (the interpretation to be placed on the image); and *iconology*, denoting the intrinsic meaning of the image.

In a generalization of Panofsky's analytic modes beyond the realm of fine art, Shatford (1986) drew a useful distinction between what a picture is *of* and what it is *about*. These correspond, respectively, with the factual (objective) and expressional (subjective) components of pre-iconography and, in iconographical mode, isolate the objective "of-ness" from the mythical, abstract, or symbolic "about-ness" of a picture.

The Panofsky-Shatford conceptual model has been represented as a mode/facet matrix, wherein each of the Panofsky modes (represented more simply as "generic," "specific," and "abstract") are coordinated with "who," "what," "where," and "when" facets. It offers a convenient formalism for the notion that an image is not a single semantic unit but an amalgam of generic, specific, and, possibly, abstract semantic content.

Jaimes and Chang (2000) have described a more elaborate conceptual framework, based on the same principles, called the Pyramid. This structure contains ten levels, the first four of which refer to perceptual ("syntactic") visual content. Of these, the first describes physical typology, the remainder describe visual primitives of color, texture, and shape. These perceptual, pre-conceptual attributes are interpretation-free responses to a visual stimulus, whereas the remaining six levels describe semantic or interpretive attributes that invoke inferential reasoning in the viewer. The six semantic layers are defined in terms of generic, specific, and abstract objects—which are local visible features—and generic, specific, and abstract scenes, which are global features of the image.

These conceptual models undoubtedly have merit, and the functionality of the Pyramid has been attested by experimentation (Jörgensen, Jaimes, Benitez, & Chang, 2001), but, in reality, categorization of non-abstract semantic content to "generic" or "specific" classes is a considerable over-simplification. In the natural order of physical existence, an entity can be interpreted into a hierarchy of related super-concepts and sub-concepts. As one navigates a path through such a concept hierarchy it may not be obvious at what level one crosses the threshold from generic to specific. For example, "carnivals" is as clearly generic as "the Rio Carnival, 2006" is specific; "Rio carnivals" straddles the two uneasily (Armitage & Enser, 1997).

The conceptual indexing model, which is believed to be more realistic, presented here replaces the simple generic–specific dichotomy by an informal generic–specific "continuum." The model also adopts Shatford Layne's (1994) specification of the "subject" cataloging component as a composite of object, spatial, temporal, and activity/event facets. The object facet, the structural properties of which are illustrated in Figure 1.2, enables "Rio carnivals" to be a member of a Specifically Named Object Class, whereas "the Rio Carnival, 2006" is a Specifically Named Object Instance; "carnival" is located within a Generic Object Class

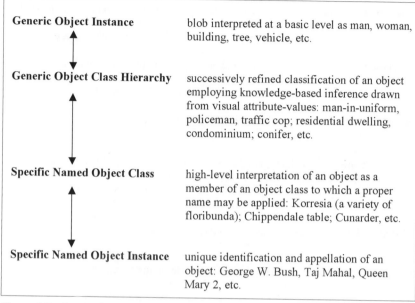

Generic Object Instance blob interpreted at a basic level as man, woman, building, tree, vehicle, etc.

Generic Object Class Hierarchy successively refined classification of an object employing knowledge-based inference drawn from visual attribute-values: man-in-uniform, policeman, traffic cop; residential dwelling, condominium; conifer, etc.

Specific Named Object Class high-level interpretation of an object as a member of an object class to which a proper name may be applied: Korresia (a variety of floribunda); Chippendale table; Cunarder, etc.

Specific Named Object Instance unique identification and appellation of an object: George W. Bush, Taj Mahal, Queen Mary 2, etc.

Figure 1.2 A generic-specific object "continuum."

Hierarchy, which might include more highly generic objects such as "fête" and "festival."

At any level within the object hierarchy affiliated concept classes may be encountered. These complement an object with those (non-visible) concepts with which it has a semantic relationship; for example, a picture of St. Paul's Cathedral in London has a relationship with the concept Church of England. In addition, attributes other than those needed to locate an object at a particular level within the object hierarchy may be associated with the object by the addition of adjectives such as "elderly," "bearded," "beautiful," etc.

The spatial, temporal, and activity/event facets, which may also exhibit hierarchical properties, are formally defined in Figures 1.3, 1.4, and 1.5, respectively.

In addition to any local features to which the four facet specifications may apply, the global semantic content of an image—its "abstract scene" (Jaimes & Chang, 2000)—may be interpreted in terms of affective content or intrinsic meaning, corresponding with Panofsky's (1962) expressional pre-iconographic and iconologic levels of analysis, respectively.

Indexing an image's local and global facets at the appropriate level of specificity demands of the human indexer increasing domain knowledge and inferential ability as one moves toward the high-specificity end of the generic–specific continuum.

Generic Location	the background to the image, i.e., the spatial context in which the object(s) within the image are placed; such as inside, outside, urban, countryside, field, lake, kitchen, stage
Specific Location	a hierarchy of increasing specificity of geographical area, identified by proper name; for example, Europe, Britain, England, London, Tottenham, Higham Road

Figure 1.3   Specification of the spatial facet in image indexing.

Generic Time	natural periods; for example, day, night, winter, summer; artificial periods of time including epochs, eras, centuries, years, decades; for example, Renaissance, Pleistocene, medieval, Victorian, twenty-first century, 1950s
Specific Time	exact year, or part thereof; for example, 1896, September 2005, 12 June 2006

Figure 1.4   Specification of the temporal facet in image indexing.

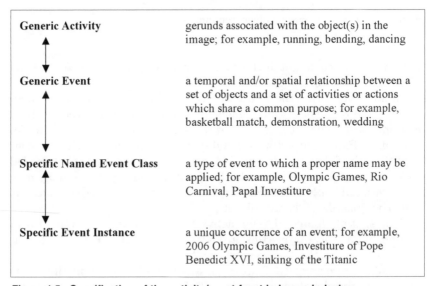

Generic Activity	gerunds associated with the object(s) in the image; for example, running, bending, dancing
Generic Event	a temporal and/or spatial relationship between a set of objects and a set of activities or actions which share a common purpose; for example, basketball match, demonstration, wedding
Specific Named Event Class	a type of event to which a proper name may be applied; for example, Olympic Games, Rio Carnival, Papal Investiture
Specific Event Instance	a unique occurrence of an event; for example, 2006 Olympic Games, Investiture of Pope Benedict XVI, sinking of the Titanic

Figure 1.5   Specification of the activity/event facet in image indexing.

In the case of film and video the intellectual and practical challenges posed by semantic indexing can exceed even those of the still image. Moving imagery is divisible into semantic structures, the smallest of which—the frame—corresponds with a still image and is usually sampled at 25 or 30 frames per second. A set of frames between a camera turn-on and a camera turn-off or other editing effect is an image composite known as a shot (Del Bimbo, 1999). A set of shots that share a common background or global spatial property are interpreted as a scene, defined more formally by Del Bimbo as a collection of consecutive shots that share the three Aristotelian properties of simultaneity in space, time, and action. The film or video stream as a complete entity is an image composite constructed from one or more scenes, although other contributory structures—"clips" and "episodes"—may be present (Del Bimbo, 1999, p. 10). In the particular case of news video footage—an application upon which heavy emphasis has been placed by the research community—the complete entity consists of a series of stories, where each story is a semantically coherent video sequence on a specific news event (Yang & Hauptmann, 2006).

Typically, the semantic content of the film or video stream as a complete entity is represented as a synopsis, outline, or abstract. This is a brief description of the action, purpose, or meaning of the whole presentation and is the approach usually adopted for feature films in sources of reference such as the Movie Database (Internet Movie Database Inc., 2007), and Halliwell (2005). The minimalist nature of this content representative is illustrated in Figure 1.6, in which the entire 97 minutes of a film that offers *en passant* a rich visual representation of 1950s urban Britain, encompassing objects throughout the generic–specific "continuum," together with generic and specific spatial and activity facets, is encapsulated in just forty words.

"A gang planning a 'job' find themselves living with a little old lady, who thinks they are musicians. When the gang set out to kill Mrs Wilberforce, they run into one problem after another, and they get what they deserve."

Figure 1.6 Plot summary for the film *The Ladykillers* **(Ealing Studios, 1955) (Hartill, 2007).**

In sharp contrast, a shot list is an exhaustive, often time-coded representation of the objects and actions in each shot, including technical detail such as camera angles and shot types. An example of this very different type of indexing device is shown in Figure 1.7.

The synopsis and the shot list are the only frequently encountered subject indexing devices for moving images, and neither is well adapted to provide access to an important, but difficult to verbalize, aspect of the semantic content of such images, namely, the spatio-temporal properties, or motion, associated with indexable objects.

Although, as has been noted, there are published cataloging standards for moving imagery, these provide little in the way of advice on subject description. Many archives have developed their own standards for content description, and in a recent study little consistency was found in the approaches adopted by a number of significant screen archives (Sandom & Enser, 2002).

DATABASE NAME: HISTORIC FILMS FILE NUMBER: VM-305 GENRE:
NEWSREELS YEAR: 1927-1929 COLOUR: B&W LENGTH: 29 MINUTES
FORMAT: BETA, 1/2TCBI

... 8 ls plane in flight
00 31 23   Aerial crowd on field in Paris (night scene)
00 31 38   Montage ticker tape parade New York city
00 32 11   England holds out her hand to u.s.
00 32 36   cu Arthur Henderson, England's powerful labor leader & aide to premier
            Macdonald makes speech about U.S. English diplomacy
00 34 05   Naval conference of world powers ends in London
00 34 14   ms England's premier Macdonald gives news conference on naval treaty
00 35 19   Mr. Macdonald says goodbye to u.s. delegates in garden of 10 Downing
            Street
00 36 18   cu President Hoover receives London naval treaty from from Mr. Stimson
00 36 50   Hoover accepts treaty & makes speech (in garden)
00 37 32   cu Mr. Stimson explains London naval treaty (naval disarmament)
00 38 21   New device cuts plane fire risk U.S.. bureau of standards tests sprinkler
            system at Washington Airport
00 38 54   montage Plane & hangar is engulfed in steam as sprinkler system proceeds
            in extinguishing fire
00 39 38   Briand ask for united Europe
00 40 11   montage Foreign minister Stresemann of Germany greets Macdonald of
            Great Britain & Briand of France at league of nations session in Geneva
00 40 45   Premier Briand of France makes speech advocating a united Europe
00 42 00   montage Briand leaves podium under thunderous applause and hand
            shakes
00 42 32   ms Stresemann of Germany makes speech
00 43 35   First sound films of India's revolt for Independence
00 43 59   aerial Thousands of people in street in boycott of English goods
00 44 00   montage Crowds mill around Bombay streets
00 44 18   Great masses of people express patriotism but observe non-violence
            counsel of Gandhi in jail
00 45 53   Crowds flock to Wall Street in market crisis
00 46 09   montage Crowd gathers outside stock exchange in crash

**Figure 1.7   Shot list from Film Images (London) Ltd. (2005). Retrieved January 7,
2007, from www.film-images.com.**

There are, nevertheless, a number of standard indexing languages in
common use to assist the human indexer in the translation of an image's
interpreted semantic content into textual annotations. Significant
among these are the *Art and Architecture Thesaurus* (*AAT*) (J. Paul
Getty Trust, 2000a), *Library of Congress Thesaurus for Graphic
Materials* (*TGM*) (Library of Congress, 2006), the *Union List of Artist
Names* (*ULAN*) (J. Paul Getty Trust, 2000c), the *Thesaurus of
Geographic Names* (*TGN*) (J. Paul Getty Trust, 2000b), and the icono-
graphic classification scheme ICONCLASS (Rijksbureau voor
Kunsthistorische Documentatie, 2007). A few years ago we would not

have expected such tools as these to be making an appearance in the research literature in image retrieval. We consider this interesting phenomenon later in this chapter.

The size, contents, and consistency of the indexing vocabulary can be controlled to some extent by such tools; in some applications the indexer need allocate only the most specific terms, and broader (and, possibly, related) terms are added automatically. Figure 1.8 shows one such example, where keywords such as "facial hair," "elderly," "James Keir Hardie," "public speaker," and "conviction" would have been allocated manually; "Europe," "Britain," and "England" would have been acquired automatically from the in-house thesaurus and recur frequently in that collection (see also Figure 1.9). Of particular note is the very important role played by a free text description or caption in representing the contextual information that facilitates the viewer's reasoning about the image's semantic content. Also evident in this example is a "Subject" field, which represents the global semantic content using concept terms from a controlled vocabulary.

It is clear from the foregoing that, for the professional practitioner in image retrieval, semantic indexing is demanding in both intellectual and economic terms. Although it is fundamental to the success of image and video retrieval, semantic indexing is not performed to any consistent standard. For an explanation of this apparent anomaly one need look no further than Shatford's (1986, p. 42) oft-quoted observation that "the delight and frustration of pictorial resources is that a picture can mean different things to different people." A picture can mean different things to the same person at different times or under different circumstances of need, moreover. The conclusion to which one is inevitably drawn is that the retrieval utility of an image is inherently unpredictable (Enser, 1995).

Besser (1990) amplifies the point in considering how a set of photographs of a busy street scene a century ago might be useful to a variety of people drawn from different occupations, each of whom might find different features of interest in the photograph, few—if any—of which are represented in the indexing. By the same token, when the images were first created their future interest could not have been predicted, and the annotation applied at that time would have reflected only a current perception of the scene. Similarly unpredictable is the retrieval utility of images that depict objects or activities too commonplace to have attracted the indexer's attention, but that acquire interest when such objects or activities gain significance for some reason. We return to the issue of significance later.

Under these circumstances of unpredictable retrieval utility and the innately entropic nature of images, the appropriate level of indexing exhaustivity is indeterminate. Only in those scenarios where the clients are well defined and their needs well understood can the negative impact of this unpredictability be lessened. In such scenarios, furthermore, the impact of indexer subjectivity which, following Markey (1984),

James Keir Hardie © Getty Images

Subject Metadata

Title	James Keir Hardie
Date	circa 1914
Description	Scottish Labour politician James Keir Hardie (1856–1915), addressing a peace meeting in Trafalgar Square, London, from the plinth of Nelson's Column. Keir Hardie was born in Legbrannock, in Lanarkshire, and worked in a coalpit from the age of 10. After working as a journalist he turned to politics. The founding Chairman of the Scottish Labour Party (1888), which was the first independent labour party in Britain, Keir Hardie was elected to Parliament in 1892 for West Ham South, and then in 1900 for Merthyr Tydfil. He was one of the founders of the new Independent Labour Party in 1893 and also established the socialist journal, *The Labour Leader*. Hardie was a pacifist and strenuously opposed the Boer War. He was the first leader of the Labour Party in Parliament (1906–07).
Subject	Personality, Politics & Government, Rallies & Public Speaking, Marches & Demonstrations, Civil Rights, Law Enforcement
Keywords	black & white, format landscape, Europe, Britain, England, clothing, uniform, audience, crowd, male, single, facial hair, elderly, addressing, pointing, British, Scottish, James Keir Hardie, Politician, public speaker, conviction

Figure 1.8 Example of archival image with semantically rich metadata using both controlled and uncontrolled vocabularies (Edina, 2007).

one might expect to be especially pronounced in the visual medium, may be reduced. Such scenarios also mitigate Besser's (1990, p. 788) observation that "historically, text-based intellectual access systems have been woefully inadequate for describing the multitude of access points from which the user might try to recall the image."

All such observations have also to take into consideration the fact that the annotation of images is a translation of documents cast in a non-textual medium into a textual surrogate. In a treatise on the lack of translatability of subject indexing between media, Svenonius (1994) has claimed that subject indexing presupposes a referential or propositional use of language: that what is depicted can be named. However, there are messages addressed to our visual and aural perceptions, the content or aboutness of which, she suggests, cannot be named; in such cases "It is useless to attempt to point to unspeakable reality with an index term" (Svenonius, 1994, p. 605).

Furthermore, although the multimedia properties of many images have been noted earlier in this chapter, subject indexing tends to focus largely, if not exclusively, on content represented in the visual modality. In the case of film and video, for example, manual indexing focuses on the visual content; little—if any—provision is made for subject access to the audio content.

The *hybrid picture* provides a rare example of a type of document in which complementary modalities do tend to be represented in the subject indexing. This is because the caption or other embedded text is as significant as the graphical content in this form of picture retrieval. The Centre for the Study of Cartoons and Caricatures in the U.K., for example, includes Embedded Text as a metadata element in its cataloging scheme (University of Kent at Canterbury, 2007). In other forms of visual surrogate, such as engineering drawings and diagrams, the embedded annotation may not be fully conveyed in the metadata, and in the case of maps and charts it is most unlikely that it would be. This seriously constrains opportunities for the user to recover such documents on the basis of their semantic *content*, as opposed to their *identity*.

Turning briefly from the professionally managed, subscription image collections to the vast aggregations of images generated by Web crawlers, we note a very sharp contrast between the effort invested by the professional image management community in subject indexing, and metadata construction in general, and the Web search engines' use of collateral text data, such as image filenames, Web page content, or alternate text tags as a means of automatically indexing (sometimes erroneously) the vast assemblies of images now available on the Web. A further contrast is starkly made by the appearance of facilities for "social tagging," whereby indexing terms can be added to images by members of the public without mediation by collection managers. Such a procedure has been advocated by Jörgensen (1999) as a means of enhancing access to under-described image collections. The most extreme example is Flickr (Yahoo! Inc., 2007a), a Web application in which members can upload photographs, annotate ("tag") them without structural or lexical limitation, and permit anyone else to add further tags. More recently still, Google (2007a) has introduced *Image Labeler*, a game in which a player is paired randomly with another player, both of whom are shown a number of images to which they are invited to supply indexing terms. There is no direct communication between the two players. When the same keyword is chosen by both players this term is added to any others by which the image is already annotated. This consensual and cooperative indexing strategy offers greater authority than Flickr, but it is interesting to conjecture whether the effect is other than to add some highly generic terms to the proffered images.

In the particular environment of television production, metadata construction has traditionally been the preserve of archivists working "behind the scenes" after the work of the production staff has been completed. That scenario is changing, as a paradigm shift in media production sees the integration of metadata creation and (re)use throughout the media production process (Davis, 2003; C. Wilkie, personal communication, December 1, 2004).

The increasing tendency for the domestic digital camera automatically to ascribe basic temporal and spatial data to images should also be noted, given the observation that people are reluctant to annotate their photo collections and show unwillingness to invest time in labeling images with text descriptions (Christel & Conescu, 2005). Notably, Google (2007c) provides a free software download called *Picasa* that assists users in the management of their personal image collections, including the construction of textual metadata in accordance with the IPTC (International Press Telecommunications Council) standard.

Users and Their Requirements

In the previous section the observation was made that the appropriate level of indexing exhaustivity is rendered indeterminate by the unpredictability of demand for the semantic content of still and moving images. Only in those scenarios where the clients' needs are well understood and, therefore, more predictable, can this disadvantage be lessened. A number of studies, in reporting on queries addressed by different types of users to a variety of image and video collections, have contributed to our better understanding of clients' needs.

Smeulders, Worring, Santini, Gupta, and Jain's (2000) categorization of image search behavior provides a useful framework in which to consider these user studies. Three types of search are identified, which they label "target search," "category search," and "search by association." The first aims to find a specific image, identified by title or other unique identifier. In a "category search" the client has no specific image in mind but is able to locate the request at some point within the generic–specific continuum of semantic content. In a "search by association" the client may approach an image collection with no particular semantic content requirement in mind, and is content to browse in order to retrieve images serendipitously. This last type of search has points of contact with Fidel's (1997) notion of a search spectrum, delimited by a "data pole" and an "objects pole," the latter conforming with "search by association" by focusing on the image as an ideas-conveying artifact.

The "category search" is the traditional focus of effort within the professional practitioner community in image retrieval. Within the context of this type of search Jörgensen has reviewed a number of user studies and identified four basic types of image query:

1. Requests for a specific item (the picture of Rouen Cathedral painted by Monet) or a specific piece of information (who painted …?)

2. Requests for a specific instance of a general category (Rouen Cathedral)

3. Requests for a general topical or subject category of images (cathedrals)

4. Requests for images communicating a particular abstract concept or affective response (pictures of cathedrals that show their role and influence in the daily life of an ordinary person of the Middle Ages) (Jörgensen, 2003, p.127)

The first three requests conform to the Specific Named Object Instance, Specific Named Object Class, and Generic Object Class elements, respectively, of Figure 1.2. The fourth type of request relates to the global semantic content of an image.

The relative proportions of queries that fall into the four categories will reflect the nature of the collections and their clientele. In the case of archival collections many requests are likely to lie at the highly specific end of the continuum. This reflects both the role of the archive in curating images as sources of information (the "data pole" in Fidel [1997]), and the specificity enhancement to be expected from the query mediation performed by expert picture library/archive staff (Chen, 2001; Hollink, Schreiber, Wielinga, & Worring, 2004; Jörgensen, 2003). One of the earliest studies to confirm this expectation analyzed some 2,700 requests addressed by a variety of client types to the Hulton Deutsch collection—a major picture archive (now part of Getty Images) (Enser, 1993; Enser & McGregor, 1992). Several other studies have confirmed the relatively high incidence of requests for specific, named features (Armitage & Enser, 1997; Chen, 2001; Gordon, 1996), and, in the particular context of journalists' requests to newspaper picture archives, see Markkula and Sormunen (2000) and Ornager (1995).

The further one moves away from the specialist archival collection, expert mediation, and experienced user scenario toward less constrained environments, and from "data pole" toward "objects pole" (Fidel, 1997), the more pronounced becomes the emphasis on queries located at the more generic end of the continuum and/or addressing the global semantic content of the image. Evidence for this may be found in user studies reported by Hollink et al. (2004), Hertzum (2003), Choi and Rasmussen (2002), Jörgensen (1998), Frost and Noakes (1998), Hastings (1995), Keister (1994), and Bakewell, Beeman, and Reese (1988). In a review of published studies of user behavior, Pisciotta (2005) provided further commentary on the wide variation in user needs for, and usage of, digital image resources.

Various approaches have been aimed at formalizing the description of the queries and search behavior collected in these user studies. The Panofsky-Shatford matrix has been used in some analyses to allow requests for both still and moving image subjects to be stratified in terms of their specific, generic, or abstract nature, and the number of different facets to be recognized and used as a measure of complexity (Armitage & Enser, 1997; Chen, 2001; Sandom & Enser, 2002; Yang, Wildemuth, & Marchionini, 2004).

Eakins and Graham (1999) used a similar approach for the categorization of queries, but employed only three levels corresponding with visual primitives, logical or "derived" features, and abstract features.

Evidence available thus far about Web-based searching of image collections points to the added significance of browsing (Goodrum, Bejune, & Siochi, 2003). In an analysis of the transaction logs of over 33,000 image requests submitted to the Excite search engine by 10,000 searchers whose characteristics were unknown, Goodrum and Spink (2001) found a high rate of search modification, with sexual or adult content terms dominating the hundred most frequently occurring terms. Jörgensen and Jörgensen (2005) studied the search behavior of image professionals involved in advertising, marketing, and graphic design, by analyzing search logs from a commercial subscription service image provider. For this user group a very low proportion of the requests were located at the specific end of the continuum; a heavy recourse to browsing and the use of descriptive, thematic terms characterized the findings.

The Concept-Based Image Retrieval Paradigm

Within the practitioner community of picture librarians and archivists the traditional paradigm of image retrieval involves textual string matching between the client's verbal search request statement and the subject annotations embedded within the image collection metadata. Any matching expression (or one that matches sufficiently closely to satisfy some similarity threshold) results in the recovery of its associated image, which is then displayed to the client for consideration. Such an approach effectively ignores the fact that the information need is in the visual domain and translates the problem into a traditional text retrieval operation.

In this *concept-based image retrieval* paradigm the matching may be effected against keywords within a controlled vocabulary, or against natural language components of the image metadata, such as subject description, caption, or title. Enser, Sandom, and Lewis (2005b) report on a project in which a number of picture archives and libraries provided sample requests addressed to their holdings, together with the images selected manually or automatically in response to those requests and the metadata associated with each such image. Inspection of the metadata showed how different textual components within the metadata could provide a match with the query—as in the example shown in Figure 1.9—or where the absence of any matching textual annotation indicated that the image had been selected as a result of mediation by image archive staff. Semantic layering is also evident in the metadata shown in Figure 1.9, which would have enabled the same image to be retrieved

---

Request: A photo of a 1950s fridge
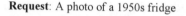

Roomy Fridge© Getty Images

Subject Metadata:

Title	Roomy Fridge
Date	circa 1952
Description	An English Electric 76A Refrigerator with an internal storage capacity of 7.6 cubic feet, a substantial increase on the standard model.
Subject	Domestic Life
Keywords	black & white, format landscape, Europe, Britain, England, appliance, kitchen appliance, food, drink, single, female, bending

---

Figure 1.9 Example of an image request, retrieved image, and its metadata (Edina, 2007).

had the request been couched in terms of a Specific Named Object Instance ("English Electric 76A Refrigerator"), a Specific Named Object Class ("English Electric refrigerator"), a Generic Object Class ("refrigerator, fridge, kitchen appliance, ..."), or semantic concept ("domestic life").

The Researcher Environment

The manifest difficulties associated with manual indexing of visual images have fueled some fifteen years of intense research activity and a voluminous literature directed toward the content-based image retrieval (CBIR) paradigm. The research environment is quite different from that of the practitioner. Absolved of any responsibility for the various aspects of collection management and service provision, the research community is enabled to focus exclusively on technical aspects of the retrieval paradigm; indeed, it is identified by the CBIR paradigm. There is an engagement with collections, but generally only in the form of relatively small-scale datasets that are used as test collections. Among the most frequently cited are the Corel image dataset (e.g., Duygulu, Barnard, de Freitas, & Forsyth, 2002), although no longer available, and the Washington dataset (University of Washington, 2007); the Brodatz (1966) album has figured prominently in the particular context of textural analysis.

Queries, similarly, have to date been artificial collections assembled as a test bed. The research community shares with the practitioner community a deep involvement with metadata construction, but in this case as an exercise in automatic indexing in which human vision and reasoning are replaced by computer vision and algorithms.

Several experimental CBIR systems have been built; comprehensive surveys of these may be found in Johansson (2000) and Kherfi et al. (2004) and a comparative evaluation has been reported by Veltkamp and Tanase (2001). One of the earliest, and certainly best known, of these systems is QBIC (Query By Image Content) (Flickner, Sawhney, Niblack, Ashley, Huang, Dom, et al., 1995), which retains a "commercial" presence on the State Hermitage Museum, St. Petersburg, Web site (State Hermitage Museum, 2003). QBIC and other experimental systems such as Blobworld, Excalibur, MARS, Photobook, and VisualSeek (Johansson, 2000; Veltkamp & Tanase, 2001) have provided an evaluative framework within which retrieval performance has been tested. The only comparable performance measure within the practitioner environment would appear to be that of economic performance.

The CBIR Paradigm—Still Images

To achieve full functionality, CBIR requires three processing tiers. The first mimics human pre-conceptual image processing by means of syntactic operations that extract low-level features from the digital domain of a document. Within the second tier generic object, scene, and activity detection is undertaken as a statistical classification procedure, and at the third tier there is an attempt to span the conceptual distance between object/scene/activity labeling and the high-level reasoning that situates those objects, scenes, or activities appropriately within the user's sociocognitive space.

At the first tier the aim is to generate a representation of the pixel domain of the digitized image automatically in the form of visual feature vectors (known as "descriptors" in MPEG-7) (Martinez, 2004). These vectors are generated from quantifiable attributes of the image, namely, the visual primitives of color, texture, and the spatial distribution of blobs, shapes, or regions detectable within the pixel domain of the digitized image. Many such feature-vectors are described in the literature; these range from the simple formulations such as histograms of pixel values that represent the global distribution of color within the image, to advanced features generated from salient interest regions within the image. In the latter case the frequently encountered use of wavelet analysis to find relevant pixels located on sharp region boundaries is motivated by observing that multi-resolution, orientation, and frequency analysis are of prime importance for the human visual system and has proven efficiency in vision applications (Ros, Laurent, & Lefebvre, 2006).

The set of feature vectors by which an image collection may be surrogated in this manner, when stacked, form a matrix, typically of high dimensionality (Rui, Huang, & Chang, 1999). Jörgensen (2003, pp. 157–159) provides an accessible overview of data reduction techniques in common use for image representation by means of which the dimensionality may be reduced. A frequently reported technique is Latent Semantic Indexing (LSI), a procedure borrowed from the traditional, theoretical model of text retrieval (Deerwester, Dumais, Furnas, Landauer, & Harshman, 1990). LSI is a linear algebraic manipulation that uses the technique of singular value decomposition (Berry, Dumais, & O'Brien, 1995) to generate a matrix of lower rank in which the latent semantics of the collection are exposed. Dumais (2004) provides an overview of LSI in a previous *ARIST* chapter and the matrix algebra is clearly explained by Hare, Lewis, Enser, and Sandom (2006a).

For the second tier of CBIR processing a variety of statistical classification techniques has been reported, among which Hidden Markov Models (HMM), Gaussian Mixture Models (GMM), Support Vector Machines (SVM), and Bayesian Networks (BN) are particularly prevalent. Eakins (2002) provides an overview of such statistical and knowledge-based techniques, which make it possible under controlled conditions to effect limited automatic scene classification and generic object recognition.

The current limitations of these techniques are considerable. Only a restricted set of object types can be handled, the knowledge is domain-specific, and machine learning of that knowledge typically requires large training sets; scalability is uncertain, and, most obviously, the search output often reveals a frustrating lack of semantic integrity. As Christel and Conescu (2005) have observed, a color-based CBIR algorithm will match busy city scenes containing beige brick backgrounds with scenes of desert sand. More sophisticated CBIR algorithms may return images of the Statue of Liberty in response to example queries seeking images of starfish—the so-called "rhyming image" phenomenon (Johansson, 2000, online). Among the practitioner community working with *direct pictures*, an image retrieval paradigm that retrieves for the user's consideration a set of images bereft of any semantic resemblance to the query image will always fail to impress.

The testing of CBIR features has revealed that users do not find low-level features intuitive to search or relevant to their queries (Chang, Smith, Beigi, & Benitez, 1997), and "as the palette of search options broadens with imagery, the potential for greater user confusion broadens as well" (Christel & Conescu, 2005, p. 75). Jörgensen (2003, p. 197) puts the matter plainly: "the emphasis in the computer science literature has been largely on what is computationally possible, and not on discovering whether essential generic visual primitives can in fact facilitate image retrieval in 'real-world' applications."

With developing maturity has come the realization that the content-based image retrieval paradigm, operating on the low-level, syntactic properties of an image, has a practical value that, currently, appears to be limited to those specialized applications in which the verbalization of either the user's query or the content of the image is problematic. Although specialized, these applications are, nonetheless, important; they include any situation where it is difficult for the perceptual saliency of some visual features to be captured in text, such as the perceptual elements of a texture, the outline of a form, and the visual effects in a video sequence (Del Bimbo, 1999). Practical applications include the interrogation of output from continuous video and satellite monitoring operations, where the focus of interest might lie in the presence, absence, or movement of non-specific features; and image comparison on the basis of textural or chromatic properties, with applications in fashion design, medicine, and fine art, among others (Eakins & Graham, 1999).

A particular characteristic of such applications is their employment of image types other than the *direct picture*. Müller et al. (2004) provide an overview of literature about content-based applications to medical imagery; specific examples include the use of computed tomography and magnetic resonance images (Hollink, Little, & Hunter, 2005; Liu, Dellaert, & Rothfus, 1998) and mammograms (Hu, Dasmahapatra, Lewis, & Shadbolt, 2003). Trademarks (Alwis & Austin, 1998; Eakins, Graham, Boardman, & Shields, 1996); engineering drawings (Eakins, 1993); maps, charts, and diagrams (Brunskill & Jörgensen, 2002) are examples of other types of images that have figured in CBIR experimental systems.

For the more traditional image retrieval activity of operating on *direct pictures*, however, the manifest limitations of CBIR are characterized as the "semantic gap," a now-familiar feature of the image retrieval landscape that has been formally defined as "the lack of coincidence between the information that one can extract from the visual data and the interpretation that the same data have for a user in a given situation" (Smeulders et al., 2000, p. 1353).

The increasing interest in finding the means to overcome this barrier is evident in Smeulders et al.'s (p. 1375) observation that "the aim of Content-Based Image Retrieval must be to provide maximum support in bridging the semantic gap between the simplicity of available visual features and the richness of the user semantics."

Most attempts at bridging the semantic gap do not address third tier CBIR processes, and the conceptual distance between object labeling and the high-level reasoning that situates those objects appropriately within sociocognitive space. In effect, the semantic gap is a two-part fracture and the focus of attention has been on only the first part (Hare, Lewis, Enser, & Sandom, 2006b). Central to these endeavors is the integration of text-based and CBIR methods for the indexing and retrieval of visual images. Zhao and Grosky (2002) have provided a useful overview of techniques for finding the latent correlation between low-level visual features and high-level semantic concepts, such approaches reflecting the view that "it is becoming clear in the image retrieval community that Content-Based Image Retrieval is not a replacement of, but rather a complementary component to, the text-based image retrieval. Only the integration of the two can result in satisfactory retrieval performance" (Rui et al., 1999, pp. 54–55).

Automatic Annotation

Automatic annotation of images has come to the fore as a means to integrate content-based and text-based image retrieval. In an overview of the techniques used in auto-annotation, Hare et al. (2006b) note two basic approaches. The first treats the issue as an unsupervised statistical inference problem wherein statistical links between regions and words are discovered by estimating the joint probability distribution between regional image features and words (Barnard, Duygulu, Forsyth, de Freitas, Blei, & Jordan, 2003). The second approach treats the problem as a supervised learning task in which a set of labeled training images is used to associate image features with words; annotation is performed by comparing visual features and propagating words (Hare et al., 2006b).

Central to the latter technique is the creation of a training set of pre-annotated images, each surrogated as a vector with elements corresponding with the allocation of keywords drawn from the indexing vocabulary. To this textual term vector is appended a "visual term" vector, with elements drawn from the image's quantized visual primitives. The matrix formed by stacking these composite, textual-and-visual term vectors provides a representation of the training set of images. Typically, this matrix is transformed by Latent Semantic Indexing in order to generate a less sparse matrix in which the latent semantics of the collection are exposed.

Vectors of visual terms from a test set of un-annotated images can be compared with the visual term constituents of the training set. This is achieved by projecting the visual term vectors of the un-annotated images into the semantic space created by the LSI process. This semantic space can be queried by keyword. Promising results have been achieved employing a Corel-derivative training set of 4,500 images and test set of 500 images described by Duygulu et al. (2002) and training and test sets of images derived from the Washington dataset (University of Washington, 2007).

Nevertheless, there are limitations to the efficacy of automatic annotation techniques in representing the semantic content of image material. These relate to the limited perception of objects permitted by the highly constrained vocabularies associated with the image datasets typically used in experimental systems to date. Figure 1.10 shows a typical example from the Washington dataset, in which the annotation is pitched at a low level in the Generic Object Class Hierarchy.

The major limitation of automatic annotation concerns the dependency on visual cues. Search engines are trained to recognize features that are actually visible in the image. Reference has been made earlier to spatial, temporal, and activity/event facets in *direct pictures*. A particularly challenging aspect of these facets is that they frequently have no visual presence in an image: they represent "extrinsic semantics."

Image source:
www.cs.washington.edu/research/imagedatabase/groundtruth/barcelona/Image16.jpg

Annotation associated with this image: **buildings; people; sky; street; trees; cathedral; steps**

Annotation source:
www.cs.washington.edu/research/imagedatabase/groundtruth/annotation.txt

Figure 1.10   Sample image and annotation from the Washington dataset.

Requests, however, very frequently incorporate such facets; Enser, Sandom, Hare, and Lewis (in press) show examples drawn from user studies within the practitioner environment.

In the case of the temporal facet, apart from those generic values related to chromaticity, such as "daytime," "night," or "autumn," the temporal constituent of an image's semantic content is not directly visible. A similar situation is encountered with the spatial facet. The presence of generic spatial features, such as water, landscape, and mountains, can be inferred by global color analysis (Li & Wang, 2003). A search engine could be trained to recognize Specific Named Object Instances, such that inferences could be made about the location shown in the image, but, in general, elements within the Specific Location Hierarchy (see Figure 1.3) can be inferred only by a learning process underpinned by some definitional textual annotation. In principle, such a learning process could migrate from human to machine-based reasoning, but, for the present at least, the resolution of image requests that include a spatial facet, such as "typical English country scene, woodlands," and "New York buses" (Enser et al., in press), is facilitated by textual annotation.

The activity/event facet presents similar difficulties. Because, in Figure 1.5, an event is defined in terms of temporal and/or spatial facets, the implication is that an event is not directly interpretable from the visual evidence in an image. Retrieval of pertinent images in response to such requests needs the support of textual metadata, by means of which an event can be interpreted "into" the image.

The activity/event facet often occurs in association with the concept of significance. Significance frequently takes the form of the first, last, or only instantiation of some physical object or event. Clearly, significance is a non-visible attribute, which can be anchored to an image only by means of some explanatory text; it has no counterpart in low-level features of an image (Enser, Sandom, & Lewis, 2005a).

Abstract concepts and affective semantic content clearly belong in the realm of human, rather than computer, vision (Enser, 2000), and those searchers who specify features that must *not* be present in the retrieved image (e.g., "George V's coronation but not procession or any royals") also place themselves beyond the reach of auto-indexing.

Ontologies

In a bid to gain a richer representation of the semantic content of images than that afforded by the associations between image features and semantic labels, the CBIR research community has demonstrated a rapidly developing interest in ontologies. One of the earliest applications of ontologies for image annotation and retrieval images was described by Schreiber, Dubbeldam, Wielemaker, and Wielinga (2001), and subsequently extended to experimentation in the generation of semantic inferencing rules, formulated by domain experts, that link low-level visual features to domain concepts. The domain was pancreatic cells, using *indirect pictures* in the form of CT scans (Hollink, Little et al., 2005).

In another medical images application, image annotation tools for region delineation, feature extraction, and image analysis were integrated with an ontology to capture the semantics involved in mammography (Hu et al., 2003). In a different applications environment, museum multimedia object metadata have been mapped to an ontology based on the CIDOC Conceptual Reference Model (CRM) (International Council of Museums, 2007) and an integrated content, metadata, and concept based image retrieval facility developed for a number of major European museums (Addis, Martinez, Lewis, Stevenson, & Giorgini, 2005).

As a result of the adoption of ontologically supported experimental image retrieval processes, tools that are well established within the image practitioner environment, such as AAT, ULAN, ICONCLASS, and WordNet (Princeton University, Cognitive Science Laboratory, 2007), are beginning to penetrate the research environment (Hollink, Schreiber, Wielemaker, & Wielinga, 2003). Such a development is to be welcomed as a step toward a greater degree of shared understanding between the two communities. More generally, the thrust toward "semantic retrieval" that is being propelled by the harnessing of ontologies is the first tentative step toward spanning the second part of the semantic gap.

There can be no doubting that this second part of the semantic gap is very wide indeed. Consideration of the complexity of real-user queries and the rich semantic content of expertly annotated images, such as those shown in Figures 1.8 and 1.9, makes abundantly clear the limitations of even the ontologically supported approaches currently under development within the research environment. In essence, these limitations reflect two constraints. First, building an ontology—albeit assisted by the adoption of standard knowledge organization and representation tools such as XML, RDF, OWL, and SKOS (Mikhalenko, 2005)—is technically demanding; domain experts, who "rarely enjoy constructing XML syntax" (Hollink, Little, et al., 2005, p. 94), find very challenging the task of specifying the rules for ontology construction. Second, ontologies tend to be domain specific but the semantic layering, which may be inferred in any given image, may not be. No doubt, as ontology engineering advances, lexicon size will expand greatly, ever-larger numbers of concepts will be handled, and the effect of these limitations may be felt less keenly. However, the danger of retrieval precision degradation due to over-exuberant automatic propagation of hierarchically related and associative-concept keywords in ontologically supported automatic indexing should be noted in this context.

The CBIR Paradigm—Moving Images

The research community has expended a great deal of effort on the development of content-based retrieval techniques that operate on either the visual content alone or the full audiovisual content of video documents. A particular characteristic of this research effort has been the emphasis placed on the evaluation of these techniques through the medium of the TRECVID competition, a video track offshoot of the Text REtrieval Conference (TREC), which began in 2001 as an open, metrics-based evaluation of content-based video retrieval (Smeaton, 2005).

By providing a forum for organizations interested in comparing their results, a large video test collection with corpora ranging from documentaries to advertising films and broadcast news, together with uniform scoring procedures, TRECVID has stimulated the research community to make continuing progress in video retrieval (Christel & Conescu, 2006).

In a previous *ARIST* chapter Smeaton (2004) provides a rich contextualization of video retrieval, encompassing technical aspects of video coding and metadata standards, indexing, searching, browsing, and summarization techniques for digital video. Some of the earliest applications of these techniques operated on only the visual content of video; more recently, research has concentrated on exploiting the multimedia properties of this documentary form.

Automatic segmentation of a video stream into shots using shot boundary detection techniques was an early focus. Automatic detection of shots inter alia makes available all the frames associated with each shot. Particular members of this frame set are selected on some consistent basis to act as keyframes—single bitmap images by which the shot may be surrogated. "Storyboards" are formulated from the simultaneous presentation on a computer screen, often as thumbnails, of a chronological ordering of these keyframes; various commercial and research systems now provide this facility (Christel & Conescu, 2005).

An entire film or video can be represented as a storyboard; this confers a benefit on the film cataloger, who is absolved from the time-consuming necessity of viewing the entire footage. The searcher is also advantaged, not only from the saving of time but also because, when a shot relevant to a query is found, there is a high probability that neighboring shots, which have a temporal relationship with the relevant shot in the same broadcast, will also be relevant.

Storyboards are particularly useful for the fast detection of events in news footage and sports broadcasts—programs that are time-consuming to watch after recording and for which program compilers and editors often wish to retrieve only the highlights.

In performing a syntactic segmentation of the video stream, shot boundary detection is a first tier CBIR process. Naphade and Smith (2004) provide an account of related techniques used for low-level visual feature extraction from video, and Martinez (2004) defines the equivalent Visual Description Tools provided in MPEG-7. The application of Latent Semantic Indexing in the context of a video object retrieval system has been described by Hohl, Souvannavong, Merialdo, and Huet (2004), and Hollink, Nguyen, Koelma, Schreiber, and Worring (2005) report its use with news video, when an 18,117 dimensional vector space was reduced to 400 dimensions.

Analysis of keyframes does not exploit the motion content of video, and more sophisticated techniques are needed if the activity/event facet of the semantic content is to be indexed. Event-based indexing of video sequences is demanding. The appearance of participating objects is highly variable due to partial occlusion or varying capture conditions (such as lighting and point of view), and the scale of the object occurrence may vary spatially and/or temporally (Moënne-Loccoz, Bruno & Marchand-Maillet, 2006).

Petkoviç and Jonker (2004) describe the use of object and event grammars to formalize spatio-temporal descriptions of high-level concepts. A tennis video case study is used to show how automatically detected features can be mapped to high-level concepts, which in this case take the form of domain-specific events such as rallies, lobs, and longest points. However, the creation of primitive object and event descriptions in the object grammar is challenging. So, too, is the application of statistical classification techniques—in this case Hidden Markov Models—in the formalization of complex actions by non-rigid objects so as to differentiate a smash from other kinds of tennis strokes, for example. As with many other such experimental, content-based systems, the experimentation prescribes the user transactions; such are the intellectual and computational demands of the formal modeling of such information retrieval scenarios that the system can address only a highly constrained set of predefined queries.

Much recent research into video retrieval has sought to exploit the multimedia nature of video documents, particularly by harnessing the audio channel as a means of generating textual annotations of the complementary video channel. Use of Automatic Speech Recognition (ASR) to enable automatic indexing of video in this way has attracted the attention of the practitioner community as well as the research community; the Informedia Digital Video Library project, begun in 1994, is the most widely reported example (Carnegie Mellon University, 2007). This landmark project seeks to make multimedia material searchable by means of ASR-enabled transcripts and to integrate speech recognition, natural language processing, image analysis, and information retrieval in order to mitigate the deficiencies of these individual technologies when applied in isolation within a multimedia context (Whitbrock & Hauptmann, 1998). Informedia operates its news stories from television broadcasts; automatically generated metadata and indexes to multiple terabytes of video are continuously available online to local users.

A system called Físchlár-News, which is very similar in principle to the Informedia project, captures Irish broadcast television news nightly and automatically analyzes and structures the broadcast into an MPEG-7 annotation (Smeaton, O'Connor, & Lee, 2005). Both systems enable the user to inspect keyframes, play the associated video, and carry out other retrieval and browsing operations. Analytic functions in both cases include program start/end identification and advertisement detection, the outputs from which are fed into a trained statistical classifier that segments the broadcast into discrete news stories that are then available as units of retrieval. Another common requirement is anchorperson shot detection, which has been successfully met using a combination of visual features (face and cloth detection) and audio features (voice shots), a description of which may be found in the work of Kim, Hwang, Kim, and Seo (2005).

From the wealth of experimental results, notably from the Informedia project, it has been found that speech transcripts provide the single most important clue for successful video retrieval. In a detailed study using TRECVID 2004 topics, Christel and Conescu (2005) showed that retrieval performance is significantly better on both specific and generic topics in news broadcasts when transcripts are available for searching. In Hauptmann's (2005, p. 7) words: "It has been disappointing for us to repeatedly find that none of the multimedia analysis and retrieval techniques provide a significant benefit over retrieval using only textual information such as ASR transcripts or closed captions ...We have found that most research from computer vision has not been robust enough to be usable."

One particular capability in broadcast news video with which the CBIR community has been challenged is the automatic detection and annotation of the geographic location of every shot within a video sequence. The problem has been investigated by Yang and Hauptmann (2006) with a view to satisfying such queries as "Find the scenes showing the flood in California caused by El Nino." Although news video may have transcripts from closed-captions or ASR in which reference is made to most of the locations shown in the footage, any given geographic location can have numerous visually different scenes, making determination of location from the visual content of a shot highly problematic. Nevertheless, within experiments conducted on the TRECVID dataset, Yang and Hauptmann report 85 percent accuracy in correctly labeling the location of any shot in news video.

Finding specific people in news videos is a further challenge that has figured in TRECVID evaluation. Searching for names in speech transcript text is a common approach, but a shot might include many other people, especially a reporter or anchorperson. Face recognition is inherently challenging, but in news videos especially so because of the variety of poses, expressions, and illumination conditions that perturb the target face. Ozkan and Duygulu (2006) report much enhanced average precision values returned by a technique that automatically detects, and discounts, anchorpersons.

ASR technology has advanced to the point where the best recognizers trained for broadcast news currently have a word error rate of about 15 percent on studio-recorded anchor speech. Performance degrades as constraints on identified speaker and comprehensiveness of vocabulary are relaxed; other noise factors, such as an interviewee crying, further degrade performance (Hauptmann, 2005).

The audio channel may convey more than just speech, of course. Crowd noise at soccer matches has been used to index key events in soccer broadcasts automatically using an audio-based, noise-level classification (Baillie & Jose, 2003). Highlights in Formula 1 motor racing broadcasts have been retrieved by automatic analysis of the audio signal and detection of the commentator's excited speech (Petkoviç & Jonker, 2004). Dimitrova, Barbieri, and Agnihotri (2004) provide an overview of theory and practice in the generation of video highlights, together with video summarization and video skim, which is a temporally condensed form of the video stream comprising a set of short video sequences composed of automatically selected portions of the original video. Audio-assisted video segmentation techniques have also been investigated by Cao, Tavanapong, Kim, and Oh (2003) for scene detection in narrative film. In this case an audio scene boundary is detected when a change occurs in speakers or in types of audio segments (speech replaced by music or silence replaced by music, for example).

Audio scene boundary detection performance is likely to be compromised, however, by a lack of synchronicity between the different modes in the multimodal data stream. It is a common technique in film, for example, for the sound track to cut to a new scene several seconds before the visual mode, so that there is no common boundary between the modalities.

Conclusion

In this chapter the attempt has been made to present an overview of current image retrieval activity within both the practitioner and research environments. Behind that attempt lies an awareness of the communication gap that separates those involved in the professional practice of visual asset management and use from those engaged in computer science and computer vision research who seek new functionalities in image retrieval. The activities of the latter community have brought forth an intimidatingly technical and voluminous literature directed toward the content-based image retrieval paradigm. The rate of publication and its abstruse nature go a long way toward explaining the communication gap between the researchers and the practitioners. The challenge of bridging that gap is at least as important, and probably no less challenging, than bridging the semantic gap in image retrieval. In looking ahead from the current position it seems clear that both gaps will remain very significant barriers to real progress in bringing the fruits of the research community's endeavors more positively into the practitioners' arena.

The scale of the challenge is not lost on those whose outlook extends beyond the computer laboratory to embrace people and the reality of their visual information needs. For some of these observers true semantic retrieval is believed to be unachievable (Santini & Jain, 1997), a view expressed more forcibly in a recent keynote address: "True semantic labelling will never be solved and do not waste your time working on it!" (Delp, 2005). Equally unequivocal is another research leader's advice to "give up on general, deep understanding of video—that problem is just too hard for now" (Hauptmann, 2005, p. 8).

In the meantime our thoughts about the effective representation of the semantic content of large-scale image resources have to be adjusted to accommodate new cultures of informal, user-supplied manual indexing and search engine-supplied automatic indexing. These issues contribute to the challenge that some observers confront in gaining a greater understanding of users' needs and searching behavior (Jörgensen & Jörgensen, 2005). It is certainly the case that we know little about how people want to use the rapidly burgeoning sources of still and moving images available freely or by registration on the Web, or created by themselves using their digital and cell phone cameras. The added emphasis that this cornucopia brings to interface design in support of browsing and relevance feedback would seem clear, however (Rui & Huang, 2001).

We can readily envisage, furthermore, that image retrieval will increasingly be exercised in multimodal contexts: Gilles (in Jaimes, Christel, Gilles, Sarukkai, & Ma, 2005), for example, foresees a medical imaging scenario in which a practitioner might want to query a medical video database with an ultrasound heart video, search the database for heart sequences with similar movements and noises, and seek to view the corresponding diagnoses.

Adding functionality in this way will strengthen the argument advanced by some that real progress in bridging the semantic gap will be achieved only through interdisciplinary research: "A successful solution to the problems of semantic image retrieval (if one exists at all) may well require a significant paradigm shift, involving techniques originally developed in other fields" (Eakins, 2002, p. 4).

For Greisdorf and O'Connor (2002) those techniques may have to be drawn from an eclectic mix of information science, perception, cognition, imaging, communication, and visual arts, as well as the computer sciences. Such an expanded research community will bring even greater vibrancy, no doubt. For its members to achieve the greatest likelihood of success in tackling the further reaches of the semantic gap, however, there will need to be a more effective engagement with the practitioner community; for among the latter are those who have, for a very long time, been putting the "semantic" in semantic image retrieval.

Acknowledgments

I am grateful to my colleagues Christine Sandom, Paul Lewis, and Jonathan Hare for their support in the preparation of this chapter. My thanks also to the reviewers of this chapter for their helpful comments.

References

Addis, M. J., Martinez, K., Lewis, P., Stevenson, J., & Giorgini, F. (2005). New ways to search, navigate and use multimedia museum collections over the Web. *Proceedings of Museums and the Web 2005*. Retrieved January 7, 2007, from www.archimuse.com/mw2005/papers/addis/addis.html

Alwis, S., & Austin, J. (1998). A novel architecture for trademark image retrieval systems. In J. P. Eakins, D. J. Harper, & J. Jose (Eds.), *The Challenge of Image Retrieval: Workshop on Image Retrieval, University of Northumbria, Newcastle upon Tyne, U.K.* Retrieved January 24, 2007, from www.bcs.org/upload/pdf/ewic_im98_paper10.pdf

Angelini, S. (Ed.). (2006). *The researcher's guide: Film, television, radio and related documentation collections in the UK* (7th ed.). London: British Universities Film and Video Council.

Armitage, L. H., & Enser, P. G. B. (1997). Analysis of user need in image archives. *Journal of Information Science, 23*(4), 287–299.

Baca, M., & Harpring, P. (Eds.). (2005). *Categories for the description of works of art.* Los Angeles: J. Paul Getty Trust & College Art Association. Retrieved January 7, 2007, from www.getty.edu/research/conducting_research/standards/cdwa

Baillie, M., & Jose, J. (2003). Audio-based event detection for sports video. *Image and video retrieval: Proceedings of the Second International Conference* (Lecture Notes in Computer Science, 2728), 300–309.

Bakewell, E., Beeman, W. O., & Reese, C. M. (1988). *Object-image-inquiry: The art historian at work* (M. Schmitt, Ed.). Santa Monica, CA: Getty Art History Information Program.

Barnard, K., Duygulu, P., Forsyth, D., de Freitas, N., Blei, D. M., & Jordan, M. I. (2003). Matching words and pictures. *Journal of Machine Learning Research, 3*, 1107–1135.

Berry, M. W., Dumais, S. T., & O'Brien, S. T. (1995). Using linear algebra for intelligent information retrieval. *SIAM Review, 37*(4), 573–595.

Besser, H. (1990). Visual access to visual images: The UC Berkeley Image Database Project. *Library Trends, 38*(4), 787–798.

Boll, S. (2005). Image and video retrieval from a user-centered mobile multimedia perspective. *Image and Video Retrieval: Proceedings of the Fourth International Conference* (Lecture Notes in Computer Science, 3568), 18–27.

British Association of Picture Libraries and Agencies. (2004). *Directory of picture libraries and agencies.* London: The Association.

British Broadcasting Corporation. (2006). *BBC news online, 10 October 2006.* Retrieved January 7, 2007, from news.bbc.co.uk/1/hi/business/6034577.stm

British Broadcasting Corporation. (2007). *BBC motion gallery about us.* Retrieved January 7, 2007, from www.bbcmotiongallery.com/Customer/AboutUs.aspx

Brodatz, P. (1966). *Textures: A photographic album for artists and designers.* New York: Dover.

Brunskill, J., & Jörgensen, C. (2002). Image attributes: A study of scientific diagrams. *Proceedings of the Annual Meeting of the American Society for Information Science and Technology*, 365–375.

Cao, Y., Tavanapong, W., Kim, K., & Oh, J. (2003). Audio-assisted scene segmentation for story browsing. *Image and video retrieval: Proceedings of the Second International Conference* (Lecture Notes in Computer Science, 2728), 446–455.

Carnegie Mellon University. (2007). *Informedia digital video library*. Retrieved January 7, 2007, from www.informedia.cs.cmu.edu

Cawkell, A. E. (1992). Selected aspects of image processing and management: Review and future prospects. *Journal of Information Science, 18*(3), 179–192.

Chang, S.-F., Smith, J. R., Beigi, M., & Benitez, A. (1997). Visual information retrieval from large distributed online repositories. *Communications of the ACM, 40*(12), 63–71.

Chen, H. (2001). An analysis of image queries in the field of art history. *Journal of the American Society for Information Science and Technology, 52*(3), 260–273.

Choi, Y., & Rasmussen, E. M. (2002). Users' relevance criteria in image retrieval in American history. *Information Processing & Management, 38*(5), 695–726.

Christel, M. G., & Conescu, R. M. (2005). Addressing the challenge of visual information access from digital image and video libraries. In *Proceedings of the 5th ACM/IEEE-CS Joint Conference on Digital Libraries*, 69–78.

Christel, M. G., & Conescu, R. M. (2006). Mining novice user activity with TRECVID interactive retrieval tasks. *Image and Video Retrieval: Proceedings of the 5th International Conference* (Lecture Notes in Computer Science, 4071), 21–30.

Davis, M. (2003). Editing out video editing. *IEEE MultiMedia Archive, 10*(2), 54–64.

Deerwester, S., Dumais, S. T., Furnas, G. W., Landauer, T. K., & Harshman, R. (1990). Indexing by latent semantic analysis. *Journal of the American Society for Information Science, 41*(6), 391–407.

Del Bimbo, A. (1999). *Visual information retrieval*. San Francisco: Morgan Kaufmann.

Delp, E. (2005, November). *Are low level features too low for indexing?* Keynote address presented at the 2nd European Workshop on the Integration of Knowledge, Semantics and Digital Media Technology, London.

Dimitrova, N., Barbieri, M., & Agnihotri, L. (2004). Providing rapid access to video content through automatic summaries. In R. Raeli & P. Innocenti (Eds.), *MMIR MultiMedia Information Retrieval: Metodologie ed esperienze internazionali di content-based retrieval per l'informazione e la documentazione* (pp. 281–300). Rome: AIDA.

Dublin Core Metadata Initiative. (2006). *The Dublin Core Metadata Initiative*. Retrieved January 7, 2007, from dublincore.org

Dumais, S. T. (2004). Latent semantic analysis. *Annual Review of Information Science and Technology, 38*(1), 188–230.

Duygulu, P., Barnard, K., de Freitas, J. F. G., & Forsyth, D. A. (2002). Object recognition as machine translation: Learning a lexicon for a fixed image vocabulary. *Proceedings of the 7th European Conference on Computer Vision – Part IV* (Lecture Notes in Computer Science, 2353), 97–112.

Eakins, J. P. (1993). Design criteria for a shape retrieval system. *Computers in Industry, 21*(2), 167–184.

Eakins, J. P. (2002). Towards intelligent image retrieval. *Pattern Recognition, 35*(1), 3–14.

Eakins, J. P., & Graham, M. E. (1999). *Content-based image retrieval: A report to the JISC Technology Applications Programme.* Newcastle upon Tyne, UK: Institute for Image Data Research, University of Northumbria at Newcastle.

Eakins, J. P., Graham, M. E., Boardman, J. M., & Shields, K. (1996). *Retrieval of trade mark images by shape feature* (British Library Research and Innovation Report 26). London: British Library Research and Innovation Centre.

Edina. (2007). *Education image gallery.* Retrieved January 7, 2007, from edina.ac.uk

Enser, P. G. B. (1993). Query analysis in a visual information retrieval context. *Journal of Document and Text Management, 1*(1), 25–52.

Enser, P. G. B. (1995). Pictorial information retrieval. *Journal of Documentation, 51*(2), 126–170.

Enser, P. G. B. (2000). Visual image retrieval: Seeking the alliance of concept-based and content-based paradigms. *Journal of Information Science, 26*(4), 199–210.

Enser, P. G. B., & McGregor, C. G. (1992). *Analysis of visual information retrieval queries. Report on Project G16412 to the British Library Research & Development Department.* London: The Department.

Enser, P. G. B., Sandom, C. J., Hare, J. S., & Lewis, P. H. (in press). Facing the reality of semantic image retrieval. *Journal of Documentation.*

Enser, P. G. B., Sandom, C. J., & Lewis, P. H. (2005a). Automatic annotation of images from the practitioner perspective. *Image and video retrieval: Proceedings of the Fourth International Conference* (Lecture Notes in Computer Science, 3568), 497–506.

Enser, P. G. B., Sandom, C. J., & Lewis, P. H. (2005b). Surveying the reality of semantic image retrieval. In S. Bres & R. Laurini (Eds.), *Visual Information and Information Systems: 8th International Conference, revised selected papers* (Lecture Notes in Computer Science, 3736) (pp. 177–188). Berlin: Springer-Verlag.

Evans, H., & Evans, M. (2003). *Picture researcher's handbook* (7th ed.). Leatherhead, UK: PIRA.

Fidel, R. (1997). The image retrieval task: Implications for the design and evaluation of image databases. *The New Review of Hypermedia and Multimedia, 3,* 181–199.

Film Images (London) Ltd. (2005). *Film images advanced search.* Retrieved January 7, 2007, from www.film-images.com/advance_search.jsp

Flickner, M., Sawhney, H., Niblack, W., Ashley, J., Huang, Q., Dom, B., et al. (1995). Query by image and video content: The QBIC system. *IEEE Computer*, *28*(9), 23–32.

Frost, C. O., & Noakes, A. (1998). Browsing images using broad classification categories. *Proceedings of the 9th ASIS SIGCR Classification Research Workshop*, 71–89.

Goodrum, A., Bejune, M., & Siochi, A. C. (2003). A state transition analysis of image search patterns on the Web. *Image and Video Retrieval: Proceedings of the Second International Conference* (Lecture Notes in Computer Science, 2728), 281–290.

Goodrum, A., & Spink, A. (2001). Image searching on the Excite Web search engine. *Information Processing & Management*, *37*(2), 295–311.

Google. (2007a). *Google image labeler*. Retrieved January 7, 2007, from images.google.com/imagelabeler

Google. (2007b). *Google video U.K.* Retrieved January 7, 2007, from video.google.co.uk

Google. (2007c). *Picasa*. Retrieved January 7, 2007, from picasa.google.com

Gordon, C. (1996). Patterns of user queries in an ICONCLASS database. *Visual Resources*, *12*, 177–186.

Graves, A., & Lalmas, M. (2002). Video retrieval using an MPEG-7 based inference network. *Proceedings of the 25th Annual International ACM SIGIR Conference on Research and Development in Information Retrieval*, 339–346.

Greisdorf, H., & O'Connor, B. (2002). Modelling what users see when they look at images: A cognitive viewpoint. *Journal of Documentation*, *58*(1), 6–29.

Halliwell, L. (2005). *Halliwell's film, video & DVD guide 2006* (Ed. J. Walker). London: Harper Collins.

Hare, J. S., Lewis, P. H., Enser, P. G. B., & Sandom, C. J. (2006a). A linear-algebraic technique with an application in semantic image retrieval. *Image and Video Retrieval: Proceedings of the 5th International Conference* (Lecture Notes in Computer Science, 4071), 31–40.

Hare, J. S., Lewis, P. H., Enser, P. G. B., & Sandom, C. J. (2006b). Mind the gap: Another look at the problem of the semantic gap in image retrieval. *Proceedings of Multimedia Content Analysis, Management and Retrieval* (SPIE vol. 6073) 607309-1–607309-12.

Harper, D. J., & Eakins, J. P. (Eds.). (1999). *The challenge of image retrieval: Papers presented at CIR99–Second UK Conference on Image Retrieval*. Newcastle upon Tyne, UK: University of Northumbria at Newcastle.

Harrison, H. W. (Ed.). (1991). *The FIAF cataloguing rules for film archives*. Munich, Germany: Saur.

Hartill, R. (2007). Plot summary for *The Ladykillers* (1955). *Internet movie database*. Retrieved January 7, 2007, from www.imdb.com/title/tt0048281/plot summary

Hastings, S. K. (1995). Query categories in a study of intellectual access to digitized art images. *Proceedings of the 58th Annual Meeting of the American Society for Information Science*, 3–8.

Hauptmann, A. G. (2005). Lessons for the future from a decade of Informedia video analysis research. *Image and Video Retrieval: Proceedings of the Fourth International Conference* (Lecture Notes in Computer Science, 3568), 1–10.

Hertzum, M. (2003). Requests for information from a film archive: A case study of multimedia retrieval. *Journal of Documentation, 59*(2), 168–186.

Hohl, L., Souvannavong, F., Merialdo, B., & Huet, B. (2004). Using structure for video object retrieval. *Image and Video Retrieval: Proceedings of the Third International Conference* (Lecture Notes in Computer Science, 3115), 564–572.

Hollink, L., Little, S., & Hunter, J. (2005). Evaluating the application of semantic inferencing rules to image annotation. *Proceedings of the 3rd International Conference on Knowledge Capture*, 91–98.

Hollink, L., Nguyen, G. P., Koelma, D. C., Schreiber, A. T., & Worring, M. (2005). Assessing user behaviour in news video retrieval. *IEE Proceedings on Vision, Image and Signal Processing, 152*(6), 911–918.

Hollink, L., Schreiber, A. T., Wielinga, B. J., & Worring, M. (2004). Classification of user image descriptions. *International Journal of Human Computer Studies, 61*(5), 601–621.

Hollink, L., Schreiber, A. T., Wielemaker, J., & Wielinga, B. J. (2003). Semantic annotation of image collections. In S. Handschuh, M. Koivunen, R. Dieng, & S. Staab (Eds.), *Knowledge Capture 2003: Proceedings Knowledge Markup and Semantic Annotation Workshop* (pp. 41–48). New York: ACM.

Hu, B., Dasmahapatra, S., Lewis, P., & Shadbolt, N. (2003). Ontology-based medical image annotation with description logics. *Proceedings of the 15th IEEE International Conference on Tools with Artificial Intelligence*, 77–82.

Infotrends/CAP Ventures. (2005). *News*. Retrieved January 7, 2007, from www.infotrends-rgi.com/home/Press/itPress/2005/1.11.05.html

International Council of Museums. (2007). *The CIDOC conceptual reference model*. Retrieved January 7, 2007, from cidoc.ics.forth.gr

Internet Movie Database Inc. (2007). *The Internet movie database*. Retrieved January 7, 2007, from www.imdb.com

J. Paul Getty Trust. (2000a). *Art & architecture thesaurus online*. Retrieved January 7, 2007, from www.getty.edu/research/conducting_research/vocabularies/aat

J. Paul Getty Trust. (2000b). *Getty thesaurus of geographic names online*. Retrieved January 7, 2007, from www.getty.edu/research/conducting_research/vocabularies/tgn

J. Paul Getty Trust. (2000c). *Union list of artist names online*. Retrieved January 7, 2007, from www.getty.edu/research/conducting_research/vocabularies/ulan

Jaimes, A., & Chang, S.-F. (2000). A conceptual framework for indexing visual information at multiple levels. *Internet Imaging* (SPIE proceedings vol. 3964). Retrieved January 14, 2007, from www.ee.columbia.edu/~ajaimes/Pubs/spie00_internet.pdf

Jaimes, A., Christel, M., Gilles, S., Sarukkai, R., & Ma, W.-Y. (2005). Multimedia information retrieval: What is it, and why isn't anyone using it? *Proceedings of the 7th ACM SIGMM International Workshop on Multimedia Information Retrieval*, 3–8.

Joint Steering Committee for Revision of AACR. (2005). *Anglo American cataloguing rules* (2nd ed., 2002 Revision [with 2003, 2004, and 2005 updates]). Chicago: American Library Association.

Johansson, B. (2000). *A survey on: Contents based search in image databases*. Retrieved January 7, 2007, from www.cvl.isy.liu.se/ScOut/TechRep/PaperInfo/bj2000.html

Jörgensen, C. (1998). Attributes of images in describing tasks: An investigation. *Information Processing & Management, 34*(2/3), 161–174.

Jörgensen, C. (1999). Access to pictorial material: A review of current research and future prospects. *Computers and the Humanities, 33*(4), 293–318.

Jörgensen, C. (2003). *Image retrieval: Theory and research*. Lanham, MD: Scarecrow Press.

Jörgensen, C., Jaimes, A., Benitez, A. B., & Chang, S.-F. (2001). A conceptual framework and empirical research for classifying visual descriptors. *Journal of the American Society for Information Science, 52*(11), 938–947.

Jörgensen, C., & Jörgensen, P. (2005). Image querying by image professionals. *Journal of the American Society for Information Science and Technology, 56*(12), 1346–1359.

Keister, L. H. (1994). User types and queries: Impact on image access systems. In R. Fidel, T. B. Hahn, E. M. Rasmussen, & P. J. Smith (Eds.), *Challenges in indexing electronic text and images* (pp. 7–22). Medford, NJ: Learned Information.

Kherfi, M. L., Ziou, D., & Bernardi, A. (2004). Image retrieval from the World Wide Web: Issues, techniques, and systems. *ACM Computing Surveys, 36*(1), 35–67.

Kim, S.-K., Hwang, D. S., Kim, J.-Y., & Seo, Y.-S. (2005). An effective news anchorperson shot detection method based on adaptive audio/visual model generation. *Image and Video Retrieval: Proceedings of the Fourth International Conference* (Lecture Notes in Computer Science, 3568), 276–285.

Krause, M. C. (1998). Intellectual problems of indexing picture collections. *Audiovisual Librarian, 14*(2), 73–81.

Li, J., & Wang, Z. (2003). Automatic linguistic indexing of pictures by a statistical modelling approach. *IEEE Transactions on Pattern Analysis and Machine Intelligence, 25*(9), 1075–1088.

Library of Congress. (2005). *MARC standards*. Retrieved January 7, 2007, from www.loc.gov/marc

Library of Congress. (2006). *Thesaurus for graphic materials I: Subject terms*. Retrieved January 7, 2007, from www.loc.gov/rr/print/tgm1

Liu, Y., Dellaert, F., & Rothfus, W. E. (1998). *Classification driven semantic based medical image indexing and retrieval: A technical report of the Robotics Institute at Carnegie Mellon University* (CMU-RI-TR-98-25). Pittsburgh, PA: The Institute.

Markey, K. (1984). Interindexer consistency tests: A literature review and report of a test of consistency in indexing visual materials. *Library & Information Science Research, 6*(2), 155–177.

Markkula, M., & Sormunen, E. (2000). End-user searching challenges indexing practices in the digital newspaper photo archive. *Information Retrieval, 1*(4), 259–285.

Martinez, J. M. (Ed.). (2004). *MPEG-7 overview* (version 10). Palma de Mallorca, Spain: International Organisation for Standardisation.

Mikhalenko, P. (2005). *Introducing SKOS.* Retrieved January 7, 2007, from www.xml.com/pub/a/2005/06/22/skos.html

Moënne-Loccoz, N., Bruno, E., & Marchand-Maillet, S. (2006). Local feature trajectories for efficient event-based indexing of video sequences. *Image and Video Retrieval: Proceedings of the 5th International Conference* (Lecture Notes in Computer Science, 4071), 82–91.

Moving Image Collections. (2006a). *Cataloging and metadata portal.* Retrieved January 7, 2007, from mic.imtc.gatech.edu/catalogers_portal/cat_unicatlg. htm

Moving Image Collections. (2006b). *Moving image collections.* Retrieved January 7, 2007, from mic.loc.gov

Müller, H., Michoux, N., Bandon, D., & Geissbuhler, A. (2004). A review of content-based image retrieval systems in medical applications: Clinical benefits and future directions. *International Journal of Medical Informatics, 73*(1), 1–23.

Naphade, M. R., & Smith, J. R. (2004). On the detection of semantic concepts at TRECVID. *Proceedings of the 12th annual ACM international conference on Multimedia,* 660–667.

Optibase, Inc. (2007). *Video archiving at CNN.* Retrieved January 7, 2007, from www.optibase.com/content.aspx?id=395

Ornager, S. (1995). The newspaper image database: Empirical supported analysis of users' typology and word association clusters. *Proceedings of the 18th Annual International ACM SIGIR Conference on Research and Development in Information Retrieval,* 212–218.

Ozkan, D., & Duygulu, P. (2006). Finding people frequently appearing in news. *Image and Video Retrieval: Proceedings of the 5th International Conference* (Lecture Notes in Computer Science, 4071), 173–182.

Panofsky, E. (1962). *Studies in iconology.* New York: Harper & Row.

Petkoviç, M., & Jonker, W. (2004). *Content-based video retrieval: A database perspective.* Boston: Kluwer.

Pisciotta, H. (2005). Understanding the picture user. *Advances in Librarianship, 29,* 223–245.

Princeton University, Cognitive Science Laboratory. (2007). *WordNet a lexical database for the English language.* Retrieved January 7, 2007, from wordnet. princeton.edu

Rasmussen, E. M. (1997). Indexing images. *Annual Review of Information Science and Technology, 32,* 169–196.

Rijksbureau voor Kunsthistorische Documentatie. (2007). *Iconclass home page*. Retrieved January 7, 2007, from www.iconclass.nl

Ros, J., Laurent, C., & Lefebvre, G. (2006). A cascade of unsupervised and supervised neural networks. *Image and Video Retrieval: Proceedings of the 5th International Conference* (Lecture Notes in Computer Science, 4071), 92–101.

Rui, Y., & Huang, T. S. (2001). Relevance feedback techniques in image retrieval. In M. S. Lew (Ed.), *Principles of visual information retrieval* (pp. 219–258). New York: Springer.

Rui, Y., Huang, T. S., & Chang, S.-F. (1999). Image retrieval: Current techniques, promising directions, and open issues. *Journal of Visual Communication and Image Representation, 10*, 39–62.

Sandom, C. J., & Enser, P. G. B. (2002). *VIRAMI: Visual information retrieval for archival moving imagery* (Library and Information Commission Research Report 129). London: The Council for Museums, Archives and Libraries.

Santini, S., & Jain, R. C. (1997). Do images mean anything? *Proceedings of IEEE International Conference on Image processing*, 564–567.

Schreiber, G., Dubbeldam, B., Wielemaker, J., & Wielinga, B. (2001). Ontology-based photo annotation. *IEEE Intelligent Systems, 16*(3), 2–10.

Shatford, S. (1986). Analyzing the subject of a picture: A theoretical approach. *Cataloging & Classification Quarterly, 5*(3), 39–61.

Shatford Layne, S. (1994). Some issues in the indexing of images. *Journal of the American Society for Information Science, 45*(8), 583–588.

Smeaton, A. F. (2004). Indexing, browsing and searching of digital video. *Annual Review of Information Science and Technology, 38*, 371–407.

Smeaton, A. F. (2005). Large scale evaluations of multimedia information retrieval: The TRECVid experience. *Image and Video Retrieval: Proceedings of the Fourth International Conference* (Lecture Notes in Computer Science, 3568), 11–17.

Smeaton, A. F., O'Connor, N. E., & Lee, H. (2005). Físchlár-News: Multimedia access to broadcast TV news. *ERCIM News, 62*. Retrieved January 7, 2007, from www.ercim.org/publication/Ercim_News/enw62/smeaton.html

Smeulders, A. W. M., Worring, M., Santini, S., Gupta, A., & Jain, R. C. (2000). Content-based retrieval at the end of the early years. *IEEE Transactions on Pattern Analysis and Machine Intelligence, 22*(12), 1349–1380.

State Hermitage Museum. (2003). *Digital Collection: QBIC colour and layout searches*. Retrieved January 7, 2007, from monarch.hermitage.ru/fcgi-bin/db2www/qbicSearch.mac/qbic?selLang=English

Sundaram, H., Naphade, M., Smith, J. R., & Yong, R. (Eds.). (2006). *Image and Video Retrieval: Proceedings of the 5th International Conference* (Lecture Notes in Computer Science, 4071).

Svenonius, E. (1994). Access to nonbook materials: The limits of subject indexing for visual and aural languages. *Journal of the American Society for Information Science, 45*(8), 600–606.

Technical Advisory Service for Images. (2007). *Resources: Case studies of digitisation projects*. Retrieved January 7, 2007, from www.tasi.ac.uk/resources/casestudies.html

Trant, J. (2004). *Image retrieval benchmark database service: A needs assessment and preliminary development plan: A report prepared for the Council on Library and Information Resources and the Coalition for Networked Information*. Retrieved January 7, 2007, from www.clir.org/PUBS/reports/trant04.html

University of California at Los Angeles. (2007). *UCLA film and television archive: About us*. Retrieved January 7, 2007, from www.cinema.ucla.edu/about/aboutus.html

University of Kent at Canterbury. (2007). *Centre for the Study of Cartoons and Caricatures*. Retrieved January 7, 2007, from library.kent.ac.uk/cartoons

University of Washington. (2007). *Index of /research/imagedatabase/ground truth*. Retrieved January 7, 2007, from www.cs.washington.edu/research/imagedatabase/groundtruth

Veltkamp, R. C., & Tanase, M. (2001). *CBIR system survey*. Retrieved January 7, 2007, from www.aa-lab.cs.uu.nl/cbirsurvey/cbir-survey/cbir-survey.html

Visual Resources Association. (2002). *Core categories* (version 3). Retrieved January 7, 2007 from www.vraweb.org/vracore3.htm

Whitbrock, M. J., & Hauptmann, A. G. (1998). Speech recognition for a digital video library. *Journal of the American Society for Information Science, 49*(7), 619–632.

White-Hensen, W. (2000). *Archival moving image materials: A cataloging manual* (2nd ed.). Washington, DC: Library of Congress, Cataloging Distribution Service.

Yahoo! Inc. (2007a). *Flickr*. Retrieved January 7, 2007, from www.flickr.com

Yahoo! Inc. (2007b). *Yahoo! Video*. Retrieved January 7, 2007, from video.yahoo.com

Yang, J., & Hauptmann, A. G. (2006). Annotating news video with locations. *Image and Video Retrieval: Proceedings of the 5th International Conference* (Lecture Notes in Computer Science, 4071), 153–162.

Yang, M., Wildemuth, B. M., & Marchionini, G. (2004). The relative effectiveness of concept-based versus content-based video retrieval. *Proceedings of the 12th Annual ACM International Conference on Multimedia*, 368–371.

YouTube Inc. (2007). *YouTube*. Retrieved January 7, 2007, from www.youtube.com

Zhao, R., & Grosky, W. I. (2002). Bridging the semantic gap in image retrieval. In T. K. Shih (Ed.), *Distributed multimedia databases: Techniques and applications* (pp. 14–36). Hershey, PA: Idea Group Publishing.

CHAPTER 2

Interactive Information Retrieval

Ian Ruthven
University of Strathclyde

Introduction

Information retrieval is a fundamental component of human information behavior. The ability to extract useful information from large electronic resources not only is one of the main activities of individuals online but is an essential skill for most professional groups and a means of achieving competitive advantage.

Our electronic information world is becoming increasingly complex with more sources of information, types of information, and ways to access information than ever before. Anyone who searches for information is required to make more decisions about searching and expected to engage with an increased number and variety of search systems. Even a standard desktop personal computer comes equipped with numerous search tools (desktop search, e-mail search, browsers to help search the Internet, embedded search tools for specific file formats such as PDF [portable document format] or Word, and specific document types such as help manuals). A standard day, if one is electronically enabled, may involve many searches across different search systems accessing different electronic resources for different purposes. The Internet, in particular, has revolutionized the ability to search, especially in the commercial arena where we have the choice of using different search systems to search essentially the same electronic resources but with different interactive functionalities. The search decisions a human is required to make before encountering any information involve not only how to search *this* resource using *this* system but also how to choose a system or resource to search in the first place. These decisions are complicated because skills learned using one type of system do not always transfer simply to searching a different type of system (Cool, Park, Belkin, Koenemann, & Ng, 1996). Neither does information literacy in one domain of expertise necessarily help when searching on unfamiliar topics.

The variability of data available, and the explicit or implicit structures of the data, also place a burden on both the searchers and system designers. How does searching within a Weblog, for example, differ from searching within technical manuals; or does all searching involve the same activities and require the same user support? As research shows (e.g., Florance & Marchionini, 1995; Ford & Ford, 1993; Kim & Allan, 2002) people often come to information retrieval (IR) systems with existing approaches to information seeking and processing and develop strategies for using specific systems. Neither search success nor a searcher's satisfaction with a system necessarily depends solely on what interactive features a system offers or on how it encourages searchers to employ these features; success and satisfaction instead depend on how well the system supports the searcher's personal strategies and how well it leads the searcher to understand how the system operates (Cool et al., 1996). Many authors have pointed out that individual differences affect interaction with information and information systems (e.g., Chen, Czerwinski, & Macredie, 2000; Ford, Miller, & Moss, 2005; Slone, 2002), that different stages of the search process require different kinds of assistance (Belkin, Cool, Stein, & Thiel, 1995; Kuhlthau, 1991), and that differences in the search context affect the interactive support required—for example searching in secondary languages requires more support in the process of document assessment and querying (Hansen & Karlgren, 2005; López-Ostenero, Gonzalo, & Verdejo, 2005).

The area of interactive information retrieval (IIR) covers research related to studying and assisting these diverse end users of information access and retrieval systems. IIR itself is shaped by (a) research on information seeking and search behavior and (b) research on the development of new methods of interacting with electronic resources. Both approaches are important; information seeking research provides the big picture on the decisions involved in finding information that contextualizes much of the work in IIR; research on methods of interacting with search systems promotes new understandings of appropriate methods to facilitate information access. The latter aspect of IIR is the main area covered in this chapter, the aim of which is to study recent and emerging trends in IIR interfaces and interactive systems.

Scope

People can find or become aware of useful information in many ways. We can receive recommendations through information filtering (Robertson & Callan, 2005) or collaborative filtering (Konstan, 2004), both of which push information toward us based on some model of our information preferences. We can follow information paths by traversing a series of items that have been manually or automatically linked to provide a narrative (Shipman, Furuta, Brenner, Chung, & Hsieh, 2000) or by creating our own information paths through browsing (Cove & Walsh, 1988). We can, of course, also find information by chance: looking for one piece of information and uncovering an unexpected piece of useful information. As Foster and Ford (2003, p. 337) note: "Perceptions [of the study participants] of the extent to which serendipity could be induced were mixed. While it was felt that some element of control could be exercised to attract 'chance encounters,' there was a perception that such encounters may really be manifestations of the hidden, but logical, influences of information gatekeepers—inherent in, for example, library classification schemes." This suggests that IIR systems could be designed to help find useful information by chance by reusing existing techniques for purposely finding information.

More commonly, electronic support for information seeking and retrieval consists of two types of systems: query-based and browse-based. Query-based systems differ from filtering systems as they force searchers to pull information out of the stored resource by expressing a request. Browsing systems—systems that are designed to support as opposed to simply permit browsing—help searchers understand and navigate an information space. In this chapter I deal with both types of systems, concentrating more on querying systems.

Dealing with the interactive issues involved in all types of information access is too wide an area to cover in one chapter. I focus specifically on the idea of a person interacting with a dedicated search system and the interaction engendered and supported by the system and interface design rather than discussing general search behavior, although, as will be seen, these two areas are linked. So, although this chapter discusses issues such as assessment of relevance and information behavior where appropriate, it does not discuss, in depth, issues such as work tasks or general information seeking behavior. The aim is to produce a chapter that is complementary to those by Vakkari (2002) on task-based information searching and Case (2006) on information seeking.

Scoping research on IIR is also problematic because research on developing better interactive systems often has an impact not only at the interface or dialogue level but also on the design of the whole system. Similarly, many articles discuss systems that have a novel interface, from which we can learn something about interaction, but the main aim of the research is neither the interface nor interaction. Finally, one could argue that almost all IR is interactive; most IR systems have some kind of interface and searchers are required to engage in some form of interaction. In deciding what to cover, I have tried to concentrate on systems where the novel features are interface- or interaction-related or where there is a human-centered evaluation to assess the interactive quality of the system; that is, where the intention behind the research is to investigate new forms of interaction, evaluate existing forms, or exploit user interaction for improved search effectiveness. Much of the research reviewed in this chapter is evaluated by experiments or studies with human participants. The variability of the experimental details and participants involved in these studies makes it difficult to compare directly, at a quantitative level, the results obtained. Therefore, although I discuss the relative success or failure of various approaches, I mostly compare the studies at a qualitative level.

Because IR is not an isolated field, another scoping issue arises as developments outside IR naturally have an impact on solutions to interactive IR questions. The rise of ontologies, for example, as part of the

Semantic Web initiative in artificial intelligence has provided new impetus to the area of knowledge-based query expansion (e.g., Legg, 2007; Navigli & Velardi, 2003). Similarly, technological advances in mobile computing have stimulated research in the area of contextual information retrieval, where context includes location, user tasks, and personal preferences. I do not touch on the technical sides of these developments but consider, where appropriate, the interactive issues raised.

The chapter concentrates on research published since 2000, mentioning early influences on current research where relevant.

Sources of Information

Interactive information seeking and retrieval is of interest to many communities and, as a result, work in this area is diffused across academic and practitioner fora. The main IR journals such as *Journal of the American Society for Information Science and Technology*, *Information Processing & Management*, *Journal of Documentation*, *Journal of Information Retrieval*, and *ACM Transactions on Information Systems* all regularly present high-quality research articles on IIR as do the leading journals in human–computer interaction (HCI), including *ACM Transactions on Computer–Human Interaction*, *Interacting with Computers*, and, to a lesser extent, *Human–Computer Interaction*.

Conferences are also a good source of material. The main IR conferences, the Association for Computing Machinery (ACM) Special Interest Group on Information Retrieval (SIGIR), the European Conference on Information Retrieval (ECIR), the International Conference on Information and Knowledge Management (CIKM) contain work on IIR, although the emphasis of late has been less on interfaces and more on system components such as relevance feedback, personalization, and techniques that could form part of an interface (e.g., summarization or clustering). The ACM Special Interest Group on Computer–Human Interaction (CHI), the Annual Meeting of the American Society for Information Science and Technology (ASIST), the World Wide Web (WWW) and Digital Library conferences, notably the Joint Conference on Digital Libraries (JCDL), and the European Conference on Digital Libraries (ECDL) also contain work on interactive information retrieval.

TREC (Text REtrieval Conference, trec.nist.gov) has dedicated efforts on interactive searching, notably the Interactive Track (1995–2003) and the HARD track (2003–2005), although tracks such as the video TREC-VID (from 2001) have also influenced interactive work in TREC. All TREC proceedings are available from the TREC Web site, and Dumais and Belkin (2005) provide a useful history of the TREC approach to interaction updating the previous history by Over (2001). Other initiatives such as CLEF (Cross-Language Evaluation Forum, www.clef-campaign.org) and INEX (INitiative for the Evaluation of XML [Extensible Markup Language] Retrieval, inex.is.informatik.uni-duisburg.de) also contain regular interactive tracks.

These are the main sources of materials on IIR, the ones I have used primarily for this chapter, but most conferences in the wide areas of IR, information science, librarianship, HCI, and the Web, as well as other less obvious places, such as conferences on social computing, will include occasional papers reflecting the pervasive nature of information access. There is no single monograph dealing solely with IIR although there are a number of dedicated monographs or collections of edited works addressing related areas. Numerous "how-to" books on optimizing end-user searching strategies and awareness (e.g., Hill, 2004) indicate the need for user support in searching. Hearst's (2000) chapter in *Modern Information Retrieval* is still worth reading. *The Turn*, by Ingwersen and Järvelin (2005), serves as a companion to Ingwersen's (1992) earlier work, which set out to provide a cognitive account of interactive information seeking. Other contributions teach us about information seeking and behavior, which, in turn, help specify the role of IIR and define the broader context in which these systems are used. Examples include the two recent collections edited by Spink and Cole on human information behavior (Spink & Cole, 2005b) and cognitive information retrieval (Spink & Cole, 2005a). Cognitive information retrieval, in this context, is focused on the human's role in information retrieval.

The question does arise of whether IIR is a distinct research area or simply a subfield of HCI (Beaulieu, 2000). Obviously one's own position does lend a particular view; but it is clear that interactive IR is more than simply developing interfaces for searching (Shneiderman, Byrd, & Croft, 1998) and that the strength of good research in IIR comes not only from a technical knowledge of interactive systems development but also from a knowledge of people's search behavior and search context, including the environmental factors that influence behavior (Fidel & Pejtersen, 2004). A particular strength of information seeking and retrieval as a hybrid domain is the awareness of the importance of the information objects themselves; not simply the media type being searched but also the generation, use, and storage of these objects (Blair, 2002). The notion of an information collection as more than simply a searchable grouping of objects is a powerful concept often under-utilized in IIR systems.

HCI and IIR come from different traditions; HCI, for example, places more emphasis on the published literature on usability whereas IR emphasizes effectiveness. Both, of course, are important, as a system with low usability will typically have low effectiveness and we probably care little about the usability of a poor system. Interactive IR does not stop at the interface and, as Bates (2002) and others point out, IIR system design is a coherent whole rather than a set of units. However, the two fields can learn from each other and the best research in IIR often reflects best practice in HCI as well as IR.

Themes

All research fields have stereotypes, idealized views of the aims and role of the activities within the field that are used to focus its intellectual debates and research agendas. Interactive information retrieval is no exception. The idealized IIR session is conceptually and practically simple: An end user creates some form of information request; this request is put to an electronic search system that retrieves a number of information objects, or references to these objects; the end user then assesses the set of retrieved results and extracts the relevant objects or information. For many searches, especially for straightforward types of Web search, this idealized view suffices and the interactive process is simple for the searcher. However, for the system designer, even this most simple view of searching raises interactive design issues—how does the system facilitate good queries or make it easier for the searcher to assess the retrieved material, for example?

A simplistic account of the interaction involved in searching eliminates many of the aspects that make interactive searching difficult for both searchers and designers of search systems. It also ignores the fact that information seeking and retrieval are usually only part of some larger activity and not ends in themselves. This larger activity, variously termed the task, domain task, or work task (Ingwersen, 1992, p. 131), influences our interaction with a system and our expectations of the interaction.

Although searches are commonly viewed and described at the session level—a series of interactive steps within a fixed time frame or terminated by a specific action such as the searcher leaving the system—we often repeat searches at different intervals (Spink, 1996; Vakkari, 2001). This can be to re-find the same information (Dumais, Cutrell, Cadiz, Jancke, Sarin, & Robbins, 2004), to update ourselves on new information provided within a dynamic information resource (Ellis, 1989; Ellis, Cox, & Hall, 1993), or because we are engaged in an ongoing activity and require additional information on the same topic (Vakkari, 2001; Vakkari & Hakala, 2000; Vakkari, Pennanen, & Serola, 2003). We may also be forced to repeat searches across different systems because no single source can completely satisfy an information need (Bhavnani, 2005). A repeated search can, therefore, be a request for the same information, for new information, or for different information—even though the search requests may appear very similar. Lin and Belkin (Lin, 2005; Lin & Belkin, 2005) demonstrate elegantly how complex is the nature of successive searching compared to the idealized one-iteration model.

Even within a single search session, the individual steps involved in completing a search may be interactively simple but not cognitively simple. We do not, for example, always know what information we require in advance of creating an information request or we may find it difficult to express our need for information as a searchable request (Belkin, 1980). The material retrieved may be too large to analyze easily and may require refinement resulting in a need for multiple query iterations. These refinements may be difficult to create and, even if the retrieval system offers the capability, it may be difficult to recognize good refinements (Ruthven, 2003). Assessing the retrieval results to select relevant material may be simple if we can easily recognize the relevant, or correct, information. On the other hand, it may be much more difficult if we have less certainty regarding the quality or accuracy of the information returned; and here the tasks that initiated the search in the first place may affect which criteria we use to assess the retrieval material (Barry & Schamber, 1998).

Searching involves a series of decisions; each decision may be influenced by the task, the collection, and factors relating to the person engaged in the search. Consequently, designing interactive systems that support how people search and, more importantly, how they want to search raises many intellectual challenges. Historically, there have been two dominant lines of research on helping people search for information: a major research thrust on automating or semi-automating tasks that humans may find difficult to perform on their own, and an equally important line of research on providing enhanced interactive functionality to allow humans more control over and input into their own search process. Both of these fields are still very much evident in recent research in IIR and the discussion presented here focuses on the research in both areas.

Improving Interaction

In the first line of research—improving interactive support for searchers—we see both novel interfaces and novel interactive functionality that help users organize information, structure their investigation of an information resource, or make interactive decisions.

The rise of the World Wide Web and the availability of Internet search engines such as MSN Search, Google, and AltaVista have radically changed perceptions of searching. Web search engines have changed the search landscape by making the ability to search more widely available than before. The effects of this availability have raised new challenges not least because the users of these systems are extremely diverse. The popularity and availability of Web search engines are particularly important in creating users' models of how search engines operate and users' expectations of search engines in general (Muramatsu & Pratt, 2001).

Web search engines, although freely available, are driven by commercial interests. This means that user interfaces developed for this type of searching may well have different aims than more traditional interfaces, but the search engine providers have an unparalleled opportunity to test new interactive techniques on a very large sample of end users. The dominance of particular behaviors in Web searching, for example, short queries, few page accesses, and little use of advanced search features, translate into new interactive challenges (Jansen & Spink, 2006). If, for example, most people use very short queries, how do we gain better representations of their information needs? Techniques such as query intention analysis have been suggested for this purpose (Kang & Kim, 2003). Similarly, if people look at only a very few results on a search page, what techniques will help users optimize the information they obtain? Here, techniques such as clustering and novel surrogates have attracted great attention.

Designing interfaces that support more difficult interactive decisions, such as selecting good query refinements, is also challenging for searchers who have learned to expect easy answers via the Web. The rise of the Web itself has had a huge impact on the development of new interactive retrieval systems and interfaces, with much of the recent work on general search interfaces using the Web as a source collection.

The prevailing model has been the query-driven approach in which a human enters a query and retrieves a list of references to information objects; this is the model favored by most search systems. Consequently, this section starts with a discussion of query formulation/reformulation and also of surrogates. These two areas represent the inputs and outputs of the querying approach: how to obtain queries and how to present the results of the retrieval. I then discuss the major alternatives to query models such as clustering, categorization, and visualization approaches incorporating some notion of information organization at the interface level. Finally, I discuss some newer trends in the literature, specifically work on personal information management, subobject retrieval, and systems for specialized retrieval tasks.

Query Formulation

Searchers often begin with a query and query-driven search interfaces rely on searchers being able to form an information request in a manner understandable by the underlying search engine. The typical querying interface accepts as a query a natural language keyword-based statement, one without operators such as Boolean connectives. Creating a good initial query is regarded as important for many reasons; it can increase search effectiveness and searcher satisfaction (Belkin, Kelly, Kim, Kim, Lee, Muresan, et al., 2003) and it facilitates automatic techniques for improving query quality such as pseudo-relevance feedback (Lynam, Buckley, Clark, & Cormack, 2004; Ruthven & Lalmas, 2003).

A system definition of a good query is one that helps discriminate objects that the searcher will judge relevant from those that the searcher will judge non-relevant, and can prioritize retrieval of the relevant material. A more human interpretation of a good query is one that returns appropriate or expected results. Depending on the user's stage of the search process, the notion of appropriate search results may be very different. Individuals carrying out an initial search, or with little knowledge of the topic being searched, may be satisfied with results that inform them about the information space being searched (Kuhlthau, 1991). Alternatively, a searcher who has good topical knowledge, good knowledge of the information problem being tackled, and a clear view of what information is required may have very specific criteria in mind for the end result (Kuhlthau, 1991). A good retrieval result, therefore, is related to the searcher's expectations of the search.

Interactive systems can help searchers construct good queries in various ways. Options include automatically modifying the searcher's query by relevance or pseudo-relevance feedback or, more radically, by replacing the searcher's query through query substitution (Jones, Rey, Madani, & Greiner, 2006; Kraft, Chang, Maghoul, & Kumar, 2006). Other options allow queries to develop through interaction, as in faceted browsing interfaces. Yet others are more interactive—either offering query suggestions to searchers or allowing searchers to be more precise in how they construct queries by developing complex querying languages or using advanced search features.

Complex Query Languages

Complex, or structured, query languages can facilitate more precise access to complex objects. Complex languages can be useful where the searcher wants to be very precise through the use of a detailed query (e.g., Pirkola, Puolamäki, & Järvelin, 2003) or where the data themselves are complex, for example, music data, which comprise different attributes such as timbre, tone, and pitch (Downie, 2004), each of which might be expressed as individual query components. Niemi, Junkkari, Järvelin, and Viita (2004) provide an example of the latter approach.

Structured query languages have attracted attention through the increased use of XML as a general description language for Web information (Chinenyanga & Kushmerick, 2001; Führ & Großjohann, 2001). Evidence for the success of complex querying languages is mixed. Järvelin and Kekäläinen (2000) have shown that structuring the content of the query is generally beneficial and that good structures can facilitate additional techniques such as query expansion. However, query languages that allow for mixing content and structural information about the document are often not easy for searchers to create and, as explained by Kamps, Marx, de Rijke, and Sigurbjörnsson (2005) and O'Keefe and Trotman (2004), query languages that are difficult to conceptualize can lead to more semantic mistakes within the query, especially if the searcher is not aware of the document structures being searched.

"Advanced" Search

An alternative to complex query languages is to offer form-based support in which searchers are asked questions about the material they wish to retrieve. Answering these questions, always assuming the searchers can answer them, produces a more sophisticated and precise query than a simple keyword request. The most common instantiation of interactive support is the advanced search features of search engines, which allow for the inclusion of metadata reflecting non-content aspects of the objects being searched. Google and AltaVista, for example, offer date range, file type, and domain restrictions among their advanced search features. Typically these restrict the objects returned in some way, cutting down the number of results rather than prompting the searcher with new ideas for queries or the content of queries. As such, these search facilities may not seem very advanced but I retain this term as the one most commonly advertised by search engine interfaces. Typically, search engines will also offer query operators such as phrase matching and Boolean-like operators ("all of these words," "none of these words," etc.).

Interestingly, the intended effect of these operators does not always match their actual effect on retrieval (Eastman & Jansen, 2003), meaning the searcher may have problems using these operators effectively. The effect of any particular operator is dependent on the implementation of the individual system, which can vary. Such lack of consistency between operators reflects earlier concerns about the usability of Boolean IR systems (Borgman, 1996). Topi and Lucas (2005a, 2005b) suggest that interfaces that support a greater number of query operators and independent training on using such operators *generally* help in improving query quality; however, this improvement is not consistent and it can be difficult to predict what training will help. Of course, most Web searchers do not have any training in online searching.

It is commonly reported that searchers often do not use advanced search features, such as Boolean operators or relevance feedback, to any great extent (e.g., Spink & Jansen, 2004). This could be because they do not understand how to use them, are not aware that they are available, or because the actual support is not viewed as being useful. However, even if the utilization is low, the fact that people try these features suggests that users often want *something* to support query formulation. Whatever the reason for the low use of advanced search features, we have to consider different styles of interactive query support or automating this support to be in the area of query intention analysis.

Asking for More Information

A common finding in Web studies is that users enter short queries, perhaps one to three query terms, which may require immediate reformulation. Belkin et al. (2003) consider the degree to which this might be a problem and how to persuade users to enter longer and more effective queries. Simply asking users for more information on their tasks helps them enter longer queries and results in shorter searches, although with equal effectiveness. Kelly et al. in a robust follow-up ask searchers for more information regarding their prior knowledge of the topic, the intended purpose of the information being sought, and additional search terms (Kelly, Deepak, & Fu, 2005). The results show such an approach—

simply asking for more information—to be very successful, outperforming pseudo-feedback approaches.

The key here is that searchers often know more about what information they want than they provide in a query. By asking good questions, interfaces that prompt searchers to enter more information can improve retrieval effectiveness. Determining which questions are good, however, can vary according to the task being performed or the domain being searched (Toms, 2002); and specialized interfaces for searching within individual domains may be more appropriate than generic one-size-fits-all interfaces.

Offering Suggestions

The system itself can offer suggestions for query creation. Google's Suggest feature proposes queries using a form of predictive text entry. As the searcher types a query, the system tries to match it to previously submitted queries. White and Marchionini (2007) attempted to replicate and evaluate Google's Suggest facility. Their comparison was similar to Koenemann and Belkin's (1996) investigation of the effects of offering query suggestions either before or after running a query. As with the Koenemann and Belkin study, offering query suggestions before running a query improves results, but not all suggestions prove to be good suggestions. Nevertheless, such a mechanism would seem to be a useful step in supporting query creation.

Query Reformulation

Queries are often reformulated by searchers after an initial, perhaps tentative, query has been run. Interactive reformulation—where the searcher controls how the query is reformulated—is a core area for IIR and a stream of research has investigated how to select good reformulation suggestions. Recently, the trend has been toward more complex refinement suggestions instead of single query terms. Kruschwitz and Al-Bakour (2005) automatically extract concepts, essentially phrases, to provide a domain model of a corpus. These concepts are mixed with terms from top-ranked documents (the terms providing new information not present in the domain model) for presentation to the searcher. The results are mixed but clearly show that the participants are willing at least to experiment with the novel interface. However, searcher attitude is important. Some participants appreciate the attempt to support query reformulation but others appear to have a low tolerance of inappropriate reformulation suggestions.

Query reformulation is supported on some Web search engines but less than the advanced search features mentioned earlier. Although Web search engines are very influential and contribute heavily to developing people's experiences of searching, the actual mechanisms are often not described or evaluated in the public literature and we must infer their design principles. There are some exceptions; for example Anick (2003) examines terminological support—suggesting key phrases derived from a pseudo-relevance feedback approach—on AltaVista. This implementation is similar in spirit to Koenemann and Belkin's (1996) notion of transparent interactive query expansion—showing expansion units for user selection after a query has been run. In this case the phrases are based on linguistic analysis, not derived from user-identified relevant documents. A major finding is that people use this terminological support, continue to use it in later searches, and generally use it successfully. However, most query reformulations continue to be manual.

As with many large-scale analyses, these findings are based on log analysis, using cookies to track individual users; deeper analysis shows that people can become confused about the nature and role of the phrases offered. This confusion can be resolved in part by providing more information about the reformulations (Ruthven, 2002) but a limiting factor in any interface is screen space. In Web or commercial interfaces, extra screen space may come at the expense of advertisements (hence revenue), requiring developers to be even more imaginative in deciding how to support searchers.

Bruza, McArthur, and Dennis (2000) compare interfaces that offer linguistically well-formed phrases for refinement with more traditional search interfaces and make two points generalizable to any method of suggesting refinements. First, although refinement suggestions can make searchers aware of useful search concepts, searchers also must realize the benefits of such refinement. That is, searchers will need to understand why refining a query could be a useful undertaking (Dennis, McArthur, & Bruza, 1998). Support for assessing the effect of any particular refinement on a search would also be useful (Ruthven, 2003). Second, a given individual interactive technique may lead to more effective searching; it also needs to be attractive to searchers—a technique that entails more work may not be used unless the benefits are very clear (Bruza et al., 2000).

Phrases are not the only unit that can be offered to searchers, although they are easy for searchers to interpret. Historically single terms have been the most studied means for interactive query expansion. Efthimiadis (2000) demonstrates the general effectiveness of interactive query suggestion and expansion and also its power in stimulating new ideas for search requests. D. He and Demner-Fushman (2004) also indicate that interactive query refinement is useful in cases where few relevant documents are available. This strength of interactive query refinement—its ability to support difficult search tasks—is endorsed by Fowkes and Beaulieu (2000) who show interactive refinement to be more effective and appropriate for complex tasks. Sihvonen and Vakkari (2004), investigating suggestions from a thesaurus rather than relevance information, find an increased use of terms for difficult tasks. This study indicates strongly that topical knowledge improves thesaurus use in that searchers are better at selecting which aspects of a topic are important and are more informed about which terms are likely to be appropriate.

How to offer reformulation suggestions has been less investigated, with most interface approaches simply presenting lists of suggestions. These may be structured in some way, for example using facets (Hearst, 2006b), but generally do not support much decision making on the quality or appropriateness of the suggestions. Rieh and Xie (2006), while examining query reformulation, note that most interaction takes place at the surface level; that is dealing with queries and results rather than deeper cognitive aspects such as searcher intent or attitude. However, the intent behind formulation is obviously important and needs support. Using a log analysis and original coding scheme, Rieh and Xie attempt to categorize query reformulation behavior and find, perhaps not surprisingly, that content reformation is most common and strict synonym replacement is rare. Specialization of queries and parallel movements, tackling different aspects of a query, are much more common—the latter being essentially multitasking (see Spink et al., 2006); this reinforces the call for more interactive support for this type of searching. If we can reliably recognize different types of query reformulation behavior, then it would be useful to see if we can predict query reformulations that support this behavior and make these suggestions clearer at the interface level.

An alternative to interactive query reformulation is, of course, to provide automatic support to refine queries, using either some form of knowledge-based query reformulation (Liu, Lieberman, & Selker, 2002; Pu, Chuang, & Yang, 2002) or techniques such as pseudo-relevance feedback (Crouch, Crouch, Chen, & Holtz, 2002). True user relevance feedback—searchers giving explicit feedback on the relevance of retrieved items—has remained popular, especially for non-textual objects such as images where the required objects are easy to recognize although perhaps harder to describe. There has been less work recently on the usability of relevance feedback, as opposed to the underlying algorithms, but also much more work on implicit feedback, to be discussed later.

Surrogates

After submitting a search request one is usually presented with a set of results; an important aspect of searching is assessing these results. For some objects, such as images, the complete objects themselves are displayed and assessed. More often surrogates are employed—keyframes for video; sentences, titles, or abstracts for documents; thumbnails for Web pages; and so on—and these can be created manually (document titles) or automatically (such as summaries).

The design and role of these surrogates within searching is of interest to IIR, especially to facilitate quick review of retrieval results and access to useful information. Novel elicitation methods such as eyetracking allow us to learn more about how people use such surrogates in searching. Lorigo et al. (2006) indicate that, in more than half of the Web searches they investigated, users reformulate queries based on scanning the surrogates without examining any pages and that navigational (Web site-finding) queries are often answered by surrogates alone. Surrogates can be useful in these cases if searchers are willing to accept occasional false hits. False hits in this case are pages appearing to be relevant because the surrogate misrepresents a page's content; this can arise from surrogates being created from cached pages (automatically generated surrogates) or deliberate misrepresentation of the page's content (Lynch, 2001). False hits can occur with most types of surrogates and also in non-Web environments; for example, Ruthven, Tombros, and Jose (2001) report a similar finding with query-biased summaries. The quick response speeds of most search engines may mean that such mistakes are not important because people can recover from them with little cost.

Summarization approaches are particularly popular for creating surrogates (e.g., Chuang & Yang 2000; Tombros & Sanderson, 1998; White, Jose, & Ruthven, 2003). Most summaries are text-based, although summaries are also possible for non-textual and mixed media, such as music videos (Xu, Shao, Maddage, & Kankanhalli, 2005). In Web research several studies have compared the relative effectiveness of the standard text-based summaries and summaries that incorporate more visual aspects commonly found in Web pages. Woodruff, Faulring, Rosenholtz, Morrison, and Pirolli (2001) report that different types of surrogates work well for different types of search task. However, some form of aggregate surrogate, incorporating Web page thumbnails and text, is best for most tasks and appears to be a safe default. Dziadosz and Chandrasekar (2002) also find that certain types of surrogates work better for certain tasks (e.g., thumbnails can be less effective than textual summaries when searching for unknown items) and report that the presence of both thumbnails and text lead to more predictions of relevant material but also more incorrect predictions of relevance.

This issue of prediction is important; a good surrogate should allow searchers to make informed decisions about the content of the object being represented. Vechtomova and Karamuftuoglu (2006) examine the quality of query-biased sentences as surrogates: assessors being asked to predict the decisions they would make on the relevance of documents based on sentence surrogates. Assessors are generally fairly good at predicting relevance, although the actual results may vary depending on the quality of the sentence selection mechanism. In a separate study Ruthven, Baillie, and Elsweiler (in press) show that sentences, in this case leading sentences from newspapers, can result in good prediction of relevance but this depends on the personal characteristics of the individual making the assessment. When given the choice, some assessors would rather not make a prediction and variation in characteristics such as the assessor's knowledge level can lead to very poor predictions. However, Bell and Ruthven (2004) show that sentence surrogates are useful in reducing the complexity of searches by allowing searchers to see an overview of the retrieved material without having to access individual documents serially.

Where summaries are particularly useful is in the area of mobile IR, or more precisely IR performed on hand-held devices with small screens and requiring different methods of information presentation. Thumbnails can be used here as well as typical text summaries, which may (Buyukkokten, Kalijuvee, Garcia-Molina, Paepcke, & Winograd, 2002) or may not use information on the structure of the document being summarized (Sweeney & Crestani, 2006).

Sweeney and Crestani (2006) point to an interesting distinction between effectiveness and preference. In their study of optimal summary length for handheld device presentation they find that people prefer longer summaries on larger devices but this does not make them more accurate at using summaries to predict relevance. Radev, Jing, Styś, and Tam (2004), also looking at summary length, find that assessors can be in agreement on the most important sentences in a summary, but longer summaries can, in certain cases, reduce agreement. As summaries become longer less important sentences are included. Document retrieval provides a similar analogy. Typical IR systems will first retrieve documents upon whose relevance most people would agree followed by more marginally relevant documents (unanimity is lacking) (Voorhees, 2000). What makes a good surrogate, then, depends on the searcher's context.

Evaluation of summarization systems follows two approaches: so-called intrinsic evaluations measure the quality of summaries directly (e.g., by comparison to a manually created *ideal* summary) and extrinsic methods evaluate how well the summaries support a person or system in some predefined task such as searching (Mani, 2001). The latter is more of interest to current work within IIR although intrinsic tasks are used in the annual Document Understanding Workshops (duc.nist.gov). Evaluating what makes an effective summary or surrogate for searching is not trivial; the idea of a good summary depends very much on the role the summary is intended to play within the search process. The authors of manually created summaries or abstracts perhaps had a similar aim—to construct one good, objective summary that would represent the content of an object for all potential (and unknown) readers and with unknown search tasks and personal differences. Such a summary may be sub-optimal for all readers but would be usable by them all.

We could argue that what searchers really want is a surrogate that will help them make decisions about the represented material: Should I read this document? Can I safely ignore it? Is it different from these other retrieved documents? These decisions may be very subjective and personal. As we can automatically create many different representations of the same object, we can potentially create different surrogates at different points in a search and for different purposes. White and Ruthven's (2006) interface for Web searching presents a layered approach to using multiple surrogates. In their interface, shallow sentence surrogates are used to give an overview of the retrieved set of pages and more detailed surrogates are employed to drill down into searcher-selected parts of the page content. Such an approach is useful in increasing the effectiveness of a search and, as a side effect, in characterizing stages within a search based on the level of use of different surrogates (White, Ruthven, & Jose, 2005).

Surrogates need not always be representations of a single object but can be representations of multiple objects. Multi-document summarization (e.g., Harabagiu & Lacatusu, 2005; McKeown, Passonneau, Elson, Nenkova, & Hirschberg, 2005; Radev et al., 2004) is a popular technique although the evaluation is decidedly non-trivial. McKeown et al. (2005) compared a number of methods for creating summaries; the results indicate the positive effect of high-quality summaries in a task-based evaluation.

Maña-López, DeBuenga, and Gómez-Hidalgo (2004) use a mixture of techniques centered on instance recall tasks: finding as many aspects of a topic as possible. Their approach also combines summaries of multiple document sets and the results show some behavioral improvements—more useful interaction may have taken place because of the combined summarization and clustering. More importantly, they indicate that such a supportive interface, one that structures access to information, helps searchers who have little familiarity with the search topic.

Surrogates for specific collections can be very inventive. For selected books, Amazon offers an intriguing range of surrogates (all of which can be used as search keys) such as a concordance of the 100 most frequently used words in the book, a list of statistically improbable phrases (phrases common to an individual book but uncommon in a collection of books) and capitalized phrases (phrases consisting of capitalized words occurring often within the text). These kinds of surrogates may, or may not, be as useful for searching and assessment as traditional surrogates. However, their presence does add to the sense of fun and engagement with the material being assessed. Norman (2004) points to such emotional appeal as a core factor in the success of search engines such as Google.

Clustering, Categorization, and Browsing

Surrogates not only are useful to help searchers assess individual objects but also to understand relationships among a collection of items or to structure their investigation of an information space. Such approaches typically assist a searcher either by presenting information before searching to aid request creation or after searching to aid interpretation of the results or provide suggestions for search refinement. For both tasks, clustering and categorization are popular approaches. Although the terminology is not always used consistently, categorization typically refers to the manual or automatic allocation of objects to predefined labels, whereas clustering generally refers to automatic groupings of objects through inter-object similarity.

One of the advantages of offering searchers information on the collection being searched *before* any other interaction takes place is that searchers may find browsing easier than producing search terms (Borgman, Hirsch, Walter, & Gallagher, 1995). Browsing is usually initiated by some information display; services such as Yahoo! (dir.yahoo.com) and Wikipedia (en.wikipedia.org) offer browsable categories as well as freetext searching to inform searchers of the location of additional information. A particularly useful form of categorization is faceted search (Yee, Swearingen, Li, & Hearst, 2003) in which metadata is organized into categories to allow searchers to explore objects interactively and drill down to an area, or set of objects, of interest (Hearst, 2006b). Such faceted approaches also facilitate the creation of complex queries through natural interaction and exploration (Hearst, Elliot, English, Sinha, Swearingen, & Yee, 2002). In situations where the searcher is less certain of the information required or is less informed about the information space, such as the area of exploratory search (White, Kules, Drucker, & Schraefel, 2006), categorization and browsing could be particularly useful to help the searcher structure the investigation.

As summarized by Hearst (2006a), clustering and categorization have advantages and disadvantages. Clustering requires no manual input, it can adapt to any genre of data, and there is a range of good, well-understood algorithms for implementation. Unfortunately, the labels assigned to clusters may not be semantically intuitive and, depending on the algorithm used, the clusters may be badly fragmented. Depending on the nature of the clustering—what objects are being clustered and how many are being clustered—clustering algorithms can also result in interaction delays. Categorization, on the other hand, generally results in superior quality groupings of objects, has clearer and better motivated semantic relationships, and is popular with end users (Hearst, 2006a). A drawback to categorization approaches is the need for an external categorization scheme, although some work has examined automatically creating hierarchies of concepts (Joho, Sanderson, & Beaulieu, 2004).

Clustering approaches can be used to select better sets of objects for presentation to the searcher; work in this area has shown the effectiveness of clustering approaches that use the query as an additional input (e.g., Iwayama, 2000; Tombros, Villa, & van Rijsbergen, 2002) rather than clustering independently of the query. Tombros et al. also report that query-biased clustering approaches can improve retrieval effectiveness over standard inverted file searches (Tombros et al., 2002). However, the interface, in particular the intuitiveness of the information display, is important in maximizing these benefits; a searcher needs to be able to understand the relationships being presented by the clustering to avoid losing the potential benefits of the clustered organization (Wu, Fuller, & Wilkinson, 2001b).

This use of clustering and categorization for displaying search results is also helpful. In particular, clustering for visualization—automatically detecting similarities between objects for graphical representations—is popular. Where the objects being clustered are easy to assess for relevance, such as images or video key-frames, the objects themselves are usually displayed (e.g., Heesch & Rüger, 2004). Where the objects are more complex, clusters will typically have some form of surrogate to label the grouping and aid the searcher's understanding of the grouping (Roussinov & Chen, 2001). Visualizations can be useful but can also create usability problems if there is insufficient support for navigation and searchers' decisions about their own search process (Wiesman, van den Herik, & Hasman, 2004). However, solid work has been done to investigate usability issues in category systems based on a searcher's criteria for using categories (e.g., Hearst, 2006b). Systems such as Kartoo (www.kartoo.com) that integrate multiple interactive features—clustering and visualization, summarization, and query refinement suggestions—may be more robust in supporting the searcher's decision making. Toms (2002) evaluated a novel interface to Google that combined Google's query interface with its directory categories. Their subjects preferred different interaction models for different types of searches (in this case, searches in different domains), with travel or shopping searches favoring the category-based approach and research-style searches favoring querying.

Although clustering can be used for visualization, clusters are more commonly used to facilitate other types of interactive support. For example, both the Wisenut (www.wisenut.com) and Vivisimo (vivisimo.com) Web search engines use clustering approaches to extract and display query refinements. Käki's (2005) Findex system offers categories with which to filter search results; a longitudinal study indicates that searchers will use categories, although not as a default mechanism. However, even if the categories were used only in a minority of searches, the categories could help in more difficult searches—searches where the queries are poor. In Käki's interface, categories are displayed alongside search results; in an earlier study Chen and Dumais (2000) use categories to structure the display of search results. Their study also hints at the utility of categories for more difficult searches; this is more readily apparent in a later study (Dumais, Cutrell, & Chen, 2001).

Visualization

As noted, visualization of information can help the searcher understand relationships among objects or sets of objects. Visualizations can be useful at many different levels. Visual representations of documents, for example, can aid the searcher by graphically representing some information about the content of the document. These representations can be representations of the document such as Hearst's (1995) TileBars, which represent the shift in a document's topical structure; representations that are relative to the query, such as Reid and Dunlop's (2003) RelevanceLinkBar; or within document representations, that is, visual representations to aid searchers as they read a document (Harper, Koychev, Sun, & Pirie, 2004). Although the mechanisms behind these visual representations are different, they share a common aim of helping searchers find which documents are most likely to be useful, identifying where in a document relevant information may be located, and giving the searcher short cuts to accessing the most useful parts of a document. With highly structured documents, especially those that have an explicitly pre-defined structure, such as plays, even more complex visual representations are possible. Crestani, Vegas, and de la Fuente (2002) present a layered ball metaphor by exploiting a rich collection-specific structure.

Visualization of multiple objects can be useful in representing relationships among objects, grouping together images with similar colors, for example, or linking the content of multiple Web sites through shared concepts as in the case of Kartoo. One particular use of visualization is to help understand similarities and differences among complex objects. Liu, Zhao, and Yi (2002) examined visualization approaches for comparing Web sites. Web sites are complex objects consisting of multiple pages and are difficult to compare using query-driven approaches. Visualizations can help by presenting overviews of Web site content, showing where information is located in a Web site, and presenting comparative views, showing which Web site contains more information on a topic or covers more areas of interest.

How information is visualized is usually decided by the system designer. However, approaches that allow searchers to manipulate and organize information while they are searching can also be useful. Interfaces such as the pile metaphor suggested by Harper and Kelly (2006)—searchers develop piles of documents as they search—help searchers by visualizing what aspects of a search they have covered and how much material they have collected. Buchanan, Blandford, Thimbleby, and Jones (2004) also find spatial displays and metaphors useful when searchers can organize their own search activities and outputs. Such visualizations are not restricted to being passive displays of information, as these interactions with the visualizations can be used to mine useful information about the searcher's interests. Heesch and Rüger (2004) use a searcher's interactions with image visualizations, for example, as a way of neatly gaining information for relevance feedback.

Visualizations may also help searchers remember search interactions. In complex searches involving a series of interactions it may be difficult for searchers to remember what objects they have already seen or where they saw a particular piece of information. Harper and Kelly's pile metaphor allows searchers to organize relevant material as it is encountered. Often, however, a previously viewed document is realized to be useful and the searcher must backtrack to re-find it. Milic-Frayling, Jones, Rodden, Smyth, Blackwell, and Sommerer

(2004) consider interface support for such backtracking on Web search engines. Their system demonstrates how even such an apparently simple concept as going back to a previous page is far from trivial and can benefit from good interface design. Campbell's (1999) path-based browser also supports session-based searching through the use of retrieval paths, which visualize the order in which objects were selected and viewed. This interface was particularly successful in allowing for multiple paths, each representing a different thread in the retrieval session.

As noted, visualizations can be applied to many stages of the interactive retrieval process. As with browsing approaches, the strength of visualization is allowing people to identify useful relationships or relevant information rather than having to recall pertinent keywords as in the querying approaches.

These techniques can be applied to most data sets and used for most retrieval tasks. Recently, new research directions have opened up to deal with novel retrieval tasks and methods of retrieval. In the remainder of this section, I discuss three in detail: support for re-finding information, part-of-object retrieval, and task specific support.

Re-Finding Information

The ability to store so much information electronically on personal computers means that we have to manage the information in such a way as to be able to re-find it later. Our ability to manage our information space constructively and our willingness to devote time to creating useful structures such as folder hierarchies are doubtful (e.g., Whittaker & Sidner, 1996). Hence the attention on how personal re-finding should be supported.

Re-finding personal information is part of personal information management (PIM) and covers the retrieval of information previously stored or accessed by an individual searcher. PIM was covered in detail in an *ARIST* chapter by Jones (2007), so here I summarize some of the features of PIM as they relate to IIR.

Re-retrieval is different from most retrieval scenarios in that what is being retrieved is not new information but information objects one has previously encountered and therefore can be partially recalled. Hence, even though the queries put to PIM systems may appear similar to those put to standard search engines, they describe what one remembers about an information object and are not a description of the information one requires. Features that can be remembered and used for searching may not be features typically supported by standard interfaces, for example, temporal information or information on previous use. Rodden and Wood (2003), in a study on personal image management, show that people can remember many different features of images (context, color, objects, semantic associations), which can be used as query components. Gonçalves and Jorge (2004), in a study based on textual documents rather than images, also indicate the range of features that people can remember including time, task, and related documents. In their QUILL system, Gonçalves and Jorge (2006) acknowledge such contextual clues by allowing searchers to tell stories (e.g., narratives describing the documents they would like retrieved). Contextual elements in the narratives, such as time or authorship information, were used to trigger retrievals. Apart from being easy to use, the interface increased the length of queries (the narratives) submitted to the system.

Personal information objects are more heavily influenced by their surrounding context than are non-personal objects. The surrounding context can contain elements from the context of the information object's creation (e.g., personal documents), their access (e.g., Web bookmarks), or their use and reuse. Such context can be used to aid retrieval as in the Haystack system (Adar, Kargar, & Stein, 1999). Successfully re-finding an object often depends on a searcher being able to step out of his current task context and remember previous contexts in which he stored or used an object—"What was I doing, or thinking, when I stored that e-mail?" How people think about their personal objects can affect the kind of retrieval support that might be effective.

Boardman and Sasse (2004) note that different personal media have different characteristics that affect how people store and retrieve objects. Bookmarks, for example, are often seen as being less personal than e-mail and as being pointers to information rather than containers of information. E-mails and files and folders, on the other hand, are often seen as more personal. Boardman and Sasse describe how people use different strategies for managing different media types. This raises the question of whether we want different tools for different media or unified interface support for all personal information objects, regardless of media type. Historically, the preference may have been for the former—media-dependent systems—but more recently the trend is toward comprehensive systems that work across all genres of personal information. There is a range of desktop search systems such as Google's (desktop. google.com) or MSN's Desktop Search (toolbar.msn.com). A common and popular theme in these systems is to relieve the searcher of having to remember *where* an item may be stored (Cutrell, Robbins, Dumais, & Sarin, 2006).

Elsweiler, Ruthven, and Jones (2005) describe an interface for retrieval of personal images, which they claim exploits features of human memory to aid the re-retrieval of personal information. Their interface displays *clues* on context, stored as object annotations, to help people remember additional features of the images they want to retrieve and also create better queries. As the searcher interacts with the information objects, the interface prompts the user with clues on previous contexts. The authors claim that the interface can help create so-called "retrieval journeys," one piece of information aiding in the recall of other useful contextually related information.

Dumais et al. (2004) employ the unified systems approach in their system, Stuff I've Seen, which presents a unified index over all information objects stored on a desktop machine. At the interface, Stuff I've Seen shows contextual information such as file type, date of access, and author. A large-scale, longitudinal evaluation of Stuff I've Seen showed positive results especially for hard-to-find items and vague recollections.

Cutrell et al. (2006) expand the Stuff I've Seen unified data approach but consider more of the user interface issues involved in facilitating access to personal information archives. As with Elsweiler et al., their system, Phlat, exploits the idea that people may remember various attributes of objects such as date, file type, or author information. Supporting searching by these attributes helps make the process more flexible. Phlat also allows for user-defined tags representing searchable concepts, which can be used to filter objects in searching, although at present it allows tagging only of objects already retrieved. Phlat's filtering and tagging allow searchers to create complex queries very simply.

Part-of-Retrieval

Information objects can be complex. Entities such as Web pages may be constructed from more than one component (images, tables, text) whereas objects such as documents, video, or speech frequently have some internal structure: video samples can be deconstructed into component scenes, documents into sections, speech into speakers. The complexity of these objects raises challenges for searchers; documents may be long and contain multiple topics, meaning that the searcher may have to perform extra work to find relevant material contained within them. Surrogates aid searchers in making initial assessments—I may want to investigate an object in more detail and summarization techniques, in particular, permit a quick overview of content but, as documents become longer or more complex, summaries may be less useful.

However, explicit structures within retrievable objects can be utilized to facilitate quick access to complex objects and an alternative to whole object retrieval is to allow the retrieval system to deal with sub-object units, returning parts of objects instead of complete ones. The two most common media types for sub-object retrieval are video and text. Smeaton (2004) has elegantly summarized the retrieval of video components including interactive video browsing and retrieval, so in this section I concentrate on retrieval of document components.

Previously, passage retrieval—retrieving the best window of text (Callan, 1994)—was the most common technique for retrieving parts of documents. Currently, thanks to the INEX initiative, structured document retrieval is receiving more attention (inex.is.informatik.uni-duisburg.de). Structured document retrieval, unlike simple passage retrieval, acknowledges the author-defined structure of the document (sections, subsections, title, etc.) to select and display the best component of the document to the searcher; the best component in INEX is the one that covers as many aspects of the query as possible with the minimum of non-relevant information.

Structured document retrieval raises a number of interesting retrieval and interaction questions. When searching, does the notion of the best component change if the search situation changes? How should an interface relate different components from the same document in an intuitive way for the searcher? Recent research in interactive retrieval from complex objects such as structured documents has followed three approaches: first, visualization approaches such as that of Harper, Muresan, Liu, Koychev, Wettschereck, and Wiratunga (2004), which aim to help searchers assess complex objects, in particular navigating to the most relevant parts of objects; second, employing complex querying languages, which, as noted before, can help searchers specify more precisely how the content and structure of an object should be used to retrieve objects (e.g., Kamps et al., 2005); and third, good interface development can help people interact with complex objects.

Research in this area is heavily influenced by behavioral studies of how people interact with structured documents. Reid, Lalmas, Finesilver, and Hertzum (2006a, 2006b) make a useful distinction between the concepts of most relevant component and the best entry points (BEPs) for accessing documents. Whereas the most relevant component may be the part of the document that contains the most relevant information, BEPs are the best place for a searcher to start investigating an individual document. A searcher may, for example, obtain an answer from a short, relevant section but prefer to be shown the containing section (BEP) to contextualize the information given in the relevant section. Reid et al. (2006b) propose different types of BEPs. A container BEP, for example, is a component that contains at least one relevant object, whereas a context BEP is a component that, although not containing any relevant information itself, provides contextual information for a subsequent relevant object.

Reid et al. (2006a, 2006b) empirically investigate these BEPs and general information search behavior in a number of small studies. Although the BEP types are shown to be not useful, it is clear that searchers themselves distinguish, conceptually and behaviorally, the notion of relevance and BEP. Searchers grasped the difference between relevant objects and the interactive steps necessary to access and recognize these objects. Furthermore, which BEP is seen as being useful depended on the search task, and to an extent, the nature of the data being searched.

This behavioral study of interaction in structured document retrieval continues in the Interactive Track of INEX (Tombros, Malik, & Larsen, 2005), still concentrating more on behavior than interface support. Investigating search behavior provides insights into possibly useful interface designs. For example, once users have investigated one component, there is a tendency to examine components of similar granularity (e.g., section followed by section). Whether this is because of preferred size of component or because some components are more useful at different points in the search is not clear. Knowledge of where components are located within documents is usefully presented at the interface level, and information on overlapping components from the same document may reduce redundancy in searching. However, as Betsi, Lalmas, and Tombros (2006) acknowledge, searchers often want different forms of interactive support for different reasons—they want relevant sections from different documents, especially if one document cannot completely satisfy the information need, but also want information on how components are linked within an individual document.

Research on novel interfaces within this area have typically exploited the structure of documents either by displaying their tables of contents (Malik, Klas, Führ, Larsen, & Tombros, 2006; Szlavik, Tombros, & Lalmas, 2006) or presenting location information as part of the surrogates in the results lists (Gövert, Führ, Abolhassani, & Großjohann, 2003).

Task-Specific Support

As retrieval tasks become more specialized and better defined, so too do the systems to support these tasks. IR now provides solutions for a range of retrieval problems, not just reference retrieval. Dedicated initiatives such as TREC have enabled the development of specialized retrieval systems and also facilitated work on interfaces for specialist retrieval tasks. As a result, there are systems for question answering, topic detection, topic distillation (selecting a good set of home pages for a given topic), large scale retrieval, and cross-language retrieval.

Specialized retrieval systems fall into two broad groups. First, we have systems that perform a specialized retrieval task. The underlying system is designed to handle particular data (e.g., genomic retrieval or people-finding systems) or the task itself is specialized and involves more than simply retrieval (e.g., topic detection, novelty detection, task distillation). Second, there are systems where the interaction is specialized in some way (e.g., structured document retrieval). Naturally this is a rough categorization, as specialized tasks often require specialized interaction and specialized interaction often results from a nonstandard retrieval model.

Each of these retrieval tasks necessitates a different type of retrieval system and also influences the type of searcher interaction that is appropriate or necessary. Cross-language retrieval interfaces often require support for user querying and document analysis (Hansen & Karlgren, 2005), whereas question answering will require support for contextualizing the typically short answers given by such a system (Lin, Quan, Sinha, Bakshi, Huynh, Katz, et al., 2003). These specialized systems contribute to both research themes—automating search processes by developing systems to help searchers perform specific tasks and improving interaction by developing novel interfaces for such tasks.

Wu, Muresan, McLean, Tang, Wilkinson, Li, et al. (2004) consider topic distillation, that is, sourcing and creating a list of resources that can be assembled into a single page to act as an entry point to a topic. In such a task, Web site home pages will be preferred to low level pages, and relevant information may be split across resources rather than contained within one site (Bhavnani, 2005). Wu et al. tackled the general question of whether a dedicated interface to a topic distillation task would perform better than traditional ranked-list interfaces. The results are inconclusive. Although participants tend to prefer a dedicated search interface, employing a specialized search engine improves search results. In a separate study on question answering, however, Wu, Fuller, and Wilkinson (2001a) show that a specialized interface can increase both searcher performance and preference.

Specialized systems increasingly cater to both information organization and retrieval tasks. Swan and Allan (2000) present an interface for browsing events in news articles. Their timeline-based interface supports discovery activities (what events are covered in the corpus, how long these events have been discussed in the corpus, which are surprising events) and organization (which terms are associated with each event, which events are most important) that may be important to people browsing news events. Smith (2002) tackles retrieval of historical data using maps to help visualize important information and recent work on geographical information retrieval has relied heavily on visualization techniques for searching (Jones & Purves, 2005).

Unfortunately, novel interfaces for specialized tasks often lack a corresponding user evaluation, concentrating only on algorithmic measures of effectiveness. A recurring question remains: What types of novel evaluation metrics are appropriate for new retrieval solutions? Wu et al. exemplify attempts to determine whether interfaces that are designed to fit a specialist task can outperform standard retrieval interfaces. The question is not as trivial as it might seem, as people do learn strategies in order to use familiar interfaces for new tasks. As Turpin and Hersh (2001) point out, people can compensate for sub-optimal retrieval systems by adopting different interaction styles. Similarly, as Muramatsu and Pratt (2001) claim, humans are very adaptable and can operate successfully even with a certain lack of understanding of how retrieval systems actually operate.

Automating Search Processes

The second theme of this chapter, automating search processes, deals with research that attempts to provide technical support for search activities that searchers find either difficult or time-consuming. This involves a wide range of solutions, from traditional approaches such as automatic query reformulation and relevance feedback to newer techniques such as collaborative filtering. Conventional techniques like relevance feedback have been treated in the research literature for decades and basic questions surrounding their use (how to use relevance information to modify a query, how to encourage searchers to engage in feedback, what relevance evidence is useful, and so on) are still being actively investigated, with the questions changing both subtly and radically as the environment in which their use changes.

Investigating how to deploy relevance feedback successfully in Web search environments has opened up new lines of research on the use of implicit search modeling. The large scale use of Web search engines (and related usage data) has also facilitated work on searcher classification, query intention analysis, and prediction of relevant items. Older research questions are still relevant to new IR environments because, even if contexts change, the problems faced by searchers often do not. Creating queries can be difficult whether we are searching bibliographic databases or the Web. Web search engine query constructors can exhibit the same usability problems as Boolean operators, and assessing relevance is affected by the reasons for the search, irrespective of the medium being searched.

In this section I select four main areas for discussion reflecting the increased attention given to them in the recent literature: implicit feedback, query intention analysis, personalization, and automated assistance.

Implicit Feedback

Explicit approaches to relevance feedback require a searcher to make explicit an assessment of (non-)relevance on retrieved information objects and also to request the system to use such assessments. These approaches rely on obtaining sufficient assessments to generalize a good model of the searcher's underlying information need. The notion of sufficient information, the amount of information required to produce a good generalized model, will generally be topic- and collection-dependent.

Early experiments indicated that standard methods of relevance feedback could perform reasonably well with small numbers of feedback documents; at least, small amounts of relevant information were better than no relevance information (Spärck Jones, 1979). However, the amount of evidence supplied by searchers is still sparse and feedback approaches that have access to multiple examples of relevant information tend to outperform those optimizing very little information (Smucker & Allan, 2006). Without sufficient relevance evidence, the system may make weak query modification decisions resulting in poor effectiveness and—potentially worse from an interactive perspective—low levels of confidence in relevance feedback as a useful technique (Beaulieu & Jones, 1998; Ruthven, 2002).

One method of overcoming the lack of evidence available from traditional explicit approaches is to exploit *implicit* evidence as a substitute for explicit feedback. The use of implicit evidence is not new in itself; however, the approach has gathered momentum due partly to the ease with which Web browsers, in particular, can be adapted or extended to capture such evidence. Recent research in the use of implicit evidence has centered around three questions: What evidence about a searcher's interaction is useful to know, how reliable is implicit evidence, and what can we do with such evidence to provide better retrieval or better interaction?

Implicit Evidence and Indicators of Interest

Evidence for implicit feedback could potentially be any evidence gained from the system–searcher interaction, including physiological evidence such as heart rates or brain wave tracing. Evidence is commonly restricted to that available from the human–system interaction. Types of evidence and proposed categorizations are summarized by Claypool, Le, Waseda, and Brown (2001); Oard and Kim (2001); and Kelly and Teevan (2003). A common distinction is between direct and indirect evidence.

Direct evidence—such as bookmarking, printing, or saving a document—represents distinct, and usually discrete, actions performed on an object by a searcher, which could be taken as an indication that the object is of interest to the searcher. Click-through behavior could also be considered as direct evidence, depending on whether the system uses the link clicked or the object clicked to as an indicator of interest. Such direct evidence is usually treated as evidence of the searcher's interest in some information object or, at least, evidence that the object is significant in some way to the search or searcher. Most researchers do not go beyond this and equate interest with relevance; the position is usually that implicit evidence tells us something about the potential significance of an object, not necessarily about its relevance to a search. However, whether we can treat implicit interest as synonymous with relevance information (implicit evidence as a substitute for explicit relevance decisions) is an important question and one that has been investigated in a number of ways.

Direct evidence is usually less abundant than indirect evidence but represents deliberate, objectively observed actions performed by a searcher on a system or object. Indirect evidence, on the other hand—such as scrolling behavior, reading time, or repeat visits to a page—is typically continuous evidence that could be interpreted as evidence of interest if it differs from some form of average behavior. That is, the system could make an inference of searcher interest based on differences in the searcher's behavior from normal behavior. For example, long reading time relative to the length of a document, scrolling the length of a document, or repeated visits to the same Web page might imply that the searcher is interested in the content of the page. Equally, these actions could say nothing about searcher interest. Long reading time might imply that the reader is unfamiliar with the content of the document being read, repeated visits might mean that the page is dynamically updated, and scrolling might mean the searcher is failing to find any useful information within the document.

The available research on good, implicit indicators suggests that direct evidence is usually more reliable; the more plentiful indirect evidence is more nebulous and requires more careful handling, in two ways. Firstly, we need to perform more validation experiments on our hypotheses regarding useful indicators of interest and, secondly, we need to construct additional components in our systems to handle the reasoning about this evidence. However, the sheer quantity of implicit information, especially indirect evidence, is one of the reasons for the attractiveness of implicit feedback.

Implicit evidence can also supply useful information about general searching behavior for investigative purposes. Lorigo, Pan, Hembrooke, Joachims, Granka, and Gay (2006) demonstrate that new methods of collecting information about the search process can uncover important aspects of how people search. Methods such as eye-tracking can uncover patterns of information assessment previously possible only through log analysis or verbal reporting. There are interesting indications that men and women have different assessment strategies, for example. Lorigo et al.'s study, examining how searchers view surrogates when searching on Google, reveals how little information searchers actually view before reformulating a query. Their findings are important in assessing what type of information searchers actually want presented on results pages (based on what they look at) and also on refining our assumptions underpinning traditional algorithms. We should not, for example, assume that pages that have not been visited by searchers are not relevant; the searcher may not even have considered a page or its surrogates.

Joachims, Granka, Pan, Hembrooke, and Gay (2005) use eye-tracking to show that people look at the top-ranked results far more than any other position, prefer visible ("above-the-fold") results and make decisions very quickly on relatively little information. However, the decisions as to which documents to click depend on the relative quality of the overall results. It is suggested, in line with earlier findings (e.g., Florance & Marchionini, 1995) that implicit judgments of relevance are best viewed as relative rather than absolute.

Reliability of Implicit Information

Several studies have probed which indicators of implicit interest are reliable and can be used for predictive algorithms such as relevance feedback or information filtering. Claypool et al. (2001), in an early study on Web browsing, found strong correlations between time taken to read Web pages, scrolling behavior, and explicit interest in a Web page. White, Ruthven, and Jose (2002) report a relationship between reading time and relevance, but Kelly and Belkin (2004) find no correlation.

Kelly and Belkin's longitudinal study was less artificial than the empirical work of Claypool et al. and White et al. and investigated the general search behavior of a small number of participants. Kelly and Belkin note the importance of the task relative to search behavior: The tasks an individual searcher performs affect his behavior and consequently the interpretations that should be made of the behavior. This raises the general question of whether implicit evidence should be treated as personal—*this* searcher typically behaves in *this* way in the presence of interesting information—or general evidence—*most* people behave *this* way.

Claypool et al. note the importance of task in implicit feedback and also the context in which the evidence appears. Reading time might be more reliable, for example, when differentiating between documents of a similar type or documents from a similar domain but less reliable for documents such as Web pages, which may vary greatly in style and readability. Similarly, relatively coarse evidence such as repeated visits to a resource might be seen as a more reliable indicator of interest or trust in the resource if the searcher has a choice as to which resource to visit.

Whether quantity of evidence can substitute for quality of evidence is not clear, although quality of evidence can perhaps be established through careful analysis of a sufficiently large data set. As has been noted, Joachims et al. (2005), in a direct comparison of explicit and implicit evidence, produced results indicating that implicit evidence can indeed substitute for explicit evidence, if handled as *relative* evidence rather than absolute evidence.

So, although implicit evidence has the potential to be effective, it often does not display the potential benefits, because it either is poor or needs to be contextualized with other information. In particular, implicit evidence can have a signal-to-noise ratio, with little useful information being presented (Shen, Tan, & Zhai, 2005). However, additive context—context from multiple sources added together—appears to be beneficial; Shen et al. (2005) use query histories and click-through data. In a relatively large sample investigation, Fox, Karnawat, Mydland, Dumais, and White (2005) also investigate interaction; they consider interaction only with the results of a search engine rather than whole searching behavior to compare explicit judgments of satisfaction with implicit feedback indicators. They also show that, overall, combinations of implicit evidence perform better than single pieces of evidence. The impression from most work in this area is that simple measures of implicit evidence may not suffice and some combination of evidence will be necessary to make robust predictions of interest (Fox et al., 2005; Shen et al., 2005; Teevan, Dumais, & Horvitz, 2005).

The area is progressing quickly and there is a move to look at the bigger picture of searching by considering more than isolated units of behavior. Fox et al., for example, analyze temporal actions—sequences of actions modeled by state transitions. Such a holistic approach to modeling implicit behavior could provide more useful clues to searcher satisfaction than simply modeling individual pieces of information.

Use of Implicit Feedback

Once we have evidence, either indirect or direct, we can use it to improve either retrieval performance or user interaction. Often this takes the form of query support, using evidence of interest to suggest new query formulations (White & Ruthven, 2006) or re-ranking of search results for presentation of retrieved material to searchers (Teevan et al., 2005). Teevan et al.'s personalized ranking study demonstrates that such approaches can be successful but not for all queries. Agichtein, Brill, and Dumais (2006) find that, for a large set of Web queries, incorporating implicit factors into the original ranking process is more effective than re-ranking the results. Agichtein et al. observe that some queries benefited from implicit feedback whereas others, particularly navigational queries, did not.

White et al. (2002) also employ implicit feedback, based on time-to-read information, to re-rank sentence surrogates. The use of implicit feedback largely failed in this experiment due to usability issues rather than the effectiveness of the feedback. Teevan et al. (2005) make a similar point—the effects of personalization should be interpretable by the searcher and not work against current user strategies.

Implicit evidence can also be used to direct the system response—what is an appropriate system reaction for this searcher at this point in a search (Ruthven et al., 2003)? White and Ruthven (2006), using a newer interface, employ implicit feedback to determine the level of system response based on a system model of the change in the user's information need as reflected in the interaction. Small estimated changes in an information need would result in modest changes, such as re-ranking of search results; large changes in the perceived information need would result in a more radical response such as running a new search.

As part of the study they investigate factors that can affect the utility of implicit versus explicit feedback using a novel Web search interface, specifically the complexity of a search task, the experience of the searcher, and search stage. Implicit feedback performs well when searchers have difficulty deciding on the relevance of individual items but explicit feedback is preferred in simpler search situations (where it is easy to decide on relevance and easy to choose new query terms). More importantly for implicit modeling, the investigation shows different search behaviors with tasks of varying complexity; searchers spend longer on initial browsing of search results before focusing their search. However, the question still remains of how reliably we can move implicit feedback from a descriptive to a predictive tool—at what level can implicit relevance feedback be consistently useful (White et al., 2005)?

Query Intention Analysis

Jansen and Spink (2006) present findings suggesting that low use of advanced search features is part of a long-term trend in Web searching. If this is the case, then a solution to improving retrieval performance might be to provide some form of support to improve searcher queries automatically.

An approach that is gaining in popularity, especially in Web research, is query intention analysis: ascertaining the searcher's goal behind the query and generating an appropriate response. For example, Broder (2002) proposes three types of Web search: informational (which corresponds to normal ad hoc search and which was the most common in Broder's study), navigational (home page finding to locate a particular site), and transactional service finding (finding a site where the user can accomplish a particular task such as shopping). Depending on how one gathers and analyzes the data, the proportion of searches within each group can vary; Broder's study on query logs estimates approximately 20 percent of searches as navigational, 30 percent transactional, and almost 50 percent as informational. This classification itself is not static—Rose and Levinson (2004) extended and revised Broder's original classification to produce one comprising twelve search goals. If a system could work out which type of search a searcher was engaged in, then it could optimize retrieval for that kind of search.

In a sense, query intention analysis, or identification, is not fundamentally new to IR. Earlier work in the area of user modeling (e.g., Ingwersen, 1992, chapter 7) tended to stress some notion of user need analysis and it has always been known that searchers carry out different types of search and want different types of responses. What is new is the work toward automatic identification of these goals.

Kang and Kim (2003, 2004) concentrate on informational and navigational searches and show that using various types of scoring techniques gives different results for different types of searches. They propose a method, based on a mixture of techniques, for classifying a query as either navigational or informational based on properties of the query terms used and how these terms have been used in Web pages. Lee, Liu, and Cho (2005) investigate navigational and informational searches but concentrate on link information and searcher clicking behavior. Both studies show reasonable success for some types of queries, especially when combinations of evidence are used, but the more difficult informational queries require more effort to detect. The difficult nature of informational queries is also noted in the TREC Web track (Craswell & Hawking, 2005).

As Azzopardi and de Rijke (2006) note, the query is not the only thing we can try to infer; other possible attributes of the search include the expertise of searcher, unit of document desired, or document type. Liu, Yu, and Meng (2006) try to infer which category of information is most appropriate for a searcher's query; Azzopardi and de Rijke try to infer query structure (or fields) with reasonable success although they note that query ambiguity causes significant problems for retrieval performance.

Personalization

Most retrieval systems assume nothing about the people who use the system. That is, each search iteration is analyzed purely on the session-based interaction with no input about the searcher, his history of interaction, or preferences. IIR systems could help improve retrieval effectiveness automatically by personalizing retrieval for individual searchers or tasks.

An awareness of the wider search context is important because it is not only the interface that affects one's ability to conduct a successful search. Attitude to searching, for example, affects interaction and not all people will react to the same tasks in the same way (Ford et al., 2005; Heinström, 2005). However, Savolainen and Kari (2006) note that, although we have many studies on various factors that might affect searching behavior (age, gender, experience, domain expertise), we have fewer tools (methodological or practical) for carrying out these analyses.

In the HARD track of TREC (Allan, 2005) and the follow-on ciqa (complex interactive question answering) track (Kelly & Lin, 2007), a central interest was how personal information about a searcher could help personalize retrieval for that individual. That is, rather than assuming that there was one average result list that would be good for all searchers, HARD and ciqa investigate whether employing information from individual searchers (in this case TREC assessors) could be used to personalize and improve retrieval performance. In different years, the tracks operated with different information that could be used to personalize retrieval, for example, metadata reflecting personal preferences toward types of article or personal information such as level of topic familiarity.

Both HARD and ciqa are unusual in that they allow limited interaction with the TREC assessors through the use of clarification (HARD) or interaction (ciqa) forms to ask for information from the assessors or to ask the assessor to judge information. Various groups (e.g., Belkin, Cole, Gwizdka, Li, Liu, Muresan, et al. [2005]; Tan, Velivelli, Fan, & Zhai, [2005]; Vechtomova & Karamuftuoglu [2005]) use the forms to investigate interactive query expansion approaches. Others tried novel interfaces; for example, Evans, Bennett, Montgomery, Sheftel, Hull, and Shanahan (2004) investigate a clustering approach and Kelly, Dollu, and Fu (2004) simply ask the assessors more about their information needs.

Topic familiarity was an area that sparked interest in many of the participating groups: How would the results of retrieval differ if the searchers, in this case the TREC assessors, had a high or low level of topical knowledge? Here groups propose and evaluate different hypotheses centered on issues such as readability of documents or the degree to which documents contain specialized vocabularies.

The Rutgers group, for example, show some benefit in presenting highly readable documents, as measured by the Flesch Reading Ease score, for assessors with low topical knowledge (Belkin, Chaleva, Cole, Li, Liu, Liu, et al., 2004) whereas the Robert Gordon group find some benefit in presenting more specific documents to assessors with high topic familiarity (Harper, Muresan, et al., 2004). Researchers at the University of Strathclyde investigate assessor confidence and interest in the topic being searched, as well as topic familiarity, trying different retrieval algorithms for assessors with different characteristics. Few of these personalized techniques work well, although there are indications that some are more effective for individual assessors though not for individual topics (Baillie, Elsweiler, Nicol, Ruthven, Sweeney, Yakici, et al., 2006).

Input to personalized retrieval systems can come from outside the searcher's own interaction. The interactive issues associated with newer systems are not as well defined as in the more traditional information access models, nor have they received sufficient research attention as yet, although the evaluation issues and profiling issues are interesting (see, for example, the special issues edited by Konstan, 2004, and Riedl & Dourish, 2005). However, collaborative or social filtering systems can be effective in mapping a searcher's interaction to that of other searchers to suggest new material. Systems such as Amazon, which recommends new items to customers based on their previous purchases, are the most visible examples; other researchers, for example Boydell and Smyth (2006), have shown collaborative techniques to be effective in increasing retrieval effectiveness by group-based filtering of useful material. Further, collaborative approaches can help identify related communities so that searchers can obtain recommendations from outside their normal group (Freyne & Smyth, 2006).

Automated Assistance

As has been noted, searchers can and do adapt to the search tools provided. However, such adaptation is not guaranteed. Searchers may simply give up using a search tool, and a lack of understanding and support can lead to poor search strategies (Muramatsu & Pratt, 2001). Savolainen and Kari's (2006) study of Web searching indicates that people face more problems in searching than simple use of search engines. We need to examine search behavior in relation to search interfaces. The area of automated assistance—offering search help—is popular in part to compensate for most searchers' lack of training.

What support should be provided in searching and what form this support should take is not yet clear. Jansen (2005) investigates the role of automated assistance in interactive searching, specifically a system that offers assistance in different aspects of search process (e.g., when issuing a query, the system offers thesaural refinements; when bookmarking or printing a document, the system implements relevance feedback based on the bookmarked or printed document and suggests terms). Jansen reports that the presentation of assistance is important; searchers will take automatic assistance and it is better to provide assistance than have it requested. Ruthven (2002) also demonstrates a preference for assistance that is offered as default rather than requested. There is, of course, a balance to be struck between increased support and cognitive load. The more complex the interaction becomes, the less useful the support. Not all interactive support is equally useful to all searchers, and for some it could become a distraction rather than a help.

Brajnik, Mizzaro, Tasso, and Venuti (2002) employ a rule-based expert system for offering suggestions to searchers on query reformulation and search tactics such as searching by author. The results are similar to Jansen (2005) and Ruthven (2002), in that automated assistance can be popular and effective but also needs to avoid being too generic. Searchers in all studies request very personal and situation-specific assistance rather than just general search advice.

The notion of situation-specificity is not only important to the area of automated assistance—mobile information seeking, for example, depends very much on a good model of the local context in which searches are being made—but automated assistance also needs to be precise enough to be of use. Studies like those of Jansen and Brajnik help benchmark the quality of other solutions.

Discussion

I started this chapter by contrasting two approaches to supporting end-user searching: automating difficult, interactive tasks and improving interactive functionality. In a sense this is a not a clear-cut distinction but two ends of a spectrum. At one end the IIR system assumes little, if any, knowledge of the person on the other side of the interface and the research objective has been to develop interactive functionality to allow the searcher to make better decisions about searching. At the other end there are approaches (such as query intention analysis) where the searcher sees no difference in the interaction and the research effort is focused on the retrieval machinery.

One way to characterize the difference between these two poles is by how extensively they use contextual information. In situations where the system has access to a variety of contextual information (the searcher's previous interactions, preferences, knowledge, etc.), it is best to develop systems that exploit this context to adapt the system's interaction or retrieval results to the needs of individual searchers. The examples presented in this chapter—implicit feedback, automated assistance, personalization—depend, in some sense, on knowledge about the person searching. Query intention analysis may not reveal what a searcher intends but tries to make an informed guess about what the searcher wants.

At the other end of the spectrum we have situations with very little contextual information; here the IIR system tries to augment the searcher's abilities to access information and there is increased interaction. Techniques such as the development of appropriate surrogates or specially designed interfaces are intended to make the most of the interaction.

Of course, novel approaches can contribute to both areas. Part-of-object retrieval research, for example, may try to automate the task of finding the most useful section of an object but the interfaces that present these sections allow searchers to interact in new and useful ways. It can also work the other way: Speech-driven interfaces avoid the need for typing and result in more convenient querying (Gilbert & Zhong, 2001), but can also make it easier to think about querying, which results in better initial queries (Du & Crestani, 2004).

Integrated solutions—solutions that combine multiple techniques within a single interface—are becoming more prevalent. Maña-López et al. (2004) use text segmentation, clustering, and summarization in their interface. Similarly, there are trends to combine information organization and retrieval techniques. These have the potential to be useful because, as Xie (2002) notes, people often engage in multiple information-seeking strategies. That is, people adopt varied methods of seeking information or interacting with an interface. Instead, they develop strategies to achieve specific goals and base these strategies on the (often low level) interactive functionality of the systems used. Interfaces that offer more flexible methods to create such strategies could provide more room for individual approaches to retrieval and allow the inclusion of personal information seeking strategies, which might otherwise be hampered by rigid interactions.

Integrating multiple searches within a session, or multitasking (Ozmutlu, Ozmutlu, & Spink, 2003; Spink 2004; Spink, Park, Jansen, & Pederson, 2006), is not well supported by the design of search engine interfaces (although Campbell's [1999] Ostensive Browser allowed multiple search threads within a single search session but not distinct subsearches). As Spärck Jones (2005) reminds us, searching is not a discrete interactive activity and we naturally integrate other activities such as spell-checking within a search. Providing more functionality to support decision making and information management activities within searching raises the overall utility of search systems. This functionality itself does not have to be very sophisticated to be useful—the spelling variation feature in Google is a simple, intuitive, and useful feature.

The move from small studies of isolated interactive features to systems that take a more realistic view of how people search is beneficial. A particular theme that has been gaining popularity, and one that has been central to the information seeking literature for some time, is that of task. As elucidated in an earlier *ARIST* chapter (Vakkari, 2002), task is a concept that has many definitions and uses within the information search and retrieval literature. However, we can point to two general aspects of task that are important to IIR: the work task (or the background activity that initiates the need to search) and the task to be fulfilled by the search itself (to answer a question, to gain as much information as possible, to obtain a useful resource, etc.).

Query intention analysis is a particular attempt to understand what the searcher means by a query—what type of response might be most appropriate—but systems that support user tasks suggest systems with a wider consideration of how people search for information. Many authors point to the importance of individual types of interactive support, either for different tasks, different stages within a search, or different search activities (e.g., Allan, Leuski, Swan, & Byrd, 2001; Kim & Allan, 2002; McDonald, Lai, & Tait, 2001; McDonald & Tait, 2003; White & Ruthven, 2006). Systems that offer the wrong support can work against the decisions a searcher must make. Ranked-list approaches to results presentation, for example, do not offer support for searchers trying to understand the structure of an information space, something that is better handled with visualizations (van der Eijk, van Mulligen, Kors, Mons, & van den Berg, 2004).

Classification and understanding of search tasks can help clarify which research directions might bear most fruit and which interactive functionality might best support these tasks. The more general concept of search task complexity is also interesting as such work provides clues about why retrieval systems are not used (Byström & Järvelin, 1995), why they might appear to be less successful for some tasks than others (Bell & Ruthven, 2004), and why certain interactive features might be preferred to others (Fowkes & Beaulieu, 2000). Examining specific types of search and the support required for successful searching appears to be a useful step forward in IIR design.

Allan, Carterette, and Lewis (2005) suggest that difficult search tasks, or at least difficult search topics, are where the most gains could be expected in IIR system performance; the argument being that today's IR systems perform well with simple tasks and we should look at ways of supporting more difficult tasks. This was the basis of the TREC HARD track (Allan, 2005), which investigated search topics where current IR systems performed poorly and where increased interaction might be the only way of improving the search performance. Search tasks that are difficult for IR systems lead to increased interaction. Research such as that of Kim (2006) show increased interaction, especially increased query reformulation, for difficult tasks. However, we could simplify the interaction by developing systems that respond better. This might mean better presentation of information, as in the case of specialist retrieval systems, or incorporation of more personal (searcher) information into the retrieval process.

In this chapter I have tried to represent the areas of IIR activity with the most recent impetus, the balance of discussion being decided by the amount of published activity within the area. The solutions proposed in searching range from complex sets of components to simpler changes in an interface or algorithm; simple changes can make a big difference. Even persuading searchers to examine more search results can increase retrieval effectiveness (White et al., 2003). What resources searchers are searching is also important and the lessons we learn from how people search can be used to determine the information architecture of these resources (Rosenfeld & Morville, 2002; Toms, 2002). This ability of human searchers to inform and surprise us is one reason to continue studying IIR as a dedicated field.

References

Adar, E., Kargar, D., & Stein, L. A. (1999). Haystack: Per-user information environments. *Proceedings of the 8th International Conference on Information and Knowledge Management*, 413–422.

Agichtein, E., Brill, E., & Dumais, S. (2006). Improving Web search ranking by incorporating user behavior information. *Proceedings of the 29th Annual International ACM SIGIR Conference on Research and Development in Information Retrieval*, 19–26.

Allan, J. (2005). HARD track overview in TREC 2004: High accuracy retrieval from documents. *Proceedings of 13th Text REtrieval Conference*, 24–37.

Allan, J., Carterette, B., & Lewis, J. (2005). When will information retrieval be "good enough"? *Proceedings of the 28th Annual International ACM SIGIR Conference on Research and Development in Information Retrieval*, 433–440.

Allan, J., Leuski, A., Swan, R., & Byrd, D. (2001). Evaluating combinations of ranked lists and visualizations of inter-document similarity. *Information Processing & Management, 37*, 435–458.

Anick, P. (2003). Using terminological feedback for Web search refinement: A log-based study. *Proceedings of the 26th Annual International ACM Conference on Research and Development in Information Retrieval*, 88–95.

Azzopardi, L., & de Rijke, M. (2006). Query intention acquisition: A case study on automatically inferring structured queries. *Proceedings of the 6th Dutch-Belgian Information Retrieval Workshop*, 3–10.

Baillie, M., Elsweiler, D., Nicol, E., Ruthven, I., Sweeney, S., Yakici, M., et al. (2006). University of Strathclyde at TREC HARD. *Proceedings of the 13th Text REtrieval Conference*. Retrieved January 4, 2007, from trec.nist.gov/pubs/trec14/papers/ustrathclyde.hard.pdf

Barry, C. L., & Schamber, L. (1998). Users' criteria for relevance evaluation: A cross-situational comparison. *Information Processing & Management, 34*, 219–236.

Bates, M. J. (2002). The cascade of interactions in the digital library interface. *Information Processing & Management, 38*, 381–400.

Beaulieu, M. (2000). Interaction in information searching and retrieval. *Journal of Documentation, 56*, 431–439.

Beaulieu, M., & Jones, S. (1998). Interactive searching and interface issues in the Okapi best match probabilistic retrieval system. *Interacting with Computers, 10*, 237–248.

Belkin, N. J. (1980). Anomalous states of knowledge as a basis for information retrieval. *Canadian Journal of Information Science, 5*, 133–143.

Belkin, N. J., Chaleva, I., Cole, M., Li, Y.-L., Liu, L., Liu, Y.-H., et al. (2004). Rutgers' HARD Track Experiences at TREC 2004. *Proceedings of the 13th Text REtrieval Conference*. Retrieved January 4, 2007, from trec.nist.gov/pubs/trec13/papers/rutgers-belkin.hard.pdf

Belkin, N. J., Cole, M., Gwizdka, J., Li, Y.-L., Liu, J.-J., Muresan, G., et al. (2005). Rutgers Information Interaction Lab at TREC 2005: Trying HARD.

Proceedings of the 14th Text REtrieval Conference. Retrieved January 4, 2007, from /trec.nist.gov/pubs/trec14/papers/rutgersu.hard.murensan.pdf

Belkin, N. J., Cool, C., Stein, A., & Thiel, U. (1995). Cases, scripts and information-seeking strategies: On the design of interactive information retrieval systems. *Expert Systems with Applications, 9,* 379–395.

Belkin, N. J., Kelly, D., Kim, G., Kim, J.-Y., Lee, H.-J., Muresan, G., et al. (2003). Query length in interactive information retrieval. *Proceedings of the 26th Annual International ACM Conference on Research and Development in Information Retrieval, 205–212.*

Bell, D. J., & Ruthven, I. (2004). Searchers' assessments of task complexity for Web searching. *Proceedings of the 26th European Conference in Information Retrieval, 57–71.*

Betsi, S., Lalmas, M., & Tombros, A. (2006). XML retrieval: User expectations. *Proceedings of the 29th International ACM SIGIR Conference on Research and Development in Information Retrieval, 611–612.*

Bhavnani, S. K. (2005). Why is it difficult to find comprehensive information? Implications of information scatter for search and design. *Journal of the American Society for Information Science and Technology, 56,* 989–1003.

Blair, D. C. (2002). The challenge of commercial document retrieval, part 1: Major issues and a framework based on search exhaustivity, determinacy of representation and document collection size. *Information Processing & Management, 38,* 273–291.

Boardman, R., & Sasse, M. A. (2004). "Stuff goes into the computer and doesn't come out": A cross-tool study of personal information management. *Proceedings of the SIGCHI Conference on Human Factors in Computing Systems, 583–590.*

Borgman, C. L. (1996). Why are online catalogs still hard to use? *Journal of the American Society for Information Science, 47,* 493–503.

Borgman, C. L., Hirsh, S. G., Walter, V. A., & Gallagher, A. L. (1995). Children's searching behavior on browsing and keyword online catalogs: The Science Library Catalog Project. *Journal of the American Society for Information Science, 46,* 663–684.

Boydell, O., & Smyth, B. (2006). Capturing community search expertise for personalized Web search using snippet-indexes. *Proceedings of the 2006 ACM CIKM International Conference on Information and Knowledge Management,* 277–286.

Brajnik, G., Mizzaro, S., Tasso, C., & Venuti, F. (2002). Strategic help in user interfaces for information retrieval. *Journal of the American Society for Information Science and Technology, 53,* 343–358.

Broder, A. (2002). A taxonomy of Web search. *SIGIR Forum, 36*(2), 3–10.

Bruza, P., McArthur, R., & Dennis, S. (2000). Interactive Internet search: Keyword, directory and query reformulation mechanisms compared. *Proceedings of the 23rd Annual International ACM SIGIR Conference on Research and Development in Information Retrieval, 280–287.*

Buchanan, G., Blandford, A., Thimbleby, H., & Jones, M. (2004). Integrating information seeking and structuring: Exploring the role of spatial hypertext in a digital library. *Proceedings of Hypertext 2004, 15th Annual Conference on Hypertext and Hypermedia, 225–234.*

Buyukkokten, O., Kaljuvee, O., Garcia-Molina, H., Paepcke, A., & Winograd, T. (2002). Efficient Web browsing on handheld devices using page and form summarization. *ACM Transactions on Information Systems, 20,* 82–115.

Byström, K., & Järvelin, K. (1995). Task complexity affects information seeking and use. *Information Processing & Management, 31*, 191–213.

Callan, J. P. (1994). Passage level evidence in document retrieval. *Proceedings of the 17th Annual International ACM SIGIR Conference on Research and Development in Information Retrieval*, 302–310.

Campbell, I. (1999). Interactive evaluation of the Ostensive Model, using a new test-collection of images with multiple relevance assessments. *Journal of Information Retrieval, 2*, 89–114.

Case, D. (2006). Information seeking. *Annual Review of Information Science and Technology, 40*, 293–327.

Chen, C., Czerwinski, M., & Macredie, R. D. (2000). Individual differences in virtual environments: Introduction and overview. *Journal of the American Society for Information Science, 51*, 499–507.

Chen, H., & Dumais, S. (2000). Bringing order to the Web: Automatically categorizing search results. *Proceedings of the SIGCHI Conference on Human Factors in Computing Systems*, 145–152.

Chinenyanga, T. T., & Kushmerick, N. (2001). Expressive retrieval from XML documents. *Proceedings of the 24th Annual international ACM SIGIR Conference on Research and Development in Information Retrieval*, 163–171.

Chuang, W. T., & Yang, J. (2000). Extracting sentence segments for text summarization: A machine learning approach. *Proceedings of the 23rd Annual International ACM SIGIR Conference on Research and Development in Information Retrieval*, 152–159.

Claypool, M., Le, P., Waseda, M., & Brown, D. (2001). Implicit interest indicators. *Proceedings of the 6th International Conference on Intelligent User Interfaces*, 33–40.

Cool, C., Park, S., Belkin, N. J., Koenemann, J., & Ng, K. B. (1996). Information seeking behavior in new searching environment. *Proceedings of the 2nd International Conference on Conceptions of Library and Information Science*, 403–416.

Cove, J. F., & Walsh, B. C. (1988). Online text retrieval via browsing. *Information Processing & Management, 24*, 31–37.

Craswell, N., & Hawking, D. (2005). Overview of the TREC 2004 Web Track. *Proceedings of the Thirteenth Text REtrieval Conference*. Retrieved January 4, 2007, from trec.nist.gov/pubs/trec13/papers/WEB.OVERVIEW.pdf

Crestani, F., Vegas, J., & de la Fuente, P. (2002). A graphical user interface for the retrieval of hierarchically structured documents. *Information Processing & Management, 40*, 269–289.

Crouch, C. J., Crouch, D. B., Chen, Q., & Holtz, S. J. (2002). Improving the retrieval effectiveness of very short queries. *Information Processing & Management, 38*, 1–36.

Cutrell, E., Robbins, D. C., Dumais, S. T., & Sarin, R. (2006). Fast, flexible filtering with Phlat: Personal search and organization made easy. *Proceedings of the ACM SIGCHI Conference on Human Factors in Computing Systems*, 261–270.

Dennis, S., McArthur, R., & Bruza, P. D. (1998). Searching the World Wide Web made easy? The cognitive load imposed by query refinement mechanisms. *Proceedings of the 3rd Australian Document Computing Symposium*, 65–71.

Downie, J. S. (2004). A sample of music information retrieval approaches. *Journal of the American Society for Information Science and Technology, 55*, 1033–1116.

Du, H., & Crestani, F. (2004). Retrieval effectiveness of written and spoken queries: An experimental evaluation. *Proceedings of 6th International Conference on Flexible Query Answering Systems*, 376–389.

Dumais, S. T., & Belkin, N. J. (2005). The Interactive TREC Track: Putting the user into search. In E. Voorhees & D. Harman (Eds.), *TREC: Experiment and evaluation in information retrieval* (pp. 123–152). Boston: MIT Press.

Dumais, S., Cutrell, E., Cadiz, J. J., Jancke, G., Sarin, R., & Robbins, D. C. (2004). Stuff I've Seen: A system for personal information retrieval and re-use. *Proceedings of the 27th Annual International ACM Conference on Research and Development in Information Retrieval*, 72–79.

Dumais, S., Cutrell, E., & Chen, H. (2001). Optimizing search by showing results in context. *Proceedings of the ACM SIGCHI Conference on Human Factors in Computing Systems*, 277–283.

Dziadosz, S., & Chandrasekar, R. (2002). Do thumbnail previews help users make better relevance decisions about Web search results? *Proceedings of the 25th Annual International ACM Conference on Research and Development in Information Retrieval*, 365–366.

Eastman, C. M., & Jansen, B. J. (2003). Coverage, relevance and ranking: The impact of query operators on Web search engine results. *ACM Transactions on Information Systems, 21*, 383–411.

Efthimiadis, E. N. (2000). Interactive query expansion: A user-based evaluation in a relevance feedback environment. *Journal of the American Society for Information Science and Technology, 51*, 989–1003.

Ellis, D. (1989). A behavioural approach to information retrieval system design. *Journal of Documentation, 45*, 171–212.

Ellis, D., Cox, D., & Hall, K. (1993). A comparison of the information seeking patterns of researchers in the physical and social sciences. *Journal of Documentation, 49*, 356–359.

Elsweiler, D., Ruthven, I., & Jones, C. (2005). Dealing with fragmented recollection of context in information management. *Context-Based Information Retrieval: Workshop in Fifth International and Interdisciplinary Conference on Modeling and Using Context*. Retrieved January 5, 2007, from ftp.informatik. rwth-aachen.de/Publications/CEUR-WS/Vol-151/CIR-05_4.pdf

Evans, D. A., Bennett, J., Montgomery, J., Sheftel, V., Hull, D. A., & Shanahan, J. G., (2004). TREC 2004 HARD Track experiments in clustering. *Proceedings of the 13th Text REtrieval Conference*. Retrieved January 4, 2007, from trec.nist.gov/pubs/trec13/papers/clairvoyance.hard.pdf

Fidel, R., & Pejtersen, A. M. (2004). From information behaviour research to the design of information systems: The Cognitive Work Analysis framework. *Information Research, 10*. Retrieved January 5, 2007, from InformationR. net/ir/10-1/paper210.html

Florance, V., & Marchionini, G. (1995). Information processing in the context of medical care. *Proceedings of the 18th Annual International ACM SIGIR Conference on Research and Development in Information Retrieval*, 158–163.

Ford, N., & Ford, R. (1993). Towards a cognitive theory of information accessing: An empirical study. *Information Processing & Management, 29*, 569–585.

Ford, N., Miller, D., & Moss, N. (2005). Web search strategies and human individual differences: A combined analysis. *Journal of the American Society for Information Science and Technology, 56*, 757–764.

Foster, A., & Ford, N. (2003). Serendipity and information seeking: An empirical study. *Journal of Documentation, 59*, 321–340.

Fowkes, H., & Beaulieu, M. (2000). Interactive searching behaviour: Okapi experiment for TREC8. *Proceedings of the IRSG 2000 Colloquium on Information Retrieval Research*, 47–56.

Fox, S., Karnawat, K., Mydland, M., Dumais, S., & White, T. (2005). Evaluating implicit measures to improve Web search. *ACM Transactions on Information Systems*, *23*, 147–168.

Freyne, J., & Smyth, B. (2006). Further experiments in case-based collaborative Web search. *Proceedings of the 8th European Conference on Case-Based Reasoning*, 256–270.

Führ, N., & Großjohann, K. (2001). XIRQL: A query language for information retrieval in XML documents. *Proceedings of the 24th Annual International ACM SIGIR Conference on Research and Development in Information Retrieval*, 172–180.

Gilbert, J. E., & Zhong, Y. (2001). Speech user interfaces for information retrieval. *Proceedings of the 10th International Conference on Information and Knowledge Management*, 77–82.

Gonçalves, D., & Jorge, J. A. (2004). "Tell me a story": Issues on the design of document retrieval systems. *Proceedings of Engineering Human Computer Interaction and Interactive Systems: Joint Working Conferences* (Lecture Notes in Computer Science), 129–145.

Gonçalves, D., & Jorge, J. A. (2006). Evaluating stories in narrative-based interfaces. *Proceedings of the 11th International Conference on Intelligent User Interfaces*, 273–275.

Gövert, N., Führ, N., Abolhassani, M., & Großjohann, K. (2003). Content-oriented retrieval with HyREX. *Proceedings of the 1st Initiative for the Evaluation of XML Retrieval Workshop*, 26–32.

Hansen, P., & Karlgren, J. (2005). Effects of foreign language and task scenario on relevance assessment. *Journal of Documentation*, *61*, 623–639.

Harabagiu, S., & Lacatusu, F. (2005). Topic themes for multi-document summarization. *Proceedings of the 28th Annual International ACM SIGIR Conference on Research and Development in Information Retrieval*, 202–209.

Harper, D. J., & Kelly, D. (2006). Contextual relevance feedback. *Proceedings of the 1st International Conference on Information Interaction in Context*, 129–137.

Harper, D. J., Koychev, I., Sun, Y., & Pirie, I. (2004). Within document retrieval: A user-centred evaluation of relevance profiling. *Information Retrieval*, *7*, 265–290.

Harper, D. J., Muresan, G., Liu, B., Koychev, I., Wettschereck, D., & Wiratunga, N. (2004). The Robert Gordon University's HARD Track experiments at TREC 2004. *Proceedings of the 13th Text REtrieval Conference*. Retrieved January 4, 2007, from trec.nist.gov/pubs/trec13/papers/rutgers-belkin.hard.pdf

He, D., & Demner-Fushman, D. (2004). HARD experiment at Maryland: From need negotiation to automated HARD process. *Proceedings of the 12th Text REtrieval Conference*, 707–714.

Hearst, M. (1995). TileBars: Visualization of term distribution information in full text information access. *Proceedings of the ACM SIGCHI Conference on Human Factors in Computing Systems*, 59–66.

Hearst, M. (2000). User interfaces and visualization. In R. Baeza-Yates & B. Ribeiro-Neto (Eds.), *Modern information retrieval* (pp. 257–324). New York: Addison-Wesley Longman.

Hearst, M. (2006a). Clustering versus faceted categories for information exploration. *Communications of the ACM*, *49*(4), 59–61.

Hearst, M. (2006b). Design recommendations for hierarchical faceted search interfaces. *ACM SIGIR Workshop on Faceted Search*. Retrieved January 5, 2007, from flamenco.berkeley.edu/papers/faceted-workshop06.pdf

Hearst, M., Elliot, A., English, J., Sinha, R., Swearingen, K., & Yee, K.-P. (2002). Finding the flow in Web site search. *Communications of the ACM, 45*(9), 42–49.

Heesch, D., & Rüger, S. (2004). Three interfaces for content-based access to image collections. *Proceedings of International Conference on Image and Video Retrieval* (Lecture Notes in Computer Science), 491–499.

Heinström, J. (2005). Fast surfing, broad scanning and deep diving: The influence of personality and study approach on students' information-seeking behaviour. *Journal of Documentation, 61*, 228–247.

Hill, B. (2004). *Google for dummies*. Indianapolis, IN: Hungry Minds.

Ingwersen, P. (1992). *Information retrieval interaction*. London: Taylor Graham.

Ingwersen, P., & Järvelin, K. (2005). *The turn: Integration of information seeking and retrieval in context*. Dordrecht, The Netherlands: Springer.

Iwayama, M. (2000). Relevance feedback with a small number of relevance judgements: Incremental relevance feedback vs. document clustering. *Proceedings of the 23rd Annual International ACM SIGIR Conference on Research and Development in Information Retrieval*, 10–16.

Järvelin, K., & Kekäläinen, J. (2000). IR evaluation methods for retrieving highly relevant documents. *Proceedings of the 23rd Annual International ACM SIGIR Conference on Research and Development in Information Retrieval*, 41–48.

Jansen, B. J. (2005). Seeking and implementing automated assistance during the search process. *Information Processing & Management, 41*, 909–928.

Jansen, B. J., & Spink, A. (2006). How are we searching the World Wide Web? A comparison of nine search engine transaction logs. *Information Processing & Management, 42*, 248–263.

Joachims, T., Granka, L., Pan, B., Hembrooke, H., & Gay, G. (2005). Accurately interpreting clickthrough data as implicit feedback. *Proceedings of the 28th Annual International ACM SIGIR Conference on Research and Development in Information Retrieval*, 154–161.

Joho, H., Sanderson, M., & Beaulieu, M. (2004). A study of user interaction with a concept-based interactive query expansion support tool. *Proceedings of the 26th European Conference in Information Retrieval*, 42–56.

Jones, C. B., & Purves, R. (2005). GIR '05 ACM workshop on geographical information retrieval. *SIGIR Forum, 40*(1), 34–37.

Jones, R., Rey, B., Madani, O., & Greiner, W. (2006). Generating query substitutions. *Proceedings of the 14th World Wide Web Conference*, 387–396.

Jones, W. (2007). Personal information management. *Annual Review of Information Science and Technology, 41*, 453–504.

Käki, M. (2005). Findex: Search result categories help users when document ranking fails. *Proceedings of the Conference on Human Factors in Computing Systems*, 131–140.

Kamps, J., Marx, M., de Rijke, M., & Sigurbjörnsson, B. (2005). Structured queries in XML retrieval. *Proceedings of the 14th ACM International Conference on Information and Knowledge Management*, 4–11.

Kang, I.-H., & Kim, G. (2003). Query type classification for Web document retrieval. *Proceedings of the 26th Annual International ACM Conference on Research and Development in Information Retrieval*, 64–71.

Kang, I.-H., & Kim, G. (2004). Integration of multiple evidences based on a query type for Web search. *Information Processing & Management, 40*, 459–478.

Kelly, D., & Belkin, N. J. (2004). Display time as implicit feedback: Understanding task effects. *Proceedings of the Annual International ACM Conference on Research and Development in Information Retrieval*, 377–384.

Kelly, D., Deepak, V., & Fu, X. (2005). The loquacious user: A document-independent source of terms for query expansion. *Proceedings of the 28th Annual International ACM SIGIR Conference on Research and Development in Information Retrieval*, 457–464.

Kelly, D., Dollu, V. D., & Fu, X. (2004). University of North Carolina's HARD Track experiments at TREC 2004. *Proceedings of the 13th Text REtrieval Conference*. Retrieved January 4, 2007, from trec.nist.gov/pubs/trec13/papers/unorthcarolina.hard.pdf

Kelly, D., & Lin, J. (2007). Overview of the TREC 2006 ci QA task. *SIGIR Forum, 41*(1), 107–116.

Kelly, D., & Teevan, J. (2003). Implicit feedback for inferring user preference: A bibliography. *SIGIR Forum, 37*(2), 18–28.

Kim, J. (2006). Task difficulty as a predictor and indicator of Web searching interaction. *Proceedings of the Conference on Human Factors in Computing Systems*, 959–964.

Kim, K.-S., & Allan, B. (2002). Cognitive and task influences on Web searching behavior. *Journal of the American Society for Information Science and Technology, 43*, 109–119.

Koenemann, J., & Belkin, N. J. (1996). A case for interaction: A study of interactive information retrieval behavior and effectiveness. *Proceedings of the ACM SIGCHI Conference on Human Factors in Computing Systems*, 205–212.

Konstan, J. A. (2004). Introduction to recommender systems: Algorithms and evaluation. *ACM Transactions on Information Systems, 22*, 1–4.

Kraft, R., Chang, C. C., Maghoul, F., & Kumar, R. (2006). Searching with context. *Proceedings of the 14th World Wide Web Conference*, 477–486.

Kruschwitz, U., & Al-Bakour, H. (2005). Users want more sophisticated search assistants: Results of a task-based evaluation. *Journal of the American Society for Information Science and Technology, 56*, 1377–1393.

Kuhlthau, C. C. (1991). Inside the search process: Information seeking from the user's perspective. *Journal of the American Society for Information Science, 42*, 361–371.

Lee, U., Liu, Z., & Cho, J. (2005). Automatic identification of user goals in Web search. *Proceedings of the 13th World Wide Web Conference*, 391–400.

Legg, C. (2007). Ontologies on the semantic Web. *Annual Review of Information Science and Technology, 41*, 407–451.

Lin, J., Quan, D., Sinha, V., Bakshi, K., Huynh, D., Katz, B., et al. (2003). What makes a good answer? The role of context in question answering. *Proceedings of the 9th International Federation for Information Processing TC13 International Conference on Human–Computer Interaction*, 25–32.

Lin, S-j. (2005). Internetworking of factors affecting successive searches over multiple episodes. *Journal of the American Society for Information Science and Technology, 56*(4), 416–436.

Lin, S-j., & Belkin, N. J. (2005). Validation of a model of information seeking over multiple search sessions. *Journal of the American Society for Information Science and Technology, 56*(4), 393–415.

Liu, B., Zhao, K., & Yi, L. (2002). Visualizing Web site comparisons. *Proceedings of the 11th Annual WWW Conference*, 693–703.

Liu, F., Yu, C., & Meng, W. (2006). Personalized Web search by mapping user queries to categories. *Proceedings of the 11th ACM International Conference on Information and Knowledge Management*, 558–565.

Liu, H., Lieberman, H., & Selker, T. (2002). GOOSE: A goal-oriented search engine with common sense. *Proceedings of the 2nd International Conference on Adaptive Hypermedia and Adaptive Web-Based Systems*, 253–263.

López-Ostenero, F., Gonzalo, J., & Verdejo, F. (2005). Noun phrases as building blocks for cross-language search assistance. *Information Processing & Management, 41*, 549–568.

Lorigo, L., Pan, B., Hembrooke, H., Joachims, T., Granka, L. & Gay, G. (2006). The influence of task and gender on search and evaluation behavior using Google. *Information Processing & Management, 42*, 1123–1131.

Lynam, T. R., Buckley, C., Clark, C. L. A., & Cormack, G. V. (2004). A multi-system analysis of document and term selection for blind feedback. *Proceedings of the 13th ACM International Conference on Information and Knowledge Management*, 261–269.

Lynch, C. A. (2001). When documents deceive: Trust and provenance as new factors for information retrieval in a tangled Web. *Journal of the American Society for Information Science and Technology, 52*, 12–17.

Malik, S., Klas, C.-P., Führ, N., Larsen, B., & Tombros, A. (2006). Designing a user interface for interactive retrieval of structured documents: Lessons learned from the INEX Interactive Track. *Proceedings of the 10th European Conference on Digital Libraries*, 75–86.

Maña-López, M. J., De Buenaga, M., & Gómez-Hidalgo, J. M. (2004). Multidocument summarization: An added value to clustering in interactive retrieval. *ACM Transactions on Information Systems, 22*, 215–241.

Mani, I. (2001). Recent developments in text summarization. *Proceedings of the 10th International Conference on Information and Knowledge Management*, 529–531.

McDonald, S., Lai, T., & Tait, J. (2001). Evaluating a content based image retrieval system. *Proceedings of the 24th Annual International ACM SIGIR Conference on Research and Development in Information Retrieval*, 232–240.

McDonald, S., & Tait, J. (2003). Search strategies in content-based image retrieval. *Proceedings of the 26th Annual International ACM Conference on Research and Development in Information Retrieval*, 80–87.

McKeown, K., Passonneau, R. J., Elson, D. K., Nenkova, A., & Hirschberg, J. (2005). Do summaries help? A task-based evaluation of multi-document summarization. *Proceedings of the 28th Annual International ACM SIGIR Conference on Research and Development in Information Retrieval*, 210–217.

Milic-Frayling, N., Jones, R., Rodden, K., Smyth, G., Blackwell, A., & Sommerer, R. (2004). SmartBack: Supporting users in back navigation. *Proceedings of the 13th Annual WWW Conference*, 63–71.

Muramatsu, J., & Pratt, W. (2001). Transparent queries: Investigating users' mental models of search engines. *Proceedings of the 24th Annual International ACM SIGIR Conference on Research and Development in Information Retrieval*, 217–224.

Navigli, R., & Velardi, P. (2003). An analysis of ontology-based query expansion strategies. *Workshop on Adaptive Text Extraction and Mining*, 42–49.

Niemi, T., Junkkari, M., Järvelin, K., & Viita, S. (2004). Advanced query language for manipulating complex entities. *Information Processing & Management, 40*, 869–889.

Norman, D. A. (2004). *Emotional design: Why we love (or hate) everyday things.* New York: Basic Books.

Oard, D., & Kim, J. (2001). Modeling information content using observable behavior. *Proceedings of the 64th Annual Meeting of the American Society for Information Science and Technology,* 38–45.

O'Keefe, R. A., & Trotman, A. (2004). The simplest query language that could possibly work. *Proceedings of the 2nd INEX Workshop,* 167–174.

Over, P. (2001). The TREC interactive track: An annotated bibliography. *Information Processing & Management,* 37, 369–381.

Ozmutlu, S., Ozmutlu, H. C., & Spink, A. (2003). Multitasking Web searching: Implications for design. *Proceedings of the 66th Annual Meeting of the American Society for Information Science and Technology,* 416–421.

Pirkola, A., Puolamäki, D., & Järvelin, K. (2003). Applying query structuring in cross-language retrieval. *Information Processing & Management,* 39, 391–402.

Pu, H-T., Chuang, S.-L., & Yang, C. (2002). Subject categorization of query terms for exploring Web users' search interests. *Journal of the American Society for Information Science and Technology,* 53, 617–630.

Radev, D. R., Jing, H., Styś, M., & Tam, D. (2004). Centroid-based summarization of multiple documents. *Information Processing & Management,* 40, 919–938.

Reid, J., & Dunlop, M. D. (2003). Evaluation of a prototype interface for structured document retrieval. *Proceedings of the 17th Annual Human–Computer Interaction Conference,* 73–86.

Reid, J., Lalmas, M., Finesilver, K., & Hertzum, M. (2006a). Best entry points for structured document retrieval, part I: Characteristics. *Information Processing & Management,* 42, 74–88.

Reid, J., Lalmas, M., Finesilver, K., & Hertzum, M. (2006b). Best entry points for structured document retrieval, part II: Characteristics. *Information Processing & Management,* 42, 89–105.

Riedl, J., & Dourish, P. (2005). Introduction to the special section on recommender systems. *ACM Transactions on Computer–Human Interaction,* 12, 371–373.

Rieh, S. Y., & Xie, H. (2006). Analysis of multiple query reformulations on the Web: The interactive information retrieval context. *Information Processing & Management,* 42, 751–768.

Robertson, S., & Callan, J. (2005). Routing and filtering. In E. M. Voorhees & D. K. Harman (Eds.), *TREC: Experiments and evaluation in information retrieval* (pp. 99–121). Boston: MIT Press.

Rodden, K., & Wood, K. R. (2003). How do people manage their digital photographs? *Proceedings of the SIGCHI Conference on Human Factors in Computing Systems,* 409–416.

Rose, D. E., & Levinson, D. (2004). Understanding user goals in Web search. *Proceedings of the 12th World Wide Web Conference,* 13–19.

Rosenfeld, L., & Morville, P. (2002). *Information architecture for the World Wide Web: Designing large-scale Web sites.* Sebastopol, CA: O'Reilly.

Roussinov, D. G., & Chen, H. (2001). Information navigation on the Web by clustering and summarizing query results. *Information Processing & Management,* 37, 789–816.

Ruthven, I. (2002). On the use of explanations as a mediating device for relevance feedback. *Proceedings of the 6th European Conference on Digital Libraries,* 338–345.

Ruthven, I. (2003). Re-examining the potential effectiveness of interactive query expansion. *Proceedings of the 26th Annual International ACM SIGIR Conference on Research and Development in Information Retrieval*, 213–220.

Ruthven, I., Baillie, M., & Elsweiler, D. (in press). The relative effects of knowledge, interest and confidence in assessing relevance. *Journal of Documentation*.

Ruthven, I., & Lalmas, M. (2003). A survey on the use of relevance feedback for information access systems. *Knowledge Engineering Review, 18*, 95–145.

Ruthven, I., Lalmas, M., & van Rijsbergen, C. J. (2003). Incorporating user search behavior into relevance feedback. *Journal of the American Society for Information Science and Technology, 54*, 528–548.

Ruthven, I., Tombros, A., & Jose, J. M. (2001). A study on the use of summaries and summary-based query expansion for a question-answering task. *Proceedings of the 2nd European Conference on Information Retrieval*, 1–14.

Savolainen, R., & Kari, J. (2006). Facing and bridging gaps in Web searching. *Information Processing & Management, 42*, 519–537.

Shen, X., Tan, B., & Zhai, C. (2005). Context sensitive information retrieval using implicit feedback. *Proceedings of the 28th Annual International ACM SIGIR Conference on Research and Development in Information Retrieval*, 43–50.

Shipman, F. M., Furuta, R., Brenner, D., Chung, C.-C., & Hsieh, H.-w. (2000). Guided paths through Web-based collections: Design, experiences, and adaptations. *Journal of the American Society for Information Science, 51*, 260–272.

Shneiderman, B., Byrd, D., & Croft, W. B. (1998). Sorting out searching: A user-interface framework for text searches. *Communications of the ACM, 41*(4), 95–98.

Sihvonen, A., & Vakkari, P. (2004). Subject knowledge improves interactive query expansion assisted by a thesaurus. *Journal of Documentation, 60*, 673–690.

Slone, D. J. (2002). The influence of mental models and goals on search patterns during Web interaction. *Journal of the American Society for Information Science and Technology, 53*, 1152–1169.

Smeaton, A. (2004). Indexing, browsing and searching of digital video. *Annual Review of Information Science and Technology, 38*, 371–407.

Smith, D. A. (2002). Detecting and browsing events in unstructured text. *Proceedings of the 25th Annual International ACM SIGIR Conference on Research and Development in Information Retrieval*, 73–80.

Smucker, M., & Allan, J. (2006). Find-Similar: Similarity browsing as a search tool. *Proceedings of the 29th Annual International ACM SIGIR Conference on Research and Development in Information Retrieval*, 461–468.

Spärck Jones, K. (1979). Search term relevance weighting given little relevance information. *Journal of Documentation, 35*, 30–48.

Spärck Jones, K. (2005). Epilogue: Metareflections on TREC. In E. M. Voorhees & D. K. Harman (Eds.), *TREC: Experiment and evaluation in information retrieval* (pp. 421–448). Boston: MIT Press.

Spink, A. (1996). Multiple search sessions model of end-user behavior: An exploratory study. *Journal of the American Society for Information Science, 47*, 603–609.

Spink, A. (2004). Multi-tasking information behavior and information task switching: An exploratory study. *Journal of Documentation, 60*, 336–351.

Spink, A., & Cole, C. (2005a). *New directions in cognitive information retrieval*. Dordrecht, The Netherlands: Springer.

Spink, A., & Cole, C. (2005b). *New directions in human information behavior*. Dordrecht, The Netherlands: Springer.

Spink, A., & Jansen, B. J. (2004). A study of Web search trends. *Webology, 1*(2). Retrieved December 22, 2006, from www.webology.ir/2004/v1n2/a4.html

Spink, A., Park, M., Jansen, B. J., & Pederson, J. (2006). Multitasking during Web search sessions. *Information Processing & Management, 42*, 264–275.

Swan, R., & Allan, J. (2000). Automatic generation of overview timelines. *Proceedings of the 23rd Annual International ACM SIGIR Conference on Research and Development in Information Retrieval*, 49–56.

Sweeney, S., & Crestani, F. (2006). Effective search results summary size and device screen size: Is there a relationship? *Information Processing & Management, 42*, 1056–1074.

Szlavik, Z., Tombros, A., & Lalmas, M. (2006). Investigating the use of summarisation for interactive XML retrieval. *Proceedings of the 21st ACM Symposium on Applied Computing, Information Access and Retrieval Track*, 1068–1072.

Tan, B., Velivelli, A., Fan, H., & Zhai, C. (2005). Interactive construction of query language models: UIUC TREC 2005 HARD Track experiments. *Proceedings of the 14th Text REtrieval Conference*. Retrieved January 4, 2007, from trec.nist.gov/pubs/trec14/papers/uillinois-uc.hard.pdf

Teevan, J., Dumais, S. T., & Horvitz, E. (2005). Personalizing search via automated analysis of interests and activities. *Proceedings of the 28th Annual International ACM SIGIR Conference on Research and Development in Information Retrieval*, 449–456.

Tombros, A., Malik, S., & Larsen, B. (2005). Report on the INEX 2004 interactive track. *SIGIR Forum, 39*(1), 43–49.

Tombros, A., & Sanderson, M. (1998). Advantages of query biased summaries in information retrieval. *Proceedings of the 21st Annual International ACM SIGIR Conference on Research and Development in Information Retrieval*, 2–10.

Tombros, A., Villa, R., & van Rijsbergen, C. J. (2002). The effectiveness of query-specific hierarchic clustering in information retrieval. *Information Processing & Management, 38*, 559–582.

Toms, E. G. (2002). Information interaction: Providing a framework for information architecture. *Journal of the American Society for Information Science and Technology, 53*, 855–862.

Topi, H., & Lucas., W. (2005a). Mix and match: Combining terms and operators for successful Web searches. *Information Processing & Management, 41*, 801–817.

Topi, H., & Lucas, W. (2005b). Searching the Web: Operator assistance required. *Information Processing & Management, 41*, 383–403.

Turpin, A. H., & Hersh, W. (2001). Why batch and user evaluations do not give the same results. *Proceedings of the 24th Annual International ACM SIGIR Conference on Research and Development in Information Retrieval*, 225–231.

Vakkari, P. (2001). A theory of the task-based information retrieval process: A summary and generalisation of a longitudinal study. *Journal of Documentation, 57*, 44–60.

Vakkari, P. (2002). Task-based information searching. *Annual Review of Information Science and Technology, 37*, 413–464.

Vakkari, P., & Hakala, N. (2000). Changes in relevance criteria and problem stages in task performance. *Journal of Documentation, 56*, 540–562.

Vakkari, P., Pennanen, M., & Serola, S. (2003). Changes of search terms and tactics while writing a research proposal: A longitudinal case study. *Information Processing & Management, 39*, 445–463.

van der Eijk, C. C., van Mulligen, E. M., Kors, J. A., Mons, B., & van den Berg, J. (2004). Constructing an associative concept space for literature-based discovery. *Journal of the American Society for Information Science and Technology, 55,* 436–444.

Vechtomova, O., & Karamuftuoglu, M. (2005). Experiments for HARD and Enterprise Tracks. *Proceedings of the 14th Text REtrieval Conference.* Retrieved January 4, 2007, from trec.nist.gov/pubs/trec14/papers/uwaterloo-vechtomova.hard.ent.pdf

Vechtomova, O., & Karamuftuoglu, M. (2006). Elicitation and use of relevance feedback information. *Information Processing & Management, 42,* 191–206.

Voorhees, E. M. (2000). Variations in relevance judgments and the measurement of retrieval effectiveness. *Information Processing & Management, 36,* 697–778.

White, R. W., Jose, J. M., & Ruthven, I. (2003). A task-oriented study on the influencing effects of query-biased summarisation in Web searching. *Information Processing & Management, 39,* 707–733.

White, R. W., Kules, B., Drucker, S. M., & Schraefel, M. C. (2006). Supporting exploratory search. *Communications of the ACM, 49*(4), 36–39.

White, R. W., & Marchionini, G. (2007). Examining the effectiveness of real-time query expansion. *Information Processing & Management, 43*(3), 685–704.

White, R. W., & Ruthven, I. (2006). A study of interface support mechanisms for interactive information retrieval. *Journal of the American Society for Information Science and Technology, 57,* 933–948.

White, R. W., Ruthven, I., & Jose, J. M. (2002). Finding relevant documents using top ranking sentences: An evaluation of two alternative schemes. *Proceedings of the 25th Annual International ACM SIGIR Conference on Research and Development in Information Retrieval,* 57–64.

White, R. W., Ruthven, I., & Jose, J. M. (2005). A study of factors affecting the utility of implicit relevance feedback. *Proceedings of the 28th Annual International ACM SIGIR Conference on Research and Development in Information Retrieval,* 35–42.

Whittaker, S., & Sidner, C. (1996). Email overload: Exploring personal information management of email. *Proceedings of the ACM SIGCHI Conference on Human Factors in Computing Systems,* 276–283.

Wiesman, F., van den Herik, H. J., & Hasman, A. (2004). Information retrieval by metabrowsing. *Journal of the American Society for Information Science and Technology, 55,* 565–578.

Woodruff, A., Faulring, A., Rosenholtz, R., Morrison, J., & Pirolli, P. (2001). Using thumbnails to search the Web. *Proceedings of the SIGCHI Conference on Human Factors in Computing Systems,* 583–590.

Wu, M., Fuller, M., & Wilkinson, R. (2001a). Searcher performance in question answering. *Proceedings of the 24th Annual International ACM SIGIR Conference on Research and Development in Information Retrieval,* 375–381.

Wu, M., Fuller, M., & Wilkinson, R. (2001b). Using clustering and classification approaches in interactive retrieval. *Information Processing & Management, 37,* 459–484.

Wu, M., Muresan, G., McLean, A., Tang, M.-C., Wilkinson, R., Li, Y., et al. (2004). Human versus machine in the topic distillation task. *Proceedings of the 27th Annual International ACM Conference on Research and Development in Information Retrieval,* 385–392.

Xu, C., Shao, X., Maddage, N. C., & Kankanhalli, M. S. (2005). Automatic music video summarization based on audio-visual-text analysis and alignment.

Proceedings of the 28th Annual International ACM SIGIR Conference on Research and Development in Information Retrieval, 361–368.

Xie, H. (2002). Patterns between interactive intentions and information-seeking strategies. *Information Processing & Management, 38*, 55–77.

Yee, P., Swearingen, K., Li, K., & Hearst, M. (2003). Faceted metadata for image search and browsing. *Proceedings of the SIGCHI Conference on Human Factors in Computing Systems*, 401–408.

CHAPTER 3

Multitasking Behavior

Amanda Spink
Queensland University of Technology

Charles Cole
McGill University

Mary Waller
Maastricht University

Introduction

This chapter does not attempt to furnish an overview of multitasking research in every scientific discipline. Rather, we highlight the importance of multitasking in the cognitive and information sciences and the need for further research on multitasking, particularly within the context of information behavior.

Why are we interested in multitasking? Why is multitasking an important theoretical and practical phenomenon for the cognitive and information sciences, and particularly for theories and models of information behavior? Multitasking has no doubt always been an essential human behavior. However, unlike earlier research on micro-analyses of brain and memory structure/capacity (Miller, 1956), multitasking pushes brain and memory research into a more global consideration of human existence. Reasons for our increased interest in the phenomenon are society's heightened interest in security concerns, the evolution of a workplace with workers now required to perform tasks formerly performed by others, and above all the pervasiveness of communication devices in both work and leisure activities.

Citations to multitasking research in the cognitive sciences have recently appeared in the popular press. The ubiquity of digital devices such as mobile phones, messaging devices, video games, and desktop and laptop computers has helped create the impression that today's young people behave differently from previous generations in their simultaneous use of multiple devices, with the result that attention is diverted from the task at hand (Scott, 2006). In response to the numerous published studies indicating the negative effects of telephone use on automobile driver performance (Strayer & Johnston, 2001), many local and state governments have adopted laws to curtail this kind of multi-tasking behavior. Employers and organizational behaviorists are also concerned about multitasking in work environments, in part because of the proliferation of information devices (Holstein, 2006). They ask questions such as: How can we keep employees focused? (Hafner, 2005). Citing former Microsoft Vice President Linda Stone's (2006) phrase "continuous partial attention," *New York Times* columnist Thomas L. Friedman (2006) labels our multitasking age "The Age of Interruption."

However, we start by considering multitasking as a human ability; the ability to handle the competing demands of multiple tasks. A task is defined as "a distinct work activity carried out for a distinct purpose" (Cascio, 1978, p. 133). Multitasking can be defined narrowly or broadly. For example, is multitasking the human ability to deal with more than one task at the same time, or is multitasking actually the ability to switch quickly from one task to the next in a rapid sequence of tasks? We here define multitasking broadly. Waller (1997, p. 225) states that "individual-level multitasking processes involve a person's allocation of his or her own scarce cognitive resources among several tasks and the moderating impact of task elements, task processes, and task resources on individual multiple-task performance."

Multitasking occurs at different levels of human behavior, including the individual and group levels (Waller, 1997). When humans multitask, they work on two or more tasks and switch between those tasks, either as individuals or within groups (Waller, 1997). Multitasking and task switching are mechanisms that help humans deal with the complex environment in which they live. People often switch among different types of tasks such as talking on the telephone, computing, reading, and information seeking. There is a growing and crucial need to extend our understanding of multitasking behavior, particularly within the context of cognitive and information behavior.

In spite of the importance of multitasking in the cognitive sciences, until recently the field of information science devoted limited attention to understanding multitasking within the context of the field's research issues and problems. Previous *ARIST* chapters on information behavior touched only parenthetically on multitasking (e.g., multitasking will increase as a result of increased collaboration in the work environment [Foster, 2006]; see also, Courtright's [2007] chapter on information use environments; Davenport [2002] on distributed cognition; Finholt [2002] on the organization of work; Garcia, Dawes, Kohne, Miller, and Groschwitz [2006] on the workplace and technological change; Jones [2007] on management of tasks; Rogers [2004] on human–computer interaction [HCI]; and Vakkari [2003] on task-based information searching).

However, recently, multitasking research has grown in theoretical and practical significance for information scientists. Multitasking is emerging as a fundamental process that underpins information behavior. As with other information science concepts, such as relevance, uncertainty, or feedback, multitasking is now an important and complex concept that is crucial if we are to understand information behavior fully.

The purpose of this chapter is to develop a framework for clarifying the relationship between information behavior and multitasking. Because cognitive science research affects information behavior studies, we first outline multitasking concepts and models within the cognitive sciences, broadly defined.

Cognitive Sciences

Various cognitively oriented fields regard multitasking as an important element of their theories and models to explain cognitive behaviors. In this section we explore the nature of multitasking from the perspectives of cognitive science, communication studies, human factors, human–computer interaction, and organizational behavior. We examine the contribution each field has made to our understanding of multitasking.

Cognitive Science

Cognitive scientists have for decades studied many aspects of multitasking or task switching (Carlson & Sohn, 2000; Miyata & Norman, 1986). The growing complexity of the global information environment means that people are increasingly engaged in multitasking and task-switching behaviors. But only now is this research being applied. Many interactive technologies still do not provide effective support for managing multitasking behaviors (Wickens, 1992).

Cognitive psychologists have an extensive research literature on multitasking, concurrent information processing, task switching (Burgess, 2000; Pashler, 2000), and sequential actions (Carlson & Sohn, 2000) at the microsecond level. Complex task switching can include three phases: desire to task switch, task switch, and switching back to a previous task. The finding that multitasking over different types of tasks can reduce productivity (Rubinstein, Meyer, & Evans, 2001) is further supported by the single channel theory, which suggests that the ability of humans to perform concurrent mental operations is limited by the capacity of a central mechanism (Schweickert & Boggs, 1984). A major understanding from cognitive science research has to do with both the positive and negative aspects of multitasking. Rubinstein et al. (2001) found that multitasking between different types of tasks can reduce productivity. Wickens (1992), on the other hand, suggests that *time sharing* allows the simultaneous performance of multiple tasks and *time swapping* allows the sequential performance of tasks.

Psychologists have also identified differences between prioritized and unprioritized multitasking situations (Ishizaka, Marshall, & Conte, 2001) and a model of group multitasking behavior (Waller, 1997). Aasman (1995) and Just, Carpenter, Keller, Emery, Zajac, and Thulborn

(2001) analyzed multitasking and dual tasking during driving. Hunt and Joslyn (2000) identified characteristics of individuals who do well in situations characterized by multitasking and decision making under considerable time pressure. Bainbridge (2002) described processes underlying human multitasking behaviors in complex task situations. Lee and Taatgen (2002) argued that multitasking behaviors can be best understood as a product of skill acquisition.

Grady, Springer, Hongwanishkul, McIntosh, and Winocur (2006) noted a "seesaw imbalance" in multitasking and aging; when we are younger there is a seesaw balance between two regions in the brain's frontal lobes. Tasks that require concentration evoke high activity in the dorsolateral prefrontal cortex, while tasks not related to the central task (such as monitoring one's surroundings) evoke low-level activity in the medial frontal and parietal regions of the brain. Seesaw imbalance occurs in older adults who find it difficult to inhibit distracting information, including interference from other tasks; thus for older people activity in the dorsolateral prefrontal cortex decreases while the medial frontal and parietal regions show less activity for focusing on the task. For aging effects on attentional control in multitasking, see Bherer, Kramer, Peterson, Colcombe, Erickson, and Becic (2005), and for aging effects on multitasking in employment, see Taylor, O'Hara, Mumenthaler, Rosen, and Yesavage (2005).

The Stroop effect in psychology denotes interference in a time-task experiment due to an incongruence between the semantic meaning of a test word and some other factor—for example, the word "blue" printed in a different color—slowing reaction times and increasing errors. In multitasking time-reaction experiments, the Stroop-like interference from the other task(s) in spite of preparation is perplexing (Meiran, 2000), requiring new research methods (neuroimaging, electrophysiology, etc.) in the important areas of study of the effects of aging (Mayr, 2001), brain damage (Keele & Rafal, 2000), and individual differences in function (Miyake, Friedman, Emerson, Witzki, Howerter, & Wagner, 2000). On the other hand, Meyer, Glass, Mueller, Seymour, and Kieras (2001) and Glass, Schumacher, Lauber, Zurbriggen, Gmeindl, Kieras, et al. (2000) did not find that degradation in performance during multitasking for people less than 70 years of age was due to decreased "hardware" functionality.

Task Switching

Task switching has been recognized as an important element of multitasking. Monsell (2003) reviews the notion of task switching in cognitive science research, which began with Jerslid (1927) but developed into a full paradigm only in the mid-1990s (Rogers & Monsell, 1995). Because it sees multitasking as switching from one task to another in rapid succession rather than the concurrent performance of two or more tasks, cognitive science research focuses on the costs to the individual of switching tasks compared to non-switch or task-repetition trials.

In experiments for deriving switching costs, subjects are asked to perform alternating different tasks so that their response times can be measured. When compared to non-switch or task-repetition trials, subjects performing switching trials take longer and make more errors. These switching costs can be reduced if the subjects are allowed to prepare for the task (Allport, Styles, & Hsieh, 1994; Meiran, 1996; Rogers & Monsell, 1995), but the costs cannot be reduced to zero—residual costs remain (De Jong, 2000; Kimberg, Aguirre, & D'Espisito, 2000; Sohn, Ursu, Anderson, Stenger, & Carter, 2000). Furthermore, even when the task switching occurs only once at the beginning of the trial and is subsequently eliminated, the single task switch at the beginning creates long-term mixing costs (mixing costs may capture executive control functioning processes in the experiment) (Rubin & Meiran, 2005).

Meyer and colleagues describe the executive control processes and cognitive architecture involved in rapid task sequencing/switching during multitasking in Rubinstein et al. (2001). Executive control provides a supervisory function controlling other perceptual/motor and cognitive processes when switching from one task to another. The three theories of executive control processes are:

1. The attention-to-action (ATA) model (Norman & Shallice, 1986), which envisages three subcomponents: action schemas, contention scheduling, and a supervisory attentional system.

2. The frontal-lobe executive (FLE) model (Duncan, 1986), which also envisages three subcomponents: goal lists, means–ends analysis procedures, and action structures.

3. The strategic response-deferment (SRD) model (Meyer & Kieras, 1997a, 1997b), which envisages three sets of production rules governing: Task 1 responses to stimulus, Task 2 responses to second stimulus, and executive process rules that obey task priorities allowing Task 2 responses to be stored temporarily in working memory until Task 1 priority is completed.

The three models "incorporate separable subcomponents that enable task switching" (Rubinstein et al., 2001, p. 765).

Logan (2004) describes the role of working memory in executive control during task switching. Theories of working memory are summarized by Miyake and Shah (1999) and Baddeley, Chincotta, and Adlam (2001). Working memory has capacity limitations (Anderson, Reder, & Lebiere, 1996); and in task switching, information is lost from working memory due to either decay (Anderson, Reder, & Lebiere, 1996) or interference (Waugh & Norman, 1965). Evidence for these two theories is mixed (Nairne, 2002). Two proposals describe how long-term memory and working memory combine together during task switching: They may be joined together, with working memory the active part (Anderson, Reder, & Lebiere, 1996), or they may be separate but interactive (Baddeley & Logie, 1999; Kieras, Meyer, Mueller, & Seymour, 1999). Does cognitive reconfiguration during task switching emphasize working memory (i.e., changing goals and stimulus-response mapping rules) (Rubinstein et al., 2001) or does it emphasize working memory plus cognition system outside working memory (Logan & Gordon, 2001; Meiran, 2000)? (See also the two opposing theoretical proposals for explaining time costs [Monsell, 1996], emphasizing either the task processing level or the executive control level.)

Multitasking continues to be an important concept for cognitive scientists. The next section examines how multitasking is represented in communication studies' models and theories.

Communication Studies

Communication studies observe multitasking from a multi-channel or multi-media perspective. In multitasking, the user of one medium or channel may also be engaging with other media at the same time. This phenomenon attracts particular interest because of the prevalence of multitasking behavior among today's media-savvy young people, who engage with television, music listening devices, instant messaging, and the telephone while surfing the Internet (Waxman, 2006). Using the term Concurrent Media Exposure (CME) to identify multitasking, Holmes, Papper, Popovich, and Bloxham (2005) state that CME behavior was indicated by 96 percent of their studies' participants, constituting 30.7 percent of the participants' total media exposure per day.

Communication scholars are interested in the user's "engagement" vis-à-vis the following four elements: (1) medium (channel), (2) content (genre), (3) audience (incidence of media exposure, time spent with media, audience demographics), and (4) context (location, hour of day, day of the week, mode of exposure, life activity, episodic structure, primary and secondary attention). These four elements constitute two study perspectives: either a media/content and/or an audience/context-centered viewpoint (Holmes, Papper, Popovich, & Bloxham, 2006). The media/content viewpoint can, in turn, have either a media channel or media content emphasis. The channel emphasis is an attribute of the particular medium: Different media channels have different potentials to engage their audience; a content emphasis focuses on the content delivered by the medium. Different media are associated with different formats, such as passive versus interactive or short episodic duration versus long episodic duration (Holmes et al., 2006).

Although CME is controlled primarily by the audience/context dimension, it is also influenced by the medium/content. For example, the combination of TV and the Internet is the dominant CME pairing, with CME occurring during 80 percent of Internet exposure (Internet as primary task) but only 28.5 percent during TV exposure (TV as primary task). For CME, Holmes et al. (2006) distinguish between active and passive engagement on the part of the user. This is illustrated on the passive side by the user shopping in a mall with radio in the background, where engagement/attention is shared; on the active side is the restless attention-shifting behavior that takes place in multitasking activities that occur in parent–child interactions.

The next section of the chapter examines multitasking research within the field of human factors.

Human Factors

Multitasking in human factors research is of pivotal concern in creating cognitive models that allow a human operator to supervise, control, and act appropriately in multidimensional environments. In human factors, multitasking is "the ability to integrate, interleave, and perform multiple tasks and/or component subtasks of a larger complex task" (Salvucci, Kushleyeva, & Lee, 2004, p. 267). There are examples of cognitive architecture/modeling and multitasking for driving (Aasman, 1995; Salvucci, Boer, & Liu, 2001), piloting combat aircraft (Jones, Laird, Nielsen, Coulter, Kenny, & Koss, 1999), and air traffic control (Lee & Anderson, 2001). Chou and Funk (1990) have proposed a Cockpit Task Management (CTM) system. Cognitive modeling for multitasking has increasingly involved studying complex domains, with unified cognitive architectures such as ACT-R (Adaptive Control of Thought-Rational) (Anderson, Bothell, Bryne, Douglass, Lebiere, & Qin, 2004), EPIC (Executive Process/Interactive Control) (Meyer & Kieras, 1997a, 1997b), and Soar (Newell, 1990).

Human factors researchers are beginning to develop supervisory and control interfaces based on cognitive modeling or cognitive architecture. Anderson and his associates (Anderson & Lebiere, 1998; Anderson, Taatgen, & Byrne, 2005; Gerjets, Scheiter, & Schoor, 2003; Schoor, Gerjets, & Scheiter, 2003; Taatgen, 2005) propose a general executive control model based on the ACT-R cognitive architecture. They have explored this cognitive architecture model for both discrete (Byrne & Anderson, 2001; Meyer & Kieras, 1997a, 1997b; Sohn & Anderson, 2001) and continuous tasks (Kieras, Meyer, Ballas, & Lauber, 2000). But they have used customized executives for multitasking that are appropriate only for the particular human activity being considered, ranging from list memory to mathematical problem solving, to air traffic control (Salvucci, Boer, & Liu, 2001).

Salvucci, Kushleyeva, and Lee (2004) provide a dedicated buffer supervising and controlling an automobile driver's goal set for multitasking, attached to the general executive. Driving a car is extremely complex and unpredictable; the higher level cognitive components maintain situation awareness, determine strategies for navigation, decide when to initiate and terminate maneuvers, and manage lower level cognitive components such as changing radio stations, conversations, and eating and drinking. Integrated driver cognitive models thus require "task prioritization and attention management to handle the multitasking nature of the driving task" (Salvucci, Boer, & Liu, 2001, p. 10).

Handheld devices provide unique challenges to user multitasking behavior. For a description of the special constraints of handheld devices (small screen size, slow processors, noisy physical environment, etc.), see Vaananen-Vainio-Mattila and Ruuska (2000). Nagata (2003) reports findings from a study that looks at multitasking while using a pocket PC (iPAQh3800). Following Preece, Rogers, and Benyon's (1994) definition of multitasking as alternating between tasks, Nagata (2003) looks at multitasking in terms of an interruption task resulting in a degradation of main task performance.

The next section outlines the role of multitasking in human–computer interaction studies.

Human–Computer Interaction Studies

The fundamentals of multitasking in human–computer interaction (HCI) studies are given by Tsukada, Okada, and Matsushita (1994), Card, Moran, and Newell (1983), and Preece et al. (1994). The issue of multitasking in HCI is approached via the concept of interruption. Interruptions are "unanticipated requests for switching between different tasks during multitasking" (McFarlane, 1997, p. 9). However, HCI differs slightly from cognitive science, which equates multitasking with task switching in repetitive tasks (see the cognitive science section of this chapter). In HCI, concurrent multitasking is acknowledged in the notion of the self being divided between internal (cognition) and external (observable behaviors) (Tsukada et al., 1994).

The information processing tasks that are internal to the person (cognition and perception) and external to the person (motor or actions) are different, creating a common situation in which a person can in fact be engaging concurrently in multiple tasks (Tsukada et al., 1994). A bottleneck may occur because people's external actions are undertaken in sequence (i.e., not concurrently) but tasks undergoing internal processing leading up to the action can in fact be performed concurrently or in parallel (McFarlane, 1997). Card et al. (1983) depict a model of two kinds of internal processing (perception and cognition) with only one motor processor for controlling external actions. Even in sequential actions, there can be an appearance of concurrent multitasking because external actions are defined as a series of 70 millisecond discrete actions that comprise all tasks, big or small. Thus, although motor actions are performed sequentially in chains of actions, the smallness of an action's discrete units means a task can be interrupted anywhere, at odd places, then returned to suddenly, giving the appearance of concurrent multitasking.

Relying on the idea that human actions are "discretizable," GOMS (Goals, Operators, Methods, and Selection rules) models have been developed (Card et al., 1983). A modification of the GOMS Model, called CPM-GOMS (Cognitive Perceptual Motor/Critical Path Method-GOMS), was created by John and Gray (1995) to model performance on subtasks and tasks. Chains of subtasks are scheduled on the three separate human processors (perception, cognition, and motor), each on a separate time track. The central idea is that people can do some things on one of the other processors while they are waiting to finish other things (McFarlane, 1997). The problem with multitasking on these parallel tracks is that people are interrupted and must return to the first task, often forgetting where they are in the subtask, which leads to wasted time and energy.

HCI research has focused on multitasking, task switching, interruptions and their effects on task performance, and on the ameliorative effects of interruptions on efficiency and safety. For example, research indicates a decrease in performance speed (Gillie & Broadbent, 1989; Kreifeldt & McCarthy, 1981) and observed differences in how people perform on interrupted tasks (Cabon, Coblentz, & Mollard, 1990) (for a review of the interruption and multitasking literature in HCI, see McFarlane, 2002). However, interruption of simple tasks has been found actually to increase performance efficiency (Brumistrov & Leonova, 2003; Speier, Valacich, & Vessey, 1997).

Information workers who engage in multitasking often suffer what is termed *prospective memory failure* when they return to a task. Prospective memory failure is the inability to remember the task that they must perform (Ellise & Kvavilashvili, 2000). Prospective memory failure has been shown to be a significant fact of life (Czerwinski & Horvitz, 2002; Dey & Abowd, 2000; Sellen, Louie, Harris, & Wilkins, 1996; Terry, 1988). Task interruptions at work are one of the most cited reasons for prospective memory failure (O'Connail & Frohlich, 1995). Accordingly, Card and Henderson (1987) propose a computer interface design to manage interruptions in multitasking and help people avoid prospective memory failure. McCrickard, Chewar, Somervell, and Ndiwalana (2003) propose a notification system, which they define as an interface used "in a divided-attention, multitasking situation," that delivers on time information to the user that is "parallel ... extraneous or supplemental to a user's attention priority" (McCrickard et al., 2003, pp. 312, 315).

The next section explores the nature of multitasking within organizational behavior research.

Organizational Behavior

Current interest concerning multitasking behavior is reflected in three general areas of the organizational behavior literature: individual differences or preferences that motivate multitasking behavior, the relationships between multitasking behavior and a variety of individuals' work-related outcomes, and multiple-task performance at the group level of analysis. Although some work on multitasking behavior across a wide range of organizations can be found in other organization-focused literatures such as management science (e.g., Eppen, Gould, Schmidt,

Moore, & Weatherford, 1998), labor economics, economic history, and occupational health (e.g., multitasking in French automobile firms [Gorgeu & Mathieu, 2005], among Dutch farm women [Bock, 2004], and in nineteenth-century Australian banks [Seltzer, 2000]), this section focuses on work published in core organizational behavior and applied psychology outlets.

It has been suggested that task environments have become more complex and workers' preferences have also changed in favor of greater task variety and more challenging work environments (Lindbeck & Snower, 2000). It thus seems reasonable to conclude that, in general, individuals are creating, encountering, and accepting more multitasking situations at work. Some workers succeed and even thrive in such environments but others do not cope well with task-juggling, experiencing instead increased levels of stress and stress-related injury and illness (Robinson & Smallman, 2006). As performance differences linked to multitasking behavior become more consequential to individuals and organizations, researchers have begun exploring the antecedents of multitasking behavior. This research eschews cognitive psychology's focus on the cognitive mechanisms of multitasking or the cognitive capability to multitask in favor of an emphasis on personality and preference.

Research on time urgency and multitasking is one such area of inquiry. Time urgency is a relatively stable individual difference variable and a subcomponent of the Type A behavior pattern (Conte, Landy, & Mathieu, 1995; Conte, Mathieu, & Landy, 1998; Landy, Rastegary, Thayer, & Colvin, 1991; Rastegary & Landy, 1993). Time urgency, like the Type A behavior pattern, has been associated with several health problems (Conte, Mathieu, & Landy, 1998). Time-urgent individuals carefully attend to the passage of time; they perceive time as their enemy and set themselves in opposition to it (Price, 1982; Waller, Conte, Gibson, & Carpenter, 2001). Time urgency is associated with time-related task strategies such as multitasking; time-urgent individuals are chronically hurried due to their tendency to schedule more activities than fit into the time available (Friedman & Roseman, 1974).

The issue of polychronicity has received slightly more attention in organizational behavior literature than time urgency, although the two concepts are closely related. Originally construed—along with monochronicity—as a characteristic of cultures (Hall, 1983), polychronicity in the organizational behavior literature refers chiefly to "the extent to which people (1) prefer to be engaged in two or more tasks or events simultaneously and are actually so engaged (the preference strongly implying the behavior and vice versa), and (2) believe their preference is the best way to do things" Bluedorn (2002, p. 51). Bluedorn cites significant positive relationships between polychronicity and extraversion (Lieberman & Rosenthal, 2001), favorable inclination toward change, tolerance for ambiguity, formal education, striving for achievement, impatience and irritability, and frequency of lateness and absenteeism (Bluedorn, 2002).

Other research focuses on the role of polychronicity in workers' outcomes in specific contexts. Slocumbe and Bluedorn (1999) found that the congruence between individuals' levels of polychronicity and amount of polychronicity they perceived in their workplaces to be positively related to (1) the individuals' organizational commitment, (2) their perceived performance, and (3) their perceptions of performance evaluation fairness. Similarly, Hecht and Allen's (2005) field study found that the fit between an individual's preference to engage in polychronic behavior and the opportunities to do so afforded by his or her work context significantly predicted worker well being (i.e., satisfaction, affect, self-efficacy, and psychological strain); however, these findings did not appear in data from their laboratory study of students. And, although Bluedorn (2002) found a negative relationship between the level of polychronicity and stress among dentists, he found no relationship between polychronicity and outcomes for other dental office workers. Additionally, in a study of delivery drivers, Francis-Smythe and Robertson (2003) found a significant positive influence of polychronicity on job-related well being. It would seem that at least for some types of work contexts, multitasking (polychronic) workers are "happy" workers. In sum, this area of research provides evidence of both positive and negative effects of multitasking behavior on workers' outcomes.

An additional and specific area of the organizational behavior literature addresses tensions between work and family roles, again providing evidence of both positive and negative influences of multitasking on workers. Research in this area generally conceptualizes multitasking as the switching by an individual between work-related and family-related roles. Ruderman, Ohlott, Panzer, and King (2002) found that managerial women with multiple life roles (job and non-job roles) successfully transferred their non-job multitasking skills to their work environments, ultimately enhancing their leadership qualities at work. This research provides support for the more general theory of work–family enrichment, which suggests "experiences in one role (can) improve the quality of life in the other role" (Greenhouse & Powell, 2006, p. 72). However, in a study based on data collected from 2,109 respondents, Voydanoff (2005) found that work–family multitasking (i.e., bringing work home and job contacts at home) were positively related to work–family conflict and perceived stress.

Most work is accomplished in groups of people in organizations; some organizational behavior scholars have therefore investigated multitasking behaviors specifically in group settings. Waller (1996, 1997) suggested that groups, like individuals, can choose different task performance strategies such as time swapping (performing one task at a time, en masse), or time sharing (performing multiple tasks simultaneously by distributing tasks across different group members). Marks, Mathieu, and Zaccaro (2001, p. 356) have likewise conceptualized teams as "multitasking units that perform multiple processes simultaneously and sequentially to orchestrate goal-directed task work."

In subsequent empirical work, Wagner, Meyer, Humphrey, and Hollenbeck (2005) argue that the choice between simultaneous (time sharing) or sequential (time swapping) task performance strategies in teams produces equivocal results. They suggest that different combinations of individualistic and collectivistic action influence how much multitasking behavior occurs in teams, reflecting team members' ability to recognize the different tasks needing to be performed and allocating them across team members. A limited amount of work in organizational behavior has also investigated individual influence on team multitasking behaviors.

Waller, Giambatista, and Zellmer-Bruhn (1998) studied the influence of highly time-urgent individuals (as compared to other group members) on group-level multitasking in small groups working toward a strict deadline. They found that the presence of a highly time-urgent member depressed group multitasking behavior, ostensibly because these individuals were able to keep their groups focused on one primary task at a time and thus monitor progress toward the deadline. Other work in the area suggests that groups comprised of individuals who are time urgent and hold a goal-oriented future- (rather than past- or present-) time orientation are more likely than other groups to "cram" more work into an allotted amount of time and that they cope by engaging in multitasking behavior (Waller et al., 2001).

The organizational behavior literature on multitasking paints a rather equivocal picture of multitasking's outcomes for workers. On the one hand, being able to switch among various tasks is regarded as a way for workers to enjoy enriched jobs and avoid monotonous, repetitive tasks that lead to boredom and dissatisfaction. Creating multitasking work environments is seen by many organizations as an arrangement that allows workers to be more flexible and responsive to unpredictable external organizational environments (Whitfield, 2000).

On the other hand, research in this area also suggests that for some workers, multitasking leads to increased levels of stress and health-related problems. Several studies have found indications that individuals are differentially motivated to and/or capable of engaging in multitasking behavior. Future research in organizational behavior should improve our understanding by more deeply investigating at least three issues.

First and as previously mentioned, the issue of volition in multitasking contexts should be carefully addressed. What different behaviors occur when workers choose to multitask and regulate their own pace of work as compared with being placed in a job context that requires near-constant multitasking? Additionally, previous research indicates that information regarding deadlines and time pressure can significantly affect individuals' task-pacing efforts (Waller, Zellmer-Bruhn, & Giambatista, 2002). Does the interaction of pacing volition and deadline imposition influence individuals' multitasking behaviors? How does information regarding task priorities (Ishizaka et al., 2001) affect pacing and multitasking under such conditions?

Second, existing work on multitasking in terms of person-job fit should be augmented. What *types* of multitasking requirements seem to be better suited to which individuals? Finally, issues of training multitasking behavior at both individual and group levels should be addressed in the organizational behavior literature, drawing upon pertinent research in human performance, cognitive psychology, and other disciplines. If the choice of task performance strategies is equivocal (Wagner et al., 2005), then what cues trigger multitasking behavior in high-performing individuals and groups in complex, time-pressured, task-performance contexts? Notwithstanding existing predilection and ability, it is conceivable that the *timing* of multitasking behavior, in addition to simultaneous task performance itself, could be improved for some individuals and groups.

Summary

Overall, in the cognitive sciences we see the development of two major themes. The first is that multitasking is, more often than not, studied within cognitive science and its associate disciplines in terms of interruption; thus, it is defined as a behavior that decreases efficiency and wastes time. Secondly, research acknowledges that with the proliferation of communication and information devices, multitasking while using these devices is facilitated and probably increasing. Is multitasking a negative or positive side effect of the advance of communication technology? Is it a behavior that is more important to us than we know?

In the next section we examine how multitasking is understood within information science.

Information Science

Until recently, information science devoted little attention to understanding multitasking within the context of the research issues and problems of the field. Multitasking research is now growing in theoretical and practical importance in information behavior research. We next examine how multitasking informs research on the Web and information retrieval.

Web and Information Retrieval Studies

Recent studies suggest that users' searches may have multiple goals or topics and that they occur within the broader context of information-seeking behaviors (Spink, 2004; Spink, Ozmutlu, & Ozmutlu, 2002). People may pool their topics and interact with an information retrieval (IR) system on multiple related or unrelated topics. Overall, a user's single session with an IR system consists of seeking information on single or multiple topics and also switching among topics (Spink et al., 2002).

Spink, Bateman, and Greisdorf (1999) found respondents in a Web-based survey reporting multitasking searches.

Spink et al. (2002) show that IR searches often include multiple topics during a single search session. They found that multitasking information seeking and searching are common human behaviors. Many IR system users conduct information seeking and searching on both related and unrelated topics. In addition, Web or IR multitasking search sessions are longer than single topic sessions, with mean topics per Web search ranging from 1 to more than 10 topics and a mean of 2.1 topic changes per search session.

Recent studies have examined multitasking searching on the Excite and AlltheWeb.com Web search engines (Ozmutlu, Ozmutlu, & Spink, 2003, 2004). Ozmutlu et al. (2003) provided a detailed analysis of multitasking sessions on AlltheWeb.com. They found that almost one third of AlltheWeb.com users performed multitasking Web searching. Multitasking Web search sessions often included more than three topics per session; were longer in duration than regular searching sessions; and most of the topics in multitasking searches involved switching among general information, computers, and entertainment. Ozmutlu et al. (2004) found that one tenth of Excite users and one third of AlltheWeb.com users conducted multitasking searches. Multitasking Web search sessions were longer than regular search sessions in terms of queries per session and duration, with both Excite and AlltheWeb.com users searching for about three topics per multitasking session and submitting about four to five queries per topic.

Typical Web search sessions are two queries; some comprise three or more (Spink & Jansen, 2004). Spink, Park, Jansen, and Pedersen (2006) conducted two studies of multitasking during Web searching; a study of two-query search sessions on the AltaVista Web search engine and a study of three-or-more-query search sessions on the AltaVista Web search engine. They examined the degree of multitasking search and information task switching during the two sets of AltaVista Web search sessions. A sample of two-query and three-or-more-query sessions were filtered from AltaVista transaction logs from 2002 and qualitatively analyzed. Sessions ranged in duration from less than a minute to a few hours. Findings included: (1) 81 percent of two-query sessions included multiple topics, (2) 91 percent of three-or-more-query sessions included multiple topics, (3) there was a broad variety of topics in multitasking search sessions, and (4) three-or-more-query sessions sometimes contained frequent topic changes.

The next section explores how multitasking is viewed within information behavior studies.

Information Behavior Studies

Spink and Park (2005) studied both multitasking information and non-information behaviors by business consultants. Key findings included: (1) seeking information formed 10.5 percent of business consultant daily tasks, (2) information-seeking tasks occurred within multitasking and task switching sequences with computing and communication tasks, and (3) information-seeking tasks were often conducted to support or respond to communication or computing tasks. Spink and Park (2005) provided a model of multitasking and task switching during information behavior that included cognitive, cognitive style, and individual differences variables. Spink, Alvarado-Albertorio, Naragan, Brumfield, and Park (2007) investigated the multitasking information behaviors of public library users at the Brentwood and Wilkinsburg Public Libraries in Pittsburgh through diary questionnaires. Some 63.5 percent of the 96 library users engaged in multitasking information behaviors, with a mean of 2.5 topic changes and 2.8 topics per library visit. A major finding was that many people in libraries seek information on multiple topics and engage in multitasking behaviors.

Spink and Cole (2005, 2006a, 2006b) have argued that, when information is added into the mix, the concept and process of multitasking takes on an added layer of complexity. Information behavior may involve a combination of cognitive and physical actions, on dual or multiple tasks concurrently or sequentially, including switching between different information tasks. Cognitively, humans sequence their information tasks and information task switching at different levels of complexity and speed. They argue that people's information behaviors are embedded within multitasking information behaviors that occur when users juggle multiple topics during the same search session.

Spink and Cole (2005, 2006a, 2006b) highlight how humans cognitively coordinate their information-seeking behaviors with their interactive searching (human–system interaction) behaviors; this includes recognizing and making sense of and cognitively articulating an information problem or a gap in their knowledge. In other words, information seekers have to coordinate a number of factors, including their cognitive state, level of knowledge, and understanding of their information problem, into a coherent series of sustained activities that include seeking, searching, retrieving, and using information. We know that hand-eye coordination is a physiological process that humans develop from childhood. But how do humans learn the process of coordinating their information needs into coherent processes of human information seeking, searching, retrieving, and use behaviors?

Rather than seeing this as a negative, like driving while engaging in another task, within information behavior research (Just et al., 2001; Rubinstein et al., 2001) we see multitasking as an essential element of the information-behavior process that must be carefully examined, allowed for, and facilitated in the design of IR systems (Spink, Park, & Cole, 2006).

Conclusion and Further Research

What have we learned from our examination of the cognitive and information sciences view of multitasking? The cognitive sciences are moving forward with research on interruption behavior that decreases efficiency and wastes time and on the positive and negative effects of multitasking while using information and communication technology.

Multitasking has been found to be beneficial in only a few cases (Brumistrov & Leonova, 2003; Speier, Valacich, & Vessey, 1997). Research in cognitive science and human factors sees multitasking as having negative consequences (i.e., producing a slow-down in performance of a principal task and increased errors). Cognitive science research views multitasking in terms of task switching, which causes inefficiencies in performance because of the residual costs when one returns to the primary task after having performed a secondary task. Because it sees multitasking as switching from one task to another in rapid succession rather than the concurrent performance of two or more tasks, cognitive science's research focus is on the costs to the individual of switching tasks compared to non-switch or task-repetition trials.

Although some cognitive science research indicates that there may be positive aspects to multitasking, the overall feeling is that further system design modifications are needed to protect against the negative effects of multitasking. A more nuanced view is possible if tasks are considered primary or secondary and requiring active or passive attention on the part of the user. An example of a primary-active task is a pilot engaged in active flying (e.g., steering) while monitoring safety-related alarm systems; an example of a secondary-passive task is listening to music while doing housework or studying for an exam. Although primary-active tasks are considered a positive form of multitasking that system design can augment, secondary-passive tasks and even secondary-active tasks (such as using a cell phone while driving) are considered impediments to the primary-active task of the user. This four-cell division of multitasking in cognitive science research between primary and secondary tasks and active and passive attention is revealingly expressed in a study of the differing placement of child-caring and housework by men and women (Michelson, 2005). The four-cell way of looking at multitasking also highlights the issue of imposed tasks versus voluntary multitasking, such as checking e-mail (secondary) while writing a business report (primary) for such beneficial reasons as resting the mind, collecting one's thoughts, or alleviating tedium—all of which serve to focus the mind when the user returns to the primary task.

Research on multitasking in organizational behavior focuses chiefly on developing a deeper understanding of the antecedents of multitasking behavior. Polychronicity seems to be the central variable of interest, for both individual and group-level multitasking behavior. Researchers are divided as to the positive and negative effects of workplace multitasking.

Many workers profess a preference for work environments that offer multitasking opportunities; however, many others report detrimental effects such as stress after working in demanding, multitasking-oriented settings. Finally, researchers report fairly consistent findings regarding the stress associated with multitasking connected to concurrent work–family demands.

Information behavior research, however, is developing the view that multitasking is an essential information behavior that enables us to adapt to our surroundings and survive. In other words, when we are engaged in performing a main task, communication devices facilitate a multitasking behavior that has always been present but becomes more obvious when we use these devices; that is, we constantly engage in a low-level scanning or monitoring of the environment. This low-level monitoring alerts us to danger and may set in motion other important information behavior phenomena that relate to human sensitivity and adaptation to both the social and physical environment in which we live (Spink & Cole, 2006a). This analysis provides hints of the importance of multitasking to human survival (Brumistrov & Leonova, 2003; Monsell, 2003; Speier, Valacich, & Vessey, 1997).

In addition, this chapter proposes that, both theoretically and practically, multitasking is an important concept for information behavior research. However, in the context of information behavior, multitasking is still largely under-researched. Task analysis in cognitive IR is a new arena of research. In spite of the new focus on tasks (Vakkari, Pennanen, & Serola, 2003), few information behavior models and theories take account of multitasking behaviors. Humans knowingly construct the information behavior-related processes that constitute our information behavior as a series of tasks. In the stop-and-go of everyday life, however, we are not in total control of how multiple tasks interact with each other; nor are we in control of how stages of an uncompleted task interact with or somehow become embedded in a task that is in focus at a given moment. Understanding and modeling multitasking information behaviors requires a greater understanding of the coordination and interplay among information seeking/foraging/sense-making, organizing, and use tasks.

We need to reconceptualize information behavior as the interplay of multitasking processes that require information coordinating behavior to work effectively (Spink, Park, Jansen, & Pedersen, 2006). Current information behavior models are also based on a single information task paradigm. But, information behaviors are often accomplished in complex fashion. Conceptualizing multitasking and coordination behaviors as suggested offers a relatively new, heuristic direction for information behavior research. The authors are currently conducting further studies to extend our understanding of the nature, patterns, and impacts of information behavior within a multitasking and coordinating framework. These include implications of multitasking in Web searching (Spink, Park, Jansen, & Pedersen, 2006) and also the development of new searching tools for more efficient IR system design (Spink & Cole, 2005).

Further research is being conducted to investigate the interplay between information and non-information tasks (Spink & Park, 2005). In particular, the concept of *information coordinating behavior* (ICB) is an important area of study for information science because it investigates how we intertwine tasks while sustaining momentum for completing individual tasks. The development of information behavior necessitates a theoretical and empirical explication of the important nature and role of information behaviors, including ICB. In information behavior, humans *coordinate* a number of elements, including their cognitive state, level of domain knowledge, and understanding of their information problem, into a coherent series of activities that may include seeking, searching, interactive browsing, retrieving, and constructing information.

Information seekers perform *interdependent activities* to achieve *goals* or solve problems. These activities may also require or create *resources* of various types. In this view, information seekers *coordinate information tasks* arising from dependencies that constrain how tasks can be performed. These dependencies may be inherent in the structure of the problem (e.g., components of a system may interact with each other, constraining the kinds of changes that can be made to a single component), or they may result from decomposition of the goal into activities or the assignment of activities to other actors and resources.

References

Aasman, J. (1995). *Modelling driver behaviour in Soar*. Leidschendam, The Netherlands: KPN Research.

Allport, A., Styles, E., & Hsieh, S. (1994). Shifting intentional set: Exploring the dynamic control of tasks. In C. Umita & M. Moscovitch (Eds.), *Attention and performance XV: Conscious and nonconscious information processing* (pp. 421–452). Cambridge, MA: MIT Press.

Anderson, J. R., Bothell, D., Byrne, M. D., Douglass, S., Lebiere, C., & Quin, Y. (2004). An integrated theory of the mind. *Psychological Review, 111*(4), 1036–1060.

Anderson, J. R., & Lebiere, C. (1998). *The atomic components of thought*. Mahwah, NJ: Erlbaum.

Anderson, J. R., Reder, L. M., & Lebiere, C. (1996). Working memory: Activation limitations on retrieval. *Cognitive Psychology, 30*(3), 221–256.

Anderson, J. R., Taatgen, N. A., & Byrne, M. D. (2005). Learning to achieve perfect time sharing: Architectural implications of Hazeltine, Teague, & Ivry (2002). *Journal of Experimental Psychology: Human Perception and Performance, 31*, 749–761.

Baddeley, A., Chincotta, D., & Adlam, A. (2001). Working memory and the control of action: Evidence from task switching. *Journal of Experimental Psychology: General, 130*(4), 641–657.

Baddeley, A., & Logie, R. H. (1999). Working memory: The multiple-component model. In A. Miyake & P. Shah (Eds.), *Models of working memory:*

Mechanisms of active maintenance and executive control (pp. 28–61). Cambridge, UK: Cambridge University Press.

Bainbridge, L. (2002). Processes underlying human performance. In D. J. Garland & J. A. Wise (Eds.), *Handbook of aviation human factors: Human factors in transportation* (pp. 107–171). Mahwah, NJ: Erlbaum.

Bherer, L., Kramer, A. F., Peterson, M. S., Colcombe, S., Erickson, K., & Becic, E. (2005). Training effects on dual-task performance: Are there age-related differences in plasticity of attentional control? *Psychology and Aging, 20*(4), 695–709.

Bluedorn, A. C. (2002). *The human organization of time.* Stanford, CA: Stanford University Press.

Bock, B. B. (2004). Fitting in and multi-tasking: Dutch farm women's strategies in rural entrepreneurship. *Sociologia Ruralis, 44*(3), 245–260.

Brumistrov, I., & Leonova, A. (2003). Do interrupted users work faster or slower? The micro-analysis of computerized text editing task. In J. Jacko & C. Stephanidis (Eds.), *Human–computer interaction: Theory and practice* (Part I) (Proceedings of HCI International 2003) (pp. 621–625). Mahwah, NJ: Erlbaum.

Burgess, P. W. (2000). Real-world multitasking from a cognitive neuroscience perspective. In S. Monsell & J. Driver (Eds.), *Control of cognitive processes: Attention and performance XVIII* (pp. 465–472). Cambridge, MA: MIT Press.

Byrne, M. D., & Anderson, J. R. (2001). Serial modules in parallel: The psychological refractory period and perfect time-sharing. *Psychological Review, 108,* 847–869.

Cabon, P., Coblentz, A., & Mollard, R. (1990). Interruption of a monotonous activity with complex tasks: Effects of individual differences. *Proceedings of the Human Factors Society 34th Annual Meeting,* 912–916.

Card, S. K., & Henderson, A., Jr. (1987). A multiple, virtual-workspace interface to support user task switching. In J. M. Carroll & P. P. Tanner (Eds.), *Proceedings of the SIGCHI/GI Conference on Human Factors in Computing Systems and Graphics Interface* (pp. 53–59). New York: ACM Press.

Card, S. K., Moran, T. P., & Newell, A. (1983). *The psychology of human–computer interaction.* Hillsdale, NJ: Erlbaum.

Carlson, R. A., & Sohn, M.-Y. (2000). Cognitive control of multistep routines: Information processing and conscious intentions. In S. Monsell & J. Driver (Eds.), *Control of cognitive processes: Attention and performance XVIII* (pp. 443–464). Cambridge, MA: MIT Press.

Cascio, W. (1978). *Applied psychology in personnel management.* Reston, VA: Reston Publishing.

Chou, C., & Funk, K. (1990). Management of multiple tasks: Cockpit task management errors. *Proceedings of the 1990 IEEE International Conference on Systems, Man, and Cybernetics,* 470–474.

Conte, J. M., Landy, F. J., & Mathieu, J. E. (1995). Time urgency: Conceptual and construct development. *Journal of Applied Psychology, 80,* 178–185.

Conte, J. M., Mathieu, J. E., & Landy, F. J. (1998). The nomological and predictive validity of time urgency. *Journal of Organizational Behavior, 19*(1), 1–13.

Courtright, C. (2007). Context in information behavior research. *Annual Review of Information Science and Technology, 41,* 273–306.

Czerwinski, M., & Horvitz, E. (2002). An investigation of memory for daily computing events. In X. Faulkner, J. Findlay, & F. Détienne, (Eds.), *People and computers XVI: Memorable yet invisible: Proceedings of HCI 2002* (pp. 229–245). London: Springer-Verlag.

Davenport, E. (2002). Organizational knowledge and communities of practice. *Annual Review of Information Science and Technology*, *36*, 171–227.

De Jong, R. (2000). An intention-activation account of residual switch costs. In S. Monsell & J. Driver (Eds.), *Control of cognitive processes: Attention and performance XVIII* (pp. 357–376). Cambridge, MA: MIT Press.

Dey, A. K., & Abowd, G. D. (2000). CyberMinder: A context aware system for supporting reminds. *Proceedings of the 2nd International Symposium on Handheld and Ubiquitous Computing*, 172–186.

Duncan, J. (1986). Disorganization of behaviour after frontal-lobe damage. *Cognitive Neuropsychology*, *3*, 271–290.

Ellise, J., & Kvavilashvili, L. (2000). Prospective memory in 2000: Past, present and future directions. *Applied Cognitive Psychology*, *14*(7), 1–9.

Eppen, G. D., Gould, F. J., Schmidt, C. P., Moore, J. H., & Weatherford, L. R. (1998). *Introductory management science: Decision modeling with spreadsheets*. Upper Saddle River, NJ: Prentice Hall.

Finholt, T. A. (2002). Collaboratories. *Annual Review of Information Science and Technology*, *36*, 73–107.

Foster, J. (2006). Collaborative information seeking and retrieval. *Annual Review of Information Science and Technology*, *40*, 329–356.

Francis-Smythe, J. A., & Robertson, I. T. (2003). The importance of time congruity in the organization. *Applied Psychology: An International Review*, *52*(2), 298–321.

Friedman, M., & Roseman, R. (1974). *Type A behavior and your heart*. New York: Knopf.

Friedman, T. L. (2006, July 5). The age of interruption. *New York Times*, p. A19.

Garcia, A. C., Dawes, M. E., Kohne, M. L., Miller, F. M., & Groschwitz, S. F. (2006). Workplace studies and technological change. *Annual Review of Information Science and Technology*, *40*, 393–437.

Gerjets, P., Scheiter, K., & Schoor, T. (2003). Modeling processes of volitional action control in multiple-task performance: How to explain effects of goal competition and task difficulty on processing strategies and performance within ACT-R. *Cognitive Science Quarterly*, *3*, 355–400.

Gillie, T., & Broadbent, D. (1989). What makes interruptions disruptive? A study of length, similarity, and complexity. *Psychological Research*, *50*, 243–250.

Glass, J. M., Schumacher, E. H., Lauber, E. J., Zurbriggen, E. L., Gmeindl, L., Kieras, et al. (2000). Aging and the psychological refractory period: Task-coordination strategies in young and old adults. *Psychology and Aging*, *15*(4), 571–595.

Gorgeu, A., & Mathieu, R. (2005). Teamwork in factories within the French automobile industry. *New Technology, Work and Employment*, *20*, 88–101.

Grady, C. L., Springer, M. V., Hongwanishkul, D., McIntosh, R., & Winocur, G. (2006). Age-related changes in brain activity across the adult lifespan. *Journal of Cognitive Neuroscience*, *18*(2), 227–241.

Greenhouse, J. H., & Powell, G. N. (2006). When work and family are allies: A theory of work–family enrichment. *Academy of Management Review*, *31*(1), 72–92.

Hafner, K. (2005, February 10). You there, at the computer: Pay attention. *The New York Times*, p. E1.

Hall, E. T. (1983). *The dance of life: The other dimension of time*. Garden City, NY: Anchor Press.

Hecht, T. D., & Allen, N. J. (2005). Exploring links between polychronicity and well-being from the perspective of person–job fit: Does it matter if you prefer to do only one thing at a time? *Organizational Behavior and Human Decision Processes, 98*, 155–178.

Holmes, M. E., Papper, R. A., Popovich, M. N., & Bloxham, M. (2005). *Middletown media studies II: Concurrent media exposure.* Muncie, IN: Ball State University Center for Media Design.

Holmes, M. E., Papper, R. A., Popovich, M. N., & Bloxham, M. (2006). *Engaging the ad-supported media: Middletown Media Studies: Observing consumers and their interactions with media* (Middletown Media Studies Whitepaper). Muncie, IN: Ball State University Center for Media Design.

Holstein, W. J. (2006, June 7). The workplace. *International Herald Tribune*, p. 22.

Hunt, E., & Joslyn, S. (2000). A functional task analysis of time-pressured decision making. In J. M. Schraagen, S. F. Chipman, & V. L. Shalin (Eds.), *Cognitive task analysis* (pp. 119–134). Mahwah, NJ: Erlbaum.

Ishizaka, K., Marshall, S. P., & Conte, J. M. (2001). Individual differences in attentional strategies in multitasking situations. *Human Performance, 14*(4), 339–358.

Jerslid, A. (1927). Mental set and shift [Special issue]. *Archives of Psychology, 89*.

John, B. E., & Gray, W. D. (1995). GOMS analysis for parallel activities. In J. Miller, I. Katz, R. Mack, & L. Marks (Eds.), *ACM Conference on Human Factors in Computing Systems: Conference companion on human factors in computing systems*, 395–396.

Jones, R. M., Laird, J. E., Nielsen, P. E., Coulter, K., Kenny, P., & Koss, F. (1999). Automated intelligent pilots for combat flight simulation. *AI Magazine, 20*, 27–42.

Jones, W. (2007). Personal information management. *Annual Review of Information Science and Technology, 41*, 453–504.

Just, M. A., Carpenter, P. A., Keller, T. A., Emery, L., Zajac, H., & Thulborn, K. R. (2001). Interdependence of non-overlapping cortical systems in dual cognitive tasks. *Neuroimage, 14*, 417–426.

Keele, S. W., & Rafal, R. D. (2000). Deficits of attentional set in patients with left prefrontal cortex lesions. In S. Monsell & J. Driver (Eds.), *Attention and performance XVIII: Control of cognitive processes* (pp. 627–651). Cambridge, MA: MIT Press.

Kieras, D. E., Meyer, D. E., Ballas, J. A., & Lauber, E. J. (2000). Modern computational perspectives on executive mental processes and cognitive control: Where to from here? In S. Monsell & J. Driver (Eds.), *Control of cognitive processes: Attention and performance XVIII* (pp. 681–712). Cambridge, MA: MIT Press.

Kieras, D. E., Meyer, D. E., Mueller, S., & Seymour, T. (1999). Insights into working memory from the perspective of the EPIC architecture for modeling skilled perceptual-motor and cognitive human performance. In A. Miyake & P. Shah (Eds.), *Models of working memory: Mechanisms of active maintenance and executive control* (pp. 183–223). Cambridge, UK: Cambridge University Press.

Kimberg, D. Y., Aguirre, G. K., & D'Espisito, M. (2000). Modulation of task-related neural activity in task switching: An fMRI study. *Cognitive Brain Research, 10*(1–2), 189–196.

Kreifeldt, J. G., & McCarthy, M. E. (1981); Interruption as a test of the user-computer interface. *Proceedings of the 17th Annual Conference on Manual Control*, 655–667.

Landy, F. J., Rastegary, H., Thayer, J., & Colvin, C. (1991). Time urgency: The construct and its measurement. *Journal of Applied Psychology, 76*, 644–657.

Lee, F. J., & Anderson, J. (2001). Does learning of a complex task have to be complex? A study in learning decomposition. *Cognitive Psychology, 42*, 267–316.

Lee, F. J., & Taatgen, N. A. (2002). Multitasking as skill acquisition. *Proceedings of the 24th Annual Meeting of the Cognitive Science Society*, 572–577.

Lieberman, M. D., & Rosenthal, R. (2001). Why introverts can't always tell who likes them: Multitasking and nonverbal decoding. *Journal of Personality and Social Psychology, 80*(2), 294–310.

Lindbeck, A., & Snower, D. J. (2000). Multitask learning and the reorganization of work: From Tayloristic to holistic organization. *Journal of Labor Economics, 18*(3), 353–376.

Logan, G. D. (2004). Working memory, task switching, and executive control in the task span procedure. *Journal of Experimental Psychology: General, 133*(2), 218–236.

Logan, G. D., & Gordon, R. D. (2001). Executive control of visual attention in dual-task situations. *Psychological Review, 108*, 393–434.

Marks, M. A., Mathieu, J. E., & Zaccaro, S. J. (2001). A temporally based framework and taxonomy of team processes. *Academy of Management Review, 26*(3), 356–376.

Mayr, U. (2001). Age differences in the selection of mental sets: The role of inhibition, stimulus ambiguity, and response-set overlap. *Psychology and Aging, 16*, 96–109.

McCrickard, D. S., Chewar, C. M., Somervell, J. P., & Ndiwalana, A. (2003). A model for notification systems evaluation: Assessing user goals for multitasking activity. *ACM Transactions on Computer–Human Interaction, 10*(4), 312–338.

McFarlane, D. C. (1997). *Interruption of people in human–computer interaction: A general unifying definition of human interruption and taxonomy.* Washington, DC: Naval Research Laboratory, The United States Navy. Retrieved July 28, 2006, from interruptions.net/literature/McFarlane-NRL-97.pdf

McFarlane, D. C. (2002). Comparison of four primary methods for coordinating the interruption of people in human–computer interaction, *Human–Computer Interaction, 17*(1), 63–139.

Meiran, N. (1996). Reconfiguration of processing mode prior to task performance. *Journal of Experimental Psychology: Learning, Memory, and Cognition, 22*, 1423–1442.

Meiran, N. (2000). Modeling cognitive control in task-switching. *Psychological Review, 63*(3–4), 234–239.

Meyer, D. E., Glass, J. M., Mueller, S. T., Seymour, T. L., & Kieras, D. E. (2001). Executive-process interactive control: A unified computational theory for answering twenty questions (and more) about cognitive aging. *European Journal of Cognitive Psychology, 13*, 123–164.

Meyer, D. E., & Kieras, D. E. (1997a). EPIC: Computational theory of executive cognitive processes and multiple-task performance: Part 1. Basic mechanisms. *Psychological Review, 104*, 3–65.

Meyer, D. E., & Kieras, D. E. (1997b). EPIC: A computational theory of executive cognitive processes and multiple-task performance: Part 2. Accounts of psychological refractory period phenomena. *Psychological Review, 104*, 749–791.

Michelson, W. (2005). *Time use: Expanding explanation in the social sciences.* Boulder, CO: Paradigm.

Miller, G. A. (1956). The magical number seven, plus or minus two: Some limits on our capacity for processing information. *Psychological Review*, *63*, 81–97.

Miyake, A., Friedman, N. P., Emerson, M. J., Witzki, A. H., Howerter, A., & Wager, T. D. (2000). The unity and diversity of executive functions and their contributions to complex "frontal lobe" tasks: A latent variable analysis. *Cognitive Psychology*, *41*, 49–100.

Miyake, A., & Shah, P. (Eds.). (1999). *Models of working memory: Mechanisms of active maintenance and executive control*. Cambridge, UK: Cambridge University Press.

Miyata, Y., & Norman, D. A. (1986). Psychological issues in support of multiple activities. In D. A. Norman & S. W. Draper (Eds.), *User centered design* (pp. 265–284). Hillsdale, NJ: Erlbaum.

Monsell, S. (1996). Control of mental processes. In V. Bruce (Ed.), *Unsolved mysteries of the mind: Tutorial essays in cognition* (pp. 93–148). Hove, England: Erlbaum, Taylor & Francis.

Monsell, S. (2003). Task switching. *Trends in Cognitive Neuroscience*, *7*(3), 134–140.

Nagata, S. F. (2003). Multitasking and interruptions during mobile Web tasks. *Proceedings of the Human Factors and Ergonomics Society 47th Annual Meeting*, 1341–1345.

Nairne, J. S. (2002). Remembering over the short term: The case against the standard model. *Annual Review of Psychology*, *53*, 53–81.

Newell, A. (1990). *Unified theories of cognition*. Cambridge, MA: Harvard University Press.

Norman, D. A., & Shallice, T. (1986). Attention to action: Willed and automatic control of behavior. In R. J. Davidson, G. E. Schwartz, & D. Shapiro (Eds.), *Consciousness and self-regulation* (Vol. 4, pp. 1–18). New York: Plenum.

O'Connail, B., & Frohlich, D. (1995). Time space in the workplace: Dealing with interruptions. *Conference on Human Factors in Computing Systems*, 262–263.

Ozmutlu, S., Ozmutlu, H. C., & Spink, A. (2003). Multitasking Web search: Implications for design. *Proceedings of the Annual Meeting of the American Society for Information Science and Technology*, 416–421.

Ozmutlu, S., Ozmutlu, H. C., & Spink, A. (2004). Are people asking questions on general Web search engines? *Online Information Review*, *6*, 396–406.

Pashler, H. (2000). Task switching and multitask performance (tutorial). In S. Monsell & J. Driver (Eds.), *Control of cognitive processes: Attention and performance XVIII* (pp. 277–309). Cambridge, MA: MIT Press.

Preece, J., Rogers, Y., & Benyon, D. (1994). *Human–computer interaction*. Workingham, England: Addison-Wesley.

Price, V. A. (1982). *Type A behavior pattern: A model for research and practice*. New York: Academic Press.

Rastegary, H., & Landy, F. J. (1993). The interactions among time urgency, uncertainty and time pressure. In O. Svenson & A. J. Maule (Eds.), *Time pressure and stress in human judgment and decision making* (pp. 217–239). New York: Plenum.

Robinson, A. M., & Smallman, C. (2006). The contemporary British workplace: A safer and healthier place? *Work, Employment, and Society*, *20*(1), 87–107.

Rogers, R., & Monsell, S. (1995). The costs of a predictable switch between simple cognitive tasks. *Journal of Experimental Psychology: General*, *124*, 207–231.

Rogers, Y. (2004). New theoretical approaches for human–computer interaction. *Annual Review of Information Science and Technology*, *38*, 87–143.

Rubin, O., & Meiran, N. (2005). On the origins of task mixing cost in the cuing task-switching paradigm. *Journal of Experimental Psychology: Learning, Memory and Cognition, 31*(6), 1477–1491.

Rubinstein, J. S., Meyer, D. E., & Evans, J. E. (2001). Executive control of cognitive processes in task switching. *Journal of Experimental Psychology: Human Perception and Performance, 27*(4), 763–797.

Ruderman, M. N., Ohlott, P. J., Panzer, K., & King, S. N. (2002). Benefits of multiple roles for managerial women. *Academy of Management Journal, 45*(2), 369–386.

Salvucci, D. D., Boer, E. R., & Liu, A. (2001). Toward an integrated model of driver behavior in a cognitive architecture. *Transportation Research Record, 1779,* 9–16.

Salvucci, D. D., Kushleyeva, Y., & Lee, F. J. (2004). Toward an ACT-R general executive for human multitasking. *Proceedings of the Sixth International Conference on Cognitive Modeling,* 267–272.

Schoor, T., Gerjets, P., & Scheiter, K. (2003). Volitional action control in multiple-task performance: Modeling effects of goal competition and task difficulty in ACT-R. *Proceedings of the Fifth International Conference on Cognitive Modeling,* 183–188.

Schweickert, R., & Boggs, G. J. (1984). Models of central capacity and concurrency. *Journal of Mathematical Psychology, 28*(3), 223–281.

Scott, M. (2006, June 17). Tuned out. *The Gazette* [Montreal], pp. H1, H4.

Sellen, A. J., Louie, G., Harris, J. E., & Wilkins, A. J. (1996). What brings intentions to mind? An in situ study of prospective memory. *Memory, 5*(4), 483–507.

Seltzer, A. J. (2000). Controlling and motivating the workforce: Evidence from the banking industry in the late nineteenth and early twentieth centuries. *Australian Economic History Review, 40*(3), 219–238.

Slocumbe, T. E., & Bluedorn, A. C. (1999). Organizational behavior implications of the congruence between preferred polychronicity and experienced work-unit polychronicity. *Journal of Organizational Behavior, 20,* 75–99.

Sohn, M.-H., & Anderson, J. R. (2001). Task preparation and task repetition: Two-component model of task switching. *Journal of Experimental Psychology: General, 130,* 764–778.

Sohn, M.-H., Ursu, S., Anderson, J. R., Stenger, V. A., & Carter, C. S. (2000). The role of prefrontal cortex and posterior parietal cortex in task switching. *Proceedings of the National Academy of Science, 97*(24), 13448–13453.

Speier, C., Valacich, J. S., & Vessey, I. (1997). The effects of task interruption and information presentation on individual decision making. In *Proceedings of the XVIII International Conference on Information Systems,* 21–36.

Spink, A. (2004). Everyday life multitasking information behavior: An exploratory study. *Journal of Documentation, 60*(4), 336–345.

Spink, A., Alvarado-Albertorio, F., Naragan, B., Brumfield, J., & Park, M. (2007). *Multitasking information behavior: An exploratory study.* Manuscript submitted for publication.

Spink, A., Bateman, J., & Greisdorf, H. (1999). Successive searching behavior during mediated information seeking: An exploratory study. *Journal of Information Science, 25*(6), 439–449.

Spink, A., & Cole, C. (2005). Multitasking framework for interactive information retrieval. In A. Spink & C. Cole (Eds.), *New directions in cognitive information retrieval* (pp. 99–112). Berlin: Springer.

Spink, A., & Cole, C. (2006a). *New directions in human information behavior.* Berlin: Springer.

Spink, A., & Cole, C. (2006b). Human information behavior: Integrating diverse approaches and information use. *Journal of the American Society for Information Science and Technology, 57*(1), 25–35.

Spink, A., & Jansen, B. J. (2004). *Web search: Public searching of the Web.* Berlin: Springer.

Spink, A., Ozmutlu, H. C., & Ozmutlu, S. (2002). Multitasking information seeking and searching processes. *Journal of the American Society for Information Science and Technology, 53*(8), 639–652.

Spink, A., & Park, M. (2005). Information and non-information task interplay. *Journal of Documentation, 61*(4), 548–554.

Spink, A., Park, M., & Cole, C. (2006). Multitasking and coordinating framework for information behavior. In A. Spink & C. B. Cole (Eds.), *New directions in human information behavior* (pp. 137–154). Berlin: Springer.

Spink, A., Park, M., Jansen, B. J., & Pedersen, J. (2006). Multitasking during Web search sessions. *Information Processing & Management, 42*(1), 264–275.

Stone, L. (2006, March). Attention: The real aphrodisiac. Conference Keynote Address. *O'Reilly Emerging Technology Conference,* San Diego, CA. Retrieved on July 8, 2006, from conferences.oreillynet.com/cs/et2006/view/e_sess/8290

Strayer, D. L., & Johnston, W. A. (2001). Driven to distraction: Dual-task studies of simulated driving and conversing on a cellular telephone. *Psychological Science, 12*(6), 462–466.

Taatgen, N. A. (2005). Modeling parallelization and speed improvement in skill acquisition: From dual tasks to complex dynamic skills. *Cognitive Science, 29,* 421–455.

Taylor, J. L., O'Hara, R., Mumenthaler, M. S., Rosen, A. C., & Yesavage, J. A. (2005). Cognitive ability, expertise, and age differences in following air-traffic control instructions. *Psychology and Aging, 20*(1), 117–133.

Terry, W. S. (1988). Everyday forgetting: Data from a diary study. *Psychological Reports, 62,* 299–303.

Tsukada, K., Okada, K. I., & Matsushita, Y. (1994). The multi-project support system based on multiplicity of task. *Eighteenth Annual International Computer Software and Applications Conference,* 358–363.

Vaananen-Vainio-Mattila, K., & Ruuska, S. (2000). Designing mobile phones and communicators of consumers' needs at Nokia. In E. Bergman (Ed.), *Information appliances and beyond: Interaction design for consumer products* (pp. 169–204). San Francisco: Morgan Kaufman.

Vakkari, P. (2003). Task-based information searching. *Annual Review of Information Science and Technology, 37,* 413–464.

Vakkari, P., Pennanen, M., & Serola, S. (2003). Changes of search terms and tactics while writing a research proposal: A longitudinal case study. *Information Processing & Management, 39*(3), 445–463.

Voydanoff, P. (2005). Consequences of boundary-spanning demands and resources for work-to-family conflict and perceived stress. *Journal of Occupational Health Psychology, 10*(4), 491–503.

Wagner, J. A., Meyer, C. J., Humphrey, S. E., & Hollenbeck, J. R. (2005). The effects of utilitarian and ontological individualism-collectivism on multitask performance in teams. *Academy of Management Best Conference Paper Proceedings,* OB:B1–OB:B6.

Waller, M. J. (1996). Multiple-task performance in groups. *Academy of Management Best Papers Proceedings,* 303–306.

Waller, M. J. (1997). Keeping the pins in the air: How work groups juggle multiple tasks. In M. M. Beyerlein & D. A. Johnson (Eds.), *Advances in interdisciplinary studies of work teams* (Vol. 4, pp. 217–247). Stamford, CT: JAI Press.

Waller, M. J., Conte, J. M., Gibson, C. B., & Carpenter, M. A. (2001). The effect of individual perceptions of deadlines on team performance. *Academy of Management Review, 26*(4), 586–600.

Waller, M. J., Giambatista, R. C., & Zellmer-Bruhn, M. E. (1998). The effects of individual time urgency on group polychronicity. *Journal of Managerial Psychology, 14*(3/4), 244–256.

Waller, M. J., Zellmer-Bruhn, M. E., & Giambatista, R. C. (2002). Watching the clock: Group pacing behavior under dynamic deadlines. *Academy of Management Journal, 45*, 1046–1055.

Waugh, N. C., & Norman, D. A. (1965). Primary memory. *Psychological Review, 72*, 89–104.

Waxman, S. (2006, May 15). At an industry media lab, close views of multitasking. *New York Times*, pp. C1, C5.

Whitfield, K. (2000). High-performance workplaces, training, and the distribution of skills. *Industrial Relations, 39*(1), 1–25.

Wickens, C. D. (1992). *Engineering psychology and human performance.* New York: HarperCollins.

CHAPTER 4

Activity Theory and Information Seeking

T. D. Wilson
University of Sheffield

Introduction

One needs a fairly broad definition of "information science" in order to consider applications of activity theory in the field, and, fortunately, as evidenced by the range of topics *ARIST* has covered over the years, the editors have encouraged a wide definition. As we shall see, to restrict the definition in any way would result in a very short chapter indeed.

Consequently, this review ranges widely, from aspects of psychology (where the theory was first formulated) through education, to information systems and human–computer interaction, digital library development, and information-seeking behavior. The paucity of contributions in what might be labeled "library and information science" is curious. It is common in this broad field to identify "activities" of numerous kinds in academic and practitioner writing. Reference service, information seeking, cataloging, children's services, and online searching are all described as "activities" and yet "activity theory" has made very little impact.

Why would activity theory be needed in library and information science? At present, research in this area is conducted within separate silos, sometimes defined by problem areas such as information retrieval (IR) and information-seeking behavior, sometimes defined by institutional type, such as research libraries, college and university libraries, school libraries, and so on. There is no overarching paradigm for research in these areas and the divisions are perpetuated in different sets of journals related to the different fields. The consequence is that researchers in one area may not understand the problem areas defined by another, may have no awareness of differences in research methodologies, and may have no common language within which to exchange ideas and results. Activity theory could provide that overarching paradigm.

The aim of this chapter, therefore, is to review the development of the concept and its application in related fields and to suggest how those applications might find their way into library and information science.

The chapter is structured as follows. First, the historical background and nature of activity theory are presented. This is followed by an analysis of its use in some fields of interest to information science, and then the implications of these developments for information science are presented. In this section, "information literacy" is used as an example of how activity theory can help to develop a research agenda. Finally, brief conclusions on the significance of activity theory for information science are presented, together with an activity-theoretical expansion of information science to include related disciplines.

Although activity theory has not been dealt with previously as a topic in its own right in *ARIST*, some authors have drawn attention to its value in other fields. Van House (2004), reviewing the field of science and technology studies, commented on the significance of activity theory in workplace studies. In the same volume, Rogers (2004) explored activity theory as one of the new approaches to human–computer interaction research.

The Origins of Activity Theory

Activity theory had its origins in psychology in the Soviet Union as a Marxist alternative to the prevailing Western psychological orthodoxy of behaviorism. It was originally proposed as a theory of human consciousness and as an explanation of the nature of human behavior. Human behavior consists of activities of one kind or another, and at the root of activity theory is the proposition that consciousness is formed through activity. In fact, as Bedny, Seglin, and Meister (2000) point out, because of the cultural impacts on consciousness, human behavior is not reducible to a variety of animal behavior; the term chosen to describe human behavior in Russian, therefore, was *deyatel'nost*, which is translated as "activity." However, as Kuutti (1996, p. 41) points out, the Russian term has connotations of acting to transform something, which the English word does not convey. In essence, therefore, "activity theory" connotes the study of the mode of human behavior that acts upon objects to transform them.[1]

The key names in the early stage of the development of activity theory were those of Lev Semyonovich Vygotsky (1896–1934), whose ideas are still widely applied in developmental psychology and educational research (e.g., Kozulin, Gindis, Ageyev, & Miller, 2003), and Sergei Leonidovich Rubinshtein (1889–1960). Rubinshtein tends to be rather ignored in the history of the theory in the West, although Zinchenko (1995, p. 42) notes (without providing a citation[2]) that: "In 1922 Sergei Rubinshtein transplanted the philosophical category of 'activity' into psychological soil." However, the research most closely associated with the development of the theory beyond Vygotsky was that of one of his students and subsequently fellow researcher, Alexei Nikolaevich Leont'ev (1903–1979). The diagrammatic representation of activity theory shown in Figure 4.1 emerged from Vygotsky's early work.

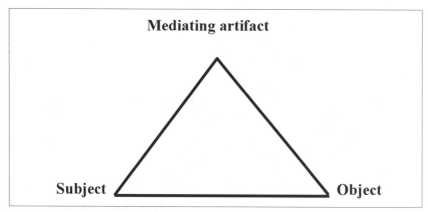

Figure 4.1   Vygotsky's activity theory.

In Vygotsky's original formulation, "mediating artifacts" are replaced by "psychological tools," by which he meant language, writing, mathematics, maps, and other symbol structures, although his later work was concerned mainly with signs and words, with other symbolic structures receiving less attention (Zinchenko, 1995, p. 38). Consequently, "artifacts" should be understood as including these tools as well as the physical tools that figure more commonly in current, Western research employing activity theory.

Because so many of the early researchers on activity theory were students and subsequently coworkers of Vygotsky, developments in the field were, to a significant degree, the result of collective endeavor. However, we can attribute many of the key ideas of the theory to Leont'ev (1977, 1978), who developed the cultural-historical dimension, notions of division of labor in the performance of activity, and, importantly, the hierarchical relationships of activity, actions, and operations. As Zinchenko (1995, p. 44) has pointed out, Vygotsky was concerned with "the problem of ideal mediators that exist between humans and between humans and the world," that is, the abstract tools of language and so on, but "the psychological theory of activity was concerned with the problem of real (i.e., concrete) tools and objects that humans ... place between themselves and nature." In essence, it is Leont'ev's activity theory that is represented in Engeström's diagrammatic representation, shown in Figure 4.2.

Engeström adds to Vygotsky's formulation the concepts of *rules and norms*, *community*, and *division of labor*. The *rules and norms* constitute the formal and informal, legal, and traditional limits on and specification of the activity being undertaken. For example, a social worker will undertake an activity of, say, evaluating a potential foster parent under the organization's procedures and guidelines for fostering, which may themselves be derived from statute law. The *community* can be elaborated at different levels; it may be the immediate work group or team of

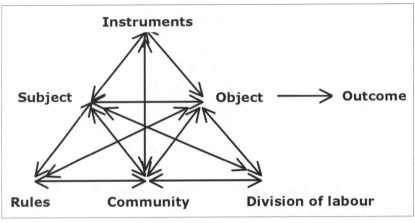

Figure 4.2   Leont'ev's activity theory as represented by Engeström (1987).

which the *subject* is part, or the wider organizational community, or the society at large. The *division of labor* simply relates to the extent to which the performance of the activity involves collaboration and the sharing of tasks with others. These extensions, in effect, move the focus of activity theory from the individual and consciousness, to activities within a community and a concern for development.

Alexandria Luria, the other former student and coworker of Vygotsky, was predominantly interested in the cultural-historical dimension of human behavior and "psychological activity" and subsequently went on to, in effect, found the study of neuropsychology.

Since the collapse of communism and the dissolution of the Soviet Union, activity theory (or "the activity approach" as it tended to be called in Russia) has lost some of its appeal as philosophers and social scientists have been exposed to ideas on phenomenology, hermeneutics, and post-modernism. Even as the name of Marx has gathered negative associations (Lektorskii, 2004, pp. 13–14), it is ironic that interest in activity theory in the West has increased.

The Nature of Activity Theory

For a proper understanding of activity theory it is necessary to look further into its origins. First, the connection to cultural-historical psychology is important. The goal of cultural-historical psychology, more recently termed "sociocultural" psychology, is defined by Wertsch, del Rio, and Alvarez (1995, p. 3):

> to explicate the relationships between human mental functioning, on the one hand, and the cultural, institutional, and

historical situations in which this functioning occurs, on the other.

The idea of the cultural-historical context has its origins, as we might suspect, in the Marxist view of society, although connections to Fichte and Hegel are also evident (Lektorskii, 2004, p. 15) and Leont'ev, driven by the fact that Vygotsky's writings were declared ideologically unsound and proscribed under Stalin, used the term *societal-historical* instead (Veer & Valsiner, 1991).

Zinchenko (1995, p. 41) notes that Leont'ev, in developing activity theory (following his move, along with Luria and Zaporozhets, from Moscow to Khar'kov), moved away from the study of consciousness to the study of object-oriented activity. The connection is derived through the Marxist position that consciousness is formed through human engagement in activities. Nardi (1996, p. 7) expresses this very well:

> Activity theorists argue that consciousness is not a set of discrete disembodied cognitive acts ... and certainly it is not the brain; rather, consciousness is located in everyday practice: you are what you do. And what you do is firmly and inextricably embedded in the social matrix of which every person is an organic part.

Although Leont'ev changed the focus of his work from consciousness to activity, the connection remained: Zinchenko (1995, p. 41) notes that "while for Vygotsky consciousness was mediated by culture, for Leont'ev mind and consciousness were mediated by tools and objects."

Reviewing a biography of Luria, Stetsenko (2003) notes that the cultural-historical context of the work of Vygotsky and his colleagues was central to the *production* of their cultural-historical theory:

> A history of the Vygotsky-Leont'ev-Luria school would have to reveal how the cultural-historical context of their work, specifically the revolutionary project of changing society based on ideals of equality and social justice that these scholars clearly espoused (all the subsequent dramatic failings of this project notwithstanding), instead of being an outside source of influence, became integrated *right into the body* of their work, into its methodology, and the very knowledge it produced.

It would be difficult to find a more telling example of the influence of the cultural-historical context on a human activity.

From this consideration of cultural-historical psychology as the foundation of activity theory, we can move on to examine its general principles, of which six are customarily described: the unity of consciousness and activity, object orientation, internalization/externalization, mediation, the hierarchical structure of activity, and development (Kaptelinin & Nardi, 1997).

The principle of *the unity of consciousness and activity* stems directly from the early work on consciousness by Vygotsky's group in Moscow. The key notion is that consciousness, or "mind" in a more generic sense, emerges in evolution through human activity in relation to the external world, or, as Kaptelinin (1995, p. 107) puts it:

> The most fundamental principle of activity theory is that of the unity of consciousness and activity. "Consciousness" in this expression means the human mind as a whole, and "activity" means human interaction with the objective reality. This principle, therefore, states that the human mind emerges and exists as a special component of human interaction with the environment. Mind is a special "organ" that appears in the process of evolution to help organisms to survive. Thus, it can be analyzed and understood only within the context of activity.

The principle of *object orientation* is simply that human activity is directed toward objects that have a scientifically determinable "reality" and/or a socioculturally determined reality. Thus, we have "real world" objects such as the raw material of, say, the woodcarver, whose activity is to act upon the block of wood to transform it into a carving, and we have the socially constructed objects of, for example, the peer group, which individual members may seek to transform by introducing new potential members.

The third principle, that of *internalization / externalization*, derives directly from the first two. Given the unity of consciousness and activity, and object-orientation, then our mental processes must be created as a consequence of our external activities being internalized. Our consciousness of the world around us is formed by our acting upon it and, reciprocally, our internal conception of the world is fixed through our activity in the world. According to Vygotsky (1978), language is the means we employ to internalize our externally derived experience.

The principle of *mediation* is, initially at least, straightforward. It is that activity is mediated by tools. However, "tool," (as already noted) is a complex concept, involving not simply, for example, chisels and planes to work on wood but also our mental tools of language and symbol. Furthermore, the kinds of sociocultural phenomena such as rules, norms, and the division of labor, identified in Engeström's version of activity theory (and earlier by Leont'ev), can also be viewed as tools in the sense that they are constructs through which our interaction with the object may be constrained or assisted (Wilson, 2006).

The principle of the *hierarchical structure of activity* is a major contribution of Leont'ev, who defined *activity, actions*, and *operations* and related them to *motives, goals*, and *conditions* as shown in Figure 4.3.

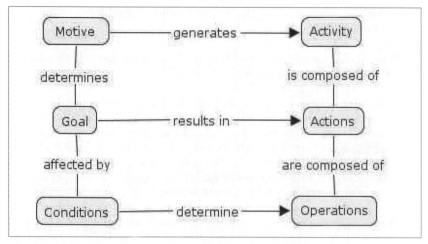

Figure 4.3   Activity, actions, and operations (Wilson, 2006).

Leont'ev (1978, section 3.5) sets out the relationships as follows:

> The concept of activity is necessarily connected with the concept of motive. Activity does not exist without a motive; "non motivated" activity is not activity without a motive but activity with a subjectively and objectively hidden motive. Basic and "formulating" appear to be the actions that realize separate human activities. We call a process an action if it is subordinated to the representation of the result that must be attained, that is, if it is subordinated to a conscious purpose. Similarly, just as the concept of motive is related to the concept of activity, the concept of purpose is related to the concept of action.

and:

> Actions are not special "units" that are included in the structure of activity. Human activity does not exist except in the form of action or a chain of actions. For example, work activity exists in work actions, school activity in school actions, social activity in actions (acts) of society, etc. If the actions that constitute activity are mentally subtracted from it, then absolutely nothing will be left of activity.

and, finally,

> The action also has its operational aspect (how, by what means this can be achieved), which is determined not by the

goal in itself but by the objective-object conditions of its achievement.

It should be noted that these hierarchical levels are not immutable: Leont'ev (1978, section 3.5) notes:

> Activity may lose the motive that elicited it, whereupon it is converted into an action realizing perhaps an entirely different relation to the world, a different activity; conversely, an action may turn into an independent stimulating force and may become a separate activity; finally, an action may be transformed into a means of achieving a goal, into an operation capable of realizing various actions.

The idea of the hierarchy, activity–actions–operations, does not find universal approval. For example, Chaiklin (2007, p. 184) suggests that "decomposing activity (or practices) into different levels destroys important conceptual advantages that a systemic activity perspective offers to the analysis of computer-based systems in a practice." He supports this view by a quotation from Leont'ev (1978, p. 68): "No type of transformation of separate 'splinters' of activity is possible in general since this would mean not a transformation of activity but its destruction."

Finally, the principle of *development* implies the need to understand how an activity has developed over time in its cultural-historical context, as well as how the actions taken on the object affect that development. This principle is sometimes referred to as "Vygotsky's principle of development" because it arose out of his work on the educational development of the child. However, in current research in many sectors, the development of activity systems other than the child's mind are at the center.

At the operational level, the nature of activity theory is neatly encapsulated by Barthelmess and Anderson (2002, p. 34), in a statement that might be taken as a gloss on Figure 4.2:

> *Activities* are undertaken by *subjects*, motivated by a purpose, transforming an *object* into an *outcome*. The object may be shared by a *community* of actors, that work together to reach a desired *outcome*. *Tools*, *rules*, and *division of labor* mediate the relationship between subjects, community, and object.

Engeström (1999, online) writes of three generations of activity theory. The first, centered upon Vygotsky, "created the idea of *mediation*" but was limited by its focus upon the individual, a limitation removed by Leont'ev in the second generation in showing "how *historically evolving division of labor* has brought about the crucial differentiation between an individual action and collective activity." The third generation, the present, "needs to develop conceptual tools to understand dialogue, multiple perspectives and voices, and networks of interacting activity systems." In the fields of application under review, we may see some of these conceptual tools in process of development.

Engteström has also been responsible for drawing attention to the contradictions that exist in and between activity systems, building upon Leont'ev and, ultimately, Marx. In *Learning by Expanding* (Engeström, 1987), he sets out four levels of contradictions. (1) Primary contradictions *within* each component of an activity, which is seen as a clash between the individual action and the overall activity. (2) Secondary contradictions between the elements of the activity—Engeström notes that, "The stiff hierarchical division of labor lagging behind and preventing the possibilities opened by advanced instruments is a typical example" (Engeström, 1987, Ch.1, online). (3) Tertiary contradiction between the dominant form of an activity and a culturally more advanced form. For example, "a tertiary contradiction arises when, say, the administrators of the medical care system order the practitioners to employ certain new procedures corresponding to the ideals of a more wholistic [sic] and integrated medicine. The new procedures may be formally implemented, but probably still subordinated to and resisted by the old general form of the activity" (Engeström, 1987, Ch. 1, online). (4) Quaternary contradictions between the elements of an activity and what Engeström calls its "neighbour activities;" thus, the rules and norms according to which an activity is carried out are produced by the neighboring "rule-producing activity," which the instruments or tools employed are produced by the neighboring "instrument-producing activity." Engeström notes that it is the contradictions in activity systems that bring about their development. "New qualitative stages and forms of activity emerge as solutions to the contradictions of the preceding stage or form" (Engeström, 1987, Ch. 2, online). Barab, Barnett, Yamagata-Lynch, Squire, and Keating (2002, p. 80) comment:

> Contradictions are best understood as tensions among the components of the activity system. ... Tensions are critical to understanding what motivates particular actions and in understanding the evolution of a system more generally. These tensions can be thought of as system dualities, and it is through understanding the interplay within and among these dualities that one can best understand and support the continued innovation of the system.

Fields of Application

The fields of application discussed here are all interrelated. Psychology shades into the psychology of education and educational development generally. Information systems development and human–computer interaction shade into online learning and information literacy, as well as into the design of library systems and online information services. All of these are related to aspects of information science such as interactive information retrieval and human information behavior research. Consequently, the disciplinary divisions used are somewhat artificial and the interactions among the fields are of more significance than the disciplinary differences.

Clearly, additional fields could also have been chosen; for example, work studies (Bedny & Karwowski, 2004; Engeström, 2000a) and organization studies (Blackler, Crump, & McDonald, 2000) are areas in which activity theory is used. However, these subject fields, although important for a consideration of the context of information activities, do not bear, to my mind, quite as close a relationship to information science as the topics discussed here. In addition, this is a selective review, rather than an exhaustive text.

Psychology

Given the origins of activity theory, psychology is the appropriate field in which to begin a consideration of the application areas; the field is so diverse, however, that a thorough review would be virtually impossible. Currently, most work appears to be in applied areas of psychology such as ergonomics, work studies, computer-supported cooperative work, and educational psychology. In any event, this chapter aims to explore those aspects of the application areas of activity theory that may have some implication for information science. From this perspective, most of the *psychological* work of relevance falls within educational psychology and in the information systems aspects of collaborative learning. Consequently, attention is given to these matters in the appropriate sections.

Psychology makes its appearance in information science in the guise of cognitive science, employed, for example, by Ingwersen (1996) in the area of interactive information retrieval; in the study of personality, for example, in Heinström's (2003) research on personality dimensions in relation to information seeking behavior; and in a number of papers (and one book) by Hjørland alone and with coworkers (Hjørland, 1997, 2002, 2004; Hjørland & Albrechtson, 1995; Hjørland & Christensen, 2002). Of these authors, only Hjørland makes any reference to activity theory (in papers relating to classification, domain analysis, and the socio-cognitive approach to information science) although often without explicit reference to the theory. Hjørland's academic background is in psychology and his aim is to draw attention to psychological and social psychological theories and epistemological positions that may have value in information science. Hence, the promotion of the idea of domain analysis as a new paradigm in information science:

The domain-analytic paradigm in information science (IS) states that the best way to understand information in IS is to study the knowledge-domains as thought or discourse communities, which are parts of society's division of labor. Knowledge organization, structure, cooperation patterns, language and communication forms, information systems, and relevance criteria are reflections of the objects of the work of these communities and of their role in society. The individual person's psychology, knowledge, information needs, and subjective relevance criteria should be seen in this perspective. (Hjørland & Albrechtson, 1995, p. 400)

and the advocacy of philosophical realism:

A realist conception of relevance, information seeking, information retrieval, and knowledge organization is outlined. Information systems of all kinds, including research libraries and public libraries, should be informed by a realist philosophy and a realist information science. (Hjørland, 2004, p. 488)

In all of Hjørland's work, activity theory is seen as one of the underpinning ideas that can provide information science with models of reality that will lead to fruitful investigation.

Education

From psychology, the move to education is a natural one because Vygotsky's work on the development of consciousness and learning was central to much of modern educational psychology. A key concept in Vygotsky's work is the Zone of Proximal Development or ZPD (Vygotsky, 1978), which is the "zone" in the learning process where the help of an adult (or a more advanced peer) can move a child from the existing level of understanding to a more advanced level. However, Tolman (1999, p. 75) points out that:

Too often … it has been interpreted simply as a way in which the teacher can aid the learning of a pupil. This completely misses its theoretical intent, which is to reveal the essentially mediated nature of human learning.

Tolman (1999, p. 75) quotes Engeström as coming "closer to the mark" when he describes the ZPD as the difference between what individuals may achieve in an existing state of everyday life and what can be achieved as a result of collective action. This original and wider intention of Vygotsky's work clearly has potential in many areas of life, including, for example, decision making in organizations. It is well known that collective problem solving can generate many more answers to a problem than any one individual alone is capable of achieving (a phenomenon known in education from Piaget, 1923/1959 onward; see also Surowiecki, 2004) and this can be seen as working within the ZPD to establish a new state of organizational "everyday life." A formal understanding of the ZPD could enable organizations to determine when collaborative action is needed.

The area within information science to which the ZPD is most obviously applicable is the study of "information literacy" and it was rather surprising to find that a search on all of the ISI databases for "zone of proximal development AND information literacy" produced no results; nor did "activity theory AND information literacy." A search on Google Scholar proved more successful, although most of the references found do not put the ZPD in the context of activity theory or cultural-historical psychology. One of few studies that embraces activity theory in its totality is a doctoral dissertation (Peach, 2003), which examines learning assistance programs and, through the activity theory approach, demonstrates the contradictions and tensions among the different groups and university units involved.

As has been noted, there is more work using the ZPD concept without reference to activity theory. Haltunen (2003) is typical of this approach, where Vygotsky and the concept receive a token citation but the paper itself deals with other issues—in this case, a constructivist learning framework.

More generally, in education, the work of Engeström has been of major significance. From his base as Professor of Adult Education and Director of the Centre for Activity Theory and Developmental Work Research at the University of Helsinki, Engeström has developed theories of learning, in both the school and the workplace, based on activity theory and the concept of *expansive learning*. He draws upon the work of Bateson (1972), who set out four levels of learning, in which Learning 3 equates to *expansive learning*. In an interview at the University of Lancaster (UK), Engeström (2002, online) commented:

> Learning by expanding, or Learning 3, is very much going beyond the information given to construct a new set of criteria, a broader picture, a broader object for your activity, in which … it liberates you from the constraints of the particular setting in which you are functioning and enables [you] to create new settings. So, Learning 3, or expansive learning, is very much about learning something which is not yet there, by constructing a new activity.

Almost all of Engeström's early work in education, from 1967 to the early 1980s, was in Finnish and concerned the development of the Finnish educational system, motivation to learn, and other aspects of learning in the school context. From about 1987, however, when

Learning by Expanding was published, he has also given attention to other forms of activity, specifically work activity, and the nature of learning in work activity systems and other organizational activity systems. In the introduction to the German edition of his book (published as part of the online version) he noted his construction of *"developmental work research* as a methodology for applying activity theory, specifically the theory of expansive learning, in the world of work, technology, and organizations" (Engeström, 1987, online).

Computer-Mediated Learning

Other major areas of education in which activity theory has had an impact are *collaborative learning* and *online learning*. For example, Baker, Hansen, Joiner, and Traum (1999) explored the concept of *grounding*, or the development of mutual understanding among learners, within an activity theory framework. They conclude that students experience difficulties in appropriating the learning *tools* (both the tools of the scientific discourse and the tools of collaborative learning) and conclude:

> Collaborative learning is associated with the increased cognitive-interactional effort involved in the transition from learning to understand each other to learning to understand the meanings of the semiotic tools that constitute the mediators of interpersonal interaction.
>
> Understanding how and when grounding leads to collaborative learning therefore requires detailed analysis of learners' *goals* in specific *situations* that motivate them to go further in their attempt to gain mutual understanding, of the extent to which the *material and semiotic tools* that they use can be appropriated, and, especially, the different forms of mutual understanding that will need to be achieved by the learners with respect to these "objects." It is precisely these aspects of collaborative learning situations that our analytical framework is designed to highlight. (Baker et al., 1999, p. 55)

Related research by Fjuk and Ludvigsen (2001) explores Engeström's (1987) concept of *contradictions,* the historically evolving problems, breakdowns, and tensions that occur in an activity system. They show that, as a result of the different perceptions of collaborative systems held by those who design and use them, contradictions occur and must be resolved through the development of the system, if *collaborative* learning is to take place. The authors conclude:

> Past designs concerning distributed collaborative learning seem to have been marked by an approach of using networked computers as add-ons to existing pedagogical and

organisational practice. However, we need to know the principles of educational traditions in order to change them with respect to new technologies and concepts. Creative and new ways of thinking that will work in practice are dependent on prior understanding of the knowledge, experience, and principles that underpin that tradition of praxis. This reality of new distributed learning situations clearly indicates that the learners' social interactions towards a shared learning environment must be viewed in terms of interconnected activity systems. It is therefore crucial to explore which conditions the distributed environment imposes on the social interactions that are found crucial for developing a common learning environment. (Fjuk & Ludvigsen, 2001, p. 5)

Berge and Fjuk (2006) used activity theory in seeking an understanding of the role of online meetings in a distance-learning, Web-based course on object-oriented programming. They note that the meetings, which involved instant messaging and streamed video recordings of the lessons, did not play out as intended; that is, they did not appear to contribute significantly to the students' learning but, nevertheless, were viewed as useful by the students. The authors suggest that the meetings facilitated the development of a "community of practice" among the students and that this function should be noted in the future design of computer-assisted learning.

Mørch and Wasson (1999) used activity theory (as one element in a multi-modal study) to guide the research process in understanding how students and instructors organized their work in using and providing material for telelearning, using the TeamWave Workplace groupware system. The authors noted that:

> Our experience with Activity Theory is that it provides a lens through which we can see the world. It is useful to orient thoughts and research questions. It provides a number of methods/tools shaped by a general theoretical approach. It can be used to guide methodological decisions regarding evaluation (how technology is used) and to a lesser extent regarding design (how technology will be used). (Mørch & Wasson, 1999, p. 4)

In a study of Australian distance learning students Fåhræus (2004) employed activity theory to analyze interviews with teachers and students regarding an online learning capability that was just emerging from what had previously been paper correspondence courses. The study revealed the inner contradictions in the situation, caused by both teachers' and students' perceptions of learning as individual and formed by the pre-existing situation, resulting in a failure to take advantage of the potential of the new technologies to enable collaborative learning.

In these different studies authors point to some common advantages of activity theory: It is used in guiding the development of research instruments, in providing a framework for the analysis of data (whether the data were gathered on an activity theory basis or not), in providing an understanding of user behavior that can help in the design of systems, and in providing understanding of the wider contextual issues that affect system use and usability.

It may appear obvious, but there are lessons in this kind of research for those involved in information literacy programs that involve computer-based learning: The students must be suitably motivated to engage in the activity, they must see the program as helping them to satisfy a personal goal, and attention must be given to ensuring that the abstract concepts associated with information searching and other information skills are appropriated and internalized, as well as the *practical* skills of actually using the computer-based learning package and any subsidiary systems (e.g., search engines and databases). There are many areas of potential contradiction in such systems: The nature of the information to be acquired by students, the extent to which that information must be implemented in practice for internalization to take place, the suitability of the pedagogical model and its harmony with the pedagogy that prevails in the students' disciplines, the effectiveness of the system's design, its integration with other systems, and so on. Resolving these contradictions through continuous development of the activity system of *computer-based information literacy instruction* will not be an insignificant task.

Information Systems

Defining *information systems* rather widely, but to maintain the distinction from computer science more generally, we can take it to include all subsidiary studies that have to do with the development of information processing systems within the organizational, work domain or human context. Under this definition, the main areas for the application of activity theory in the information systems field have been computer-supported cooperative work (CSCW), human–computer interaction, and information systems development.

Computer-Supported Cooperative Work

With the spread of computing in organizations of all kinds much more work is now computer-supported and, because of widespread global distribution and the necessity for teamwork in knowledge-intensive enterprises, much work is both cooperative and computer-supported. CSCW is dealt with first in this subsection because, like human–computer interaction, it has significant relationships to activity theory in education and learning theory. To make effective use of cooperative computer systems, the users and teams must develop a common understanding not only of the nature of the tasks they share but also of the artifacts made available to them to assist and support their work on those tasks. By artifacts we mean not simply the networked computers they employ but also the communication tools associated with those computers, for example, Voice over Internet Protocol (VoIP) telephony and video-telephony as well as the more usual e-mail and chat services and the group-work software. In addition there are the psychological tools of language and symbolism that must also be shared and, in multi-disciplinary (and often multi-cultural) teams, problems relating to these tools are not uncommon. In other words, participants have to learn how to use the system and, crucially, to share that learning and the languages of learning. With intensively interacting teams one may see Engeström's *expansive learning* take place, with new uses being developed for established systems and new ways of working evolving.

Computer-mediated learning and computer-supported cooperative work are clearly closely connected; learning activity may be considered a rather specialized mode of work and work activity involves learning. Consequently, we find that the technologies employed in CSCW have much in common with those involved in collaborative learning and computer-mediated learning generally. Collis and Margaryan (2004) investigated this close connection in a study of work-based learning in Shell International Exploration and Production. Activity theory was used as the basis for the design of online courses (following suggestions made by Jonassen and Rohrer-Murphy, 1999) and the course was delivered using a framework developed by the authors, WBA-CSCL (Work Based Activity-Computer-Supported Collaborative Learning), which, itself, was analyzed as an activity system. In other words, the learning was work-related. The authors conclude that activity theory served the purpose of course development well and that its analytical use revealed contradictions in the organization that prevented the full benefits from being derived. Specifically, learning on the job was not perceived as true learning by the participants in the course, who saw education as "going on a course." Also, although company policy favored skills development, the policy had not been translated into action regarding making time available for learning or changing the reward and promotion systems. The authors conclude:

> Thus, the WBA-CSCL Framework based on activity theory and the associated course-design approach appear to help in structuring the introduction of new forms of learning for professionals in corporate settings. However, much stills [*sic*] needs to change in the social climate of the workplace (the community, the rules, and the division of labor) before the potential of the approach will be realized in widespread practice in corporate settings. (Collis & Margaryan, 2004, p. 50)

Heeren and Lewis (1997) connect work and learning in their study of communication media employed by three different, distributed research communities. Using a combination of activity theory and media richness theory (Daft & Lengel, 1984), they note that collaborative activities evolve in such settings and, although the study concerned collaborative research groups, draw conclusions for computer-aided collaborative learning. They observe that "communications technology can provide support at certain phases of activity in the context of work. However, there is little evidence that this support assists learning communities *except* where those activities are structured so as to reflect working practices" and specifically draw attention to the need to establish a common understanding of the motive for learning, to provide opportunities for face-to-face interaction, and to understand the need for group leadership, if the learning objectives are to be attained (Heeren & Lewis, 1997, p. 96).

Fjeld, Lauche, Bichsel, Voorhorst, Krueger, and Rauterberg (2002) explore the process of establishing shared understanding in an interesting fashion. They point out that groupware systems are often developed from single-user systems and that effective development of software that is to be used in virtual circumstances needs to be developed in a common physical space, or, as they put it, the developers must be co-located. To this end, they employed an augmented reality system, called BUILD-IT, which involved the developers in manipulating physical objects to develop virtual tools for physical planning. Activity theory was employed as the framework for the study, with an emphasis on the objectification of virtual tools. The notion of co-located development of virtual systems would appear to have much to offer, especially if, as in this example, the system is to be used by a limited number of individuals working as a team.

In a study of process-centered software development environments, Barthelmess and Anderson (2002) study software development as a collaborative activity from an activity theory perspective. One of their key points is that such environments often do not incorporate a means of communication among the collaborating system designers. This draws attention to the essentially communicative nature of interaction within an activity system.

Inevitably, given the character of CSCW, the notion of *communities of practice* will appear in conjunction with other concepts, and Cluts (2003) used this idea in association with activity theory to examine how shared understanding of a groupware system for sales and customer contact management was established in an organization. Using the activity theory checklist developed by Kaptelinin, Nardi, and Macauley to guide interviews and observation, the study concerned

> the installation of a major CSCW software package ... [which] was implemented to facilitate sharing of information and customer contacts among the customer service team. The software included central information file and contact management, sales management, and profitability analysis

capabilities, all of which were new functions for the organization. (Cluts, 2003, p. 144)

This was a major technological innovation for the bank and the author concludes that:

This information [i.e., the findings of the study] and the language of activity theory and communities of practice can then be used to describe implications for developers and implementation managers. The implications themselves are not new, but the language of activity theory and communities of practice provide a richer context for understanding and making sense of development principles. (Cluts, 2003, p. 150)

Paradoxically, cooperative work requires not simply collaboration among individuals, but also considerable *individual* dedication to the success of the collaborative enterprise. For example, Cluts noted the extent to which intended users of the system watched to discover the extent to which others were using it in deciding their own participation. This paradox was also explored within an activity theory framework by Nardi, Whittaker, and Schwarz (2002), who define *intensional networks* as the social networks formed, as conditions and tasks require, by people working within and across organizations. The implication for activity theory of the rise of such networks is the need to consider the subject not as an individual but as a collective. (This suggestion is not new; for example, in his famous discussion of the prehistoric hunting party, Leont'ev clearly envisages the subject as the group.) The idea of the intensional network also has implications for the kinds of systems needed to support work of this kind.

Human–Computer Interaction (HCI)

As already noted, Rogers (2004) has surveyed activity theory as a new theoretical direction in HCI research sufficiently recently (her references take us up to 2002) for her analysis to act as a starting point. In reviewing work, she concludes that, "… to achieve a level of competence in understanding and applying activity theory requires considerable learning and experience. … When given to others not familiar with the original theory, the model's utility is limited" (p. 106). This problem, however, would be common to any community of researchers who have been trained in other sets of methodological approaches; it does not appear to have inhibited interest in applying activity theory in relation to HCI.

In an earlier review, Kuutti painted a picture of HCI as a field in which the dominant paradigm of cognitive psychology was failing to deliver results that benefited information system design. He suggested activity theory as a means of remedying the situation, suggesting that its main strengths were its attention to multiple levels of interaction, the social context of interaction, and its concepts of development and the "dynamic features of human practices" (Kuutti, 1996, p. 38).

In HCI, the dominant model of activity theory is Engeström's, introduced to the field by the Danish researcher Bødker (1989); however, an alternative, promoted by Bedny (e.g., Bedny, Seglin, & Meister, 2000) and known as systemic-structural activity theory has also been applied. Bedny emphasizes the importance of Rubinshtein (e.g., 1957) in the development of this variant of activity theory; specifically noting the distinction between Vygotsky's perception of the formation of intellect through social interaction and the psychological tools such as language, gesture, and sign, and that of Rubinshtein (and the later writings of Leont'ev) in which the formation of intellect through work activity is also emphasized (Bedny, Karwowski, & Bedny, 2001).

The ability to relate the general conceptual framework of activity theory to other theories is evident in HCI as elsewhere; for example, Widjaja and Balbo (2005) marry activity theory with structuration theory (Giddens, 1984) to propose *structuration of activity* as an alternative to both in explaining human work activity in general and HCI in particular. The connections between activity theory and structuration theory are readily apparent; however, whether combining the two frameworks provides much improvement over activity theory alone is not as clear.

Activity theory has also been combined with *genre theory*, most notably by Spinuzzi (1999, 2002). In this work, the notion of *genres*, familiar to us from literary studies, is extended to include *screen genres* (such features as dialog boxes and drop-down menus) and associated *documentation genres*, which could include, for example, the formal documentation associated with a system as well as the informal genres developed by the user in interaction with, or in preparing to use the system. The latter might include, for example, hand-written notes of data to be entered into the system or data cut from the screen record and pasted into an electronic document. *Usability* then becomes a matter not simply of screen design of an application but also of ensuring the usability of the system in the wider context of interacting screen and non-screen genres.

A related piece of work, which does not use genre theory (although it would have been appropriate to do so) and which is concerned not simply with human-computer interaction, but with more general human–ICT interaction, explored the nature of command and control in two ambulance services in the U.K. Activity theory was used as a framework to explore factors such as the differences in division of labor in the two services, together with differences in artifacts (computer-based in one and manual in the other). The study led to the conclusion that: "software support for ambulance control should take the form of a set of tools (e.g., gazetteer, electronic map, notepad) to be used differently by different users for different purposes. Such a configuration would support the emergence of situated, well adapted, collaborative practices over time" (McCarthy, Wright, Healey, Dearden, & Harrison, 1997, p. 110).

Similarly, work by Hart-Davidson (2002), dealing with *document-mediated interaction*, mentions genres without using genre analysis and adopts an activity theory perspective in examining how a specific type of document, engineering students' design reports, might be best designed for on-screen interaction by a teacher assigning a grade. The analysis leads to a design that calls up specific parts of the document for review, with a panel showing the grade possibilities and their criteria. A document design of this kind, tailored to a particular use, is more appropriate in the specialized circumstances than would be a normal word-processed document. In other words, exploration of the *activity* leads to changes in design structure.

Recently, human–computer interaction researchers have been using the term "interaction design," perhaps as a consequence of understanding that interacting with computers does not define the whole of a work task, even though that task is completed largely through the help of computers. An excellent introductory text on activity theory and interaction design, which could become the standard work in the field, was recently published by Kaptelinin and Nardi (2006).

Information Systems Development

Several researchers have been responsible for introducing activity theory into information systems development or systems design generally. For example, the Danish researcher Susanne Bødker (1991, p. 551) argues:

> Present systems design is really in a conflict situation for a number of reasons including that
>
> - the material that is worked with (computers) become [*sic*] more and more flexible, and that the tools and techniques used in systems design today are insufficient for that kind of material and for the challenges posed by ready-made software,
>
> - and, that real user influence is necessary in more and more cases

and urges the adoption of activity theory as a conceptual framework for a variety of reasons, including:

> An analysis of systems design as an activity system allows for a focus on many different levels of the total activity. We can look at the materials and tools used by a couple of programmers, or we can look at the total project group in relation to the surrounding organizational units. What is the purpose of

their activity, what do they do to fulfill this purpose, and how do they do it? What are the actual social and physical conditions for their work? In particular this analysis points at the many different levels where systems design tools and techniques comes [*sic*] in. And it points at the many parts played by computer technology in the design process. (Bødker, 1991, p. 559)

Bødker's paper would be essential reading for anyone in the information science world who wishes to understand why activity theory might be appropriate for our field.

Quek and Shah (2004) compared five activity theory-based methods of systems design: Activity Analysis and Development (ActAD) (Korpela, 1997); the Activity Checklist (Kaptelinin, Nardi, & Macaulay, 1999); the Activity-Oriented Design Method (AODM) (Mwanza, 2002); the Jonassen and Rohrer-Murphy (1999) framework; and the Martins and Daltrini (1999) framework. Quek and Shah (2004, p. 8) conclude:

> It is found that within the AT-based methods that have emerged from the survey, there is a lack of comprehensive treatment regarding coverage of development phases as well as coverage of AT concepts. It is also found that only one of the methods [Mwanza's AODM] has been validated in a real life systems development.

Korpela, Mursu, and Soriyan (2002, p. 115) develop the ActAD framework referred to previously, defining information system development as:

> the process by which some collective work activity is facilitated by new information-technological means through analysis, design, implementation, introduction, and sustained support, as well as process management.

The authors illustrate the application of the framework by reference to a number of studies, noting the importance of the network of activities into which the information systems development activity must fit. Thus, even within a single organization, the activity addressed by the development process will be related more or less intimately to other activities that are not the subject of systems development but which may affect or be affected by that development. They conclude, "the concept of activity network is useful in analyzing work practice in context but network analysis has not received sufficient attention in previous activity-theoretical studies" (Korpela, Mursu, & Soriyan, 2002, p. 125).

In an interesting study, Irestig, Eriksson, and Timpka (2004) compared two methods of contextual design by examining the prototypes resulting from participatory design and user-centered design. Case studies of the two systems were analyzed using an activity theory framework. Significant differences emerged with user-centered design focusing more upon the individual user interface and the computer systems generally and the participatory design process producing a system that was more focused on organizational tasks and the political reality of the system, which was pragmatic and easy to install and maintain.

There could be lessons from work of this kind for the design of, for example, digital library systems and organizational intranets. The idea of user-centered systems is strongly rooted in information science in areas such as interactive information retrieval and in the field of information-seeking behavior research. However, the shortcomings of the prototype resulting from the application of user-centered design suggest that, if the system (digital library or whatever) is to respond pragmatically to organizational issues, a participatory design process is likely to be more effective.

More generally, and linking information systems development and education, a study from Singapore (Lim & Hang, 2003) used activity theory to explore the integration of information and communication technology (ICT) in schools. Specifically, the authors sought to answer the question, "How has ICT been integrated in Singapore schools such that students engage in higher order thinking?"—akin to asking whether "expansive learning" takes place. The activity theory approach provided a broad contextual framework, allowing the researchers to explore contradictions in the system that inhibited the effective use of ICT. They noted, for example, that teachers continued to teach as previously and did not use the technology to stimulate student self-learning; also, the lessons on the use of ICT did not extend to the use of ICT for learning but, rather, were an end in themselves. Once these contradictions were recognized, the school was able to take action to overcome them. The authors conclude:

> By adopting an activity-theoretical approach to the study, we will be able to document and describe the activity systems across schools and classrooms with the integral contextual understanding of how larger entities such as policymakers have on them. Not only can we understand the various processes within and between activity systems, we can construct pedagogical models and approaches of ICT integration for schools based on that understanding. (Lim & Hang, 2003, p. 62)

One area of information systems design that is close to information behavior research is the study of information requirements. Here Turner, Turner, and Horton (1999) have applied activity theory as a framework for organizing ethnographic data and thereby arriving at fresh insights in the context of requirements. The authors employ the activity theory concept of *contradictions* to show how these reveal requirements for systems design. An example of a contradiction occurred in the updating activity of the observed research project: The authors comment that updating required the transcription of information from team-members' notebooks to the whiteboard used in the updating session. An artifact designed to present notebook pages would have resolved this contradiction.

Information Science

As has been noted, activity theory appears not to have had a significant influence in information science, at least in the West. It would be surprising, however, if such a significant development in the Soviet Union had not had its effect on research in library and information science in that country. Indeed, such was the case, as the next subsection shows.

The Activity Approach in Soviet Library and Information Science Research

Although, from the 1950s onward, there was an attempt by publishers to reveal the nature of the Soviet Union's research activities in a number of fields through the production of translations of Russian journals, librarianship and information science were not beneficiaries of this effort, except for some occasional studies included in *ARIST* reviews. Added to this, Western researchers' language skills rarely extended to a knowledge of Russian.

Consequently in the West, an understanding of what was going on in this area has been lacking. Not surprisingly, however, activity theory or the activity approach was widely applied in the Soviet Union and East European countries. In Marxist terminology the term "activity" is closely associated with the terms of "labor" and "practice." "Practical activity" is supposed to be the main criterion of scientific truth in Marxist methodology and was treated as one of generic cognitive means in science, including the social sciences. Therefore, "practical activity" was a widely used category and central research concept in different sciences and disciplines.

Activity in general is understood as the primary means of human existence and is divided into several major areas (practical, cognitive and educational, and organizational) according to its goals and results. All these activity areas are closely interrelated. As such, the activity approach was always explicitly or implicitly present in Soviet library and information science research. Korshunov (1975, pp. 5–33) provides a fairly exhaustive review of the development of the activity approach in bibliography from the 1920s until the beginning of the 1970s. However, the conscious and qualitatively different application of the activity approach as a research tool in the information disciplines (bibliography, information science, and librarianship) is related to the development of the theory of bibliography and mainly to the concept of bibliography as a special activity (or a system of related activities) developed during the 1970s. This concept was extended to information activities and librarianship.[3]

In bibliography research, the activity approach was treated as a means for the holistic integration of the data produced by different methods and means of research. Its advantage is that investigation is not limited to the relations between a subject and an object. On the contrary, this approach demands that other components of an activity (such as needs, goals, means, and tools) be taken into account. Therefore, the activity approach facilitates deeper, multi-aspect, and more systemic research into bibliography as a complex social phenomenon. A combination of the activity and system approaches was used and bibliography was treated as a system of practical, managerial, and cognitive (scientific and educational) activities. This system guarantees the production, dissemination, preservation, and use of bibliographic information in society.

Russian bibliographers have created a definition of bibliography through the category of activity. In addition to the traditional (ontological) approach, the new activity approach was used in Russia from the 1970s onward. The conception of bibliography as a system of activity (or activities) was created by Barsuk (1975), Korshunov (1975), Tugov (1977), Fomina (1976), Bespalova (1980, 1982), Vochrysheva (1989), and others. Maceviciute and Janonis (2004) present an account of the Russian concept of bibliographic activity. The activity approach was also incorporated into the standard bibliographic terms (Gosstandart, 1985). The definition of bibliography as an activity system was a significant step forward in recognition of bibliography as a coherent social phenomenon.

One of the most important issues within this approach was an attempt to follow the requirement of the activity approach and to distinguish two main structural levels of bibliography: the essential internal and the empirical external (see the discussion on externalization/internalization). The structure of an activity consists of needs, motives, interests, goals, subject, object, processes, means and methods, conditions, and results. The essential internal structures of bibliography are constructed from the first three motivational components. The essential initial element of the activity and the driver or source of all kinds and forms of activity are a need and a motive. An interest is a concrete form in which the need is expressed; it is a measure of perception of the need. Needs and interests are transformed into a goal (an ideal model of the expected result). This is a cause and a regulator of a conscious activity. The goal has to be adequate to the possibilities and demands the selection of effective means and methods. Each kind of activity is determined by objective and subjective conditions (such as material and human resources). Conscious application of the activity approach requires that a scholar investigate all components of the activity in interdependent, mutual relation to one another.

The essential internal structure of bibliographic activity determines the coherence and continuity of it in time (history) and space. It is expressed in the deep functions of bibliography as they relate to societal needs and the motives of the activity. The empirical external level is expressed in the variety that bibliographic phenomena, tools, methods, processes, results, goals, and such can take in concrete sociocultural-historical contexts (Bespalova, 1982, p. 21; Korshunov, 1975, p. 119). This position provided the possibility of revealing the historical development of bibliography, bringing together various forms of bibliographic information from early bibliographic lists and library catalogs to the complex social and technological phenomenon that bibliography has become.

The concept of activity is also applied to information activity. It is centered upon the category of information need, with human information activity being treated as an integrative part of any activity (Kogan 1981; Kogan & Ukhanov 1991; Ukhanov 1996). This concept of scientific information activity was also used by the authors working in information science in Russia (e.g., Michailov, Chernyj, & Giliarevskij, 1968, 1976). The authors often make a distinction between information activity as a part of everyday work or life and a professional information activity system that is characterized by consciously formulated goals and results (information products or services) (Maceviciute, 2004).

The search for the essential functions of library work that would bring together a variety of libraries and other related institutions stimulated the use of the combination of the activity and system approaches in library science. This approach was used by Stoliarov (1981), Vaneev (2004), Cherniak (1981), Sokolov (1984), among others.

The activity approach in the library and information science disciplines in Russia and in other East European countries at present is regarded as self-evident. The definitions of librarianship, bibliography, and information work in encyclopedias (e.g., Glosienë, 1997), intergovernmental terminological standards in the region (e.g., Intergovernmental Council of Standardization, Metrology, and Certification, 1999), and special dictionaries are based on the concept of activity. On the other hand, it is obvious that empirical research has not used the full potential of activity theory and, perhaps as a consequence, within the fields of practice the theories are often regarded as inconsequential and removed from practical concerns.

Why was activity theory ignored in Western information science research when educational and other researchers took it into their fields? One can only speculate about this, but the migration of ideas seems to have happened in two ways. First, Engeström is Finnish and (for geopolitical reasons) Russian has long been more widely taught in Finland than in other Western European countries; consequently, it is likely that in pursuing his initial research in education, his attention would be drawn to Russian sources that would be accessible to him. Secondly, expatriate Soviet researchers, such as Bedny, took their activity theory background with them when they moved West and spread their ideas as they gained academic positions and began publishing in English. I know of no such scholars in the library and information science field.

It can be seen that the activity approach in Soviet library and information science serves as a conceptual framework that brings together virtually all research in the field. There is no such conceptual framework in the West; however, a few writers have explored the relevance of activity theory in a variety of areas, and Spasser (1999, p. 1137), in a short paper, concludes that it "can provide information science with a rich, unifying, and heuristically valuable vocabulary and conceptual framework that will facilitate both the continual betterment of practice and the secure transferability and cumulation of knowledge."

The limited application of activity theory in a number of areas of information science is explored next.

Digital Library Development

The research literature on digital libraries is largely concerned with technological issues and with the nature of the information resources included in such libraries (the European DigiCULT project [European Commission. Directorate-General for the Information Society, 2002] may be taken as an example of the latter). Elliot and Kling's (1997, p. 1023) definition of "digital library" is very wide, and perhaps usefully so, as attempts to restrict the definition do not appear to serve any particularly useful purpose: "information systems (IS) and services that provide electronic documents—text files, digital sound, digital video—available in dynamic or archival repositories." Examples range from the Association for Computing Machinery (ACM) Digital Library, an electronic store of ACM publications including journals and conference proceedings, to individual organizational intranets, which are sometimes described as digital libraries, and to more restricted collections such as that explored by Spasser (2002).

Spasser's work is one of very few in information science that fully employs an activity theory perspective (it is published in *Computer Supported Cooperative Work*, rather than one of the information science journals). The study concerns the Flora of North America digital library, an enormously ambitious project to describe the more than 27,000 species in America north of Mexico. It is, at one and the same time, a paper publishing project, with thirty volumes planned by Oxford University Press; a collaborative work effort on the part of more than 800 participants; a collaborative research project; and a digital library under development. The focus of Spasser's (2002, p. 88) paper is on the reorganization of the project from one based on traditional publishing methods, which proved inadequate:

> While the Project has moved forward (the first three volumes have been published, and intensive work is well under way on volumes 22–24 and volume 4), with its 800+ participants

scattered across North America involved in a decades-long effort and with hundreds of manuscripts in various stages of review by different sets of participants at any one time, traditional publishing methods have proved inadequate and inefficient.

Accordingly, a move was made from traditional publishing methods to the use of a computer-based system, Collaborative Publishing Services (Spasser, 2002, p. 88) which:

> attempts to integrate communication, information sharing (through creation of a common information object repository), and coordination support features and is accessible by unmodified Web browsers across heterogeneous, autonomous, and distributed information technology infrastructures.

Interactive Information Retrieval

On the face of things, one would expect that, if any area within information science were to be an early adopter of activity theory, it would be the field of interactive information retrieval. The subject overlaps with other areas, such as human–computer interaction (indeed it might be described as a subfield of HCI) and information systems development. However, although there are still some key researchers in the interactive IR field (in spite of much of the work having migrated to computer science), such as Ingwersen at the Royal School of Library and Information Science in Copenhagen, Järvelin at the University of Tampere, and Belkin and Saracevic at Rutgers University, activity theory appears to have made little, if any impact.

A search on Scholar Google (with the equivalent of the Boolean construction (("interactive information retrieval" OR "interactive IR") AND "activity theory") revealed nothing of interest, nor did the same search on the *Web of Knowledge*. The same search on Google revealed only one project at Rutgers (under the direction of Belkin): doctoral candidate Muh-Chuyn Tang is employing activity theory in a study of user reaction to a novel "faceted information space." In a dissertation proposal, Tang (n.d., p. 4) notes:

> The first group of research questions involves users' perception and acceptance of the display tool, as compared with the tool they have been accustomed to. This will entail the investigation of users' assimilation of the display tool over time. This part of the inquiry will be directed by activity theory where the internalization of the external tool is highlighted.

Overall, therefore, it appears that interactive information retrieval researchers have not yet engaged with activity theory to any significant extent and perhaps they and those in human–computer interaction have not yet engaged with one another.

Information-Seeking Behavior

Although Kuhlthau (2004) does not make reference to activity theory in her work, it is worth drawing attention to her conception of the Zone of Intervention, which is "modeled on Vygotsky's ... zone of proximal development" (Kuhlthau, 2004, p. 128):

> The zone of intervention is that area in which an information user can do with advice and assistance what he or she cannot do alone or can do only with difficulty. ... Intervention within this zone enables users to progress in the accomplishment of their task. (Kuhlthau, 2004, p. 129)

It would be relatively straightforward to incorporate this idea of the zone of intervention into a study of, for example, information seekers' use of various technological tools. Kuhlthau uses the idea in the development of school librarians' skills in dealing with information users but its use in information literacy programs generally would also be feasible.

Jin's (2004) poster at the 2004 ASIST Annual Meeting set out a program of research to explore the information behavior of competitive intelligence practitioners. This is evidently a doctoral research project and appears not yet to have been fully reported. However, the activity theory framework is clearly presented and adapted to a consideration of the competitive intelligence activity and the author notes (p. 2) "within the framework, [the] overall activity system, rather than individual CI practitioners, becomes the unit of analysis for research on information behavior." It is not clear, however, how the activity theory framework will help to provide answers to the research questions, which appear to be rather traditional in character and not influenced by activity theory.

Wilson (2006) has explored the relevance of activity theory for research in information-seeking behavior by revisiting previous research and retrospectively applying the framework. He shows, for example, how information flows in the social welfare activity of taking a child into protective care involve multiple activity systems in different agencies and how information seeking can be a collaborative activity, involving division of labor. Information exchange among interacting agencies may be one of the conceptual tools for which Engeström (1999) identified a need in the third generation of activity theory. Wilson also shows how the rather static diagrammatic models of activity theory might be converted to a process model, which also embodies rules, norms, and the division of labor as tools in activity.

Other researchers in this field have occasionally mentioned activity theory in their work without, however, taking the analysis very far. For example, Attfield and Dowell (2003) briefly mention activity theory in their study of the information-seeking behavior of journalists, drawing attention to the fact that search behavior is often related not to a single goal but to multiple goals. However, as a whole, their paper does not employ activity theory as an analytical framework.

Lessons for Information Science?

What do we learn from this review of the applicability of activity theory to research in librarianship and information science? As shown, to date there has been relatively little research in these fields performed within an activity theory framework—the fingers of both hands would not been needed to count the number of papers. True, Hjørland has written quite extensively on realism in information science and on domain analysis and usually mentions activity theory as one of his sources of influence, but research within a specific activity theory framework is rare. We can cite Spasser (1999, 2000, 2002) as one of the main researchers within the tradition and, in addition to the work by Jin (2004) and Wilson (2006), as also has been noted, Talja, Tuominen, and Savolainen (2005) draw attention to activity theory in their consideration of the "isms" of information science, as part of "collectivism" and mainly through reference to the work of Hjørland and Albrechtson. Overall, however, we must conclude that information science research, at least as traditionally defined in the library and information science community, has been little affected by the burgeoning interest in activity theory in cognate disciplines.

This leads to the question: What influence ought activity theory to have in information science?

The field of education, having arguably the most experience of activity-theory-based research is a fruitful area for synergy. Two subdisciplines can build upon the discoveries and models in education: information literacy and computer-based collaborative learning. As has been noted, information literacy is already a topic of research in education and the key recommendation would be for information science researchers to form strategic alliances with colleagues in education, who are likely to have a greater awareness of activity theory. Considering research itself as an activity collaboration can offer considerable benefits, not least because a division of labor would be possible—the information scientist being concerned with the development of skills in searching for and accessing information resources and the educationalist interested in the pedagogical issues relating to the teaching of these skills. Both would be interested in how information on information skills is best presented to naïve information searchers and how the student's activity could benefit from the wider contextual framework of pedagogical development that activity theory can provide. Also, Engeström's concept (1987) of *expansive learning* could lift information literacy research out of a relatively mundane concern with skills development to deal with how the acquisition of those skills helps the student (and which students and how) to "go beyond the information given" to the creative use of that information.

As has been noted, a search for research on information literacy with an activity theory perspective had only very limited success and, in general, the field does not yet appear to have engaged with activity theory. In this section, to exemplify the potential of activity theory for information-related research, we explore what benefits there might be in adopting an activity theory framework for information literacy research. Using Engeström's triangle (Figure 4.2), we can consider each of the nodes in turn to discover the research questions to which activity theory gives rise, thereby illustrating the value of the theory as a conceptual framework for the development of research.

To begin with the "subject," most information literacy research is concerned with programs developed for students, to equip them with the skills of information searching and information use that will serve them well not only in their current roles but in relation to life-long learning. But what of the teachers of those students? Is it assumed that they have all the necessary skills and do not require further development? And what of the librarians who serve those students and teachers? They may be involved in information literacy programs themselves but, often, the persons involved are not necessarily those who serve the students and teachers daily. Should information literacy programs, then, be developed and taught collaboratively? Should there be collaboration in learning, so that fast-learning students can help teachers gain a better understanding of the complexities of search engines? Should librarians be involved as learners so that they discover what resources are thought to be most useful by both teachers and students? In other words, simply asking, "Who is the subject of this activity?" gives rise to these questions and probably many more. And these questions relate only to the world of education: what of the world of work? What questions arise when we consider that context?

Turning to the "object," the core question is, "What is the object of information literacy development?" Is it to provide the individual student with a specific range of information discovery and information use skills? Or is it to develop the competencies of the target group (students, teachers, librarians, or whomever) collectively? If the latter, the implications would be very different. When we turn to work organizations, information literacy development might focus on teams or communities of practice, where a decision might be taken that a division of labor might be most effective and only one member of the team or community should become expert in information searching, analysis, and delivery to colleagues. Interestingly, this was Farradane's (1953) original definition of the information scientist. Is the world of connected, distributed information resources driving us back to that original concept?

"Tools" are generally considered to be computers and the associated software systems, but the work on genre theory, as well as activity theory itself, suggests that "tools" can be interpreted as a much more diverse set of phenomena. There is considerable attention in information literacy research and programs to the physical tools of computing and to the software, but people use a variety of additional tools, from other programs such as word-processors to personal digital assistants (PDAs) and paper resources, such as files and notebooks. How these various tools, and others such as thesauri and classification systems (including those devised by individuals for their own purposes), are integrated by the learner is an intriguing subject for research.

Considering the "rules and norms," there is a clear link between information seeking, information use, and information ethics that needs exploration in the context of information literacy. Students, in particular, need to be aware of the conventions of citation and quotation, in order to avoid charges of plagiarism, for example. At the collective level, there may also be informal rules and norms of behavior with respect to information use; for example, in a student project team, the necessity to share information freely may need to be reinforced.

How the nature of the "community" influences information literacy has not been explored, to my knowledge at least. In the education sector, a particular peer group of students may hold that information literacy is irrelevant and not to be pursued, but another group, bound together by the need to finish a joint project, may have a completely different perspective. In work organizations, similar divergences of view may prevail and different levels within the community may give more or less support to the development of information literacy in the organization. If, for example, senior management hold that time should not be wasted on information searching and Internet use, those who actually need the training and development may be forced into self-learning. This may be an example of the *contradictions* in activity systems, with the goals of one group, the senior managers, being in conflict with the goals of the team or the work group.

"Division of labor" has already been mentioned as a factor in teamwork and, in certain situations, training individuals rather than groups may be an appropriate strategy. The trained individuals might then operate as trainers themselves for other members of the work group or community of practice. In the educational environment one would expect information literacy programs to apply to everyone, however, and the division of labor may refer to the distribution of teaching and mentoring roles over the different parties involved in the process—teachers, students, and librarians.

Finally, we consider the "outcomes": This implies conducting evaluation research on the success (or otherwise) of information literacy programs. Longitudinal research on the efficacy of information literacy programs is often called for but rarely accomplished, and yet the long-term effects may be their most useful feature. The acquisition of certain personal information management competencies may well serve a useful purpose in relation to, for example, the conduct of project work in an educational institution, but, if thoroughly learned and internalized into everyday performance, they may have a lasting benefit on an individual's career outside of education.

It is also recognized that actions have intended and unintended consequences. What are the unintended consequences of information literacy development?

This brief and very incomplete review of activity theory as a conceptual framework for a subfield of information science reveals its power as a tool for developing a research program. When applied to a specific project, there is at least equal potential.

There are also synergies between education and information seeking behavior, as the reference to the work of Kuhlthau demonstrates. Many researchers, however, use the educational sector simply as an arena in which to carry out their research and do not develop the connections in ways that would be fruitful for education. An exception is the work of Limberg and her colleagues at the Swedish School of Library and Information Science. Beginning with her doctoral study (outlined in Limberg, 1999) and subsequently moving into project-based research with a strong educational component (e.g., Hultgren & Limberg, 2003; Limberg & Alexandersson, 2003), Limberg (like Kuhlthau) has demonstrated the value that information-seeking behavior research can have for education. Limberg has adopted a sociocultural approach (Alexandersson & Limberg, 2004) (which is closely related to the activity theory perspective) and, as with Kuhlthau, it would be interesting to map her work directly into such a perspective and discover what additional insights might be obtained.

The area of online learning and online information use is closely related and depends upon developments in information skills formation and information literacy. At root, these activities depend on distributed information systems and activity theory has contributed to this area. The role of library and information services in such learning systems is often limited to ensuring the availability of resources. The wide variety of interfaces available and the considerable variation in the design of library intranets is sufficient evidence that little has been done to ensure that the networked learner (who may actually be on the same university campus as the library) understands the role of the intranet and the significance of different kinds of information resources. This would require, again, a synergy with research in education and human–computer interaction. George, Bright, Hurlbert, Linke, St. Clair, and Stein (2006) investigated the information behavior of masters' and doctoral students engaged in research. They found that, although such students were not new to library and information use, few were fully aware of the range of resources available through the library intranet and the means available to discover those resources.

Information literacy has been the focus of this discussion because of its strong inter-disciplinary character but other areas of information research might also benefit from the application of an activity theory perspective. For example, in relation to the management and use of information in organizations, there is a great deal of research from a variety of directions. The "Tampere School" of studies on task analysis (Byström, 2002; Byström & Hansen, 2005; Byström & Järvelin, 1995; Vakkari, 2001, 2003) has shown that the nature of individual tasks and their performance is significant for various aspects of information science, from information searching to information retrieval; the incorporation of these studies into an activity theory perspective might lead to the investigation of interesting relationships between tasks and the wider activities of which they are a part. Also, it would direct attention to the contextual aspects through a consideration of the rules and norms of the organization in which the tasks are performed; the community affected by, or engaged in the tasks; the performance of those tasks; and the extent of the division of labor in activities, which raises issues of the coordination of tasks for the accomplishment of the wider activity. Very interesting research in the area of work task analysis is being carried out at the VTT Technical Research Centre in Finland by Norros and her colleagues (see, for example, Norros, 2004).

Davenport and Hall (2002) have drawn attention to the use of activity theory in research on communities of practice and organizational learning. However, there appears to be very little in organizational studies journals that adopts such a perspective. In fact a search on *Web of Knowledge* for "activity theory AND (communities of practice OR organizational learning)" across the six major organization theory journals resulted in only three items, only one of which, Blackler (1995), actually concerns this specific subject. This is a little odd because there are certainly two other papers in the journal *Organization* on the topic (Blackler, Crump, & McDonald, 2000; Engeström, 2000b). There is also a very interesting third paper (Thompson, 2004), which suggests that, in applying activity theory to organizational life, researchers have moved away from Vygotsky's original concept. Thompson (2004, p. 580) argues that:

> this original formulation, which emphasized the mediation of human consciousness by tools and signs ... has been replaced by a concern with the interrelationships between social groupings, which, not being conscious, are incapable of mediated experience in the manner Vygotsky proposes.

Although critical of work by Blacker and Engeström, Thompson does not wish to dispose of activity theory altogether. He seeks, as his title states, rather to strengthen organizational activity theory by drawing in ideas from the Russian philosopher and literary theorist, Mikhail Bakhtin, to ground activity theory more securely in its Vygotskian origins.

Interestingly, in his comments on Blacker, Engeström (2000b) also draws attention to the value of Bakhtin's work.

Activity theory may not be an appropriate research framework for every area within library and information science but on the basis of this analysis, it would be appropriate for any investigation of library and information *practice*—and the greater part of research is concerned with practice: how things are done, how to do them more effectively or efficiently, and how to develop systems that support the doing.

A sign of an increasing interest in the application of activity theory can be found in the thematic issue on the subject in the April, 2007 issue of the open access journal, *Information Research*, with papers on information sharing and organizational learning (Widén-Wulff and Davenport, 2007), distributed information behaviour (von Thaden, 2007), and school library programs (Meyers, 2007), which fall squarely into the information science field, together with papers on accessibility in social Web site design (Kane, 2007) and information systems development (Mursu, Minkkinen and Korpela, 2007), which extend the field in the manner suggested in the conclusion to this chapter.

Conclusion

Although this review of possible influences may be satisfactory from the perspective of a narrow definition of information science, it might actually be more interesting to redefine the field to cover the totality of the disciplines covered by this review. The latter would be a more radical approach and one that is justified, in this author's mind, by two factors. First is the extent to which the original idea of information science has been eroded by the acceptance by other disciplines of many of the key concerns of information science. We can point, for example, to information retrieval, research on which has migrated almost entirely to computer science; to the obvious relationships between information requirements in information systems and information behavior in information science; to the fact that studies in information literacy, which began as user education in librarianship, are now part of the research agenda in education; and to the increasing tendency for information services to be computer-based and, hence, to require the disciplines of information systems development. Apart from the continuing concern with the management of the physical record in the form of books and archive materials, information delivery has become more and more a matter of *electronic* information delivery and the tendency for information science to merge into the wider world of information disciplines generally shows no sign of reversal or containment.

The second factor is that by reviewing activity theory as a common conceptual framework for the range of information-related disciplines reviewed here, one's attention is drawn to the artificiality of the distinctions. Very often, common phenomena are being explored through activity theory but in different academic subcultures, in different journals, and not always with the degree of interdisciplinarity that might be appropriate.

It appears, in fact, that information science would be a useful term under which to subordinate all of the information research areas reviewed here (excluding psychology and education), leading to what Engeström (1987) calls the expansive transformation of the field. We can use Engeström's model of the activity system to suggest the kind of transformation that could take place through an integration of the information disciplines. Figure 4.4 owes something to Figures 2.10 and 2.12 in Engeström (1987). The figure is fairly readily readable and the explanation is straightforward. The arrows show the expansive character of the changes, and the small activity theory diagram shows the new information science research system as the outcome of the transformation. At all points in the figure, we suggest an expansion of concerns and motives that shifts the model from one that is related to individual information science disciplines or subdisciplines (such as HCI, information systems development, and collaborative learning systems) to one that is based on the implications of adopting activity theory as a common conceptual framework for research across the disciplines, providing a common language and enabling a common understanding of research issues.

Such a solution to the fragmentation of research across disciplines will not be easy to accomplish, but the more the interrelated concerns are shown in *ARIST*, the more likely it is that a solution of this kind will ultimately enable us to define "information science" as a coherent and useful research area.

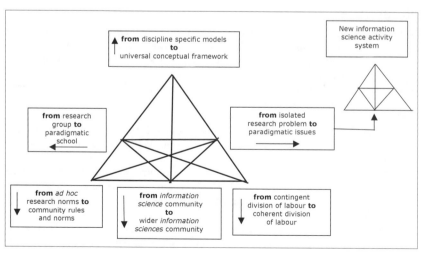

Figure 4.4 The expansive development of information science.

Acknowledgments

I am grateful to Professor Elena Maceviciute for her contribution of the section on activity theory in the USSR and for earlier discussions on the Russian literature on activity theory. I also thank the anonymous referees whose comments on the original draft enabled something better to emerge; I am, of course, entirely responsible for the imperfections that remain.

Endnotes

1. The problem of translating Russian terms used in activity theory is also dealt with by Kaptelinin and Nardi, 2006, chapter 6.
2. Although Zinchenko provides no citation, he may have in mind Rubinshtein's (1922) "Principle of creative personal activity." Intriguingly, Rubinshtein worked as Director of the Research Library of Odessa from 1922 to 1930 (see www.ido.edu.ru/psychology/psychophysiology/biograf27.html) and then as Assistant Director of the City Libraries of St. Petersburg before returning to academic psychology in the same city (Don, 2004).
3. The term "bibliography" or "bibliographic science" has a much broader connotation in Soviet literature than in the West; Maceviciûtë and Janonis (2004, p. 32) note:

   Bibliographic practice is the practical creation of bibliographic information and bibliographic services in society, supporting practically every other human activity through a wide range of institutions (libraries, archives, museums, information services, indexing and abstracting centres, publishing, science communication, etc. …) or beyond them.

   In other words, it embraces the whole of library and information science, and more.

References

Alexandersson, M., & Limberg, L. (2004). *Textflytt och sökslump: Informationssökning via skolbibliotek*. [Text transport and random searching: Information seeking via the school library.] Stockholm, Sweden: Myndigheten för skolutveckning.

Attfield, S., & Dowell, J. (2003). Information seeking and use by newspaper journalists. *Journal of Documentation*, 59(2), 187–204.

Baker, M. J., Hansen, T., Joiner, R., & Traum, D. (1999). The role of grounding in collaborative learning tasks. In P. Dillenbourg (Ed.), *Collaborative learning: Cognitive and computational approaches* (pp. 31–63). Amsterdam: Elsevier Science.

Barab, S. A., Barnett, M., Yamagata-Lynch, L., Squire, K., & Keating, T. (2002). Using activity theory to understand the systemic tensions characterizing a technology-rich introductory astronomy course. *Mind, Culture, and Activity*, 9(2), 76–107.

Barsuk, A. I. (1975). *Библиографоведение в системе книговедческих дисциплин*. [Science of bibliography in the system of book research disciplines]. Moscow: Kniga.

Barthelmess, P., & Anderson, K. M. (2002). A view of software development environments based on activity theory. *Computer Supported Cooperative Work, 11*(1), 13–37.

Bateson, G. (1972). *Steps to an ecology of mind.* New York: Ballantine Books.

Bedny, G. Z., & Karwowski, W. (2004). Activity theory as a basis for the study of work. *Ergonomics, 47*(2/5), 134–153.

Bedny, G. Z., Karwowski, W., & Bedny, M. (2001). The principle of unity of cognition and behavior: Implications of activity theory for the study of human work. *International Journal of Cognitive Ergonomics, 5*(4), 401–420.

Bedny, G. Z., Seglin, M. H., & Meister, D. (2000). Activity theory: History, research and application. *Theoretical Issues in Ergonomic Science, 1*(2), 168–206.

Berge, O., & Fjuk, A. (2006). Understanding the roles of online meetings in a net-based course. *Journal of Computer Assisted Learning, 22*(1), 13–23.

Bespalova, E. K. (1980). Библиография как деятельность [Bibliography as activity]. *Советская библиография* [Soviet Bibliography], no. 6, 10–18.

Bespalova, E. K. (1982). *Структура советской библиографии как области деятельности.* [Structure of the Soviet bibliography as a field of activity]. Moscow: Kniga.

Blackler, F. (1995). Knowledge, knowledge work and organizations: An overview and interpretation. *Organization Studies, 16*(6), 1021–1046.

Blackler, F., Crump, N., & McDonald, S. (2000). Organizing processes in complex activity networks. *Organization, 7*(2), 277–300.

Bødker, S. (1989). A human activity approach to user interfaces. *Human-Computer Interaction, 4*(3), 171–195.

Bødker, S. (1991). Activity Theory as a challenge to systems design. In H.-E. Nissen, H. K. Klein, & R. Hirschheim (Eds.), *Information systems research: Contemporary approaches and emergent traditions* (pp. 551–564). Amsterdam: North-Holland.

Byström, K. (2002). Information and information sources in tasks of varying complexity. *Journal of the American Society for Information Science and Technology, 53*(7), 581–591.

Byström, K., & Hansen, P. (2005). Conceptual framework for tasks in information studies. *Journal of the American Society for Information Science and Technology, 56*(10), 1050–1061.

Byström, K., & Järvelin, K. (1995). Task complexity affects information seeking and use. *Information Processing & Management, 31*, 191–213.

Chaiklin, S. (2007). Modular or integrated?—An activity perspective for designing and evaluating computer-based systems. *International Journal of Human–Computer Interaction, 22*(1 & 2), 173–190.

Cherniak, A. J. (1981). О предмете библиотековедения [About the subject of library science]. *Научно-технические библиотеки СССР* [Research and technical libraries of the SSSR], no. 2, 3–11.

Cluts, M. M. (2003). The evolution of artifacts in cooperative work: Constructing meaning through activity. *Proceedings of the International ACM SIG Group Conference on Supporting Group Work,* 144–152.

Collis, B., & Margaryan, A. (2004). Applying activity theory to computer-supported collaborative learning and work-based activities in corporate settings. *Educational Technology Research and Development, 52*(4), 38–52.

Daft, R. L., & Lengel, R. H. (1984). Information richness: A new approach to managerial behavior and organization design. *Research in Organizational Behavior, 6*, 191–233.

Davenport, E., & Hall, H. (2002). Organizational learning and communities of practice. *Annual Review of Information Science and Technology, 36*, 171–227.

Don, E. (2004). Sergey Rubinshtein, 1889–1960. *Historical Times, 24*(3). Retrieved July 27, 2006, from www.erickson-foundation.org/news/Archives/Acrobat%20Files/24_3%20 acrobat.pdf

Elliott, M., & Kling, R. (1997). Organizational usability of digital libraries: Case study in legal research in civil and criminal courts. *Journal of the American Society for Information Science, 48*(11), 1023–1035.

Engeström, Y. (1987). *Learning by expanding: An activity-theoretical approach to developmental research.* Helsinki, Finland: Orienta-Konsultit. Retrieved May 20, 2006, from communication.ucsd.edu/LCHC/MCA/Paper/Engestrom/expanding/toc.htm

Engeström, Y. (1999). *Learning by expanding: Ten years after* (Trans. F. Seeger). Retrieved December 22, 2006, from lchc.ucsd.edu/MCA/Paper/Engestrom/expanding/intro.htm

Engeström, Y. (2000a). Activity theory as a framework for analyzing and redesigning work. *Ergonomics, 43*(7), 960–974.

Engeström, Y. (2000b). Comment on Blacker et al. Activity theory and the social construction of knowledge: A story of four umpires. *Organization, 7*(2), 301–310.

Engeström, Y. (2002). *A video interview with Yryö Engeström, University of California and University of Helsinki.* Lancaster, UK: Lancaster University, Centre for Studies in Advanced Learning Technology. Retrieved May 20, 2006, from csalt.lancs.ac.uk/alt/engestrom

European Commission. Directorate-General for the Information Society. (2002). *The DigiCULT Report: Technological landscapes for tomorrow's cultural economy: Unlocking the value of cultural heritage. Full report.* Luxembourg, Belgium: Office for Official Publications of the European Communities. Retrieved July 25, 2006, from tinyurl.com/hphz8.

Fåhræus, E. R. (2004). Distance education students moving towards collaborative learning: A field study of Australian distance education students and systems. *Educational Technology & Society, 7*(2), 129–140.

Farradane, J. E. L. (1953). Information service in industry. *Research, 6*, 327–330.

Fjeld, M., Lauche, K., Bichsel, M., Voorhorst, F., Krueger, H., & Rauterberg, M. (2002). Physical and virtual tools: Activity theory applied to the design of groupware. *Computer Supported Cooperative Work, 11*(1–2), 153–190.

Fjuk, A., & Ludvigsen, S. (2001). *The complexity of distributed collaborative learning: Unit of analysis.* Paper presented at the European Conference on Computer-Supported Collaborative Learning, Maastricht, the Netherlands. Retrieved May 18, 2006, from www.telenor.no/fou/program/nomadiske/articles/CSCL-ASFinal.pdf

Fomina, E. N. (1976). Рекомендательное библиографоведение – вид продуктивной творческой деятельности [Science of recomendatory bibliography as a kind of productive and creative activity]. *Рекомендательная библиография в системе пропаганды книги в СССР* [Recomendatory bibliography in the system of book propaganda in the SSSR], вып. 14, 5–56.

George, C., Bright, A., Hurlbert, T., Linke, E. C., St. Clair, G., & Stein, J. (2006). Scholarly use of information: Graduate students' information seeking behaviour. *Information Research, 11*(4), paper 272. Retrieved July 15, 2006, from InformationR.net/ir/11-4/paper272.html

Giddens, A. (1984). *The constitution of society: Outline of the theory of structuration.* Cambridge, UK: Polity Press.

Glosienë, A. (1997). Bibliotekininkystë [Librarianship]. In *Knygotyra: Enciklopedinis žodynas* (pp. 56–57). Vilnius, Lithuania: Alma Littera.

Gosstandart SSSR. (1985). *ГОСТ 7.0-84. Библиографическая деятельность. Основные термины и определения.* [Bibliographic activity. Main terms and definitions] åoskva: Izdatel'stvo standartov.

Haltunen, K. (2003). Students' conceptions of information retrieval: Implications for the design of learning environments. *Library & Information Science Research*, 25(3), 307–322.

Hart-Davidson, W. (2002). Modeling document-mediated interaction. *Proceedings of the 20th Annual International Conference on Computer Documentation*, 60–71.

Heeren, E., & Lewis, R. (1997). Selecting communication media for distributed communities. *Journal of Computer Assisted Learning*, 13(2), 85–98.

Heinström, J. (2003). Five personality dimensions and their influence on information behaviour. *Information Research*, 9(1), paper 165. Retrieved May 18, 2006, from InformationR.net/ir/9-1/paper165.html

Hjørland, B. (1997). *Information seeking and subject representation: An activity theoretical approach to information science.* Westport, CT: Greenwood Press.

Hjørland, B. (2002). Epistemology and the socio-cognitive perspective in information science. *Journal of the American Society for Information Science and Technology*, 53(4), 257–270.

Hjørland, B. (2004). Arguments for philosophical realism in library and information science. *Library Trends*, 52(3), 488–506.

Hjørland, B., & Albrechtson, A. (1995). Toward a new horizon in information science: Domain-analysis. *Journal of the American Society for Information Science*, 46(6), 400–425.

Hjørland, B., & Christensen, F. S. (2002). Work tasks and socio-cognitive relevance: A specific example. *Journal of the American Society for Information Science and Technology*, 53(11), 960–965.

Hultgren, F., & Limberg, L. (2003). A study of research on children's information behaviour in a school context. *New Review of Information Behaviour Research*, 4(1), 1–15.

Ingwersen, P. (1996). Cognitive perspectives of information retrieval interaction: Elements of a cognitive IR theory. *Journal of Documentation*, 52(1), 3–50.

Intergovernmental Council of Standardization, Metrology, and Certification. (1999). *ГОСТ 7.0-99. Библиографическая деятельность. Основные термины и определения.* [Bibliographic activity. Main terms and definitions]. Moscow: IPK Izdatel'stvo standartov.

Irestig, M., Eriksson, H., & Timpka, T. (2004). The impact of participation in information system design: A comparison of contextual placements. *Proceedings of the Eighth Participatory Design Conference*, 102–111.

Jin, T. (2004). *Using activity theory framework to study information behavior of competitive intelligence (CI) practitioners.* Poster presented at the Annual Meeting of the American Society for Information Science and Technology. Retrieved December 21, 2006, from www.asis.org/Conferences/AM04/posters/222.doc

Jonassen, D., & Rohrer-Murphy, L. (1999). Activity theory as a framework for designing constructivist learning environments. *Educational Technology Research and Development*, 47(1), 61–79.

Kane, S. (2007). Everyday inclusive Web design: An activity perspective. *Information Research*, 12(3), paper 309. Retrieved April 15, 2007, from InformationR.net/ir/12-3/paper309.html

Kaptelinin, V. (1995). Activity theory: Implications for human–computer interaction. In B. Nardi, (Ed.), *Context and consciousness: Activity theory and human–computer interaction* (pp. 102–121). Cambridge, MA: MIT Press.

Kaptelinin, V., & Nardi, B. A. (1997). *Activity theory: Basic concepts and applications.* Retrieved May 17, 2006, from www.acm.org/sigchi/chi97/proceedings/tutorial/bn.htm

Kaptelinin, V., & Nardi, B. A. (2006). *Acting with technology: Activity theory and interaction design.* Cambridge, MA: MIT Press.

Kaptelinin, V., Nardi, B., & Macaulay, C. (1999). The activity checklist: A tool for representing the "space" of context. *Interactions, 6*(4), 27–39.

Kogan, V. Z. (1981). *Человек в потоке информации* [A human being in the flow of information]. Novosibirsk, USSR: Nauka, Sib. Dpt.

Kogan, V. Z., & Ukhanov, V. A. (1991). *Человек: информация, потребность, деятельность* [Human beings: Information, need, activity]. Tomsk, Russia: Tomsk University Press.

Korpela, M. (1997). *Activity analysis and development in a nutshell.* Retrieved July 24, 2006, from www.uku.fi/atkk/actad/nutshell.html

Korpela, M., Mursu, A., & Soriyan, H. A. (2002). Information systems development as an activity. *Computer Supported Cooperative Work, 11*(1–2), 111–128.

Korshunov, O. P. (1975). *Проблемы общей теории библиографии* [Problems of general theory of bibliography]. Moscow: Kniga.

Kozulin, A., Gindis, B., Ageyev, V. S., & Miller, S. M. (Eds.). (2003). *Vygotsky's educational theory in cultural context.* Cambridge, UK: Cambridge University Press.

Kuhlthau, C. C. (2004). *Seeking meaning: A process approach to library and information services.* Westport, CT: Libraries Unlimited.

Kuutti, K. (1996). Activity theory as a potential framework for human–computer interaction research. In B. Nardi, (Ed.), *Context and consciousness: Activity theory and human–computer interaction* (pp. 17–44). Cambridge, MA: MIT Press.

Lektorskii, V. A. (2004). The activity approach: Death or rebirth? *Journal of Russian and East European Psychology, 42*(2), 12–29.

Leont'ev, A. N. (1977). Activity and consciousness. In *Philosophy in the USSR: Problems of dialectical materialism* (pp. 180–202). Moscow: Progress Publishers. Retrieved July 15, 2006, from www.marxists.org/archive/leontev/works/1977/leon1977.htm

Leont'ev, A. N. (1978). *Activity, consciousness, and personality* (M. J. Hall, Trans.). Englewood Cliffs, NJ: Prentice Hall. Retrieved July 15, 2006, from www.marxists.org/archive/leontev/works/1978/index.htm

Lim, C. P., & Hang, D. (2003). An activity theory approach to research of ICT integration in Singapore schools. *Computers & Education, 41*(1), 49–63.

Limberg, L. (1999). Experiencing information seeking and learning: A study of the interaction between two phenomena. *Information Research, 5*(1), paper 68. Retrieved July 25, 2006, from informationr.net/ir/5-1/paper68.html

Limberg, L., & Alexandersson, M. (2003). The school library as a space for learning. *School Libraries Worldwide, 9*(1), 1–15.

McCarthy, J. C., Wright, P. C., Healey, P., Dearden, A., & Harrison, M. D. (1997). Locating the scene: The particular and the general in contexts for ambulance control. *Proceedings of the International ACM SIGGROUP Conference on Supporting Group Work*, 101–110.

Maceviciute, E. (2004). *Informacinės veiklos struktūra: komponentų sàveika : Habilitacijai teikiamų darbų apþvalga.* [Structure of information activity:

Interaction of components: Habilitation review]. Vilnius, Lithuania: Vilnius University.

Maceviciute, E., & Janonis, O. (2004). Conceptions of bibliography in the Russian Federation: The Russian phenomenon of bibliographic theory. *Libri, 54*(1), 30–42.

Martins, L. E. G., & Daltrini, B. M. (1999). An approach to software requirements elicitation using precepts from activity theory. *Proceedings of the 14th IEEE International Conference on Automated Software Engineering*, 15–23.

Meyers, E. M. (2007). From activity to learning: Using cultural historical activity theory to model school library programmes and practices. *Information Research, 12*(3), paper 313. Retrieved April 15, 2007, from InformationR. net/ir/12-3/paper313.html

Michailov, A. I., Chernyj, A. I., & Giliarevskij, R. S. (1968). *Основы информатики.* [Foundations of informatics]. Moscow: Nauka.

Michailov, A. I., Chernyj, A. I., & Giliarevskij, R. S. (1976). *Научные коммуникации и информатика* [Scholarly communications and informatics]. Moscow: Nauka.

Mørch, A., & Wasson, B. (1999). *Dynamics of groupware use in a collaborative telelearning scenario.* Position paper submitted to Workshop on Evolving Use of Groupware at ECSCW'99. Retrieved September 16, 2006, from www.telin.nl/events/ecscw99evo/PDFpapers/Morch.PDF

Mursu, A., Minkkinen, I., & Korpela, M. (2007). Activity Theory in information systems research and practice: Theoretical underpinnings for an information systems development method. *Information Research, 12*(3), paper 311. Retrieved April 15, 2007, from InformationR.net/ir/12-3/paper311.html

Mwanza, D. (2002). *Towards an activity-oriented design method for HCI research and practice.* Unpublished doctoral dissertation, The Open University, United Kingdom. Retrieved July 25, 2006, from iet.open.ac.uk/pp/d.mwanza/Phd.htm

Nardi, B. (1996). Activity theory and human–computer interaction. In B. Nardi, (Ed.), *Context and consciousness: Activity theory and human–computer interaction* (pp. 8–16). Cambridge, MA: MIT Press.

Nardi, B. A., Whittaker, S., & Schwarz, H. (2002). NetWORKers and their activity in intensional networks. *Computer Supported Cooperative Work, 11*(1–2), 205–242.

Norros, L. (2004). *Acting under uncertainty: The core task analysis in ecological study of work.* (VTT Publications 546). Helsinki, Finland: VTT Technical Research Centre of Finland. Retrieved December 23, 2006, from virtual.vtt.fi/inf/pdf/publications/2004/P546.pdf

Peach, D. (2003). *Improving the provision of learning assistance services in higher education.* Unpublished doctoral dissertation, Griffith University, Queensland, Australia. Retrieved June 13, 2006, from www4.gu.edu.au: 8080/adt-root/uploads/approved/adt-QGU20040319. 163140/public/02Whole. pdf

Piaget, J. (1959). *The language and thought of the child* (3rd ed.). London: Routledge & Kegan Paul. (First published 1923).

Quek, A., & Shah, H. (2004). A comparative survey of activity-based methods for information systems development. *Proceedings of ICEIS: 6th International Conference on Enterprise Information Systems.* Retrieved June 13, 2006, from www-lih.univ-lehavre.fr/Intranet/proceedings/ICEIS2004/ICEIS%25202004/ Area%25205%2520-%2520Human-Computer%2520Interaction/Oral%2520 Presentations/Short %2520Papers/C5_371_Quek.pdf

Rogers, Y. (2004). New theoretical approaches for HCI. *Annual Review of Information Science and Technology, 38*, 87–143.

Rubinshtein, S. L. (1922). *Принцип творческой самодеятельности.* [Principle of creative personal activity]. Odessa, Ukraine: University of Odessa.

Rubinshtein, S. L. (1957). *Existence and consciousness.* Moscow: Academy of Pedagogical Science.

Sokolov, A. V. (1984). Социальные функции библиотечной и библиографической деятельности [Social functions of library and bibliography activity]. *Научно-технические библиотеки СССР* [Research and technical libraries of the SSSR], no. 6, 19–27.

Spasser, M. A. (1999). Informing information science: The case for activity theory. *Journal of the American Society for Information Science, 50*(12), 1136–1138.

Spasser, M. A. (2000). Articulating collaborative activity: Design-in-use of collaborative publishing services in the Flora of North America Project. *Scandinavian Journal of Information Systems, 12*(1), 149–172.

Spasser, M. A. (2002). Realist activity theory for digital library evaluation: Conceptual framework and case study. *Computer Supported Cooperative Work, 11*(1/2), 81–110.

Spinuzzi, C. (1999). Grappling with distributed usability: A cultural-historical examination of documentation genres over four decades. *Proceedings of the 17th Annual International Conference on Computer Documentation,* 16–21.

Spinuzzi, C. (2002). Modelling genre ecologies. *Proceedings of the 20th Annual International Conference on Computer Documentation,* 200–207.

Stetsenko, A. (2003). Alexander Luria and the cultural-historical activity theory: Pieces for the history of an outstanding collaborative project in psychology. [Book review.] *Mind, Culture and Activity, 10*(1), 93–97.

Stoliarov, J. N. (1981). *Библиотека: структурно-функциональный подход* [A library: Structural-functional approach]. Moscow: Kniga.

Surowiecki, J. (2004). *The wisdom of crowds.* New York: Doubleday.

Talja, S., Tuominen, K., & Savolainen, R. (2005). "Isms" in information science: Constructivism, collectivism and constructionism. *Journal of Documentation, 61*(1), 79–101.

Tang, M.-C. (n.d.). *Dissertation proposal. Browsing in a faceted information space: A longitudinal study of users' interaction with a novel display tool.* Retrieved July 13, 2006, from www.scils.rutgers.edu/~muhchyun/description_of_the_research.pdf

Thompson, M. P. A. (2004). Some proposals for strengthening organizational activity theory. *Organization, 11*(5), 579–602.

Tolman, C. W. (1999). Society versus context in individual development: Does theory make a difference? In Y. Engeström, R. Miettinen, & R.-L. Punamäki (Eds.), *Perspectives on activity theory* (pp. 70–86). Cambridge, UK: Cambridge University Press.

Tugov, J. M. (1977). Об исходном пункте теоретического воспроизведения библиографии [On the starting point of the theoretical reconstruction of bibliography]. *Советская библиография* [Soviet Bibliography], no.1, 50–67.

Turner, P., Turner, S., & Horton, J. (1999). From description to requirements: An activity theoretic perspective. *Proceedings of the International ACM SIG-GROUP Conference on Supporting Group Work,* 286–295.

Ukhanov, V. A. (1996). *Информационная деятельность человека: Социально-философский анализ.* [Human information activity : Social and philosophical analysis]. Chabarovsk, Russia: Izdatel'stvo Chabarovskogo technologicheskogo universiteta.

Vakkari, P. (2001). A theory of the task-based information retrieval process: A summary and generalisation of a longitudinal study. *Journal of Documentation, 57*(1), 44–60.

Vakkari, P. (2003). Task-based information searching. *Annual Review of Information Science and Technology, 37,* 413–464.

Van House, N. (2004). Science and technology studies and information studies. *Annual Review of Information Science and Technology, 38,* 3–86.

Vaneev, A. N. (2004). *Библиотечное дело. Теория. Методика. Практика : [сб. тр.] : к 80-летию со дня рождения автора.* [Library work. Theory. Methodology. Practice]. St. Petersburg: Professija.

Veer, R. v. d., & Valsiner, J. (1991). *Understanding Vygotsky: A quest for synthesis.* Oxford, UK: Blackwell.

Vochrysheva, M. G. (1989). *Библиографмческая деятельность: Структура и эффективность.* [Bibliographic activity: Structure and effectiveness]. Moscow: Knizhnaja palata.

Von Thaden, T. (2007). Building a foundation to study distributed information behaviour. *Information Research, 12*(3), paper 312. Retrieved April 15, 2007, from InformationR.net/ir/12-3/paper312.html

Vygotsky, L. S. (1978). *Mind in society: The development of higher psychological processes.* Cambridge, MA: Harvard University Press.

Wertsch, J. V., del Rio, P., & Alvarez, A. (1995). Sociocultural studies: History, action, and mediation. In J. V. Wertsch, P. del Rio, & A. Alvarez (Eds.), *Sociocultural studies of mind* (pp. 1–34). Cambridge, UK: Cambridge University Press.

Widén-Wulff, G., & Davenport, E. (2007). Activity systems, information sharing and the development of organizational knowledge in two Finnish firms: An exploratory study using Activity Theory. *Information Research, 12*(3), paper 310. Retrieved April 15, 2007, from InformationR.net/ir/12-3/paper310.html

Widjaja, I., & Balbo, S. (2005). Structuration of activity: A view on human activity. *Proceedings of the 19th Conference of the Computer–Human Interaction Special Interest Group (CHISIG) of Australia,* 1–4.

Wilson, T. D. (2006). A re-examination of information seeking behaviour in the context of activity theory. *Information Research, 11*(4). Retrieved July 15, 2006, from InformationR.net/ir/11-4/paper260.html

Zinchenko, V. (1995). Cultural-historical psychology and the psychological theory of activity: Retrospect and prospect. In J. V. Wertsch, P. del Rio, & A. Alvarez (Eds.), *Sociocultural studies of mind* (pp. 37–55). Cambridge, UK: Cambridge University Press.

The Nature of Academic Disciplines

CHAPTER 5

Scholarship and Disciplinary Practices

Carole L. Palmer
Melissa H. Cragin
University of Illinois at Urbana-Champaign

Introduction

Research on disciplinary practice has been growing and maturing in the social sciences in recent decades. At the same time, disciplinary and practice-oriented studies in information science have also increased. In particular, disciplinary structures have been a common analytical framework in studies of scientific and scholarly communication; studies of information seeking and use have frequently examined the information practices of scholars working within or across disciplines. This chapter reviews a range of literature on the disciplinary nature of scholarly work practices. Most but not all of the research discussed takes information practices as the object of study and all the literature identified contributes to our understanding of scholarly information practices and how they vary among disciplines or, more precisely, among communities of scholars. Our aim is to trace the development of what we refer to throughout this review as the "information practices approach," our shorthand for research that recognizes the social dimension of disciplines as a primary influence on the information activities of scholars and scientists. The first two sections of the chapter provide an orientation to this approach with an overview of practice-oriented and discipline-oriented research in the social sciences and associated trends in information science.

Understanding the nature of information practices and their relation to the production of scholarship is important for both theoretical and applied work in library and information science (LIS). Research on scholarly practices provides a foundation for the development of information systems, services, and tools to support scholarship and science, especially as we strive to manage the escalating stores of digital literature and data for use by current and future researchers. As forecast in de Jong and Rip's (1997) discussion of the future of computer-supported discovery environments, the practice of e-research is evolving in many fields. That paper envisaged the biomedical discovery process as a series of unfolding problems solved by a group of physically distributed scientists supported primarily by electronically networked collections of literature, data, and analysis tools. This scenario was no doubt provocative at the time but such research work is now an accepted and desirable—and seemingly obtainable—objective in many fields of research. Thus, as Hine (2005, p. 3) notes,

> In the contemporary context of e-science, aiming directly to reshape scientific endeavours and provide new infrastructures to support them, this goal of studying the detail of actual practice takes on a new significance. In particular, the sociological perspective can add an attention to the ways that scientists work with objects, both material and virtual, and an understanding of the way that fields of science differ.

Of course, e-research trends are not restricted to the sciences, and, as a metascience (Bates, 1999), information science should be equally concerned with information work practices in the humanities and the social sciences.

Information science (IS) has long been concerned with scholarship, especially with scholarly literature as a resource for research and academia. This is evident in a series of early *ARIST* chapters titled "Information Needs and Uses" covering the communication and application of scientific and technical information by scientists, engineers, and technologists (Allen, 1969; Crane, 1971; Herner & Herner, 1967; Menzel, 1966; Paisley, 1968). These chapters were largely concerned with the effects and uses of various forms and channels of information and, to some degree, disciplinary practices were a latent theme. Menzel's (1966, p. 43) review included studies about "what is actually going on in the course of scientific and technological activity" and each of these early chapters reported general methodological improvements in studies of information behavior. Paisley (1968, p. 2) expressed concern with the "shallow conceptualization" of many studies that failed to grasp factors such as "the uses to which information will be put, the social, political, economic and other systems that powerfully affect the user and his work, and the consequences of information use—e.g., productivity." Perhaps most pertinent was Paisley's (p. 1) exclusion of studies on "systems tests that do not take place in the user's natural working environment."

Chapters reviewing the growing base of research on information needs and uses and information behavior have continued to include studies of scholarly groups; more recent reviews on scholarly communication and electronic publishing have also offered some perspective on scholarly research practices. Hills (1983, p. 100) presented a general model of the scholarly communication process as a system of "flows of information, ... actions and interactions among" interdependent constituents, including the scholar, the publisher, the product, the librarian, learned societies, and new communication technologies. He situated the scholar as "the central point of ... concern without whom there can be no scholarly communication" and asserted the need "to examine the ways in which scholars carry out their research, how they record this work, and how it is disseminated, received, and used" (p. 101). Although his review was only generally about practice, Hills did highlight roles and responsibilities of the various constituents in the scholarly communication process and specifically emphasized scholars' involvement in the dissemination and publishing process. King and Tenopir's (1999, p. 424) chapter is the most comprehensive on the topic, presenting a thorough overview of research on the "demand, use and readership of scholarly literature."

Framework and Scope

This chapter comprises seven sections:

- The Practice Turn in Social Science
- Disciplinary Structures and Cultures
- Information Work and Domains
- Domain Comparisons
- Information Work Processes and Primitives
- Collaboration and Data Practices
- Digital Scholarship

The two opening sections serve as background to the review, introducing the practice perspective and the concept of "discipline" and related characterizations of scholarly communities. These sections begin with a general social science view and then draw together selected IS work that, over time, has taken an increasingly socio-disciplinary approach to understanding scholarly practices. The Information Work and Domains section reviews primarily domain analytic user studies from LIS, concentrating on research with applications to information systems and services development. The Domain Comparisons section follows with comparative studies that have advanced our understanding of significant distinctions among scholarly communities. The next section on Information Work Processes and Primitives reviews studies on searching and writing processes and introduces our concept of "information work primitives" as a category of basic, more discrete scholarly activities. The Collaboration and Data Practices section first covers a selection of studies related to collaborative activities as they pertain to scholarly communication, with the second segment highlighting research concerning data practices. The concluding section reviews recent work from LIS, IS, and cognate fields that suggests the future direction of research on scholarly information practices in the digital age. Taken as a whole, this chapter presents a body of research on how communities of scholars and scientists work with information to produce scholarship.

Most of the material reviewed is empirical research, but we have also included critiques and commentaries that have paved the way for the emergence of the practice approach in IS. Throughout the review, we do not strive to be comprehensive but rather to show the trajectory of literature that is building our knowledge of information work in scholarly practice. As a result, both quantitative and qualitative studies are covered, although ethnographic methods are increasingly favored in IS and have been more standard among practice researchers in the social sciences generally. At various points we highlight frameworks and concepts developed in other social science fields—especially the sociology of science, the sociology of knowledge, and science and technology studies (STS)—that have provided a theoretical base for IS studies or that we believe have particular potential to inform studies of information practices. Throughout our discussion we use the STS abbreviation to generally refer to these fields.

Because of the inclusion of the STS literature, and because of the early and abundant work on scientific information and communication in IS, studies of the sciences are well represented in the review. For balance, we have made a particular effort to include studies of the humanities, although there are considerably fewer works to be found outside of LIS. The social sciences are only selectively represented here due to the more limited body of recent work on the research processes and information use of social scientists (Hobohm, 1999; Line, 2000).

The Practice Turn in Social Science

There is a growing body of research in the social sciences that takes a practice approach to studying knowledge production and research processes. The "practice turn" has influenced a broad range of social research such that "references to practices await the contemporary academician in diverse disciplines, from cultural theory and history to sociology, anthropology, and science and technology studies" (Schatzki, 2001, p. 1). To this list we would add IS and LIS, fields that have long been concerned with mobilizing information to support the work of researchers in academia and industry. In his important critique of frameworks for studying information, Frohmann (2004) painstakingly analyzes the shortcomings of LIS research on scientific and scholarly information and the detrimental absence of the practice approach as applied in STS. We agree that theoretically based studies of practice are rare in LIS. However, in this chapter we identify a body of information research that contributes to social studies of scholarly practice that, over time, demonstrates more sophisticated, practice-oriented frameworks and methods. As Frohmann asserts, these practice-based analyses stand to make a greater contribution to our understanding of information phenomena in relation to the real world of scholarly work than traditional information-centric approaches.

The term "practice" is used widely, generically, and imprecisely in the literature, not unlike the term "information," as detailed by Frohmann (2004). And, although the turn to practice as an analytical perspective is evident in the social sciences, there is no unified practice approach, only some common ideas about the concept across fields (Schatzki, 2001). Practices are "arrays of human activity" that are "materially mediated" and "organized around shared practical understanding" (p. 2). Therefore, the practice concept also encompasses how and why an activity is performed. Phenomena such as "knowledge, meaning, human activity, science, power, language, social institutions, and historical transformation occur within and are products of the *field of practices*. The field of practices is the total nexus of interconnected human practices" and is seen by practice scholars as the most productive place "to study the nature and transformation of their subject matter" (p. 2).

Like much practice oriented research, the disciplinary practices approach covered in this review is concerned with what Schatzki refers to as "subdomains"—disciplines, specialties, research areas, for example, and their shared understandings, skills, and work activities—within the more global field of practices. And, because the practice approach is "materialist" in nature, these understandings and activities involve information artifacts used and created in the work situation. Although practice researchers share a conviction that the field of practices offers the best site for developing insights on science and scholarship, among other social phenomena, "practice thought encompasses multifarious and often conflicting intuitions, conceptions, and research strategies" (Schatzki, 2001, p. 14). As a result, across the literature we see interesting juxtapositions such as strong social constructionist perspectives along with arguments that "the practice approach is compatible with a robust form of realism" (Schatzki, 2001, p. 12).

The practice approach has been especially prominent in STS, where qualitative and ethnographic methods and historical case studies have been widely applied to investigate how science and scholarship are produced. These approaches have been necessary for investigators to go beyond analysis of the end products created by scholars to follow the ongoing processes of research work where it takes place. Selected STS authors whose methods and ideas have been important for inquiry into "information practices" are identified in this chapter. However, for more systematic reviews of research on practices, techniques, and instrumentation at the local level of disciplinary culture, we refer readers to Sismondo (2004) for a recent STS overview and to Van House's (2004) *ARIST* chapter on STS and information studies. Also, Frohmann (2004) presents a sustained analysis of STS work with particular relevance to research questions in IS, emphasizing the perspectives of Knorr Cetina (1981, 1999), Latour (1987), Latour and Woolgar (1986), Pickering (1992), Rouse (1996), and numerous other important STS authors.

Information scientists, however, have been slow to move their data collection efforts into the laboratories, institutes, departments, and offices where scholars and scientists work, to conduct the kinds of local case studies common in STS. In fact, survey research is still widely applied in IS studies of scholarly information practices. But, because surveys offer a limited view of the information work of scholarly communities (Savolainen, 1998; Talja & Maula, 2003), our emphasis in this chapter is on more qualitative approaches, especially those that strive to document scholarly activities situated in the workplace. As we move our discussion from foundational work in scientific communication to studies of information and communication technologies (ICTs) and digital scholarship, the trend is toward more rigorous application of an evolving information practices approach that applies STS perspectives and methods.

The Practice Approach and IS

The holistic and materialist practice approach is well suited to research aimed at understanding the diversity of resources and activities involved in the scholarly process, but it has been thinly applied in IS. This may reflect the nature of the field, which strives to both understand information phenomena in a fundamental sense and also respond to a profession (with its own ingrained practices and responsibilities to constituencies) and its associated application areas. This creates something of a paradox. Taking an analytical approach that scrutinizes the complex range of activities involved in research production may on the surface seem too broad in scope for IS researchers, who are concerned with the documents, retrieval systems, and the users of those resources. But, the practice approach prioritizes the material aspects of how work gets done. Therefore, information sources and technologies are necessarily studied as constituent components of the scientific and scholarly enterprise. Books, articles, reports, bibliographic records, data, e-mail messages, digital documents, ICTs, and databases are as much a part of research as the ideas, methods, instruments, people, and institutions. As Frohmann (2004) notes, information objects are not the only, and generally not the most prominent, components of research practice. Nonetheless, they are diverse and variable in their roles and inextricably linked to the situations and contexts in which researchers do their work. The information practices approach offers empirical means for interrogating how scholarly information resources and tools can best support researchers' activities and goals.

The IS literature has been reporting on scholarly information activities for decades but explanations of the social dimensions of researchers' practices have been limited. Tacit acceptance of the social nature of scholarship is represented in how groups of researchers are demarcated in the design of research studies. Basically, disciplines are seen as meaningful units on which to base analysis. Often, there is also an unarticulated assumption as to how results are theorized. For instance, in qualitative studies of information seeking and use, results based on small, purposeful, representative samples are accepted *because* we understand that particular activities, skills, meanings, and perspectives are shared by social communities of scholars.

Over the past few decades there has been a slow emergence of what might best be called "practice awareness" in IS. As has been noted, studies of scholars have often examined information sources, channels, and technologies with the associated practices remaining implicit in the analysis. Stone's (1982) and Watson-Boone's (1994) LIS reviews on information use in the humanities, however, highlighted activities and resources associated with the physical work of producing scholarship, demonstrating that research processes were within scope for some studies. "Practices" highlighted by Stone (1982) included researchers' tendencies to: work alone, perform their own literature searches, rely on browsing, use books more than journals, employ retrospective materials, and prefer originals over facsimiles. Humanities scholars were also described as adopting a range of research methods, which may be drawn from different disciplines and working with a wide variety of materials. These conclusions do not fully consider the context of disciplinary practice but they do reveal a fundamental concern with both the materials and information work involved in the production of scholarship.

In an early, exceptional study, produced by the Art History Information Program of the J. Paul Getty Trust and the Institute for Research in Information and Scholarship of Brown University, researchers investigated the actual work processes of art historians (Bakewell, Beeman, & Reese, 1988). Their anthropological approach produced rich descriptions of art-history inquiry as well as case studies of research projects of two art historians. A few examples of similar studies that have built directly on STS frameworks include Ruhleder's (1994) investigation of classical scholars' use of computing packages, which drew on the enculturation model promoted by Collins (1987) and Henderson's (1991) visual culture perspective, among others. Palmer and Neumann (2002) applied Latour's (1987) concepts of "accumulation" and "translation" of knowledge to explain the information gathering and interpretation activities of interdisciplinary humanities scholars. Building on Becher's (2000) cultural identity approach to academic disciplines, Fry (2004) examined the relationship between research culture and information technology adoption in corpus-based linguistics. Other studies taking a firm information practices approach will be covered in the subsequent sections.

Information Work

For IS, the practice approach offers a vantage point from which to assess what scholars do and what they value in their daily work. Thinking about scholarship as work with materials and people is central to this perspective, and certain STS studies of research practice offer specific insights into this work as it relates to information. For example, much information work can be understood as a type of "articulation work"—the planning, organizing, evaluating, adjusting, coordinating, and integrating activities involved in getting work done (Corbin & Strauss, 1993; Fujimura, 1987; Strauss, 1988). By extension, information work is the actual labor of locating, gathering, sorting, interpreting, assimilating, and producing information. Without successful information work, many other types of work cannot be completed. As Gerson argued, "Every kind of work involves some kind of information production/construction/consumption/use" (as cited by Strauss, Fagerhaugh, Suszek, & Wiener, 1985, p. 253). Information work is connected to both the work itself and to the structural contexts in which that work is situated (Strauss et al., 1985).

In her study of medical research Fujimura (1987) showed how research projects depend on articulation devoted to aligning work at three levels—the experiment, the laboratory, and the social world. Successful alignment takes place largely by "articulating—collecting, coordinating, and integrating"—between the levels. Most of the articulation tasks identified by Fujimura are information work or require information work. For example, between the experiment and laboratory level, the activities include integrating data and results, surveying the literature, and writing research reports. Talking and corresponding with other scientists are primary alignment tasks between the laboratory and social world levels. Many IS studies discussed in this review are designed specifically to identify and understand these kinds of information work activities. However, not all information work is articulation work. The research process may also involve information work that is less about coordination and more of a sustained process of problem solving (MacMullin & Taylor, 1984; Simon, Langley, & Bradshaw, 1981; Vakkari, 1999). And certain classes of information work have been associated with specific stages of research. For example, based on their study of brain researchers, Palmer, Cragin, and Hogan (2007) and Palmer (2006) developed the concept of "weak information work" to represent difficult information activities that share characteristics with weak methods in scientific problem solving. The identification of different types of information work and assessment of their relative impact on research production are interesting open research questions in IS that will require application of an information practices approach.

Disciplinary Structures and Cultures

The term "discipline" is commonly used to describe and differentiate knowledge, institutional structures, researchers, and resources in the working world of scholarship and science. In IS, disciplines have been a standard framework for bibliometric analyses of bodies of literature and studies of scholarly communication and user communities. In accordance with this trend, we deploy the term readily throughout this review. However, we do so with full understanding of its gloss on the complexity of how research is socially organized and conducted. Disciplines serve an important function—they represent subject areas, tools, procedures, concepts, and theories of stable epistemic communities (Klein, 1990). But because the boundaries of scholarship are progressively shifting and dissolving, disciplines can be misleading simplifications of research work and the material and intellectual configurations that sustain it (Becher, 1990; Geertz, 1983; Pinch, 1990). Real-world research problems and solutions rarely arise within orderly disciplinary categories: "Disciplines now routinely experience the push of prolific fields and the pull of strong new concepts and paradigms" (Klein, 1996, p. 56). The resulting interaction between disciplinary domains keeps scholarship from becoming partitioned and stagnant (Becher, 2000; Chubin, 1976; Crane, 1972), increasing the utility and worth of the collective body of knowledge (Boulding, 1968; Campbell, 1969).

The interdisciplinary nature of knowledge and research practice has been portrayed in many ways—as overlapping, blurring, displaced, and shifting boundaries; merging, fusing, and intersecting territories; and mingling and migrating individuals (Campbell, 1969; Hoch, 1987; Klein, 1993; Mulkay, 1974; Palmer, 2001b). None of these descriptions completely explains all the levels of activity and the interplay among scholarly communities, yet how we conceive of disciplinary dynamics has a significant influence on what we can learn about research practice. As will be discussed further, Hjørland asserts that domain groupings are the soundest unit of study for information science research (Hjørland & Albrechtsen, 1995; Hjørland & Hartel, 2003), but questions remain as to how best to define a scholarly domain (Palmer, 1999a). This is a critical research design and sampling concern for studies of information practices, but unfortunately many researchers do not adequately justify the groups they choose to investigate. The most valid units of study and analysis for a practices approach would reflect communities of scholars and scientists with real working connections in their research activities, which could take the form of a well established disciplinary culture, an emergent interdisciplinary domain, or a collaborative work group.

Traweek's (1988) exploration of the high energy physics community is an exemplary case study of a stable, discipline-based community with a deep, well-established culture. Members of the discipline have a shared past, hope for a shared future, the means of acquiring new members and of recognizing and maintaining differences from other communities. With her anthropological approach, Traweek was able to show, for instance, how the exchange of disciplinary stories contributes to making science happen by helping members reach agreement on what machines, people, and facts count. Only the scientists immersed in the culture know what is to be said, what should be written, and how to navigate the information channels restricted to insiders.

Studies of research work as culture in the tradition of Traweek (1988), and widely associated with Pickering (1992), describe patterns, actions, means, meanings, and tools within a social environment. Structures of work are a fundamental part of this environment, as are material resources and the practices used for gathering, using, and transmitting materials to other members of a culture and novices on the periphery. Information is, of course, a vital resource, and certain cultural practice scholars have focused their analytical lens on the scientific literature. For example, Bazerman (1988), Knorr Cetina (1981), Latour (1987), and Myers (1993) each examined the creation and function of the journal article in the production of science, albeit in very different ways. Others have looked at a wider realm of information materials, such as Henderson (1999), who illustrated the influence of the "visual culture" of design engineers on how they aggregate, store, and manipulate information and the critical role of paper drawings, even after the adoption of computer applications, for the communication and teamwork involved in the design process.

Some domains of interest may not be sufficiently well established to have developed a genuine culture. For example, in his study of the development of computer simulation techniques during and after World War II, Galison (1996) demonstrated how nuclear weapons scientists integrated a novel cluster of skills, highly diverse subject matter, and common activities into a new research domain grounded in statistics, game theory, sampling, and computer coding. The new mode of inquiry addressed problems too complex for theory and too remote from lab materials for experiment. The emergent domain developed, in part, through what Galison (p. 119) refers to as a "trading zone," the conceptual space where raw materials and information are exchanged, cross-disciplinary languages evolve, and the new communities form around research problems.

Disciplinary cultures and trading zones are very different kinds of units of social and scholarly analysis, but each provides important insights into the role and value of information within the larger context of the process of conducting science. Some IS researchers have been applying relevant frameworks and concepts from STS but there is still need for greater integration of method and content knowledge into studies of information work and scholarly communication. As Cronin (2003, p. 16) notes, "what is missing is a compelling analysis of the structural dynamics of the scholarly communication marketplace, one that focuses upon the array of stakeholder dynamics, technological drivers, and competitive forces (and their interactions) that are reconfiguring the ecosystem." The information practices approach has made contributions to this end and holds considerable promise for gaining further insights into the base of scholarly production that underpins this marketplace. In the next two sections we discuss two genres of LIS studies, one that works to identify or define scholarly social structures and one that uses disciplinary or domain structures as a priori analytic units.

Social Structures of Scholarship and IS

A range of socially based work in IS has been concerned with structures of scholarship and more macro-disciplinary patterns of practice. Here we introduce Jesse Shera's social epistemological approach to information science, early work on scientific communication, and contributions made by bibliometric studies as key areas that have helped set the foundation for the information practices approach. These approaches are largely distinguished by their focus on how scholars interact with each other, albeit sometimes only through associations represented in the literature. Nevertheless, the results from these studies add to our understanding of the structures of interactive scholarly groups and relationships among groups.

Jesse Shera's writings on the purpose and theoretical basis of LIS drew the profession's attention away from the individual served by libraries toward the collective behavior of society at large. Recognizing the value of empirical work from sociology of knowledge concerned with the impact of social processes on the intellectual sphere, Shera and his colleague Margaret Egan (Egan & Shera, 1952) proposed a new discipline of social epistemology to provide a theoretical foundation for librarianship (Fallis, 2002; Furner, 2002). They conceived of LIS as much more than a service profession, calling for further exploitation of graphic communication and bibliographic tools to analyze the state and dynamics of knowledge. One aim of social epistemology would be to use documentary sources as a base of evidence for building a comprehensive body of knowledge on "intellectual integration and differentiation" that recognized the associated "complex social structure" of knowledge (Shera, 1972, p. 132). The LIS profession, according to Shera (1972, p. 111), is essentially about how "knowledge is coordinated, integrated, and put to work," how knowledge is shaped by what social groups do and how they interact. Anticipating the need for an empirical approach to understanding processes of knowledge production, Egan and Shera (1952, pp. 133–135) proposed "situational analysis" as a means for studying the "production, distribution, and utilization of intellectual products."

A more broadly developed foundation for the current information practices approach is found in the large corpus of studies on formal and informal scientific communication, work that was also concerned with more effective distribution and use of intellectual content. These studies took root in a series of meetings and projects on scientists' information needs, uses, and communication that began in the mid-20th century. Proceedings or major reports were generated from the Royal Society Scientific Information Conference (1948), the Chicago School symposium on special information in 1952 (Egan, 1954), the International Conference on Scientific Information in 1958, the American Psychological Association (1963) project on scientific information exchange in psychology, and a large body of research by Garvey and Griffith (e.g., 1963, 1964, 1968). Also of note is Allen's (1966) landmark study, identifying the variance between scientists' and technologists' patterns of information seeking, channel selection, and use. His study was one of the first to draw attention to important disciplinary differences.

Price's (1963) and Crane's (1972) classic studies of social relationships in scientific fields and the "invisible college" are emblematic of early approaches to mapping science through bibliometric and other quantitative measures of social and intellectual dynamics. Within the realm of scholarly communication, bibliometric studies have been concerned with identifying patterns using indicators such as citations, authors, textual content (Borgman, 1990), and acknowledgments (Cronin, 1995). Information science has produced a substantial body of such research dating back to Hulme's (1923) and Bradford's (1948) early work in statistical bibliography; bibliometric studies have since been instrumental for illustrating the landscape of literatures and trends in growth and interaction across scholarly domains. Citation analysis techniques (Smith, 1981), in particular, have been widely applied to examine the interaction among intellectual domains (e.g., Hurd, 1992; McCain, 1986b; White & McCain, 1998).

Although they are not practice oriented per se—that is, they do not provide data on the actual scholarly activities of locating, selecting, or applying the literature referenced—bibliometric analyses are grounded in our understanding of the social nature of scholarly writing. Scholars use bibliographic references to connect themselves to the works of other scholars. As Small (1978) argued, citation analysis assumes that citations have important symbolic value, and that making reference to a text is a significant social act. These acts are governed by rules of sociocognitive behavior within a field, leading authors to select their references with care to signal the originality of their own work in relation to what others have done before (Turner, 1994). Bibliometric studies contribute to our understanding of the "socioecology of scholarship" by exposing the combinations of resources used and the associations developed among fields of research, as scholars synthesize new information into their existing base of knowledge (Sandstrom, 1994, p. 444).

Current bibliometric studies continue to elaborate previous results on scholarly structures. For example, building on Merton (1967) and others (Cole, 1983; Griffith & Small, 1983; Line, 1981; Small & Crane, 1979), Hargens (2000) investigated two prototypical disciplinary modes of literature use: authors in the first mode focus on recently published literature, incorporating past work without acknowledging original sources and authors in the second mode tend to ignore recent work in favor of foundational texts. Applying reference network analysis to compare seven research areas, he found that behavioral science networks were distinctive of the second mode in their overcitation of foundational papers. Moreover, IS researchers have begun to concentrate on advancing techniques for visualizing the results of such quantitative network studies (e.g., Börner, Chen, & Boyack, 2003; Chen & Paul, 2001). But the relationship between representations of the intellectual world generated by bibliometric patterns and those produced by other social network techniques is not yet well understood (Lievrouw, Rogers, Lowe, & Nadel, 1987; Mullins, Hargens, Hecht, & Kick, 1977; Pierce, 1990; White, 2001; Zuccala, 2006).

Social networks are generally represented by associations, or ties, among individuals or groups of people. These ties correspond to some interaction among the participants and can be measured by range, density, and boundedness (Wellman, 1996). Data are generally collected using some combination of survey and possibly interviews, or with bibliometric techniques. Interestingly, White, Wellman, and Nazer's (2003) analysis of both bibliometric and social network measures of an interdisciplinary research organization indicated no strong association between citing practices and social ties, with citation motivated primarily by disciplinary perspective and related aspects of subject and method. For the members of the work group studied, friendship and acquaintance mattered but "content-laden networks" appeared to be the origin of intercitation (p. 125). That is, "who you know pays off only if the people you know have something worth knowing" (p. 125).

The activities involved in the intellectual work of scholarship are clearly complex, and bibliometric and social network techniques have provided key insights on both structural dynamics and more global patterns of practice. Quantitative measures are best used to classify and present statistical data to show where to look to gain a better understanding of activities and materials involved in knowledge development (Turner, 1994). Additional methods are needed to investigate the scholarly process more fully (Edge, 1979; Lievrouw, 1990).

Domain Analytic Distinctions

Domain analytic studies of scholarly information behavior have become common and, as we will see at the end of this chapter, this is a trend in new studies of digital scholarship. Similar to Shera's position, the domain analytic approach is concerned with "problems in the theory of knowledge," which, according to Hjørland and Albrechtsen (1995, p. 411), are "more fundamental than knowledge about the users of information systems." In other words, knowledge of domains strengthens our grasp of what constitutes consensus among communities of scholars, providing more explanatory power than studies of interactions between individuals and the information systems and sources they use. Of course, determining what constitutes a meaningful domain is no easy task because the parameters can be interpreted in many different ways. In fact, Hjørland and Albrechtsen discussed various units, including specialties, disciplines, and discourse communities; and they use studies of the humanities, social sciences, applied science, and interdisciplinary studies as their examples of important contributions to the domain analytic program. In a recent issue of *Knowledge Organization* devoted to domain analysis, individual papers on circumscribed domains covered nursing, art studies, music, and hobbies (Abrahamsen, 2003; Hartel, 2003; Ørom, 2003; Sundin, 2003).

Domains can be defined in several ways—in terms of intellectual association, for example, or links in the literature, or by more practice-based relationships such as communication networks or groups of collaborators. Hjørland and Albrechtsen's (1995) discussion mentioned *environment* as a domain based concept, invoking Taylor's (1991, p. 217) practice oriented "information use environment" (IUE) framework. IUEs are a way of conceptualizing a domain in terms of people in their work setting, their day-to-day activities, and the types of problems encountered and solutions accepted. Taylor's model has proven to be a productive framework for user studies but unfortunately has rarely been applied to scholarly domains. Other criteria can be equally well justified for determining domains of interest, such as problem areas where specialty terrains intersect or where researchers cooperate in sharing data, tools, and expertise. The heterogeneity of units of analysis obviously makes it difficult to integrate results from the growing number of domain based studies (Palmer, 1999a; Tennis, 2003). Further development of the approach is needed for more effective application to the study of scholarly information practices (Talja, 2005).

Overall, scholarly domains vary considerably in their representations in the literature, ranging in size and scope from general classes such as the social sciences (Cronin, 1982; Line, 1971), to disciplinary divisions such as art history (Stam, 1984) and atmospheric science (Hallmark, 2001), and interdisciplinary fields such as women's studies (Westbrook, 2003). Moreover, papers characterized as being about scientists, social scientists, or humanities scholars sometimes use a representative discipline as their base for data collection. For example, Palmer's (1991) study titled "Scientists and Information" investigated a sample of agricultural researchers. Analyses of specific research areas, such as the study of stateless nations (Meho & Haas, 2001) and biblical studies (Michels, 2005), are less common; Fry and Talja (2004) defend such "specialisms" as the most effective unit for the domain analytic approach.

Information Work and Domains

In spite of the lack of uniformity in analytical unit, domain-based user studies, especially those focusing on integral components of the research process or the range of activities involved in scholarship, have made a substantive contribution to information practices research in IS. The model of information seeking developed by Leckie, Pettigrew, and Sylvain (1996) is a good example in its emphasis on work roles and related information activities, although their analysis was based primarily on professional rather than scholarly domains. Ellis's (1993) widely cited information seeking model was based on studies of scholars and scientists; it is discussed further in the section on domain comparisons. It has been influential in research on scholarly information seeking and also in information use studies more generally. Studies that have considered shifts in the nature of scholarly practices over time have also been important. For example, Wiberley tracked changes in humanities research practice during the early adoption of electronic resources (Wiberley, 1991; Wiberley & Jones, 1989, 1994). Among a small sample of humanities scholars, Wiberley and Jones (2000) found that some senior researchers were employing a more diverse range of technologies than the junior scholars. Covi (2000) also found that senior scientists were interested in exploring electronic communication tools and that differences in adoption rates were associated with instances when doctoral students were able to bring new technologies into a lab or discipline.

Within the general class of the humanities, Bates and her colleagues produced a sequence of reports from the "Getty Online Searching Project" in which a small group of scholars was given an opportunity to do searches of DIALOG databases over a two-year period in the early 1990s (Bates, 1994, 1996a, 1996b; Bates, Wilde, & Siegfried, 1993, 1995; Siegfried, Bates, & Wilde, 1993). Notable results in terms of information work included limited use of online searching and frequent searching of names, places, titles of works, and other proper nouns. As previous research had suggested, scholars continued to identify citations to secondary materials via books and articles, reviews, and recommendations from colleagues. These studies stand as authoritative contributions on aspects of scholarly information work but they are also limited in the insights they can provide. As Manoff (1997) noted, the test databases made available to the participants were not strong in humanities content and therefore not the type of resource naturally favored by humanities scholars.

White and Wang (1997) and Wang and White (1999) also followed the development of research projects over time, tracking the reading and citing decisions of a group of agricultural economists. They were primarily interested in the cognitive criteria for citing behavior, but they did make interesting observations about the declining number of documents (relative to the number of documents retrieved) used during the course of a project.

Research on interdisciplinary scholarship, which tends to investigate new, or emerging domains, has been an area of special interest in IS. As Bates (1996c, p. 163) observed, interdisciplinary researchers "constitute a significant and distinctive class of scholars." They often work in research areas not well represented in university departments or other systems of knowledge organization. The move toward interdisciplinary specialization and synthesis in research practice has long been recognized as a critical problem for research libraries and for the organization of information resources (Berthel, 1968; Palmer, 1996b). Bibliometric techniques have been a standard approach for mapping cross-disciplinary information transfer and use (Borgman, 1990; Borgman & Furner, 2002; Chubin, Porter, & Rossini, 1986), and the variety of techniques and measures has been increasing in recent years

(Hurd, 1992; McCain, 1986a; Morillo, Bordons, & Gómez, 2003; Perry, 2003; Pierce, 1999; Rinia, van Leeuwen, Bruins, van Vuren, & van Raan, 2002; Steele & Stier, 2000).

Qualitative studies of interdisciplinarity have tended to investigate not domains per se, but rather interdisciplinary researchers as a class of scholar, to identify how this research orientation influences information practices. Spanner (2001) extended his investigation beyond distinct information activities to consider the complex environment of interdisciplinary work, including the impact of disciplinary acculturation and time management. Studies by Palmer (1996a, 1999b, 2001b) and Palmer and Neumann (2002) examined interdisciplinary scientists and humanities scholars, combining bibliometric and qualitative practice-based approaches to identify the interplay of modes of research, collaboration, knowledge development, and information practices. Using a naturalistic interviewing technique, Foster (2004) developed a nonlinear model of interdisciplinary information seeking that accounted for the social and organizational structures of research, as well as aspects of the specific projects undertaken by researchers.

Content analyses of documents have complemented domain-based studies of scholars' information work processes and added an important dimension to our theoretical understanding of the contexts of practice within domains. For example, Frost's (1979) analysis of functions of citations showed that literary scholars tended to cite in order to support their work or to refer readers to additional readings. Scientists used citations more for introducing the object of research and providing factual information. Green's (2000) study empirically demonstrated that bibliographic chaining or footnote chasing from "seed documents" was used to identify sources not listed in standard indexes. Tibbo's (1992) work on scholarly indexing and abstracting highlighted the inconsistencies in ANSI/ISO abstracting standards for scholarly and scientific writing and across indexing for historical journal articles and dissertations. Tibbo (1994) attributed the lag in indexing and abstracting services for humanities to more complex and expensive indexing needs in the humanities.

Journal Practices

Document types have also been a focus of domain analytic studies (Hjørland, 2002a). The journal article is a commonly studied format and an area of inquiry that serves as an interesting case for contrasting STS and IS orientations to practice. From the STS perspective promoted by Frohmann (2004), the content of information resources is secondary to how they support scholarly practice. Thus the importance of journal literature lies more in its strategic role positioning research in an ongoing narrative of a particular science than in its intellectual content. Journal articles are more than just an end product; they are intertwined with other practices that together constitute science (Bazerman, 1988; Knorr Cetina, 1981; Myers, 1993). Therefore, Frohmann (2004) argued that IS should be investigating not the role of the journal in communication among researchers but rather how journal articles stabilize scientific phenomena and contribute to the maintenance and development of a research program. Both types of studies can, however, contribute to determining whether, when, and how objects, such as databases, collections, and information infrastructures, actually stabilize (Cragin & Shankar, 2006). As with all resources used in scholarship, the journal article must be placed in the context of the many assemblages of people, things, social relations, and documentary practices that sustain research.

A few user studies researchers have taken a concerted information practices approach to the journal literature. Fry and Talja's (2004) comparative study, discussed in the next section, is a good example, as is Bishop's (1999) analysis of how scientists work with components of journal articles in relation to their intellectual work processes and strategies. However, most journal studies in IS have tended to look at access and use in isolation from the many other activities involved in the research process. This has necessarily been the case in studies that have relied on log data (e.g., Davis & Solla, 2003; Nicholas, Huntington, Jamali, & Watkinson, 2006; and numerous studies reviewed by Jamali, Nicholas, & Huntington, 2005), which cannot represent research process or context. Survey studies and other qualitative follow-ups to log analyses have gone further in capturing scholars' preferences and practices in looking for and using journal literature (e.g., Eason, Richardson, & Yu, 2000), but these, too, are generally limited in how much they can reveal about situated practice. It is true, nonetheless, that the cumulative journal studies have provided substantial insight into some social dimensions of journal use. Tenopir's (2003) comprehensive report presents results from major e-journal initiatives and the series of longitudinal survey studies produced by Tenopir and King and their colleagues. In particular, the synthesis confirms different patterns of use by faculty members in different subject disciplines.

Domain Comparisons

As the previous section suggests, the growth of domain-based information use studies has created a need to integrate the many findings and multiple models that are being generated from that research. On the other hand, there has been a productive trend in comparative studies of domains that work toward more systematic explanations of the differences among domain cultures and practices. As Bates (1998, p. 1200) noted, scholarly communication and social processes "function differently" across domains and we should be assuming that "these many differences *do* make a difference" in information access and use. Comparing communication for fields including high energy physics, computer science, molecular biology, and astrophysics, Kling and McKim (2000) argued for a work practice approach to move beyond vague notions that conflate the varying activities and interests of intellectual communities (see also, Kling, McKim, & King, 2003). Other commentators have affirmed that to support researchers effectively, information system development will need to take into account the many types of research information and their divergent roles in different fields (Agre, 1995; Borgman, 2000).

The influential information seeking model developed by Ellis (1989, 1993) and Ellis, Cox, and Hall (1993) was based on a comparative analysis of scholars in the social sciences, physical sciences, and literature. Using a grounded theory approach, their research was directed much more toward investigating scholarly practices than was the research of many previous information seeking studies. However, the results indicated only minor, mostly terminological, differences, leading to the conclusion that a uniform process—starting, chaining, browsing, differentiating, monitoring, and extracting—was applicable across the fields. And, as Meho and Tibbo (2003) pointed out, the model was consistent with previous user studies in the social sciences (Line, 1971; Skelton, 1973). However, others have since shown that the Ellis model could be better adapted to reflect disciplinary variation. Meho and Tibbo (2003) extended Ellis's model based on e-mail interviews with a distinct group of social scientists working in the research area of stateless nations, adding accessing, networking, verifying, and information managing to the information seeking framework. They also identified a number of obstacles unique to stateless nations research. Palmer and Neumann (2002) showed that, for interdisciplinary humanities scholars, such a model needs to reflect the diversity of materials used, the work of interpreting information from far afield, and the exchange of information among scholars. The browsing and monitoring activities Ellis identified were evident but more aligned with Sandstrom's (1994) description of how researchers "forage" (p. 415) for resources in "patchy information environments" (p. 432). These findings reinforce the observation made by Bates (1996c) about the distinctive quality of interdisciplinary information seeking processes.

Differences between science and engineering have long been recognized (Allen, 1966, 1969), but more recent studies have looked at variations within the sciences. Brown's (1999) comparative questionnaire study of astronomers, chemists, mathematicians, and physicists revealed that scientists use different information from mathematicians, who were more influenced by conference and invisible college communication and tended to rely on a variety of documentary materials in addition to journals. However, Brown's results showing scientists' preference for print journals has quickly become outdated. Using a personalized, open-ended questionnaire approach, Hallmark (2004) contrasted data from 1998 and 2002 to show scientists' consistent use of the Internet to access journals and data over that period, with the later set of data showing a high dependence on e-journals for retrieval of articles.

Covi and Kling produced a series of comparative reports on the information practices of academic researchers (Covi, 1999; Kling & Covi, 1995, 1997). Covi's (1999, p. 294) approach was explicitly materialist in its application of the concept of "material mastery" as a framework for analyzing disciplinary aspects of working with documents. Based on a large set of interviews with researchers in molecular biology, literary theory, sociology, and computer science, she identified clear disciplinary influences on work characteristics. Unlike most LIS studies, Covi (1999) investigated not just the use of information resources by scholars but also what constitutes a scholarly contribution in the various fields.

Palmer (2005) examined both use and creation of digital resources by scholars in a more generalized comparative analysis based on two studies of scientists and two studies of humanities scholars. The report identified new Internet-based information seeking and use patterns but also emphasized how the digital resources developed by researchers can inform the development of digital libraries to fit different disciplinary cultures. Fry and Talja (2007) addressed scholar-produced digital resources in a paper integrating results from their separate comparative studies (Fry, 2006a; Talja & Maula, 2003). Applying Whitley's (2000) ideas on mutual dependence and task uncertainty, they covered seven fields, ranging from physics to literature, and provided function and audience descriptions for five kinds of resources. Fry (2006a) detailed the coordination, collaboration, ICT appropriation, and cultural aspects of physics, linguistics, and geography. This work showed, for instance, that physics was most effective in the production of digital resources even though it is the largest and most distributed field.

Recent practice-oriented studies of journal use with a comparative domain approach have complemented the previous work on e-journal use. Fry and Talja (2004, p. 20) asserted the need for models that explain patterns of e-journal adoption and "practices within the overarching context of domain difference." They adapted Becher's (2000) disciplinary culture distinctions related to hard/soft and pure/applied sciences and aspects of Whitley's (2000) theory of the social organization of "fields" to show how cultural identity factors relate to research, communication, and information practices. They also correctly criticized the lack of studies on non-use of e-journals as a major weakness in the body of e-journal research.

The study by Talja and Maula (2003) is one of the few to investigate explicitly the phenomenon of non-use along with use patterns of scholars. Building on earlier studies that suggested influences from domain size (Bates, 1996a; 2002), degree of scatter (Mote, 1962; Packer & Soergel, 1979), and relevance type (Hjørland, 2002b), they contrasted e-journal use in literature/cultural studies, history, nursing science, and ecological environmental science. Not surprisingly, they found non-use highest within the humanities and, supporting Eason et al. (2000), they identified clear differences in directed searching, browsing, chaining, and sharing across fields. Interestingly, chaining was highly associated with literary studies scholars and browsing with history scholars, challenging hypotheses proposed by Bates (1996a; 2002). In a large Web survey of users of the Finnish National Electronic Library, Vakkari & Talja (in press) found that search methods varied significantly among disciplinary groups and interesting shifts in information practices were identified that point to important areas for further study. For example, the social sciences, economics, and natural sciences were found to be more dependent on chaining and browsing than the humanities, with humanists moving more toward keyword searching than shown in past studies.

Communication technologies have also been a focus of comparative study. Talja and her colleagues identified field variations in the mailing list use and sharing practices of scholars (Talja, 2002; Talja, Savolainen, & Maula, 2004). Literature and history scholars were found to be more dedicated mailing list followers because of the intellectually and geographically dispersed nature of their fields; environmental and nursing scientists, however, were tied to local groups and collaborations. Overall, the impact of mailing lists, especially for making personal contacts, was limited across fields and the only common sharing approach identified across groups was "social sharing." Nursing had the most diverse range of sharing practices, which included both strategic and directive approaches. In relation to interpersonal information sharing, Vakkari and Talja (in press) reported markedly low reliance on colleagues as sources of information and especially surprising low levels in the natural sciences, which is inconsistent with the findings of many other studies.

Walsh, Kucker, Maloney, and Gabbay (2000) tested some very specific hypotheses on the uses of e-mail for professional and research-related tasks in biology, mathematics, physics, and sociology. They found that physicists used e-mail for many professional tasks but that use was lower for the sociologists and even more limited for biologists. E-mail was the medium of choice for carrying out several research activities, such as coordinating work and interacting on "quick questions" or decisions. Examining e-mail in relation to productivity, the number of refereed papers published in a two-year period was significantly correlated with "publishing an e-mail address, number of e-mail messages sent, and to the likelihood of using e-mail for professional tasks" (p. 1304).

Barjak (2006) was also interested in the use of the Internet for informal communication and relationships to productivity. Drawing on a broad base of previous work in the sociology of science and the sociology of knowledge, he surveyed five academic disciplines as well as private, not-for-profit R&D organizations, distributed across seven European countries. His results were comparable with U.S.-based studies in finding ubiquitous uptake of the Internet, although "the intensity of use" varied across countries (p. 1363). He also found a correlation between the number of conference presentations and the practice of including manuscripts on home pages, which was particularly notable in such disciplines as chemistry and psychology "that were found hesitant in adopting electronic manuscript repositories" (p. 1363). Moreover, productive scientists were more likely to use the Internet for all the investigated purposes (social communication, information retrieval, and dissemination). Barjak observed, however, that the "Internet–productivity relationship ... may be a trade-off between communicating and performing other research work" (p. 1363).

Information Work Processes and Primitives

Thus far we have emphasized studies that have taken a contextual, process-oriented view of information practices. Process models of scholarly work allow us to grasp the breadth of practices that require information support and the nuances of their disciplinary culture and requirements. And, although the aim of this chapter is primarily to distinguish and show the value of this approach for IS, it is also important to recognize the need for a thorough understanding of specific scholarly activities to inform development of information resources and tools. After all, as discussed earlier, practices are arrays of activities (Schatzki, 2001), but not all activities are of equal importance to the scholarly process or to the interests of IS. Any given activity is best studied and understood as part of a larger field of disciplinary practice, but there is also a need for a more thorough synthesis of results on what we have learned about specific activities.

Of particular interest are what Unsworth (2000, online) has referred to as "scholarly primitives"—common, discrete activities integral to how scholars create new works. Unsworth identified discovering, annotating, comparing, referring, sampling, illustrating, and representing as scholarly primitives in the humanities, claiming that these are the activities digital resource and tool developers should be working to support. However, there has been limited empirical research investigating units of scholarly work at this level of granularity. Instead, what we have learned about such activities tends to be distributed across numerous studies of broader scope. In this section we bring together results on two components of the scholarly process, searching and writing, drawing attention to what we consider to be the more finely grained "information work primitives"—activities such as chaining, browsing, and annotating—associated with these activities. In cumulating results on selected processes and primitives, we are not suggesting they should be extracted and generalized across domains. Instead, we wish to present a base of findings from which to determine directions for further research on how these activities can be better supported with information technologies customized for distinct scholarly applications.

Two other scholarly processes, collecting and reading, are not well represented in the research literature and therefore not covered here. However, Soper's (1976) and Case's (1986) studies of scholars' use of personal collections stand as important contributions to the little studied area of collecting. In addition, reading patterns have been well documented in general terms, such as time spent, number of papers read, and preferences for digital format, as in the e-journal studies by Tenopir discussed previously. However, few studies have examined the actual scholarly nature of the activity of reading, that is, how researchers interact directly with content and apply it in the research process (Palmer, 2004). Both collecting and reading processes are in particular need of close empirical investigation as sites of information work primitives, especially as they relate to the use of digital materials.

Searching

There is considerable literature in information retrieval and information use that examines scholarly searching. Here we discuss selected domain-based studies in the tradition of Bates's Getty project mentioned previously, considering primarily empirical work that applies qualitative techniques such as interviews (structured personal account, semi-structured, in-depth) and open-ended questionnaires, sometimes combined with interviews and observations. Because e-journal searching, particularly by scientists, has already been discussed, this section looks at practices primarily in the humanities where journal use is less prominent.

Chaining continues to be confirmed as one of the most popular searching techniques (Buchanan, Cunningham, Blandford, Rimmer, & Warwick, 2005; Ileperuma, 2002; Westbrook, 2003) and is probably one of the best examples of what we consider to be an information work primitive. Scholars depend on bibliographic listings, particularly those found in scholarly books, journals, and Web sites on target topic areas to develop chains of selected readings. But as Duff and Johnson (2002) show in their holistic description of the process of searching for archival information, other searching approaches are critical to the research process, including collecting names of individuals and organizations and conducting provenance searches. Moreover, contextual information, such as knowledge of relationships among documents or the way the records are organized, is necessary for interpretation.

Browsing is another information work primitive that is especially important in the humanities (Ellis & Oldman, 2005) and for scholars working in new and rapidly developing interdisciplinary fields. Browsing becomes more complicated as scholars attempt to find information scattered across domains (Mote, 1962; Weisgerber, 1993) and interdisciplinary researchers use "probing" (Palmer, 2001b, p. 31) and "exploring" (Palmer & Neumann, 2002, p. 106) strategies to gather sources distributed outside their core research areas. Disparity in vocabulary and inadequate indexing require distinct database search techniques (White, 1996) and other ad hoc strategies for gathering information. For instance, women's studies scholars have relied heavily on browsing both publisher catalogs and the shelves of libraries and bookstores (Westbrook, 2003).

Scholars working in more established, non-interdisciplinary fields may also perform relatively high levels of out-of-domain searching, often using chaining and browsing techniques (Brockman, Neumann, Palmer, & Tidline, 2001; Palmer, 2001a). According to Case (1991) and Brown (2002), both historians and music scholars search for materials from the social sciences, including philosophy, anthropology, art history, criticism, literature, statistics, sociology, and criminology and sciences such as geography and physiology. As Buchanan et al. (2005) reported, success with more uncertainty-laden conceptual searches depends on the searcher's level of domain knowledge and experience in using particular digital resources. Their study of a range of humanities scholars found that subject classifications were almost never used because they did not match scholars' conceptual models of their fields. Browsing was still highly valued in physical libraries, but it was seen as problematic in digital libraries.

Humanities scholars often search for primary sources, many of which may not be formally published (Brockman et al., 2001; Brown, 2002). For example, historians use documents such as diaries, wills, letters, and manuscripts and visual materials such as photographs, portraits, architectural drawings, and films, as well as other types of objects. Although they prefer working with original materials, scholars often have access only to reproductions (Case, 1991). In a relatively short period of time, scholars have shifted away from the use of print bibliographic tools. None of the 20 U.S. historians Case (1991) studied reported using any bibliographic databases, but by 2001 Brockman et al. found a growing dependence on digitally accessible resources. For historians, digitized archival databases have proven invaluable for identifying materials that had previously been nearly impossible to find but print-based archival finding aids are still preferred by some historians and music scholars (Brown, 2002; Duff & Johnson, 2002). The greatest displacement seems to be with encyclopedia sources, where the Web has essentially replaced the use of print (Buchanan et al., 2005; Ellis & Oldman, 2005).

Literature on searching that takes the research project as an important construct provides a helpful information practices perspective. Ileperuma (2002) found that humanists search mainly to support their project work, unlike social scientists who search mainly to keep up with current developments in their fields. The greatest amount of searching in digital libraries takes place at the initial stages of a project (Buchanan et al., 2005). Chu's (1999) study of literary criticism also identified the "preparation" stage (p. 261) as search dependent, as well as the "analysis and writing" (p. 261) and "further writing and dissemination" (p. 262) stages. Within these stages searching served a range of purposes, including supporting an argument, clarification, identifying new developments, following up on leads, and finding a critical work to incorporate. For economists, White (1975, p. 340) found searching to be prominent in the "problem or idea" phase but most purposive in the "methodology and data collection" stage. There is overlap among Chu's and White's phases but the emphasis on searching to support writing in Chu's study is significant. Although it has received limited attention in

IS research, writing, and its associated primitives, is at the heart of scholarly work in the humanities.

Writing

A number of books has been published recently examining the social aspects of academic writing in general (e.g., Brodkey, 1987) and in specific domains: molecular biology, magnetic physics, mechanical engineering, electronic engineering, philosophy, sociology, marketing, and applied linguistics (Hyland, 2000); and biology, physics, chemistry, psychology, and philosophy (Cronin, 2005). Hyland focused on texts as disciplinary practices, employing textual and genre analysis to trace how various disciplines have been produced and reproduced through writing practices. Cronin concentrated on the effects of collaboration on scholarly writing and the political economy of authorship. In IS, writing practices have been of interest in terms of tracking the processes of knowledge exchange through formal channels, often with a focus on scholarly publishing; however, our understanding of writing activities in scholarly production is still quite limited. In the sciences, for example, we know very little about the "scribbling" and "jotting" of ideas, recording of data, and other informal writing that is performed at the bench (Rheinberger, 2003, p. 314). Yet, these activities are "nearer to the materialities of scientific work than are research communications" and therefore play a key role in mediating information (p. 314). It follows that, as was the case with the searching activities discussed previously, primitives and project stages are important constructs for understanding writing activities.

Writing is an integral part of any research process and is involved at multiple project stages. Two of the stages in Chu's (1999) model are predominately about writing: the fourth stage of analysis and writing, when a paper is first drafted, and the sixth stage, further writing and dissemination, when rewriting takes place. Taking notes occurs in the second stage of preparation and a series of writing processes—mapping, sketching, and outlining—is involved in the third, elaboration, stage. In music research, Brown (2002) identified similar activities associated with more general stages. In particular, the preparing and organizing stage involved the creation of notes, outlines, tables, lists, timelines, and chronologies, later followed by a standard writing and dissemination stage. Similar to the jottings of scientists, note taking and annotation are information work primitives used to manage the physical and intellectual articulation work of coordinating sources and the interpretive work that generates original research in the humanities (Brockman et al., 2001; Case, 1991).

O'Hara, Taylor, Newman, and Sellen (2002) observed how scholars marked up multiple source materials in tacit and informal ways (see also Marshall, 1998a, 1998b) as they performed real-world writing tasks. Both abbreviated notes and extensive structured notes were continually manipulated in the production of print and electronic logs and databases to support project work. This process has parallels with the elaborate writing rituals Case (1991) documented, with historians taking a chronological approach to annotation and music scholars using notes to capture explicit musical examples—particularly important in writing about music (Brown, 2002). Annotation work is of growing research interest, especially for application to the development of reading devices and writing software (e.g., Marshall, 1998b; Marshall & Brush, 2004; Schilit, Golovchinsky, & Price, 1998), but little work has yet been done specifically on their unique contribution to the production of scholarship.

Supporting Bishop's (1999) findings on how scientists use document components, Hartley's (2006) international survey of researchers indicated that natural scientists place high importance on incorporating tables, diagrams, and other illustrative images in their writings, and when writing book reviews value the presence of these components in the works of others. Hutto's (2003, p. 215) ethnographic study found that scientists' writing process is guided by the standard science reporting format, with authors producing content in the sequence that sections appear because it helps them to see "where they are going." Thus, some scientists have difficulty writing in nonstandard formats for highly influential journals such as *Science* or *Nature*. Disciplinary conventions, especially in biology, for example, staying in passive voice and not including negative results in the manuscript, also shape writing and sometimes force authors to make revisions with which they do not agree (see also Myers, 1990). Biologists characterized science writing as "'almost formulaic; every scientific paper sounds like every other one'" (Hutto, 2003, p. 212). In contrast, historians consider style to be an important feature because "subject and expression are inextricably intertwined" (Case, 1991, p. 78).

In terms of format, generalizations about the prominence of the journal article in science and the continued important role of the book in the humanities are well founded. But it is the variations in scholarly products that are perhaps most worthy of further investigation. For example, Varghese and Abraham (2004) analyzed books produced by active researchers in linguistics, psychology, and sociobiology. Book-length essays were the most common book genre, and the format is seen as vital in transferring scientific knowledge to the general public and for moving knowledge beyond disciplinary boundaries. Book reviews are produced by scholars across fields and require a very different writing process, appreciated by both social scientists and scientists for allowing them more freedom to air their views (Hartley, 2006).

In recent decades, the practice of co-authorship has been evolving and its escalation in science has sometimes been controversial. In extreme cases, multiple authors of scientific journal articles can number over a hundred, particularly in high energy physics and biomedicine where large, distributed collaborations are common (Biagioli, 2003; Cronin,

2001). But as Cronin (2001) observed, most of the researchers listed as authors of any given article never took part in the actual writing of the paper. Because those responsible for preparing a publication must work together effectively, the actual writing process typically involves small groups (Kim & Eklundh, 2001). Interdisciplinary writing is particularly difficult for co-authors. Spanner (2001) reported that varying vocabularies made it hard for collaborators in computer science and biology to understand each other's contributions and that writing a document required hours on tasks such as translating terminologies and negotiating sentence structure and general format. Making decisions on what needs to be explained to different audiences is also burdensome writing work for interdisciplinary authors (Palmer, 2001b). Even when researchers jointly writing a paper come from the same disciplinary background, scientific writing tends to produce a "pasteurized prose of collaboration" (Cronin, 2001, p. 561).

In the humanities, sole authorship still dominates, but scholars do commonly consult and collaborate with others while writing (Brockman et al., 2001). Collaborators of this sort are well characterized by Cronin's (2003) idea of the cognitive partner whose contributions are generally recognized in the acknowledgment section of a paper. This type of interaction around the writing process is a classic kind of invisible college practice observed across the humanities (Case, 1991; Chu, 1999; Ellis & Oldman, 2005).

Collaboration and Data Practices

Scientific collaboration has received considerable attention in recent years and research on data management practices is increasing (Sonnenwald, 2007). Both areas have tended to be examined in relation to computing, networks, and e-research, with fewer studies considering collaboration's role in knowledge production or scholarly communication. Studies of data management work practices are of particular importance because of the emerging need for digital data curation expertise to support science operations. Moreover, with the drive toward data sharing and big, data-intensive science, collaboration continues to be a critical area of interest. Accordingly, the studies covered here are discussed in some detail and selected from a range of fields, including computer-mediated communication (CMC), social networking, LIS, and the area of collaboratory research. We omit some cognate disciplines because they tend not to study scholarly work; these should be noted, however, because they make significant contributions to our understanding of systems, work flow processes, environments, and organizational practices that are also important for understanding information work. Research in computer supported cooperative work (CSCW) and organizational science, for example, help situate information use in a larger contextual frame; as such, they are often referenced.

Various terms are used to describe or stand for socio-technical infrastructures and distributed computing tools that support research, such as "networks," "CMC," or "collaboratories." But there is a fairly consistent distinction that sets collaboratories apart from the components involved in distributed computing networks described in the CMC research. For example, Walsh and Bayma (1996a, 1996b) studied a broad range of CMC tools, including e-mail, fax, and ftp (file transfer protocol), as well as online data and bibliographic databases, but did not include systems and tools that were directly involved in experimental activities. Collaboratories imply research "centers without walls," (National Research Council, 1993, p. 7) and therefore specifically include resources, systems, and tools to support distributed collaboration in the execution of experimental activities, including data collection, management, and analysis. These differences have obvious implications for research on scholarly information work. The focus of CMC, for example, allows investigation of searching as well as informal exchange of information. Collaboratory research, on the other hand, is better positioned to develop our understanding of shared use of instruments, curation activities such as data management and preservation, and also collaborative writing.

Collaborative Research

The common theme of the studies presented here is the focus on direct interactions among researchers that are integral to the production of scholarship. By direct interaction we intend purposeful social or communicative practices that have an impact on some research product or project, some shared, some not, or as Haythornthwaite (2006, p. 1079) states, "the kinds of actions that sustain collaborations." Her social network study showed that information exchange is important in maintaining research collaborations. Analyzing the kinds of "knowledge," or information, given and received among three research teams, two highly interdisciplinary (science and social science) and one less so (education), she showed that "learning is a substantial part of what supports interdisciplinary research relationships" (p. 1091). In addition to reporting more standard sociometric statistics on who communicates (giver/receiver) which types of information, she used qualitative data to identify nine types of information exchanged: fact, process, method, research, technology, idea generation, socialization, and administration. For the social science team, "fact" or discipline-specific content was the type of information most frequently given and received, but "method" information concerning how to apply or use a technique was most frequently exchanged by the science team. For the education team, "fact" information was given most frequently but "process" information was deemed most important to receive.

Several recent studies have addressed the changing nature of collaboration due in part to ICT use. These authors pointedly state that technologies are not the "sole or even primary force" (Walsh, Kucker, Maloney, & Gabbay, 2000, p. 1296) in producing the changes apparent in both individual work practices and the organization of scientific work more broadly. Their view is that science and collaboration are social activities that do not change due to the mere existence of CMC tools. Changes depend on which technologies are chosen and how they are used (see also Hara, Solomon, Kim, & Sonnenwald, 2003) and such choices are influenced by various social factors. Thus adoption and application of technologies across scholarly communities will not be uniform.

For example, in their mixed-methods study of the effects of computer network use in mathematics, chemistry, physics, and experimental biology, Walsh and Bayma (1996a, 1996b) documented variations in CMC use across fields. They identified changing collaboration patterns, specifically an increase in group size and remote (primarily international) collaborations (Walsh & Bayma, 1996b). A number of findings pertained to specific disciplines: For example, in math "the introduction of CMC was associated with a dramatic increase in joint-authored papers" (Walsh & Bayma, 1996b, p. 347); and use of electronic mail and group mail (bulletin boards, distributed lists) was more common in mathematics and physics than in experimental biology or chemistry, where network use appeared to be "largely limited to using on-line bibliographic databases" (Walsh & Bayma, 1996a, p. 689). Some of their findings have more general implications as well. Participants reported that CMC cannot replace face-to-face communication and has functioned mainly to support the extension, or "reproduction," of local practices across distributed collaborations (Walsh & Bayma, 1996b, p. 350). Additionally, although CMC has served to reduce some communication barriers and open participation to some peripheral participants, it has not significantly affected the status of those on the periphery (p. 359).

These studies show that CMC has been used successfully in some disciplines to coordinate and carry out research activities; Cummings and Kiesler (2005), however, made interesting observations about complications in use (or non-use) of communication tools by research groups distributed across disciplines and universities. They found that "multi-university projects were less successful, on average, than projects located at a single university," even when several disciplines were involved (p. 714). Moreover, projects that "used more coordination mechanisms were more successful" (p. 714), yet projects that included a higher number of universities tended to use fewer such mechanisms, leading them to conclude that "the work arrangements that make these collaborations possible require a deliberate strategy for coordination" (p. 717).

Sonnenwald, Maglaughlin, and Whitton (2004) developed a framework to facilitate the design of collaboratory systems to support a kind of information work termed situation awareness. As they define it, situation awareness includes several socio-cognitive activities such as the gathering, incorporation, and utilization of environmental information.

For geographically distributed collaborations, situation awareness is mediated by technology. They found that group practices need to be developed that will permit and maintain shared understanding of space, domain knowledge, and articulation work strategies; and contextual, task/process, and socio-emotional information are required to support immediate and future interactions. In terms of technological intervention, they observed that no one system or set of tools universally facilitates situation awareness and as yet there is no theory to support situation-specific design.

Several studies have proposed conceptual frameworks for analyzing collaborative research. Hara et al. (2003) investigated the nature of collaboration in the research life of members of an administratively constructed team. Based on sociometric, interview, and observational data, they developed a typology that construes collaboration as a continuum. One end represents complementary work, such as research projects being divided into discrete tasks that scientists do independently; at the other end is integrative work, in which all the activities are done together. The framework includes factors known to influence the several types of collaboration found along the continuum: Compatibility is composed of work style and management style; work connections relate to expertise; incentives concern resources; and socio-technical infrastructure includes awareness, access (to other collaborators), and communication systems. Their model has parallels with that developed in Palmer's (1999b; 2001b) study of information work and boundary crossing in interdisciplinary science. She identified several research modes that represent the communication and information activities of interdisciplinary scientists, the collaborator, the team leader, and the generalist. Collaborators were found to approach research problems by working with colleagues from other domains and tend to focus on finding specific information and expertise to move their research forward. They also adopt a particular knowledge strategy, termed consulting (as opposed to recruiting or learning), for seeking information and guidance from knowledgeable people and information sources (Palmer, 2001b).

Work with Data

Data activities include the collection, transformation, processing, managing, sharing, preservation and archiving, accessing, and re-use of data. As with other types of information work, variations are rooted in structures and processes of local agreement, disciplines and subdisciplines, and other organizational or social structures, such as project-based collaborations. These practices will necessarily shape the development and use of digital data collections and how these collections intersect with computing networks and information infrastructures (Bowker & Star, 2000). Currently, there is limited research on these practices, but studies focused on data will be imperative to improve our understanding of both the epistemological bases and the actual practices that arise from new forms of collaboration and novel approaches to data management. Here we summarize a few of the more pertinent studies on data practices.

Taking an STS perspective, Van House, Butler, and Schiff (1998) considered data sharing a particular kind of collaboration and were concerned with credibility and trust in the development of shared information resources, particularly the implications for digital library development. Although not focused explicitly on work practices, this study was one of the first in IS to consider domain-based data issues and factors of trust. They studied the cooperative work of developing environmental planning data sets for a digital library, applying communities of practice, boundary objects, and assemblages as conceptual frameworks for informing the design of tools to support cooperative knowledge work. Using interviews, observations of meetings, and analysis of pertinent documents, they analyzed the social arrangements for deciding what is known and who is to be trusted, while assessing the impact that a new Web-based resource had on this heterogeneous group of public and professional stakeholders with varying skills, vocabulary, and long-term interests. They observed changes in the environment of data collection and control due to pressure from public sector constituencies for open access to the data and analyses and found that shared sets of practices were forged by participants working together and making collective sense of evidence.

Also concerned with the design of collaborative tools, Birnholtz and Bietz's (2003) analysis compared when and how data were collected by three different disciplines: earthquake engineering, space physics, and HIV/AIDS research. Based on Latour's proposition that scientists regard data as accurate representations of the physical world and as evidence to support claims, they argued that data are different from documents in important and fundamental ways and warrant separate study. Although they did not provide a deep analysis of this distinction, they identified characteristics of socially structured scientific practices that shape data activities. They noted, for example, that for the earthquake engineers and the space physicists, experimentalists and modelers were increasingly negotiating collaborative relationships around larger projects that satisfied the needs of both groups, rather than working separately and trying to develop a sharing relationship after the fact. And, drawing on Whitley (2000) and Fuchs (1992), they determined that in disciplines involving high task uncertainty there was more variation among researchers. More generally they observed that the creative effort involved in the conduct of research goes into design of the experiment itself and conceiving novel ways to collect data.

Data editing practices, perhaps one of the least visible aspects of data management and analysis, require agreements within a work site about what constitutes acceptable and unacceptable data (Star, 1983) and include deleting or altering aspects of data. Leahey, Entwisle, and Einaudi (2003) documented general data editing rules or approaches across subdisciplinary groupings, following a Web-based survey of tenured faculty in sociology, psychology, and anthropology from U.S. research universities. Using a vignette scenario to ask qualitative questions in the proper use of data, they found variation related to discipline and experience with different types of data and data collection methods. Controlling for a number of demographic and informal learning variables, they found that field researchers were more likely than those who used flexible interviewing strategies to object to proposed edits presented in the vignette. Researchers who were accustomed to using archival data were more likely to propose dropping problematic cases. In addition to discipline, other social communities, such as those surrounding data collections methods, influenced respondents' attitudes toward editing standards. This suggests that practice researchers might look at data-related practices as indicators of social structures not visible or prominent in typical domain or disciplinary foci.

Zimmerman (2003) specifically studied secondary use through in-depth interviews with ecologists who used data they did not collect themselves, noting that ecological research has a strong tradition of data sharing, yet data are not easy to share (see also Bowker, 2000). As with many scientific fields, data sharing in ecology has not generally been recognized for reward in promotion and tenure systems and the re-use of other scientists' data has not always been a legitimate approach to research. Ecologists' methods for locating key data, defined as that most critical to a research project, included inquiries made directly to museums, referrals from other scientists to survey data or databases, personal knowledge, and searches of peer-reviewed literature. Highlighting the work required to apply domain knowledge and experience to resolve ambiguities in data collection or analysis, Zimmerman's findings are consistent with Leahey et al. (2003). Personal experiences in collecting data, along with the informal knowledge gained in fieldwork, helped to inform assessment practices involved in data re-use.

Using bibliometric measures, case studies, and surveys, Brown (2003) investigated the integration and use of genomic and proteomic databases (GPD) into the research and publication practices of scientists at the University of Oklahoma. The case studies reveal that all the scientists agree that sharing of genomic and proteomic data is fundamental to the advancement of science and all submit data as part of the peer-review publishing process. The scientists were both pleased and comfortable with the data resources, which had a positive impact on research work. However, the specific roles and functions of information resources such as GPDs, as instruments per se (Hine, 2006), and their impact on research practices, have yet to be investigated. Beaulieu (2004) explored this type of informational turn in neuroscience and its two primary and dynamic components: digital information and networks. Contrasting wet lab neuroanatomy practices with brain imaging, she tracked the changes taking place in the respective experimental systems, showing an increased reliance on visualization and automated, quantitative methods in neuroscience and how databases build on the tradition of pathological paper atlases. Differentiating the brain as an information object (based in what might be called neuroinformatics epistemology) from the brain as wet object (based in wet laboratory epistemic practices), she showed how a new research program devoted to the study of variability has developed out of the shift of anatomical brain research toward digital data collections.

Digital Scholarship

In this concluding section we consider digital scholarship and e-research more generally and, unless specified, we will mean these to include e-science, e-social science, digital humanities, and cyberinfrastructure. As noted previously, the base of empirical research on scholarly practices in the humanities and especially the social sciences is not as prevalent as that on the sciences. However, development of digital and computing applications that support digital scholarship has been steadily increasing in those areas. In 1997 the American Council of Learned Societies reported little production of authentic digital scholarship or scholarly research that could not have been achieved without a computer (Pavliscak, Ross, & Henry, 1997), but this is clearly no longer the case (see, e.g., Burton, 2002; Schreibman, Siemens, & Unsworth, 2004). And a new American Council of Learned Societies (2006) report, *Our Cultural Commonwealth*, provides a practice-based working definition of digital scholarship. Digital scholarship in recent practice has meant several related things:

- Building a digital collection of information for further study and analysis
- Creating appropriate tools for collection-building
- Creating appropriate tools for the analysis and study of collections
- Using digital collections and analytical tools to generate new intellectual products
- Creating authoring tools for these new intellectual products, either in traditional forms or in digital form

As the authors note, using digital collections and tools to create new knowledge will likely remain the most widely recognized purpose of cyberinfrastructure; yet the other elements are necessary to allow and support basic and applied intellectual work. That is, the development and maintenance of collections and tools are a large part of what makes digital scholarship possible and, as such, will require allocation the of resources, cooperative arrangements, and recognition and credit for undertaking this type of work.

Two other recent studies from IS on academic researchers and digital scholarly communication offer a common perspective on the need to understand the work of established researchers to guide policies for future development. Rowlands and Nicholas's (2005) population of interest was authors recently published in a top (ISI-indexed) journal; Houghton, Steele, and Henty (2004, p. 231) applied more purposeful sampling, stating, "it is only by understanding the evolving needs of leading researchers that we can effectively support their activities in the future." They examined three aspects of digital scholarship: communication and collaboration, information search and access, and dissemination and publication. Basing initial findings on in-depth interviews, followed by workshops with scientists to further develop their results, they found that the existing information infrastructure was better suited to supporting the traditional than the new mode of knowledge production and that a re-alignment of developmental forces, such as rights management and evaluation systems, will require a holistic approach that treats these as parts of a single research information and scholarly communication system. Rowlands and Nicholas (2005), who concentrated on open access publishing and institutional repositories, determined that system development has been based on a data vacuum that does not adequately account for the views and practices of scholars.

In recent discourse on approaches to studying e-science, the variability of research practices across disciplines and the rapidly changing nature of the research environment have been central themes. These themes are clearly applicable beyond science, to studies of e-research more generally. Arguments made by Hine (2005) and Wouters (2006) about e-science hold for all of e-research. Because research is fragmented and many facets of the research process require scrutiny, a combination of methods will be necessary to understand how disciplinary practice and culture are evolving. Woolgar and Coopmans (2006) have proposed that the relationship between ethnomethodologically oriented workplace studies and science and technology studies be investigated as e-science and e-social science applications evolve. Historical approaches can provide a view of how something has unfolded over a period of time; contemporary discourse, however, can illuminate the ordering and social shaping of Grid technologies. They stress that we will need both and more of such approaches but "whatever the focus of the research, ... it needs to embrace a form of analytic skepticism. Rather than adopting a received view of the central components of e-research, their currency and meaning need interrogation and analysis" (pp. 19–20).

Their point is similar to Hine's (2006), who states that the work of science goes on simultaneously in many places and moves faster than an ethnographer can keep up. Novel ethnographic strategies for pursuing both the locations of scientific work and the connections among them are likely to be increasingly important in the future. The ethnography of contemporary science can still usefully focus on laboratory life but needs to be able to take other forms of ordering, including digital ordering, into account. It will be necessary not only to focus on activities that are explicitly promoted as e-research but also to examine other areas where use of ICTs is expanding (Wouters, 2006; see also Hine, 2005). In fact, as

Wouters (2006) claims, the digital realm is only one dimension of the scientific practices to be studied and prematurely conceived general notions of e-science are suspect. He considers practices at the level of the individual researcher, the research group, or the institution the most valid. But, focusing on these units raises the challenge of also capturing the networked nature of present-day research. For this, Wouters (2006) suggests social network analysis and virtual ethnography (Hine, 2000) for mapping of relationships among groups and adding critical distance in perspective. Websphere studies (Fry, 2006b) also hold considerable promise.

Conclusion

By tracing the emergence of the information practices approach in IS and cognate fields, we have brought into relief a valuable body of research for informing the development of information technologies for scholars and scientists. These studies have investigated many aspects of information work, taking into account and explicating the social dimension of scholarly practice and its influence on how information is gathered and used by researchers. Yet, there is still much to learn about the differences among scholarly communities, specifically which differences really make a difference in terms of managing and mobilizing literature and data over the long term for scholarly purposes. This review has provided an overview of the relevant literature but more comprehensive reviews that integrate research on specific domains are needed to draw out firm conclusions and set a solid foundation for future research.

The unit of analysis complication discussed previously remains an ongoing problem for studies of scholarly information work. It is necessary to move beyond the individual level of analysis to develop information systems that support active groups of scholars and scientists. Such groups, however, will need to be representative of real materially and intellectually based research communities. Thus an important aspect of future IS research will be to develop domain definitions that reflect populations of scholars that have formal and informal research connections. That is, samples need to be drawn from functioning scholarly networks or pools of researchers who have relationships either through direct communication and collaboration channels or extended links in the literature or the networked world. These, we would argue, are the domains of interest for information resource and tool development. They represent where the trading zones exist, where communities of inquiry will become established, and where the evolution of shared practice and culture can best be observed.

Studies of scholarly information work practices are essential for understanding how to develop digital content and functionality for the actual daily and long-term needs of researchers. However, it can be difficult to translate results of such studies for direct application, especially if the investigators are not enculturated into the scholarly communities under investigation or if the scope of a study is too broad. Directly engaging domain scholars as collaborators or partners in research design and interpretation of results is important for reducing the chain of inference required to determine implications for the design and development of technologies for specific research communities. Moreover, identifying and directly investigating information work primitives will focus attention on the activities of the highest priority for the production of new scholarship. In fact, studies that directly examine how information technologies are being developed by scholars and scientists for themselves are probably the most direct route to understanding the problems and potentials of scholarly work with information technologies.

Acknowledgments

The authors wish to thank Oksana Zavalina for her extensive research assistance and the *ARIST* reviewers for their valuable comments.

References

Abrahamsen, K. T. (2003). Indexing of musical genres: An epistemological perspective. *Knowledge Organization, 30*(3/4), 144–169.

Agre, P. E. (1995). Institutional circuitry: Thinking about the forms and uses of information. *Information Technology and Libraries, 14*(4), 225–230.

Allen, T. J. (1966). *Managing the flow of scientific and technical information.* Cambridge, MA: MIT Press.

Allen, T. J. (1969). Information needs and uses. *Annual Review of Information Science and Technology, 4,* 3–30.

American Council of Learned Societies. (2006). *Our cultural commonwealth: The report of the American Council of Learned Societies Commission on Cyberinfrastructure for Humanities and Social Science.* New York: The Council.

American Psychological Association. (1963). *Project on scientific information exchange in psychology.* Washington, DC: The Association.

Bakewell, E., Beeman, W. O., & Reese, C. M. (1988). *Object, image, inquiry: The art historian at work* (M. Schmitt, Ed.). Santa Monica, CA: J. Paul Getty Trust.

Barjak, F. (2006). The role of the Internet in informal scholarly communication. *Journal of the American Society for Information Science and Technology, 57*(10), 1350–1367.

Bates, M. J. (1994). The design of databases and other information resources for humanities scholars: The Getty online searching project report no. 4. *Online and CDROM Review, 18*(6), 331–340.

Bates, M. J. (1996a). Document familiarity, relevance, and Bradford's law: The Getty online searching project report no. 5. *Information Processing & Management, 32*(6), 697–707.

Bates, M. J. (1996b). The Getty end-user online searching project in the humanities: Report no. 6: Overview and conclusions. *College & Research Libraries, 57*(6), 514–523.

Bates, M. J. (1996c). Learning about the information seeking of interdisciplinary scholars and students. *Library Trends, 45*(2), 155–164.

Bates, M. J. (1998). Indexing and access for digital libraries and the Internet: Human, database, and domain factors. *Journal of the American Society for Information Science, 49*(13), 1185–1205.

Bates, M. J. (1999). The invisible substrate of information science. *Journal of the American Society for Information Science, 50*(12), 1043–1050.

Bates, M. J. (2002). Speculations on browsing, directed searching, and linking in relation to the Bradford distribution. *Emerging frameworks and methods: Proceedings of the fourth International Conference on Conceptions of Library and Information Science*, 137–149.

Bates, M. J., Wilde, D. N., & Siegfried, S. (1993). An analysis of search terminology used by humanities scholars: The Getty online searching project report no. 1. *Library Quarterly, 63*(1), 1–39.

Bates, M. J., Wilde, D. N., & Siegfried, S. (1995). Research practices of humanities scholars in an online environment: The Getty online searching project report no. 3. *Library & Information Science Research, 17*(1), 5–40.

Bazerman, C. (1988). *Shaping written knowledge: The genre and activity of the experimental article in science*. Madison: University of Wisconsin Press.

Beaulieu, A. (2004). From brainbank to database: The informational turn in the study of the brain. *Studies in History and Philosophy of Biological and Biomedical Sciences, 35*(2), 367–390.

Becher, T. (1990). The counter-culture of specialization. *European Journal of Education, 25*(3), 333–346.

Becher, T. (2000). *Academic tribes and territories: Intellectual enquiry and the culture of disciplines* (2nd ed.). Buckingham, UK: Society for Research into Higher Education and Open University Press.

Berthel, J. H. (1968). Twentieth century scholarship and the research library: A marriage of convenience. *University of Tennessee Library Lectures, 20*, 15–31.

Biagioli, M. (2003). Rights or rewards?: Changing frameworks of scientific authorship. In M. Biagioli & P. Galison (Eds.), *Scientific authorship: Credit and intellectual property in science* (pp. 253–279). New York: Routledge.

Birnholtz, J. P., & Bietz, M. J. (2003). Data at work: Supporting sharing in science and engineering. *Proceedings of the 2003 International ACM SIGGROUP Conference on Supporting Group Work*, 339–348.

Bishop, A. P. (1999). Document structure and digital libraries: How researchers mobilize information in journal articles. *Information Processing & Management, 35*(3), 255–279.

Borgman, C. L. (Ed.). (1990). *Scholarly communication and bibliometrics*. Newbury Park, CA: Sage.

Borgman, C. L. (2000). Digital libraries and the continuum of scholarly communication. *Journal of Documentation, 56*(4), 412–430.

Borgman, C. L., & Furner, J. (2002). Scholarly communication and bibliometrics. *Annual Review of Information Science and Technology, 36*, 3–72.

Börner, K., Chen, C., & Boyack, K. W. (2003). Visualizing knowledge domains. *Annual Review of Information Science and Technology, 37*, 179–255.

Boulding, K. E. (1968). Knowledge as a commodity. In K. E. Boulding, *Beyond economics: Essays on society, religion, and ethics* (pp. 141–150). Ann Arbor: University of Michigan Press.

Bowker, G. C. (2000). Biodiversity datadiversity. *Social Studies of Science, 30*(5), 643–683.

Bowker, G. C., & Star, S. L. (2000). *Sorting things out: Classification and its consequences*. Cambridge, MA: MIT Press.

Bradford, S. C. (1948). *Documentation*. London: Crosby Lockwood.

Brockman, W. S., Neumann, L., Palmer, C. L., & Tidline, T. (2001). *Scholarly work in the humanities and the evolving information environment*. Washington, DC: Digital Library Federation and the Council on Library and Information Resources.

Brodkey, L. (1987). *Academic writing as social practice*. Philadelphia: Temple University Press.

Brown, C. D. (2002). Straddling the humanities and social sciences: The research process of music scholars. *Library & Information Science Research, 24*(1), 73–94.

Brown, C. M. (1999). Information seeking behavior of scientists in the electronic information age: Astronomers, chemists, mathematicians, and physicists. *Journal of the American Society for Information Science, 50*(10), 929–943.

Brown, C. M. (2003). The changing face of scientific discourse: Analysis of genomic and protein database usage and acceptance. *Journal of the American Society for Information Science and Technology, 54*(10), 926–938.

Buchanan, G., Cunningham, S. J., Blandford, A., Rimmer, J., & Warwick, C. (2005). Information seeking by humanities scholars. *Proceedings of the 9th European Conference on Research and Advanced Technology for Digital Libraries* (Lecture Notes in Computer Science, 3652), 218–229.

Burton, O. V. (Ed.). (2002). *Computing in the social sciences and humanities*. Urbana: University of Illinois Press.

Campbell, D. (1969). Ethnocentrism of disciplines and the fish-scale model of omniscience. In M. Sherif & C. W. Sherif (Eds.), *Interdisciplinary Relationships in the Social Sciences* (pp. 328–348). Chicago: Aldine.

Case, D. O. (1986). Collection and organization of written information by social scientists and humanists: A review and exploratory study. *Journal of Information Science, 12*(3), 97–104.

Case, D. O. (1991). The collection and use of information by some American historians: A study of motives and methods. *Library Quarterly, 61*(1), 61–82.

Chen, C., & Paul, R. J. (2001). Visualizing a knowledge domain intellectual structure. *Computer, 34*(3), 65–71.

Chu, C. M. (1999). Literary critics at work and their information needs: A research-phases model. *Library & Information Science Research, 21*(2), 247–273.

Chubin, D. E. (1976). The conceptualization of scientific specialties. *Sociological Quarterly, 17*(4), 448–476.

Chubin, D. E., Porter, A. L., & Rossini, F. A. (Eds.). (1986). *Interdisciplinary analysis and research: Theory and practice of problem-focused research and development*. Mt. Airy, MD: Lomond.

Cole, S. (1983). The hierarchy of the sciences? *American Journal of Sociology, 89*, 111–139.

Collins, H. M. (1987). Expert systems and the science of knowledge. In W. E. Bijker, T. P. Hughes, & T. J. Pinch (Eds.), *The social construction of technological systems: New directions in the sociology and history of technology* (pp. 329–348). Cambridge, MA: MIT Press.

Corbin, J. M., & Strauss, A. S. (1993). The articulation of work through interaction. *Sociological Quarterly, 34*(1), 71–83.

Covi, L. M. (1999). Material mastery: Situating digital library use in university research practices. *Information Processing & Management, 35*(3), 293–316.

Covi, L. M. (2000). Debunking the myth of the Nintendo generation: How doctoral students introduce new electronic communication practices into university research. *Journal of the American Society for Information Science, 51*(14), 1284–1294.

Cragin, M. H., & Shankar, K. (2006). Scientific data collections and distributed collective practice. *Computer Supported Cooperative Work, 15*(2/3), 185–204.

Crane, D. (1971). Information needs and uses. *Annual Review of Information Science and Technology, 6*, 3–39.

Crane, D. (1972). *Invisible colleges: Diffusion of knowledge in scientific communities.* Chicago: University of Chicago Press.

Cronin, B. (1982). Invisible colleges and information transfer: A review and commentary with particular reference to the social sciences. *Journal of Documentation, 38*(3), 212–236.

Cronin, B. (1995). *The scholar's courtesy: The role of acknowledgements in the primary communication process.* London: Taylor Graham.

Cronin, B. (2001). Hyperauthorship: A postmodern perversion or evidence of a structural shift in scholarly communication practices? *Journal of the American Society for Information Science and Technology, 52*(7), 558–569.

Cronin, B. (2003). Scholarly communication and epistemic cultures. *New Review of Academic Librarianship, 9*, 1–24.

Cronin, B. (2005). *The hand of science: Academic writing and its rewards.* Latham, MD: Scarecrow Press.

Cummings, J., & Kiesler, S. (2005). Collaborative research across disciplinary and organizational boundaries. *Social Studies of Science, 35*(5), 703–722.

Davis, P. M., & Solla, L. R. (2003). An IP-level analysis of usage statistics for electronic journals in chemistry: Making inferences about user behavior. *Journal of the American Society for Information Science and Technology, 54*(11), 1062–1068.

de Jong, H., & Rip, A. (1997). The computer revolution in science: Steps towards the realization of computer-supported discovery environments. *Artificial Intelligence, 91*(2), 225–256.

Duff, W. M., & Johnson, C. A. (2002). Accidentally found on purpose: Information-seeking behavior of historians in archives. *Library Quarterly, 72*(4), 472–496.

Eason, K., Richardson, S., & Yu, L. (2000). Patterns of use of electronic journals. *Journal of Documentation, 56*(5), 477–504.

Edge, D. O. (1979). Quantitative measures of communication in science: A critical review. *History of Science, 17*(2), 102–134.

Egan, M. E. (Ed.). (1954). *The communication of specialized information.* Chicago: Distributed by the American Library Association for the University of Chicago Graduate Library School.

Egan, M. E., & Shera, J. H. (1952). Foundations of a theory of bibliography. *Library Quarterly, 22*(2), 125–137.

Ellis, D. (1989). A behavioral approach to information retrieval system design. *Journal of Documentation, 45*(2), 171–212.

Ellis, D. (1993). Modeling the information-seeking patterns of academic researchers: A grounded theory approach. *Library Quarterly, 63*(4), 469–486.

Ellis, D., Cox, D., & Hall, K. (1993). A comparison of the information seeking patterns of researchers in the physical and social sciences. *Journal of Documentation, 49*(4), 356–369.

Ellis, D., & Oldman, H. (2005). The English literature researcher in the age of the Internet. *Journal of Information Science, 31*(1), 29–36.

Fallis, D. (2002). Introduction: Social epistemology and information science. *Social Epistemology, 16*(1), 1–4.

Foster, A. (2004). A nonlinear model of information-seeking behavior. *Journal of the *American Society for Information Science and Technology, 55*(3), 228–237.

Frohmann, B. (2004). *Deflating information: From science studies to documentation.* Toronto: University of Toronto Press.

Frost, C. O. (1979). The use of citations in literary research: A preliminary classification of citation functions. *Library Quarterly, 49*(4), 399–414.

Fry, J. (2004). The cultural shaping of ICTs within academic fields: Corpus-based linguistics as a case study. *Literary and Linguistic Computing, 19*(3), 303–319.

Fry, J. (2006a). Scholarly research and information practices: A domain analytic approach. *Information Processing & Management, 42*(1), 299–316.

Fry, J. (2006b). Studying the scholarly Web: How disciplinary culture shapes online representations. *International Journal of Scientometrics, Informetrics and Bibliometrics, 10*(1), paper 2. Retrieved July 19, 2006, from www.cindoc. csic.es/cybermetrics/articles/v10i1p2.html

Fry, J., & Talja, S. (2004). The cultural shaping of scholarly communication: Explaining e-journal use within and across academic fields. *Proceedings of the Annual Meeting of the American Society for Information Science and Technology,* 20–30.

Fry, J., & Talja, S. (2007). The intellectual and social organization of academic fields and the shaping of digital resources. *Journal of Information Science, 33*(2), 115–133.

Fuchs, S. (1992). *The professional quest for truth: A social theory of science and knowledge.* Albany: State University of New York Press.

Fujimura, J. H. (1987). Constructing do-able problems in cancer research: Articulating alignment. *Social Studies of Science, 17*(2), 257–293.

Furner, J. (2002). Shera's social epistemology recast as psychological bibliology. *Social Epistemology, 16*(1), 5–22.

Galison, P. (1996). Computer simulations and the trading zone. In P. Galison & D. J. Stump (Eds.), *The disunity of science: Boundaries, contexts, and power* (pp. 118–157). Stanford, CA: Stanford University Press.

Garvey, W. D., & Griffith, B. C. (1963). The American Psychological Association project on scientific information exchange in psychology. *Journal of Counseling Psychology, 10,* 297–302.

Garvey, W. D., & Griffith, B. C. (1964). The effect of convention presentations on information exchange behavior and subsequent research. *Proceedings of the American Documentation Institute,* 201–213.

Garvey, W. D., & Griffith, B. C. (1968). Informal channels of communication in the behavioral sciences: Their relevance in the structuring of formal or bibliographic communication. In E. B. Montgomery (Ed.), *The foundations of access to knowledge.* Syracuse, NY: Syracuse University.

Geertz, C. (1983). *Local knowledge: Further essays in interpretive anthropology.* New York: Basic Books.

Green, R. (2000). Locating sources in humanities scholarship: The efficacy of following bibliographic references. *Library Quarterly, 70*(2), 201–229.

Griffith, B. C., & Small, H. G. (1983). *The structure of the social and behavioral sciences literature.* Stockholm, Sweden: Royal Institute of Technical Libraries.

Hallmark, J. (2001). Information-seeking behavior of academic meteorologists and the role of information specialists. *Science and Technology Libraries, 21*(1/2), 53–64.

Hallmark, J. (2004). Access and retrieval of recent journal articles: A comparative study of chemists and geoscientists. *Issues in Science and Technology*

Librarianship, 40, article 1. Retrieved July 7, 2006, from www.istl.org/04-summer/article1.html

Hara, N., Solomon, P., Kim, S.-L., & Sonnenwald, D. H. (2003). An emerging view of scientific collaboration: Scientists' perspectives on collaboration and factors that impact collaboration. *Journal of the American Society for Information Science and Technology, 54*(10), 952–965.

Hargens, L. (2000). Using the literature: Reference networks, reference contexts, and the social structure of scholarship. *American Sociological Review, 65*(6), 846–865.

Hartel, J. (2003). The serious leisure frontier in library and information science: Hobby domains. *Knowledge Organization, 30*(3/4), 228–238.

Hartley, J. (2006). Reading and writing book reviews across the disciplines. *Journal of the American Society for Information Science and Technology, 57*(9), 1194–1207.

Haythornthwaite, C. (2006). Learning and knowledge networks in interdisciplinary collaborations. *Journal of the American Society for Information Science and Technology, 57*(8), 1079–1092.

Henderson, K. (1991). Flexible sketches and inflexible data bases: Visual communication, conscription devices, and boundary objects in design engineering. *Science, Technology, & Human Values, 16*(4), 448–473.

Henderson, K. (1999). *On line and on paper: Visual representations, visual culture, and computer graphics in design engineering.* Cambridge, MA: MIT Press.

Herner, S., & Herner, M. (1967). Information needs and uses in science and technology. *Annual Review of Information Science and Technology, 2*, 1–34.

Hills, P. J. (1983). The scholarly communication process. *Annual Review of Information Science and Technology, 18*, 99–125.

Hine, C. (2000). *Virtual ethnography.* London: Sage.

Hine, C. (2005). Material culture and the shaping of e-science. *First International Conference on E-Social Science.* Retrieved July 24, 2006, from www.ncess.ac.uk/events/conference/2005/papers/papers/ncess2005_paper_Hine.pdf

Hine, C. (2006). Databases as scientific instruments and their role in the ordering of scientific work. *Social Studies of Science, 36*(2), 269–298.

Hjørland, B. (2002a). Domain analysis in information science: Eleven approaches—traditional as well as innovative. *Journal of Documentation, 58*(4), 422–462.

Hjørland, B. (2002b). Epistemology and the socio-cognitive perspective in information science. *Journal of the American Society for Information Science and Technology, 55*(6), 557–560.

Hjørland, B., & Albrechtsen, H. (1995). Toward a new horizon in information science: Domain-analysis. *Journal of the American Society for Information Science, 46*(6), 400–425.

Hjørland, B., & Hartel, J. (2003). Ontological, epistemological and sociological dimensions of domains. *Knowledge Organization, 30*(3/4), 239–245.

Hobohm, H.-C. (1999). Social science information and documentation: Time for a state of the art? *INSPEL, 3*, 123–130.

Hoch, P. K. (1987). Institutional versus intellectual migration in the nucleation of new scientific specialties. *Studies in History and Philosophy of Science, 18*(4), 481–500.

Houghton, J. W., Steele, C., & Henty, M. (2004). Research practices and scholarly communication in the digital environment. *Learned Publishing, 17*(3), 231–249.

Hulme, E. W. (1923). *Statistical bibliography in relation to the growth of modern civilization*. London: Butler and Tanner Crafton.

Hurd, J. M. (1992). Interdisciplinary research in the sciences: Implications for library organization. *College & Research Libraries, 53*(4), 283–297.

Hutto, D. (2003). When professional biologists write: An ethnographic study with pedagogical implications. *Technical Communication Quarterly, 12*(2), 207–223.

Hyland, K. (2000). *Disciplinary discourses: Social interactions in academic writing*. Harlow, UK: Longman.

Ileperuma, S. (2002). Information gathering behaviour of arts scholars in Sri Lankan universities: A critical evaluation. *Collection Building, 21*(1), 22–31.

International Conference on Scientific Information (1959). *Proceedings of the International Conference on Scientific Information*. Washington, DC: National Academy of Sciences, National Research Council.

Jamali, H. R., Nicholas, D., & Huntington, P. (2005). The use and users of scholarly e-journals: A review of log-analysis studies. *Aslib Proceedings, 57*(6), 554–571.

Kim, H.-C., & Eklundh, K. S. (2001). Reviewing practices in collaborative writing. *Computer Supported Cooperative Work, 10*, 247–259.

King, D. W., & Tenopir, C. (1999). Using and reading scholarly literature. *Annual Review of Information Science and Technology, 34*, 423–477.

Klein, J. T. (1990). *Interdisciplinarity: History, theory, and practice*. Detroit, MI: Wayne State University.

Klein, J. T. (1993). Blurring, cracking, and crossing: Permeation and the fracturing of discipline. In E. Messer-Davidow, D. R. Shumway, & D. J. Sylvan (Eds.), *Knowledges: Historical and critical studies in disciplinarity* (pp. 185–211). Charlottesville: University Press of Virginia.

Klein, J. T. (1996). *Crossing boundaries: Knowledge, disciplinarities, and interdisciplinarities*. Charlottesville: University Press of Virginia.

Kling, R., & Covi, L. (1995). Electronic journals and legitimate media in the systems of scholarly communication. *The Information Society, 11*(4), 261–271.

Kling, R., & Covi, L. (1997). *Digital libraries and the practices of scholarly communication: Report of a project* (CSI Working Paper No. WP-97-03). Bloomington: Indiana University, Center for Social Informatics. Retrieved July 20, 2006, from rkcsi.indiana.edu/archive/CSI/WP/wp97-03B.html

Kling, R., & McKim, G. (2000). Not just a matter of time: Field differences and the shaping of electronic media in supporting scientific communication. *Journal of the American Society for Information Science, 51*(14), 1306–1320.

Kling, R., McKim, G., & King, A. (2003). A bit more to it: Scholarly communication forums as socio-technical interaction networks. *Journal of the American Society for Information Science and Technology, 54*(1), 47–67.

Knorr Cetina, K. (1981). *The manufacture of knowledge*. Oxford, UK: Pergamon Press.

Knorr Cetina, K. (1999). *Epistemic cultures: How sciences make knowledge*. Cambridge, MA: Harvard University Press.

Latour, B. (1987). *Science in action: How to follow scientists and engineers through society*. Cambridge, MA: Harvard University Press.

Latour, B., & Woolgar, S. (1986). *Laboratory life: The social construction of scientific facts*. Princeton, NJ: Princeton University Press.

Leahey, E., Entwisle, B., & Einaudi, P. (2003). Diversity in everyday research practice: The case of data editing. *Sociological Methods & Research, 32*(1), 64–89.

Leckie, G. J., Pettigrew, K. E., & Sylvain, C. (1996). Modeling the information-seeking of professionals: A general model derived from research on engineers, health care professionals, and lawyers. *Library Quarterly, 66*(2), 161–193.

Lievrouw, L. A. (1990). Reconciling structure and process in the study of scholarly communication. In C. L. Borgman (Ed.), *Scholarly communication and bibliometrics* (pp. 59–69). Newbury Park, CA: Sage.

Lievrouw, L. A., Rogers, E. M., Lowe, C. U., & Nadel, E. (1987). Triangulation as a research strategy for identifying invisible colleges among biomedical scientists. *Social Networks, 9,* 217–248.

Line, M. B. (1971). The information uses and needs of social scientists: An overview of INFROSS. *Aslib Proceedings, 21*(8), 412–434.

Line, M. B. (1981). The structure of social science literature as shown by a large-scale citation analysis. *Social Science Information Studies, 1,* 67–87.

Line, M. B. (2000). Social science information: The poor relation. *IFLA Journal, 26*(3), 177–179.

MacMullin, S. E., & Taylor, R. S. (1984). Problem dimensions and information traits. *The Information Society, 3*(1), 91–111.

Manoff, M. (1997). Cyberhope or cyberhype?: Computers and scholarly research. *Canadian Journal of Communication, 22*(3), 197–212.

Marshall, C. C. (1998a). *The future of annotation in a digital (paper) world.* Paper presented at the 35th Annual GSLIS Clinic: Successes and Failures of Digital Libraries, University of Illinois at Urbana-Champaign. Retrieved February 26, 2007, from www.csdl.tamu.edu/~marshall/uiuc-paper-complete.pdf

Marshall, C. C. (1998b). Toward an ecology of hypertext annotation. *Proceedings of the Ninth ACM Conference on Hypertext and Hypermedia,* 40–49.

Marshall, C. C., & Brush, A. J. B. (2004). Exploring the relationship between personal and public annotations. *Proceedings of the 4th ACM/IEEE-CS Joint Conference on Digital Libraries,* 349–357.

McCain, K. (1986a). Cocited author mapping as a valid representation of intellectual structure. *Journal of the American Society for Information Science, 37*(3), 111–122.

McCain, K. (1986b). Cross-disciplinary citation patterns in the history of technology. In J. M. Hurd & C. H. Davis (Eds.), *Proceedings of the Annual Meeting of the American Society for Information Science and Technology,* 194–198.

Meho, L. I., & Haas, S. W. (2001). Information-seeking behavior and use of social science faculty studying stateless nations: A case study. *Library & Information Science Research, 21*(1), 5–25.

Meho, L. I., & Tibbo, H. R. (2003). Modeling the information-seeking behavior of social scientists: Ellis's study revisited. *Journal of the American Society for Information Science and Technology, 54*(6), 570–587.

Menzel, H. (1966). Information needs and uses in science and technology. *Annual Review of Information Science and Technology, 1,* 41–69.

Merton, R. (1967). *Social theory and social structure.* Glencoe, IL: Free Press.

Merz, M. (2006). Embedding digital infrastructure in epistemic culture. In C. M. Hine (Ed.), *New infrastructures for knowledge production: Understanding e-science* (pp. 99–119). Hershey, PA: Information Science Publishing.

Michels, D. H. (2005). The use of people as information sources in biblical studies research. *Canadian Journal of Information and Library Science, 29*(1), 91–109.

Morillo, F., Bordons, M., & Gómez, I. (2003). Interdisciplinarity in science: A tentative topology of disciplines and research areas. *Journal of the American Society for Information Science and Technology, 54*(13), 1237–1249.

Mote, L. J. B. (1962). Reasons for the variations in the information needs of scientists. *Journal of Documentation, 18*(4), 169–175.

Mulkay, M. (1974). Conceptual displacement and migration in science. *Science Studies, 4*(3), 205–234.

Mullins, N. C., Hargens, L. L., Hecht, P. K., & Kick, E. L. (1977). The group structure of cocitation clusters: A comparative study. *American Sociological Review, 42*(4), 552–562.

Myers, G. (1990). *Writing biology: Texts in the social construction of scientific knowledge.* Madison: University of Wisconsin Press.

Myers, G. (1993). The social construction of two biologists' articles. In E. Messer-Davidow, D. R. Shumway, & D. J. Sylvan (Eds.), *Knowledges: Historical and critical studies in disciplinarity* (pp. 327–367). Charlottesville: University Press of Virginia.

National Research Council. (1993). *National collaboratories: Applying information technologies for scientific research.* Washington, DC: National Academy Press.

Nentwich, M. (2006). Cyberinfrastructure for next generation scholarly publishing. In C. M. Hine (Ed.), *New infrastructures for knowledge production: Understanding e-science* (pp. 189–205). Hershey, PA: Information Science Publishing.

Nicholas, D., Huntington, P., Jamali, H. R., & Watkinson, A. (2006). The information-seeking behaviour of the users of digital scholarly journals. *Information Processing & Management, 42*(5), 1345–1365.

O'Hara, K., Taylor, A., Newman, W., & Sellen, A. J. (2002). Understanding the materiality of writing from multiple sources. *International Journal of Human–Computer Studies, 56*(3), 269–305.

Ørom, A. (2003). Knowledge organization in the domain of art studies: History, transition and conceptual changes. *Knowledge Organization, 30*(3/4), 128–143.

Packer, K. H., & Soergel, D. (1979). The importance of SDI for current awareness in fields with severe scatter of information. *Journal of the American Society for Information Science, 30*(3), 125–135.

Paisley, W. J. (1968). Information needs and uses. *Annual Review of Information Science and Technology, 3*, 1–30.

Palmer, C. L. (1996a). Information work at the boundaries of science: Linking information services to research practices. *Library Trends, 45*(2), 165–191.

Palmer, C. L. (1996b). Introduction. *Library Trends, 45*(2), 129–133.

Palmer, C. L. (1999a). Aligning studies of information seeking and use with domain analysis. *Journal of the American Society for Information Science, 50*(12), 1139–1140.

Palmer, C. L. (1999b). Structures and strategies of interdisciplinary science. *Journal of the American Society for Information Science, 50*(3), 242–253.

Palmer, C. L. (2001a). The information connection in scholarly synthesis. In R. G. McInnis (Ed.), *Discourse synthesis: Studies in historical and contemporary social epistemology* (pp. 125–141). Westport, CT: Praeger.

Palmer, C. L. (2001b). *Work at the boundaries of science: Information and the interdisciplinary research process.* Dordrecht, The Netherlands: Kluwer.

Palmer, C. L. (2004). Thematic research collections. In S. Schreibman, R. Siemens, & J. Unsworth (Eds.), *Companion to digital humanities* (pp. 348–365). Oxford, UK: Blackwell. Retrieved January 17, 2007, from www.digitalhumanities.org/companion

Palmer, C. L. (2005). Scholarly work and the shaping of digital access. *Journal of the American Society for Information Science and Technology, 56*(11), 1140–1153.

Palmer, C. L. (2006). Weak information work and "doable" problems in interdisciplinary science. *Proceedings of the Annual Meeting of the American Society for Information Science and Technology*. Retrieved February 26, 2007, from eprints.rclis.org/archive/00008183/01/Palmer_Weak.pdf

Palmer, C. L., Cragin, M. H., & Hogan, T. P. (2007). Weak information work in scientific discovery. *Information Processing & Management, 43*(3), 808–820.

Palmer, C. L., & Neumann, L. J. (2002). The information work of interdisciplinary humanities scholars: Exploration and translation. *Library Quarterly, 72*(1), 85–117.

Palmer, J. (1991). Scientists and information: Using cluster analysis to identify information style. *Journal of Documentation, 47*(2), 105–129.

Pavliscak, P., Ross, S., & Henry, C. (1997). *Information technology in humanities scholarship: Achievements, prospects, and challenges: The United States focus* (ACLS Occasional Paper no. 37). New York: American Council of Learned Societies. Retrieved July 24, 2006, from www.acls.org/op37.htm

Perry, C. A. (2003). Network influences on scholarly communications in developmental dyslexia: A longitudinal follow-up. *Journal of the American Society for Information Science and Technology, 54*(14), 1278–1295.

Pickering, A. (1992). *Science as practice and culture*. Chicago: University of Chicago Press.

Pierce, S. J. (1990). Disciplinary work and interdisciplinary areas: Sociology and bibliometrics. In C. L. Borgman (Ed.), *Scholarly communication and bibliometrics* (pp. 46–58). Newbury Park, CA: Sage.

Pierce, S. J. (1999). Boundary crossing in research literatures as a means of interdisciplinary information transfer. *Journal of the American Society for Information Science, 50*(3), 271–279.

Pinch, T. (1990). The culture of scientists and disciplinary rhetoric. *European Journal of Education, 25*(3), 295–304.

Price, D. J. D. (1963). *Little science, big science*. New York: Columbia University Press.

Rheinberger, H.-J. (2003). Discourses of circumstance: A note on the author in science. In M. Biagioli & P. Galison (Eds.), *Scientific authorship: Credit and intellectual property in science* (pp. 309–323). New York: Routledge.

Rinia, E. J., van Leeuwen, T. N., Bruins, E. E. W., van Vuren, H. G., & van Raan, A. F. J. (2002). Measuring knowledge transfer between fields of science. *Scientometrics, 54*(3), 347–362.

Rouse, J. (1996). *Engaging science: How to understand its practices philosophically*. Ithaca, NY: Cornell University Press.

Rowlands, I., & Nicholas, D. (2005). Scholarly communication in the digital environment: The 2005 survey of journal author behaviour and attitudes. *Aslib Proceedings, 57*(6), 481–497.

Royal Society Scientific Information Conference (1948). *Report and papers submitted*. London: The Society.

Ruhleder, K. (1994). Rich and lean representations of information for knowledge work: The role of computing packages in the work of classical scholars. *ACM Transactions on Information Systems, 12*(2), 208–230.

Sandstrom, P. E. (1994). An optimal foraging approach to information seeking and use. *Library Quarterly, 64*(4), 414–449.

Savolainen, R. (1998). Use studies of electronic networks: A review of empirical research approaches and challenges for their development. *Journal of Documentation, 54*(3), 332–351.

Schatzki, T. R. (2001). Introduction: Practice theory. In T. R. Schatzki, K. Knorr Cetina, & E. Von Savigny (Eds.), *The practice turn in contemporary theory* (pp. 1–14). New York: Routledge.

Schilit, B. N., Golovchinsky, G., & Price, M. N. (1998). Beyond paper: Supporting active reading with free form digital ink annotations. *Proceedings of the SIGCHI Conference on Human Factors in Computing Systems,* 249–256.

Schreibman, S., Siemans, R., & Unsworth, J. (Eds.). (2004). *A companion to digital humanities.* Malden, MA: Blackwell.

Shera, J. H. (1972). An epistemological foundation for library science. In J. H. Shera, *The foundations of education for librarianship* (pp. 109–134). New York: Becker and Hayes.

Siegfried, S., Bates, M. J., & Wilde, D. N. (1993). A profile of end-user searching behavior by humanities scholars: The Getty online searching project report no. 2. *Journal of the American Society for Information Science, 44*(5), 273–291.

Simon, H. A., Langley, P. W., & Bradshaw, G. L. (1981). Scientific discovery as problem solving. *Synthese, 47*(1), 1–27.

Sismondo, S. (2004). *Introduction to science and technology studies.* Malden, MA: Blackwell.

Skelton, B. (1973). Scientists and social scientists as information users: A comparison of results of science user studies with the investigation into information requirements of the social sciences. *Journal of Librarianship, 5*(2), 138–156.

Small, H. G. (1978). Cited documents as concept symbols. *Social Studies of Science, 8,* 327–340.

Small, H. G., & Crane, D. (1979). Specialties and disciplines in science and social science: An examination of their structure using citation indexes. *Scientometrics, 1,* 445–461.

Smith, L. C. (1981). Citation analysis. *Library Trends, 30*(1), 83–106.

Sonnenwald, D. H. (2007). Scientific collaboration. *Annual Review of Information Science and Technology,* 643–681.

Sonnenwald, D. H., Maglaughlin, K. L., & Whitton, M. C. (2004). Designing to support situation awareness across distances: An example from a scientific collaboratory. *Information Processing & Management, 40*(6), 989–1011.

Soper, M. E. (1976). Characteristics and use of personal collections. *Library Quarterly, 46*(4), 397–415.

Spanner, D. (2001). Border crossings: Understanding the cultural and informational dilemmas of interdisciplinary scholars. *Journal of Academic Librarianship, 27*(5), 352–360.

Stam, D. C. (1984). How art historians look for information. *Art Documentation, 3*(1), 117–119.

Star, S. L. (1983). Simplification in scientific work: An example from neuroscience research. *Social Studies of Science, 13*(2), 205–228.

Steele, T. W., & Stier, J. C. (2000). The impact of interdisciplinary research in the environmental sciences: A forestry case study. *Journal of the American Society for Information Science, 51*(5), 476–484.

Stone, S. (1982). Humanities scholars: Information needs and uses. *Journal of Documentation, 38*(4), 292–313.

Strauss, A. (1988). The articulation of project work: An organizational process. *Sociological Quarterly, 29*(2), 163–178.

Strauss, A., Fagerhaugh, S., Suszek, B., & Wiener, C. (1985). *Social organization of medical work*. Chicago: University of Chicago Press.

Sundin, O. (2003). Towards an understanding of symbolic aspects of professional information: An analysis of the nursing knowledge domain. *Knowledge Organization, 30*(3/4), 170–181.

Talja, S. (2002). Information sharing in academic communities: Types and levels of collaboration in information seeking and use. *New Review of Information Behavior Research, 3*, 143–160.

Talja, S. (2005). The domain analytic approach to scholars' information practices. In K. Fisher, S. Erdelez, & L. McKechnie (Eds.), *Theories of information behavior* (pp. 123–127). Medford, NJ: Information Today.

Talja, S., & Maula, H. (2003). Reasons for the use and non-use of electronic journals and databases: A domain analytic study in four scholarly disciplines. *Journal of Documentation, 59*(6), 673–691.

Talja, S., Savolainen, R., & Maula, H. (2004). Field differences in the use and perceived usefulness of scholarly mailing lists. *Information Research, 10*(1), paper 200. Retrieved July 18, 2006, from InformationR.net/ir/10-1/paper200.html

Taylor, R. S. (1991). Information use environments. *Progress in Communication Sciences, 10*, 217–255.

Tennis, J. T. (2003). Two axes of domains for domain analysis. *Knowledge Organization, 30*(3/4), 191–195.

Tenopir, C. (2003). *Use and users of electronic library resources: An overview and analysis of recent research studies*. Washington, DC: Council on Library and Information Resources.

Tibbo, H. R. (1992). Abstracting across the disciplines: A content analysis of abstracts from the natural sciences, the social sciences, and the humanities with implications for abstracting standards and online information retrieval. *Library & Information Science Research, 14*, 31–56.

Tibbo, H. R. (1994). Indexing for the humanities. *Journal of the American Society for Information Science, 45*(8), 607–619.

Traweek, S. (1988). *Beamtimes and lifetimes: The world of high energy physicists*. Cambridge, MA: Harvard University Press.

Turner, W. A. (1994). What's in an R: InfoRmetrics or infometrics? *Scientometrics, 30*(2/3), 471–480.

Unsworth, J. (2000, May). Scholarly primitives: What methods do humanities researchers have in common, and how might our tools reflect this? In *Symposium on Humanities Computing: Formal Methods, Experimental Practice*. King's College, London. Retrieved July 19, 2006, from www.iath.virginia.edu/~jmu2m/Kings.5-00/primitives.html

Vakkari, P. (1999). Task complexity, information types, search strategies and relevance: Integrating studies on information seeking and retrieval. *Information Processing & Management, 35*(6), 819–837.

Vakkari, P., & Talja, S. (in press). Search methods of e-journal articles for academic tasks: A case study of FinELib. *Information Research*.

Van House, N. A. (2004). Science and technology studies and information studies. *Annual Review of Information Science and Technology, 38*, 1–86.

Van House, N. A., Butler, M., & Schiff, L. (1998). Cooperative knowledge work and practices of trust: Sharing environmental planning data sets. *Proceedings of the 1998 ACM Conference on Computer Supported Cooperative Work*, 335–343.

Varghese, S. A., & Abraham, S. A. (2004). Book-length scholarly essays as a hybrid genre in science. *Written Communication, 21*(2), 201–231.

Walsh, J. P., & Bayma, T. (1996a). Computer networks and scientific work. *Social Studies of Science, 26*(3), 661–703.

Walsh, J. P., & Bayma, T. (1996b). The virtual college: Computer-mediated communication and scientific work. *The Information Society, 12*(4), 343–363.

Walsh, J. P., Kucker, S., Maloney, N. G., & Gabbay, S. (2000). Connecting minds: Computer-mediated communication and scientific work. *Journal of the American Society for Information Science, 51*(14), 1295–1305.

Wang, P., & White, M. D. (1999). A cognitive model of document use during a research project. Study II. Decisions at the reading and citing stages. *Journal of the American Society for Information Science, 50*(2), 98–114.

Watson-Boone, R. (1994). The information needs and habits of humanities scholars. *RQ, 34*(2), 203–216.

Weisgerber, D. W. (1993). Interdisciplinary searching: Problems and suggested remedies. A report from the ICSTI Group on Interdisciplinary Searching. *Journal of Documentation, 49*(3), 231–254.

Wellman, B. (1996). For a social network analysis of computer networks: A sociological perspective on collaborative work and virtual community. *Proceedings of SIGCPR/SIGMIS Conference on Computer Personnel Research*, 1–11.

Westbrook, L. (2003). Information needs and experiences of scholars in women's studies: Problems and solutions. *College & Research Libraries, 64*(3), 192–209.

White, H. D. (1996). Literature retrieval for interdisciplinary syntheses. *Library Trends, 45*(2), 239–264.

White, H. D. (2001). Authors as citers over time. *Journal of the American Society for Information Science and Technology, 52*(2), 87–108.

White, H. D., & McCain, K. W. (1998). Visualizing a discipline: An author-cocitation analysis of information science, 1972–1995. *Journal of the American Society for Information Science, 49*(4), 327–355.

White, H. D., Wellman, B., & Nazer, N. (2003). Does citation reflect social structure? Longitudinal evidence from the Globenet interdisciplinary research group. *Journal of the American Society for Information Science and Technology, 55*(2), 111–126.

White, M. D. (1975). The communication behavior of academic economists in research phases. *Library Quarterly, 45*(4), 337–354.

White, M. D., & Wang, P. (1997). A qualitative study of citing behavior: Contributions, criteria and metalevel documentation concerns. *Library Quarterly, 67*(2), 122–154.

Whitley, R. (2000). *The intellectual and social organization of the sciences* (2nd ed.). Oxford, UK: Clarendon Press.

Wiberley, S. E. (1991). Habits of humanists: Scholarly behavior and new information technologies. *Library Hi Tech, 9*(1), 17–21.

Wiberley, S. E., & Jones, W. G. (1989). Patterns of information seeking in the humanities. *College & Research Libraries, 50*(6), 638–645.

Wiberley, S. E., & Jones, W. G. (1994). Humanists revisited: A longitudinal look at the adoption of information technology. *College & Research Libraries, 55*(6), 499–509.

Wiberley, S. E., & Jones, W. G. (2000). Time and technology: A decade-long look at humanists use of electronic information technology. *College & Research Libraries, 61*(5), 421–431.

Woolgar, S., & Coopmans, C. (2006). Virtual witnessing in a virtual age: A prospectus for social studies of e-Science. In C. M. Hine (Ed.), *New Infrastructures for Knowledge Production: Understanding e-science* (pp. 1–25).

Hershey, PA: Information Science Publishing.

Wouters, P. (2006, July). What is the matter with e-science? Thinking aloud about informatisation in knowledge creation. *Pantaneto Forum, 23*. Retrieved July 26, 2006, from www.pantaneto.co.uk/issue23/wouters.htm

Zimmerman, A. (2003). *Data sharing and secondary use of scientific data: Experiences of ecologists*. Unpublished doctoral dissertation, University of Michigan, Ann Arbor.

Zuccala, A. (2006). Modeling the invisible college. *Journal of the American Society for Information Science and Technology, 57*(2), 152–168.

CHAPTER 6

Mapping Research Specialties

Steven A. Morris
Oklahoma State University

Betsy Van der Veer Martens
University of Oklahoma

Introduction

Research specialties consist of relatively small self-organizing groups of researchers that tend to study the same research topics, attend the same conferences, publish in the same journals, and also read and cite each others' research papers. Specialties are important in science because of their crucial role in the creation and validation of scientific knowledge.

This chapter is divided into two sections. The first reviews in detail the science of modeling research specialties, following the history of the study of specialties from Chubin's (1976) seminal work of thirty years ago, and further covering current approaches to studying specialties: sociological, bibliographical, communicative, and cognitive.

In the second section the mapping of specialties is reviewed in terms of a simple working model of a specialty that includes the network of researchers, base knowledge, and the specialty's formal literature. We review goals and processes of mapping and, using a network model of a specialty-specific collection of papers, discuss bibliometric methods of extracting information about the specialty: 1) researchers and research teams, 2) experts and authorities, 3) research subtopics, 4) groups of references representing base knowledge, 5) research vocabularies, 6) archival journals for research reports, and 7) archival journals for base knowledge. We review methods of characterizing individual bibliographic entities: authors, papers, journals, references, and index terms. We further review methods to identify and characterize entity groups in a specialty and methods to visualize those groups and the overlapping relations among them.

Imagine the following scenario, played out in a corporate environment: an emerging technology promises to disrupt the economics of the company's core business, potentially leading to enormous riches through exploitation of a new technology, or leading to company failure when its core products suddenly become obsolete. A research manager assembles a small team to investigate and make recommendations. The team quickly gathers relevant and useful data: 1) What are the research topics in the new technology? 2) Who are the experts? 3) Where are the centers of excellence? 4) What journals should be monitored? 5) What is a recommended reading list? 6) What is the technical jargon? The team quickly pulls this information together, in effect summarizing all the important aspects of the new technology into a mental map that can be presented to research managers for assessment and decision making.

In another scenario, a university researcher looking for funding opportunities sees a request for a proposal on a topic within his area of expertise, which requires the use of ancillary technology with which he is unfamiliar. The researcher calls in a graduate assistant, who spends a day in the university library running queries and tracking down papers on the topic of interest. He sketches out a map of the subtopics and how they are related and sketches a second map of research teams in the specialty and how they appear to be linked. He copies key papers that announce recent discoveries in the technology, along with some well-regarded review papers. He puts these papers and maps into a binder and presents it to the researcher, who uses the information for both technical information about the topic and also to assess the research area in terms of other researchers and institutions that will submit competing proposals.

In a third scenario, an historian of science has spent considerable time interviewing key figures in the development of a well known theory regarding the papers they consider most relevant to that theory's development. Upon consulting the bibliographic references in these papers, she discovers that many refer to works not mentioned in the interviews. She maps the actual connections among the network of papers and, based on those data, develops a new set of questions regarding the theory's development that may enrich her historical account.

The scenarios given here illustrate activities associated with mapping research specialties in which it is necessary to find the structure and dynamics of a research specialty: 1) a map of the network of researchers and research teams involved with the specialty, 2) a map of the base knowledge supporting research in the specialty, and 3) a map of current research topics in the specialty. Such a mapping activity, more often than not, does not actually produce visualizations, but may rather involve building mental maps for the investigator, who uses them to make policy or personnel decisions, or who may present those results to managers who fund research and make policy decisions.

Definition of a Research Specialty

The easiest way to define a research specialty is through its social embodiment: *a research specialty is a self-organized network of researchers who tend to study the same research topics, attend the same conferences, read and cite each other's research papers and publish in the same research journals*. A research specialty produces, over time, a cumulating corpus of knowledge, embodied in educational theses, books, conference papers, and a permanent journal literature. Members of a research specialty also tend to share and use, to some degree, a framework of *base knowledge*, which includes knowledge of theories, experimental data, techniques, validation standards, exemplars, worrisome contradictions, and controversies.

Definition of a Model

We define a model here in the sense of a utilitarian tool: *a model is a simplified representation of a system that provides the user with insight into the structure and function of that system*. A second definition of a model, again given in a utilitarian sense, is that of a simplified representation that allows a user to perform quantitative analysis of the system's structure and behavior. In this review we explicitly present two models useful for mapping specialties: 1) a simple model of a research specialty, its base knowledge, and its formal literature; and 2) a model of a specialty-specific collection of papers as a complex network of interconnected entities.

Definition of a Map

We define a map as *a representation of the structure and interconnection of known elements of a system*. Cartographic maps, for example, use known elements associated with geographic landscapes: roads, rivers, lakes, cities, towns, and political borders. The user of the map knows what these elements represent. In another example, an electrical schematic serves as a map of an electronic circuit: It shows the interconnection of known circuit elements such as resistors, transistors, and capacitors. To use the schematic properly, the user must already know the function of each type of element that appears on the schematic.

A map of a specialty is a representation of the structure and interconnection of known elements of the specialty, which include: research topics, researcher teams, base knowledge concepts, authorities, archival journals, research institutions, and technical vocabularies. It is important to define such a map as a representation rather than a diagram, for we do not wish to limit such maps to visualizations; we include simple mental maps and verbal descriptions in our definition of a map.

Motivation for a Review of Specialty Mapping

Reviews and books covering bibliometric techniques, for example, the recent book by Moed (2005), tend to emphasize *evaluative bibliometrics*, the assessment of the importance and influence of researchers, journals, institutions, and nations. In this review, we emphasize *descriptive bibliometrics*, that is, mapping of social and knowledge structures in science. We also focus narrowly on research specialties, which, because of their small size, can be studied at a level of detail not normally considered suitable for mapping science. This is important because, as we explain, research specialties are the agents of change in science—the units in science where new discoveries and developments are picked up, assessed, validated, and knitted into the fabric of scientific knowledge.

Another motivation for writing this review lies in the consolidation and extension of bibliometric techniques as they relate to the mapping of research specialties. In this sense, we aim to present a consolidated framework of mapping techniques and then review existing techniques in the context of that framework. It is well known that several bibliometric methods can be applied to mapping specialties: reference co-citation analysis, bibliographic coupling analysis, co-authorship analysis, author co-citation analysis, co-word analysis, paper to paper citation analysis, journal to journal citation analysis, and journal co-citation analysis. All of these techniques are similar in applications and interpretation, yet they measure distinctly different aspects of the research specialty. We intend to catalog and consolidate the application and interpretation of these techniques.

Motivation for Reviewing the Modeling of Research Specialties

A primary motivation for this chapter is to provide a comprehensive review of the study of research specialties. This is important in that it specifically addresses the question of what is being mapped in specialty mapping. The literature covering the study of specialties is vast and dispersed, and studies have branched into several differing approaches. We discuss the current state of research in each of these approaches and present those discussions as an integrated review.

Organization of the Chapter

The remainder of the chapter is divided into two main sections. First, the section on models of research specialties reviews in detail the science of modeling research specialties, starting with the history of the study of specialties and then discussing major approaches to modeling research specialties: sociological, bibliographical, communicative, and cognitive. Second, the section on mapping research specialties describes: the important characteristics of specialties in the context of mapping, a simple working model of a specialty, the goals of mapping, the process of mapping, modeling of specialty-specific collections of papers, bibliographic tokens, characterization of bibliographic entities, characterization of entity groups, and visualization techniques.

It is hoped that, in the end, this review will provide a consolidated perspective on modeling and mapping specialties, giving the reader detailed information about what a specialty is, what its basic parts are, and how they are linked. Using this knowledge of the model of a specialty, the reader can understand a unified approach to mapping the specialty and appreciate mapping of specialties in terms of how they manifest their structure and processes in their literature, and how those manifestations are analyzed to uncover the original structure and processes that produced them.

Models of Research Specialties

History of the Study of Research Specialties

Although the study of research specialties has increased in viability and visibility over the past half century, it has not yet become a cohesive and coherent specialty itself due to the variety of backgrounds, interests, and goals of those pursuing such research. As Chubin (1985) pointed out in the second of his two reviews of the state of research specialties, this is reflected in the number of terms that are used to denote different areas of emphasis within the concept: research groups (Shepard, 1954), scientific reference groups (Ben-David, 1960), scientific communities (Hagstrom, 1965), invisible colleges (Crane, 1969b; Price & Beaver, 1966), epistemic communities (Holzner, 1968), scientific reference groups (Paisley, 1968), research networks (Mulkay, 1971; Mulkay, Gilbert, & Woolgar, 1975), coherent social groups in science (Griffith & Mullins, 1972), theory groups (Mullins, 1973), co-citation clusters (Small, 1973), scientific networks (Collins, 1974), scientific specialties (Chubin, 1976), scientific collectivities (Woolgar, 1976), thought collectives (Fleck, 1979), and dispersed research schools (Geison, 1993).

Wray (2005, p. 151) remarked that there has been a loss of interest in scientific specialization in recent years; we disagree, but note that the work is being continued under various auspices and under various nomenclatures, which makes comparisons of these investigations difficult. The section on research approaches to research specialties provides a short introduction to these investigations in order to show that they are all connected to the key questions Chubin (1976, p. 449) asked in his seminal review of the field:

> What are the social and intellectual properties of a specialty?
> How do specialties grow, stabilize, and decline?
> What are the temporal and spatial dimensions of a specialty?
> How do specialties vary in size, scope, and life expectancy?
> What are the institutional arrangements that support
>   specialties?
> What impact does funding have on the kind and volume of
>   research produced in a specialty?

The significant role of science in society and, accordingly, the role of scientists themselves, began to be recognized in the aftermath of the First World War (Bernal, 1939). The internal workings of science received wider attention, however, only after the end of the Second World War (Barber 1952; Merton, 1957; Shepard, 1956), in large part due to the increasing influence and importance of the scientific enterprise in the twentieth century (Price, 1963; Storer, 1966). Perhaps ironically in the era of "big science" symbolized by the creation of the National Science Foundation and the scientific information explosion symbolized by the creation of the National Federation of Science Abstracting and Indexing Services, this attention focused primarily on small communities of no more than 100 or so scientists working on related theoretical problems. These specialist communities, whether working on molecular biology (Mullins, 1972), radio astronomy (Mulkay & Edge, 1976), leukemia (Oehler, Snizek, & Mullins, 1989), superstring theory (Budd & Hurt, 1991; Hurt & Budd, 1992), or nanotechnology (Calero, Butler, Valdés, & Noyons, 2006) are seen as foundational to the growth of scientific knowledge. Their workings are examined in an attempt to discover how and why their communicative practices (Hagstrom, 1965) and cognitive processes (Kuhn, 1970) so differ from other groups as to constitute a communication system (Garvey & Griffith, 1967) whose components appear to compose what has been termed the "fish-scale model of omniscience" (Campbell, 1969, p. 328). Or, as phrased by the late Thomas Kuhn (2000, p. 250), "Proliferation of structures, practices and worlds is what preserves the breadth of scientific knowledge, intense practice at the horizons of individual worlds is what increases its depth."

Cole (2000, p. 109) notes that scientific activity was previously seen, as a well structured hierarchy of the sciences that represented "a uniquely rational activity in which evaluation of new contributions was based upon the objective analysis of empirical evidence." Today it is seen as "a much more chaotic endeavor in which the objective analysis of new contributions is frequently difficult or impossible. Rather than the evaluation of new knowledge being based upon the application of agreed upon rules, consensus is influenced by the interaction of a set of social processes and the cognitive content of science itself" (Cole, 2000, p. 109).

The importance of the communication network of science can be attributed to its elements (the scientists) being interconnected through partially disturbed channels of information, the channel "noise" representing some specific dissensus against a general background of consensus regarding shared knowledge (Freudenthal, 1984, p. 289). The noise is important in that it may signal novel knowledge: that is, scientific discovery. Studying the communication network of science as a whole is difficult because it is so vast, rapidly changing, and complicated that neither the participants nor the observers can attend to more than an isolated few of the communicative events at any given time. Moreover, the communicative practices overlie the cognitive processes, and these not only vary by field, but also are open to a wide variety of interpretations.

Storer's (1966) remains one of the best known interpretations noting that the social system of science differs from that of other formal and informal organizations in that, after recruitment, the roles occupied by the members are much less hierarchical and differentiated than roles in other human activities. "The integration of the social system of science is based primarily upon the existence of relatively clear-cut 'channels of implication,' that is, channels of relevance and communication through which the implications of one body of work for another are indicated. It is the office of theory to point out these channels of implication, and as such, theory is vitally important as a means for integrating the scientific community. Yet theory not only organizes and integrates research findings, but also opens up new questions and new areas for study" (Storer, 1966, p. 146).

Fuchs and Spear (1999, p. 38) reiterate the point: "science does not cumulate as such because it has no essential unity. Sociology must look for cumulation-events in active and circumscribed scientific networks, not in science itself. Science cannot cumulate toward anything because it has no unified and active center which could 'do' anything." Focusing on the research specialty concept is in itself a simplified model of the complex sociocognitive interactions of a changing set of scientific actors and their intellectual artifacts in a particular attention space (Collins, 1989, 1998) over time. The value of the research specialty concept, therefore, lies in its very limitations: the focusing of attention on specific phenomena. We assume that a research specialty is the largest homogeneous unit in the self-organizing systems of science, in that each specialty tends to have its own set of problems; a cohesive core of researchers; and shared knowledge, vocabulary, and archival literature. When studying science at so-called higher levels, such as fields, these local homogeneities are mixed together and cannot be studied in local terms. In weather parlance, specialties are local phenomena analogous to thunderstorms but fields of science are global phenomena analogous to regional climate. The two must be separated and studied on their own terms.

The definition of research specialty adopted in this review is that of both Kuhn (1970, p. 178), who suggested "communities of one hundred members, sometimes considerably less," and of Price (1986, p. 64), who posited an "invisible college" of approximately 100 "core" scientists, assuming an average scientist who monitors the work of those individuals who are rivals and peers, and whose workload allows "about 100 papers read for every one published." Although Lievrouw (1990, p. 66) has proposed a revised definition for the invisible college as "a set of informal communication relations among scholars or researchers who share a specific common interest or goal," the nature of science is such that, without the published papers, the informal communication relations of most scholars appear of limited interest. Although scientific progress cannot be achieved without informal communication, scientific progress cannot be verified without formal communication. In his review of the role of journals in the growth of scientific knowledge, Cole (2000, p. 111) comments that "the journals only provide a place for new work to be published: it is the communication and evaluation system of the scientific community that tells the scientist which articles to pay attention to." Even after completion of the important journal refereeing and editing process (Zuckerman & Merton, 1971), that attention is paid in the form of subsequent references to those works deemed of importance to the specialty.

We prefer to use Chubin's term, "research specialty," rather than "invisible college," because it does not presuppose that the researchers are in frequent informal contact with one another as is often implicit in the use of the invisible college rubric. The distinction also recognizes that, although science is viewed as global and universal, this view has been from a privileged perspective: scientists outside the mainstream of Western scientific circles have always had difficulty in contributing and having their contributions recognized (Hwang, 2005). A research specialty, therefore, is defined by the "consensual structure of concepts in a field, employed through its citation and co-citation network" (Small, 1980, p. 183) rather than by a selection or self-selection of scientists themselves. Or, more tersely: "a research specialty evolves over time as a kind of family tree in which earlier studies influence later studies" (Rogers, Dearing, & Bregman, 1993, p. 74).

Regardless of its imperfections, the concept of research specialty has survived, largely because research specialties, although undoubtedly disparate in many ways (such as explanatory goals, level of consensus, and formalized methodologies) continue to be the primary representatives of the collective cognition that embraces and embodies the scientific method as the best approach to understanding the animate and inanimate world.

Research Approaches to Research Specialties

Crane (1970, p. 28) noted early that three separate research approaches are involved in the study of science as a communication system: 1) studies of scientific literature itself, 2) studies of how scientists obtain and use the information needed for their research, and 3) studies of the relationships among scientists who conduct research in the same areas. These approaches converge in the realization that scientific information differs from other information types in that it shows recurrent patterns beyond the standard statistical regularities identified by various power laws, such as those of Lotka, Zipf, and Bradford. Therefore the specific relationships of scientific information, scientific information transfer, and scientific information production may also be of value. As more scientific information about scientific information became available, it reinforced the growing interest in these more scientific approaches to science itself (Narin, 1975).

In his 1976 review of the study of scientific specialties, Chubin (1976) briefly noted the particular importance of the following approaches: the sociological (p. 448), the bibliographical or bibliometric (p. 451), the communicative (p. 453), and the cognitive (p. 455). The remainder of this section will describe and briefly summarize developments in each of Chubin's four categories.

The Sociological Approach

As Chubin (1976) observed, the study of research specialties originated in sociology, with special emphasis on their social structure. Sociologists Jonathan Cole and Harriet Zuckerman (1975, p. 143) expressed this well in their comment that, although the development of scientific specialties is highly variable, "development and elaboration of the cognitive structure of new specialties appear to depend in part on correlative development of their social structures—on the routinization of an evaluation and reward system, procedures of communication, acquisition of resources and the socialization of new recruits. In short, the tandem development of both cognitive and social structures of specialties seems central to their institutionalization and establishment as legitimate areas of inquiry."

Sociological avenues to research specialty studies may be usefully approached from any of four different directions: 1) exploration of how and why science as a social system might be different from other contemporary institutions, 2) investigation of how and why it might be the same, 3) probing its connections with the wider environment, and 4) observing how science maintains its boundaries within that wider environment. All four directions are still being explored, although some paths are better trodden than others.

Mertonian Sociology of Science

The first direction, so-called classic sociology of science, is famously associated with Merton, whose pioneering work on priorities in scientific discoveries (Merton, 1957), the norms of science (Merton, 1973), and the accumulation of advantage in scientific publication (Merton, 1968, 1988) were all focused on the functioning of science as a social system. Zuckerman's work on scientific stratification (1970, 1977) and the referee system (Zuckerman & Merton, 1971), Jonathan and Stephen Cole's work on scientific output and recognition (Cole, 1989; J. R. Cole & Cole, 1972; S. Cole, 1970; S. Cole & Cole, 1967, 1973), and Crane's (1976) work in comparing the reward systems in science, art, and religion were all originally based on collaborations with Merton.

Other representatives of this functionalist framework include: studies of the social system of science (Storer, 1966), role hybridization in science (Ben-David & Collins, 1966), competition and social control in science (Collins, 1968), the functioning of the reward system within the British scientific community (Gaston, 1970, 1973), stratification in science as exemplified by citation distributions (Hargens & Felmlee, 1984), achievement and ascription processes in scientific publication (Stewart, 1983), scientific life-cycle productivity (Diamond, 1984), the economic value of citations to the cited author (Diamond, 1985, 1986), and scientific norms in discovery disputes (Cozzens, 1989a).

Merton's contributions have been enormously influential both in themselves (Cronin, 2004; Garfield, 2004a, 2004b; Hargens, 2004) and as catalysts for challenge (Knorr Cetina, 1982; Whitley, 1972) and change (S. Cole, 1993; Small, 2004). Kim (1994, pp. 6–7) comments that:

> The Mertonian model of consensus formation hinges on the functionalist theory of social stratification. Presupposing consensus upon evaluative criteria, the Mertonians have proceeded to analyze how research is differentially rewarded according to its scientific merit, that is, according to universal criteria. The differential rewards, therefore, explain the existence of various strata in the social system of science. In this process of social stratifications, scientific "stars" are born who can legitimately exercise cognitive authority over the mass of average and below-average scientists. However, unless the Mertonian model can demonstrate how consensus emerges from previous dissensus, the model becomes "circular" ... and its weakness [is] its inability to explain, to use Kuhn's term, the transition from scientific crisis to normal science. In short, Merton and his associates have consistently regarded the existence of the high degree of consensus in natural sciences as the natural state and have assumed that it is established and maintained by the scientific elites.

Social Studies of Science

The second direction, generally known as social studies of science or science and technology studies, is popularly associated with the so-called strong program (Bloor, 1991, 1997), which sharply differentiated itself from earlier work by making the central assumption that consensus in science is part of the problem. The strong program's central tenet is that the study of science and scientific beliefs cannot be bracketed from the study of everyday practices and cognitions. It includes such defining concepts as: causality (beliefs must be explained causally), symmetry (the same analysis should explain both success and failure in science), impartiality in respect to truth or falsity, and reflexivity (the program must apply its methods to itself). The strong program has weakened considerably in recent years, as the evidence mounts that in spite of the importance of shared knowledge in science, no scientist takes a purely social attitude toward scientific pursuits. Nevertheless, it is now generally accepted that science does indeed possess a culture that can be studied by non-scientists (Freudenthal, 1984; Rouse, 1993) and that in-depth studies of actual scientific practices can provide invaluable insights into how research activities translate into scientific findings (Knorr-Cetina, 1981, 1991; Latour & Woolgar, 1986).

Open Systems

The third direction is an open systems approach to the sociology of science; it represents less of an abrupt departure from the Mertonian approach than does science and technology studies. This approach has gradually evolved from the functionalist emphasis on the relationship between stratification and the reward system in science to a recognition that scientific innovation is usually the result of collaboration. Thus the organization of collaboration and competition among groups in a research specialty may have important explanatory outcomes (Hargens, Mullins, & Hecht, 1980). For example, Pao's (1992) study of co-authorship in schistosomiasis found that increased co-authorship was associated with increased research funding, and that there appeared to be two types of co-authors: highly productive *globals* who collaborated with numerous individuals beyond their own groups and lower rank *locals* who were more limited in their formal collaborations.

Whitley (1976) was arguably the first to propose a comparative approach to the organization of scientific production and concomitant variations in knowledge structures, which have an impact on processes of legitimization, recruitment, resource allocation, social control, and interaction with major societal institutions. The degree of mutual functional dependence among scientists and the degree of both technical and strategic task uncertainty determine the organizational structure of scientific fields and, ultimately, the internal structure of their specialty groups (Whitley, 2000). Fuchs extends this approach to the examination of scientific communication (Fuchs, 1986), change (Fuchs, 1993), and cumulation (Fuchs & Spear, 1999).

On a broader scale, Shrum (1984) has pointed out the importance of considering the larger technical and economic environment when studying the systems of basic science in order to provide a more realistic picture of how scientific specialties actually operate. Diamond's (2000) work is an example of a study that heeds these considerations; it provides a comprehensive review of the complementarity of scientometrics and economics. Latour's (2005) actor-network systems approach now incorporates an even more holistic view of the social as it is embedded in both science and technology.

Etzkowitz (1983, 1989) has discussed the effects of the growth of entrepreneurial science in academe and its continuing effect on scientific norms. Much policy-oriented (Gibbons, Limoges, Nowotny, Schwartzman, Scott, & Trow, 1994; Nowotny, Scott, & Gibbons, 2001) and innovation-oriented work (Etzkowitz & Leydesdorff, 2000; Leydesdorff & Etzkowitz, 1996, 1998), focusing on applied science and technology, takes this approach to a national policy level beyond the concerns of research specialties in basic science (Shinn, 1999, 2002).

Generalized Demarcation

Finally, the fourth direction in the sociology of science focuses on the boundaries of science (the so-called generalized demarcation problem) and how they are maintained against: anti-science (Holton, 1993), non-science (Gieryn, 1983, 1999; Kinchy & Kleinman, 2003; Mellor, 2003), heterodox science (Simon, 2002), and religion (Forrest & Gross, 2003; Stahl, Campbell, Petry, & Diver, 2002). One vital way in which these boundaries are routinely maintained is by non-citation (Scott & Cole, 1985). Mukerji and Simon (1998) discuss how discredited communities employ alternative methods of communication when denied access to the mainstream scientific communication system.

Each of these approaches takes into account the existence of the scientific paper as a central medium of communication among scientists and the existence of the citation of previous papers in such works. The Mertonian approach considers them as integral to the scientific social structure, science and technology studies as the traces or inscriptions of making science, open systems as the critical nodes in a larger network of communication, and the demarcation perspective as the place holders for truth claims within social epistemology.

The Bibliographical Approach

Although Chubin (1976, 1985) focused on the bibliometric aspect of the study of research specialties, the so-called bibliographical universe (Wilson, 1968, pp. 6–19) is considerably larger, with multiple dimensions that may slowly be converging. This universe has always been divided; research by the classification community and research by the citation community have had little in common. Wilson (1968, pp. 20–40) proposed that the two major forms of so-called bibliographical control over the universe of "writings and recorded sayings" are descriptive control and exploitative control. Although both controls can be exercised through the library catalog, through cataloging and information retrieval functions, Wilson pointed out that the intentions behind such controls are often quite distinct. Descriptive control aims to provide a complete listing of all members of a class: exploitative control aims to provide those members of a class most textually relevant to a specified need. Descriptive control is rooted in librarianship; exploitative control is rooted in information science. Smiraglia (2002b) provides an excellent review of the historical issues involved. Garfield (1968, p. 179) also expressed this perceived division:

> Conventional bibliography essentially describes the structure of man's accumulated knowledge simply as a neatly piled brick wall. It is primarily descriptive of what man has

created—a simple inventory of publications without regard to the interrelationships between the items in the inventory. In contrast, in citation indexing the conception of man's knowledge is a huge graph or network.

Descriptive control's ideal is a comprehensive classification of all works on a subject; exploitative control's ideal is the relevant set of works on a subject precisely pertinent to a particular user's perceived need. Descriptive control is most often associated with cataloging, the hierarchical structure of knowledge, and the so-called nature of the work (Smiraglia, 2001, 2002a). Descriptive control is not often engaged with the study of research specialties, but exploitative control very often is. Our suggestion here is that the connection between the two is stronger than is commonly understood, and should become even stronger over time, with the development of so-called next-generation cataloging systems that move beyond traditional bibliographic structures.

Miksa (1998, pp. 40–41) observed the inaccuracy of the widely held belief that bibliographic classification and scientific classification share a similar background and philosophy. Bibliographic classification systems such as that of Melvil Dewey merely adopted the utility of the method used by the classificationists of knowledge and the sciences (which, in the nineteenth century, was still assumed to be a natural hierarchy of the sciences) and proceeded to develop their own hierarchically classified structure of subject categories. This history has had a clear impact on the development of bibliographic classification (Smiraglia, 2002b).

Building on Cutter's concepts of catalog access as refined by Lubetzky (1969), Tillett (1991, 2001) provided a taxonomy of seven bibliographic relationships, of which only the last (a shared-characteristic relationship, which holds between a bibliographic item and other bibliographic items that are not otherwise related but coincidentally have a common author, title, subject, or other characteristic) can be considered to include reference/citation relationships.

However, this relationship offers an often-overlooked connection among parts of the bibliographic universe. Furner (2003) points out that this shared-characteristics category may include: relevance relationships (as communicated by document users), citation relationships (as communicated by document authors), and bibliographic relationships (as communicated by document catalogers). These can all be viewed as properties that may be analyzed for purposes of improved classification and control. For the study of research specialties, in our opinion, the lack of communication in recent years among those who focus on relevance relationships, those who focus on citation relationships, and those who focus on bibliographic relationships has impeded progress in all three areas.

Relevance Relationships

In their article on relevance relationships, Bean and Green (2001, p. 115) note that:

> Relevance is widely acknowledged to be the most fundamental issue of information science as a discipline and the most central concern of information and document retrieval as applications. From a practical point of view, the purpose of such systems is commonly considered to be the retrieval of relevant information or at least the retrieval of citations to documents in which relevant information can be found. But from a theoretical point of view, about the only aspect of relevance that is agreed upon is how difficult it is to predict what information or documents will be found relevant to a given user need.

They note also (p. 117) that relevance has many dimensions, not simply "two diametrically opposed views of relevance, an objective system view, based on topicality or aboutness, and a subjective user view, based on contextual factors, including, for example, novelty, source characteristics, and availability. ... It's not a case of either/or, but of both/and." Saracevic's (1975, p. 323) framework for considering relevance in terms of both objective and subjective criteria emphasized that information science's focus on relevance originated in its importance in scientific communication: "The systematic and selective publication of fragments of works—items of knowledge related to a broader problem rather than complete treatises, the selective derivation from and selective integration into a network of other works; and an evaluation before and after publication." Relevance, thus, is defined by what a particular scientist perceives as pertinent to a particular unsolved problem in his search for information. Although Case (2002, p. 234) has pointed out in his review of information seeking that "the once-common investigation of scientists' use of sources is much less common today than it was in past decades," nonetheless, there is clearly still interest in the study of particular scientific communities' use of sources, particularly electronic ones.

Recent examples of such work include Brown's (1999) comparative study of the use of information sources by astronomers, chemists, mathematicians, and physicists; Yitzhaki and Hammerschlag's (2004) study of computer scientists; and Tenopir, King, Boyce, and Grayson's (2005) study of astronomers. As information infrastructure evolves, merging both formal and informal channels of transmission, knowledge of these studies in terms of relevance relationships would clearly provide an additional dimension to the other approaches. Zuccala's (2006) innovative model integrating Taylor's (1986) concept of the information environment and the information behavior of invisible college members provides a suggestion of how effective such integration might be.

Citation Relationships

The large-scale study of citation relationships was made possible by Garfield's (1955, p. 108) development of the *Science Citation Index*, which he termed an "association-of-ideas index," tying this approach to the bibliographical tradition, but moving beyond its original focus on bibliographical control and into a new focus on bibliometrics. Garfield's original intention was to provide a selective dissemination of information service for working scientists that was not limited by the presuppositions of human indexers. However, the broader implications of this current-awareness commercial service in writing the history of science soon became apparent (Garfield, Sher, & Torpie, 1964). The *Science Citation Index*'s creation marked the start of what Wouters (1999, p. 2) has called "the citation culture": a situation in which the machine indexing of the written representations of scientific activity has had both intended and unintended consequences on the practice of science itself.

The array of interrelationships among citations, which is more evident through tools such as the *Science Citation Index*, also made it apparent that the scientists who created these citation networks through their use of references in their own papers were taking a very different approach to the task than would have been employed by librarians as subject indexers. These idiosyncrasies in citation practice had been noted earlier (Chubin & Moitra, 1975; Moravcsik & Murugesan, 1975), but their prevalence was not obvious until comparisons of reference lists became a routine part of citation analysis (Garfield, 1955) and also formed a basis for the critique of citation analysis itself (Edge, 1979; MacRoberts & MacRoberts, 1989).

Garfield (1955, p. 109) introduced the notion of studying references to preceding work as a potential measure of one document's influence on subsequent ones and sparked studies on the distributions and contributions of such influential documents (Oppenheim & Renn, 1979), the associated issues of how quickly a document is likely to be cited (Burrell, 2002b), and how quickly its influence is likely to wane (Egghe & Rousseau, 2000).

Co-Occurrence Relationships

The study of co-occurrence among references can be dated to Kessler's (1963) concept of bibliographic coupling, which suggested that two documents that cited one or more documents in common were more related in topic than those that did not. Small (1973) introduced the term *co-citation* to describe what he posited as a stronger relationship: two documents are said to be co-cited if they appear simultaneously in the reference list of a third document. Martyn (1964, 1975) raised the same objection to both approaches: The mere fact that a mention has been made of a previous document could not be taken as an objective measure of influence of the earlier document on the latter.

Regardless of this criticism, Small (1974) noted that both co-citation and multiple citation connections appear to have significance, especially in indicating the existence of research specialties (Small & Greenlee, 1980) and disciplines (Small & Crane, 1979). At an even higher level of abstraction, Price (1965) used ISI data to theorize science itself through the exploration of networks of scientific papers indicating the existence of so-called research fronts. Cozzens (1985) observed that co-citation studies appear to confirm Price's (1970) hypotheses regarding significant areas of intellectual focus as shown by referencing patterns within active specialty groups, but without showing sharp differences between levels of immediacy and obsolescence in hard science, soft science, technology, and non-science. However, both Hedges (1987) and H. M. Collins (1998) have pointed to the largely unacknowledged role that different evidentiary cultures may play in these publication practices.

Specific to the study of research specialties has been work on: reference networks (Baldi & Hargens, 1997; Price, 1965); the codification and accumulation of knowledge in various fields (Cozzens, 1985; Lewis 1980); the use of journal to journal citation data to identify specialty emergence and change (Van den Besselaar & Leydesdorff, 1996); and the development (Krauze, 1972; Stokes & Hartley, 1989), intersections (Ennis, 1992; Persson & Beckmann, 1995), non-intersections (Swanson, 1986, 1987), and decline (Fisher, 1966, 1967) of areas of specialization. All of these have obvious implications for information storage, retrieval, and dissemination in addition to their role as science indicators.

Author Co-Citation Relationships

A second stream of important bibliometric work has come from White and Griffith (1981, 1982), who translated the co-citation network framework from documents to the authors themselves as author co-citation analysis (ACA). This is another approach to the problem of studying research specialties by visualizing their implicit structures through co-citation of authors and co-authors. White (1990) also credits the inspiration of Rosengren (1968) for having developed a system of author co-mentions earlier in the sociology of literature, using a very similar approach. The value of author co-citation analysis is that, as White (1990, p. 85) states, "The use of authors as the unit of analysis opens the possibility of exploring questions concerning both perceived cognitive structure and perceived social structure of science." Accordingly, the ACA mapping technique has been adopted not only by bibliometric practitioners (McCain, 1990; White & McCain, 1998) but also by a variety of researchers in other disciplines. These studies range from identifying key figures in the emergence of a new specialty such as medical informatics (Andrews, 2003) or entrepreneurship research (Reader & Watkins, 2006) to studies of pioneering researchers in established specialties such as game theory (McCain & McCain, 2002) or social psychology (Marion, 2004).

Co-Word Analysis

Another key bibliometric approach deliberately differentiated from that of classic co-citation analysis by its inventors is that of co-word analysis (He, 1999). This technique, introduced by Callon, Courtial, Turner, and Bauin (1983), makes use of the terms used in indexing documents (in both manual and automatic indexing systems) to generate lists of the documents in which specific technical terms occur. These data are then used to create maps of those documents with the view that the co-occurrence of specific terms provides a more objective measure of document similarity than either co-citation analysis or subject cataloging. This technique has been employed to study: biotechnology (Rip & Courtial, 1984), artificial intelligence (Courtial & Law, 1989), cancer research (Oehler et al., 1989), polymer chemistry (Callon, Courtial, & Laville, 1991), acidification research (Law & Whitaker, 1992), scientometrics (Courtial, 1994), information retrieval research (Ding, Chowdhury, & Foo 2001), and software engineering (Coulter, Monarch, & Konda, 1998). Criticisms leveled at the technique center around the mutable nature of words (Leydesdorff, 1997), but advocates note that words are famously carriers of scientific change and development (Courtial, 1998).

Network Relationships

Some of the more interesting bibliometric variations stem from differing perspectives on networks themselves. The two major perspectives are those of methodological individualists and methodological collectivists (Sawyer, 2001). Methodological individualists view the emergent qualities of science as arising from the actions of individual agents (scientific papers, citations, or scientists), but methodological collectivists view them as resulting from interactions of the feedback loops inherent in the systems dynamics of science. Constructuralism (Kaufer & Carley, 1993), information foraging (Sandstrom, 2001), and Latour's actor-network theory (Latour, 1987; Luukkonen, 1997), all represent agent-based views. Conversely, most of the work by Leydesdorff on specialty structure and dynamics (Leydesdorff, 2001a, 2001b), and by Newman (2000, 2001a, 2001b, 2001c, 2004) on scientific co-authorship employs the systems dynamics perspective. Obviously, both perspectives have much to offer in terms of an integrated view of research specialty bibliometrics.

Bibliographic Relationships

Furner's (2003) third shared-characteristic relationship, bibliographic relationships created by catalogers, has received little attention within the cataloging community. Most attention there has been focused on the first six relationships, as they are the most significant in terms of describing any particular work. Leazer and Smiraglia (1999, pp. 205–206) point out that "current catalog design is inadequate in part because design principles regarding bibliographic relationships are weak and undertheorized for two major reasons. First, the catalog and its code fail to provide the cataloger with the proper concepts to recognize and express bibliographic relationships. Second, catalogers cannot express or control the relationships that they manage to perceive. Catalog designs force catalogers to list works in a prescribed linear order that does violence to the robust and complex structures of bibliographic families."

However, many of these bibliographic relationships, or bibliographic tokens, are already being mapped for purposes of exploitative control for the study of research specialties, as will be discussed in the section on mapping research specialties. Such innovations, in the form of metadata, could form the basis of new descriptive control mechanisms in next-generation library catalogs as well. Markey (2007) provides a very useful account of the past and possible future of library catalog development.

Beghtol (2001) argues that every bibliographic classification system is a theoretical construct imposed on reality, and the classificatory relationships that are assumed to be valuable have generally received much less attention than the particular topics included in each system. She proposes that such relationships are functions of both the syntactic and semantic axes of classification systems; she further asserts that both the explicit and implicit relationships, internal to the system and external to other systems, require much more specific research. Olson (1998), Green (2001), Hjørland and Nielsen (2001), Beghtol (2003), Jacob (2004), Mai (2004), Svenonius (2004), and Hjørland and Pedersen (2005) provide excellent reviews of the many pragmatic and philosophical issues that may be required for the eventual reintegration of the bibliographic universe to provide both descriptive and exploitative control.

The Communicative Approach

The importance of the communicative approach is highlighted by Chubin's (1976, pp. 451–452) suggestion that the nature of the communication relationship used to link specialty members represents the key to conceptualizing the structure of specialties. He quoted Crane's (1972, p. 20) dictum that "the use of citation linkages between scientific papers is an approximate rather than an exact measure of intellectual debts." Clearly, both Chubin and Crane agree that the study of citation in isolation provides a very limited perspective on communication in scientific specialties, which should be supplemented by other tools of communicative analysis.

The two communicative approaches most relevant to scientific specialties, therefore, involve the study of communication among specialty members and the study of the content of specialty papers themselves. These two approaches may be termed the diffusionist approach, focusing on the communicative process, and the discursive approach, focusing on the communicative content.

Knowledge Diffusion

The diffusion perspective is the earlier one, in that Paisley (1968) provided a structured model of the communication environment in which the scientist operates. He noted the importance of both the invisible college as a transient communication group and the more permanent importance of the research specialty itself in developing formal communication channels such as journals. Both Crane (1969b) and Crawford (1971) explored the invisible college hypothesis in conjunction with the diffusion of innovations perspective (Rogers, 1962) in studying the diffusion of theories in rural sociology, mathematics, and sleep research. Within the field of communications itself, Valente and Rogers (1995) studied the spread of the diffusion of innovations paradigm through various areas of communications research, using a framework based on the work of Kuhn, Crane, and Price, and found that it presented an important exception to the Kuhnian model in that the paradigm diffused widely outside its original area of application even after it seemed to be exhausted there.

Michaelson (1993) proposed a diffusion process model based on both invisible college communication processes and scientific publication processes. In her study of role analysis she found that personal contacts were influential in the decision of scientists to enter the specialty throughout its existence, but published articles became influential only later in the period. She noted that this was contrary to Price's (1986) assertion that scientific papers do not serve as sources of influence within an invisible college, but speculated that her findings reflected her focus on an evolving, rather than an established, invisible college.

Lievrouw (1992) also proposed a model for the relationship between communication and the growth of specialties from the communicative perspective based on her study of lipid metabolism research. Her model has been utilized primarily in studies of the diffusion of scientific information outside the scientific community, which is the current area of emphasis in most science communication studies (Zehr, 1999).

Lievrouw commented (1990) that the very invisibility of invisible colleges makes it more difficult to study them directly than to infer their existence from the networks of their papers. As has been noted, informal communication is at the heart of the invisible college, but only recently, as informal communication channels such as e-mail, preprint repositories, wikis, and blogs become easily observable, has their study been poised to become as prevalent as the study of more formal communication channels (Cronin, 2005).

Since the time of Chubin's review, the study of discourse (or rhetoric) in its written form has become an increasingly popular approach to the study of research specialties. This borrows, from communication science, the technique of content analysis and the idea that persuasion is an important communicative goal (Chubin & Moitra, 1975; Gilbert, 1977). However, Cozzens (1989b, p. 444) correctly noted that this approach also draws from both the sociological and cognitive approaches, in that it can view the citation as both a "reward" within the social system of scientists and a "relationship" within the cognitive system of science texts. In Small's (1978) development of the idea of citation as concept symbol—defining the phrases in the text that discuss each reference as the citation context of the reference—he showed that, for highly cited references, citation context becomes codified by authors for use when discussing specific ideas and techniques (concepts). Although others have pointed out that there is limited uniformity in citation etiquette (Ravetz, 1971), Small's citation-as-concept-symbol framework has provided a theoretical underpinning for much ensuing research on so-called citation behavior (Allen, 1997; Brooks, 1985, 1986; Case & Higgins, 2000) and its social and rhetorical implications beyond its obvious impact on effective information retrieval.

White (2004b) reviewed the growing importance of interdisciplinary ties among citation researchers from discourse analysis, sociology of science, and information science in the past twenty years. The new emphasis on the research article as a specific genre (Bazerman, 1988; Sinding, 1996) gives these metadiscourse analysts the opportunity to make new observations about such issues as: how textual conventions vary among research areas (Hyland, 2004), how novice scholars learn citation practices (Rose, 1996), how scientists craft citations as part of their argument (Myers, 1990), how research articles are received by their prospective audiences (Budd, 2001; Leydesdorff & Amsterdamska, 1990; Swales, 1990, 2004), and why citing practices should be considered as a social act rather than one of private consciousness (Nicolaisen, 2003, 2007). Clearly, both the diffusionist and discursive perspectives contribute to a deeper interpretation of how citations and their connections can be interpreted in terms of research specialties.

The Cognitive Approach

Chubin's (1976, p. 455) statement that "how structure crystallizes around intellectual events (e.g., the 'intrusion' of a discovery, new technique or theory) is still unknown" remains accurate more than thirty years later. As he also noted, the so-called cognitive turn (Fuller, De Mey, Shin, & Woolgar, 1989) in the study of scientific specialties was originally taken from deep within the history of science by Kuhn's (1970) *The Structure of Scientific Revolutions*, with its groundbreaking implications regarding the practice of science in the present as well as in the past. Although it has now been recognized that Kuhn's work was in itself grounded in previous work in the history and philosophy of science and also drew from a wide variety of other disciplines (Hoyningen-Huene, 1993, pp. xviii–xix), his short explication of the structure of scientific change has become deeply embedded in both scholarly and popular views of the topic. Kuhn explicitly tied changes in so-called paradigms to cognitive developments within scientific specialties. Moravcsik and Murugesan (1979) were the first to apply citation context analysis and

Small (1980) was the first to apply co-citation analysis to study paradigmatic shifts within specialties.

Later commentators have observed that Kuhn's concept of paradigm shift is ambiguous (Masterman, 1970, pp. 61–65), that he over-simplifies and over-generalizes their occurrence in much of science (Fuchs, 1993, p. 934), and that other philosophers of science have offered more compelling theses regarding the cognitive-oriented problems of specialty differentiation, development, and decay that have not received nearly as much attention (Laudan, Donovan, Laudan, Barker, Brown, Lepllin, et al., 1986).

In spite of this, Kuhn's work on paradigms is as foundational to the cognitive approach in the study of scientific specialties as Merton's work on the reward system of science is to the sociological approach. In her author co-citation analysis of scholarly communication in sociology of science and in information science, Kärki (1996, p. 329) found that, for Kuhn and Merton, "The scholarly community has thus virtually agreed that you cannot deal with one without taking into account the other." Briefly stated, a research specialty, following Price and Kuhn, is a self-organized social group defined by study of a shared research topic and contributions to a common literature. The members of a research specialty also tend to have informal communication channels with one another, and to cite and co-author with one another more often than with those outside the research specialty. They tend to attend the same research conferences, publish in the same journals, and cite the same references in their papers. Specialties, in summary, are self-organizing.

As the point of interest regarding research specialties is the growth of reliable knowledge through collective cognition rather than simply the modeling of the formation of social groups in general, however, the cognitive structure of the group is considered the factor that most distinguishes it from, for example, a community of practice (Cox, 2005) in which the management and use of knowledge is considered more important than its creation. Although much work has been done on the so-called stages of research specialties, which can be viewed qualitatively as stages of social group formation or quantitatively as stages of cluster formation, this work does not draw from the social psychology model of "forming, storming, norming, performing, and adjourning" phases within small groups (Tuckman & Jensen, 1977, pp. 425–426), but is rather a more cognitively oriented sequence of events, although the social element is also of importance.

The three best-known models of specialty cognitive change are those of Kuhn, Mulkay, and De Mey, briefly described in the following paragraphs. Kuhn's model, of course, has attracted far more notice than the others.

Kuhn's model (1970, pp.181–186) can be summarized as follows: First there is a pre-specialty phase in which competing conceptualizations of phenomena and rival hypotheses contend for dominance among the researchers working in a general area of interest. Second, there is the establishment of a so-called paradigm or disciplinary matrix around which the emerging specialty forms a consensus: 1) symbolic generalizations capture specific disciplinary language through logic or mathematics, 2) metaphysical commitments represent belief in particular models, 3) validation standards used in judging the relative worth of evidence such as experiments, and 4) exemplars represent the sharing of successful solutions to disciplinary problems or puzzles and provide a generic way of looking at unsolved problems or puzzles. These four elements represent the unproblematic base knowledge of a particular specialty. This is the phase of formal science for a specialty and its literature expands in a relatively organized fashion as its research puzzles and problems are attacked. Discontinuities occur when theoretical or empirical anomalies arise that cannot be resolved within the paradigm, precipitating a crisis that causes researchers to question the basic paradigm itself. The crisis is resolved when a new discovery or theory can satisfactorily resolve the crisis. This results in a paradigm shift, leading to the abandonment of old base knowledge and the extension of the new theory into a paradigm for a new round of puzzle solving. This revolutionary change results in the birth of a new specialty.

However, critics such as Toulmin (1970, p. 41) have complained that scientific change is not nearly as binary as Kuhn suggests. Rheingold (1980, p. 477) observed that investigators in areas close to Kuhn's own research interests simply did not find confirmation of his views. As Fuchs (1993, p. 934) points out, "The major failure underlying these various problems with Kuhn's theory is the failure to allow for more variations in scientific practice." Solomon (1994, p. 290) adds: "Multivariate models of scientific change have rarely been offered in the science studies literature. Philosophers of science generally discuss only a few of the variables, historians of science tell narratives of scientific change which are qualitative accounts featuring a few variables and sociologists of science have generally (especially recently) eschewed quantitative methods in favor of qualitative ethnographic work."

The competing models of specialty development, however, have to date received little attention. For example, Mulkay (1975, p. 517) proposed a "branching model," driven by discoveries, "which are unexpected but which are not incompatible with existing scientific assumptions. Such discoveries reveal 'new areas of ignorance' to be explored, in many cases, by means of the extension and gradual modification of established conceptual and technical apparatus." These "new areas of ignorance" lead to growth areas for existing specialties and, in many cases, the branching off of new specialties by participants seeking new problems. Mulkay (p. 520) suggests that this "fluid and amorphous web" is a more realistic model of scientific growth and change than is Kuhn's "model of closure" or Merton's "model of openness." However, this model has not received empirical testing.

De Mey (1982, pp. 150–168) put forward an even more inclusive set of research specialty life cycle models based on diffusion models. He also considers cognitive content, social structure, methodological orientation, institutional forms, and literature in connection with the life-cycle model. Although some of the models, such as the fashion cycle, are less useful than they appear at first glance, largely because of the special epistemic considerations involved in scientists' adoption of any innovation (Crane, 1969a), the fact that De Mey's more inclusive approach, like that of Mulkay, has not entered into most discussions of scientific specialty development suggests that the popularity of Kuhn's approach may be because it identifies a limited set of cognitive and social mechanisms rather than because of its comprehensiveness.

Other additions to the current cognitive approach in the study of scientific specialties include Kim's (1994, 1996) model of consensus formation, Chen's work on the mapping of paradigms (Chen, Cribbin, Macredie, & Morar, 2002), Budd's (1999) emphasis on citations as knowledge claims, and Wray's (2005) work on changes in taxonomy as indicators of paradigmatic change. All of these represent potentially important contributions to a better understanding of "the primary site of crystallization, of scientists organizational response to new knowledge, ... the specialty" (Chubin, 1976, p. 455).

Mapping Research Specialties

Introduction

The previous section addressed the history and current state of the study of research specialties and their social and cognitive processes. We discussed the four main approaches to studying and modeling specialties: sociological, bibliographical, communicative, and cognitive. The literature on the topic, although enormous, is diffuse and only partially cumulative. Nevertheless, the progress in specialty studies has been substantial and sufficient for our purpose, which is to lay out a consolidated framework of the underlying models and processes used to map research specialties.

We have defined a model as "a simplified representation of a system that provides the user with insight into the structure and function of that system" and we further defined a map as "a representation of the structure and interconnection of known elements of a system." From these definitions we see that the model of the research specialty defines the specialty's structural elements and the map of a specific research specialty defines the instantiation and interconnection of those elements. Given this, the model of the specialty is vitally important to mapping and shapes both the construction and use of maps of specialties. It is impossible to construct or interpret a geographic map without knowing the underlying model of the earth's surface and that surface's structural elements: rivers, lakes, mountains, coastlines, roads, and cities. By analogy, it is impossible to construct and interpret a map of a scientific specialty without an underlying model of the specialty and its elements, both social and cognitive.

This section will review the techniques used to map specialties, discussing the following topics in order:

- The characteristics of specialties that are particularly important in the context of mapping
- A simple working model of a research specialty for mapping purposes
- A review of the goals of mapping
- A review of the process of mapping
- A review of modeling of collections of journal papers
- A discussion of bibliographic entities and bibliographic links and their function as tokens when mapping
- A discussion of entity groups as tokens when mapping
- A review of visualization of maps of research specialties

In this section we review existing theory and techniques of descriptive bibliometrics in the context of modeling and mapping of research specialties. Each bibliometric technique, be it bibliographic coupling, or author co-citation analysis, provides a limited view of one or more elements within the specialty, just as the projection of a three dimensional object on a plane reveals some features of the object but not others. In the process of this review, we attempt to catalog the usefulness of each descriptive bibliometric technique for mapping specific research specialty elements.

Important Characteristics of Specialties in the Context of Mapping

Before proceeding with the review, it is useful to discuss briefly some characteristics of specialties that are important in the context of mapping. First, the size of a specialty is important in defining the scope of mapping and its level of detail. Second, overlap and scatter determine the limits of specificity that can be attained in defining structure and in classification of groups while mapping. Third, homogeneity of the specialty, in terms of both social and cognitive structure, also determines the scale of the mapping exercise.

The Size of Specialties

There has been little formal discussion after Kuhn and Price on the actual size of specialties. As noted in the section on models of research specialties, Price, by estimating the maximum number of research papers that could be reasonably read and followed by a single researcher, produced an estimate of 100 researchers as the size of a specialty. Morris (2005a), assuming membership in a specialty to be 100 *core* members, used Lotka's law and back-of-envelope style calculations to estimate that a specialty could consist of about 1,000 core and scatter members, with a specialty literature of from 100 to 5,000 papers.

The limited size of specialties keeps their analysis manageable in terms of computational scale and allows information to be interpreted, visualized, and discussed in great detail. This yields actionable information such as specific topics of important papers or specific expertise of researchers and research teams. Bibliometric analysis of research at levels above the specialty, that is, analysis of disciplines and fields, is usually summarized as indicators, in order to avoid computational complexity and information overload for the users of such analysis.

Core and Scatter Phenomena

Core and scatter is the "distinctive pattern of concentration and dispersion" (White & McCain, 1989, p. 124) that appears in collections of papers when relative frequencies of entities are counted. For example, a frequency table of papers per paper author in a collection of papers covering a specialty will typically yield a core of highly productive authors who produce a significant percentage of the papers in the collection, together with a large scatter group of authors who produce only a small number of papers each. This type of dispersion is often called a *center-periphery* pattern (Mullins, Hargens, Hecht, & Kick, 1977); it is a manifestation of both social organization within the specialty (Crane, 1969b) and decision processes by individual authors and editors as they select references, journals, terms, and other items that become associated with papers (White & McCain, 1989).

Core and scatter is usually associated with relative frequencies that can cumulate as the specialty's literature grows; it generally forms long-tailed power-law distributions. These are typically "papers per X" distributions within the collection, where X is some other entity type in the collection. Most studied of these phenomena are the "papers per paper author" distribution, characterized as Lotka's law (Lotka, 1926), "papers per paper journal" distribution, characterized as Bradford's law (White & McCain, 1989), and "papers per reference" distribution, the reference power law noted by Price (1965), Naranan (1971), and Seglen (1992).

In the context of mapping specialties, core and scatter has a significant effect on gathering a collection of papers to cover the specialty. On the one hand, it is usually easy to find a group of highly relevant papers that cover the core of the specialty, but on the other, it becomes increasingly laborious to gather all papers with some significant relevance, and impossible to gather all papers that are marginally relevant to the specialty. Core and scatter also significantly affects clustering analysis that is applied to a collection of papers, as will be discussed.

Overlap Phenomena

Overlap considers the correspondence of entities to classes of interest in a specialty. Entities can possess multiple membership in many classes or, in the sense of fuzzy sets, entities can possess fractional membership of varying magnitude in a number of classes. In the case of specialties, researcher membership tends to overlap extensively across various related specialties. This phenomenon was discussed by Campbell (1969), who asserted that, although there is a great deal of overlap of specialty membership within disciplines, there is little overlap of that membership between disciplines.

The concept of overlapping membership of entities in classes occurs in several contexts in collections of papers covering specialties: papers possess overlapping membership when classified by topic, paper authors possess overlapping membership when classified by the journals they use, references possess overlapping membership when classed by the groups of papers that cite them.

Overlap can be thought of as a phenomenon that occurs with core and scatter, as Figure 6.1 illustrates. Assume a continuum of members against some family of classes, for example, where members are researchers and classes are different research specialties. As illustrated in the figure, the core membership in each class tends to be distinct and easily distinguishable. However, scatter members, whose membership in any particular class is weak, are not easy to distinguish and can be thought of as belonging partially to two adjacent classes.

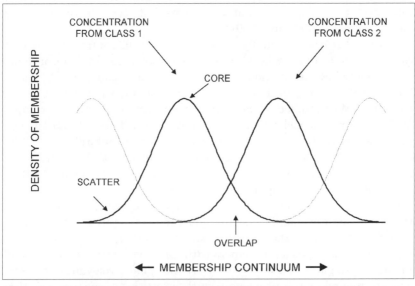

Figure 6.1   Illustration of "core and scatter" and "overlap" of membership over classes in a research specialty.

Overlap and core and scatter phenomena affect mapping of specialties. When classifying entities in the collection of papers, whether by manual sorting or statistical clustering, overlapping membership is difficult to discriminate and also difficult to interpret, visualize, and report. Generally, statistical clustering is based on co-occurrence counts. For example, papers are clustered by counts of common references. Core and scatter phenomena produce skewed distributions of such co-occurrence counts, greatly reducing the ability of clustering algorithms to discriminate among groups of entities.

Homogeneity of Specialties

Specialties contain social and cognitive elements that share a large number of common characteristics; a specialty is homogeneous in terms of these characteristics. The researchers tend to work on a related set of problems, adopt a common paradigm, publish in the same set of journals, use a common technical jargon, attend the same technical conferences, and cite the same set of core references in their papers. Homogeneity of specialties is seldom discussed by scientists who study specialties, but homogeneity is an implicit assumption in all discussions of specialties.

We assert that units in science larger than specialties are not homogeneous in this sense, that is, research specialties are the largest units in science that possess enough homogeneity to warrant detailed mapping. Restating Ziman's (1968, p. 9) definition of the function of science as the "production of public knowledge" we can view the function of science as the production of "validated knowledge." From this, it is easy to reason that specialties are the self-organized units in science that provide knowledge validation. In this sense specialties are the primary agents of change in science: Any scientific discovery, no matter how earthshaking, has no measurable impact until it is taken up by the members of a specialty, examined, cross-examined, extended, and adopted as a base for further research.

The communication requirements inherent in this validation process limit the size of specialties to 100 or so core members. Units in science larger than this, disciplines and fields, perform infrastructure functions, that is, recruitment, training, funding, and the institutional provision of libraries, laboratories, and offices.

Given the discussion on core and scatter and overlap, we expect some limits in the homogeneity of specialties as we map them. We accept this as in the nature of the thing being mapped and qualify our interpretations accordingly. Nevertheless, given the preceding discussion, it is evident that specialties, as primary generators of validated knowledge in science, are sufficiently important to be mapped. Furthermore, the homogeneity and limited size of specialties make the mapping computationally manageable and the results interpretable without the burden of information overload.

A Simple Working Model of a Scientific Specialty
Basic Model of a Research Specialty

Figure 6.2 shows a simple working model, useful for the purpose of explaining the process of mapping a research specialty. This model of the specialty is comprised of three parts: 1) a network of *researchers*, 2) a system of *base knowledge*, and 3) a *formal literature*. These three parts model the social, cognitive, communicative, and bibliographic processes in the specialty.

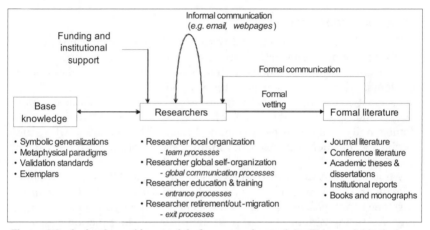

Figure 6.2 A simple working model of a research specialty. This model includes the researchers as a social network, the base knowledge they use, funding, informal communications, and archival literature.

In Figure 6.2, we show a basic input into the specialty as funding and institutional support for researchers. Research is almost always conducted by professionals in academic, institutional, corporate, or governmental settings. Scientists need money for salaries and equipment, and also need infrastructural support for laboratories, libraries, and offices. Specialties live and die on their funding; analysis of such funding is a useful tool when mapping a specialty (Boyack & Börner, 2003).

Researchers tend to conduct research as individuals or in small teams. The researchers can be characterized by their local organization (team processes) and their interaction with other outside teams and other researchers working in the specialty. This is a self-organized and global process of establishing links and communicative infrastructure within the specialty: organizing conferences and workshops, editing journals, vetting journal papers, and initiating the creation of journals as appropriate. We define communication among scientists on specific research tasks as *research collaboration*.

Mapping the structure of collaboration within a specialty is useful for identifying information dissemination patterns in a specialty and for identifying central researchers, research teams, and institutions that serve as communication hubs in the specialty.

The researchers perform their work using *base knowledge*—theories, experimental data, techniques, validation standards, worrisome contradictions, controversies, and theory limitations, comprising the shared knowledge that is often used by researchers in the specialty. This definition of base knowledge does not address either consensus or proven knowledge. It is strictly limited to concepts that are *shared* and *often used*. Terms that are typically used to denote the concept of base knowledge, such as paradigm and consensus, are difficult to define (Knorr, 1975; Kuhn, 1970). Base knowledge often changes discontinuously, either, according to Kuhn (1970), as a paradigm shift generated by a crisis, or according to Mulkay (1976), as the result of discoveries that generate new specialties as branches from existing specialties.

Researchers engage in various informal communication activities: conversations at conferences, workshops, letters, e-mails, and viewing Web pages. Informal communication is unvetted, transitory, and undocumented, so it has heretofore not been extensively studied as a tool of mapping research specialties. Recently, however, it has become practical to automate the gathering of data from Web pages, and much research activity has been directed toward the use of Web pages as a tool for mapping research specialties (Thelwall, Vaughan, & Björneborn, 2005).

As research proceeds in the specialty, individual researchers and research teams produce reports that, upon submission to research journals, are vetted through the refereeing process and finally published in journals. These journal papers, along with books, monographs, conference papers, educational theses, and institutional reports, comprise the *specialty literature*, a collection of formal reports and texts that contains the cumulating written record of research conducted in the specialty. The specialty literature, by virtue of its vetting and permanence, provides an audit trail of knowledge claims in the specialty; it is therefore usually the best source data for mapping the specialty.

We have seen in the section on models of research specialties that such modeling is a complex and difficult task, fraught with interpretational problems. Four approaches have been used to study specialties: sociological, bibliographical, communicative, and cognitive. The simple model of the specialty presented in Figure 6.2 can accommodate each of these approaches, as has been explained. Being a simple model, it is necessarily incomplete. It does not model some social elements, such as authority, credibility, and consensus; it also ignores dynamic phenomena such as growth and cumulative advantage. Nevertheless it functions as a simple structural model of research specialties that facilitates a review of the process of mapping specialties.

The Goals of Mapping Research Specialties

We can define five general goals of the mapping of specialties: mapping social structure, mapping base knowledge, mapping research subtopics, mapping overlapping relations among the elements of the specialty, and mapping changes occurring in the specialty. A detailed discussion of each of these goals and their motivations follows.

Mapping the Social Network of Researchers

The specific goal is to identify and characterize individual researchers, teams of researchers, and their sponsoring institutions in terms of both productivity and impact of research results. A further goal is to investigate the structure of communication among scientists: inside their teams and through their weak ties (Granovetter, 1973). This reveals who is working in the specialty, their levels of participation, and their collaborators. This is useful information for investigators looking for experts, possible research partners, and centers of excellence within the specialty.

Mapping the Structure of the Base Knowledge in the Specialty

Specific goals for mapping base knowledge are to:

- Identify and characterize important concepts used by members of the specialty: theories, models, mathematical techniques, empirical evidence, experimental techniques, validation standards, exemplars, controversies, alternate theories, and worrisome contradictions.
- Group and arrange base knowledge: show how pieces of base knowledge are related and show the hierarchical structure of such relations.
- Identify borrowings of base knowledge from other specialties.
- Identify loans of base knowledge to other specialties.

Specific textual description of pieces of base knowledge cannot be automated. Labeling is subjective and must be done by a human analyst. In mapping, investigators rely on well-cited references to point to journal papers and texts that analysts can use to produce such labels. Furthermore, the patterns of use and co-use of such references reflects the structural pattern of base knowledge used in the specialty (Small, 1986). Maps of these patterns can greatly aid analysts and subject matter experts in their extraction and interpretation of base knowledge. Such analysis is typically used to monitor for emergence of disruptive research developments, such as discoveries and new applications that represent potential new directions for research, and that represent new opportunities and threats for government and commercial endeavors. Analysis of base knowledge may help analysts to interpret which elements of that knowledge are trusted, that is, accepted as generally indisputable knowledge, and which elements are considered by researchers in the specialty to be poorly developed, contradictory, or controversial. This interpretation of "trusted," "disputed," and "provisional" knowledge allows some assessment of risk of success or failure of research and helps researchers and policy makers to perform cost–benefit analysis of research and funding decisions.

Mapping the Topic Structure of the Research in the Specialty

Topics are the labels of specific research problems in the specialty. The goal is to identify research subtopics within the specialty, and to group and arrange research subtopics to show how subtopics are related and to show the hierarchical structure of those relations. This reveals the problems in the specialty that researchers and their funders consider central, an important piece of knowledge for funding organizations, reviewers, students, and other researchers preparing to enter the specialty. Early detection of emerging subtopics is information that can represent economic opportunity and competitive advantage to commercial organizations.

Mapping the Relations and the Overlap of Relations among the Elements of the Specialty

Mapping the overlapping relations among the elements of the research specialty—the researchers, base knowledge, and research subtopics—identifies which researchers are working on which subtopics and what pieces of the base knowledge they apply to their problems. This is useful information for identifying possible collaborators and partners; it can also help an investigator focus on the subtopics and experts that bear on the problem of interest. Investigation of overlap is important for finding where borrowing and lending of base knowledge is occurring across subspecialties and from outside the specialty. Armed with this information, researchers may identify new base knowledge to apply to their own research problem or, alternately, they may find research problems where they can apply their own base knowledge. Borrowing and lending of base knowledge in this way can produce economic opportunity and competitive advantage for commercial organizations.

Mapping the Changes Occurring in the Specialty

Specific goals for mapping changes include:

- Identifying trends in the specialty: 1) gradual changes in base knowledge, 2) shifts in research subtopics—including subspecialization and branching of topics into lower level subtopics, and 3) changes in the social structure of the researchers.
- Identifying discontinuous events in the specialty: 1) discoveries that lead to new subtopics and obsolescence of old subtopics, 2) emergence and retirement of productive researchers and research

teams, and 3) discontinuous changes in funding and regulatory policy, for example, massive new injections or redirection of research funds that may cause significant migration of researchers into or out of a specialty.

Mapping change reveals what is current in the specialty in terms of researchers, base knowledge, and research topics; it further shows what is "hot" in terms of recent discoveries or events. Newly emerging discoveries can signal the impending obsolescence of specific subtopics, information that is extremely important in terms of making funding and career decisions for research managers and researchers themselves.

In the previous paragraphs we outlined a working definition of research specialties and discussed the goals of mapping research specialties and the uses of mapping. We have shown that research specialties themselves are important in that they are the agents of change in science, where discoveries are validated, extended, and applied; where the landscape of science is continuously redefined at the local level. We have shown that the goals of mapping research specialties are complex and go beyond mapping of knowledge. Specifically, mapping specialties is a mapping of social structure, base knowledge, topic structure, and how those three elements are interrelated.

The Process of Mapping Research Specialties
Techniques of Mapping

The methods of mapping research specialties can generally be divided into either survey techniques or bibliometric techniques. The former requires the participation of subject matter experts; the latter is based strictly on the analysis of data. These two types of techniques can be used separately or together when mapping a research specialty.

Survey Techniques

Survey techniques encompass a number of methods for eliciting information from subject matter experts (SME), who are drawn from the membership of the specialty. Investigators may interview selected members of the specialty to gain information, asking them to supply, from their personal knowledge, information about the specialty. This can include: sub-topics, base knowledge, productive researchers and research teams, authorities, centers of excellence, preferred journals, or hot topics. The investigator consolidates and summarizes this information when mapping. An example of this type of study was reported by Crane (1980).

Another useful survey technique is card-sorting, where names of entities—such as researchers, or terms, or sub-topic labels—are placed on cards and SMEs are asked to sort the cards into stacks based on their similarity. McCain, Verner, Hislop, Evanco, and Cole (2005) give an example of the use of card sorting, combined with bibliometric techniques, to map software engineering related specialties.

Survey forms of fixed questions can be distributed to SMEs to acquire specific information in a form suitable for statistical analysis. Survey forms can be distributed and returned through postal mail but currently such surveys are increasingly conducted through e-mail and Web-based methods.

Panels of SMEs can also be used to acquire information, using group facilitation methods such as the Delphi method, to gain information about the state of research in a specialty and to forecast trends or impending discoveries (Porter, Roper, Mason, Rossini, & Banks, 1991).

Survey techniques are of limited use in mapping for several reasons. It is difficult to find SMEs to participate in such surveys, which can result in small numbers of participants and cause problems of sampling bias and statistical significance. Surveys are also expensive to conduct, time-consuming for the investigator, and are subjective in their interpretation. Note, however, that maps of the cognitive structure of a specialty must necessarily be validated by SMEs. It is therefore impossible to avoid the use of surveys and interviews, even when purely bibliometric techniques are used for mapping (Kostoff, del Rio, Hunenik, Garcia, & Ramirez, 2001). Van der Veer Martens and Goodrum (2006) provide an informative diagram of the use of such multiple techniques in their work on the emergence of groups around particular theories. Noyons (2001) addresses the topic of validation of mapping by SMEs and notes that developments in Web-based feedback tools, combined with interactive visual mapping, hold great promise for developing techniques that produce well-validated maps that can be used easily by policy makers.

Bibliometric Techniques

Bibliometric mapping techniques use data taken from written communications in the specialty. Two such sources are available: Web pages maintained by the researchers and institutions and the formal specialty literature. Funding records are also sometimes used as a source of data.

Analysis of Web Content

Specialty mapping based on Web pages is a developing technique; it is still not well defined in its application and interpretation (Thelwall et al., 2005). Web pages are not uniformly formatted, so it is difficult to extract information from them. They are also transitory and unvetted, leading to interpretational problems in mapping (Bar-Ilan, 2001). However, several studies have shown that it is possible to infer parts of the collaboration structure in a specialty from analyzing hyperlinks in Web pages. For example, Kretschmer, Hoffmann, and Kretschmer (2006), studying collaboration of German immunology institutions, compared results of Web-content derived mapping to Web of Science (WoS) derived bibliometric mapping and found good correspondence. Some researchers have conducted limited studies of specialties using data gathering techniques very similar to that employed in author co-citation analysis (Leydesdorff & Vaughan, 2006). Manual scanning of Web pages by an investigator for specific information about specific research groups or topics is a useful, widespread practice. Other emerging sources of Web-based data are online collaborative encyclopedias such as Wikipedia (Holloway, Bozicevic, & Börner, 2007) and online indexers of journal papers such as Google Scholar (Neuhaus, Neuhaus, Asher, & Wrede, 2006) and CiteSeer (ResearchIndex) (Feitelson & Yovel, 2004; Zhao & Logan, 2002). In all, it is evident that *Webometrics* (the bibliometric analysis of Web pages and other Web-based content) will continue to develop and will be increasingly applied to tasks in mapping of research specialties.

Analysis of Formal Literature

Bibliometric analysis of a specialty's formal literature is technically the best developed and most commonly applied method of mapping a specialty. Data is generally acquired from online abstracting services in the form of bibliographic records corresponding to abstracts of individual journal papers.

Journal literature has an exceptional communication and archival function in science. Ziman (1969, p. 318) wrote: "The results of research only become completely scientific when they are published." Journal literature has developed into its present form in answer to specific requirements: the need for a permanent body of vetted reports in semi-standard format that can be indexed and that can provide an audit trail of knowledge claims. Because of this, primary journal papers have grown to acquire a specific set of characteristics (Ziman, 1984). Specifically, journal papers are: vetted, permanently accessible, publicly accessible, unchangeable, formal, attributable, citable, abstracted and indexed, limited in scope, limited in length, and original in content.

Journal literature, because of its unique characteristics, because of its role as repository of the specialty's research results and reviews, and because of the easy access and gathering of specialty-specific abstracts in electronic form, makes an excellent data source for mapping specialties. There is extensive research on journal-paper-based mapping and bibliometric analysis. Several books and major reviews have appeared over the last 30 years (Borgman & Furner, 2002; Egghe & Rousseau, 1990; Moed, 2005; Narin, 1975; Nicholas & Ritchie, 1978; White & McCain, 1989). The remainder of this chapter will focus on mapping using bibliometric techniques whose input data is derived from journal papers.

Specialty Literatures

We define a *specialty literature* as the collection of journal papers, conference papers, academic theses, and books generated by the researchers in a specialty that pertain to research topics within the specialty. Of course, there will be varying amounts of overlap in research topics covered by the specialty literature with topics from other related specialties; mapping such overlap is one of the tasks of mapping a specialty.

Collections of Papers

Assume a list of journal (and possibly conference) papers that constitutes a comprehensive sample of a specialty's literature. A *collection of papers* is a database of papers in such a list. Each record in the database corresponds to one paper and each record contains a list of bibliographic entities, usually paper authors, paper journal, references cited, and index terms that are associated with the paper. In some collections of papers, each record may also contain the abstract text or body text from its corresponding paper. A collection of papers must be built by sampling the specialty's literature (Borgman & Furner, 2002; Börner, Chen, & Boyack, 2003; Moed, 2005; White & McCain, 1989).

Query-Derived Occurrence and Co-Occurrence Matrices

An occurrence matrix contains counts of the number of times a pair of bibliographic entities is associated through a common paper. For example, in a paper-to-reference-author matrix, the rows correspond to papers and the columns correspond to reference authors. The element at position i,j in this matrix gives the number of times paper i cites reference author j. A co-occurrence matrix contains counts of the number of times two bibliographic entities of the same entity type are associated with a common entity of some other entity type. For example, an author co-citation matrix relative to papers lists the co-occurrence counts of reference authors in papers. The element at position i,j in this matrix is the count of the number of papers that are linked to reference author i and reference author j, that is, the number of papers in which reference author i and reference author j are cited together.

Query-derived occurrence and co-occurrence matrices are derived through a series of queries using an online abstracting service such as Dialog. The lists of entities of interest can be derived from subject matter experts, or they can be derived from ranked lists of entities extracted from queries designed to retrieve a specialty-specific list of papers. For example: 1) a query is used to generate a list of papers covering a specialty, 2) a list of reference authors ranked by the number of times cited is extracted from this list, and 3) the top twenty authors are used for building occurrence or co-occurrence matrices. This data gathering technique was pioneered by White and Griffith (1981) for author co-citation analysis and can be extended to analysis of journals. Query derived occurrence matrices are time-consuming to build but, once acquired, are small enough to be easily analyzed using statistical software packages (McCain, 1990).

Manifestations of Research Specialties in Specialty Literatures

Figure 6.3 shows a simple conceptual diagram of mapping of research specialties through their literature. In both the social and cognitive processes of the research specialty there is static structure and dynamic activity that is of interest to the investigator. The static structure and dynamic activity appear as manifestations in the specialty's research literature. For example, a research team will manifest itself in the specialty literature as a group of authors that tends to consistently co-author papers. The job of the investigator is to analyze these manifestations in the specialty literature and build a map of the cognitive and social structure of the specialty, in both the static and dynamic sense.

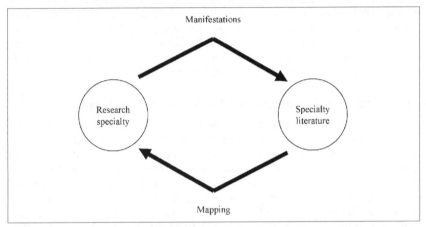

Figure 6.3 **A simple conceptual diagram of mapping a research specialty. The social and cognitive elements of interest in the research specialty are manifested in various ways in the specialty's literature. Mapping is the process of inferring the static structure and dynamic changes of those social and cognitive elements from their manifestations in the literature.**

The Mapping Process

Figure 6.4 shows the mapping process in greater detail. On the left we see that the cognitive processes and social processes in the specialty produce *manifestations*, that is, evidence of themselves, in the specialty literature. The investigator uses a sampling scheme to build a collection of papers covering the specialty. Once a collection of papers is constructed and its coverage of the specialty verified, the investigator applies bibliometric techniques to extract maps of the social and cognitive structures of the research specialty from the manifestations found within the collection of papers. Alternately, as shown in Figure 6.4, the investigator builds one or more query-based occurrence or co-occurrence matrices and applies bibliometric analysis to these data.

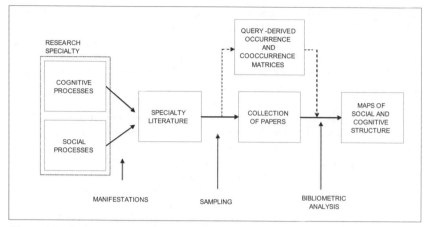

Figure 6.4   A simple diagram showing the steps of mapping a specialty.

General Work Flow when Mapping a Specialty

The work flow for mapping a specialty is fairly straightforward, although the details of analysis can change from one investigator to the next. Assuming that the investigator uses a collection of papers for mapping, an illustrative sequence of tasks is given here:

The investigator defines the specialty to be mapped. This is done in accordance with the project definition and may involve interviews with subject matter experts to help define the scope of the specialty. It is important at this stage to determine, from the subject matter experts, candidate index terms and seed references that can be used to gather the collection of papers in order to assemble a comprehensive sample of the specialty's literature.

The investigator gathers the collection of papers. Bibliographic records are typically gathered from ISI's Web of Science, but other sources may be used, for example, *Chemical Abstracts*. The collection of papers is usually gathered using an iterative process, checking coverage of index term queries and seed references and exploring the gathered papers for signs of problems, such as query terms that capture papers from unwanted specialties.

The investigator performs an analysis to classify the papers by subtopic. Bibliographic coupling can be used for this purpose as Morris, Yen, Wu, and Asnake (2003) discussed. Other techniques for classifying papers by subtopic typically use one of two techniques for finding research fronts from clusters of highly cited references (Chen, 2006; Persson, 1994). Once identified, clusters of papers will need to be labeled. Automated methods of labeling exist, but do not work very well (White & McCain, 1997). Manual labeling can be accomplished by scanning titles of papers in each cluster for themes. In a typical study with fewer than fifty clusters of papers, this is a manageable task; it additionally serves the invaluable function of familiarizing the investigator with the subtopics in the specialty.

The investigator performs analysis to identify the structure of the base knowledge in the specialty. This involves using co-citation analysis to cluster the highly cited references in the collection of papers. A cross-mapping technique (Morris & Yen, 2004) can be used to associate the co-citation clusters with subtopic labels generated from bibliographic coupling. Other methods, such as the Braam-Moed-van Raan (BMV) technique, label co-citation clusters by associating reference clusters with index term clusters (Braam, Moed, & van Raan, 1991).

The investigator may perform author co-citation analysis. This technique, which clusters reference authors by co-citation in papers, tends to map broad base knowledge concepts in the specialty. It is useful to think of clusters of reference authors found using author co-citation analysis as *co-used authorities*, groups of reference authors whose work is used together in common research topics.

The investigator performs analysis to identify the structure of the social network of researchers. This is usually done by performing co-authorship analysis to cluster authors by common papers, a method that identifies teams of authors in the specialty and the weak ties among those teams (Subramanyam, 1983).

The investigator may analyze index terms using term co-occurrence analysis. This produces clusters of index terms that tend to occur together in papers. Such clusters can be thought of as subtopic vocabularies. These vocabularies can be correlated with groups of papers or groups of references for labeling purposes (Braam et al., 1991).

The investigator may perform journal co-citation analysis. This analysis clusters reference journals that tend to be cited together in papers or cited together in journals. Such clusters can be thought of as base knowledge archives and their analysis helps to identify the key journals and specialties from which base knowledge is drawn.

The investigator will perform analysis to find the relations among research subtopics, base knowledge structures, and research teams. This can be done using crossmap analysis (Morris & Yen, 2004), or by manually matching groups of subtopic labeled papers to co-citation clusters of reference as was done by Chen and Morris (2003).

The investigator will analyze dynamic trends and events in the specialty. This can be done using techniques such as Pathfinder visualization (Chen, 2006) or the cluster string techniques of Small and Greenlee (1989). Timeline techniques can be applied to papers, references, or reference authors (Morris & Boyack, 2005) or analysis of data from fixed progressive time intervals can be analyzed to reveal trends (White & McCain, 1998). Analysis of specialty dynamics reveals emerging and declining subtopics, base knowledge, and research teams. For an investigator newly studying a specialty, this analysis quickly reveals obsolete base knowledge and subtopics that need not be studied in depth; it also shows events corresponding to discoveries, which may not be of primary importance to the investigator.

Modeling Collections of Papers

Importance of Modeling Collections of Papers

Given the mapping process just outlined, it is important to have a good working model of a collection of papers covering a specialty. Such a model facilitates the mapping of specialties from collections of papers by allowing the investigator to understand the nature of the information stored in the collection. A model facilitates the application of quantitative mathematical tools to be applied to the collection for revealing structure and deriving metrics of specialty processes.

Requirements of a Model of a Collection of Papers

There are several requirements for a good general model of a collection of papers:

- The model should describe, as fully as possible, all the information in the collection of papers.
- The model should be concise and understandable.
- The model should facilitate quantitative analysis. Specifically, this means that the model should be easily adaptable to co-occurrence clustering of papers, references, authors, terms, and journals and should further be adaptable to calculation of quantitative indicators and metrics, easily yielding distributions usually studied in relation to collections such as Lotka's law, Bradford's law, and the reference power law.
- The model should be readily adaptable to characterize growth of the literature.
- The model should be readily adaptable to visualize the structure of basic elements of a specialty, the relation among those elements, and further facilitate the visualization of dynamics within the specialty.

In this section we discuss some previous models of collections of papers and introduce a general model of collections of papers that addresses many of the requirements outlined.

Existing Models of Specialty Literatures and Collections of Papers

Many models of collections of papers have appeared over the history of bibliometrics. Most of these are ancillary to well established bibliometric techniques and usually describe the connections among a single type of entity in the collection of papers. Perhaps the earliest model of literature was Price's (1965) model of papers citing papers. Price's model covers all of science and does not consider literatures associated with homogeneous specialties. Remarkably, Price's paper introduces a series of conjectures and concepts that later developed into complete subtopics of the specialty of bibliometrics. He introduces statistical metrics such as the reference-per-paper distribution and gives perhaps the earliest discussion of the now well-known reference power law (Naranan, 1971; Redner, 1998; Seglen, 1992). He also discusses the conditional probability of a paper being cited repeatedly, which presages the "nth-citation" distribution subtopic of informetrics (Burrell, 2002a). He introduces the concept of literature obsolescence and the concept of a research front (Chen, 2006; Garfield, 1994; Morris et al., 2003; Persson, 1994).

Garfield (1979), in his well-known book on citation indexing, uses the paper-citing-papers model and applies this model to small topics covering our definition of research specialties. Garfield's model is focused on finding the evolution of concepts. Citations are assumed to represent the transfer of a concept from the cited paper to the author of the citing paper. From this model a "historiograph," a diagram of the genealogy of concept growth as a specialty grows, can be derived (Garfield, Pudovkin, & Istomin, 2003, p. 184).

Salton (1989), in his classic book, models a collection of papers as a weighted bipartite network of papers connected to index terms, expressed as a term matrix. This model was applied to methods of retrieving documents using queries.

Our goal is to present a model of a collection of papers that incorporates the various models given here and consolidates them in a useful way. To this end, we review a unified model of a collection of papers that serves for previously introduced types of bibliometric analysis: citation analysis (Garfield, 1979), co-citation analysis (Small, 1973), author co-citation analysis (White & Griffith, 1981), journal co-citation analysis (McCain, 1991), bibliographic coupling analysis (Kessler, 1963), co-word analysis (Callon, Law, & Rip, 1986), co-authorship analysis (Beaver, 1979; Subramanyam, 1983), and journal citation analysis (Leydesdorff, 1994, 2006; Narin, 1975).

A Framework for Modeling Collections of Papers

Figure 6.5 shows a working model of a collection of papers. This model consists of a collection of entities of seven different entity types: 1) papers, 2) index terms, 3) references, 4) paper authors, 5) reference authors, 6) paper journals, and 7) reference journals. The base entity type in this model is the paper. Each paper is linked to the index terms that are associated with it, the authors that authored the paper (paper authors), the journal in which it appeared (paper journal), and the references that it cited. Each reference is linked to the authors that are associated with it (reference authors), and the journal that is associated with it (reference journals). In Web of Science records, only the first author of the cited reference is recorded; this leads to interpretational problems that will be discussed later in this section. The diagram in Figure 6.5 models associations between entities as links, yielding a system of six coupled bipartite networks: 1) papers to paper authors, 2) papers to references, 3) papers to paper journals, 4) papers to index terms, 5) references to reference authors, and 6) references to reference journals.

Another way of thinking about the model in Figure 6.5 is as an entity-relationship model, a database modeling technique introduced by P. Chen (1976). A simplified entity-relationship diagram is shown in Figure 6.6. Each of the lines connecting two entity types on the diagram denotes relations and can be thought of as a table in the database holding the collection of papers. The entity-relationship model can be expanded to add other entity types in the collection of papers, but the seven entity types shown in Figure 6.6, along with *paper year* and *reference year*, are

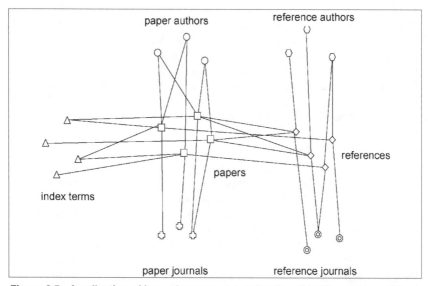

Figure 6.5   A collection of journal papers as a collection of bibliographic entities.

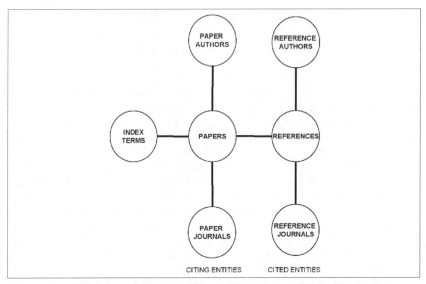

Figure 6.6 **Diagram of an entity-relationship model of a collection of journal papers.**

the most easily extracted from downloaded WoS files. Acquiring additional entities of other types requires special *entity extraction* routines (Thompson, 2005) that are difficult to create and often unreliable. Examples of such entity types include: title terms, abstract terms, body text terms, author institution, paper country, and country of origin.

Paper country denotes country names that appear in the address lines of paper authors. In Web of Science files, the author addresses (which are not linked to their specific authors) can be linked only to the paper in which they appear. This leads to operational and interpretational difficulties when conducting collaboration studies (Katz & Martin, 1997). *Country of origin* is the originating country of a researcher or student, without regard to the country in which he or she is working (Basu & Lewison, 2006; Jin, Rousseau, Suttmeier, & Cao, 2007).

Bibliographic Entities

We define *bibliographic entities* as objects of interest that are instanced in bibliographic records. Each entity is of a specific *entity type*. In the simple coupled bipartite model of Figure 6.5 the bibliographic entity types are: papers, index terms, references, paper authors, reference authors, paper journals, and reference journals. We also define *physical entities* as objects of interest in the real world. Generally, we expect physical entities to *correspond* to one or more bibliographic entities. For example, a researcher, a physical entity, can correspond to two bibliographic entities: a paper author and a reference author. Given the practical limitation of size and retrieval of collections of papers, it is common for some physical entities of interest to have no corresponding bibliographic entity in a collection of papers used to map a specialty.

Bibliographic entities and their links are representations of the bibliographic data that occur in collections of papers, representations that allow those data to be described in network terms and expressed mathematically as a collection of matrices. Entities should not be confused with *units of analysis*, a term with multiple definitions that is often used by bibliometricians. Smith (1981, p. 86) uses the term to denote aggregation levels for citation analysis and states that "units of analysis can be individual articles or books, journals, authors, industrial organizations, academic departments, universities, cities, states, nations, and even telescopes." Börner et al. (2003) use the term to denote the types of objects being mapped as part of bibliometric analysis. White and McCain (1989, p. 124) use the term to denote the type of record of source data, usually articles: "articles—or other writings—are the true unit of analysis in many bibliometric studies, and authors' names and journal names are *variables*, not units of analysis."

The Difference between Papers and References

Papers correspond to the bibliographic records stored by abstracting services; they are the base records in collections of papers. If the records contain citation data, these are supplied as a list of references cited by the paper. There are no pointers between records that denote citation relationships, nor is it necessary to have such pointers for most types of bibliometric analysis. Such pointers in a collection would form an incomplete set in two ways: papers cite many items that are not indexed by abstracting services (textbooks, monographs, Web pages, and doctoral dissertations, for example). In some fields, particularly in the social sciences, most references do not correspond to journal papers (Nicholas & Ritchie, 1978, p. 125). These cited items are not indexed and so will have no corresponding records in the collection.

Specialties are subject to overlap and the core and scatter phenomenon previously discussed. Most collections of papers exhibit a reference power law (Naranan, 1971) of papers per reference with an exponent of about 3. Assuming about 25 references per paper, it is easy to calculate from this power law that the number of references will be about 20 times more than the number of papers in a collection of papers. Because of this, 95 percent or more of the references in the collection will not have a corresponding record in the collection. Also, many of the papers in the collection will have no corresponding reference in the collection because a significant number of papers are not cited by papers in the collection.

It is also necessary, for mapping purposes, to distinguish *citing items* from *cited items*. Citing items, as papers, are reports that are connected to the specialty's research topics in some way. We can, for example, infer a list of subtopics by browsing paper titles and abstracts for themes or by extracting terms using co-word analysis (Callon et al., 1986). Cited items (references) are connected to the base knowledge of the specialty in some way. For example, we can infer the concepts represented by highly cited references by analyzing the phrasing used when they are cited (Schneider, 2006; Small, 1986). Because papers tend to show manifestations of a specialty's research topics and references tend to show manifestations of base knowledge, they must be separated for mapping purposes.

The terms *citation* and *reference* are often used interchangeably. Some researchers define them as two complementary actions, "reference" as "acknowledgement to" and "citation" as "acknowledgment from" (Narin, 1975, p. 3; see also Egghe & Rousseau, 1990). Here we define a reference as an object (entity) that is instanced in the reference list of a paper. We define a citation as an action, that is, a citation is the inclusion of a reference, by a paper, in its reference list. Papers *cite* references.

Mapping References to Papers

Some types of bibliometric mapping use networks of like entities citing each other. There are paper-citing-paper models (Börner, Maru, & Goldstone, 2004; Garfield, 1979), and journal-citing-journal models (Leydesdorff, 2006). These types of models are needed when mapping information flow or concept flow, or when analyzing images and identities (White, 2001).

Dropping index terms in the model of Figure 6.6 and adding physical entities and their correspondence links to bibliographic entities (papers, references, paper authors, reference authors, paper journals, and reference journals) yields the model in Figure 6.7. The correspondence links shown in Figure 6.7 can be expressed in three tables in the collection of papers database: 1) a paper to reference correspondence table, 2) a paper journal to reference journal correspondence table, and 3) a paper author to reference author correspondence table. In these tables there will be a large number of missing correspondences. For example, for papers and references, there will be many papers that have no corresponding reference entities and a great many references that have no corresponding paper entity. Correspondence tables are built by matching attributes in paper bibliographic records to reference attributes such as author name, journal name, and volume number and page number.

Figure 6.8 shows the mechanics of building networks of entities that cite each other. Papers cite references that are linked through a paper-reference correspondence table back to papers. Paper authors author papers, which cite references, which are associated with reference authors, which are linked back to paper authors through a paper author to reference author correspondence. The same process describes finding a journal citing journal network from paper journal to paper to references to reference journals to paper journals. Building such networks may involve a great deal of effort in cleaning up the multiple names of highly cited references and authors, a time-intensive process (Moed, 2005, chapters 13 and 14).

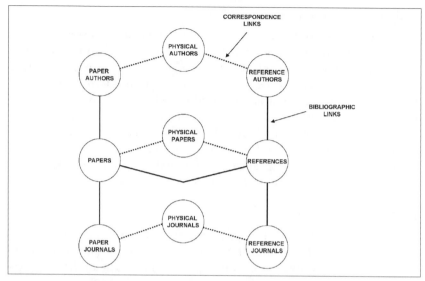

Figure 6.7 Model of the relation between bibliographic entities and physical enti-ties for papers, references, authors, and journals.

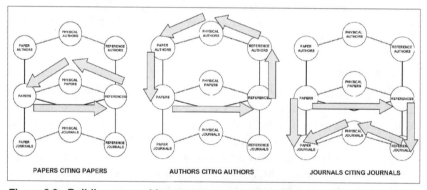

Figure 6.8 Building paper-citing-paper networks, author-citing-author networks, and journal-citing-journal networks by tracing correspondence links.

Direct Bibliographic Links

In a network sense, bibliographic entities are connected by *direct links* through the association of papers with their dependent entities and references with their dependent entities. In the model presented in Figure 6.6, there are six types of direct links: 1) papers to paper authors, 2) paper to index terms, 3) paper to paper journals, 4) paper to refer-ences, 5) reference to reference authors, and 6) reference to reference journals.

Indirect Bibliographic Links

Indirect links are formed by a path of two or more direct links. For example, when a paper author is linked to a paper, which is linked to a cited reference, which is linked to a particular reference author, there is an indirect link between the paper author and that reference author. In the model in Figure 6.6, assuming undirected links, there are 14 possible types of indirect links that can exist in a collection of papers. Among the most useful types of indirect links are paper author to reference author, used for author co-citation analysis, and paper journal to reference journal, used for journal co-citation analysis. Indirect links can be computed using matrix multiplication.

Co-Occurrence Links

Given a pair of like entities, a co-occurrence link is a link whose weight is a count of the number of common links of the pair to an entity of some other entity type. For example, two paper authors that have co-authored four papers would have a co-occurrence link of weight 4 relative to papers (co-authorship count). Two references that are cited together in twenty papers would have a co-occurrence link of weight 20 relative to papers (the co-citation count). Two papers that cite three common references would have a co-occurrence link of 3 relative to references (bibliographic coupling count).

Link Weights

Bibliographic links can be considered to have a strength, known as the *link weight*. In the model in Figure 6.6 all direct links are assumed to be *unweighted* and those links are always considered to have unity weight. If we use a model with term entities based on title terms, abstract terms, or body text terms, the direct links from papers to such term entities can be weighted by the number of times such entities occur in the title, abstract, or paper body respectively. Link weights for indirect links can be easily calculated by matrix multiplication of the occurrence matrices that define the bipartite networks that comprise the paths of indirect links of interest. Co-occurrence link weights are similarly calculated. In some situations, when calculating links based on weighted co-occurrence matrices, it is necessary to use a generalized matrix multiplication (Morris, 2005b) that implements the overlap function (Jones & Furnas, 1987; Salton, 1989) or some other link weight function, such as the harmonic mean. Examples of situations requiring such techniques are when calculating occurrence and co-occurrence weights related to abstract or title terms, or when calculating co-citation weights of reference authors relative to paper authors.

Similarity Links

Similarity links are normalized co-occurrence links. Similarity links range in weight from zero for no similarity to unity for identical similarity. Normalizing co-occurrence links to similarities greatly attenuates the influence of heavily occurring entities on clustering algorithms. Several well known algorithms exist for computing similarities, including the dice coefficient, the cosine coefficient, the Jaccard coefficient (Börner et al., 2003; Salton, 1989). Pearson's correlation coefficient, often referred to as r_{xy} and often used for author co-citation analysis (McCain, 1990), is problematic as a similarity measure. It assumes values from -1 to +1 and is typically converted to similarity by adding 1 and dividing the sum by two. This gives zero correlation a similarity value of one half, introducing interpretational problems. Other interpretational problems can be identified but further discussion is beyond the scope of this chapter. A discussion of the use of r_{xy} in author co-citation analysis can be found in the work of Ahlgren, Jarneving, and Rousseau (2004), White (2004a), and Leydesdorff (2005). For collections of papers, where co-occurrence matrices are usually very sparse, it is easy to show that the value of r_{xy} approaches the value of the cosine coefficient.

Bibliographic Tokens

We assert that entities, links, and groups of related entities in a collection of papers are *manifestations* of the social and cognitive processes in a specialty. As such, we will use the entities, links, and entity groups as *tokens* of objects in the specialty. We define bibliographic tokens as bibliographic entities, links, or entity groups that represent some object, concept, or event in a research specialty. Note that, although the interpretation of papers, paper authors, and paper journals as tokens is straightforward and fairly obvious, the interpretation of cited entities is somewhat problematic. The interpretation of cited entities as tokens is based on the knowledge that authors of journal papers tend to cite well known references as concept symbols (Hargens, 2000; Small, 1978).

Bibliographic Entities as Tokens

Any of the six bibliographic entities in Figure 6.6 can function as tokens that represent objects and concepts in the specialty. For example, a paper in a collection of papers is a token representing a report on some research task but a paper author is a token of a researcher in the specialty. Table 6.1 gives a proposed list of the entity types in a collection of papers and their function as tokens representing objects in a specialty.

Considering bibliographic entities as tokens of objects in the research specialty is sometimes imprecise, as it is possible for entities to be tokens of different objects in the specialty. In the case of references, as mentioned in the section on models of research specialties, many researchers have proposed various independent and overlapping reasons that authors cite references, a topic reviewed by Cronin (1984) and

Table 6.1 Entities in a collection of papers and their significance as tokens of research specialty objects

Bibliographic entity	Token representing	Notes
Paper	Research report	Papers are the base entities in the collection of papers. The collection grows one paper at a time.
Reference	Base knowledge concepts	Heavily cited references symbolize fixed concepts associated with base knowledge in the specialty.
Paper journal	Research report archive	Paper journals function as depositories of papers and can be considered to have an archival function.
Paper author	Researcher	Paper authors perform and report on research tasks.
Reference journal	Base knowledge archive	Considering that references point to base knowledge in the specialty, reference journals have an archival function for base knowledge.
Reference author	Authorities	Considering that references point to base knowledge in the specialty, reference authors represent broad base knowledge concepts and can be considered authorities or experts.
Index term	Research topics	Author-supplied index terms may contain considerable ambiguity and overlap in meaning because authors typically do not use standardized index terms.

Nicolaison (2007). Each of these motivations represents a different concept or object in the specialty for which the reference is a bibliographic token: This confuses the task of mapping. If, however, we stay thoroughly cognizant of the limitations of the mapping process, we may talk in generalities about the function of entities as tokens. This helps considerably to clarify what is being measured by mapping.

In Table 6.1 we use papers to represent *research reports*. In particular, papers can be considered reports on specific *research tasks*. Note that papers contain no evidence of their own importance. Review papers do not usually represent research tasks and can be considered simply as summary reports of research results in the specialty.

As bibliographic entities, references can often be considered as tokens of *exemplars*, or base knowledge concepts in the specialty. This is particularly true of heavily cited references in a specialty literature; in fact, the citation counts of references can be used to infer the importance of the paper or book corresponding to a reference (Moed, 2005). There is a solid and expanding group of researchers who have explored the idea of references (or papers as references) representing base knowledge concepts in a specialty. Garfield's technique of mapping the evolution of ideas through citation analysis assumes that key papers in the specialty are cited for the concepts they contributed to the research reported on by a paper (Garfield, 1979; Garfield et al., 2003). Small (1978) produced a model of references being cited as concept symbols. He developed this idea into citation context analysis, a technique often used to identify the concepts represented by heavily cited references in a specialty literature (Small, 1985, 1986). This idea has recently been applied by other authors in specific case studies (Schneider, 2006; Schneider & Borlund, 2005). Hargens (2000, p. 860) identifies well-cited references as "short-hand 'markers' of general perspectives." Morris (2005a) proposes a model of the manifestation of base knowledge as paradigmatic exem-plars represented by highly cited references in a specialty's literature.

As noted in Table 6.1, paper journals can be considered archives of research reports. As such, paper journals represent the repository of reports on the research conducted in the specialty. One of the goals of mapping is to correlate paper journals with specific research subtopics in the specialty for monitoring purposes.

Reference journals, through their association with highly cited refer-ences that represent the specialty's base knowledge, are tokens of archives of base knowledge in the specialty. One of the goals of mapping is to find the correlation of reference journals with specific base knowl-edge in the specialty. This helps to identify fields and outside specialties that supply base knowledge. It is possible that the most widely used ref-erence journals in a specialty do not correspond to the paper journals in which most researchers publish within that same specialty. This indi-cates a specialty that borrows a great deal of its base knowledge from other specialties while publishing its research reports in its own pre-ferred journals.

Paper authors are tokens of researchers in a specialty. A great num-ber of investigators have used this assumption, starting with Lotka (1926), through Price and Beaver (1966), and most notably with the landmark three-paper series by Beaver (1978, 1979) and Beaver and Rosen (1979).

Reference authors are problematic as tokens. Highly cited references, tokens of base knowledge, have associated reference authors and we therefore assume that reference authors serve in some way as tokens of base knowledge. Note, however, that a reference author may be associ-ated with several loosely related highly cited references and, alterna-tively, a reference author may not be associated with any very heavily cited references, but still may accrue a large number of total citations across a large number of separate references. Thus the base knowledge that a reference author represents is of a higher and more abstract char-acter than the exemplars represented by highly cited references. We will consider reference authors as tokens of *broad base knowledge concepts* or as representing *authorities*, defined as past or present persons that are regarded by researchers as experts in areas of broad knowledge in the specialty.

References in WoS files contain only the first author name. Other authors in the cited papers cannot be analyzed, leading to interpretational difficulties, especially when attempting to measure the influence of specific researchers through author co-citation. This is a limitation of using query-derived author co-citation matrices. Using a collection of papers, it is possible to build an author-citing-author network, as discussed in the section on modeling collections of research papers. From this network, all-author co-citation analysis can be performed on the author-citing-author network. This analysis may be incomplete, in that influential authorities from outside the specialty may be highly cited by papers in the collection, but because few or none of their papers are in the collection, they are not found in the author-citing-author network. Eom (2003) presents detailed instructions for author co-citation analysis based on using a collection of papers. Using a collection of papers, Persson (2001) showed that the use of first authors only in author co-citation analysis did not significantly alter the mapping of research themes in a field, but that first-author-only analysis significantly distorted measures of influence of top-cited researchers in the field. Rousseau and Zuccala (2004) propose a classification scheme for author co-citation that allows better interpretation of links among reference authors.

Index terms are supplied by authors or are assigned by catalogers to denote the research problem addressed by the research reported by the paper. Generally, an index term indicates what research was performed, not what base knowledge was used. Thus, index terms can be considered as tokens representing research problems, that is, research topics.

Bibliographic Links as Tokens

Bibliographic links function as tokens that represent relationships in the specialty. For example, a link between a paper author and a paper in a collection of papers is a token representing the specific relationship that the author as a researcher has participated in the research being reported on by the paper. A listing of the most useful links in a collection of papers and their functions as tokens is shown diagrammatically in Figure 6.9.

Co-Occurrence Links as Tokens

Co-occurrence links also function as tokens of relationships between entities in a research specialty. For example, when two paper authors have a co-occurrence link through a paper they have co-authored, the assumed relationship between the authors is that they collaborated on the research task that is reported in the paper. Figure 6.10 shows the entity-relation diagram of Figure 6.6 modified to show some important types of co-occurrence links in a collection of papers. Most of these types

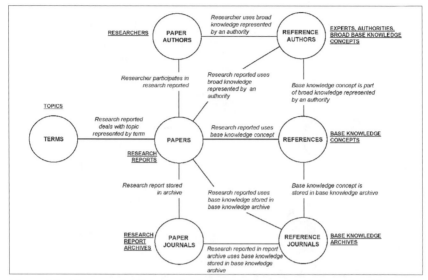

Figure 6.9　Diagram showing the function of bibliographic links and entities as tokens of physical objects and relations in a research specialty. Entity token functions are written in underlined capitals beside the entity circles; link token functions are written in lower case on or near the link lines.

of links have been previously studied: bibliographic coupling (Kessler, 1963), co-citation (Small, 1973), co-authorship (Subramanyam, 1983), author co-citation (White & Griffith, 1981), journal co-citation (McCain, 1991), and term co-occurrence (Callon et al., 1991). Table 6.2 shows a proposed list of bibliographic co-occurrence links and their functions as tokens of relationships in a research specialty.

Co-occurrence links are used extensively to map the social and cognitive structure of the research specialty. This is done by using raw co-occurrence counts or derived similarities to cluster entities into groups that tend to share some common characteristic. For example, research teams may be mapped by calculating the co-authorship links among the authors in the collection of papers and clustering them into groups that have co-authored papers. Considering that co-authorship (paper author to paper author co-occurrence relative to papers) is a token of two researchers working on the same research task, we can infer that such co-authorship groups represent research teams.

Characterization of Bibliographic Entities

Occurrence Matrix Descriptions of Collections of Papers

The information about entities and their links in a collection of papers is most conveniently stored in a series of *occurrence matrices* that list

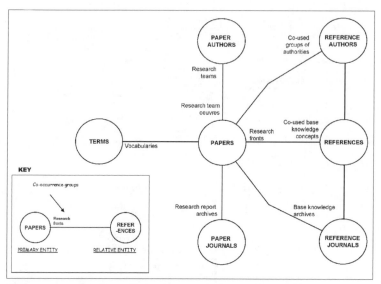

Figure 6.10   Diagram showing types of co-occurrence relations in a collection of papers using the model of Figure 6.6.

Table 6.2   Co-occurrence links between entities in a collection of papers and their significance as tokens of relationships in a specialty

Entity pair	Common entity	Name of bibliographic relation	Token of relationship
Papers	Reference	Bibliographic coupling	Two papers use common base knowledge.
References	Paper	Reference co-citation	Two pieces of base knowledge used in the research reported by the paper.
Papers	Index term	Index term coupling	Reported research in two papers addresses the research problem denoted by the index term.
Paper author	Reference author	Author co-citation (paper author)	Two researchers each use the broad base knowledge concept represented by the reference author.
Paper	Reference author	Author co-citation (paper)	Reported research in two papers uses the broad base knowledge concept represented by the reference author.
Paper journal	Reference journal	Journal co-citation (paper journal)	Reported research from two archives uses base knowledge stored in the reference journal.

the links between entities from pairs of entity types in the collection. Define the row entities as the *primary entity type* and the column entities as the *secondary entity type*. Both the rows and columns are ordered by the sequence of the appearance of their corresponding entities in the specialty. This means that for paper entities, the matrix rows, corresponding to papers, are arranged in the sequence of the publication dates of the papers. References, however, are not arranged in order of their dates, but are arranged in the order of their *first appearance* in the specialty literature when the papers are arranged in chronological order. Such ordering facilitates the study of the growth of the research specialty (Morris, 2005a).

There is an occurrence matrix corresponding to each bipartite network shown in Figure 6.5. These six matrices contain all the information about the links that characterize the network of entities in a collection of papers. Occurrence matrices corresponding to indirect links are easily computed by simple chained matrix multiplications.

Co-Occurrence Matrices in Collections of Papers

Co-occurrence matrices list the weights of co-occurrence links among the entities of a single entity type relative to some secondary entity type. For example, paper authors (primary entity type) have co-occurrence links based on the number of papers they have co-authored (papers as secondary entity type), or the number of times they have cited the same reference (references as secondary entity type), or the number of times they have cited the same reference authors (reference authors as secondary entity type). In the model in Figure 6.5, there are 42 possible co-occurrence matrices, although only a few of these are useful for bibliometric analysis.

Co-occurrence matrices are easily computed by post-multiplying the occurrence matrix of the primary entity type to secondary entity type by its transpose. For example, a co-authorship matrix can be computed by post multiplying the paper author to paper matrix by its transpose.

Entity Characterization Techniques

Bibliometric techniques that are generally applied to mapping specialties can be divided into two methods: characterization of individual entities and characterization of groups of entities that are found by co-occurrence clustering. The characterization of individual entities uses two bibliometric methods: ranking by number of occurrences and characterization by patterns of occurrence and co-occurrence.

Ranking of Entities

Ranking by occurrence is the fairly simple task of tabulating occurrences associated with an entity and putting those entities in descending order of the number of occurrence. Examples include:

- Ranking references by number of citations received.
- Ranking of reference authors by number of citations received.
- Ranking of paper authors by productivity, that is, ranking authors by the number of papers published.
- Ranking of reference journals by the number of citations received.

The calculation of rankings from collections of papers is fairly straightforward. Such rankings are often used to derive *indicators*, which are carefully normalized estimates of the influence or importance of individual entities, typically researchers and journals. Further discussion of indicators is beyond the scope of this review. Narin (1975) and also Egghe and Rousseau (1990) are good sources of information on that topic; Moed (2005) provides an excellent primer and detailed discussion on the application of evaluative bibliometrics.

Features and Feature Vectors

In the pattern recognition sense, a *feature* is a measurable observable associated with an entity that can be used to characterize an entity for purposes of clustering, mapping, and for other statistical techniques. Duda, Hart, and Stork (2001) provide a full review of features and their use in pattern recognition. A *feature vector* is a vector where each element holds a feature. Usually, feature vectors are considered as coordinates in some multi-dimensional *feature space*. Given the feature vectors for a collection of entities, many techniques, such as clustering or multi-dimensional scaling, can be applied to identify, classify, compare, or map the entities of interest.

Using Occurrence Feature Vectors to Characterize Entities in Collections of Papers

An *occurrence feature vector* shows the pattern of associations that an entity has with entities of some other entity type. Assume a pair of entity types described by an occurrence matrix. The occurrence feature vector of a primary entity, relative to the secondary entity type, corresponds to that primary entity's row in the occurrence matrix.

The occurrence vector associated with primary entity i describes the pattern of secondary entities associated with i and serves as a *characterizing pattern*, that is, a pattern of associations that helps to characterize entity i's place in the specialty. For example, for a reference author to paper author matrix, the vector listing the paper authors citing a reference author i characterizes author i by the pattern of researchers that use his or her work. Table 6.3 shows a proposed list of different types of occurrence feature vectors with their associated characterizing patterns.

Table 6.3 **Examples of occurrence feature vectors for entities in a collection of papers**

Primary entity type	Relative entity type	Characterizing pattern
Paper	Reference	Pattern of base knowledge used by research reported.
Reference	Paper	Pattern of research that uses base knowledge represented by the reference.
Paper author	Paper	A paper author's oeuvre.
Paper author	Reference author	The authorities used by the paper author. The pattern of broad base knowledge a researcher uses in his research. An author *identity* (White, 2001).
Reference author	Paper author	The pattern of researchers that use the broad base knowledge concepts that the reference author represents.
Paper journal	Reference journal	The reference journals holding base knowledge used in research reported in the paper journal.
Reference journal	Paper journal	The paper journals whose archived reported research draws base knowledge archived in a reference journal.
Paper	Index terms	A paper's research vocabulary.

Using Co-Occurrence Feature Vectors to Characterize Entities in Collections of Papers

The *co-occurrence feature vector* of a primary entity, relative to a secondary entity, is the primary entity's corresponding row from the corresponding co-occurrence matrix. Similar to occurrence feature vectors, co-occurrence feature vectors serve as a specific characterizing pattern. For example, the row i from a co-authorship matrix characterizes paper author i by the researchers with whom he or she collaborates. Table 6.4 shows a proposed list of primary entity-type to secondary entity-type pairs and the characterizing patterns that can be inferred from the associated co-occurrence feature vectors.

Occurrence and co-occurrence feature vectors characterize entities in the collection of papers and provide metrics to help find an entity's position in the research specialty in multiple ways. For example, using feature vectors, a paper author can be characterized by:

- The author's pattern of co-authorship, using the co-occurrence feature vector drawn from the co-authorship matrix (primary

Table 6.4 Examples of co-occurrence feature vectors for entities in a collection of papers

Primary entity type	Relative entity type	Characterizing pattern
Paper	Reference	A paper's pattern of papers that cite the same references that it does. (The papers that use the same base knowledge it does.)
Reference	Paper	A reference's pattern of references that are co-cited in papers with it. (The base knowledge that is co-used with the base knowledge represented by the paper.)
Paper author	Paper	A paper author's pattern of co-authors. (A researcher's pattern of collaborators.)
Paper author	Reference author	A paper author's pattern of paper authors that cite the same reference authors he or she does. (The researchers that use the same authorities he or she does.)
Reference author	Paper	A reference author's pattern of reference authors that are co-cited with him or her. (Authorities that are co-used with him or her. The *image* of a reference author [White, 2001].)
Reference journal	Paper	A reference journal's pattern of reference journals that are co-cited with it. (Base knowledge archives that are co-used with it.)
Paper	Index terms	A paper's pattern of papers that are associated with the same index terms it is. Other reported research that deals with the same research topic as that reported by the paper.
Index terms	Paper	An index term's pattern of other index terms associated with it in papers. (Research topics addressed together in reported papers with the topic represented by the index term.)

entity type = authors, secondary entity type = papers). This information will help identify the author's research team and weak ties.

- The author's pattern of cited references, using a feature vector taken from the paper author to reference matrix. This information will help identify the specific base knowledge the author uses.
- The author's pattern of cited reference authors, using a feature vector from the paper author to reference author matrix. This information helps identify the pattern of authorities that the author cites, an indication of broad knowledge concepts applied in his or her research. This vector corresponds to an author's identity as defined by White (2001).

- The author's pattern of associated index terms, using the feature vector from the paper author to index terms matrix. This helps to identify the research topics in which the researcher is performing research.

The use of feature vectors generalizes and formalizes the concept of *author image* and *author identity* proposed by White (2001). An author's identity is the pattern of the authors that he or she cites, which corresponds to the author's corresponding row in the paper author to reference author matrix. An author's image is the pattern of authors with whom he or she has been co-cited; it corresponds to a row in the reference author co-occurrence matrix relative to papers. This row lists the counts of the number of times a reference author has been cited with the other reference authors in the collection of papers. The concept of identities and images has been extended to reference journals and paper journals by Nebelong-Bonnevie and Frandsen (2006) and Bonnevie-Nebelong (2006).

Characterization of Entity Groups

Entity Groups

The previous section discussed the characterization of individual bibliographic entities in a collection of papers and further discussed methods to find the location of such entities relative to the overall social structure, base knowledge, and research subtopics in the specialty. Another task in the process of mapping the specialty is to locate and map groups of entities that correspond to important groups in the specialty: teams of researchers, groups of related references that represent subsets of base knowledge, groups of papers by subtopic, vocabularies of index terms, research team oeuvres (and importantly their associated research subtopic), groups of reference authors representing co-used authorities, groups of reference journals representing base knowledge archives, and groups of paper journals representing research report archives (especially important for deciding which journals to subscribe to and actively monitor).

Analysis of entity groups is a two part process: 1) identification of groups and 2) investigation of the relation of groups of a particular entity type to each other and to groups of differing entity types. We must also consider the overlap of relations among groups. The tasks of group identification and mapping of group relations are both non-trivial. Typically, metrics used for classification are so skewed that unambiguous classification of entities is impossible. Furthermore, it is extremely difficult to evaluate grouping algorithms meaningfully, as there are few benchmark collections of papers, with known groups, upon which to test such algorithms.

It is not within the scope of this chapter to go deeply into the details of finding groups within collections of papers. The mechanics of clustering and mapping of groups within such collections has been covered well in *ARIST* (e.g., Börner et al., 2003). In the information science literature, most examples of finding groups of entities are based on agglomerative clustering of entities based on raw co-occurrence counts or based on counts that have been normalized to similarities.

Clustering Algorithms

Generally, two clustering algorithms are applied to find entity groups, agglomerative clustering and c-means clustering (Gordon, 1999). Agglomerative clustering uses pairwise distances between entities, sometimes using vector distances computed from rows of appropriate occurrence and co-occurrence matrices. For example, clustering of papers based on bibliographic coupling may utilize vector distances between the papers rows in the paper to reference matrix. Alternatively, similarities in a similarity matrix can be converted to distances for clustering. Agglomerative clustering gathers groups by iteratively fusing clusters of entities that have the greatest similarity according to some linkage function (Gordon, 1999). Agglomerative clustering produces a dendrogram that describes the taxonomy of the groups formed in the clustering process.

C-means clustering (also called k-means) is an iterative algorithm that assigns class membership of entities by minimizing the distances of the entity-feature vectors to mean cluster centers in the vector space (Gordon, 1999). The occurrence or co-occurrence feature vectors of the entities can be used for this purpose. Fuzzy c-means algorithms exist that can be used to find overlap in group membership (Bezdek, 1981).

Co-Occurrence Clustered Entities as Tokens of Objects in the Research Specialty

When groups of entities are found by clustering that is based on co-occurrence relative to a second entity type, it is important to consider what such groups represent. Groups of entities clustered on co-occurrence share a common characteristic and these groups function as tokens of group objects within the specialty. For example, a group of authors, found by clustering using co-authorship, represents a research team in the specialty. Table 6.5 summarizes the useful co-occurrence groups and their possible functions as tokens in a collection of papers.

Bibliographic Coupling Analysis

Bibliographic coupling analysis clusters papers by common references. Assuming that highly cited references are markers of base knowledge concepts, bibliographic coupling forms groups of papers that report on research that uses the same base knowledge. Bibliographic coupling was proposed and used by Kessler (1963); it was later critiqued by Weinberg (1974), who concluded that it was not very effective as a retrieval tool but had good potential for the mapping of science. Morris

Table 6.5 **Useful groupings of bibliographic entities relative to secondary entities and the function of those groups as tokens of objects in the research specialty**

Primary entity	Secondary entity	Token representing:
Papers	References	Research fronts (groups of papers whose reported research uses the same base knowledge. This correlates to groups of papers dealing with the same research subtopic).
Paper authors	Papers	Collaboration groups (research teams).
References	Papers	Reference groups representing co-used base knowledge.
Reference authors	Papers	Groups of reference authors representing co-used authorities (co-used broad base knowledge).
Reference journals	Papers	Groups of co-used base knowledge archives.
Index terms	Papers	Groups of co-used terms (vocabularies).
Papers	Index terms	Reports grouped by similar vocabulary (correlates to groups of papers dealing with the same research subtopic).
Papers	Paper authors	Collaboration group (research team) oeuvres.

et al. (2003) found that bibliographic coupling analysis could be applied to timelines that visualized growth dynamics in a specialty. Jarneving (2001) used bibliographic coupling, along with co-citation analysis, journal co-citation analysis, and word profiles of clusters, to map the specialties of cardiovascular research. A later study by Jarneving (2005) compared bibliographic coupling clusters against paper groups that cite common co-citation clusters, two methods of forming research fronts. Word profile analysis revealed considerable difference in the research fronts that were found.

Co-Authorship Analysis

Co-authorship analysis clusters paper authors by common paper; it is used to infer teams of collaborating researchers. Beaver and Rosen (1979) first explored the origins of co-authorship and the basic relation of collaboration to co-authorship. Subramanyam (1983) produced an important review of the use of bibliometrics and co-authorship to study research collaboration, identifying types of collaboration and levels of collaboration, as well as examining basic assumptions of co-authorship analysis. Melin and Persson (1996), Katz and Martin (1997), and Laudel

(2002) also review concepts in collaboration and co-authorship, especially highlighting the inability of co-authorship to measure informal collaboration. For examples of mapping research teams and collaboration structures, see Mählck and Persson (2000) who map the research departments at two universities; Peters and van Raan (1991), who map the collaboration structure in a chemical engineering department; and Seglen and Aksnes (2000), who map research groups among Norwegian microbiologists.

Co-Citation Analysis

Co-citation analysis clusters references by common paper. Assuming highly cited references to be markers of base knowledge concepts, co-citation analysis identifies groups of co-used base knowledge concepts. Co-citation was originally applied to specialty mapping by Small and Griffith (1974) and Griffith, Small, Stonehill, and Dey (1974). Bellardo (1980) provided an early assessment of the validity of co-citation analysis. The method has been further developed and applied by Small (Small, 1973, 1997, 1998, 1999; Small & Greenlee, 1989; Small & Sweeney, 1985) both for studies of specialties and for producing maps of fields of science.

Author Co-Citation Analysis

Author co-citation analysis clusters reference authors by common papers. Assuming highly cited authors to be authorities or markers of broad base knowledge concepts, ACA identifies co-used broad base knowledge concepts in the specialty. White and Griffith (1981) originally proposed author co-citation analysis, a common technique for mapping groups of reference authors in specialties or in broader areas of science. The method, as originally proposed, uses co-citation counts from query-derived co-occurrence matrices (discussed in the section on the process of mapping research specialties). McCain (1990) gives a technical overview of this technique. It is easily adapted for use using data from collections of papers, as shown by Eom (1996, 2003). White and McCain (1998) demonstrate the use of author co-citation to map the field of information science, using factor analysis to find groups of authors as co-used markers of broad areas of base knowledge in the field.

Journal Co-Citation Analysis

Journal co-citation analysis clusters reference journals by common papers. Assuming cited journals as base knowledge archives, journal co-citation tends to form groups of journals that function as co-used archives. McCain (1991) first proposed the technique. The method has been applied to mapping information science (Ding, Chowdhury, & Foo, 2000), economics (McCain, 1991), neural networks (McCain, 1998), urban studies (Liu, 2005), and semiconductor literature (Tsay, Xu, & Wu, 2003).

Co-Word Analysis

Co-word analysis clusters index terms by common papers. This produces co-used terms, which can be interpreted as vocabularies or themes. As noted in the section on the bibliographical approach, co-word analysis was pioneered by Callon et al. (1983) and applied by various researchers to a number of mapping applications.

Word-profile analysis is another technique for extracting vocabularies (Braam et al., 1991). Clusters of papers are formed that cite common co-citation clusters. Highly occurring index terms are extracted from these clusters to form word profiles, which denote vocabularies associated with each cluster. Jarneving (2005) applied this technique to bibliographic coupling clusters in order to compare bibliographic-coupling derived research fronts with co-citation cluster-derived research fronts.

Besselaar and Heimeriks (2006) use word-reference co-occurrence clustering to cluster papers. In this technique, co-occurrences are based on two papers simultaneously being linked to a common index term AND a common reference. They applied the method to clustering papers from information science journals and found it effective in delineating specialties in the field. Clusters formed this way could be difficult to define as tokens: They are groups of papers denoting both shared topics (common index terms) and shared base knowledge (common references). Reid and Chen (2005) use co-occurrence of title and abstract terms as input to a self-organizing map program to map the structure of topics in terrorism research.

Visualization

Introduction

A research specialty is a complex system with four interacting elements to be mapped: the social network of researchers, the base knowledge used by researchers, the research subtopics, and the archival journals. The job of the investigator is to understand the structure and dynamics of each of these elements and their overlapping relations. As reported here, this can be done by mapping the specialty through its manifestations in the specialty literature. The complexity of this mapping is immense: If we use our model of a collection of papers, we are mapping the structure and dynamics through papers, references, paper authors, reference authors, paper journals, reference journals, and index terms.

When mapping specialties, visualizations help to explore, analyze, summarize, and conceptualize structure, overlapping relations, and dynamics. They are extremely useful when presenting mapping results to interested parties and when summarizing data in formal reports. Visualizations have become more automated, sophisticated, and interactive as computer workstations have advanced. Often, however, automated visualizations do not perform well, particularly in labeling entity groups, and the visualizations, being flashy and colorful, do not transfer well to written reports. Automated visualization, however, is certainly not required; it is perfectly appropriate for the investigator to summarize findings of structure and dynamics in the research specialty using manually constructed diagrams, usually entered into presentation programs such as Microsoft PowerPoint, in order to advance the audience's understanding of the complex structure, relations, and dynamics of the specialty under investigation.

Review of Selected Visualization Techniques

Tufte's (2001) book covers the basic techniques of information visualization and is especially useful for finding standards by which to judge those visualizations. White and McCain's (1997) review of literature visualization techniques is certainly still current. It contains an extensive review of visualization techniques; it catalogs the applications of visualization in library and information science and in making science policy decisions. White and McCain's "gentle critique" (p. 144) is useful reading for those who tend to get carried away with visualization as an end in itself. White and McCain identify labeling as the biggest deficiency of most visualization techniques.

Multidimensional Scaling

Multidimensional scaling (MDS) is a statistical technique (Kruskal & Wish, 1978) that accepts positions of entities in a multidimensional space and maps those positions to a two dimensional plane while minimizing the distortion in the original distances. The technique is widely used in social sciences for mapping authors. MDS is helpful for visualizing relations among small groups of entities; it is typically used for diagramming relations among reference journals or reference authors. Liu (2005), for example, uses MDS to visualize a small set of 38 reference journals in urban studies based on journal co-citation.

Landscape Visualization and Graph Layout Visualization

Börner et al. (2003) present a comprehensive overview of the mechanics of visualization: process flow in visualization, calculating similarities, clustering, and final visualization. They find two techniques particularly useful: landscape visualization and node-link network visualizations. Landscape visualizations are maps of entities positioned on a plane, where entities tend to clump together into dense groups that are closely related by some distance metric, typically co-citation similarity. When a 3-D plot of entity density is displayed, the visualization typically resembles a landscape of mountains (entity groups) separated by valleys. Landscape plots provide a grand view of a network of entities that is easily understood, although somewhat oversimplified. VxInsight (Boyack, Wylie, & Davidson, 2002) and IN-SPIRE (Hetzler & Turner, 2004) are typical programs that generate landscape visualizations.

Node-link network visualizations are typically done using a ball and stick metaphor, where entities are depicted as points or nodes and links are shown as lines that connect them. The graph layout program Pajek (Batagelj, 2003; Batagelj & Mrvar, 2003) is often used for such visualizations. This program is capable of laying out very large networks for visualization; it has been used to visualize large networks of references (Batagelj, 2003). Network visualizations are useful for displaying crucial communications pathways among disparate groups of entities.

Pathfinder Networks

The work of Chaomei Chen at Drexel University is notable in its extensive use of pathfinder networks (Schvaneveldt, Durso, & Dearholt, 1989). Pathfinder network analysis is a network pruning technique that iteratively drops weak links in a network until the backbone structure is revealed. After pruning, the network can be revealed using a layout program such as Pajek. Pathfinder visualizations are used to show the main communications links in a network; they plainly show key entities that link between sub-networks in the graph. Chen has adapted pathfinder networks to the visualization of co-citation networks (Chen, Paul, & Okeefe, 2001) and further applied co-citation analysis, augmented by Pathfinder visualizations, to study competing paradigms (Chen et al., 2002), knowledge diffusion (Chen & Hicks, 2004), detection of intellectual turning points (Chen, 2004), and author co-citation techniques (Chen, 1999). Chen's work focuses on the detection of dynamic trends and events in specialties (Chen, 2006).

Matrix-Based Mapping of Bibliographic Entities

Networks of entities can be readily visualized by displaying their adjacency matrices. Such visualizations focus on mapping relations among entities and groups of entities rather than mapping the entities themselves. Appropriate permutation of the rows and columns of the displayed matrix reveals underlying structure in the network. This visualization technique was pioneered by Bertin (2001), and is reviewed by Siirtola and Makinen (2005). Using a set of standardized tasks, Ghoniem, Fekete, and Castagliola (2005) found that, for networks of more than twenty nodes, matrix-based visualizations outperformed node-link visualizations in all of the tasks except path finding.

Matrix-based visualization techniques were applied to collections of papers by Morris and Yen (2004), who developed the crossmap technique for visualizing overlap of relations between groups of entities from two different entity types. Entity groups for both types are formed by agglomerative hierarchical clustering. The occurrence matrix of the two entity types is displayed as a bubble plot with rows and columns arranged to match the two clustering dendrograms, which are displayed on the top and left sides of the plot. Entity or entity-group labels are placed on the sides of the plot that are opposite the dendrograms. The crossmapping technique is quite useful, yielding much information in one chart. The two dendrograms show the hierarchical structure of similarity of entities of each type and the matrix bubble plot shows the overlapping relations of groups from one entity type to the other. Morris and Boyack (2005) applied this technique to mapping topics, base knowledge, and collaboration in the specialty of anthrax research.

Timelines

Timelines are maps of individual entities plotted by time; they are useful for visualizing dynamic changes in the specialty, particularly during periods of rapid growth and when a specialty breaks into subspecialties. Small and Greenlee (1989) use *cluster strings*, a timeline technique based on tracking continuity of clusters serially by year, to track the growth and diversification of AIDS research. More recently, Small (2006) applied the technique to the prediction of growth areas in specialties. Morris et al. (2003) present a timeline technique for plotting groups of papers after clustering using bibliographic coupling, a technique suitable for visualizing the effects of discontinuous events in a specialty. The technique was used to visualize the effects of the 2001 anthrax bioterror attacks on the field of anthrax research (Morris & Boyack, 2005).

Conclusion and Suggested Reading

The problem of mapping specialties is complex and poorly defined. A number of techniques have been developed and applied. Each of these techniques reveals some separate aspect of the specialty. For example, co-authorship analysis uncovers the social structure of collaboration and research teams in the specialty, co-citation analysis uncovers structure of base knowledge in the specialty, and bibliographic coupling analysis reveals research subtopics. In and of themselves, these analytic techniques are inadequate as tools to map the whole research specialty: the social structure of researchers, the base knowledge they use, and the research topics they study. As shown in Figure 6.11, the metaphor of the blind men and the elephant is appropriate, as each analytic technique reveals the specialty in some limited aspect.

Our review has covered two distinct but closely related topics: the modeling of specialties and the mapping of specialties. Modeling of specialties (the specialty of studying specialties) can be divided into four different approaches: sociological, bibliographic, communicative, and cognitive. We have noted that there are opportunities for integration in these approaches, particularly in integrating the study of relevance relationships, citation relationships, and bibliographic relationships. Reviewing the mapping of specialties, we presented the bibliometric techniques used to map specialties within a framework that shows how each technique contributes to the blind men's understanding of the elephant that is a research specialty. Each of these techniques reveals a different

Figure 6.11 **The blind men and the elephant, a metaphor for the many bibliometric analysis techniques applied to mapping research specialties.**

view; when combined, these produce a multi-faceted map of the social
structure, base knowledge, research topics, and archival journals that
are associated with the specialty.

Research specialties are the agents of change in science; as self-organized,
knowledge-validation organizations, they nurture the flowering of new discoveries and discard obsolete ideas. As complex as research specialties are,
they are still small and homogeneous. As such, the study and mapping of specialties is not a task of hopelessly large scope and complexity. It is possible to
build useful maps of specialties, and such mapping is being performed by
investigators on a routine basis.

References

Ahlgren, P., Jarneving, B., & Rousseau, R. (2004). Author cocitation analysis and
Pearson's r. *Journal of the American Society for Information Science and
Technology, 55*(9), 843.

Allen, B. (1997). Referring to schools of thought: An example of symbolic citations. *Social Studies of Science, 27*(4), 937–949.

Andrews, J. E. (2003). An author co-citation analysis of medical informatics.
Journal of the Medical Library Association, 91(1), 47–56.

Baldi, S., & Hargens, L. L. (1997). Re-examining Price's conjectures on the structure of reference networks: Results from the special relativity, spatial diffusing

modeling and role analysis literature. *Social Studies of Science*, 27(6), 669–687.

Barber, B. (1952). *Science and the social order*. New York: Free Press.

Bar-Ilan, J. (2001). Data collection methods on the Web for informetric purposes: A review and analysis. *Scientometrics*, 50(1), 7–32.

Basu, A., & Lewison, G. (2006, January). *Visualization of a scientific community of Indian origin in the US: A case study of bioinformatics and genomics.* Paper presented at the International Workshop on Webometrics, Informetrics and Scientometrics & Seventh COLLNET Meeting, Nancy, France.

Batagelj, V. (2003). *Efficient algorithms for citation network analysis.* Retrieved February 13, 2007, from arxiv.org/PS_cache/cs/pdf/0309/0309023.pdf

Batagelj, V., & Mrvar, A. (2003). Analysis and visualization of large networks. In M. Jungar & P. Mutzel (Eds.), *Graph drawing software* (pp. 77–103). Berlin: Springer.

Bazerman, C. (1988). *Shaping written knowledge: The genre and activity of the experimental article in science.* Madison: University of Wisconsin Press.

Bean, C. A., & Green, R. (2001). Relevance relationships. In C. A. Bean & R. Green (Eds.), *Relationships in the organization of knowledge* (pp. 115–132). Dordrecht, The Netherlands: Springer.

Beaver, D. D. (1978). Studies in scientific collaboration. Part I. The professional origins of scientific co-authorship. *Scientometrics*, 1(1), 65–84.

Beaver, D. D. (1979). Studies in scientific collaboration. Part II. Scientific co-authorship, research productivity and visibility in the French scientific elite. *Scientometrics*, 1(2), 133–149.

Beaver, D. D., & Rosen, R. (1979). Studies in scientific collaboration. Part III. Professionalization and the natural history of modern scientific co-authorship. *Scientometrics*, 1(3), 231–245.

Beghtol, C. (2001). Relationships in classificatory structure and meaning. In C. A. Bean & R. Green (Eds.), *Relationships in the organization of knowledge* (pp. 99–113). Dordrecht, The Netherlands: Springer.

Beghtol, C. (2003). Classification for information retrieval and classification for knowledge discovery: Relationships between "professional" and "naïve" classifications. *Knowledge Organization*, 30(2), 64–73.

Bellardo, T. (1980). The use of co-citations to study science. *Library Research, 2*, 231–237.

Ben-David, J. (1960). Roles and innovation in medicine. *American Journal of Sociology*, 65(6), 557–568.

Ben-David, J., & Collins, R. (1966). Social factors in the origin of a new science: The case of psychology. *American Sociological Review*, 31(4), 451–465.

Bernal, J. D. (1939). *The social function of science*. London: Routledge.

Bertin, J. (2001). Matrix theory of graphics. *Information Design Journal*, 10(1), 5–19.

Besselaar, P., & Heimeriks, G. (2006). Mapping research topics using word-reference co-occurrences: A method and an exploratory case study. *Scientometrics*, 68, 377–393.

Bezdek, J. C. (1981). *Pattern recognition with fuzzy objective function algorithms.* New York: Plenum Press.

Bloor, D. (1991). *Knowledge and social imagery* (2nd ed.). Chicago: University of Chicago Press.

Bloor, D. (1997). Remember the strong program? *Science, Technology, & Human Values*, 22(3), 373–385.

Bonnevie-Nebelong, E. (2006). Methods for journal evaluation: Journal citation identity, journal citation image and internationalisation. *Scientometrics*, *66*(2), 411.

Borgman, C. L., & Furner, J. (2002). Scholarly communication and bibliometrics. *Annual Review of Information Science and Technology*, *36*, 3–72.

Börner, K., Chen, C., & Boyack, K. W. (2003). Visualizing knowledge domains. *Annual Review of Information Science and Technology*, *37*, 179–255.

Börner, K., Maru, J. T., & Goldstone, R. L. (2004). The simultaneous evolution of author and paper networks. *Proceedings of the National Academy of Science of the United States*, *101*(suppl. 1), 5266–5273.

Boyack, K. W., & Börner, K. (2003). Indicator-assisted evaluation and funding of research: Visualizing the influence of grants on the number and citation counts of research papers. *Journal of the American Society for Information Science and Technology*, *54*(5), 447–461.

Boyack, K. W., Wylie, B. N., & Davidson, G. S. (2002). Domain visualization using VxInsight® for science and technology management. *Journal of the American Society for Information Society and Technology*, *53*(9), 764–774.

Braam, R. R., Moed, H. F., & van Raan, A. F. J. (1991). Mapping of science by combined co-citation and word analysis. I. Structural aspects. *Journal of the American Society for Information Science and Technology*, *42*(4), 233–251.

Brooks, T. A. (1985). Private acts and public objects: An investigation of citer motivations. *Journal of the American Society for Information Science*, *36*(4), 223–229.

Brooks, T. A. (1986). Evidence of complex citer motivations. *Journal of the American Society for Information Science*, *37*(1), 34–36.

Brown, C. M. (1999). Information-seeking behavior of scientists in the electronic information age: Astronomers, chemists, mathematicians, and physicists. *Journal of the American Society for Information Science*, *50*(10), 929–943.

Budd, J. M. (1999). Citation and knowledge claims: Sociology of knowledge as a case in point. *Journal of Information Science*, *25*(4), 265–274.

Budd, J. M. (2001). Misreading science in the twentieth century. *Science Communication*, *22*(3), 300–315.

Budd, J. M., & Hurt, C. D. (1991). Superstring theory: Information transfer in an emerging field. *Scientometrics*, *21*(1), 87–98.

Burrell, Q. L. (2002a). The nth-citation distribution and obsolescence. *Scientometrics*, *53*(3), 309–323.

Burrell, Q. L. (2002b). Will this paper ever be cited? *Journal of the American Society for Information Science and Technology*, *53*(3), 232–235.

Calero, C., Butler, R., Valdés, C. C., & Noyons, E. (2006). How to identify research groups using publication analysis: An example in the field of nanotechnology. *Scientometrics*, *66*(2), 365–376.

Callon, M., Courtial, J. P., & Laville, F. (1991). Co-word analysis as a tool for describing the network of interactions between basic and technological research: The case of polymer chemistry. *Scientometrics*, *22*(1), 155–205.

Callon, M., Courtial, J. P., Turner, W. A., & Bauin, S. (1983). From translations to problematic networks: An introduction to co-word analysis. *Social Sciences Information*, *22*, 191–235.

Callon, M., Law, J., & Rip, A. (1986). Qualitative scientometrics. In M. Callon, J. Law, & A. Rip (Eds.), *Mapping the dynamics of science and technology* (pp. 103–123). London: Macmillan.

Campbell, D. T. (1969). Ethnocentricism of disciplines and the fish-scale model of omniscience. In M. Sherif & C. W. Sherif (Eds.), *Interdisciplinary relationships in the social sciences* (pp. 328–348). Chicago: Aldine Publishing Company.

Case, D. O. (2002). *Looking for information: A survey of research on information seeking, needs, and behavior*. San Diego, CA: Academic Press.

Case, D. O., & Higgins, G. M. (2000). How can we investigate citation behavior? A study of reasons for citing literature in communication. *Journal of the American Society for Information Science, 51*(7), 635–645.

Chen, C. (1999). Visualizing semantic spaces and author co-citation networks in digital libraries. *Information Processing & Management, 35*, 401–420.

Chen, C. (2004). Searching for intellectual turning points: Progressive domain knowledge visualization. *Proceedings of the National Academy of Science of the United States, 101*(suppl. 1), 5303–5310.

Chen, C. (2006). Citespace II: Detecting and visualizing emerging trends and transient patterns in scientific literature. *Journal of the American Society for Information Science and Technology, 57*(3), 359–377.

Chen, C., Cribbin, T., Macredie, R., & Morar, S. (2002). Visualizing and tracking the growth of competing paradigms: Two case studies. *Journal of the American Society for Information Science and Technology, 53*(8), 678–689.

Chen, C., & Hicks, D. (2004). Tracing knowledge diffusion. *Scientometrics, 59*(2), 199–211.

Chen, C., Paul, R. J., & Okeefe, B. (2001). Fitting the jigsaw of citation: Information visualization in domain analysis. *Journal of the American Society for Information Science and Technology, 52*(4), 315–330.

Chen, C. M., & Morris, S. A. (2003, October). *Visualizing evolving networks: Minimum spanning trees versus pathfinder networks*. Paper presented at the IEEE Symposium on Information Visualization, Seattle, Washington.

Chen, P. (1976). The entity-relationship model: Toward a unified view of data. *ACM Transactions on Database Systems, 1*(1), 9–36.

Chubin, D. E. (1976). The conceptualization of scientific specialties. *Sociological Quarterly, 17*(4), 448–476.

Chubin, D. E. (1985). Beyond invisible colleges: Inspirations and aspirations of post-1972 social studies of science. *Scientometrics, 7*(3–6), 221–254.

Chubin, D. E., & Moitra, S. D. (1975). Content analysis of references: Adjunct or alternative to citation counting? *Social Studies of Science, 5*, 423–441.

Cole, J. R. (1989). The paradox of universal particularism and institutional universalism. *Social Science Information, 28*(1), 51–76.

Cole, J. R., & Cole, S. (1972). The Ortega hypothesis: Citation analysis suggests that only a few scientists contribute to scientific progress. *Science, 178*(4059), 368–373.

Cole, J. R., & Zuckerman, H. (1975). The emergence of a scientific specialty: The self-exemplifying case of the sociology of science. In L. A. Coser (Ed.), *The idea of social structure: Papers in honor of Robert K. Merton* (pp. 139–174). New York: Harcourt Brace Jovanovich.

Cole, S. (1970). Professional standing and the reception of scientific discoveries. *American Journal of Sociology, 76*, 286–306.

Cole, S. (1983). The hierarchy of the sciences. *American Journal of Sociology, 89*(1), 111–139.

Cole, S. (1993). *Making science: Between nature and society*. Cambridge, MA: Harvard University Press.

Cole, S. (2000). The role of journals in the growth of scientific knowledge. In B. Cronin & H. B. Atkins (Eds.), *The web of knowledge: A festschrift in honor of Eugene Garfield* (pp. 109–142). Medford, NJ: Information Today, Inc.

Cole, S., & Cole, J. R. (1967). Scientific output and recognition: A study in the operation of the reward system in science. *American Sociological Review, 32*(3), 377–390.

Cole, S., & Cole, J. R. (1973). *Social stratification in science.* Chicago: University of Chicago Press.

Collins, H. M. (1974). The TEA-set: Tacit knowledge and scientific networks. *Science Studies, 4,* 165–186.

Collins, H. M. (1998). The meaning of data: Open and closed evidential cultures in the search for gravitational waves. *American Journal of Sociology, 104*(2), 293–338.

Collins, R. (1968). Competition and social control in science: An essay in theory construction. *Sociology of Education, 41*(2), 123–140.

Collins, R. (1989). Toward a theory of intellectual change: The social causes of philosophies. *Science, Technology, & Human Values, 14*(2), 107–140.

Collins, R. (1998). *The sociology of philosophies: A global theory of intellectual change.* Cambridge, MA: Harvard University Press.

Coulter, N., Monarch, I., & Konda, S. (1998). Software engineering as seen through its research literature: A study in co-word analysis. *Journal of the American Society for Information Science and Technology, 49*(13), 1206–1223.

Courtial, J. P. (1994). A co-word analysis of scientometrics. *Scientometrics, 31*(3), 251–260.

Courtial, J. P. (1998). Comments on Leydesdorff's article. *Journal of the American Society for Information Science, 49*(1), 98.

Courtial, J. P., & Law, J. (1989). A co-word study of artificial intelligence. *Social Studies of Science, 19*(2), 301–311.

Cox, A. (2005). What are communities of practice? A comprehensive review of four seminal works. *Journal of Information Science, 31*(6), 527–540.

Cozzens, S. E. (1985). Using the archive: Derek Price's theory of differences among the sciences. *Scientometrics, 7*(3–6), 431–441.

Cozzens, S. E. (1989a). *Social control and multiple discovery in science: The opiate receptor case.* Albany: State University of New York Press.

Cozzens, S. E. (1989b). What do citations count? The rhetoric-first model. *Scientometrics, 15,* 437–447.

Crane, D. (1969a). Fashion in science: Does it exist? *Social Problems, 16*(4), 433–441.

Crane, D. (1969b). Social structure in a group of scientists: A test of the "invisible college" hypothesis. *American Sociological Review, 34,* 335–352.

Crane, D. (1970). The nature of scientific communication and influence. *International Social Science Journal, 22*(1), 28–41.

Crane, D. (1972). *Invisible colleges: Diffusion of knowledge in scientific communities.* Chicago: University of Chicago Press.

Crane, D. (1976). Reward systems in art, science, and religion. *American Behavioral Scientist, 19*(6), 719–734.

Crane, D. (1980). An exploratory study of Kuhnian paradigms in theoretical high energy physics. *Social Studies of Science, 10,* 23–54.

Crawford, S. (1971). Informal communication among scientists in sleep research. *Journal of the American Society for Information Science, 22*(5), 301–310.

Cronin, B. (1984). *The citation process: The role and significance of citations in scientific communication.* London: Taylor Graham.

Cronin, B. (2004). Normative shaping of scientific practice: The magic of Merton. *Scientometrics, 60*(1), 41–46.

Cronin, B. (2005). *The hand of science: Academic writing and its rewards.* Lanham, MD: Scarecrow Press.

De Mey, M. (1982). *The cognitive paradigm.* Boston: Kluwer Academic.

Diamond, A. M. (1984). An economic model of the life-cycle research productivity of scientists. *Scientometrics, 6,* 189–196.

Diamond, A. M. (1985). The money values of citations to single-authored and multiple-authored articles. *Scientometrics, 8,* 815–820.

Diamond, A. M. (1986). What is a citation worth? *Journal of Human Resources, 21*(2), 200–215.

Diamond, A. M. (2000). The complementarity of scientometrics and economics. In B. Cronin & H. B. Atkins (Eds.), *The web of knowledge: A festchrift in honor of Eugene Garfield* (pp. 321–336). Medford, NJ: Information Today, Inc.

Ding, Y., Chowdhury, G. G., & Foo, S. (2000). Journals as markers of intellectual space: Journal co-citation analysis of information retrieval area, 1987–1997. *Scientometrics, 47*(1), 55–73.

Ding, Y., Chowdhury, G. G., & Foo, S. (2001). Bibliometric cartography of information retrieval research by using co-word analysis. *Information Processing & Management,* 37(6), 817–842.

Duda, R. O., Hart, P. E., & Stork, D. G. (2001). *Pattern classification* (2nd ed.). New York: Wiley.

Edge, D. O. (1979). Quantitative measures of communication in science: A critical review. *History of Science, 17*(2), 102–134.

Egghe, L., & Rousseau, R. (1990). *Introduction to informetrics: Quantitative methods in library, documentation and information science.* Amsterdam: Elsevier.

Egghe, L., & Rousseau, R. (2000). Aging, obsolescence, impact, growth and utilization: Definitions and relations. *Journal of the American Society for Information Science, 51*(11), 1004–1017.

Ennis, J. G. (1992). The social organization of sociological knowledge: Structural models of the intersections of specialties. *American Sociological Review, 57*(2), 259–265.

Eom, S. B. (1996). The contributions of organizational science to the development of decision support systems research subspecialties. *Journal of the American Society for Information Science, 47,* 941–952.

Eom, S. B. (2003). *Author co-citation analysis using custom bibliographic databases: An introduction to the SAS approach.* Lewiston, NY: Edwin Mellen Press.

Etzkowitz, H. (1983). Entrepreneurial scientists and entrepreneurial universities in American academic science. *Minerva, 21,* 198–233.

Etzkowitz, H. (1989). Entrepreneurial science in the academy: A case of the transformation of norms. *Social Problems, 36*(1), 14–29.

Etzkowitz, H., & Leydesdorff, L. (2000). The dynamics of innovation: From national systems and "mode 2" to a triple helix of university-industry-government relations. *Research Policy, 29*(2), 109–123.

Feitelson, D. G., & Yovel, U. (2004). Predictive ranking of computer scientists using CiteSeer data. *Journal of Documentation, 60*(1), 44–61.

Fisher, C. S. (1966). The death of a mathematical theory: A study in the sociology of knowledge. *Archive of the History of Exact Sciences, 3,* 137–159.

Fisher, C. S. (1967). The last invariant theorists: A sociological study of the collective biographies of mathematical specialists. *European Journal of Sociology, 8*(2), 216–244.

Fleck, L. (1979). *Genesis and development of a scientific fact.* Chicago: University of Chicago Press.

Forrest, B. C., & Gross, P. R. (2003). *Creationism's Trojan horse: The wedge of intelligent design.* New York: Oxford University Press.

Freudenthal, G. (1984). The role of shared knowledge in science: The failure of the constructivist programme in the sociology of science. *Social Studies of Science, 14*, 285–295.

Fuchs, S. (1986). The social organization of scientific knowledge. *Sociological Theory, 4*, 126–142.

Fuchs, S. (1993). A sociological theory of scientific change. *Social Forces, 71*(4), 933–953.

Fuchs, S., & Spear, J. H. (1999). The social conditions of cumulation. *American Sociologist, 30*, 21–40.

Fuller, S., De Mey, M., Shinn, T., & Woolgar, S. (1989). *The cognitive turn: Sociological and psychological perspectives on science.* Boston: Kluwer Academic.

Furner, J. (2003). Bibliographic relationships, citation relations, relevance relationships, and bibliographic classification: An integrative view. *Proceedings of the 13th ASIST SIG/CR Classification Research Workshop*, 42–52.

Garfield, E. (1955). Citation index for science: A new dimension in documentation through association of ideas. *Science, 122*(3159), 108–111.

Garfield, E. (1968). World brain or "Memex": Mechanical and intellectual requirements for universal bibliographic control. In E. B. Montgomery (Ed.), *The foundations of access to knowledge: A symposium* (pp. 169–196). Syracuse, NY: Syracuse University Press.

Garfield, E. (1979). *Citation indexing: Its theory and application in science, technology, and humanities.* New York: Wiley.

Garfield, E. (1994). Research fronts. *Current Contents, 41*, 3–7.

Garfield, E. (2004a). The intended consequences of Robert K. Merton. *Scientometrics, 60*(1), 51–61.

Garfield, E. (2004b). The unintended and unanticipated consequences of Robert K. Merton. *Social Studies of Science, 34*(6), 845–853.

Garfield, E., Pudovkin, A. I., & Istomin, V. S. (2003). Mapping the output of topical searches in the Web of Knowledge and the case of Watson-Crick. *Information Technology and Libraries, 22*(4), 183–187.

Garfield, E., Sher, I. H., & Torpie, R. J. (1964). *The use of citation data in writing the history of science.* Philadelphia: Institute for Scientific Information.

Garvey, W. D., & Griffith, B. C. (1967). Scientific communication as a social system. *Science, 157*(3792), 1011–1016.

Gaston, J. (1970). The reward system in British science. *American Sociological Review, 35*(4), 718–732.

Gaston, J. (1973). *Originality and competition in science: A study of the British high energy physics community.* Chicago: University of Chicago Press.

Geison, G. L. (1993). Research schools and new directions in the historiography of science. *Osiris, 8*, 226–238.

Ghoniem, M., Fekete, J., & Castagliola, P. (2005). On the readability of graphs using node-link and matrix-based representations: A controlled experiment and statistical analysis. *Information Visualization, 4*, 114–135.

Gibbons, M., Limoges, C., Nowotny, H., Schwartzman, S., Scott, P., & Trow, M. (1994). *The new production of knowledge: The dynamics of science and research in contemporary society*. London: Sage.

Gieryn, T. F. (1983). Boundary-work and the demarcation of science from non-science: Strains and interests in professional ideologies of scientists. *American Sociological Review, 48*, 781–795.

Gieryn, T. F. (1999). *Cultural boundaries of science: Credibility on the line*. Chicago: University of Chicago Press.

Gilbert, G. N. (1977). Referencing as persuasion. *Social Studies of Science, 7*, 113–122.

Gordon, A. D. (1999). *Classification* (2nd ed.). Boca Raton, FL: Chapman & Hall/CRC.

Granovetter, M. S. (1973). The strength of weak ties. *American Journal of Sociology, 778*(6), 1360–1380.

Green, R. (2001). Relations in the organization of knowledge: An overview. In C. A. Bean & R. Green (Eds.), *Relationships in the organization of knowledge* (pp. 3–18). Dordrecht, The Netherlands: Springer.

Griffith, B. C., & Mullins, N. C. (1972). Coherent social groups in scientific change. *Science, 177*(4053), 959–964.

Griffith, B. C., Small, H. G., Stonehill, J. A., & Dey, S. (1974). The structure of scientific literatures II: Toward a macro- and microstructure of science. *Science Studies, 4*, 339–365.

Hagstrom, W. O. (1965). *The scientific community*. New York: Basic Books.

Hargens, L. L. (2000). Using the literature: Reference networks, reference contexts, and the social structure of scholarship. *American Sociological Review, 65*(6), 846–865.

Hargens, L. L. (2004). What is Mertonian sociology of science? *Scientometrics, 60*(1), 63–70.

Hargens, L. L., & Felmlee, D. H. (1984). Structural determinants of stratification in science. *American Sociological Review, 49*(5), 685–697.

Hargens, L. L., Mullins, N. C., & Hecht, P. K. (1980). Research areas and stratification processes in science. *Social Studies of Science, 10*(1), 56–74.

Hedges, L. V. (1987). How hard is hard science, how soft is soft science?: The empirical cumulativeness of research. *American Psychologist, 42*, 443–455.

He, Q. (1999). Knowledge discovery through co-word analysis. *Library Trends, 48*(1), 131–159.

Hetzler, E., & Turner, A. (2004). Analysis experiences using information visualization. *IEEE Computer Graphics and Applications, 24*(5), 22–26.

Hjørland, B., & Nielsen, L. K. (2001). Subject access points in electronic retrieval. *Annual Review of Information Science and Technology, 35*, 249–298.

Hjørland, B., & Pedersen, K. N. (2005). A substantive theory of classification for information retrieval. *Journal of Documentation, 61*(5), 582–597.

Holloway, T., Bozicevic, M., & Börner, K. (2007). Analyzing and visualizing the semantic coverage of Wikipedia and its authors. *Complexity, 12*(3), 30–40.

Holton, G. (1993). *Science and anti-science*. Cambridge, MA: Harvard University Press.

Holzner, B. (1968). *Reality construction in society*. Cambridge, MA: Schenkman.

Hoyningen-Huene, P. (1993). *Reconstructing scientific revolutions: Thomas S. Kuhn's philosophy of science* (A. T. Levine, Trans.). Chicago: University of Chicago Press.

Hurt, C. D., & Budd, J. M. (1992). Modeling the literature of superstring theory: A case study of fast literature. *Scientometrics, 24*(3), 471–480.

Hwang, K. (2005). The inferior science and the dominant use of English in knowledge production. *Science Communication, 26*(4), 390–427.

Hyland, K. (2004). *Disciplinary discourses: Social interactions in academic writing.* Ann Arbor: University of Michigan Press.

Jacob, E. K. (2004). Classification and categorization: A difference that makes a difference. *Library Trends, 52*(3), 515–540.

Jarneving, B. (2001). The cognitive structure of current cardiovascular research. *Scientometrics, 50*(3), 365–389.

Jarneving, B. (2005). A comparison of two bibliometric methods for the mapping of the research front. *Scientometrics, 65*(2), 245–263.

Jin, B., Rousseau, R., Suttmeier, R. P., & Cao, C. (2007, June). *The role of ethnic ties in international collaboration: The overseas Chinese phenomenon.* Paper presented at the International Conference on Scientometrics and Informatics, Madrid, Spain.

Jones, W. P., & Furnas, G. W. (1987). Pictures of relevance: A geometrical analysis of similarity measures. *Journal of the American Society for Information Science and Technology, 38*(6), 420–442.

Kärki, R. (1996). Searching for bridges between disciplines: An author co-citation analysis on the research into scholarly communication. *Journal of Information Science, 22*(5), 323–334.

Katz, J. S., & Martin, B. R. (1997). What is research collaboration? *Research Policy, 26*, 1–18.

Kaufer, D. S., & Carley, K. M. (1993). *Communication at a distance: The influence of print on sociocultural organization and change.* Hillsdale, NJ: Erlbaum.

Kessler, M. M. (1963). Bibliographic coupling between scientific papers. *American Documentation, 14*, 10–25.

Kim, K.-M. (1994). *Explaining scientific consensus: The case of Mendelian genetics.* New York: Guilford Press.

Kim, K.-M. (1996). Hierarchy of scientific consensus and the flow of dissensus over time. *Philosophy of the Social Sciences, 26*, 3–25.

Kinchy, A. J., & Kleinman, D. L. (2003). Organizing credibility: Discursive and organizational orthodoxy on the borders of ecology and politics. *Social Studies of Science, 33*(6), 869–896.

Knorr, K. D. (1975). The nature of scientific consensus and the case of social sciences. In K. D. Knorr, H. Strasser, & H. G. Zilian (Eds.), *Determinants and controls of scientific development.* Boston: D. Reidel.

Knorr Cetina, K. (1991). Epistemic cultures: Forms of reason in science. *History of Political Economy, 23*(1), 105–122.

Knorr Cetina, K. D. (1981). *The manufacture of knowledge: An essay on the constructivist and contextual nature of science.* Oxford, UK: Pergamon.

Knorr Cetina, K. D. (1982). Scientific communities or transepistemic arenas of research?: A critique of quasi-economic models of science. *Social Studies of Science, 12*(1), 101–130.

Kostoff, R. N., del Rio, J. A., Hunenik, J. A., Garcia, E. O., & Ramirez, A. M. (2001). Citation mining: Integrating text mining and bibliometrics for research user profiling. *Journal of the American Society for Information Science and Technology, 52*(13), 1148–1156.

Krauze, T. K. (1972). Social and intellectual structures of science: A mathematical analysis. *Science Studies, 2*, 369–393.

Kretschmer, H., Hoffmann, U., & Kretschmer, T. (2006). Collaboration structures between German immunology institutions, and gender visibility, as reflected in the Web. *Research Evaluation, 15*(2), 117–126.

Kruskal, J. B., & Wish, M. (1978). *Multidimensional scaling.* Beverly Hills, CA: Sage.

Kuhn, T. S. (1970). *The structure of scientific revolutions* (2nd, enlarged ed.). Chicago: University of Chicago Press.

Kuhn, T. S. (2000). Afterword. In J. Conant & J. Haugeland (Eds.), *The road since structure: Philosophical essays 1970–1983, with an autobiographical interview* (pp. 224–252). Chicago: University of Chicago Press.

Latour, B. (1987). *Science in action: How to follow scientists and engineers through society.* Milton Keynes, UK: The Open University Press.

Latour, B. (2005). *Reassembling the social: An introduction to actor-network theory.* New York: Oxford University Press.

Latour, B., & Woolgar, S. (1986). *Laboratory life: The construction of scientific knowledge* (2nd ed.). Princeton, NJ: Princeton University Press.

Laudan, L., Donovan, A., Laudan, R., Barker, P., Brown, H., Lepllin, J., et al. (1986). Scientific change: Philosophical models and historical research. *Synthese, 69*, 141–223.

Laudel, G. (2002). What do we measure by co-authorships? *Research Evaluation, 11*(1), 3–15.

Law, J., & Whitaker, J. (1992). Mapping acidification research: A test of the co-word method. *Scientometrics, 23*(3), 417–461.

Leazer, G. H., & Smiraglia, R. P. (1999). Bibliographic families in the library catalog: A qualitative analysis and grounded theory. *Library Resources & Technical Services, 43*(4), 191–212.

Lewis, G. L. (1980). The relationship of conceptual development to consensus: An exploratory analysis of three subfields. *Social Studies of Science, 10*(3), 285–308.

Leydesdorff, L. (1994). The generation of aggregated journal-journal citation maps on the basis of the CD-ROM version of the Science Citation Index. *Scientometrics, 31*(1), 59–84.

Leydesdorff, L. (1997). Why words and co-words cannot map the development of the sciences. *Journal of the American Society for Information Science, 48,* 418–427.

Leydesdorff, L. (2001a). *The challenge of scientometrics: The development, measurement, and self-organization of scientific communications.* Parkland, FL: Universal Publishers.

Leydesdorff, L. (2001b). *A sociological theory of communication: Self organization of the knowledge society.* Parkland, FL: Universal Publishers.

Leydesdorff, L. (2005). Similarity measures, author cocitation analysis, and information theory. *Journal of the American Society for Information Science and Technology, 56*(7), 769–772.

Leydesdorff, L. (2006). Can scientific journals be classified in terms of aggregated journal-journal citation relations using the Journal Citation Reports? *Journal of the American Society for Information Science and Technology, 57*(5), 601–613.

Leydesdorff, L., & Amsterdamska, O. (1990). Dimensions of citation analysis. *Science, Technology, & Human Values, 15*(3), 305–335.

Leydesdorff, L., & Etzkowitz, H. (1996). Emergence of a triple helix of university-industry-government relations. *Science and Public Policy, 23*, 279–286.

Leydesdorff, L., & Etzkowitz, H. (1998). The triple helix as a model for innovation studies. *Science and Public Policy, 25*(3), 195–203.

Leydesdorff, L., & Vaughan, L. (2006). Co-occurrence matrices and their applications in information science: Extending ACA to the Web environment. *Journal of the American Society for Information Science and Technology, 57*(12), 1616–1628.

Lievrouw, L. A. (1990). Reconciling structure and process in the study of scholarly communication. In C. L. Borgman (Ed.), *Scholarly communication and bibliometrics* (pp. 59–69). Newbury Park, CA: Sage.

Lievrouw, L. A. (1992). Communication, representation, and scientific knowledge: A conceptual framework and case study. *Knowledge and Policy, 5*(1), 6–28.

Liu, Z. (2005). Visualizing the intellectual structure in urban studies: A journal co-citation analysis (1992–2002). *Scientometrics, 62*(3), 385–402.

Lotka, A. J. (1926). The frequency distribution of scientific productivity. *Journal of the Washington Academy of Sciences, 16,* 317–323.

Lubetzky, S. (1969). *Principles of cataloging.* Los Angeles: University of California Institute of Library Research.

Luukkonen, T. (1997). Why has Latour's theory of citations been ignored by the bibliometric community? *Scientometrics, 38*(1), 27–37.

MacRoberts, M. H., & MacRoberts, B. R. (1989). Problems of citation analysis: A critical review. *Journal of the American Society for Information Science, 40*(5), 342–349.

Mählck, P., & Persson, O. (2000). Socio-bibliometric mapping of intra-departmental networks. *Scientometrics, 49*(1), 81–91.

Mai, J.-E. (2004). Classification in context: Relativity, reality and representation. *Knowledge Organization, 31*(1), 39–48.

Marion, L. (2004). *Of tribes and totems: Author co-citation analysis of Kurt Lewin's influence on social science journals.* Unpublished doctoral dissertation, Drexel University, Philadelphia.

Markey, K. (2007). The online library catalog: Paradise lost and paradise regained. *D-Lib, 13*(1/2). Retrieved February 4, 2007, from www.dlib.org/dlib/january07/markey/01markey.html

Martyn, J. (1964). Bibliographic coupling. *Journal of Documentation, 20*(4), 236.

Martyn, J. (1975). Citation analysis. *Journal of Documentation, 31*(4), 290–297.

Masterman, M. (1970). The nature of a paradigm. In I. Lakatos & A. Musgrove (Eds.), *Criticism and the growth of knowledge* (pp. 59–89). Chicago: University of Chicago Press.

McCain, K. W. (1990). Mapping authors in intellectual space: A technical overview. *Journal of the American Society for Information Science, 41*(6), 433–444.

McCain, K. W. (1991). Mapping economics through the journal literature: An experiment in journal cocitation analysis. *Journal of the American Society for Information Science, 42*(4), 290–296.

McCain, K. W. (1998). Neural networks research in context: A longitudinal journal cocitation analysis of an emerging interdisciplinary field. *Scientometrics, 41*(3), 389–410.

McCain, K. W., & McCain, R. A. (2002). Mapping "A Beautiful Mind": A comparison of the author cocitation PFNets for John Nash, John Harsanyi, and Reinhard Selten: The three winners of the 1994 Nobel prize for economics. *Proceedings of the Annual Meeting of the American Society for Information Science and Technology,* 552–553.

McCain, K. W., Verner, J. M., Hislop, G. W., Evanco, W., & Cole, V. (2005). The use of bibliometric and knowledge elicitation techniques to map a knowledge domain: Software engineering in the 1990s. *Scientometrics, 65*(1), 131–144.

Melin, G., & Persson, O. (1996). Studying research collaboration using co-authorships. *Scientometrics, 36*(3), 363–377.

Mellor, F. (2003). Between fact and fiction: Demarcating science from non-science in popular physics books. *Social Studies of Science, 33*(4), 509–538.

Merton, R. K. (1957). Priorities in scientific discovery: A chapter in the sociology of science. *American Sociological Review, 22*(6), 635–659.

Merton, R. K. (1968). The Matthew effect in science: The reward and communication system of science. *Science, 159*(3810), 56–63.

Merton, R. K. (1973). The normative structure of science. In N. W. Storer (Ed.), *The sociology of science: Theoretical and empirical investigations* (pp. 267–278). Chicago: University of Chicago Press.

Merton, R. K. (1988). The Matthew effect in science, II: Cumulative advantage and the symbolism of intellectual property. *Isis, 79*(4), 606–623.

Michaelson, A. G. (1993). The development of a scientific specialty as diffusion through social relations: The case of role analysis. *Social Networks, 15*(3), 217–236.

Miksa, F. L. (1998). *The DDC, the universe of knowledge, and the post-modern library*. Albany NY: Forest Press.

Moed, H. F. (2005). *Citation analysis in research evaluation*. Dordrecht, The Netherlands: Springer.

Moravcsik, M. J., & Murugesan, P. (1975). Some results on the function and quality of citations. *Social Studies of Science, 5*, 86–92.

Moravcsik, M. J., & Murugesan, P. (1979). Citation patterns in scientific revolutions. *Scientometrics, 1*(2), 161–169.

Morris, S. A. (2005a). Manifestation of emerging specialties in journal literature: A growth model of papers, references, exemplars, bibliographic coupling, co-citation, and clustering coefficient distribution. *Journal of the American Society for Information Science and Technology, 56*(12), 1250–1273.

Morris, S. A. (2005b). *Unified mathematical treatment of complex cascaded bipartite networks: The case of collections of journal papers*. Unpublished doctoral dissertation, Oklahoma State University, Stillwater.

Morris, S. A., & Boyack, K. W. (2005, July). *Visualizing 60 years of anthrax research*. Paper presented at the 10th International Conference of the International Society for Scientometrics and Informetrics, Stockholm, Sweden.

Morris, S. A., & Yen, G. (2004). Crossmaps: Visualization of overlapping relationships in collections of journal papers. *Proceedings of the National Academy of Sciences, 101*(suppl. 1), 5291–5296.

Morris, S. A., Yen, G., Wu, Z., & Asnake, B. (2003). Time line visualization of research fronts. *Journal of the American Society for Information Science and Technology, 54*(5), 413–422.

Mukerji, C., & Simon, B. (1998). Out of the limelight: Discredited communities and informal communication on the Internet. *Sociological Inquiry, 68*(2), 258–273.

Mulkay, M. J. (1971). Some suggestions for sociological research. *Science Studies, 1*, 207–213.

Mulkay, M. J. (1975). Three models of scientific development. *Sociological Review, 23*, 509–526.

Mulkay, M. J. (1976). The model of branching. *Sociological Review, 24*(1), 125–133.

Mulkay, M. J., & Edge, D. O. (1976). Cognitive, technical and social factors in the growth of radio astronomy. In G. Lemaine, R. MacLeod, M. J. Mulkay, & P. Weingart (Eds.), *Perspectives on the emergence of scientific disciplines* (pp. 153–186). Chicago: Aldine.

Mulkay, M. J., Gilbert, G. N., & Woolgar, S. (1975). Problem areas and research networks in science. *Sociology, 9*(2), 187–203.

Mullins, N. C. (1972). The development of a scientific specialty: The phage group and the origins of molecular biology. *Minerva, 10*(1), 51–82.

Mullins, N. C. (1973). *Theories and theory groups in contemporary American sociology*. New York: Harper & Row.

Mullins, N. C., Hargens, L. L., Hecht, P. K., & Kick, E. L. (1977). The group structure of cocitation clusters: A comparative study. *American Sociological Review, 42*(4), 552–562.

Myers, G. (1990). *Writing biology: Texts in the social construction of scientific knowledge*. Madison: University of Wisconsin Press.

Naranan, S. (1971). Power law relations in science bibliography: A self-consistent interpretation. *Journal of Documentation, 27*(2), 83–97.

Narin, F. (1975). *Evaluative bibliometrics*. Cherry Hill, NJ: Computer Horizons.

Nebelong-Bonnevie, E., & Frandsen, T. F. (2006). Journal citation identity and journal citation image: A portrait of the *Journal of Documentation*. *Journal of Documentation, 62*(1), 30–57.

Neuhaus, C., Neuhaus, E., Asher, A., & Wrede, C. (2006). The depth and breadth of Google Scholar: An empirical study. *portal: Libraries and the Academy, 6*(2), 127–141.

Newman, M. E. J. (2000). *Who is the best connected scientist? A study of scientific coauthorship networks* (SFI Working Paper 00-12-064). Santa Fe, NM: Santa Fe Institute.

Newman, M. E. J. (2001a). Scientific collaboration networks I: Network construction and fundamental results. *Physical Review E, 64*, 016131.

Newman, M. E. J. (2001b). Scientific collaboration networks II: Shortest paths, weighted networks, and centrality. *Physical Review E, 64*, 016132.

Newman, M. E. J. (2001c). The structure of scientific collaboration networks. *Proceedings of the National Academy of Sciences, 98*, 404–409.

Newman, M. E. J. (2004). Coauthorship networks and patterns of scientific collaboration. *Proceedings of the National Academy of Sciences, 101*(1), 5200–5205.

Nicholas, D., & Ritchie, M. (1978). *Literature and bibliometrics*. London: Clive Bingley.

Nicolaisen, J. (2003). The social act of citing: Towards new horizons in citation theory. *Proceedings of the Annual Meeting of the American Society for Information Science and Technology*, 12–20.

Nicolaisen, J. (2007). Citation analysis. *Annual Review of Information Science and Technology, 41*, 609–641.

Noyons, E. (2001). Bibliographic mapping of science in a science policy context. *Scientometrics, 50*(1), 83–98.

Nowotny, H., Scott, P., & Gibbons, M. (2001). *Rethinking science: Knowledge and the public in an age of uncertainty*. Malden, MA: Blackwell.

Oehler, K., Snizek, W. E., & Mullins, N. C. (1989). Words and sentences over time: How facts are built and sustained in a specialty area. *Science, Technology, & Human Values, 14*(3), 258–274.

Olson, H. A. (1998). Mapping beyond Dewey's boundaries: Constructing classificatory space for marginalized knowledge domains. *Library Trends, 47*(2), 233–254.

Oppenheim, C., & Renn, S. P. (1979). Highly cited old papers and the reasons why they continue to be cited. *Journal of the American Society for Information Science, 29*(5), 225–231.

Paisley, W. J. (1968). Information needs and uses. *Annual Review of Information Science and Technology, 1*, 1–30.

Pao, M. L. (1992). Global and local collaborators: A study of scientific collaboration. *Information Processing & Management, 28*(1), 99–109.

Persson, O. (1994). The intellectual base and research fronts of *JASIS* 1986–1990. *Journal of the American Society for Information Science and Technology, 45*(1), 31–38.

Persson, O. (2001). All author citations versus first author citations. *Scientometrics, 50*(2), 339–344.

Persson, O., & Beckmann, M. (1995). Locating the network of interacting authors in scientific specialities. *Scientometrics, 33*(3), 351–366.

Peters, H. P. F., & van Raan, A. F. J. (1991). Structuring scientific activities by co-author analysis: An exercise on a university faculty level. *Scientometrics, 20*(1), 235–255.

Porter, A. L., Roper, A. T., Mason, T. W., Rossini, F. A., & Banks, J. (1991). *Forecasting and management of technology.* New York: Wiley.

Price, D. J. D. (1963). *Little science, big science.* New York: Columbia University Press.

Price, D. J. D. (1965). Networks of scientific papers. *Science, 149*(3683), 510–515.

Price, D. J. D. (1970). Citation measures of hard science, soft science, technology and nonscience. In C. E. Nelson & D. K. Pollock (Eds.), *Communication among scientists and engineers* (pp. 3–15). Lexington, MA: Heath-Lexington Books.

Price, D. J. D. (1986). Invisible colleges and the affluent scientific commuter. In *Little science, big science ... and beyond* (pp. 56–81). New York: Columbia University Press.

Price, D. J. D., & Beaver, D. D. (1966). Collaboration in an invisible college. *American Psychologist, 21*, 1011–1018.

Ravetz, J. R. (1971). *Scientific knowledge and its social problems.* Oxford, UK: Oxford University Press.

Reader, D., & Watkins, D. (2006). The social and collaborative nature of entrepreneurship scholarship: A co-citation and perceptual analysis. *Entrepreneurship Theory and Practice, 30*(3), 417–441.

Redner, S. (1998). How popular is your paper? An empirical study of the citation distribution. *European Physical Journal B, 4*(2), 131–134.

Reid, E., & Chen, H. (2005). Mapping the contemporary terrorism research domain: Researchers, publications, and institutions analysis. In P. Kantor, G. Muresan, F. Roberts, D. Zeng, F.-Y. Wang, H. Chen, & R. Merkle (Eds.), *Intelligence and Security Informatics* (Lecture Notes in Computer Science 3495, pp. 322–339). Berlin: Springer.

Rheingold, N. (1980). Through paradigm-land to a normal history of science. *Social Studies of Science, 10*(4), 475–496.

Rip, A., & Courtial, J. P. (1984). Co-word maps of biotechnology: An example of cognitive scientometrics. *Scientometrics, 6*, 381–400.

Rogers, E. M. (1962). *Diffusion of innovation.* New York: Free Press.

Rogers, E. M., Dearing, J. W., & Bregman, D. (1993). The anatomy of agenda setting research. *Journal of Communication, 43*(2), 68–84.

Rose, S. K. (1996). What's love got to do with it?: Scholarly citation practices as courtship rituals. *Language and Learning Across the Disciplines, 1*(3), 34–48.

Rosengren, K. E. (1968). *Sociological aspects of the literary system.* Stockholm: Natur och Kultur.

Rouse, J. (1993). What are cultural studies of scientific knowledge? *Configurations, 1*(1), 57–94.

Rousseau, R., & Zuccala, A. (2004). A classification of author co-citations: Definitions and search strategies. *Journal of the American Society for Information Society and Technology, 55*(6), 513.

Salton, G. (1989). *Automatic text processing: The transformation, analysis, and retrieval of information by computer.* Reading, MA: Addison-Wesley.

Sandstrom, P. E. (2001). Scholarly communication as a socioecological system. *Scientometrics, 51*(3), 573–605.

Saracevic, T. (1975). Relevance: A review of and a framework for the thinking on the notion in information science. *Journal of the American Society for Information Science, 26*(6), 321–343.

Sawyer, R. K. (2001). Emergence in sociology: Contemporary philosophy of mind and some implications for sociological theory. *American Journal of Sociology, 107*(3), 551–585.

Schneider, J. W. (2006). Concept symbols revisited, naming clusters by parsing and filtering noun phrases from citation context of concept symbols. *Scientometrics, 68*(3), 573–593.

Schneider, J. W., & Borlund, P. (2005). A bibliometric-based semi-automatic approach to identification of candidate thesaurus terms: Parsing and filtering of noun phrases from citation contexts. *Proceedings of the 5th International Conference on Conceptions of Library and Information Sciences* (Lecture Notes in Computer Science, 3507), 226–237.

Schvaneveldt, R. W., Durso, F. T., & Dearholt, D. W. (1989). Network structures in proximity data. *Psychology of Learning and Motivation, 24,* 249–284.

Scott, E. C., & Cole, H. P. (1985). The elusive scientific basis of creation "science." *Quarterly Review of Biology, 60*(1), 21–30.

Seglen, P. O. (1992). The skewness of science. *Journal of the American Society for Information Science, 43*(9), 628–638.

Seglen, P. O., & Aksnes, D. W. (2000). Scientific productivity and group size: A bibliometric analysis of Norwegian microbiological research. *Scientometrics, 49*(1), 125–143.

Shepard, H. (1954). The value system of a university research group. *American Sociological Review, 19*(4), 456–462.

Shepard, H. A. (1956). Basic research and the social system of pure science. *Philosophy of Science, 23*(1), 48–57.

Shinn, T. (1999). Change or mutation? Reflections on the foundations of contemporary science. *Social Science Information, 3*(1), 149–176.

Shinn, T. (2002). The triple helix and new production of knowledge: Prepackaged thinking on science and technology. *Social Studies of Science, 32*(4), 599–614.

Shrum, W. (1984). Scientific specialties and technical systems. *Social Studies of Science, 14*(1), 63–90.

Siirtola, H., & Makinen, E. (2005). Constructing and reconstructing the reorderable matrix. *Information Visualization, 4,* 32–48.

Simon, B. (2002). *Undead science: Science studies and the afterlife of cold fusion.* New Brunswick, NJ: Rutgers University Press.

Sinding, C. (1996). Literary genres and the construction of knowledge in biology: Semantic shifts and scientific change. *Social Studies of Science, 26*(1), 43–70.

Small, H. (2006). Tracking and predicting growth areas in science. *Scientometrics, 68*(3), 595.

Small, H. G. (1973). Cocitation in scientific literature: New measure of relationship between 2 documents. *Journal of the American Society for Information Science, 24*(4), 265–269.

Small, H. G. (1974). Multiple citation patterns in scientific literature: The circle and hill models. *Information Storage & Retrieval, 10*(11–12), 393–402.

Small, H. G. (1978). Cited documents as concept symbols. *Social Studies of Science, 8*, 327–340.

Small, H. G. (1980). Co-citation context analysis and the structure of paradigms. *Journal of Documentation, 36*(3), 183–196.

Small, H. G. (1985). Citation context analysis. In B. Dervin & M. Voight (Eds.), *Progress in Communication Sciences* (pp. 287–310). Norwood, NJ: Ablex.

Small, H. G. (1986). The synthesis of specialty narratives from co-citation clusters. *Journal of the American Society for Information Science, 37*(3), 97–110.

Small, H. G. (1997). Update on science mapping: Creating large document spaces. *Scientometrics, 38*(2), 275–293.

Small, H. G. (1998). A general framework for creating large-scale maps of science in two or three dimensions: The SciViz system. *Scientometrics, 41*(1), 125–133.

Small, H. G. (1999). Visualizing science by citation mapping. *Journal of the American Society for Information Science and Technology, 50*(9), 799–813.

Small, H. G. (2004). On the shoulders of Robert Merton: Towards a normative theory of citation. *Scientometrics, 60*(1), 71–79.

Small, H. G., & Crane, D. (1979). Specialties and disciplines in science and social science: An examination of their structure using citation indexes. *Scientometrics, 1*(5–6), 445–461.

Small, H. G., & Greenlee, E. (1980). Citation context analysis of a co-citation cluster: Recombinant DNA. *Scientometrics, 2*(4), 277–301.

Small, H. G., & Greenlee, E. (1989). A co-citation study of AIDS research. *Communication Research, 16*(5), 642–666.

Small, H. G., & Griffith, B. C. (1974). The structure of scientific literature I: Identifying and graphing specialties. *Science Studies, 4*, 17–40.

Small, H. G., & Sweeney, E. (1985). Clustering the science citation index using co-citations I: A comparison of methods. *Scientometrics, 7*(3–6), 391–409.

Smiraglia, R. P. (2001). Works as signs, symbols and canons: The epistemology of the work. *Knowledge Organization, 28*, 192–202.

Smiraglia, R. P. (2002a). Further reflections on the nature of "a work": An introduction. *Cataloging & Classification Quarterly, 33*(3/4), 1–11.

Smiraglia, R. P. (2002b). The progress of theory in knowledge organization. *Library Trends, 50* (3), 530–549.

Smith, L. C. (1981). Citation analysis. *Library Trends, 30*, 83–106.

Solomon, M. (1994). Multivariate models of scientific change. *Proceedings of the Biennial Meeting of the Philosophy of Science Association* (vol. 2), 287–297.

Stahl, W. A., Campbell, R. A., Petry, Y., & Diver, G. (2002). *Webs of reality: Social perspectives on science and religion.* New Brunswick, NJ: Rutgers University Press.

Stewart, J. A. (1983). Achievement and ascriptive processes in the recognition of scientific articles. *Social Forces, 62*(1), 166–189.

Stokes, T. D., & Hartley, A. J. (1989). Coauthorship, social structure and influence within specialties. *Social Studies of Science, 19*(1), 101–125.

Storer, N. W. (1966). *The social system of science.* New York: Holt, Rinehart and Winston.

Subramanyam, K. (1983). Bibliometric studies of research collaboration. *Journal of Information Science, 6*, 33–38.

Svenonius, E. (2004). The epistemological foundations of knowledge representations. *Library Trends, 52*(3), 571–587.

Swales, J. M. (1990). *Genre analysis: English in academic and research settings.* New York: Cambridge University Press.

Swales, J. M. (2004). *Research genres: Explorations and applications.* New York: Cambridge University Press.

Swanson, D. R. (1986). Undiscovered public knowledge. *Library Quarterly, 56*(2), 103–118.

Swanson, D. R. (1987). Two medical literatures that are logically but not bibliographically connected. *Journal of the American Society for Information Science, 38*, 228–233.

Taylor, R. S. (1986). *Value-added processes in information systems.* Norwood, NJ: Ablex Publishing Corp.

Tenopir, C., King, D. W., Boyce, P., & Grayson, M. (2005). Relying on electronic journals: Reading patterns of astronomers. *Journal of the American Society for Information Science and Technology, 56*(8), 786–802.

Thelwall, M., Vaughan, L., & Björneborn, L. (2005). Webometrics. *Annual Review of Information Science and Technology, 39*, 81–135.

Thompson, P. (2005). Text mining, names and security. *Journal of Database Management, 16*(1), 54–59.

Tillett, B. B. (1991). A taxonomy of bibliographic relationships. *Library Resources & Technical Services, 35*(2), 150–158.

Tillett, B. B. (2001). Bibliographical relationships. In C. A. Bean & R. Green (Eds.), *Relationships in the organization of knowledge* (pp. 19–35). Dordrecht, The Netherlands: Springer.

Toulmin, S. E. (1970). Does the distinction between normal and revolutionary science hold water? In I. Lakatos & A. Musgrave (Eds.), *Criticism and the growth of knowledge* (pp. 39–50). New York: Cambridge University Press.

Tsay, M. Y., Xu, H., & Wu, C. W. (2003). Journal co-citation analysis of semiconductor literature. *Scientometrics, 57*(1), 7–25.

Tuckman, B. W., & Jensen, M. A. C. (1977). Stages of small-group development revisited. *Group & Organization Studies, 2*(4), 419–427.

Tufte, E. R. (2001). *The visual display of quantitative information* (2nd ed.). Cheshire, CT: Graphic Press.

Valente, T. W., & Rogers, E. M. (1995). The origins and development of the diffusion of innovations paradigm as an example of scientific growth. *Science Communication, 16*(3), 242–273.

Van den Besselaar, P., & Leydesdorff, L. (1996). Mapping change in scientific specialties: A scientometric reconstruction of the development of artificial intelligence. *Journal of the American Society for Information Science, 47*(6), 415–436.

Van der Veer Martens, B., & Goodrum, A. (2006). The diffusion of theories: A functional approach. *Journal of the American Society for Information Science and Technology, 57*(3), 330-341.

Weinberg, B. H. (1974). Bibliographic coupling: A review. *Information Storage & Retrieval, 10*, 189–196.

White, H. D. (1990). Author co-citation analysis: Overview and defense. In C. L. Borgman (Ed.), *Scholarly communication and bibliometrics* (pp. 84–106). Newbury Park, CA: Sage.

White, H. D. (2001). Authors as citers over time. *Journal of the American Society for Information Science and Technology, 52*(2), 87–108.

White, H. D. (2004a). Author cocitation analysis and Pearson's r: Reply. *Journal of the American Society for Information Society and Technology, 55*(9), 843.

White, H. D. (2004b). Citation analysis and discourse analysis revisited. *Applied Linguistics, 25*(1), 89–116.

White, H. D., & Griffith, B. C. (1981). Author cocitation: A literature measure of intellectual structure. *Journal of the American Society for Information Science, 32*(3), 163–172.

White, H. D., & Griffith, B. C. (1982). Authors as markers of intellectual space: Cocitation in studies of science, technology, and society. *Journal of Documentation, 38*(4), 255–272.

White, H. D., & McCain, K. W. (1989). Bibliometrics. *Annual Review of Information Science and Technology, 24,* 119–186.

White, H. D., & McCain, K. W. (1997). Visualization of literatures. *Annual Review of Information Science and Technology, 32,* 99–168.

White, H. D., & McCain, K. W. (1998). Visualizing a discipline: An author co-citation analysis of information science, 1972–1995. *Journal of the American Society for Information Science, 49*(4), 327–356.

Whitley, R. (1972). Black boxism and the sociology of science: A discussion of the major developments in the field. *Sociology Review Monographs, 18,* 61–92.

Whitley, R. (1976). Umbrella and polytheistic scientific disciplines and their elites. *Social Studies of Science, 6*(3/4), 471–497.

Whitley, R. (2000). *The intellectual and social organization of the sciences* (2nd ed.). Oxford, UK: Oxford University Press.

Wilson, P. (1968). *Two kinds of power: An essay on bibliographic control.* Berkeley, CA: University of California Press.

Woolgar, S. W. (1976). The identification and definition of scientific collectivities. In G. Lemaine, R. Macleod, M. Mulkay, & P. Weingart (Eds.), *Perspectives on the emergence of scientific disciplines* (pp. 233–245). Chicago: Aldine.

Wouters, P. D. (1999). *The citation culture.* Unpublished doctoral dissertation, University of Amsterdam.

Wray, W. B. (2005). Rethinking scientific specialization. *Social Studies of Science, 35*(1), 151–164.

Yitzhaki, M., & Hammerschlag, G. (2004). Accessibility and use of information sources among computer scientists and software engineers in Israel: Academy versus industry. *Journal of the American Society for Information Science and Technology, 55*(9), 832–842.

Zehr, S. C. (1999). Scientists' representations of uncertainty. In S. M. Friedman, S. Dunwoody, & C. L. Rogers (Eds.), *Communicating uncertainty: Media coverage of new and controversial science* (pp. 3–21). Mahwah, NJ: Erlbaum.

Zhao, D. Z., & Logan, E. (2002). Citation analysis using scientific publications on the Web as data source: A case study in the XML research area. *Scientometrics, 54*(3), 449–472.

Ziman, J. M. (1968). *Public knowledge: An essay concerning the social dimension of science.* Cambridge, UK: Cambridge University Press.

Ziman, J. M. (1969). Information, communication, knowledge. *Nature, 224,* 318–324.

Ziman, J. M. (1984). *An introduction to science studies: The philosophical and social aspects of science and technology.* Cambridge, UK: Cambridge University Press.

Zuccala, A. (2006). Modeling the invisible college. *Journal of the American Society for Information Science and Technology, 57*(2), 156–168.

Zuckerman, H. (1970). Stratification in American science. *Sociological Inquiry, 40*, 235–257.

Zuckerman, H. (1977). *Scientific elite: Nobel laureates in the United States.* New York: Free Press.

Zuckerman, H., & Merton, R. K. (1971). Patterns of evaluation in science: Institutionalization, structure and functions of the referee system. *Minerva, 9*, 66–100.

CHAPTER 7

Scientific Writing

Ken Hyland
University of London

Françoise Salager-Meyer
Universidad de Los Andes

Why Is Scientific Writing So Interesting?

Writing is a key element in the formation of social realities, institutions, and personal identities in almost every domain of professional life and the sciences are no exception. Although it is often regarded as simply a conventional means of conveying the results of laboratory experiments or armchair cogitation, scientific writing has come to be seen as socially constitutive of disciplines, of individual status and authority, and of knowledge itself. In research articles, monographs, textbooks, scientific letters, and popularizations, the ways writers present their topics, signal their allegiances, and stake their claims display their professional competence in discipline-approved practices. It is these practices, and not abstract and disengaged beliefs and theories, that principally define what disciplines are and how knowledge is agreed upon and codified (e.g., Bazerman, 1988; Hyland, 2000a, 2006; Myers, 1990).

Successful academic writing depends on the individual writer's projection of a shared professional context. Writers seek to embed their writing in a particular social world, which they reflect and conjure through approved discourses. As a result, the genres of the academy have attracted increasing attention as they offer a rich source of information about the social practices of academics. Kress (1989, p. 7), for example, argues that discourses are "systematically-organized sets of statements which give expression to the meanings and values of an institution." Texts, in other words, are socially produced in particular communities and depend on them for their sense so that by studying the ways academics write we learn more about disciplinary inquiry and how knowledge is constructed, negotiated, and made persuasive.

Writing is also significant to analysts for the simple reason that what academics principally do is write. Latour and Woolgar (1979), for example, have suggested that the modern research lab devotes more energy to producing papers than discoveries, and that scientists' time is spent largely in discussing and preparing articles for publication in competition with other labs. The popular view of the academic as a solitary individual experimenting in the laboratory, collecting data in the field, or wrestling with ideas in the library, and then retiring to write up the results is a modern myth (e.g., Cronin, 2005). Research is a *social* enterprise and written texts are the principal embodiment of this activity. The growing interest in academic writing has therefore been accompanied by an interest in *how* academics write rather than simply *what* they write about. When we look at academic texts closely, we see that they are distinguished not only by specialist topics and vocabularies, but also by different appeals to background knowledge, different means of establishing truth, and different ways of engaging with readers.

Scientific writing has been studied principally from four perspectives:

> Applied linguists have largely focused on the informational, rhetorical, cross-linguistic, and stylistic organization of written texts for descriptive or pedagogic purposes (e.g., Hyland, 2000a; Swales, 1990).

> Information scientists have focused on the role of texts in the classification, manipulation, retrieval, and dissemination of information (e.g., Cronin, 2005).

> Historians, together with several applied linguists, have been interested in the rhetorical evolution of the research article (Salager-Meyer, 1998a; Salager-Meyer & Defives, 1998; Shapin, 1984).

> Sociological studies have sought to explore the interactions between scientists for evidence of the processes which maintain social order (Gilbert & Mulkay, 1984; Knorr Cetina, 1981).

This review seeks to offer an analytic and critical overview of research on scientific writing from a largely linguistic perspective. This perspective, we believe, complements the interests of those working in information science, where the central concern is with the literatures involved in scholarly communication through bibliometrics, citation analysis, and information retrieval. Such studies have long drawn upon insights from linguistic theory and analysis as a means of understanding knowledge; our discussion is an attempt to systematize the sources of these insights. We leave it to readers to determine how they might appropriate and employ the approaches and research we report. In this chapter we take a broad view of *scientific* to include the natural, social, and human sciences; and we understand *writing* principally as research writing but also include instructional and student writing. We first briefly discuss the significance of writing to the academy and then examine research on its key features from generic, disciplinary, and cross-linguistic perspectives.

The Importance of Science Writing

In this section we briefly sketch the three key ways in which academic writing is important, both to academic communities and to society at large: first, in academic persuasion and the construction of knowledge; second, in legitimizing the ideological and political authority of science in the modern world; and third, in establishing an institutionalized system of hierarchy, reputation, and reward through publication.

Writing, Persuasion, and the Limits of Scientific Explanation

Scientific writing is often privileged as a unique form of argument where the text is merely the channel that allows scientists to communicate independently existing truths, relaying directly observable facts to the world. The label "scientific" confers reliability on a method and prestige on its users; it implies all that is most empirically verifiable about academic knowledge and is seen to provide a description of what the natural and human worlds are actually like. This, in turn, serves to distinguish it from the socially contingent. Academic writing, in other words, represents a discourse of "Truth" (Lemke, 1995, p. 178) and for these reasons it has been imitated by the fields of human and social inquiry, such as sociology and linguistics, which are often considered "softer," and thus less dependable forms of knowledge.

Underlying this realist model is the idea that knowledge is built on the non-contingent pillars of impartial observation, experimental demonstration, replication, and falsifiability. Unfortunately, none of these offers a reliable means of knowing the world, as all reporting occurs in a disciplinary context. Interpretation depends on what the mind allows the eye to see and this is determined by the theories and assumptions the scientist brings to the problem (e.g., Kuhn, 1970). Simply, texts cannot be seen as accurate representations of "what the world is really like" because this representation is always filtered through acts of selection and foregrounding. In other words, to discuss results and theories is not to reveal absolute proof; it is to engage in particular forms of argument.

If truth does not reside in an external reality, there will always be more than one plausible interpretation of any piece of data; this plurality of competing explanations shifts attention to the ways that academics argue their claims. Knowledge is not a privileged representation of reality but a conversation between members of academic communities who have some agreement on the ground rules for negotiating what counts as plausible. We must see knowledge as emerging from a disciplinary matrix and ground our understandings of academic persuasion in the conventional textual practices for producing agreement (Hyland, 1998b, 2005b).

The first reason for studying scientific writing therefore concerns its role in the disciplinary construction of knowledge. All academic writers must display familiarity with the persuasive practices of their disciplines: encoding ideas, employing warrants, framing arguments, and conveying an appropriate attitude to their readers and their ideas in ways that their potential audience will find most convincing (Hyland, 2000a, 2005a; Swales, 1990). In sum, persuasion in academic articles, as in other areas of professional life, involves the use of language to relate independent beliefs to shared experience. Through texts, writers galvanize support, express collegiality, resolve difficulties, and negotiate disagreement through patterns of rhetorical choices that connect their texts with their disciplinary cultures.

Writing and the Ideological Authority of the Sciences

The second reason for taking an interest in scientific writing is that the discourses of the academy are extremely valued and influential ideological systems in the wider community. Science is held in high esteem in the modern world precisely because it provides a model of rationality and detached reasoning. Of course there can be public skepticism about science, but we tend to distinguish it from the socially contingent and invest it with a cultural authority not bestowed on the more obviously partisan rhetorics of politics, journalism, and commerce. Importantly then, academic discourses possess cultural and political authority because of the control they afford over the physical and intellectual circumstances of our lives. It is a means for producing truth; and in every society power is based on truth.

This, however, is a discourse which promotes a universe in which the domination of nature is linked to the domination of humans, used to both justify power relations and to conflate a particular view of knowledge as *truth*. In other words, the discourses of the academy are not merely credible systems of making meaning but are extremely valued and influential ideological systems in the wider community. The words of science are, as Stanley Aronowitz (1988, p. 351) writes, the "discourse of the late capitalist state":

> Science is a language of power and those who bear its legitimate claims, i.e., those who are involved in the ownership and control of its processes and results, have become a distinctive social category equipped with a distinctive ideology and position in the post-war world.

The languages of the academy have, in fact, reshaped our entire world view, becoming the dominant mode for interpreting reality and our own existence. They exert a considerable, although often unnoticed, influence on all aspects of our everyday lives, as Halliday and Martin (1993, p. 11) observe:

> Every text, from the discourses of technocracy and bureaucracy to the television magazine and the blurb on the back of the cereal packet, is in some way affected by the modes of meaning that evolved as the scaffolding for scientific knowledge. In other words, the language of science has become the language of literacy.

The fact that the influence of scientific discourses has spilled into other domains of life—bureaucracy, government, commerce, etc.—means that they increasingly provide both a model for communication and a filter for perception.

Of greatest importance is the role of academic disciplines in offering schemata of what is known and how it can be known. Disciplines contain alternative, even deviant, perspectives; but dominant ideologies have tended to promote a mechanically materialist view of the world directed to utility and composed of individuals passively subject to forces outside their control. Such narratives of human and natural phenomena successfully obscure the social relations behind them because elements are abstracted from their social contexts, thereby offering little threat to existing social relations. Gould (1998), for example, has pointed to the strength of a discourse of evolution where diversity and stability are suppressed to represent a fixed progression. This helps to construct a picture of social and technological evolution as a march of uninterrupted progress to the present, supporting an ideology of comfortable progress and predictability that justifies current political and social realities.

In sum, the application of scientific discourse to justify social relations is inherently ideological as it serves to endow those relations with nature's authority. Disciplinary discourses are not only powerfully authoritative accounts of human and natural phenomena; they also have significant political consequences as they desensitize us to the socially situated nature of expert assertions.

Writing and Academic Careers

A final aspect of the significance of scientific writing we mention here is how it works to distribute social power and individual prestige within a community. When they write, academics not only negotiate community knowledge, individual contributions, and personal credibility; they also produce and sustain status relationships, exercise authority, and reproduce interests that help distribute influence and resources. The institutionalized system for both creating knowledge and distributing rewards is that of publication. A paper is judged as a contribution by an audience of colleagues who are potentially in a position to make use of it. If editors, referees, proposal readers, conference attendees, and journal readers regard it as original and significant, allow it to be published, cite it in their own work, and develop it further, then the writer receives the reward of recognition in the form of promotion, tenure, or greater access to grants and consultancies.

Hagstrom (1965) has analyzed this process as a form of barter where recognition is exchanged for a contribution of information. Latour and Woolgar (1979), shifting this market metaphor and echoing Bourdieu's (1991) notion of symbolic capital, see academics as engaged in converting different kinds of "credit" in a cycle of moves designed to maximize their credibility. A successful publication may help a researcher gain credit, which can be converted into a research grant to finance equipment and recruit colleagues. This, in turn, generates more data, which can be converted to arguments, fresh publications, and so on. This model perhaps attributes an unrealistically high degree of autonomy to individual practitioners and underestimates the effect of political and economic forces in academic life. It is true, however, that academics who excel in the publication process often gain appointments to key positions, access to economic resources, and the occupation of major gatekeeping roles for funding applications and research contracts (Becher, 1989; Cronin, 2005). They not only achieve social power within their disciplines but also form an elite as greater resources flow to them to further their work.

Writing therefore becomes both a cohesive and a competitive force, giving coherence and public prestige to disciplinary endeavor and also sanctioning rivalry among individuals, institutions, and disciplines for scarce resources. With regular research assessment exercises and the publication of university league tables in a growing number of countries around the world, publication "productivity" has become a crude measure of worthwhile individual careers hanging on the length of personal bibliographies. James Watson, Nobel laureate and a member of the biology establishment, spells this out:

> It starts at the beginning. If you publish first, you become a professor first; your future depends on some indication that you can do something by yourself. It's that simple. Competitiveness is very dominant. The chief emotion in the field. (Quoted in Judson, 1995, p. 194)

In sum, through peer review and editorial intervention, disciplines seek to ensure that accounts of new knowledge conform to the broad rhetorical practices they have established; writers, however, tend to employ these practices to get published and achieve recognition. This desire to gain a reputation therefore acts as a system of social control as it encourages conformity to the approved discursive practices of the discipline. To put it bluntly, the ideological and discursive system that reproduces knowledge also reproduces a particular arrangement of social relations. This kind of control has been shown in a number of studies, from the editorial power exercised at a major U.S. writing conference (Berkenkotter & Huckin, 1995), through the complex rhetorical strategies needed to gain a hearing for the idea of chaos theory (Paul & Charney, 1995), to the ways brilliant insights from outsiders are often neglected by scientific hierarchies (Sacks, 1998).

Restricting access to prestigious discourses is commonplace in all areas of professional life. This process of drawing on appropriate rhetorical resources to negotiate ideas is, of course, particularly difficult for writers whose native language is not English and whose academic norms may not be those of the discipline in the metropolitan center (e.g., Canagarajah, 1999, 2002b).

In the following sections we look at some of the ways that these discourses are realized in different genres, disciplines, and languages.

Genre Variation in Academic Writing

Academic communities have developed rhetorically effective and discipline-distinctive ways of constructing plausible accounts of research. Such conventional, socially recognized ways of using language are referred to as *genres* and the analysis of academic genres has been the staple of applied linguistic research into scientific writing for the past 20 years (e.g., Flowerdew, 2002; Hyland, 2000a, 2005a; Swales, 1990, 2004). Genre theories rest on the idea that texts are similar or different and can be classified as one genre or another. In order to systematize these classifications, research has set out to characterize various key linguistic and rhetorical features of particular genres.

Genre analysis is based on two central assumptions: that the features of a similar group of texts depend on the social context of their creation and use and that those features can be described in a way that relates a text to others like it and to the choices and constraints acting on text producers. Language is seen as embedded in (and constitutive of) social realities, as it is through recurrent use of conventionalized forms that individuals develop relationships, establish communities, and get things done. Genres are then, "the effects of the action of individual social agents acting *both* within the bounds of their history and the constraints of particular contexts, *and* with a knowledge of existing generic types" (Kress, 1989, p. 10).

Essentially genre analysis is the study of situated language use in institutional settings although analysts differ in the emphasis they give to either context or text: some focus on the roles of texts in social communities (e.g., Blyler & Thralls, 1993) and others on the ways texts are organized to reflect and construct these communities (Hyland, 2002a, 2002b; Johns, 2002). As a result, academic genres have been studied in three main ways. First, as typified rhetorical actions using ethnographic methods to relate language use to social structures and individual identities (e.g., Bazerman, 1988; Prior, 1998). Second, as regularities of staged, goal-oriented, social practices employing text analytic methods to explicate the distinctive rhetorical steps, or moves, of genres together with their typical lexical, grammatical, and cohesive patterns (e.g., Halliday & Martin, 1993). Third, genres have been analyzed as a class of communicative events employed by specific discourse communities whose members share broad communicative purposes (Johns, 1997; Swales, 1990, 2004).

A range of written academic genres has been studied in recent years. These include article abstracts (Salager-Meyer, 1990; Swales, 1990), scientific letters (Hyland, 2000a), acknowledgments (Cronin, 1995; Giannoni, 2002, 2006; Hyland, 2004a; Hyland & Tse, 2004b; Salager-Meyer, Alcaraz Ariza, Pabón, & Zambrano, 2006a), theses (Bunton, 2002; Hyland, 2004a; Hyland & Tse, 2004a, 2005), book reviews (Hyland, 2000a; Motta-Roth, 1998; Salager-Meyer & Alcaraz Ariza, 2004; Salager-Meyer, Alcaraz Ariza, Pabón, & Zambrano, 2006b; Tse & Hyland, 2006), conference abstracts (Swales, 1995), and student essays (Johns, 1997) as well as various occluded, or hidden, genres such as article submission letters (Swales, 1996), grant proposals (Connor, 2000; Connor & Upton, 2004), and editors' responses to journal submissions (Flowerdew & Dudley-Evans, 2002). In the following sections we briefly sketch something of what the research tells us about the key academic genres of English-written articles, textbooks, and popularizations.

The Research Article

The research article is a cultural accomplishment developed from the activities of Henry Oldenburgh in England and Denis de Sallo in France during the 17th century and emerged in embryonic form, with the establishment of the *Journal des Sçavans*, in Paris in January 1665 and the *Philosophical Transactions of the Royal Society* in London in March 1665.[1]

The genre of the scientific article developed from the informative letters that scientists used to write to each other. The early scientific article sought to establish credibility more by means of "the technology of virtual witnessing" (Shapin, 1984, p. 491), that is more through the reliable testimony of credible witnesses to secure the agreement of the scientific community than by technical details, more by qualitative experience than by quantitative experiment and observation in support of theory. Natural philosophers, or "men of science," as scientists were then called in the 17th and 18th centuries (the word *scientist* was coined in 1833 by William Whewell at the request of the poet Coleridge) were tolerant of a wide range of verificational means; they relied on the evidence of the five senses and the trust that existed between gentlemen. The end of the 18th century saw the demise of this communal gentlemanly witnessing even though the ethos of gentlemanly courtesy persisted down to the second half of the 19th century (Shapin, 1984).

However, as *The Philosophical Transactions* and subsequent journals began to provide a regular arena for discussion, the new and recurring rhetorical situation that emerged led to the creation of a new genre increasingly distinct from its letter-writing origin. Bacon and Boyle influenced the way science was communicated; they both contributed much to the "making" of a rhetoric of science and to developing a convincing style for the research report in order to reach consensus that can only be achieved through rhetorical persuasion (see Bazerman, 1984; Shapin, 1984; and Valle, 1999 for detailed analyses of the research article configurational development). Regarding the changes in style, presentation, and argumentation the genre underwent over the last four centuries, Gross, Harmon, and Reidy (2002) convincingly argue that these changes should not be taken as progress or improvement, but as an evolving response to an evolving discourse situation. More consistent, then, is an explanation of change in terms of plausible selection pressures and adaptive mechanisms, increased cognitive complexity, higher standard of proof, and greater volume of data coupled with a dramatic increase in the number of scientific articles, "a proliferation as startling as the overnight increase of bacteria in a petri dish" (Gross et al., 2002, p. 29).

A great deal of research into academic writing has focused on this most prestigious genre of scholarly writing: the research article. Considerable literature has shown that this is a rhetorically sophisticated artifact that displays a careful balance of factual information and social interaction. Indeed, academic writers need to make the results of their research not only public, but also persuasive; and their success in gaining acceptance for their work depends at least in part on the strategic manipulation of various rhetorical and interactive features (Myers, 1990; Swales, 2004).

One strand of research has sought to describe the conventional rhetorical structure of the article, or various parts of it, through a move analysis—identifying distinct rhetorical units that perform coherent communicative functions (Swales, 2004). This work was pioneered by Swales's (1990) analysis of article introductions, the three-part CARS (Creating a Research Space) model, which has proved remarkably robust. Despite terminological variations, it seems to be a prototypical structure in English-written article introductions in a range of disciplines (e.g., Lewin, Fine, & Young, 2001; Samraj, 2002) and various formal features have been identified as signalling these moves. Beyond this, descriptions have been given for the Methods, Results (Brett, 1994), and Discussion sections (Dubois, 1997; Lewin et al., 2001). Unfortunately, some of these descriptions offer an assortment of analytic schemes for what are essentially similar texts, particularly when considering the Discussion section. Although these differences are in part simply nomenclatural, this section appears to offer writers an array of rhetorical options; and this explains why Dubois (1997) abandoned altogether the attempt to offer an overall scheme.

Analyzing schematic structures has proved an invaluable way of looking at texts but the differences suggest the need to tie functions more closely to formal realizations. Many years ago Crookes (1986) raised the problem of validating analyses to ensure they are not simply products of the analyst's intuitions. Moves are, of course, always motivated outside the text as writers respond to their social context but analysts have not always been convincingly able to identify the ways these shifts are explicitly signalled by lexico-grammatical patterning. In addition to problems of intuition-driven descriptions, analysts are also increasingly aware of the dangers of oversimplification by assuming blocks of texts to be mono-functional and ignoring writers' complex purposes and "private intentions" (Bhatia, 1999).

In addition to move analyses, research has increasingly examined clusters of register, style, lexis, and other rhetorical features that might distinguish articles and other genres. One example of this work is Halliday's (1998) continuing interest in *grammatical metaphor* in physics writing. This explores how scientists reconstrue human experience by presenting processes as things—packaging complex phenomena as a single element of clause structure. Grammatical metaphor freezes an event, such as "atoms bond rapidly," and repackages it as an object, "rapid atom bonding." Adverbs become adjectives, processes become nouns, and nouns become adjectival, creating a noun phrase. Turning processes into objects in this way embodies scientific epistemologies that seek to show relationships between entities. Grammatical metaphor is also central to physics because it allows writers to highlight processes in order to say something about them and to manage the information flow of a text more effectively.

An important feature of much recent work has been a growing interest in the interpersonal dimensions of academic writing. This research has sought to reveal how persuasion in various genres is accomplished not only through the representation of ideas but also by the construction of an appropriate authorial self and the negotiation of accepted participant relationships (Hyland, 2005a, 2005b). Once again, academic articles have attracted considerable attention in this regard, with recent work looking at, for example, imperatives (Hyland, 2002b; Swales et al., 1998), personal pronouns (Hyland, 2001b; Kuo, 1999), hedging and boosting (Hyland, 1998a; Myers, 1989; Salager-Meyer, 1994), theme (Gosden, 1993), and citation practices (Cronin, 1995, 2005; Cronin, Shaw, & La Barre, 2003, 2004; Hyland, 2000a; Thompson & Ye, 1991).

Interaction in research writing essentially involves "positioning," or adopting a point of view in relation to both the issues discussed in the text and others who hold points of view on those issues. In claiming a right to be heard, and to have their work taken seriously, writers must display competence as disciplinary insiders. This competence is, at least in part, achieved through a writer–reader dialogue that situates both their research and themselves, establishing relationships between people and between people and ideas. Several different approaches have been taken to interactions in texts including the evaluation model (Hunston & Thompson, 2000) and metadiscourse[2] (Hyland, 2004b,

2005a; Hyland & Tse, 2004a); both draw on the ideas of stance and engagement (Hyland, 2001a & 2005b). *Stance* refers to the writer's textual voice or community recognized personality; the ways writers present themselves and convey their judgments, opinions, and commitments. *Engagement*, on the other hand, refers to the ways writers acknowledge and connect with their readers, pulling them along with their argument, focusing their attention, acknowledging their uncertainties, including them as discourse participants, and guiding them to interpretations. Figure 7.1 summarizes the main ways these interactional functions are realized.

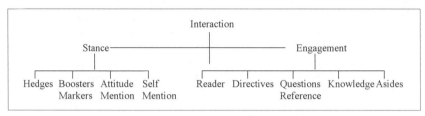

Figure 7.1   Key resources of academic interaction (Hyland, 2005a).

Together these resources have a dialogic purpose in that they refer to, anticipate, or otherwise take up the actual or anticipated voices and positions of potential readers (Bakhtin, 1986).

Textbooks

University textbooks were, until recently, something of a neglected genre, tending to have a peripheral status and frequently seen as commercial projects unrelated to research. There is a widely held view of textbooks as repositories of codified knowledge and classroom lore (Myers, 1992), which reflects Kuhn's (1970) influential belief that, at least in the sciences, textbooks are conservative exemplars of current disciplinary paradigms. They are seen as places where we find the tamed and accepted theories of a discipline, where "normal science" is defined and acknowledged fact represented. Bakhtin (1981, p. 427) refers to this as "undialogized" discourse, privileged in its absolute definition of reality. Thus, although the research article is a highly valued genre central to the disciplinary construction of new knowledge, the textbook represents an attempt to reduce the multivocity of past texts to a single voice of authority. Connors (1986, p. 190) represents the dichotomy like this:

> In most developed intellectual disciplines, the function of texts has always been essentially conservative: textbooks, which change with glacial slowness, provide stability amid the shifting winds of theoretical argument. They serve as sources for the proven truths needed for students' basic training while

advanced scholarship extends the theoretical envelope, usually in journal articles.

Textbooks are indispensable to academic life, particularly for undergraduates. Not only do they facilitate the professional's role as a teacher, but they play a major role in the learner's experience and understanding of a subject by providing a coherently ordered epistemological map of the disciplinary landscape and its textual practices. Students entering university must acquire the specialized literacy of their community and textbooks offer a model of literacy practices, how the discipline discusses what it knows (Candlin & Hyland, 1999). The practices of constructing a disciplinary image and mediating unfamiliar material, however, involve rhetorical characteristics not always shared by other genres (e.g., Love, 2002; Myers, 1992; Swales, 1993). It is thus unclear whether they can both convey scholarship to neophytes and develop the "peculiar ways of knowing, selecting, evaluating, reporting, concluding and arguing that define the discourse of the community" (Bartholomae, 1986, p. 4).

Textbooks are therefore something of a hybrid genre at the intersection of scientific and pedagogic discourse (Bondi, 1999; Hyland, 2000a). Even where paradigms compete for dominance they stand as representations of disciplinary orthodoxy while providing a medium for writers to disseminate a vision of their discipline to both experts and novices, representing a complex professional discourse that involves the writer in both pedagogic and professional interactions (Hyland, 2000a; Swales, 1995). As a result, several studies of the textbook genre have been concerned with the status of the knowledge they present, concentrating in particular on such issues as hedging and authorial comment (e.g., Halliday & Martin, 1993; Hyland, 2000a), argument structure (Bondi, 1999; Love, 2002), and the interplay of different voices in the text (Bondi, 1999; Freddi, 2005).

Writers have sought to bring together some of these features by exploring the role of metadiscourse in university textbooks (Hyland, 2000a, 2005b). Metadiscourse concerns the writer's references to the writer, the reader, or the text. It is a key dimension of genre analysis as it can help show how language choices reflect the different purposes of writers, the different assumptions they make about their audiences, and the different kinds of interactions they create with their readers (Crismore, Markkanen, & Steffensen, 1993; Hyland, 2005a; Hyland & Tse, 2004a). Metadiscourse actually refers to a diverse array of *interactive* and *interactional* (Thompson, 2001) resources used to manage textual interactions. Perhaps unsurprisingly, we find that interactive features, such as frame markers (*first, in conclusion, we will now*), transitions (*therefore, and on the other hand*), and endophoric markers (*see table, as noted above*), which are largely used to manage the information flow and assist comprehension, are more frequent in textbooks. Interactional resources like hedges (*possible, perhaps, may*), boosters (*show, definitely, demonstrate*), and self-mention (*exclusive we, I*) which focus on the participants of the interaction and are typically used to assist persuasion, are more frequent in articles (Hyland, 2000a, 2005a).

Science Popularizations

The number of journals carrying reports of scientific findings for a lay audience has dramatically increased in recent years, interesting analysts by their different use of language for different purposes and audiences. We should emphasize here that popular science belongs to Fleck's exoteric circle (Cohen & Schnelle, 1986) and should be distinguished from publications for a professional, non-specialist audience of scientists interested in developments outside their disciplines, essentially an esoteric audience with different epistemological and communicative needs. Unlike research articles—which seek to negotiate claims for new knowledge with reviewers, editors, and peers—and textbooks—which offer a model of the discipline for students—pieces written for the general public attempt to link issues in the specialist domain to those of everyday life. For some, this represents a distortion, a dumbing down of science to suggest easy comprehension and an ideology of progress; others regard the jargon and technicalities of science papers as exclusive and elitist.

Myers (1990) argues that a key difference between articles and popularizations is their contrasting views of science, with popularizations tending to focus on the *objects* of study and articles on the disciplinary *procedures* by which they are studied. The professional papers construct what he calls a "narrative of science" (p. 141) by following the argument of the scientist, arranging time into a parallel series of events, and emphasizing the conceptual structure of the discipline in their syntax and vocabulary. The discourse thus embodies assumptions of impersonality, cumulative knowledge construction, and empiricism. The popular articles, on the other hand, present a "narrative of nature" (p. 141), focusing on the (plant or animal) material rather than the scientific activity of studying them. Presentation in popularizations is therefore often chronological and the syntax and vocabulary paint a picture of nature, which is external to scientific practices. Here the scientist acts alone and simply observes nature. These different language choices not only convey different meanings of both research and science, but also mean that writers or readers of one narrative cannot easily understand the other.

Such generic language differences have been explored by a number of writers. Crismore and Farnsworth (1990), for example, have shown that science authors tend to remove hedges when they write for a lay readership as they seek to offer a sense of the uniqueness and originality of observations, confer greater certainty on claims, and stress the factual status of results. Hyland (2005b) discovered considerable variation in evidential claims and the ways that popularizations drew on external justification for statements. In research articles, attributions to other sources largely function to recognize earlier work and embed new work in a community-generated literature to demonstrate its relevance and importance (Hyland, 2000a). Popularizations, on the other hand, identify only particular scientists who are relevant to the current development and bestow credibility through their *position* in an institution. Popularizations also differ from articles in how such material is imported into the text. Popularizations appear to be more like popular journalism in their use of direct interview quotes and extensive use of the reporting verb *say*, whereas material in articles is overwhelmingly presented as a summary from a single source or as a generalization combining several studies.

There are, then, distinctive differences in the genres of the academy that are repeated for other texts as writers set out their ideas for different purposes and audiences. In this science popularization genre, information is presented as newsworthy, and language choices work to invest it with factual status, relate it to real life concerns, and present it as relevant to readers who may have little interest in the ways that findings were arrived at or in the controversies surrounding them. Such differences between genres are, as we elaborate in the following sections, also key features of academic writing in different disciplines and in different languages.

Disciplinary Variation

Although the concept of genre has been extremely productive in exploring situated language use over the past twenty years, its influence has perhaps led to an overemphasis on the resemblances between texts rather than the differences among them. This is largely because genre harnesses the power of generalization: grouping together texts that have important similarities in terms of rhetorical purpose, form, and audience and then exploring how they differ from other text types. Consequently there has been a relative neglect of the ways the same genres vary across communities. With the idea of *discourse community* we arrive at a more rounded and socially informed theory of texts and contexts. The concept draws attention to the idea that we do generally use language to communicate not with the world at large, but with individuals and with other members of our social groups. In studies of academic discourse, then, "community" provides a principled way of understanding how meaning is produced *in interaction* and has proved useful in identifying disciplinary-specific rhetorical practices.

Community and Discipline

The notion of discipline is nebulous and shifting, notoriously difficult to define and seen variously as institutional conveniences, networks of communication, domains of values, and modes of enquiry; post-modernists, however, have looked at the fragmentation of academic life and rejected the term altogether (e.g., Gilbert, 1995). The idea of academic community, or discipline, however, is central to our understanding of science and science writing. From the "invisible colleges" of the 17th century to the research groups of modern times, it has provided a way of understanding the social practices of academics acting as group members. In applied linguistics a great deal of research has confirmed the distinctiveness of discourses cohering around the concept of community, and researchers have become more sensitive to the ways genres are written, used, and responded to by individuals acting as members of social groups.

The concept of community provides a means of analyzing communication as a joint, socially situated accomplishment. The idea draws together a number of key aspects of context that are crucial to the production and interpretation of discourse: knowledge of a cultural and interpersonal situation, knowledge of interlocutors, knowledge of the world, and knowledge of texts and conventions for saying things (e.g., Swales, 1990, 1998). Emphasis, therefore, tends to be on what is shared by a community (e.g., Johns, 1997), including patterns of interaction and the "rhetorical conventions and stylistic practices that are tacit and routine for the members" (Doheny-Farina, 1992, p. 296). Although critics see the concept as too structuralist, static, and deterministic (e.g., Canagarajah, 2002a; Prior, 1998), current conceptions of community in terms of an individual's engagement in certain discourses and practices, rather than orientations to rules and goals, provide a more rounded and socially informed theory of texts and contexts (Hyland, 2000a, 2006).

When applied to academic domains, the expression of community in the notion of *discipline* offers researchers a framework for conceptualizing the expectations, conventions, and practices that influence academic communication. Disciplinary communities have been described as "tribes" (Becher, 1989, p.1), each with its own norms, categorizations, bodies of knowledge, sets of conventions, and modes of inquiry, which comprise a recognizable culture (Bartholomae, 1986; Hyland, 2000a). The important point is that it is individuals acting as *community members* who use language to engage in these practices or achieve these goals. This community-based orientation to literacy therefore focuses on the importance of communicating, and learning to communicate, as an *insider* of the community with which one wishes to engage. Textual features reveal writers' assumptions about their readers, shaped by prior texts, repeated experience, participation in various groups, and orientations to certain conventions (Tse & Hyland, 2006).

Situating Arguments in Disciplinary Conventions

Research into how writing functions in different disciplines was pioneered by Bazerman (1988) and MacDonald (1994), who showed how knowledge creation is related to key epistemological and cultural differences through the ways that writers in different fields draw on disciplinary literature, code knowledge in accepted modes of argument, and represent themselves in their texts. MacDonald, for example, suggested that psychology articles are more likely to foreground research methods and warrants and are more abstract; literature articles, however, are more particularistic and focus least on research methods and warrants.

There also appear to be considerable differences in how writers situate their work to mark their participation in their communities. In science and engineering abstracts, for instance, writers frequently offer their research as a valuable contribution to pressing real-world issues, indicating an applied dimension and the diffusion of information from the public into the scientific sphere. Constant progress is a central part of scientific cultures and writers often stress novelty, whereas engineers emphasize the utility of their research, mainly to the industrial world that relies on it. This explains why software and computer engineering article introductions do not strictly follow the CARS model we referred to in the section on the research article (Anthony, 1999; Posteguillo, 1999). Writers in marketing, applied linguistics, and sociology, by way of contrast, tend to establish an unresolved disciplinary-relevant problem (Hyland, 2000a; Samraj, 2002). We also find variations in textbooks. In hard knowledge fields the discipline appears to embody its truths and current platforms of professional activity. In the sciences (e.g., Myers, 1992) and economics (Tadros, 1994) certitude, abstract nominalizations (recasting actions as things), thematic structure, and style thus seem to reinforce existing paradigms. In philosophy and composition, on the other hand, textbooks are often regarded as important vehicles for advancing scholarship and presenting original research (e.g., Gebhardt, 1993).

One of the most obvious strategies for situating research within disciplinary expectations is through citation (Hyland, 2000a; Thompson & Ye, 1991). By acknowledging previous research, writers are able to display an allegiance to a particular orientation, create a rhetorical gap for their research, and establish a credible writer ethos (Swales, 1990). The frequency and use of citations, however, exhibit disciplinary differences. The fact that scientific knowledge tends to be highly specialized means that scientists participate in relatively discrete areas and can presuppose a certain amount of background knowledge and expertise (Hyland, 2000a). Citation therefore integrates new claims into a frame of already accredited facts. References are often sparse and bound to a particular topic, which helps to closely define a specific context and contribute to a sense of linear progression. In the social sciences, however, the literature is open to greater interpretation, and criteria for establishing claims are less clear-cut. Because readers cannot be assumed to possess the same interpretive knowledge, writers have to elaborate a context through far greater use of citation (Hyland, 2000a). This specialization of research also means that self-citation is a particularly prominent feature of writing in the hard sciences (Lawani, 1982; Rousseau, 1999; Tagliacozzo, 1977), where it comprises over 12 percent of all references (Salager-Meyer, 1998a), compared with only 4 percent in soft fields (Hyland, 2001b).

A further aspect of disciplinary variation concerns the use of key genres and their structures. Coffin, Curry, Goodman, Hewings, Lillis, and Swann (2003), for example, identify three different genres as being pivotal to each of three main domains of knowledge: project proposals in the sciences, essays in the humanities, and reports and case studies in the social sciences. But even when we identify a common genre across disciplines, we find a range of different structural patterns. Braine (1995), for instance, found that no two branches of engineering had experimental report formats that employed the same move structures. Such variations have also been found in the emphasis given to particular moves in article abstracts (Hyland, 2000a; Samraj, 2002) and articles themselves.

Such differences also occur in student writing genres. Hyland (2004a), for instance, in a study of the acknowledgments in 240 Ph.D. and M.A. dissertations, found that writers in soft fields were far more likely to offer a reflection on their research experience and to accept responsibility for the work; writers in the sciences and engineering fields, however, more often thanked individuals and institutions for funding and technical support. At the other end of the dissertation, Bunton (2005) shows that the generic structure of the conclusion chapter of Ph.D. theses in science and technology tends to be longer and have more sections than those in the humanities and social sciences. The science and technology conclusions also concentrated on broader results and claims, gave greater emphasis to future research, and referred to practical applications that the writers saw being put to immediate use in their field.

Authorial Stance and Reader Engagement

We have noted that writers must project a shared disciplinary context by expressing a stance that balances claims for the significance, originality, and plausibility of their work against the convictions and expectations of their readers (Hyland, 2005b). Comparisons show that writers in different disciplines represent themselves and their work in different ways, with those in the humanities and social sciences taking far more explicitly involved and personal positions than those in the science and engineering fields (Bondi, 2005; Hyland, 2005b). In a series of studies, Hyland addressed disciplinary variation in the use of hedges and boosters (Hyland, 1998a; 2001a; Hyland & Tse, 2004a), attitude markers (Hyland, 2000a), and self-mention (Hyland, 2001b) in research papers; he found that the more discursive (soft) fields of philosophy, sociology, applied linguistics, and marketing contained 75 percent more stance items than the engineering and science papers. Figure 7.2 summarizes these findings.

Other studies have confirmed these disciplinary variations in stance features. There seems, for example, to be far heavier use of self-mention in computer science and electronic engineering articles than in physics (Kuo, 1999) and different patterns of author representation in history

Feature	Phil	Soc	AL	Mk	Phy	Bio	ME	EE	Total
Stance	*42.8*	*31.1*	*37.2*	*39.5*	*25.0*	*23.8*	*19.8*	*21.6*	*30.9*
Hedges	18.5	14.7	18.0	20.0	9.6	13.6	8.2	9.6	14.5
Attitude Mkrs	8.9	7.0	8.6	6.9	3.9	2.9	5.6	5.5	6.4
Boosters	9.7	5.1	6.2	7.1	6.0	3.9	5.0	3.2	5.8
Self Mention	5.7	4.3	4.4	5.5	5.5	3.4	1.0	3.3	4.2

Figure 7.2   Stance features (per 1,000 words) in 240 research articles.

compared with economics articles (Bondi, 2005). Research has also noted differences in other academic genres. Motta-Roth (1998) discovered that book reviews in economics are more evaluative than those in linguistics or chemistry, perhaps because of the greater competitiveness among alternative theories in that field; and Parry (1998) observed that criticisms are more overt in humanities than science theses, ranging from caustic in philosophy to considerate in history. Busà (2005) noted the syntactic foregrounding of discourse producers (*the economist, the author, we*) in economics abstracts compared to those from physiology, which thematize discourse objects (*study, research*) and references to human subjects are replaced by objectivized discourse entities (*subjects, patients, groups*) making psychology appear to be a very impersonal discipline. Support for this kind of impersonality in the sciences was also observed in the higher frequencies of *evaluative that* structures, such as *we believe that* and *it is possible that*, in the social sciences in both articles and theses abstracts (Hyland & Tse, 2005) and in articles and book reviews (Groom, 2005).

We also find similar disciplinary differences in engagement features (Hyland, 2001a; 2002a; 2005a; Hyland & Tse, 2004a), with considerable variation in the use of reader pronouns, questions, and directives in research articles across disciplines. More than 80 percent of these occur in the soft discipline papers, particularly in philosophy, where they appeal to scholarly solidarity, presupposing a set of discipline-identifying understandings linking the writer and readers (see Figure 7.3).

Overall, these stance patterns coincide with our intuitions that the sciences tend to produce more impersonal, or at least less reader inclusive, texts. More precisely, however, they indicate how the resources of language mediate the contexts in which they are used.

The considerations discussed so far have dealt exclusively with Anglo-American scientific writing. We will now discuss the main findings of cross-linguistic research into scientific writing.

Feature	Phil	Soc	AL	Mk	Phy	Bio	ME	EE	Total
Total	**16.3**	**5.1**	**5.0**	**3.2**	**4.9**	**1.6**	**2.8**	**4.3**	**5.9**
Reader ref.	11.0	2.3	1.9	1.1	2.1	0.1	0.5	1.0	2.9
Directives	2.6	1.6	2.0	1.3	2.1	1.3	2.0	2.9	1.9
Questions	1.4	0.7	0.5	0.3	0.1	0.1	0.1	0.0	0.5
Shared know.	1.0	0.4	0.6	0.4	0.5	0.1	0.3	0.4	0.5
Asides	0.2	0.2	0.1	0.1	0.0	0.0	0.0	0.0	0.1

Figure 7.3 **Engagement features by discipline (per 1,000 words).**

Cross-Linguistic Variation

As we have noted, rhetorical analyses consider texts as social constructs and show how language reflects institutional context and organizes human knowledge. Contrastive rhetoricians, as their name indicates, focus on the comparison of academic discourses written in English with comparable discourses written in other languages (Connor, 1996, 2002; Grabe & Kaplan, 1996). These comparative studies have been concerned mainly with issues such as the structuring of the research article (e.g., Evangelisti Allori, 1998; Sa'Adeddin, 1989), the concept of coherence (e.g., Hinds, 1987, 1990), the use of hedges and modal expressions (e.g., Hyland, 1998a, 1998b; Salager-Meyer, 1994, 1998b, 2000), the use of reporting verbs (e.g., Thompson & Ye, 1991), the frequency of connectors and metadiscourse markers (e.g., Mauranen, 1992, 1993; Ventola & Mauranen, 1991), and the expression of criticism (Salager-Meyer, Alcaraz Ariza, & Zambrano, 2003).

The majority of this research compares English with Asian (mostly Chinese and Japanese) and Arabic languages, although a few deal with other Western European languages (e.g., Finnish, Spanish, Italian, and French), and more recently with the patterns characteristic of Russian and Slavic languages (Polish, Czech, Bulgarian, Slovene, Hungarian, and Ukranian). We focus next on three of the features previously mentioned that are particularly relevant to cross-linguistic/cultural studies of scientific writing: (1) the structuring of the introduction of research papers (more specifically the CARS model); (2) the phenomenon of hedges; and (3) the use of metadiscourse.

The CARS Model

Swales's (1990) CARS model has undoubtedly been the most influential model in the textual analysis of the research article. It captures the ways in which academic writers justify and highlight their own contributions to the ongoing research of a field by establishing a research topic and summarizing the key features of previous work, thus creating a gap that will accommodate the writer's claims. It is based on an ecological metaphor of populations of researchers competing for resources and visibility in tightly contested areas, not unlike populations of plants competing for light and nutrients. In other words, the CARS model assumes antagonism and competition for research space among individual members or research groups within an academic discourse community (Fredrickson & Swales, 1994). But, as Swales (2004) observes, this metaphor has produced two conflicting effects: contributing to both the model's "interestingness" and its fallibility.

These effects derive from the fact that the CARS model privileges an environment in which originality is highly prized, competition fierce, and academic self-promotion strong (Hyland, 2000b; Lindeberg, 1998). In other words, as Swales (2004) observes, the model reflects primarily research in hard fields with big journals, big names, and big libraries within large discourse communities. Incidentally, the same could be said of the sociological and anthropological accounts provided by such influential monographs as those of Latour and Woolgar (1979) and Knorr Cetina (1981) that are based on "big science"; the North American scholarly communication system with its high-speed, high bandwidth networks; and competition for influence, power, resources, and prestige.[3] But self-promotion may not have such a high priority in all academic cultures.

In Eastern European academic contexts, for example, the cultural, historical, and political proximity of languages has led to very different patterns of organization. Duszak (1994) and Golebiowski (1998, 1999) observe that Polish writers tend to downplay the "occupying a niche move," which is so frequent in English-language research paper introductions. Yakhontova (2002b, p. 292) similarly found no research gap in Russian- and Ukranian-language papers and noted the absence of self-advertisement in conference abstracts in those languages compared with the strong "promotional flavor" in English-language ones. As we have seen, the influence of a market society with its emphasis on competitiveness, attention winning, and recognition of target audiences to promote a research product inevitably influences academic discourse, making it persuasive and self-promotional.

The absence of an explicit research gap has also been observed in research papers in Spanish (López, 1982), Arabic (Najjar, 1990), Malaysian (Ahmad, 1997), and Swedish (Fredrickson & Swales, 1994). Fredrickson and Swales remark that the Swedish-language papers they examined had a story-like feature, carefully positioned at the beginning of the article as an attention-getting device, as if writers were competing for readership, not for a space on the academic stage.

Recent work reveals the complexities of comparing English with Chinese. Taylor and Chen (1991), for example, show the methodological problems in contrastive studies that result from the complex interactions of both regional and disciplinary variations. Examining the CARS model in a variety of science and engineering papers written in English by Chinese writers, in English by English-speaking writers, and in Chinese by Chinese writers, they found consistent patterns of difference across disciplines and first language speakers.

The Chinese scholars (when writing in English and even more so when writing in Chinese) were less likely to elaborate the moves, wrote less, and tended to omit or truncate discussion of previous research. In fact, the Chinese academics refrained from directly citing writers whose work was seen as deficient or incomplete. Taylor and Chen offer two speculative explanations for their findings: (1) that Chinese scientists do not have access to a wide literature and (2) a culturally oriented reason; disputation was absent in the Chinese scientific tradition for a long time and for Chinese scholars the maintenance of relationship takes precedence over content in their academic writing (Scollon, 1997).

Harrison (2002) offers similar conclusions about the lack of a knowledge gap in the introductions of Japanese scientific texts. He argues that Japanese people tend to avoid confrontation, make assumptions about shared background knowledge, and place a high value on allusion to events and situations. It has been noted that such a concept of scientific writing causes problems when Japanese scholars fail to realize that more detailed information is necessary for understanding by people from other countries.

Swales (2004) remarks that the frequent absence of a literature gap in papers written in languages other than English could reflect a kinder, more gentle and relaxed academic world in which there is less competition for research space. In this alternative world, instead of competition for readership, the need to justify doing any research at all may have higher priority than establishing some small gap in an extensive literature. As we will see later, writer–audience considerations are also important factors that must be taken into consideration when analyzing and interpreting the rhetoric of scientific writing.

Hedging

Scientific writers make decisions about the level of their knowledge claims; the higher the level of claim, the more likely it will contradict existing positions and challenge the assumptions underlying ongoing research in the area. "Claim-making is a risky practice," as Hyland (2000a, p. 93) expresses it. Researchers resort to hedges to modify the epistemic warrant of their claims. These devices allow the writer to reduce his or her commitment to the propositional content of the utterance or to open a discursive space where readers can dispute the writer's interpretations.

Hedges are among the main pragmatic features that shape the research article as the principal vehicle for new knowledge and distinguish it from other forms of academic discourse (Hyland, 1998a). They allow researchers to produce a closer fit between their statements about new discoveries and the pre-existing understandings of the scientific community. They are interactive devices in that they build a relationship between the writer and the community of readers and allow writers to anticipate audience reaction by reducing the certainty with which they present their claims, a "modesty" strategy in scientific writing, which dates back to Robert Boyle.

Because hedges can express politeness, indirectness, understatement, mitigation, commitment, and/or vagueness, they are pragmatically polyfunctional (Clemen, 1997) and have been the focus of extensive research in all kinds of discourses. An abundant literature has demonstrated the importance of this socio-pragmatic phenomenon in Anglo-American academic writing since Lakoff (1972) first discussed it, but no real consensus has been reached. This lack of consensus was exemplified in the late 1990s by the radically opposed stances adopted by Crompton (1997), who fervently defended a positivist view on the subject, and Salager-Meyer (1994, 1998b, 2000), who strongly supported a mentalistic approach and defined hedges as first and foremost the product of a mental attitude. Nonetheless, it is important to note that hedges are no longer approached from a semantic perspective but rather from a socio-pragmatic one.

Linguists and applied linguists have studied hedging in written scientific discourse in a number of other languages. Régent (1994), Crosnier (1996), and Liddicoat (2005) have analyzed the issue in French-language research papers, and all reached the conclusion that French scientists are much more prescriptive, authoritarian, and categorical than their English-speaking colleagues. Instead they use *bemol statements* (Régent, 1994, p. 58) when stating their claims and rejecting others' opinions, thus avoiding the so-called face-threatening act (Brown & Levinson, 1987). Martin (1996, p. 22) agrees that it is in the use of such *précautions oratoires* that we find the most prominent cultural difference between English and French academic writing. This led Beaufrère-Bertheux (1997, p. 232) to refer to the hyper-modesty of Anglo-American scientists and Sionis (1997, p. 211) to the "exaggerated self-confidence of French academics" who sound arrogant to their Anglo-American counterparts.

The use of fewer hedging devices has also been noted in Finnish academic writing (Ventola, 1997) and in articles written in Bulgarian and in English by Bulgarian-speaking scientists (Vassileva, 1997, 2001), indicating that Finnish and Bulgarian academic writings show a higher degree of commitment and a lower degree of deference toward the discourse community than does their English counterpart. Articles written in Spanish and in English by Spanish-speaking scientists were also found to be less modalized than those written in English by native-English-speaking scientists (Mendiluce Cabrera & Hernández Bartolomé, 2005; Oliver del Olmo, 2004), as were research articles written in Dutch by Dutch authors (Burrough-Boenisch, 2004). In contrast, articles written in German and in English by German authors (e.g.,

Clyne, 1991; Kreutz & Harres, 1997), in Polish by Polish writers (Duszak, 1994), and in Czech by Czech writers (Cmejroková & Danes, 1997) show a higher degree of tentativeness than those written by English-speaking writers.

Research into hedging in East Asian languages is more contentious. Although Hinkel (1997) claims that hedging is common in the Confucian rhetorical tradition, her study is inconclusive. Hyland and Milton's (1997) analysis of hedging in the Hong Kong University of Science and Technology's learners' corpus showed that essays written by more proficient students approached the level of those written by native English writers in their use of hedges, thus suggesting that a learner's proficiency level plays a role in the use of hedges. Hinkel's findings may have resulted from the essay prompts she used, highlighting the importance of careful research design.

These differences indicate that the convention of hedging in academic writing is culture-specific. Emphasis, however, should be given to the point made in the section on disciplinary variation, that discipline and genre play an important role in the frequency of use of hedging. Research papers in the humanities and social sciences contain more probability expressions than those in the natural sciences. Diachronic studies of hedging have also shown that the difference in the use of modalization between 19th and 20th century scientific writing lies not so much in the frequency of hedging devices but on the type of devices used (Gross et al., 2002; Salager-Meyer & Defives, 1998). Other variables could also exert an influence on the use of modalization in academic writing, such as the writer's status, age, and gender, but these variables have rarely, if ever, been taken into consideration, perhaps because of the difficulty of analyzing them.

Metadiscourse and the Concept of Reader-Writer-Responsible Languages

Contrastive rhetoric analyses of scientific discourse have also called attention to the existence of differences in explicitness between languages. English is said to lie at the higher end of a scale of explicitness of text organization: English readers expect signposts of coherence and unity as they read and writers need to provide these transitions (Crismore & Farnsworth, 1990; Hyland, 1999a, 1999b, 2004b; Hyland & Tse, 2004a, 2004b). English-written texts, which tend to contain a great deal of metadiscourse, thus reflect a more reader-oriented attitude. Other languages, though, are much less writer-responsible.[4]

Academic writing in Japanese (Hinds, 1987), Korean (Eggington, 1987) and Chinese (Jensen, 1998) is said to be characterized by non-linearity, with less use of explicit transitions and illocution markers. Readers are expected to piece together the thread of the writer's logic, which binds the composition together so as to make a coherent text. According to Hinds (1984, 1987, 1990), writing that is too explicit is not valued in many East Asian languages, where the task of the writer is not necessarily to convince but rather to stimulate readers to think for themselves and draw their own conclusions from the argument. Hinds's work has been extremely influential; but some critics have pointed out that his generalizations about Japanese expository prose are based on analyses of articles from only one newspaper and that different genres may require different styles. Hinds's point that there is a difference in the perceived coherence of Japanese and Anglo-American texts, however, remains an important and interesting issue.

Texts written in Spanish (Valero Garcés, 1996) and Portuguese (Oliveira, 1997) also lack many of the explicit signals of cohesion we expect in English-language texts. Far fewer links, previews, and reviews have also been noted in French-language scientific papers (Bachschmidt, 1999; Osborne, 1994) as well as in Slovene (Pisanski Peterlin, 2005) and German academic writing (Clyne, 1991). German academic texts are often dismissed as pretentious, digressive, propositionally asymmetrical, longwinded, and badly organized by English readers because of their non-adherence to English discourse structures and rhetorical norms. Michael Clyne characterizes German academic discourse as "cooked spaghetti" (Clyne, 1987, pp. 237–238; Skudlik, 1990) because of its sharp contrast with more linear Anglo-American writing. Clyne argued that saying a text is easy to follow may be interpreted as a compliment in an Anglo-Saxon context but it is less so among German academics whose texts conform to the primary function of *Wissensdarstellung*. Similarly, Ventola and Mauranen (1991) and Mauranen (1993) reported that Finnish scientists use less metalanguage for organizing texts, show a more negative kind of politeness, and have a greater tendency toward implicitness than Anglo-American writers. Some might consider Finnish prose aloof and uncaring toward the reader, but Mauranen has claimed that the Finnish style can be interpreted as polite and non-patronizing, as what is obvious is left unsaid.

Scientific prose in Slavic languages also tends to be more concerned with presenting knowledge than addressing the reader (Cmejrková & Danes, 1997; Golebiowski, 1998; Yakhontova, 2001), or, as Yakhontova (2002a, p. 224) aptly put it in her study of conference abstracts written by Russian and Ukrainian academics, Slavic academic writing tends to "tell" rather than "sell." This does not imply a lack of writer–reader cooperation but means that the reader is expected to invest more effort in following the writer's presentation.

Limitations of Contrastive Rhetoric Studies

Contrastive rhetoric studies of scientific writing have been criticized on a variety of grounds, the most frequently voiced referring to design flaws such as small sample size (Connor, 1996), comparing mixed genres in different contexts (Swales, 1990), and a lack of *a tertium comparationis* (Connor, 1996, p. 164). Moreover, as Swales (2004) has argued, it is increasingly difficult in today's research world to construct a corpus of non-English texts that can be considered equivalent to English ones (especially in the "bigger" fields) in terms of status, potential audience, and level of reviewing and editorial gatekeeping.

Genres, too, have to be taken into account; although many research genres seem to be universal, there may still be differences between Anglo-American genres and those of other languages (Grabe & Kaplan, 1996; Yakhontova, 2002b). Choice of language may indeed entail a change of genre (Melander, 1998, p. 217). This research is also criticized for its tendency to characterize groups as static and homogeneous (Spack, 1997).

Recent critics have blamed contrastive rhetoricians for teaching students/scientists to write for native English speakers' expectations instead of expressing their own lingual and cultural identities (Kubota, 1999; Ramanathan & Atkinson, 1999). We should distinguish the author as a social individual with a native language and an investment in a text from the author as a social construct, observing a set of rhetorical practices for which social identity is less relevant. Connor, Davies, and DeRycker (1995) have pointed out that, if Finnish scientists wish to secure European Union (EU) research grants, they need to follow EU norms and these tend to be based on Anglo-American scientific discourse.

We now examine the various cultural, socio-political, historical, and educational factors that are thought to account for the cross-linguistic rhetorical differences observed in scientific writing.

Academic Cultures, Intellectual Traditions, and Socio-Political Considerations

Traditionally, the differences in writing styles and patterns of textual organization revealed in contrasted texts are labeled "cultural" or "cultural specific differences." This umbrella term embraces diverse interpretations stemming from a wide range of possible influences, from purely intralinguistic peculiarities to socio-political factors that interplay and leave their joint imprints upon the texts created within different linguistic and cultural environments. Several interpretational perspectives thus account for the extremely complicated and intricate relationship between writing and culture. We present and compare the various standpoints from which researchers, in the last decade or so, have sought to explain the differences observed in the writing styles of different academic cultures, starting from the earliest (the influence of thought patterns) to the most recent, which calls socio-political factors into play.

Thought Patterns

The thought patterns explanation is related to the Sapir-Whorf linguistic relativity hypothesis that proposes a close connection between one's language and one's worldview. It was initiated by Kaplan (1966) through his germinal and provocative "doodles study" of the organization of paragraphs in different languages. From this study Kaplan claimed that English follows a linear model[5] and that writers from Semitic, Oriental, Russian, and Romance language backgrounds apply a more digressive or circular model. Although Kaplan's study has been criticized for its ethnocentrism, it is considered the starting point of contrastive rhetoric research. This approach suggests both that rhetorical patterns are as much a component of language as lexical, syntactical, and semantic phenomena and that a broadening of discourse analysis is required to provide wider cross-linguistic and cross-cultural comparative evidence in the area of textual studies.

Folman and Sarig (1990) took issue with the influence of thought patterns on writing style and claimed that cross-linguistic rhetorical differences lay within the realm of the professed and implanted syllabi of language arts. This argument does not seem valid, however, because syllabi are a cultural product and reflect a nation's particular thought patterns.

Influence of National Intellectual Style

Rather than referring to nations, Galtung (1979, 1985) relies on thought styles to explain different academic and intellectual traditions, hence different conceptions of academic writing. Galtung compared Teutonic intellectual style with "Saxonic," "Nipponic," and "Gallic" styles and found that Saxonic style emphasizes data analysis, description, and deductive thinking and facilitates dialogue and interaction. In contrast, scholars influenced by Teutonic intellectual styles discourage dialogue by engaging in cryptic monologism, which emphasizes theoretical issues and inductive thinking and gives greater significance to the propositional content than to form; in short, a style that institutionalizes digression or "baroqueness, associativeness and multiplicity of standpoints" (Cmejrková, 1996, p. 13). Clyne (1991, p. 65) posited that knowledge—a stimulus for thought—is idealized in the German tradition where the onus is on the reader to make the effort to understand texts. Studies conducted by Clyne (1983, 1987, 1991), Mauranen (1993), and Golebiowski (1998) on the issues of linearity, hierarchy, symmetry, and digression in academic texts written in English by German, Finnish, and Polish scholars suggested that scientific communication styles and discoursal organization are related to cultural value systems. Such generalizations, however, risk interpreting data through cultural stereotypes.

Influence of the Educational System and Writing Instruction

National intellectual traditions shape the norms and conventions of writing and these norms are transmitted and sustained by educational systems. As Mauranen (1992, p. 239) argued: "there is ample evidence that all writing is strongly anchored in the values of the writing cultures that people get socialized into as they learn to write." Writing is then an expression of culture[6] and native culture (in particular the educational system of an author's culture) influences writing habits. This view is shared by many researchers (Clyne, 1991; Le, 1999; Martin, 1996; Mauranen, 1993; Swales, 1990; Vassileva, 2000) who treat genres as a kind of social activity realized in language, existing within social, cultural, and linguistic parameters. Duszak (1994) argues that styles of intellectual debating, scientific prose, and attitudes to knowledge and academia are interconnected with cultural values, norms, and beliefs. In other words, the generic constraints on academic prose reflect the cultural habits of the writer's academic community.

It is therefore assumed that national educational styles are congruent with a general cultural value orientation and the dominant verbal style associated with it; and that this influences the "clash" (Peck MacDonald, 1990, p. 55) observed between Anglo-American and "continental" writing. In the North American educational system writing instruction is given considerable emphasis, as is evidenced in widespread college composition courses that place great emphasis on the argumentative/persuasive essay, the existence of writing centers at universities, and the numerous writing journals and textbooks that are available (see Braine, 2001; Connor, 1996; and Russell, 1992 for an historical overview of this tradition). No such tradition of writing instruction exists elsewhere in the world (Andersson & Gunnarsson, 1995; Canagarajah, 2002b; Mauranen, 1993; Petric, 2005; Salager-Meyer et al., 2003; Yakhontova, 1997, 2001), although this state of affairs is slowly changing (Petric, 2005; Salager-Meyer et al., 2003).

Influence of Other Languages and Learning Traditions

Vassileva (2001, p. 100) remarked that the "essay-like" composition style of Bulgarian academic texts is due to the long-standing impact of French and German, Russian itself being influenced by French. Similarly, Yakhontova (2001) emphasized that the Ukranian system of higher education still employs the highly theoretical stance characteristic of European (German and French) intellectualism. The emerging body of work investigating discourse-level contrasts between writing in English and in Czech, Russian, Ukranian, Polish, and Slovene can be explained by several factors:

1. Similarities in the syntactic structures of Slavic languages.
2. The German historical influence on education and academic discourse in the region, more recently transmitted via the Russian

intellectual tradition. German academic writing served as a model for Slovene academic culture until the end of World War II (Pisanski Peterlin, 2005); its influence is still present in some disciplines, especially in the humanities and the soft sciences. The cultural ties between the Slovene people and the German-speaking world remained strong even after the end of the Austro-Hungarian monarchy; German was still one of the most important foreign languages and also the language of profes-sional and scientific training well after World War II.

3. Ukranian scholarship was formed during the Soviet era (and dominated by it for over seventy years) when the communist ide-ology was considered to be the only methodological foundation of research. This ideology has obviously left its imprint on Soviet and post-Soviet academic rhetoric.

The influence of other languages and learning traditions has also been noted in the case of Finnish (Mauranen, 1993) and Swedish (Lindeberg, 1988) academic writing, two countries that have been greatly influenced by the German academic tradition. This confirms Galtung's (1979, 1985) theory, which places Eastern Europe in the sphere of historical influence of the Teutonic intellectual style.

Such external ideological influence is obviously not static but dynamic; it is socially coded and transmitted, and it changes as the soci-ety whose values it articulates changes (Atkinson, 1999a; Gross et al., 2002; Salager-Meyer et al., 2003; Valle, 1999). Changes in educational systems also bring about changes in writing styles. The latest research on Slavic languages is a case in point. It shows a growing influence of Anglo-American rhetoric on textual patterns in Slavic scientific writing (Petric, 2005; Yakhontova, 2001, 2002a). Yakhontova (2002a) argues that this is because Ukranian society (traditionally collaborative, homo-geneous, and non-conflictive) has only recently been exposed to market forces that affect its academic culture. This, of course, coincides with the growing influence of English as the global language of science and technology.

Rhetorical and stylistic changes have also been observed in Korean academic writing, which is adopting a Western-influenced linear style (Eggington, 1987), and in Chinese academic journals (Shi, 2002, p. 628), which "are changing rapidly to adopt the international (Anglo-American/Western) style and format of publication." A progressive styl-istic uniformity has also been noted in letters of application written in Flemish, Finnish, and English (Upton & Connor, 2001) covering a ten-year period: letters of the early 1990s showed greater differences between cultural groups than those of later years. A universal form of letter of application may very well be emerging in the global business environment.

The growing influence of British and American rhetoric has also been noted in Spanish academic writing in the use of causal metatext

(Moreno, 1997) and in the evolution of the linguistic formulation of criticism. Such criticism was conveyed in a very aggressive, personal, and face-threatening fashion up to the 1960s; for a number of social, historical, and political reasons it is now expressed in a much more subdued, modalized, and impersonal "Anglo-American" way (Salager-Meyer et al., 2003). Moreno and Salager-Meyer et al. explain that the similarities observed rest in part in the extent to which Spanish and Latin American education is today influenced by English-speaking academia. The majority of graduate level texts and materials in the Spanish-speaking world are translations of books originally written in English and most academics, especially those in the hard fields, resort to English language sources for teaching and research. It should be noted, however, that Salager-Meyer et al.'s research is confined to the medical field and that Moreno's work is based on a minor rhetorical feature of articles, limitations that do not permit any broad generalizations about the comparative rhetoric of text organization in Spanish and English.

In spite of the importance of socio-political and ideological factors in shaping scientific writing, there is some evidence that these factors may have less influence than purely cultural ones (Vassileva, 2000), although both are intertwined.

Influence of Audience Size

The size and local character of the discourse community are also important factors to be considered in the shaping of scientific writing conventions, as studies from sociolinguistic and sociocognitive perspectives confirm (Berkenkotter & Huckin, 1995; Golebiowski, 1998; Melander, 1998; Swales, 2004).

Ahmad (1997), for example, suggests that the reluctance of Malaysian scientists to engage in a more conflictual and challenging style of discourse is due to the small size of the Malaysian discourse community, where everybody may be familiar with the work of others. Research in Malay thus means addressing a local readership, not a large international audience. In such a constrained context, indicating a gap in others' research is not a prime concern. What is more important is justifying the study being reported as a valid and rigorous area of investigation and emphasizing the Malaysian need to develop research programs. Indeed, in a developing country such as Malaysia where research activities in many areas are only beginning, there are huge gaps wherever one turns and quite a number of areas have yet to develop a research tradition. The metaphor of competing for an ecological niche in a wider research ecosystem thus does not really apply here.

In a more recent study, Burgess (2002) found that the nature and size of the audience were more important variables than specialization or language of publication in the choice of rhetorical practices in the introductions of articles published in international linguistics journals,

Hispanic studies journals, and English language studies published in both Spanish and English.

Interplay of Disciplinary and National Cultures

A few studies of scientific discourse have suggested that cross-cultural differences may be small when compared to differences between disciplines and sub-disciplines (Taylor & Chen, 1991) or between professional and colloquial registers. This dimension has rarely been taken into consideration, even though it sometimes seems to neutralize potential cultural proclivities. For example, Clyne (1983) argued that, in some disciplines (e.g., mathematics and engineering), German scientists appear to have adopted a basically linear structure. This may be conditioned by the discipline or the leadership in the discipline of English speakers. Melander, Swales, and Fredrickson (1997) reached similar conclusions in their analysis of Swedish abstracts from three different disciplines. More recent research by Yakhontova (2002b) on abstracts in two different fields (applied mathematics and linguistics) written in Ukranian, Russian, and English also showed essentially interdisciplinary differences between the two sets of data and revealed a complex interaction of factors.

Disciplinary conventions and context thus interact with national cultural influences and these influences may be particularly prominent in fields with universal cognitive paradigms (e.g., the so-called hard sciences).

Conclusions

We have sought to emphasize in this review that research writing is a social enterprise both in the sense that it is an immediate engagement with colleagues and that it is mediated by the social cultures and institutions within which it occurs. Research papers, for example, do not simply report research but present it in ways acceptable to a discipline and a society. In today's highly competitive research world, academic writing functions to shape information for the needs of an audience, accomplish a writer's own rhetorical purposes, and establish the author within a discipline and wider context. Such writing is important because it offers a window into the values, beliefs, and practices of disciplinary communities. It shows us how disciplines help to create a view of the world through their writing and the ways that texts are influenced by the problems, social practices, and ways of thinking of particular social groups. Writing practices are deeply embedded in the epistemological and social convictions of scientific disciplines.

This is just one example of how the structures and roles of language, which have evolved in one context, are adapted for use in very different ones, providing the means for constructing knowledge in fields as diverse as medicine and mechanics. In fact, the development of literacy, with its enormous impact on mode of communication and genre, has itself helped to reshape these contexts. The spread of science in the 18th century accompanied a desire to establish a literacy of empirical enquiry, a new "univocal discourse," which could represent real events without the mediation of rhetoric. Logic was imposed on grammar, dictionaries and taxonomies emerged, and the perception that a correct use of language bestowed social prestige grew. The use of writing to capture events for analysis could, however, never establish one-to-one correspondences between words and things; but an expository and argument-oriented literacy emerged eventually to supplant in influence a more event- and narrative-oriented one.

In recent years a great deal of attention has been given to the rhetorical conventions of academic expositions in several different languages. The results of this cross-linguistic research indicate that scientific writing depends upon the milieu and the period in which it develops, and that research reporting is language/culture bound. Indeed, because social context always impinges on language, all writing is strongly anchored in the values of the cultures into which people are socialized when they learn how to write, values that are inculcated and transmitted through national educational systems. These systems are neither static nor immutable but dynamic, potentially influenced by external social, cultural, and political forces, as we have noted in connection with scientific writing in Slavic languages. These factors can alter peoples' vision of the world and, consequently, what they understand. The impact of such wider societal and ideological trends, and the political dimension underlying academic practices, therefore constitute important sources of writing change.

We are aware of the partial coverage of this chapter, despite its length. The explosion of research into scientific and academic writing over the past decade or so has meant that we have been able to mention only a few of the key genres, theories, and studies in this area. In particular, we are aware of work on other academic genres such as essays, acknowledgments, and grant applications and the growing research into Internet communications, Web-resources such as wikis, and the potential effects of grid technologies on writing and instruction. We have been able only to touch on writing in foreign language instruction and English for academic purposes teaching, and have been unable to mention the numerous contributions of information science research to our understanding of writing. In spite of these limitations, however, we hope to have provided a sufficiently broad overview of current developments and understandings of science writing from the perspective of applied linguistics.

Endnotes

1. The *Philosophical Transactions* are still published today; the *Journal des Sçavans* (renamed *Journal des Savants* in 1716) ceased publication in 1792.

2. Metadiscourse refers to those aspects of a text that explicitly refer to the organization of the discourse or the writer's stance toward its content or the reader.
3. The CARS model seems to have made its appearance in the 1960s; see Bazerman (1988) for a study of its evolution in physics article introductions, Dudley-Evans and Henderson (1990) in economics, and Gunnarsson (1989) in medicine. Valle (1999) argues that when the CARS model was used in the 17th century it was not for situating the text within the background of previous knowledge or for indicating a gap in that knowledge, but for juxtaposing and dialogizing different views.
4. The "reader-responsible" vs. "writer-responsible" typology of language was introduced by Hinds in 1987 in his comparative studies of Japanese and English scientific writing; it was later qualified as "dialogic" or expository as compared with "monologic" or contemplative (Cmejrková & Danes, 1997).
5. A linear text features propositions leading directly to those following them with each part of each proposition following the one above it in the hierarchy. *Digression* is understood as the other end of the linear scale.
6. For definitions of the "received" and the "alternative/non-standard" views of culture, see Atkinson (1999b).

References

Ahmad, U. K. (1997). Research article introductions in Malay: Rhetoric in an emerging research community. In A. Duszak (Ed.), *Culture and styles in academic discourse* (pp. 273–303). Berlin, Germany: Mouton de Gruyter.

Andersson, B., & Gunnarsson, B. L. (1995). A contrastive study of text patterns in conference abstracts. In B. Warvick, S. K. Tanskanen, & R. Hiltunen (Eds.), *Organization in discourse. Proceedings from the Türkü Conference* (pp. 139–148). Türkü, Finland: Anglicana Türküensia.

Anthony, L. (1999). Writing research article introductions in software engineering: How accurate is the standard model? *IEEE Transactions of Professional Communication, 42,* 38–46.

Atkinson, D. (1999a). *Scientific discourse in sociohistoric context.* Mahwah, NJ: Erlbaum.

Atkinson, D. (1999b). Culture in TESOL. *TESOL Quarterly, 33,* 625–654.

Aronowitz, S. (1988). *Science as power: Discourse and ideology in modern society.* London: Macmillan.

Bachschmidt, P. (1999). Contruction de l'argumentation dans l'article de recherche en mécanique: Différences entre discours du francophone et de l'anglophone. *ASp (Anglais de Spécialité), 23–26,* 197–207.

Bakhtin, M. (1981). *The dialogical imagination* (M. Holquist, Ed., C. Emerson & M. Holquist, Trans.). Austin: University of Texas Press.

Bakhtin, M. (1986). *Speech genres and other late essays.* Austin: University of Texas Press.

Bartholomae, D. (1986). Inventing the university. *Journal of Basic Writing, 5,* 4–23.

Bazerman, C. (1984). Modern evolution of the experimental report in physics: Spectroscopic articles in *Physical Review* 1893–1980. *Social Studies of Science, 14,* 163–196.

Bazerman, C. (1988). *Shaping written knowledge.* Madison: University of Wisconsin Press.

Beaufrère-Bertheux, C. (1997). L'anglais de la recherche médicale: Une grande diversité. *ASp (Anglais de Spécialité)*, *15/18*, 223–238.

Becher, T. (1989). *Academic tribes and territories: Intellectual inquiry and the cultures of disciplines*. Milton Keynes, UK: Society for Research into Higher Education and Open University Press.

Berkenkotter, C., & Huckin, T. (1995). *Genre knowledge in disciplinary communication*. Hillsdale, NJ: Erlbaum.

Bhatia, V. K. (1999). Integrating products, processes, purposes and participants in professional writing. In C. N. Candlin & K. Hyland (Eds.), *Writing: Texts, processes and practices* (pp. 21–39). London: Longman.

Blyler, N., & Thralls, C. (Eds.). (1993). *Professional communication: The social perspective*. Newbury Park, CA: Sage.

Bondi, M. (1999). *English across genres: Language variation in the discourse of economics*. Modena: Edizioni Il Fiorino.

Bondi, M. (2005). Metadiscursive practices in academic discourse: Variation across genres and disciplines. In J. Bamford & M. Bondi (Eds.), *Dialogue within discourse communities: Metadiscursive perspectives on academic genres* (pp. 3–30). Tübingen, Germany: Niemeyer.

Bourdieu, P. (1991). *Language and symbolic power*. Oxford, UK: Polity Press.

Braine, G. (1995). Writing in the natural sciences and engineering. In D. Belcher & G. Braine (Eds.), *Academic writing in a second language: Essays on research and pedagogy* (pp. 113–133). Norwood, NJ: Ablex.

Braine, G. (2001). When professors don't cooperate: A critical perspective on EAP research. *English for Specific Purposes*, *20*, 293–303.

Brett, P. (1994). A genre analysis of the results sections of sociology articles. *English for Specific Purposes*, *13*, 47–59.

Brown, G., & Levinson, S. (1987). *Politeness: Some universals in language usage*. Cambridge, UK: Cambridge University Press.

Bunton, D. (2002). Generic moves in PhD thesis introductions. In J. Flowerdew (Ed.), *Academic Discourse* (pp. 57–74). London: Longman.

Bunton, D. (2005). The structure of PhD conclusion chapters. *Journal of English for Academic Purposes*, *4*(3), 207–224.

Burgess, S. (2002). Packed houses and intimate gathering: Audience and rhetorical structure. In J. Flowerdew (Ed.), *Academic discourse* (pp. 196–215). Harlow, UK: Longman.

Burrough-Boenisch, J. (2004). NS and NNS scientists' amendments of Dutch scientific English and their impact on hedging. *English for Specific Purposes*, *24*(1), 25–39.

Busà, M. (2005). The use of metadiscourse in abstracts: A comparison between economics and psychology abstracts. In J. Bamford & M. Bondi (Eds.), *Dialogue within discourse communities: Metadiscursive perspectives on academic genres* (pp. 31–48). Tübingen, Germany: Niemeyer.

Canagarajah, S. (1999). *Resisting linguistic imperialism in English teaching*. Oxford, UK: Oxford University Press.

Canagarajah, S. (2002a). *Critical academic writing and multilingual students*. Ann Arbor: University of Michigan Press.

Canagarajah, S. (2002b). *The geopolitics of academic writing*. Pittsburg, PA: University of Pittsburg Press.

Candlin, C. N., & Hyland, K. (Eds.). (1999). *Writing: Texts, processes and practices*. London: Longman.

Clemen, G. (1997). The concept of hedging: Origins, approaches and definitions. In R. Markkanen & H. Schröder (Eds.), *Hedging and discourse: Approaches to the analysis of a pragmatic phenomenon in academic texts* (pp. 235–248). Berlin, Germany: Mouton de Gruyter.

Clyne, M. G. (1983). Linguistic and written discourse in particular languages: English and German. *Annual Review of Applied Linguistics, III*, 38–49.

Clyne, M. G. (1987). Cultural differences in the organization of academic texts: English and German. *Journal of Pragmatics, 11*(2), 211–247.

Clyne, M. G. (1991). The sociocultural dimension: The dilemma of the German-speaking scholar. In H. Schröder (Ed.), *Subject-oriented texts* (pp. 49–67). Berlin, Germany: Mouton de Gruyter.

Cmejrková, S. (1996). Academic writing in Czech and English. In E. Ventola & A. Mauranen (Eds.). *Academic writing: Intercultural and textual issues* (pp. 137–152). Amsterdam: John Benjamins.

Cmejrková, S., & Danes, F. (1997). Academic writing and cultural identity: The case of Czech academic writing, In A. Duszak (Ed.), *Culture and styles in academic discourse* (pp. 41–62). Berlin, Germany: Mouton de Gruyter.

Cohen, R. S., & Schnelle, T. (Eds.). (1986). *Cognition and fact: Materials on Ludwik Fleck*. Dordrecht, Netherlands: Reidel.

Coffin, C., Curry, M., Goodman, S., Hewings, A., Lillis, T., & Swann, J. (2003). *Teaching academic writing: A toolkit for higher education*. London: Routledge.

Connor, U. (1996). *Contrastive rhetoric*. Cambridge, UK. Cambridge University Press.

Connor, U. (2000). Variations in rhetorical moves in grant proposals of US humanists and scientists. *Text, 20*(1), 1–28.

Connor, U. (2002). New directions in contrastive rhetoric. *TESOL Quarterly, 36*(4), 493–510.

Connor, U., Davies, K., & DeRycker, T. (1995). Correctness and clarity for applying for overseas jobs: A cross-cultural analysis of US and Flemish applications. *Text, 15*, 457–475.

Connor, U., & Upton, T. (2004). The genre of grant proposals: A corpus linguistic study. In U. Connor & T. Upton (Eds.), *Discourse in the professions* (pp. 235–255). Amsterdam: Benjamins.

Connors, R. (1986). Textbooks and the evolution of the discipline. *College Composition and Communication, 37*, 178–194.

Crismore, A., & Farnsworth, R. (1990). Metadiscourse in popular and professional science discourse. In W. Nash (Ed.), *The writing scholar: Studies in academic discourse* (pp. 118–136). Newbury Park, CA: Sage.

Crismore, A., Markkanen, R., & Steffensen, M. (1993). Metadiscourse in persuasive writing: A study of texts written by American and Finnish university students. *Written Communication, 10*(1), 39–71.

Crompton, P. (1997). Hedging in academic writing: Some theoretical problems. *English for Specific Purposes, 16*(4), 271–287.

Cronin, B. (1995). *The scholar's courtesy: The role of acknowledgement in the primary communication process*. London: Taylor Graham.

Cronin, B. (2005). *The hand of science: Academic writing and its rewards*. Lanham, MD: Scarecrow Press.

Cronin, B., Shaw, D., & La Barre, K. (2003). A cast of thousands: Co-authorship and subauthorship collaboration in the 20th century as manifested in the scholarly journal literature of psychology and philosophy. *Journal of the American Society for Information Science and Technology, 54*(9), 855–871.

Cronin, B., Shaw, D., & La Barre, K. (2004). Visible, less visible and invisible work: Patterns of collaboration in 20th century chemistry. *Journal of the American Society for Information Science and Technology, 55*(2), 160–168.

Crookes, G. (1986). Towards a validated analysis of scientific text structure. *Applied Linguistics*, 7, 57–70.

Crosnier, E. (1996). L'intéret de la modalisation comme aide à la rédaction en anglais pour les scientifiques français: Méthodologie et perspective pédagogique. *ASp (Anglais de Spécialité)*, 11/14, 89–103.

Doheny-Farina, S. (1992). *Rhetoric, innovation, technology: Case studies of technical communication in technology transfers*. Cambridge, MA: MIT Press.

Dubois, B.-L. (1997). *The biomedical discussion section in context*. Greenwich, CT: Ablex.

Dudley-Evans, T., & Henderson, W. (1990). The organisation of article introductions: Evidence of change in economics writing. In T. Dudley-Evans & W. Henderson (Eds.), *The language of economics: The analysis of economics discourse* (ELT Documents 134, pp. 67–78). London: Modern English Publications and The British Council.

Duszak, A. (1994). Academic discourse and intellectual styles. *Journal of Pragmatics*, 21, 291–313.

Eggington, W. G. (1987). Written academic discourse in Korean: Implications for effective communication. In U. Connor & R. B. Kaplan (Eds.), *Writing across languages: Analysis of L2 texts* (pp. 153–168). Reading, MA: Addison-Wesley.

Evangelisti Allori, P. (Ed.). (1998). *Academic discourse in Europe*. Rome: Bulzoni.

Flowerdew, J. (Ed.). (2002). *Academic discourse*. London: Longman.

Flowerdew, J., & Dudley-Evans, T. (2002). Genre analysis of editorial letters to international journal contributors. *Applied Linguistics*, 23(4), 463–489.

Folman, S., & Sarig, G. (1990). Intellectual rhetoric differences in meaning construction. *Communication and Cognition*, 23, 45–92.

Freddi, M. (2005). How linguists write about linguistics: The case of introductory textbooks. In J. Bamford & M. Bondi (Eds.), *Dialogue within discourse communities: Metadiscursive perspectives on academic genres* (pp. 49–66). Tübingen, Germany: Niemeyer.

Fredrickson, K., & Swales, J. (1994). Competition and discourse community: Introductions from *Nysvenka Studier*. In B. L. Gunnarsson, P. Linell, & B. Nordberg (Eds.), *Text and talk in professional contexts* (pp. 9–22). Uppsala, Sweden: Association Suedoise de Linguistique Appliquée.

Galtung, J. (1979). Deductive thinking and political practice. An essay on Teutonic intellectual style. In J. Galtung (Ed.), *Papers on methodology* (Vol. 2, pp. 194–209). Copenhagen, Denmark: Ejlers.

Galtung, J. (1985). Struktur, kultur und intellektueller Stil. In A. Wierlacher (Ed.), *Das Fremde und das Eigene* [The foreign and the familiar] (pp. 151–193). Munich, Germany: Judficium.

Gebhardt, R. C. (1993). Scholarship, promotion, and tenure in composition studies. *College Composition and Communication*, 44, 439–442.

Giannoni, D. S. (2002). Worlds of gratitude: A contrastive study of acknowledgment texts in English and Italian research articles. *Applied Linguistics*, 23(1), 1–31.

Giannoni, D. S. (2006). Book acknowledgements across disciplines and texts. In K. Hyland & M. Bondi (Eds.), *Academic discourse across disciplines* (pp. 151–176). Frankfurt, Germany: Peter Lang.

Gilbert, G., & Mulkay, M. (1984). *Opening Pandora's box: A sociological analysis of scientific discourse*. Cambridge, UK: Cambridge University Press.

Gilbert, S. F. (1995). Introduction: Postmodernism and science. *Science in Context*, 8, 559–561.

Golebiowski, Z. (1998). Rhetorical approaches to scientific writing: An English-Polish contrastive study. *Text, 18,* 67–102.

Golebiowski, Z. (1999). Application of Swales' model in the analysis of research papers by Polish authors. *International Review of Applied Linguistics, 37,* 231–247.

Gosden, H. (1993). Discourse functions of subject in scientific research articles. *Applied Linguistics, 14*(1), 56–75.

Gould, S. J. (1998). Ladders and cones: Constraining evolution by canonical icons. In R. Silvers (Ed.), *Hidden histories of science* (pp. 37–67). London: Granta.

Grabe, W., & Kaplan, R. B. (1996). *Theory and practice of writing.* London: Longman.

Groom, N. (2005). Pattern and meaning across genres and disciplines: An exploratory study. *Journal of English for Academic Purposes, 4/3,* 257–277.

Gross, A. G., Harmon, J. E., & Reidy, M. S. (2002). *Communicating science: The scientific article from the 17th century to the present.* Oxford, UK: Oxford University Press.

Gunnarsson, B. L. (1989). LSP texts in a diachronic perspective. In C. Laurén & M. Nordman (Eds.), *Special language: From humans thinking to thinking machines* (pp. 243–252). Philadelphia: Multilingual Matters Ltd.

Hagstrom, W. (1965). *The scientific community.* New York: Basic Books.

Halliday, M. A. K. (1998). Things and relations: Regrammaticising experience as technical knowledge. In J. Martin & R. Veel (Eds.), *Reading science* (pp. 185–235). London: Routledge.

Halliday, M. A. K., & Martin, J. R. (1993). *Writing science: Literacy and discursive power.* London: Falmer Press.

Harrison, B. (2002). Japanese research papers: The advisability of translators performing a proactive editing role. *European Science Editing, 28*(4), 104–107.

Hinds, J. (1984). Retention of information using a Japanese style of presentation. *Studies in Linguistics, 8,* 45–69.

Hinds, J. (1987). Reader vs. writer responsibility: A new typology. In U. Connor & R. B. Kaplan (Eds.), *Writing across languages: Analysis of L2 texts* (pp. 141–152). Reading, MA: Addison-Wesley.

Hinds, J. (1990). Inductive, deductive, quasi inductive: Expository writing in Japanese, Korean, Chinese and Thai. In U. Connor & A. M. Johns (Eds.), *Coherence in writing: Research and pedagogical perspectives* (pp. 87–110). Alexandria, VA: TESOL.

Hinkel, E. (1997). Objectivity and credibility in L1 and L2 academic writing. In E. Hinkel (Ed.), *Culture and second language teaching and learning* (pp. 90–108). Cambridge, UK: Cambridge University Press.

Hunston, S., & Thompson, G. (Eds.). (2000). *Evaluation in text: Authorial stance and the construction of discourse.* Oxford, UK: Oxford University Press.

Hyland, K. (1998a). *Hedging in scientific research articles.* Amsterdam: John Benjamins.

Hyland, K. (1998b). Persuasion and context: The pragmatics of academic metadiscourse. *Journal of Pragmatics, 30,* 437–455.

Hyland, K. (1999a). Disciplinary discourses: Writer stance in research articles. In C. Candlin & Hyland, K. (Eds.), *Writing: Texts, processes and practices* (pp. 99–121). London: Longman.

Hyland, K. (1999b). Talking to students: Metadiscourse in introductory textbooks. *English for Specific Purposes, 18,* 3–26.

Hyland, K. (2000a). *Disciplinary discourses: Social interactions in academic writing.* London: Longman.

Hyland, K. (2000b). Hedges, boosters and lexical invisibility: Noticing modifiers in academic texts. *Language Awareness, 9*(4), 179–197.

Hyland, K. (2001a). Bringing in the reader: Addressee features in academic writing. *Written Communication, 18,* 549–574.

Hyland, K. (2001b). Humble servants of the discipline? Self-mention in research articles. *English for Specific Purposes, 20,* 207–226.

Hyland, K. (2002a). Directives: Power and engagement in academic writing. *Applied Linguistics, 23*(2), 215–239.

Hyland, K. (2002b). Specificity revisited: How far should we go now? *English for Specific Purposes, 21*(4), 385–395.

Hyland, K. (2004a). Graduates' gratitude: The generic structure of dissertation acknowledgements. *English for Specific Purposes, 23*(3), 303–324.

Hyland, K. (2004b). Disciplinary interactions: Metadiscourse in L2 postgraduate writing. *Journal of Second Language Writing, 13,* 133–151.

Hyland, K. (2005a). *Metadiscourse.* London: Continuum.

Hyland, K. (2005b). Stance and engagement: A model of interaction in academic discourse. *Discourse Studies, 7*(2), 173–191.

Hyland, K. (2006). Disciplinary differences: Language variation in academic discourses. In K. Hyland & M. Bondi (Eds.), *Academic discourse across disciplines* (pp. 17–45). Frankfurt, Germany: Peter Lang.

Hyland, K., & Milton, J. (1997). Qualification and certainty in L1 and L2 students' writing. *Journal of Second Language Writing, 16*(2), 183–205.

Hyland, K., & Tse, P. (2004a). Metadiscourse in academic writing: A reappraisal. *Applied Linguistics, 25*(2), 156–177.

Hyland, K., & Tse, P. (2004b). "I would like to thank my supervisor": Acknowledgements in graduate dissertations. *International Journal of Applied Linguistics, 14*(2), 259–275.

Hyland, K., & Tse, P. (2005). Hooking the reader: A corpus study of *evaluative that* in abstracts. *English for Specific Purposes, 24*(2), 123–139.

Jensen, J. V. (1998). Teaching East Asian rhetoric. *The Rhetoric Society Quarterly, 18,* 136–149.

Johns, A. M. (1997). *Text, role and context: Developing academic literacies.* Cambridge, UK: Cambridge University Press.

Johns, A. M. (Ed). (2002). *Genre in the classroom: Multiple perspectives.* Mahwah, NJ: Erlbaum.

Judson, H. (1995). *The eighth day of creation: The makers of the revolution in biology.* Harmondsworth, UK: Penguin Books.

Kaplan, R. (1966). Cultural thought patterns in intercultural education. *Language Learning, 16,* 1–20.

Knorr Cetina, K. (1981). *The manufacture of knowledge.* Oxford, UK: Pergamon Press.

Kress, G. (1989). *Linguistic processes in sociocultural practice.* Oxford, UK: Oxford University Press.

Kreutz, H., & Harres, A. (1997). Some observations on the distribution and function of hedging in German and English academic writing. In A. Duszak (Ed.), *Culture and styles of academic discourse* (pp. 181–201). Berlin, Germany: Mouton de Gruyter.

Kubota, R. (1999). Japanese culture constructed by discourse: Implications for applied linguistics research and English language teaching. *TESOL Quarterly, 33,* 9–35.

Kuhn, T. (1970). *The structure of scientific revolutions* (2nd ed.). Chicago: University of Chicago Press.

Kuo, C.-H. (1999). The use of personal pronouns: Role relationships in scientific journal articles. *English for Specific Purposes, 18*(2), 121–138.

Lakoff, G. (1972). Hedges: A study in meaning criteria and the logic of fuzzy concepts. *Proceedings of the 8th Annual Meeting of the Chicago Linguistic Society,* 183–228.

Latour, B., & Woolgar, S. (1979). *Laboratory life: The social construction of scientific facts.* Beverly Hills, CA: Sage.

Lawani, S. (1982). On the heterogeneity and classification of author self-citations. *Journal of the American Society for Information Science, 33,* 281–284.

Le, E. (1999). The use of paragraphs in French and English academic writing: Towards a grammar of paragraphs. *Text, 19*(3), 307–343.

Lemke, J. (1995). *Textual politics: Discourse and social dynamics.* London: Taylor and Francis.

Lewin, B., Fine, J., & Young, L. (2001). *Expository discourse: A genre-based approach to social science research texts.* London: Continuum.

Liddicoat, A. J. (2005). Writing about knowing in science. *LSP and Professional Communication, 5*(2), 8–27.

Lindeberg, A. C. (1988). *Cohesion, coherence, and coherence patterns in expository and argumentative student essays in EFL: An exploratory study.* Unpublished licenciate thesis, Obo Akademi, Türkü, Finland.

Lindeberg, A. C. (1998). Promotional rhetorical steps and linguistic signalling in research articles in three disciplines. In L. Lundqvist, H. Pitch, & J. Qvistgaard (Eds.), *LSP: Identity and interface research* (pp. 689–698). Copenhagen, Denmark: Copenhagen Business School.

López, G. S. (1982). *Article introductions in Spanish: A study in comparative rhetoric.* Unpublished master's dissertation, Aston University, Birmingham, UK.

Love, A. (2002). Introductory concepts and cutting edge theories: Can the genre of the textbook accommodate both? In J. Flowerdew (Ed.), *Academic discourse* (pp. 76–90). London: Longman.

MacDonald, S. P. (1994). *Professional academic writing in the humanities and social sciences.* Carbondale: Southern Illinois University Press.

Martin, J. (1996). Les enjeux du discours scientifiques: La stratégie de véridiction. *ASp (Anglais de Spécialité), 11/14,* 13–33.

Mauranen, A. (1992). Reference in academic rhetoric: A contrastive study of English and Finnish writing. In A. C. Lindberg, N. E. Enkvist, & K. Vikberg (Eds.), *Nordic research on text and discourse, Nordtext Symposium 1990* (pp. 237–250). Obo, Finland: Obo Academic Press.

Mauranen, A. (1993). *Cultural differences in academic rhetoric.* Frankfurt, Germany: Peter Lang.

Melander, B. (1998). Culture or genre? Issues in the interpretation of cross-cultural differences in scientific papers. In I. Fortanet, S. Posteguillo, C. Palmer, & J. F. Coll (Eds.), *Genre studies in English for academic purposes* (pp. 211–226). Castello de La Plana: Universitat Jaume I.

Melander, B., Swales, J., & Fredrickson, K. M. (1997). Journal abstracts from three academic fields in the United States and Sweden: National or disciplinary proclivities? In A. Duszak (Ed.), *Culture and styles of academic discourse* (pp. 252–272). Berlin, Germany: Mouton de Gruyter.

Mendiluce Cabrera, G., & Hernández Bartolomé, A. I. (2005). La matización asertiva en el artículo biomédico: Una propuesta de clasificación para los estudios contrastivos inglés-español. *Ibérica*, *10*, 63–90.

Moreno, A. (1997). Genre constraints across languages: Causal metatext in Spanish and English RAs. *English for Specific Purposes*, *16*(3), 161–179.

Motta-Roth, D. (1998). Discourse analysis and academic book reviews: A study of text and disciplinary cultures. In I. Fortenet, S. Posteguillo, J. C. Palmer, & J. F. Coll (Eds.), *Genre studies in English for academic purposes* (pp. 29–58). Castello, Spain: Universitat Jaume I.

Myers, G. (1989). The pragmatics of politeness in scientific articles. *Applied Linguistics*, *10*, 1–35.

Myers, G. (1990). *Writing biology: Texts in the social construction of scientific knowledge*. Madison: University of Wisconsin Press.

Myers, G. (1992). Textbooks and the sociology of scientific knowledge. *English for Specific Purposes*, *11*(1), 3–17.

Najjar, H. (1990). *Arabic as a research language: The case of the agricultural sciences*. Unpublished doctoral dissertation, University of Michigan, Ann Arbor.

Oliveira, L. P. (1997). Variaçao intercultural na escrita: Contrastes multidimensionais em inglês e português. Unpublished doctoral dissertation, Pontificia Universidade Católica de São Paulo, Brazil.

Oliver del Olmo, S. (2004). *Análisis contrastivo español / inglés de la atenuación retórica en el discurso médico: El artículo de investigación y el caso clínico*. Unpublished doctoral dissertation, Universitat Pompeu Fabra, Barcelona, Spain.

Osborne, J. (1994). La cohésion dans les productions écrites d'étudiants en anglais de spécialité: Un problème culturel? *ASp (Anglais de Spécialité)*, *5 / 6*, 205–215.

Parry, S. (1998). Disciplinary discourse in doctoral theses. *Higher Education*, *36*, 273–299.

Paul, D., & Charney, D. (1995). Introducing chaos (theory) into science and engineering. *Written Communication*, *12*(4), 396–438.

Peck MacDonald, S. (1990). The literary argument and its discursive conventions. In W. Nash (Ed.), *The writing scholar* (pp. 31–62). Newbury Park, CA: Sage.

Petric, B. (2005). Contrastive rhetoric in the writing classroom: A case study. *English for Specific Purposes*, *24*, 213–228.

Pisanski Peterlin, A. (2005). Text-organising metatext in research articles: An English-Slovene contrastive analysis. *English for Specific Purposes*, *24*, 307–319.

Posteguillo, S. (1999). The schematic structure of computer science research articles. *English for Specific Purposes*, *18*, 139–160.

Prior, P. (1998). *Writing / disciplinarity: A sociohistoric account of literate activity in the academy*. Mahwah, NJ: Erlbaum.

Ramanathan, V., & Atkinson, D. (1999). Individualism, academic writing, and ESL writers. *Journal of Second Language Writing*, *8*, 45–75.

Régent, O. (1994). L'article scientifique: un produit culturel. *ASp (Anglais de spécialité)*, *5 / 6*, 55–61.

Rousseau, R. (1999). Temporal differences in self-citation rates of scientific journals. *Scientometrics*, *44*(3), 521–531.

Russell, D. R. (1992). American origins of the writing-across-the-curriculum movement. In A. Herrington & C. Moran (Eds.), *Writing, teaching and learning in the disciplines* (pp. 22–42). New York: The Modern Language Association of America.

Sa'adeddin, M. A. (1989). Text development and Arabic-English negative interference. *Applied Linguistics, 10*(1), 36–51.

Sacks, O. (1998). Scotoma: Forgetting and neglect in science. In R. B. Silvers (Ed.), *Hidden histories of science* (pp. 141–188). London: Granta.

Salager-Meyer, F. (1990). Discoursal flaws in medical English abstracts: A genre analysis per research and text type. *TEXT, 10*(4), 365–384.

Salager-Meyer, F. (1994). Hedges and textual communicative function in medical English written discourse. *English for Specific Purposes, 13*(2), 149–170.

Salager-Meyer, F. (1998a). Referential behavior in scientific writing: A diachronic study (1810–1995). *English for Specific Purposes, 13*, 149–171.

Salager-Meyer, F. (1998b). Language is not a physical object. *English for Specific Purposes, 17*(3), 295–303.

Salager-Meyer, F. (2000). Procrutes' recipes: Hedging and positivism. *English for Specific Purposes, 19*(2), 175–189.

Salager-Meyer, F., & Alcaraz Ariza, M. A. (2004). Negative appraisals in academic book reviews: A cross-linguistic approach. In C. Candlin & M. Gotti (Eds.), *Intercultural aspects of specialized communication* (pp. 149–172). Frankfurt, Germany: Peter Lang.

Salager-Meyer, F., Alcaraz Ariza, M. A., & Zambrano, N. (2003). The scimitar, the dagger and the glove: Intercultural differences in the rhetoric of criticism in Spanish, French and English medical discourse (1930–1995). *English for Specific Purposes, 22*, 223–247.

Salager-Meyer, F., Alcaraz Ariza, M. A., Pabón, M., &. Zambrano, N. (2006a). Paying one's intellectual debt: Acknowledgments in conventional vs. complementary/alternative medical research. In M. Gotti & F. Salager-Meyer (Eds.), *Advances in medical discourse analysis: Oral and written contexts* (407–430). Frankfurt, Germany: Peter Lang.

Salager-Meyer, F., Alcaraz Ariza, M. A., Pabón, M., &. Zambrano, N. (2006b). Big science, internationalisation, professionnalisation et fonction sociale de la science à travers l'analyse diachronique des recensions d'ouvrage. *LSP and Professional Communication, 6*(1), 8–25.

Salager-Meyer, F., & Defives, G. (1998). From the gentleman's courtesy to the expert's caution: A diachronic analysis of hedges in academic writing (1810–1995). In I. Fortanet, S. Posteguillo, C. Palmer, & J. F. Coll (Eds.), *Genre studies in English for academic purposes* (pp. 133–171). Castellon, Spain: Universitat Jaume I.

Samraj, B. (2002). Introductions in research articles: Variation across disciplines. *English for Specific Purposes, 21*, 1–18.

Scollon, R. (1997). Contrastive rhetoric, contrastive poetics or perhaps something else? *TESOL Quarterly, 31*, 352–358.

Shapin, S. (1984). Pump and circumstance: Robert Boyle's literary technology. *Social Studies of Science, 14*, 481–520.

Shi, L. (2002). How Western-trained Chinese TESOL professionals publish in their home environments. *TESOL Quarterly, 36*(4), 625–634.

Sionis, C. (1997). Stratégies et styles rédactionnels de l'article de recherche: Les ressources de l'utilisateur non-natif devant publier en anglais. *ASp (Anglais de Spécialité), 15–18*, 207–223.

Skudlik, S. (1990). *Sprachen in den Wissenschaften: Deutsch und Englisch in der internationalen Kommunikation.* Tübingen, Germany: Gunter Narr.

Spack, R. (1997). The rhetorical construction of multilingual students. *TESOL Quarterly, 31*, 765–774.

Swales, J. (1990). *Genre analysis: English in academic and research settings.* Cambridge, UK: Cambridge University Press.

Swales, J. (1993). Genre and engagement. *Revue Belge de Philogie et Histoire, 71*(3), 689–698.

Swales, J. (1995). The role of the textbook in EAP writing research. *English for Specific Purposes, 14*(1), 3–18.

Swales, J. (1996). Occluded genres in the academy: The case of the submission letter. In E. Ventola & A. Mauranen (Eds.), *Academic writing* (pp. 45–58). Amsterdam: John Benjamins.

Swales, J. (1998). *Other floors, other voices: A textography of a small university building.* Mahwah, NJ: Erlbaum.

Swales, J. (2004). *Research genres.* Cambridge, UK: Cambridge University Press.

Swales, J., Ahmad, U., Chang, Y.-Y., Chavez, D., Dressen, D., & Seymour, R. (1998). Consider this: The role of imperatives in scholarly writing. *Applied Linguistics, 19*(1), 97–121.

Tadros, A. (1994). Predictive categories in expository text. In M. Coulthard (Ed.), *Advances in written text analysis* (pp. 69–72). London: Routledge.

Tagliacozzo, R. (1977). Self-citations in scientific literature. *Journal of Documentation, 33*(4), 251–265.

Taylor, G., & Chen, T. (1991). Linguistic, cultural and subcultural issues in contrastive discourse analysis: Anglo-American and Chinese scientific texts. *Applied Linguistics, 12*, 319–336.

Thompson, G. (2001). Interaction in academic writing: Learning to argue with the reader. *Applied Linguistics, 22*(1), 58–78.

Thompson, G., & Ye, Y. (1991). Evaluation of the reporting verbs used in academic papers. *Applied Linguistics, 12*, 365–382.

Tse, P., & Hyland, K. (2006). Gender and discipline: Exploring metadiscourse variation in academic book reviews. In K. Hyland & M. Bondi (Eds.), *Academic discourse across disciplines* (pp. 177–202). Frankfurt, Germany: Peter Lang.

Upton T., &. Connor, U. (2001). Using computerized corpus analysis to investigate the textlinguistic discourse moves of a genre. *English for Specific Purposes, 20*, 313–329.

Valero-Garcés, C. (1996). Contrastive ESP rhetoric: Metatext in Spanish English economics texts. *English for Specific Purposes, 15*(4), 279–294.

Valle, E. (1999). *A collective intelligence: The life sciences in the Royal Society as a scientific discourse community 1665–1965* (Anglicana Türküensia, 17). Turku, Finland: University of Türkü.

Vassileva, I. (1997). Hedging in English and Bulgarian academic writing. In A. Duszak (Ed.), *Culture and styles of academic discourse* (pp. 203–223). Berlin, Germany: Mouton de Gruyter.

Vassileva, I. (2000). *Who is the author? A contrastive analysis of authorial presence in English, German, French, Russian and Bulgarian academic discourse.* Asgard, Germany: Sankt Augustin.

Vassileva, I. (2001). Commitment and detachment in English and Bulgarian academic writing. *English for Specific Purposes, 20*, 83–103.

Ventola, E. (1997). Modalization: Probability—an exploration into its role in academic writing. In A. Duszak (Ed.), *Culture and styles in academic writing* (pp. 157–179). Berlin, Germany: Mouton de Gruyter.

Ventola, E., & Mauranen, A. (1991). Non-native writing and native revisiting of scientific articles. In E. Ventola (Ed.), *Functional and systemic linguistics* (pp. 457–492). Berlin, Germany: Mouton de Gruyter.

Yakhontova, T. (1997). The signs of a new time: Academic writing in ESP curricula of Ukranian universities. In A. Duszak (Ed.), *Culture and styles of academic discourse* (pp. 103–112). Berlin, Germany: Mouton de Gruyter.

Yakhontova, T. (2001). Textbooks, context and learners. *English for Specific Purposes, 20,* 397–415.

Yakhontova, T. (2002a). "Selling" or "telling"? The issue of cultural variation in research genres. In J. Flowerdew (Ed.), *Academic discourse* (pp. 216–232). Harlow, UK: Pearson Education.

Yakhontova, T. (2002b). Titles of conference presentations abstracts: A cross cultural perspective. In E. Ventola, C. Shalom, & S. Thompson (Eds.), *The language of conferencing* (pp. 277–300). Frankfurt, Germany: Peter Lang.

CHAPTER 8

The Concept of Genre in Information Studies

Jack Andersen
Royal School of Library and Information Science, Copenhagen

Introduction

Humans and human societies have always organized and transmitted knowledge, meaning, and human experience by means of particular modes of communication. Oral cultures and societies preserve their knowledge using songs, stories, genealogies, poetry, hymns, and so on. Literate cultures preserve their knowledge using, among other things, lists, e-mail, recipes, newspapers, novels, maps, journals, books, diaries, textbooks, letters, and Weblogs. Such forms of communication are an inherent part of the organization of any culture because they structure and sustain society's institutionalized means and modes of communication. The concept that covers this variety of forms of communication and human activity can be termed *genre*. Most people would probably instinctively associate genre with literary forms, such as the novel, the poem, or the drama, and there is nothing wrong with this. However, we also recognize that there are a number of communication forms pertaining to nonfictional prose and used in a variety of human activities. Genres of nonfictional prose cover the relationship between forms of communication, human activity and social organization, and how activities are typified by means of genre. Genre is thus broader than literary works. It follows that in order to understand genre we will have to look at more than mere text types. This chapter deals with genres of nonfictional prose. Although research in library and information studies (LIS) is not limited to nonfictional prose and its use in various professional or everyday life contexts, many classical LIS studies of, for instance, information use, are indeed studies of the use of nonfictional prose, in particular, scholarly literature. However, these studies seldom address textual form.

The purpose of this chapter is to critically review, discuss, and analyze the concept of genre within LIS. This results in the following chapter structure. First, a discussion of the LIS context and its relation to genre is provided. Emphasis is on the significance of genre for LIS, why

LIS should want to know (more) about it, and what exactly it is about genre that is important for LIS to know. This is followed by an overview of genre and genre-related research in LIS and its implications for LIS research and discourse. I examine the ways genre theory has been employed in LIS research and related fields. Third, a review of genre theory research is provided in order to show what scholarly traditions inform modern genre theory and its concepts. Fourth, I outline basic concepts from genre theory in order to demonstrate their usefulness in LIS research. The concluding section points to the need for further genre-oriented perspectives in LIS research.

The LIS Context and Its Relationship to Genre

Discussing what theory, schools of thought, ideas, traditions, or concepts are relevant to LIS implies a particular stance toward what LIS is as a field of research. The question of stance is beyond the scope of this chapter. It is clear, however, that there has been a social-humanistic turn in LIS during the last decade, which has led to a more interpretive-critical approach to research (in particular Andersen, 2002a, 2004, 2005, 2006; Andersen & Skouvig, 2006; Black, 1998, 2001, 2006; Budd, 2001, 2003; Buschman, 2003; Cornelius, 1996; Cronin, 2005; Dahlström, 2004; Day, 2001; Frohmann, 2004; Hansson, 2004, 2005, 2006; Hjørland, 2004; Hjørland & Albrechtsen, 1995; Mai, 2001; Olsson, 1999; Paling, 2004; Radford, 1992, 1998; Sundin, 2003; Sundin & Johannisson, 2005; Talja, 1997, 2005; Warner, 2002; Wiegand, 2003). Although the contents of these writings vary considerably regarding the notion of an *interpretive-critical* approach, they do contain a common thread. They all draw on and introduce theorists and theoretical frameworks in order to broaden our understanding of (traditional) LIS research areas. I intend to situate this chapter in this line of work.

For the sake of the argument, assume that LIS is the study of how and with what means professional, scholarly, cultural, and social knowledge as materialized in documents (print or electronic) is communicated in society and what function libraries and other similar knowledge organizing institutions or activities have, or are supposed to have, in these communication processes.[1] Professional, scholarly, cultural, and social communication as manifested in documents comprises a diversity of genres: work orders, newsletters, recipes, bibliographies, articles in literary-cultural journals, surveys, chronicles, technical reports, governmental reports, scholarly articles, book reviews, and so on. As LIS is interested in how knowledge in documents and other artifacts is organized, genre theory is a productive perspective. Studying genres would reveal how they and human activity are important organizing factors of communication and knowledge. It would tell us what kinds of genres various people and institutions in different communicative contexts prefer. A genre view of these communicative activities would provide a means to examine systematically document production and use and the organization of document production and use. Thus, using genre as an analytical concept in LIS would help us understand how professional, cultural, and social communication is carried out. It would also enable understanding of how genres organize activity, texts, knowledge, and people. Moreover, a genre perspective would not only focus on the people and the production and use of various documents, but also stress typical activities in which people are discursively engaged. From a genre point of view, then, document production and use are looked upon not as ends in themselves but in terms of how documents help people do their work (cf. Bazerman, 2004, p. 319). If LIS, by means of theoretical and empirical studies, can gain a more thorough understanding of situated and typified document production and use, then we may also be able to have a more informed understanding of the ways in which information systems help, or fail to help, people do their work. This implies that we should view information systems not as ends in themselves but rather as means to an end. We should focus on what information systems *do*, as tools to be used in goal-directed activity. Such a view may have been present in LIS but formulated in other ways. However, what has been missing is the genre perspective.

Why should LIS want to know about genre? Cornelius (2003) has pointed out that LIS needs to connect to theoretical debates in other social science and humanities fields because LIS tends to live an isolated theoretical life. A genre-theoretical approach to LIS research problems provides an opportunity to connect to other theoretical discourses, in particular in the humanities. Moreover, genre can provide LIS with a concrete object of study. In fact, Agre (1997) has suggested using genre, rather than information, as a focal point in LIS. Genre theory is not about text types in isolation, but rather about the fact that recognizing (as both producer and user) a particular text type means recognizing a particular communicative situation and activity in which that type of text (genre) is used to accomplish a given task. Bazerman (2000, p. 16) puts it this way:

> Genres help us navigate the complex worlds of written communication and symbolic activity, because in recognizing a text type we recognize many things about the institutional and social setting, the activities being proposed, the roles available to writer and reader, the motives, ideas, ideology, and expected content of the document, and where this all might fit in our life.

Take the example of the digital library. The digital library is a textual place on the Internet that helps us "navigate the complex worlds of written communication and symbolic activity" (Bazerman, 2000, p. 16). When we recognize a given digital library as such, we also know what to expect of it, that is, what it can do for users and what users can accomplish by using a digital library, as compared to other textual places on the Internet that perform similar actions. A genre understanding of digital libraries thus provides a means of understanding matters of knowledge organization, communication of symbolic activity, and information seeking. Generally, genre broadens our understanding of how knowledge is organized and communicated by means of recorded discourse as articulated through some generic form.

The most important thing for LIS to know about genre is that genre studies are not primarily concerned with text types, but with how different human activities involving the use of texts become typified as a consequence of the production and use of recorded discourse by different agents. Typified human activities reveal what kinds of paths and access to knowledge are considered legitimate or appropriate in particular contexts; this also reveals what kinds of information seeking strategies are employed and why they are employed the way they are. By adopting a genre approach, LIS is capable of producing an understanding of the institutional and social setting in which the communication and organization of knowledge, culture, or information take place.

In LIS, many user studies have been carried out over the years to determine how people use the kinds of information and information systems they do. Rarely has emphasis been put on the artifacts that materialize and configure information and the effect of those artifacts on the use of information (see Frohmann, 2004). Although genre is much more than text type, the text as a social and material object is nevertheless important for theoretical and methodological reasons. Therefore, a genre approach to LIS would imply a greater focus on the study of texts and on how and why they accomplish what they do on behalf of the people producing and using texts in human activities. In short, user studies would be genre studies.

Genre in Library and Information Studies

It is not that LIS is totally unfamiliar with the notion of genre. During the last decade, there has been a certain amount of genre-related research produced in LIS and fields related to LIS. Genre-related research in LIS has been carried out in connection with knowledge organization, Web design, and digital communication. In particular, it is interesting to note that genre-related research in LIS is closely linked to the growth of digital media.

One research field in LIS that has paid some attention to genre is knowledge organization, although the main organizing principle usually adhered to is topic rather than genre. In his book on subject analysis, Langridge (1989, p. 45) recognized what comes close to a genre aspect when talking about the role of "forms of writing" in connection with subject analysis. Such discussion of the role of forms as presented by Langridge is hard to find in the knowledge organization literature. The way "forms of writing" is understood here is, inter alia, in terms of the viewpoint from which a document is written, although what Langridge

(1989, p. 55) refers to as "bibliographic form" comes close to a genre awareness.

In classification systems and bibliographies, genre is usually treated in terms of forms of literature (e.g., textbooks, biographies, essays, anthologies). Recognizing that forms of literature create expectations on the part of users, who thereby display a certain amount of genre consciousness, Wilson and Robinson (1990, p. 38) argue that:

> Catalog users are never indifferent to genre, though they might not themselves put it that way. One never really wants just *any* kind of book on a topic, though one may not be able to say just what kind one does want. Providing content descriptions in terms both of topic and of kind is simply recognizing the ordinary relevance of information about kinds of books. (emphasis in original)

Identifying genre is a crucial part of document description. Wilson and Robinson further argue that such identification entails looking at socially recognizable forms (i.e., genre) and not only genre names that are familiar to librarians:

> Description of genre or kind is important because the idea of genre or kind is the idea of a range of *conventional procedure that guides both the performance of producers* (if only in the direction of deliberate flouting of convention) and *the expectations of users*. (Wilson & Robinson, 1990, p. 42; emphasis added)

In other words, recognizing and knowing what to do with a particular genre is not an issue to be solved on the part of producers or users. How to deal with genres is a function of what kind of socio-communicative activity in which producers and users of discourse are collectively involved; classification and indexing systems are central to this.

One of the first articles to deal with genre theory in the digital realm was Vaughan and Dillon's (1998) paper on genre and how it shapes our understanding of digital documents. They argued that genre theory, together with cognitive psychology, could provide a framework for analysis and design. Given the theoretical distance between cognitive psychology and genre theory, it is not clear how two such approaches could be successfully combined. Vaughan and Dillon (1998, p. 562) write that "To understand the significance and meaning of rules, practices, and conventions associated with a genre one cannot look simply to the artefact, one must look first to the user. Cognitive psychology's research on mental representations of structure is one avenue for pursing an understanding of digital documents grounded in user conceptions of regularity." Although it is true that to look at the artifact is not enough, it is difficult to see how cognitive psychology is a fruitful or relevant perspective when it comes to understanding user conceptions of regularity. In light of genre theory, user conceptions of regularity are social (and historical) in character. Users' ways of handling and understanding texts and their regulatory functions can be seen in their socio-textual practices; and such practices shape the use of texts. What is cognitive about this? One cannot reasonably claim to identify any kind of mental representation here; to claim to do so is to strip off the social, leaving nothing. Moreover, Vaughan and Dillon (1998) seem to settle on a notion of genre that equates it with mere text type and not as a notion that deals with the intersection of human activity and communicative situation. It does seem to limit our understanding of digital documents if we do not relate our understandings to the recurrent situations that give rise to such documents and the kinds of social action they try to accomplish.

At the Classification Research Workshop in 1999, held in connection with the annual meeting of the American Society for Information Science and Technology (ASIST), Davenport (2001) presented a paper on documentary genres. She considered documentary genres to be devices for categorization and regulation and suggested that classification research should consider ways of including genre analysis "in an agenda for classification research" (Davenport, 2001, p. 50). It is disappointing to observe, however, that genre analysis has not really become part of an agenda for classification research.

Dillon and Gushrowski (2000) argued that the personal home page could be seen as the first truly digital genre, having no equivalent in the world of print. This was decided through an empirical study asking users what they considered to be *good* home page design and what kinds of elements they believed should appear in a good personal home page. On this basis, Dillon and Gushrowski (2000, p. 205) concluded that "the shared matching of expectation and preference across this community of users suggests that the personal home page might be the first unique digital information genre." But what people *believe* should be on a home page is rather different from what they *expect*. The latter is shaped by concrete experiences with artifacts performing functions similar to a personal home page; that is, expectations are formed through social practices. To say what should be present on a home page is a normative judgment and is thus rather different from what is actually present on home pages. Genre theory is not concerned with how texts *should* perform but with how they actually perform and how they gain their regulatory power in various human activities. This is how we develop our expectations of texts. Therefore, tracing the emergence of a genre cannot be done solely on an experimental level. It also entails social and historical analysis that can account for the practices and activities constituting a given genre. Such an understanding is missing in the work reported here.

The Hawaii International Conference on System Sciences has for many years had a minitrack on genres of digital documents (www.hicss.hawaii.edu). The papers on digital document genres demonstrate the variety of ways research issues in electronic document management, organizational communication, document production and use, Web structuring, information retrieval, human-computer interaction, and e-democracy can benefit from and be informed by a genre approach (e.g., Bergquist & Ljungberg, 1999; Goldstein & Sabin, 2006; Karjalainen et al., 2000; Rehm, 2002; Roussinov, Crowston, Nilan, Kwasnik, Liu, & Cai, 2001; Sæbø & Päivärinta, 2005; Shepherd & Watters, 1998; Toms & Campbell, 1999; Tyrväinen & Päivärinta, 1999; Watters & Shepherd, 1997; Yates, Orlikowski, & Rennecker, 1997; Yates & Sumner, 1997). Many of these studies are helpful because they illustrate the depth and social and humanistic rationale with which classic LIS research topics can be approached, a depth and rationale some topics may not yet have had but nevertheless have strongly needed.

The 2000 ASIST annual meeting included a session devoted to genre. The presentations were subsequently published in the *Bulletin of the American Society for Information Science and Technology* (Document Genres, 2000/2001). The authors discussed the concept of genre (Beghtol, 2000/2001), how to recognize digital genre (Toms, 2000/2001), and how genre could contribute to improved Web search effectiveness (Kwasnik, Crowston, Nilan, & Roussinov, 2000/2001). With these discussions, the authors addressed relevant aspects of genre and its applicability to LIS research. One might have wished, however, for a more precise discussion of genre because, even though the authors relied mostly on the work of researchers arguing for a sociological understanding of genre, the articles in the *Bulletin* tended to discuss genre in terms of text type or text typology/taxonomy. The sociologically oriented scholars within genre theory (e.g., Miller, 1984) actually exclude formal text taxonomy exercises on the grounds that an understanding of genre must be based "in the conventions of discourse that a society establishes as ways of 'acting together.' *It does not lend itself to taxonomy*, for genres change, evolve and decay; *the number of genres current in any society is indeterminate and depends upon the complexity and diversity of society*" (p. 163; emphasis added). Thus, the study and understanding of genre is as much grounded in a study of society as in a study of texts and one does not gain this kind of understanding by producing pure taxonomies of texts.

Crowston and Williams (2000) studied 1,000 randomly selected Web pages and analyzed the kinds of genre to which they corresponded, arguing that Web site designers should draw on an understanding of genre. In new media, some genres are reproduced or adapted, some novel genres emerge as a consequence of the medium employed, and some simply disappear. Therefore, Crowston and Williams maintain, designing Web sites is a matter of knowing what kind of genre one is reproducing or adapting. They note how reproducing or modifying an already established genre can be an advantage because the audience with whom the particular Web site is communicating can easily recognize the genre and understand its purpose and what to expect of it. The introduction of a new genre, however, may be difficult if readers have a resistance to novel forms of communication or may mislead them if they do not have the experience and knowledge to handle new communicative forms. Therefore, according to Crowston and Williams (2000), Web site designers should develop a sense of community—although hard to define on the Web—and seek to reproduce or adapt genres appropriate for, and familiar to, such a community. Crowston and Williams have demonstrated the advantage of a genre approach to Web site design and other knowledge organization activities in the digital universe. They also underscore how Web site design is not only a matter of technical knowledge but as much a matter of understanding forms of communication (i.e., genres) and their situatedness: a basic humanistic approach to Web site design.

Crowston and Williams's analysis of the type of understanding involved in a knowledge organization activity such as Web site design shows how design activity is also a communicative activity. Another approach to using genre in connection with knowledge organization has been suggested by Crowston and Kwasnik (2003, pp. 353–354):

> The treatment of genre is limited or not very well defined. ...
> Historically, most library and information systems took genre
> for granted because most collections contained only a limited
> array of document types. The exceptions are literary genres
> (such as poetry) and publication types (such as almanacs or
> newspapers).

They contend that in the digital universe a topic approach to organizing document collections is not enough. Computerized information systems have a fundamental limitation, Crowston and Kwasnik (2003, p. 345) argue, because "they know what documents say, but not what they mean or for what purposes they might be useful." Hence their suggestion of incorporating genre in document representations because "identifying a genre provides information as to the document's purpose and its fit to the user's situation, which can be otherwise difficult to assess" (p. 350). They give the example of a university professor looking for information about computer database systems for the class he is teaching. In this kind of search the professor is looking for particular genres of educational documents (e.g., syllabi, assignments, class notes). But when the professor is writing a journal article, he would probably be looking for scholarly work on the topic (e.g., research articles). Crowston and Kwasnik (2003, p. 350) maintain that the relevant documents for these two searches are different, even though the keywords and topics might almost be the same. This is a crucial argument in favor of genre because much thinking on document representation in LIS has ignored the purpose of a document and its fit to the user's situation; that is, the information provided by genre.

In a theoretical analysis of knowledge organization as a social activity, Andersen (2004, pp. 85–95) draws on theories of genre and activity systems. The aim is to explain the complex relationship between any kind of organization and representation of documents in information systems and forms of social organization. Forms of social organization are constituted by genre and activity systems, which the knowledge organizing activity mediates. Andersen (2004) argues that the documents that are the objects of knowledge organization activity are tools in communication. Documents are expressed through particular genres to be used in particular human activities organized within structured discourses. Being part of these activities, knowledge organization is embedded in and constituted by forms of social organization. However, genre and activity systems that rely on written communication cannot function as a social activity without a means to assure this communication. Knowledge organization is the activity that assures this communication (e.g., Schryer, 1993; Yates, 1989). To further develop and exemplify Andersen's argument, more theoretical and empirical work is needed.

In 2005, the journal *Information Technology and People* published a special issue on genres of digital documents, edited by Kwasnik and Crowston, who have been among the strongest advocates of genre in LIS (Genres of Digital Documents, 2005). The four papers "address fundamental questions about genre and extend the study of genres to the environment of the World Wide Web" (Kwasnik & Crowston, 2005, pp. 76–77) in accordance with the aim of the issue, which "was to provide models of genre research" (p. 86). The papers deal with a wide range of genre issues in the digital context. Hyun-Gyung et al. (2005) address the fixity of digital genres in organizational communication and the challenges people face in working with digital genres and coordinating them at work. Askehave and Ellerup Nielsen (2005) discuss how digital genres present a challenge to traditional genre theory because medium is not usually incorporated in a traditional concept of genre. Digital genres must incorporate medium into the notion of genre because on the Web one cannot separate medium from genre (Askehave & Ellerup Nielsen, 2005). Herring et al. (2005, p. 143) examine Weblogs and seek to "characterize the properties of the emergent blog genre and situate it with respect to offline genres, as well as with respect to the broader genre ecology of the Internet." Finally, Ihlström and Henfridsson (2005) look at the evolution of the online newspaper in Scandinavia. Their study shows that "online newspapers have established a number of communicative practices significant for recognizing them as a specific group of digital genre" (p. 188). But this has not made the printed news obsolete; their study also showed "the emergence of sequential dependencies between online and printed news, suggesting a type of genre interdependency" (p. 189).

This special issue of *Information Technology and People* on genres of digital documents illustrates the potential of genre theory for approaching problems and challenges in Web-mediated communication because the Web both reproduces and creates new forms of communication and hence new forms of mediating and organizing knowledge, culture, and human experience.

Cross and Oppenheim's (2006) study of scientific abstracts provides another example of the use of genre analysis in LIS. Their move-analysis of selected abstracts from protozoological research showed that these abstracts contained five moves compared to the four-move model put forward by Swales (1990). The authors are more text-linguistically oriented than the studies reviewed here and less interested in what the abstract accomplishes as a social tool in scholarly communication.

Looking at genre change, Paling and Nilan (2006) analyzed empirically whether editors of small literary magazines used online technology to reinforce or alter the values characteristic of their genre. They found that the editors actually strengthened and reinforced their genre, that of the small literary magazine, and that the values expressed by means of this genre are not associated with print culture only. This study is one of several analyzing the interplay among information technology, social structure, human activity, and genre (e.g., Yates & Orlikowski, 1992).

To recapitulate this review section, the many analyses and studies of genre within LIS and related disciplines show that genre theory may not have gained wide recognition and impact on LIS research as the analyses and studies are very scattered, sometimes accidental, and have not always contributed significantly to theory development in genre studies. Nevertheless, the analyses and studies that have been carried out suggest that genre theory is able to strongly inform and broaden our understanding of both traditional LIS research issues and new research issues such as Web communication and organization. Thus, we should work in LIS to take up genre theory as a central research approach and ensure a line of ongoing research, through which we may contribute to its theoretical development.

The Field of Genre: Its Theory and Concepts

In this section, I introduce and discuss genre-theoretical issues and concepts. This paves the way for considering how genre theory and its concepts can be used in LIS research.

In *Genre and the New Rhetoric*, Freedman and Medway (1994, pp. 8–10) identify two major schools of thought within modern genre studies: The North American School and the Sydney School. The former derives its concept of genre from a rhetorical tradition. It is inspired by Miller's seminal essay "Genre as Social Action" in which genre is conceptualized as "typified rhetorical actions based in recurrent situations" (Miller, 1984, p. 159). This leads the North American School toward a socio-historical concept of genre, focusing on how texts become typified and how they function within a social and interactional context. Thus, genre theory in the North American tradition understands genre in relation to how people, texts, and activities interact with each other in order to produce meaning and knowledge for action. The Sydney School of genre is based on Halliday's systemic functional linguistics. It emphasizes formal textual features and that results in a more linguistically oriented concept of genre. Common to both schools, however, is the attention paid to the role of the social in conceptualizing and understanding genres and the role of context (Freedman & Medway, 1994, p. 9). The account of genre in this section is mainly based on the North American tradition because this tradition is sociologically inspired and, I believe, therefore better suited to LIS.

How to recognize and understand various types of texts, and what they accomplish in different human activities based on the production and use of texts, is a major issue in genre theory. In this way, genre theory is concerned with much more than mere text types and their formal textual features. An approach that studies only text types and their formal qualities does not allow for investigation into the activities performed by using texts or how we may arrive at an understanding of texts and their discursive activities.

We still may say that genre involves characteristics that differentiate texts (verbal or written) from each other. But this differentiation is not a matter of recognizing purely textual and formal features. The characteristics are of a social nature as well. To recognize a particular text type is to recognize a particular communicative situation and activity in which that type of text (genre) is used to accomplish a given task. In our everyday interaction with texts, whether as producers or recipients, genres are a means of orientation. Our knowledge of genres determines means and modes of textual production and what we expect of texts in our professional as well as in our everyday lives. Genre becomes a kind of *textual existentialism* and is thus connected to literacy: The more we know about the communicative activities in which we are involved, the more we know how to understand and use the texts produced by these activities. Texts and contexts are *not* considered as two distinct categories in genre theory, but text is integral to both context and action (see Winsor, 1999). To produce and use a text is to be situated in a context with socially and historically developed typified activities of producing and reading texts. For example, a scientist cannot simply invent his own way of reporting experiments to colleagues if he wants to be taken seriously. He has to know how to apply some conventions for presenting the experimental setup, evaluation methods, results, and so on. On the other hand, the reader of a scientific article has to know something about the tradition of reporting such experiments in order to understand and evaluate the work reported. This was what Bazerman (1988) showed in his study of the experimental article in science. He paid particular attention to how this genre emerged historically; and how it was, and is, shaped by the recurrent typified communicative activities of writers (scientists reporting their experiments) and readers (evaluating and learning from the experiments of others); and how the genre shaped the knowledge producing activity into a typified activity (the writing and reading of an experimental article) as a product of its history and agents. Thus, Bazerman's study demonstrates how we may conceive of genre as "typified rhetorical actions based in recurrent situations" (Miller, 1984, p. 159).

As has been mentioned, North American genre theory and its socio-logical orientation can be ascribed to Miller (1984) and her influential essay "Genre as Social Action." Here Miller broke with tradition in rhetorical genre theory, which concerned itself with the creation of tax-onomy. Instead, she argued for a rhetorical understanding of genre that was not based "on the substance or the form of discourse *but on the action it is used to accomplish*" (p. 151; emphasis added). Thus, the focus shifted from the formal qualities of genre to its function, and the notion of typification was brought in to explain why and how a genre was able to accomplish something in human discourse. Typification becomes crit-ical if genres can be said to accomplish something. Because writers and readers are separated in time and space, a mechanism is needed to com-municate in an appropriate and timely way and to avoid, or minimize, the risk of misunderstandings. In a typified communicative activity, cer-tain actions are carried out in certain situations, following certain forms of communication, leading to the ability to recognize and understand particular standardized practices and activities (Bazerman, 2004, p. 316). Typification is what allows one to recognize and identify a particu-lar context and its particular forms of communication (its genres); this would also cover the typification of social practices and human activities. We can understand genre as "typified rhetorical actions based in recur-rent situations" (Miller, 1984, p. 159) because communicative situations recur and our discursive actions become typified as a result of this recur-rence. As a consequence of genre theory's emphasis on typification, the notion of *discourse community* is also essential. Members having shared rules of producing and reading texts and ways of acting discursively characterize a discourse community. Genres are, among other things, the social and discursive resource of a discourse community—its glue, so to speak.

A concept from social theory, which has informed genre theory, is *structuration* (Giddens, 1984). With structuration, Giddens takes up an old problem in social theory, that of the relationship between social structure and human agency. Giddens's argument is that structure and agency do not represent a dichotomy, but rather both produce and repro-duce each other, a duality of structure in Giddens's terms. Humans live in a socially structured world but, at the same time, humans with all their social and cultural resources and activities shape socially struc-tured society. Structuration has informed genre theory through the writ-ings of, in particular, Yates and Orlikowski (1992) and Orlikowski and Yates (1994). Miller (1994) also discusses structuration theory as a con-tinuation of her own notion of genre. The argument is that the use of genres simultaneously constitutes and reproduces social structures. Miller (1994, p. 71) proposes that genres represent

> a specific, and important, *constituent* of society, a major aspect of its communicative structure, one of the structures of power that institutions wield. Genre we can understand specifically as that aspect of situated communication that is *capable of reproduction* ...

Understanding genre in the light of structuration theory explicitly locates genre within social theory and elevates genre beyond a decontextualized view of how to use and understand particular forms of text.

Another approach to genre, similar to structuration theory, is *activity theory* (e.g., Bazerman, 1997, 2004; Russell, 1997; Winsor, 1999). This approach has its historical roots in the cultural-historical school in psychology, which originated in the 1930s in the Soviet Union with Vygotsky, Luria, and later Leont'ev (see Wilson's chapter in the present volume). Activity theory explicates the relationship between human activity and modes of cognition. It considers social and cultural forms as objective conditions of possibilities for both cognition and human activity. Human activity is understood as intentional and object-oriented. To this end humans make use of particular tools, such as texts. Activity theory stresses that humans shape and are shaped by social structures by means of their production and use of tools in an active dialectical process. These structures are considered relatively objective insofar as they constitute the social and material circumstances with and within which humans act.

Concepts from activity theory that have influenced, and which inform, genre theory are intentionality, tools, mediation, activity, and meaning (Russell, 1997). Russell synthesizes aspects of Vygotskian activity theory and Bazerman's theory of genre systems into a framework for understanding the practice of writing as it relates to and connects school and society; that is "to understand the relation between writing in school and writing in other social practices" (p. 505). By focusing on the interaction between various genre and activity systems, the relationship between genre(s) and social organization is recognized. According to Russell (p. 520), the role of genre systems is to mediate activity systems. The social organization of society can be said to be made up of various activity systems, each interacting or conflicting with others. Tools (mediational means), subject(s), and the object/motive express the organization of the single activity system. Thus, genres indirectly influence social organization in terms of their mediation of activity systems. This again brings to the fore the notion of genre as social action and its connection with the structuring and maintenance of social organization.

Through this, activity theory's view of activity and tools comes close to rhetoric's understanding of communication as purposeful activity and texts as something humans produce and use intentionally as tools in order to change, shape, or affect a given state of affairs achieved by persuasive or strategic communication. This similarity between activity theory and rhetoric may explain why genre theory in the North American school turned to activity theory in the 1990s. The latter was capable of providing a broad conceptual and theoretical outlook for genre theory and explaining its concern for how people, texts, activities, and situations collaborate in order to produce genres as relatively stable forms of social organization.

A notion of genre similar to Miller's (1984) comes from literary theorist Mikhail Bakhtin. In his essay "The Problem of Speech Genres," Bakhtin (1986) not only criticizes structuralist linguistics for being sender-oriented, but also offers a functional understanding of what he calls *speech genres*. To facilitate and coordinate human activity by means of language use, "relatively stable types of utterances" develop in spheres of human activity (p. 60). Bakhtin calls these utterances speech genres (oral or written). To Bakhtin, the utterance is the basic unit of analysis in connection with speech communication, and it serves to illuminate the socio-historical nature of ways of uttering.

Utterances, according to Bakhtin, are always directed toward somebody, which he calls the *addressivity* of an utterance. Utterances therefore cannot exist without an addressee. In continuation of this, what is critical to Bakhtin in terms of utterances is that they are never the product of a single individual. Although it is an individual stating an utterance, an utterance is to be seen as a response to, and shaped by, another previous utterance—a responsive understanding as Bakhtin (1986, p. 68) calls it. In this way the possible reaction of the respondent is incorporated into, and implied by, the very utterance to be uttered. Bakhtin (1986, p. 91) writes:

> Every utterance must be regarded primarily as a response to preceding utterances of the given sphere. ... Each utterance refutes, affirms, supplements, and relies on the others, presupposes them to be known, and somehow takes them into account. After all, as regards a given question, in a given matter, and so forth, the utterance occupies a particular definite position in a given sphere of communication. It is impossible to determine its position without correlating it with other positions. Therefore, each utterance is filled with various kinds of responsive reactions to other utterances of the given sphere of speech communication.

With respect to the particular position occupied by an utterance, this shows Bakhtin's awareness that speech genres are produced with an intention, a purpose in mind, and that this is what determines their position in a given sphere of socially organized human activity. Moreover, the utterance is "filled with dialogic overtones" (Bakhtin, 1986, p. 92). These dialogic overtones point to the socio-historical nature of uttering (e.g., of arguing or debating), as an utterance is both a product of and a response to previous utterances in a given sphere of communication. The genre of the utterance is also determined just as particular genres are developed for particular communicative activities.

The understanding of genre in terms of the discursive action it is used to accomplish is similar to the understanding of language developed in speech act theory by Austin (1962) and Searle (1969). The main line of argument in speech act theory is that language is a communication tool, a means to accomplish something in human communication. Speech act theory distinguishes between three levels of speech acts. First is the locutionary act covering what is actually said. Second, the illocutionary act covers the intention of what is uttered; that is, the act the communicator intended the audience to recognize. Third, there is the perlocutionary act. This speech act covers the actual response of those hearing the act of the communicator. Speech act theory has also been developed and discussed within the context of genre theory by Bazerman (1994, 2004). When we want to convince a particular audience about some state of affairs and have the audience accept and act in accordance with our argument, the discursive "battle" consists largely of matching the perlocutionary act with the illocutionary act (Bazerman, 2004, p. 315).

Berkenkotter and Huckin (1995) develop the concept of genre knowledge. Having knowledge of a particular genre means that a person possesses the ability to act appropriately within a particular discourse community. It implies knowledge of writing conventions and epistemologies. The more we are involved in a discourse community and its genres, the more genre knowledge we have and vice versa. Thus, genre knowledge is a measure of how much we are socialized into a given discourse community.

Looking at one particular genre and the action it accomplishes also affects other genres in a given setting. To understand genres and their relation to each other, Devitt (1991) developed the notion of *genre sets* and Bazerman (1994) developed the notion of *genre systems*. Genre sets cover all the kinds of texts a person in a given position produces. Therefore, identifying a genre set means identifying a large part of a person's work (Bazerman, 2004, p. 318). Genre systems represent "interrelated genres that interact with each other in specific settings" (Bazerman, 1994, p. 97) and consist of the genre sets people working together are producing and using. The connection of systems of genre to social interaction is that some genres are, or must be, invoked simultaneously in order to act appropriately within a specific setting. This further demands an understanding of which genres to invoke: "Only a limited range of genres may appropriately follow upon another in particular settings" (Bazerman, 1994, p. 98). That is, the setting is a precondition for the use of genre(s).

Bazerman (1997, 2004) and Russell (1997) add the notion of *activity systems* to genre systems, opening "a focus on what people are doing and how texts help people do it, rather than on texts as ends in themselves"

(Bazerman, 2004, p. 319). Similar to genre sets and genre and activity systems, Orlikowski and Yates (1994, p. 542) introduce *genre repertoire* to designate the genres available in a given social setting:

> to understand a community's communicative practices, we must examine the set of genres that are routinely enacted by members of the community. We designate such a set of genres a community's "genre repertoire."

Accordingly, genre sets, genre and activity systems, and genre repertoires are powerful analytical tools for examining the organization of texts, work, knowledge, and human activity.

In *Tracing Genres through Organizations: A Sociocultural Approach to Information Design*, Spinuzzi (2003) discusses his concept of *genre ecologies*. This covers the complex of artifacts mediating activities and their mutual relationship; that is, that changing the condition of one genre will affect others. Critiquing user-centered design for not taking into account the unofficial genres users employ when interacting with computer systems, Spinuzzi introduces his method of *genre tracing*. This is a way of tracing the evolution of unofficial genres favored by users and using them as solutions in information design problems.

North American genre theory and its associated concepts illustrate how genre theory has broadened its theoretical and methodological perspectives. One may point to Miller's (1984) article on genre as social action as triggering this body of sociologically inspired genre theory. Any claim that genre is a means for social action must necessarily lead to an understanding of genre that connects human activity, texts, social structure, and people, making the study of genre a study of politics and knowledge, as these are mediated and shaped through forms of communication (e.g., Winsor, 2000). Much of our sense of everyday life, politics, and work in late modernity is to a large extent mediated by forms of communication; genres may provide ways of dealing with hypercomplex society (Qvortrup, 2003).

Genre and Its Use in LIS Research

The preceding sections have examined: 1) the relationship between genre and LIS research; 2) genre-related research that has been carried out in LIS; and 3) genre theory and its core concepts. This section integrates the three foregoing discussions on genre and LIS and considers ways of applying genre theory in LIS research. In particular, I emphasize genre as social action, structuration, genre knowledge, notions of genre sets, genre repertoire, and genre and activity systems.

Within LIS the domain-analytical approach recognizes the importance of genre studies (Hjørland, 1997, 2002; Hjørland & Albrechtsen, 1995). Domain-analysis is a response to those approaches tending to favor universalistic frameworks. Genre is always studied situationally.

Genres exist only where there are users organized in a community/domain/institutional setting. Because of this, studying genres means studying their domains of activity. Genre analysis is a natural component of domain analysis, as suggested by Hjørland (2002).

The Concept of Genre as Social Action in LIS Studies

As mentioned earlier, LIS studies how and through what means professional, scholarly, cultural, and social knowledge as materialized in documents (print or electronic) is communicated in society as well as what function libraries and other similar knowledge organizing institutions or activities have, or are supposed to have, in these communications. When genre is conceptualized as "typified rhetorical actions based in recurrent situations" (Miller, 1984, p. 159) we have a means to analyze various communicative practices. For instance, we might interpret citation as a typified activity. What you do in a typified activity tends to recur. So it is with citations; they are a part of social practice (i.e., reading and writing scholarly documents) and are historically constituted activites that regulate and stabilize experiences and actions in order for them to be recognized as appropriate modes of doing and knowing.

Moreover, as a genre is defined by those using it, genre studies come close to user studies. Traditional user studies have focused on how people seek information and what sources they use. Important insights have been gained here. But the starting point has been people's information needs and how they try to meet these needs. Genre studies would start with the genre and then move backward and ask questions such as: How did this particular text come to look and be used as it was? What actions, or goals, is the text intended to support? Who is involved in producing and using this text? What larger textual and activity system is the text part of? To study a genre is to study how knowledge is regulated, codified, and altered by people and their communicative activities. One might even say that a particular genre defines an information need. For instance, a fishing guide cannot solve the need for information on how to prepare a sushi dinner. The fishing guide and its informative potential, one might say, is not unlimited. This is because a genre, and the form of knowledge it materializes, is defined and constrained by the activity it is used to accomplish.

Because of the emphasis on types and type-based knowledge found in Miller's genre concept, genre is itself a knowledge organizing category. Genre understood in this way allows us to recognize types of situations where people, texts, activity, and knowledge are organized in a particular way in order to create a basis for accomplishing social actions. For knowledge organization research this implies that we should view certain sociocultural practices (e.g., blogging) as not only knowledge structuring practices but also as identity-making activities. As a consequence, genre can become a crucial concept in knowledge organization research.

Genre and Structuration Theory in LIS Studies

The notion of structuration as it is applied in genre theory derives from Giddens (1984) and his book *The Constitution of Society: Outline of the Theory of Structuration*. The basic tenet here is that structure and agency represent a duality of structure. They produce, reproduce, and/or modify each other. In light of structuration theory, genres are social institutions because they shape and are shaped by communicative action. Genres represent, at the same time, both structure and agency. Consequently, genres simultaneously constitute, regulate, produce, and reproduce social structures.

Without connecting it to genre, Solomon (2000) employed the concept of structuration in LIS in a study of how to deal with the tension between stability and dynamism in knowledge organization systems. But how can genre and structuration theory be used in LIS research? Yates and Orlikowski have applied both genre and structuration theory to analyze organizations and their communicative practices, in particular considering how electronic communication technologies are formed and form the communicative practices of organizations (e.g., Orlikowski & Yates, 1994; Yates & Orlikowski, 1992). Based on Yates's (1989) book *Control through Communication*, Yates and Orlikowski (1992) employ a genre understanding and structuration theory to explain the dynamics between structure and agency in organizations. For instance, the memo genre developed out of a need to control internal organizational communication (Yates, 1989). At the same time, when organizations started to use vertical instead of horizontal filing, this encouraged a subject approach and reinforced the need for memos to have only one subject. In line with structuration theory, we can detect a reciprocal and recursive relationship between social structure, communicative action, and filing system (a form of knowledge organization). Many studies of knowledge organization in LIS have tended to focus either on how certain social structures have an effect on knowledge organization or on how knowledge organization reproduces social structures (e.g., Wiegand, 1998). However, knowledge is not organized by itself but by a complex interaction between human activity, media, genres, technologies, ideologies, and institutional structures. A genre and structurational approach to studying and understanding knowledge organization activity would be valuable in LIS as it can produce an understanding of how, and to what extent, knowledge organization shapes and is shaped by forms of social organization, genres, and human activity and thus situates knowledge organization research at the intersection of social theory and genre theory. This is not mainstream thinking in LIS, as knowledge organization seems to be more influenced by computer science (e.g., design and evaluation of systems) in this regard.

Genre Knowledge and Its Application in LIS Research

Berkenkotter and Huckin (1993) introduced the notion of genre knowledge. They conceptualized genre knowledge as "a form of situated cognition" and for writers this means that to "make things happen, that is, to publish, to exert an influence on the field, to be cited, and so forth, they must know *how to strategically use their understanding of genre*" (p. 477; emphasis added). That is, genre knowledge encompasses the ability to act appropriately in a given communicative and typified situation that demands a particular response. In LIS, Andersen (2006) has employed the concept of genre knowledge in relation to information literacy. He argues that:

> Our knowledge of genres determines the means and modes of how we produce, use, understand, seek, and evaluate texts and what we expect of them in professional as well as everyday life. Information literacy becomes equivalent to genre knowledge, as the more we know about the communicative activities we are involved in, the more we also know how to understand, evaluate, seek, and use the texts produced by these activities. (Andersen, 2006, pp. 225–226)

For people to locate documents or information they must possess a sense of the situation that brought them into the information seeking activity. Genre knowledge can be used to explain information seeking activity in various kinds of situations and institutional settings. That is, why and how people seek and use the kinds of documents they do in a given human activity. More speculatively, genre knowledge could be used to analyze indexing. Understanding what kind of genre knowledge an indexer employs can tell us how and why particular index terms were chosen. In this way the indexer's view of the document and its use context could be revealed, and it could thus be determined whether the indexing effort corresponded with the intended goal or policy of the institutional setting.

Genre Sets, Genre Repertoire, and Activity Systems in LIS Research

The notions of genre sets (Devitt, 1991), genre repertoire (Orlikowski & Yates, 1994), and genre and activity systems (Bazerman, 1994, 1997; Russell, 1997) have all developed as a way to understand how communicative activities are organized through the use of texts. In LIS such an understanding of genre practices can be used to contextualize our understanding of knowledge organization activity.

The purpose of knowledge organization is retrieval, documentation, regulation, and stabilization of a given setting. This suggests that knowledge organization as a social activity, whether it takes place in a library, organization, or some other setting, entails socio-communicative practices. Knowledge organization is in this way part of the production, dissemination, use, and transformation of knowledge as it is materialized in a given kind of document or written genre. As Andersen (2002b) has argued, when tracing the historicity of the LIS-concept of knowledge organization, the social activity of organizing knowledge in information systems seems to have been downplayed (for further analysis of this see Andersen & Skouvig, 2006).

With these elements (genre sets, genre repertoire, genre systems, and activity systems), genre studies has developed an understanding of the communicative force of writing and its involvement in the production, dissemination, use, and transformation of written knowledge in structured social activities. However, this understanding of genre does not seem to have considered the role of the systems for knowledge organization (e.g., archives, bibliographies, or library catalogs) in these activities. Analytically, we can try to connect knowledge organization with forms of social organization insofar as this is constituted by genre and activity systems and expressed through the production and use of documents in various contexts. This connection seems important for both knowledge organization theory and theories of genre and activity systems. The documents that are the objects for knowledge organization are communicative tools with a history. They are expressed through particular genres to be used in particular human activities organized within structured discourses. Being part of these activities, knowledge organization is embedded in, and regulated and constituted by, social organization. However, genre and activity systems relying on written communication cannot function as a social activity without a mechanism to assure this communication.

What writers on genre sets, genre repertoire, and genre and activity systems all seem to emphasize is that not only is genre social action, but, more importantly, also a useful tool for analyzing and understanding how social action and social organization are accomplished in diverse (recurrent) settings/activities. However, to the extent that social organization can be defined by its means and modes of communication, the production, dissemination, and use of written genres is also dependent on an activity system securing these processes over time; that is, retrieval and documentation. A full recognition of this aspect does not seem to be apparent in the writings discussed. If theories of genre and activity systems are going to account for the complex social interaction between texts, genres, human activities, and the production and use of written genres, then it seems that knowledge organization must be incorporated into the mix. Conversely, if knowledge organization is to recognize fully its inherently social nature and responsibility and the connection to human communicative activities and social organization, then theories of genre and activity systems seem reasonable frameworks to adopt.

The notion of knowledge organization as a communicative instrument in the production, dissemination, and use of documents was indeed envisaged by Egan and Shera (1952). They saw bibliography as a form of communication and through this linked it to social action. However, they were not particularly clear about their ideas and were, unfortunately, neglected by the LIS community. Nevertheless, Egan and Shera's emphasis on bibliography as an instrument in the transmission of written knowledge was, and is, important. One can go about analyzing and synthesizing knowledge organization and theories of genre and activity systems in two ways. First, by looking at what genre and activity systems mean for knowledge organization. What kind of view of knowledge organization is implied? Second, what does knowledge organization imply for genre and activity systems? What can knowledge organization contribute that is not already encompassed or accounted for in theories of genre and activity systems? Answers to these questions should contribute to a fruitful view of the interdependence between knowledge organization and genre and activity systems, a view that in the long run may strengthen both theories.

The relationship between social organization and knowledge organization can be grasped by viewing the idea of organizing and representing documents in information systems *as a consequence* of society's attempt to organize itself through its use of the various means and modes of communication. Genre conceived of as "typified rhetorical actions based in recurrent situations" (Miller, 1984, p. 159) implies for knowledge organization not only that the rhetorical actions must be recognized, but also that knowledge organization itself is a typified rhetorical action. For instance, when there is an archive in an organization, it is there because of some recurrent situation (i.e., the performance of genre). The writing activities of the organization are carried out for a reason. They accomplish a human communicative purpose that is a part of the organization's social division of labor, its social organization, developed historically. In terms of writing as a social activity, Bazerman (1988, p. 10) notes: "Writing is a social action; texts help organize social activities and social structure; and reading is a form of social participation." It should follow from this statement that insofar as "texts help organize social activities and social structure," those activities that organize texts for retrieval and documentation are indirectly involved in organizing social activities and social structure. Thus, knowledge organization both supports and transforms social structure.

Knowledge organization is part of the larger genre and activity systems that constitute the discursive activity of knowledge organization. However, knowledge organization strikes back at this discourse. In its description of documents, knowledge organization transforms them through the use of a certain vocabulary. This in effect determines how documents are to be retrieved and also how they may be used in socially structured activities. That is, there is a constant interaction going on between genre and activity systems and knowledge organization. Genre and activity systems are sites where knowledge is produced, disseminated, used, and transformed. One important instrument for doing this is knowledge organization. Organizing knowledge in information systems can be considered a rhetorical action and thus part of a rhetorical situation. Although not writing about knowledge organization, Poster (1995, p. 85) has argued about databases that they are a discourse, a form of writing, because they effect a constitution of the subject (i.e., the individual). In much the same way it can be said that knowledge organization effects a constitution of the documents registered (and thus of the genre and activity systems they are used in) when choosing which documents to include for description and how to describe them. This choice determines which documents can be retrieved and in what ways they can be retrieved, and shows that the discourse of knowledge organization is to some extent of a rhetorical nature.

Knowledge organization and genre and activity systems depend on and affect each other. Knowledge organization cannot ignore the role played by social organization and its genre and activity systems because that is the sphere where the production, dissemination, and use of documents take place. It is where the meaning of the documents is constructed and produced historically through "typified rhetorical actions based in recurrent situations" (Miller, 1984, p. 159). Knowledge organization cannot be undertaken without taking into account the activities the documents are going to serve or support. Documents are tools that serve particular communicative needs and purposes and are used in different socio-communicative activities. These activities are to a large extent constituted by prevailing means and modes of communication and by social organization. That is, the organization and representation of documents in information systems supports these kinds of activities. This demonstrates the importance of taking social organization into account when organizing and representing documents in information systems. The whole notion of genre and activity systems, on the other hand, cannot be understood in its totality without paying attention to those activities securing and influencing the distribution of documents over time. Archives, libraries, catalogs, and bibliographies are genres of communication that have developed historically to support and maintain writing and documentation activities. In that sense they have played a crucial part in the organization of society. By incorporating the notion of the organization and representation of documents in information systems for the purpose of retrieval and documentation, theories of genre and activity systems are able to offer a rich picture for an understanding of the social role of writing and documentation activities in society. Organizing and searching for texts in information systems are just as complex as the activities of writing and reading. Indeed, as human activities, they both constitute each other.

Such analysis leads to a complex understanding of both knowledge organization as a social activity and genre and activity systems, and, not least, the connection between the two. The complexity has to be dealt with in order to recognize fully both knowledge organization and genre and activity systems as socially and historically developed activities structuring society. For this purpose, we can employ the notions of genre sets, genre repertoire, and genre and activity systems.

Conclusion

This review of the concept of genre has explored its potential utility in LIS research. This was done by discussing the LIS context and its relation to genre in order to identify possible lines of research in LIS that might benefit from genre theory. This led to an overview of genre and genre-related research in LIS and its implications for LIS research. Then, a review of genre theory research was provided and, finally, an examination of selected concepts from genre theory in order to consider their usefulness in LIS research.

As has been shown, genre is not unknown in certain areas of LIS. It is interesting, however, that a classical research area such as scholarly communication has been little informed by genre theory. One would expect this to be an obvious place for genre theory in LIS. If LIS were to adopt genre theory, then it would need to accept the full consequence of employing genre approaches in the form outlined here.

- First, genre theory is based in the humanities and qualitative social sciences. This may not be reconcilable with trends in LIS. But recognizing genre theory in LIS entails a view of users, documents, and information systems as agents and tools of culture and history involved in discursive activities. This is to say, LIS research objects are products of culture and not of nature. Moreover, LIS is an interdisciplinary field and should be able to incorporate many perspectives. Interdisciplinary fields cannot afford to exclude views that highlight relevant aspects of their research topics.

- Second, genre theory does not look for mental representations of people's actions, meaning that cognitivistic (and similar) approaches cannot be reconciled with genre theory. Studies of genre are studies of social activity as it is here and now.

- Third, LIS should also contribute to the development of genre theory, not remain just a user of genre theory. This requires more theoretical work coming from the LIS community. Obviously, such work should emerge from LIS research areas and then contribute to the generic development of genre theory. As has been demonstrated, there are some LIS research activities pointing in that direction. It also implies, however, that (classical) LIS research areas need to be reconsidered and discursively reconfigured. That is a challenge, not a threat.

Endnote

1. This conception excludes oral communication, even though we may not be able to exclude oral communication from LIS research. For the purpose of this chapter, however, I focus on written communication because modern genre theory is primarily oriented toward written communication.

References

Agre, P. (1997). The end of information & the future of libraries. *Progressive Librarian*, 12/13. Retrieved February 17, 2007, from libr.org/pl/12-13_Agre.html

Andersen, J. (2002a). Ascribing cognitive authority to scholarly documents: On the (possible) role of knowledge organization in scholarly communication. *Advances in Knowledge Organization: Proceedings of the Seventh International ISKO Conference*, 28–37.

Andersen, J. (2002b). Communication technologies and the concept of knowledge organization: A medium-theory perspective. *Knowledge Organization, 29*(1), 29–39.

Andersen, J. (2004). *Analyzing the role of knowledge organization in scholarly communication: An inquiry into the intellectual foundation of knowledge organization*. Copenhagen: Department of Information Studies, Royal School of Library and Information Science. Retrieved February 17, 2007, from www.db.dk/dbi/samling/phd/jackandersen-phd.pdf

Andersen, J. (2005). Information criticism: Where is it? *Progressive Librarian*, 25, 12–22.

Andersen, J. (2006). The public sphere and discursive activities: Information literacy as sociopolitical skills. *Journal of Documentation, 62*(2), 213–228.

Andersen, J., & Skouvig, L. (2006). Knowledge organization: A sociohistorical analysis and critique. *Library Quarterly, 76*(3), 300–322.

Askehave, I., & Ellerup Nielsen, A. (2005). Digital genres: A challenge to traditional genre theory. *Information Technology & People, 18*(2), 120–141.

Austin, J. L. (1962). *How to do things with words*. Cambridge, UK: Cambridge University Press.

Bakhtin, M. (1986). The problem of speech genres. In M. Bakhtin, *Speech genres and other late essays* (V. W. McGee, Trans., C. Emerson & M. Holquist, Eds.) (pp. 60–102). Austin: University of Texas Press.

Bazerman, C. (1988). *Shaping written knowledge: The genre and activity of the experimental article in science*. Madison: University of Wisconsin Press.

Bazerman, C. (1994). Systems of genres and the enactment of social intentions. In A. Freedman & P. Medway (Eds.), *Genre and the new rhetoric* (pp. 79–101). London: Taylor & Francis.

Bazerman, C. (1997). Discursively structured activities. *Mind, Culture, and Activity, 4*(4), 296–308.

Bazerman, C. (2000). Letters and the social grounding of differentiated genres. In D. Barton & N. Hall (Eds.), *Letter writing as a social practice* (pp. 15–29). Amsterdam: John Benjamins.

Bazerman, C. (2004). Speech acts, genres and activity systems: How texts organize activity and people. In C. Bazerman & P. Prior (Eds.), *What writing does and how it does it: An introduction to analyzing texts and textual practices* (pp. 309–339). Mahwah, NJ: Erlbaum.

Beghtol, C. (2000, December/2001, January). The concept of genre and its characteristics. *Bulletin of the American Society for Information Science and Technology, 27*(2), 17–19. Retrieved February 27, 2007, from www.asis.org/Bulletin/Dec-01/beghtol.html

Bergquist, M., & Ljungberg, F. (1999). Genres in action: Negotiating genres in practice. *Proceedings of the 32nd Hawaii International Conference on System Sciences*, 2009.

Berkenkotter, C., & Huckin, T. (1993). Rethinking genre from a sociocognitive perspective. *Written Communication, 10*(4), 475–509.

Berkenkotter, C., & Huckin, T. (1995). *Genre knowledge in disciplinary communication: Cognition/culture/power.* Hillsdale, NJ: Erlbaum.

Black, A. (1998). Information and modernity: The history of information and the eclipse of library history. *Library History, 14,* 37–43.

Black, A. (2001). The Victorian information society: Surveillance, bureaucracy and public librarianship in nineteenth-century Britain. *The Information Society, 17*(1), 63–80.

Black, A. (2006). Information history. *Annual Review of Information Science and Technology, 40,* 441–473.

Budd, J. (2001). *Knowledge and knowing in library and information science: A philosophical framework.* Lanham, MD: Scarecrow Press.

Budd, J. (2003). The library, praxis, and symbolic power. *Library Quarterly, 73,* 1–18.

Buschman, J. (2003). *Dismantling the public sphere: Situating and sustaining librarianship in the age of the new public philosophy.* Westport, CT: Libraries Unlimited.

Cornelius, I. (1996). *Meaning and method in information studies.* Norwood, NJ: Arcade Publishing.

Cornelius, I. (2003). Review of "Current Theory in Library and Information Science," issue of *Library Trends* (W. E. McGrath, Ed.). *Journal of Documentation, 59*(5), 612–615.

Cronin, B. (2005). *The hand of science: Academic writing and its rewards.* Lanham, MD: Scarecrow Press.

Cross, C., & Oppenheim, C. (2006). A genre analysis of scientific abstracts. *Journal of Documentation, 62*(4), 428–446.

Crowston, K., & Kwasnik, B. H. (2003). Can document-genre metadata improve information access to large digital collections? *Library Trends, 52*(2), 345–361.

Crowston, K., & Williams, M. (2000). Reproduced and emergent genres of communication on the World Wide Web. *The Information Society, 16*(3), 201–215.

Dahlström, M. (2004). How reproductive is a scholarly edition? *Literary and Linguistic Computing, 19*(1), 17–33.

Davenport, E. (2001). Implicit orders: Documentary genres and organizational practice. *Advances in Classification Research: Proceedings of the 10th ASIS SIG/CR Classification Research Workshop,* 39–54.

Day, R. (2001). *The modern invention of information: Discourse, history, and power.* Carbondale: Southern Illinois University Press.

Devitt, A. (1991). Intertextuality in tax accounting: Generic, referential, and functional. In C. Bazerman & J. Paradis (Eds.), *Textual dynamics of the professions: Historical and contemporary studies of writing in professional communities* (pp. 336–380). Madison: University of Wisconsin Press.

Dillon, A., & Gushrowski, B. A. (2000). Genres and the Web: Is the personal home page the first uniquely digital genre? *Journal of the American Society for Information Science, 51*(2), 202–205.

Document genres. (2000, December/2001, January). *Bulletin of the American Society for Information Science and Technology, 27*(2). Retrieved February 17, 2007, from www.asis.org/Bulletin/Dec-01/Bulletin/Aug-99/index.html

Egan, M., & Shera, J. H. (1952). Foundations of a theory of bibliography. *Library Quarterly, 22*(2), 125–137.

Freedman, A., & Medway, P. (Eds.). (1994). *Genre and the new rhetoric.* London: Taylor & Francis.

Frohmann, B. (2004). *Deflating information: From science studies to documentation*. Toronto, Canada: University of Toronto Press.

Genres of digital documents [Special issue]. (2005). *Information Technology and People*; *18*(2).

Giddens, A. (1984). *The constitution of society: Outline of the theory of structuration*. Berkeley: University of California Press.

Goldstein, J., & Sabin, R. E. (2006). Using speech acts to categorize email and identify email genres. *Proceedings of the 39th Annual Hawaii International Conference on System Sciences* (vol. 3), 50b.

Hansson, J. (2004). The social legitimacy of library and information studies: Reconsidering the institutional paradigm. In B. Rayward (Ed.), *Aware and responsible: Papers of the Nordic-International Colloquium on Social and Cultural Awareness and Responsibility in Library, Information and Documentation Studies* (pp. 49–69). Lanham, MD : Scarecrow Press.

Hansson, J. (2005). Hermeneutics as a bridge between the modern and the postmodern in library and information science. *Journal of Documentation*, *61*(1), 102–113.

Hansson, J. (2006). Just collaboration or really something else?: On joint use libraries and normative institutional change with two examples from Sweden. *Library Trends*, *54*(4), 549–568.

Herring, S. C., Scheidt, L. A., Wright, E., & Bonus, S. (2005). Weblogs as a bridging genre. *The Information Society*, *16*(3), 142–171.

Hjørland, B. (1997). *Information seeking and subject representation: An activity-theoretical approach to information science*. Westport, CT: Greenwood Press.

Hjørland, B. (2002). Domain analysis in information science: Eleven approaches—traditional as well as innovative. *Journal of Documentation*, *58*(4), 422–462.

Hjørland, B. (2004). Social and cultural awareness and responsibility in library, information and documentation studies. In B. Rayward (Ed.), *Aware and responsible: Papers of the Nordic-International Colloquium on Social and Cultural Awareness and Responsibility in Library, Information and Documentation Studies* (pp. 71–91). Lanham, MD: Scarecrow Press.

Hjørland B., & Albrechtsen, H. (1995). Toward a new horizon in information science: Domain-analysis. *Journal of the American Society for Information Science*, *46*(6), 400–425.

Hyun-Gyung, I., Yates, J., & Orlikowski, W. (2005). Temporal coordination through communication: Using genres in a virtual start-up organization. *The Information Society*, *16*(3), 89–119.

Ihlström, C., & Henfridsson, O. (2005). Online newspapers in Scandinavia: A longitudinal study of genre change and interdependency. *Information Technology & People*, *18*(2), 172–192.

Karjalainen, A., Päivärinta, T., Tyrväinen, P., & Rajala, J. (2000). Genre-based metadata for enterprise document management. *Proceedings of the 33rd Hawaii Conference on Systems Sciences*, 1–10.

Kwasnik, B. H., & Crowston, K. (2005). Introduction to the special issue: Genres of digital documents. *Information Technology & People*, *18*(2), 76–88.

Kwasnik, B. H., Crowston, K., Nilan, M., & Roussinov, D. (2000, December/2001, January). Identifying document genre to improve Web search effectiveness. *Bulletin of the American Society for Information Science and Technology*, *27*(2), 20–22. Retrieved February 27, 2007, from www.asis.org/Bulletin/Dec-01/kwasnikartic.html

Langridge, D. W. (1989). *Subject analysis: Principles and procedures*. London: Bowker-Saur.

Mai, J. E. (2001). Semiotics and indexing: An analysis of the subject indexing process. *Journal of Documentation, 57*(5), 591–622.

Miller, C. R. (1984). Genre as social action. *Quarterly Journal of Speech, 70*, 151–167.

Miller, C. R. (1994). Rhetorical community: The cultural basis of genre. In A. Freedman & P. Medway (Eds.), *Genre and the new rhetoric* (pp. 67–78). London: Taylor & Francis.

Olson, H. A. (1999). Exclusivity, teleology and hierarchy: Our Aristotelean legacy. *Knowledge Organization, 26*, 65–73.

Orlikowski, W. J., & Yates, J. (1994). Genre repertoire: The structuring of communicative practices in organizations. *Administrative Science Quarterly, 39*(4), 541–574.

Paling, S. (2004). Classification, rhetoric, and the classificatory. *Library Trends, 52*(3), 588–603.

Paling, S., & Nilan, M. (2006). Technology, genres, and value change: The case of little magazines. *Journal of the American Society for Information Science and Technology, 57*(7), 862–872.

Poster, M. (1995). *The second media age*. Cambridge, UK: Polity Press.

Qvortrup, L. (2003). *The hypercomplex society*. New York: Peter Lang.

Radford, G. P. (1992). Positivism, Foucault, and the fantasia of the library: Conceptions of knowledge and the modern library experience. *Library Quarterly, 62*, 408–424.

Radford, G. P. (1998). Flaubert, Foucault, and the bibliotheque fantastique: Toward a postmodern epistemology for library science. *Library Trends, 46*, 616–634.

Rehm, G. (2002). Towards automatic Web genre identification. A corpus-based approach in the domain of academia by example of the academic's personal homepage. *Proceedings of the Hawaii International Conference on System Sciences*, 1143–1152.

Roussinov, D., Crowston, K., Nilan, M., Kwasnik, B. H., Liu, X., & Cai, J. (2001). Genre-based navigation on the Web. *Proceedings of the Thirty-Fourth Hawaii International Conference on Systems Science*, 4013–4022.

Russell, D. R. (1997). Rethinking genre in school and society. An activity theory analysis. *Written Communication, 14*(4), 504–554.

Sæbø, Ø., & Päivärinta, T. (2005). Autopoietic cybergenres for e-democracy?: Genre analysis of a Web-based discussion board. *Proceedings of the 38th Hawaii International Conference on System Sciences*, 98–108.

Schryer, C. F. (1993). Records as genre. *Written Communication, 10*, 200–234.

Searle, J. R. (1969). *Speech acts: An essay in the philosophy of language*. Cambridge, UK: Cambridge University Press.

Shepherd, M., & Watters, C. R. (1998). The evolution of cybergenres. *Proceedings of the Thirty-First Annual Hawaii International Conference on System Sciences*, 97–109.

Solomon, P. (2000). Exploring structuration in knowledge organization: Implications for managing the tension between stability and dynamism. *Proceedings of the Sixth International ISKO Conference*, 254–260.

Spinuzzi, C. (2003). *Tracing genres through organizations: A sociocultural approach to information design*. Cambridge, MA: MIT Press.

Sundin, O. (2003). Towards an understanding of symbolic aspects of professional information: An analysis of the nursing knowledge domain. *Knowledge Organization, 30*(3/4), 170–181.

Sundin, O., & Johannisson, J. (2005). Pragmatism, neo-pragmatism and socio-cultural theory: Communicative participation as a perspective in LIS. *Journal of Documentation, 61*(1), 23–43.

Swales, J. M. (1990). *Genre analysis. English in academic and research settings.* Cambridge, UK: Cambridge University Press.

Talja, S. (1997). Constituting "information" and "user" as research objects: A theory of knowledge formations as an alternative to the information man-theory. In P. Vakkari, R. Savolainen, & B. Dervin (Eds.), *Information seeking in context* (pp. 67–80). London: Taylor Graham.

Talja, S. (2005) The social and discursive construction of computing skills. *Journal of the American Society for Information Science and Technology, 56*(1), 13–22.

Toms, E. G. (2000, December/2001, January). Recognizing digital genre. *Bulletin of the American Society for Information Science and Technology, 27*(2), 20–22. Retrieved February 27, 2007, from www.asis.org/Bulletin/Dec-01/toms.html

Toms, E. G., & Campbell, D. G. (1999). Genre as interface metaphor: Exploiting form and function in digital environments. *Proceedings of the 32nd Hawaii International Conference on System Sciences,* 1–10.

Tyrväinen, P., & Päivärinta, T. (1999). On rethinking organizational document genres for electronic document management. *Proceedings of the 32nd Hawaii International Conference on System Sciences,* 2011.

Vaughan, M., & Dillon, A. (1998). The role of genre in shaping our understanding of digital documents. *Proceedings of the Annual Meeting of the American Society for Information Science,* 559–566.

Warner, J. (2002). Forms of labour in information systems. *Information Research, 7*(4). Retrieved February 17, 2007, from InformationR.net/ir/7-4/paper 135.html

Watters, C., & Shepherd, M. A. (1997). The digital broadsheet: An evolving genre. *Proceedings of the Thirtieth Hawaii International Conference on System Sciences* (vol. 6), 22–29.

Wiegand, W. A. (1998). The "Amherst Method": The origins of the Dewey Decimal Classification scheme. *Libraries & Culture, 33*(2), 175–194.

Wiegand, W. A. (2003). To reposition a research agenda: What American studies can teach the LIS community about the library in the life of the user. *Library Quarterly, 73*(4), 369–382.

Wilson, P., & Robinson, N. (1990). Form subdivisions and genre. *Library Resources & Technical Services, 34*(1), 36–43.

Winsor, D. A. (1999). Genre and activity systems: The role of documentation in maintaining and changing engineering activity systems. *Written Communication, 16*(2), 200–224.

Winsor, D. A. (2000). Ordering work: Blue-collar literacy and the political nature of genre. *Written Communication, 17*(2), 155–184.

Yates, J. (1989). *Control through communication: The rise of system in American management.* Baltimore: Johns Hopkins University Press.

Yates, J., & Orlikowski, W. J. (1992). Genres of organizational communication: A structurational approach to studying communication and media. *Academy of Management Review, 17*(2), 299–326.

Yates, J., Orlikowski, W. J., & Rennecker, J. (1997). Collaborative genres for collaboration: Genre systems in digital media. *Proceedings of the Thirtieth Annual Hawaii International Conference on System Sciences*, (vol. 6), 50–59.

Yates, S. J., & Sumner, T. R. (1997). Digital genres and the new burden of fixity. *Proceedings of the Thirtieth Hawaii International Conference on System Sciences*, (vol. 6), 3–12.

Information Management and Systems

CHAPTER 9

Knowledge Management

Bill Martin
RMIT University

Introduction

When the initial *ARIST* chapter on knowledge management was written (MacMorrow, 2001) the field was still very much at the developmental stage. In the succeeding six years, considerable progress has been made toward raising the general level of understanding of knowledge management—its principles and components, underlying theories, and key areas of research and practice. This is not to say that all the contradictions (terminological, jurisdictional, and operational) have been resolved. The concept continues to suffer from image problems, which result from the combination of its overselling by vendors and consultants in the 1990s and the fallout from Enron and similar corporate scandals linked to untraditional accounting methods (Ekbia, 2004). The term *knowledge management* seems to have gained acceptance more by default than anything else. More significantly, although some aspects of knowledge—such as culture, organizational structure, communication processes, and information—can be managed, knowledge itself, arguably, cannot (Kakabadse, Kakabadse, & Kouzmin, 2003).

In this chapter, developments are viewed not as major paradigm shifts so much as the varied and iterative responses of management and management researchers to the need to acquire, create, organize, disseminate, manage, and account for a range of largely intangible resources—from know-how to organizational conversation—that, for good or ill, have acquired the collective designation of *knowledge management*.

A Note on Knowledge Theory

In a philosophical context, the study of knowledge involves the metaphysical, embracing issues of what can be *known* and of *truth*, matters far beyond the scope of this chapter, and indeed, the competence of the author. Nevertheless, to understand something of the meaning and nature of knowledge in an organizational sense, some grasp of theory is important, if only at the ontological and epistemological levels. Ontological and epistemological positions can be broadly categorized as positivist or objective on one hand and subjective or constructivist on the other; the former posited on the existence of a reality independent of human consciousness or knowledge, the latter viewing reality as a construct of the human mind (Flanagan, 1991; Johnson & Duberley, 2000; Rosenau, 1992; Venzin, von Krogh, & Roos, 1998; von Krogh, Ichijo, & Nonaka, 2000). To positivists, the *truth* of knowledge is understood as the degree to which inner representations correspond to the world outside, but to constructionists the world is not perceived as a fixed and objective entity because it is not possible to represent reality. In the latter position, knowledge emerges from a dynamic human process of justifying personal beliefs as part of an aspiration for *truth*; and in this context it can be validated but never attained as absolute truth (Nonaka, 1994). In this view, knowledge is an activity: the process of knowing (Blackler, 1995; Cook & Brown, 1999; Polanyi, 1966; Vera & Crossan, 2003). This positivist-constructivist dichotomy is reflected respectively in epistemologies of possession and of action. The former represents a *content* and practice perspective on knowledge management, with knowledge being viewed as an economic asset that allows predictive truth to be codified, stored, and exchanged between individuals within a firm or sold by one firm to another (Assudani, 2005; Bahra, 2001; Blackler, 1995; Bukowitz & Williams, 1999). In the latter *relationist* perspective, knowledge emerges from the practice of knowing (Cook & Brown, 1999) and, rather than being something that is possessed, is something that people do; it is a mediated, situated, provisional, pragmatic, and contested phenomenon (Assudani, 2005).

These two broad epistemological approaches encompass and to some extent reflect the key distinction between *explicit* knowledge (formal, identifiable, easy to capture and transmit) and *tacit* knowledge (informal, tied to the senses and innate personal skills, not always possible to articulate). The distinction between these two types of knowledge continues to be a major feature of knowledge management, in both theory and practice. Nonaka and Takeuchi (1995) applied Polanyi's (1966) distinction in constructing their Socialization Externalization Combination Internalization (SECI) model of knowledge conversion. They may have paid insufficient attention to *intrinsic* knowledge, that is knowledge that, although similar to tacit in that it is not explicit, nonetheless can be articulated (Firestone & McElroy, 2003). The model may also have contributed to an oversimplification of differences that, rather than being absolute, represent movement along a continuum between explicit and tacit (Choo, 1998; Küpers, 2005; Stacey, 2001; Stenmark, 2000, 2001; Styhre, 2003, 2004; Tsoukas, 1997). This tacit-explicit dichotomy has attracted renewed attention in view of the recent emphasis on the role of narrative in organizations, which involves articulation of much that is tacit and embodied—a form of *knowledge-in-use* through its constitution and reconstitution in everyday practice (Küypers, 2005; Orlikowski, 2002; Patriotta, 2003, 2004; Snowden, 2000, 2002b). Nevertheless, the depiction of a knowledge spiral where tacit knowledge is shared through a socialization process and becomes implicit through externalization, and explicit knowledge is shared through a combination process and becomes tacit through internalization (Nonaka & Takeuchi, 1995) continues to resonate with knowledge management theoreticians and practitioners alike. Their interest has been further sparked by contributions to the knowledge management corpus from, in particular, the fields of economics and management but also from the sociology of knowledge.

Contributions from the Sociology of Knowledge

Since the middle of the last century, the sociology of knowledge has emphasized the social creation of knowledge, rejecting earlier positivist and Marxist perceptions of knowledge as secondary to, and a function of, economic relations in society (McCarthy, 1996). In a sociological context, the study of knowledge is located within the broader category of *culture*, a construct that expresses the collective experiences of entire societies as well as of particular groups, classes, regions, and communities. However, culture is no longer regarded as simply a reflection of forms of social organization, but rather as a set of *practices*, where *social reality* is not a phenomenon that exists in its own right, but one that is produced and communicated, and whose meanings are derived in and through systems of knowledge (Goldman, 1986; McCarthy, 1996).

This evolutionary concept of knowledge as meaning that is continuously reproduced and potentially transformed in action is far removed from causal or explanatory positivist frameworks (McCarthy, 1996; Stacey, 2001). As a consequence, all notions of *reality, knowledge-of-reality* and *meaning* must be recognized as highly problematical. The strength of this observation can be seen in the widespread rejection of descriptions of knowledge as some kind of fundamental truth across a range of theoretical and disciplinary boundaries from post-modernism to pragmatic philosophy, with knowledge being viewed as existing in particular contexts and representations of truth and knowledge being essentially incomplete and self-referential (Assudani, 2005; Casey, 2000; McCarthy, 1996). What, then, of the perspectives of such business-related domains as economics, management, social capital, and learning theory?

Contributions from Economics

The influx of ideas from economics into knowledge management has not always followed a direct route, nor have the sources always been located within the economics mainstream. A major source of influence has been the literature on the knowledge-based economy, something that owes as much to the work of management writers as to economists (Ásgeirsdóttir, 2005; Drucker, 1994; Organisation for Economic Co-operation and Development, 1996). The connections between knowledge and economics go back to Adam Smith (1776/1861) and his interest in knowledge content and production efficiencies and, later to Alfred Marshall's (1890) views of knowledge as the most powerful engine of production. Thereafter, neoclassical economics treated knowledge as the outcome of an explicit and formal production function (Arrow & Hahn, 1971) that would facilitate market equilibrium as firms adopted the most efficient production functions through imitative learning (Hallwood, 1997). This emphasis on rationality and a search for personal utility in a contractual and transactional context (Coase, 1988; North, 1981; Williamson, 1985) has survived its predicted demise in the face of new organizational forms and boundary-spanning knowledge networks (Day & Schoemaker, 2000; Foss, 2001; Hamel, 2000; Teece, 1998; Williamson, 1985, 1991, 1999), owing in part to its continued relevance to issues of knowledge management, including those of incentives and the influence of alternative organizational arrangements on value-creation in firms characterized as knowledge-integrating institutions (Buckley & Carter, 1996; Foss & Mahnke, 2003; Jensen & Meckling, 1992; Osterloh & Frey, 2000). Nevertheless, to a substantial extent assumptions of market equilibrium have given way to acceptance of states of non-equilibrium, owing not only to uncertainty and the unequal distribution of resources, but also to differences in the ability of firms to reconfigure internal resources and processes and to create others through innovation (Hodgson, 1994; von Krogh & Grand, 2002).

Economists have been accused both of over-investing in information to the detriment of knowledge (Mayer, 2005; Yeager, 2005) and of ignoring knowledge as being too difficult to handle (Penrose, 1959). However, the issue of what is *knowledge* and what is *information* remains moot, not least where the production of knowledge-based goods and services entails the codification of knowledge into symbols for easy transmission, replication, and storage (Boisot, 1995; Cohendet & Steinmuller, 2000; Cowan, David, & Foray, 2000; Saviotti, 1998). Much really useful knowledge, being tacit in nature, is resistant to codification and is better viewed as a process or an activity than as an entity—a complex and loose pattern emerging from experience and the use of routines, which facilitates the transmission of various messages (Boulding, 1955). It is the structure rather than the signal that is knowledge (MacKay, 1969), and the symbols that emerge from codification are in fact information (Langlois, 2001). Nevertheless, both Stiglitz's (1985) work on market inefficiencies involving information asymmetries and imperfect information and that of von Hayek (1937, 1945) on competitive price systems as mechanisms for the low-cost aggregation and transmission of information contributed to awareness that within the price system much of the knowledge was tacit and was neither directly communicable nor amenable to the effects of mechanisms that elicited information (Caldwell, 1997, 2005; Yeager, 2005).

This issue of tacit knowledge links directly to developments in the theory of economic growth. In neoclassical models, economic growth was viewed as *exogenous*, coming from outside the model and dependent on assumed rates of technological progress and of growth in the labor force. It was not until the 1980s that dissatisfaction with the limits of these models resulted in the emergence of *endogenous growth theory* or *new growth theory*, where technical change was *endogenized* and knowledge was regarded not as incidental, but as something produced through the rational optimizing behavior of economic agents (Langlois, 2001). The development of the endogenous theory owed much to the earlier work of Penrose (1959) on the distinction between formal and informal (personal) knowledge, a distinction now familiar in terms of tacit versus explicit knowledge. Also important were Kaldor and Mirrlees's (1962) investigation of the relationship between technical progress, per capita investment, and learning and Arrow's (1962) association of learning with the absolute level of knowledge already accumulated within the economy.

Arrow influenced a younger generation of economists whose work on endogenous growth theory incorporated technological improvement directly into growth calculations by showing how knowledge—the combination of technology and new ideas—was created and distributed throughout the economy (Romer, 1986, 1990, 1996). The effect of new ideas expressed as technological progress, combined with appropriate scientific and market institutions, turned the traditional economics of scarcity and diminishing returns on its head (Neef, 1999). In this new perspective, the power of ideas leads to constant improvement and to the prospect that knowledge-based products, once an initial investment in R&D has been made, can be sold again and again with minimal marginal production cost (Arthur, 1990, 1994, 1996). These developments promised not only the codification and re-use of knowledge and experience, but also the prospect of increasing returns to knowledge. Questions as to the most effective mechanisms for this reuse remain, such as whether this is best achieved through knowledge transmission or, alternatively, its embodiment in technology, in organizations and institutions (Langlois, 1999a, 1999b, 2001; Nelson, 1992). At this point a number of issues derived from evolutionary economics, resource-based theory, and strategic management need to be acknowledged.

Evolutionary and Resource Based Theories

Until the middle of the 1980s, the link between economics and strategy came mainly through organizational economics, with a focus on organizational capability and on achieving the best possible fit between the organization and its environment in order to secure a competitive and sustainable market position (Porter, 1991). The presence of market imperfections in the acquisition and utilization of resources, including informational resources, provided some organizations with opportunities to deploy these resources more effectively than their rivals (Carlisle, 2000; Williamson, 1985, 1991, 1999). During the mid-1980s, the search for sustained competitive advantage began to shift from what had been an essentially external focus toward one based on the nurturing of internal resources, capabilities, and competencies (Carlisle, 2000). In this resource-based view, firms were regarded as heterogeneous bundles of imperfectly mobile *resources* (basic inputs into gaining and maintaining competitive advantage) and *capabilities* (a firm's capacity in acquiring and utilizing its resources for competitive gain) whose characteristics could predict organizational success (Barney, 1991; Hall, 1993). Organizations sought to exploit knowledge by building these capabilities and related *competencies* (the ability to do particular things well), with an emphasis on the value of heterogeneous bundles of imperfectly mobile resources that were intangible, rare, imperfectly imitable, and non-substitutable (Grant, 1996b; Hamel & Prahalad, 1989). As a resource, knowledge met all the foregoing criteria and, in addition, was causally ambiguous in that its precise form could be difficult to specify and its precise effect on performance difficult to isolate (Carlisle, 2000).

This *knowledge-based* perspective argues that organizational knowledge—such as operational routines, skills, or know-how—is emergent, evolving, dynamic, and permanently embedded in the organization (Assudani, 2005; Spender, 1996a). Firms with these capabilities can supplement them with the conversion of individual and social expertise, including shared identity and social capital (Kogut & Zander, 1996; Nahapiet & Ghosal, 1998) in the production of economically useful goods and services (Grant, 1996a; Kogut & Zander, 1996). Whether as resource-based theory per se or as its knowledge-based derivative, this treatment of knowledge represented a major advance over the standard neoclassical approach. Nevertheless, difficulties remained in the identification and separation of the resources that created the value, in characterizing what it was that made them valuable (Williamson, 1999), and in understanding the dynamic character of competence-building and destruction over time (Leonard-Barton, 1992; Teece, 1977; Teece & Pisano, 1994). Evolutionary theory provides the means by which to address some of these issues.

A key element of resource-based theory was the possibility that some firms could enjoy the benefits of *Ricardian* rents, that is, economic rent derived from a differential advantage owing to organizational resources. It is due in part to differences in productivity but chiefly to advantages of location (Montgomery, 1995; Winter, 1995). Contrary to standard neoclassical theory, which views knowledge as exogenous, and as a given, *evolutionary theory* indicates that knowledge is subject to some form of transformation as a result of searching and learning (Nelson & Winter, 1982). This represents a search for *Schumpeterian* rents as a source of competitive success, that is, rents resulting from differences in the ability of firms to create first mover advantages by proactive innovation (von Krogh & Grand, 2002). By directly addressing the origin of resource differences and how they are created, maintained, and defended over time, both as a result of deliberate problem solving and random events (Nelson, 1991; Nelson & Winter, 1982), the evolutionary perspective focuses on technological evolution and the resulting competition among firms as bundles of routines (Foss, Knudsen, & Montgomery, 1995). On the basis of key activities including adaptation, learning, and searching, firms emerge as path-dependent knowledge bases where bundles of hierarchically arranged routines aggregate persistent behavior patterns (Nelson & Winter, 1982). The evolutionary approach has made a key contribution by linking knowledge to innovation, rent creation, and strategic behavior. However, it falls short of explaining the fundamental issue of knowledge creation; and for this a new theory or theories are required (von Krogh & Grand, 2002). Such theories are emerging within the mainstream knowledge management area; but first we review some relevant advances in economic and community development and social network theory under the rubric of social capital.

Social Capital

Social capital is another topic that has received treatment in *ARIST* (Davenport & Snyder, 2005). The concept has been traced back to early economists from Smith and Ricardo to Marx and Marshall (Farr, 2003). From its modern manifestation, during the early 20th century, to a revival during the 1990s, the concept has remained ambiguous and subject to diverse interpretations from its depiction as aggregates of social resources and institutionalized relationships (Bourdieu, 1986; Coleman, 1990; Fine, 1999; Putnam, 1993), to the norms and networks that enable people to act collectively (Woolcock & Narayan, 2000) within networks of trust (Barr, 1998; Whiteley, 2000; Paldam & Svendsen, 2000), to norms of reciprocity and the strength of associative life (Buckland, 1998; Maluccio, Haddad, & May, 2000).

Generally, therefore, the subject remains contentious, at both the organizational and national levels. Many researchers are uncomfortable with the implied assumption that positive outcomes must result from the presence of social capital and, indeed, that the outcomes are always positive (Dasgupta, 2000; Portes, 1998). In the development arena, current perceptions of social capital have emerged only after decades in which social relationships were viewed as inimical to development (owing to their perceived potential for sustaining conditions of dependency and exploitation) and contrary to traditional neoclassical perspectives based on rational choices in perfect markets (Woolcock & Narayan, 2000). Although on occasion preferring to use such proxies as infrastructure, trust, and community in place of the term *social capital*, from the middle of the 1990s the World Bank has embraced the notion and the view that it is crucial to the development process and to the creation of sustainable social institutions, organizations, and communities (Fine, 1999; Gittell & Vidal, 1998; Harriss & De Renzio, 1997; Hornburg & Lang, 1998; Schulgasser, 1999; World Bank, 1999).

Social Capital in an Organizational Context

The nature and role of social capital are relevant to knowledge management when placed in an organizational context, particularly that of the many-layered networks that can operate within and between individuals, groups, and organizations (Burt, 1992; Nohria & Eccles, 1992; Cohen & Prusak, 2001).

Cohen and Prusak (2001) and Duguid (2005) have expressed reservations over a perceived tendency to treat social capital in a mechanistic and system-oriented fashion that all too often ignores the social aspects of organizations. This criticism goes to the very nature of social capital and to questions not so much about its social character as its status as capital (Farr, 2003; Fine, 2001). Some would see this use of the term *capital* as ideologically focused and, in effect, skewing perceptions of social phenomena and goods toward an economic and capitalist perspective (Cohen & Prusak, 2001); in a wider industry and market context this is, to some extent at least, only to be expected. However, even modest expectations of the concept are likely to hinge on a more realistic view of the power of social capital within communities (Durlauf, 2002) and in the context of much broader, multi-causal models of community change (Adam & Roncevic, 2003). The context-dependent nature of social capital suggests why neither attitudes (norms, trust) nor infrastructures (networks, organization) per se can be understood as social capital in isolation from the issue of access, something that is neither brokered nor distributed equitably (Edwards & Foley, 1988). One very effective means of brokering access is through the medium of Communities of Practice (COP).

Social Capital and COP Theory

Social capital theory posits the operation of networks of individuals that help to embed economic interactions in social relations (Granovetter, 1973, 1985; Polanyi, 1957). Through social exchanges, people build webs of trust (Fukayama, 1995; Putnam, 1993, 2000), and of obligation, reputation, expectations, and norms (Coleman, 1988) within which they are willing to share knowledge and coordinate action. Perhaps the most celebrated of such mechanisms for knowledge exchange are Communities of Practice. The concept of Communities of Practice emerged in the field of educational research (Lave & Wenger, 1991); it was later described as groups of people with a shared concern for a problem or topic, who deepen their knowledge and expertise by interacting on an ongoing basis (Foote, Matson, Weiss, & Wenger, 2002).

Communities of Practice constitute a form of middle ground between the macro- and micro-organizational levels; they have the ability to focus on problem identification, learning, and knowledge at such levels, while being able to adapt continuously and proactively to environmental change (Brown & Duguid, 2001). Unlike teams or work groups, Communities of Practice tend to function best when they emerge naturally from the common interests of people working on similar problems and learning from the experience. Significantly this constitutes not merely learning as situated in practice, but learning as an integral part of practice: learning as generative social practice lived in the world (Hildreth, Kimble, & Wright, 2000). Membership of a COP provides the actors involved with tacit knowledge about how to become a practitioner, about *knowing how*, rather than *knowing what*, about learning *to be* in contrast to *learning to* (Duguid, 2005). Communities of Practice can vary widely in their characteristics, being based on a single or on several disciplines, small or localized, or geographically dispersed as virtual communities that communicate primarily by telephone, e-mail, online discussion groups, and videoconferencing. They also interact with people moving from one community to another, acting as *boundary spanners*, aiding in the spread of practice and knowledge.

Knowledge flow and transfer are achieved alternately by the phenomena of *stickiness* and *leakiness*. Knowledge is more likely to leak between communities where there is some measure of similarity between them; stickiness, however, is a function of the degree of difference between communities (Brown & Duguid, 2001). Newell, Robertson, Scarborough, and Swan (2002) point out that in spite of evidence for the value of communities, it can be difficult for organizations to implement them. This is partly because the cognitive perspective, where knowledge is regarded as something possessed by individuals rather than communities, fits more neatly with established management practices. Communities are not reflected on the organization chart, are not linked into formal systems of goal setting and accountability, and do not have bosses. Another set of problems concerns how to identify, develop, and sustain these communities in a dynamic business world. This implies a need to go beyond problem solving to embrace a range of corporate issues, including the need to overcome unseen boundaries to knowledge sharing, for example, those shaped by practice and epistemic commitment, which, along with distinctions between what people *can* share and are actually *willing* to share (Duguid, 2005), can frustrate the efforts of otherwise willing collaborators (Gamble & Blackwell, 2001). Finally, there is always the risk that Communities of Practice can turn out to be inhospitable rather than welcoming, coercive rather than persuasive (Brown & Duguid, 2001) or can become insular and blinkered by the limitations of their own world view, with the further risk that core competencies can be turned into core rigidities (Leonard-Barton, 1992). On balance, however, these COPs are proven vehicles for knowledge creation and sharing, frequently exhibiting continuous and often seamless interaction between their narrative and cognitive processes and those of organizational learning (Boland & Tenkasi, 1995).

Learning

Initially, the literature on organizational learning focused on learning as either a cognitive process (Argyris & Schon, 1978; Daft & Weick, 1984) or as a function of behavioral change occurring through modification of an organization's programs, goals, decision rules, or routines (Cyert & March, 1963; Nelson & Winter, 1982). A second set of foci has been that of organizational learning and the Learning Organization. Organizational learning can be defined as the capacity or processes within an organization to maintain or improve performance based on experience (Nevis, DiBella, & Gould, 1995; Wang & Ahmed, 2003) or more recently, the process of change in individual and shared thought and action, which is affected by and embedded in the institutions of the organization (Bierly, Kessler, & Christensen, 2000; Vera & Crossan, 2003). This learning can occur by accident or design, in formal and less formal fashion, and from doing, as for instance in action learning or learning situated in organizational events (Nidumolu, Subramani, & Aldrich, 2001).

Learning organizations are those skilled at creating, acquiring, and transferring knowledge and at modifying their behavior to reflect new knowledge and insights (Armstrong & Foley, 2003; Garvin, 1993); or alternatively, are organizations where knowledge is captured and systematized to the benefit of the entire organization (Loermans, 2002). However, organizations must use this knowledge in a way that leads to action and change. Simply developing the capability to acquire and share knowledge is not sufficient to become a knowledge-based, learning organization (Albert & Picq, 2004; Watkins & Marsick, 1996). Although as a concept, the learning organization still attracts a fair amount of criticism, no organization today can afford to abstain from the processes of individual and group learning and related efforts, or ignore the need to embed the results in non-human repositories such as routines, systems, structures, culture, and strategy (Crossan, Lane, & White, 1999). A number of mechanisms for the learning process can be identified, ranging from: Argyris and Schon's (1978) original, single, and double loop learning through the exploitation of mental models within the organization (Kim, 1993); the exploitation of firm competencies and the sharing of experiences and routines (Darr et al., 1995; Murray & Donegan, 2003; Sorenson, 2003) including through the use of teams, communities, and alliances (Barrett, Cappleman, Shoib, & Walsham, 2004; Mowery et al., 1996); and changes in organizational design (Audia et al., 2001; Sorenson, 2003), the employment of After-Action reviews and Lessons Learned (Botkin, 1999), and learning by hiring (Dosi, 1988; Kim, 1997; Song, Almeida, & Wu, 2003).

Single and Double Loop Learning

The single-double loop learning dichotomy still resonates with managers. In single loop learning, the focus is on *how* to get things done and on obtaining knowledge in order to solve specific problems based on existing premises. In contrast, double loop learning involves the establishment of different premises and ways of doing things, by asking *why* questions that probe the basic assumptions and norms that underpin and explain present theories of action (Botkin, 1999). Unfortunately much of the learning that occurs in organizations remains at the single loop level, owing to the inability of practitioners, for example, to remove the kind of organizational defensive routines that ensure that espoused learning theories are diluted in practice into theories-in-use (Argyris, 2004). Nevertheless, the basic approach continues in, for example, the incremental learning and step function learning dichotomies reported from manufacturing industry (Helfat & Raubitschek, 2002) and between the practice of exploitation, based on the efficient use of existing competencies, and of exploration comprising the development of new ones (Holland, 1975; March, 1995; Uzzi & Lancaster, 2003). Put differently, such practices represent respectively, first order learning, which entails improved exploitation through the maintenance of existing identity, knowledge and practices, and control and coordination in a dominant design, and second order learning aimed at architectural change and a change of rules (Bogenrieder & Nooteboom, 2004). It is argued that in the deployment of existing knowledge in emergent situations, staff enjoying the luxury of *reflection-in-action* can be in the position to generate new knowledge and by engaging in *exploration through exploitation* (March, 1991) can participate in double loop learning. Conversely, this process of *learning-by-doing* based on refinements of existing knowledge (Argote, 1999) and being path-dependent (Levitt & March, 1988) can actually be at odds with *reflection-in-action* (Garud & Kumaraswamy, 2005). What is growing, however, is the recognition that a continuous, self-directed learning approach on the part of individual employees can offer benefits in terms of increased efficiency, effectiveness, and cost savings (Guglielmino & Guglielmino, 2001).

Whatever the form of learning in operation, the mainstream learning literature regards the transfer mechanism between individual and group learning as sitting at the heart of organizational learning. Accordingly, individual learning becomes embedded in an organization's memory and structure through the exchange of individual and shared mental models within the organization (Kim, 1993). These are an individual's assumptions, expectations, knowledge, and information about the world or other people and relationships with them, as well as about the nonhuman world in which the individual lives and acts. Mental models provide the means for individuals to process data about the world and for making a choice of actions to take. They are also linked to learning styles, both those of single loop and double loop learning. The business of articulating and sharing mental models has strategic implications through its links to potential learning gaps between what firms need to know and what they actually know. In trying to close these strategic learning gaps firms seek to share mental models to enhance both the rapidity and the effectiveness of learning (Zack, 2002). This mainstream approach has been criticized not only in relation to its perceptions of mental models, but also for the fundamental distinction between individual and group levels. Rather than being predetermined and representing a given reality, it is argued, individual minds actually construct the worlds they perceive and act on (Stacey, 2001).

Routines and Experience

Learning is also achieved on the basis of shared libraries of effective routines (Sorenson, 2003), which enable the firm to learn from its experience, select those routines and activities that can generate the desired outcomes (March, 1988; Nelson & Winter, 1982), and then distribute the knowledge gained and implement these routines across the organization (Darr et al., 1995). Through iteration, organizations can continually improve performance, until at least marginal returns begin to decline (Sorenson, 2003). Routines improve functionality by reducing uncertainty, saving time, and improving efficiency, but they can have the effect of reducing the likelihood of innovation, not least because their implementation is basically a single-loop learning activity (Argyris, 2004). Accordingly, in spite of their disruptive potential, interruptions to established routines have been identified as a possible method of knowledge acquisition (Zellmer-Bruhn, 2003) during which the breaks from normal activity can trigger change (Okhuysen & Eisenhardt, 2002).

The acquisition of knowledge is also strongly influenced by experience. Hence, whether an organization (or the relevant employees) is specialist or generalist in nature can influence the ability to learn from experience. Ingram and Baum (1997) found that specialists who concentrated in a small number of geographic areas were more likely to learn from their own experience than generalists who operated over a larger area. Nadler, Shaw, and Walton (1995) showed that experience observing someone perform a task can be more beneficial for subsequent performance than other types of experience, such as that acquired through classroom training. This can help individuals acquire tacit knowledge as well as explicit knowledge. Individuals who learn through observation may not be able to articulate what they learn, but are able to transfer the knowledge to a new task.

Changes in Organizational Design

Learning can result from changes in organizational design, where for example, regrouping into smaller units can further accelerate the learning process (Audia et al., 2001). Organizations can provide opportunities for members to learn from each other by reducing the distance, either physical or psychological between people—say by learning from observation (Nadler et al., 1995). In a structural context, there is conflicting evidence for the nature of the link to learning. Hence claims that firms that operate within integrated (Sorenson, 2003) or centralized (Chang & Harrington, 2003) structures have demonstrated an enhanced ability to learn and to transfer knowledge, at least under conditions of market volatility, are matched by others to the effect that the interdependence generated, say by vertical integration, can result in suboptimal organizational outcomes, as it interferes with activities such as learning-by-doing and impedes the implementation of new routines and their transfer throughout the firm (Rivkin, 2000; Sorenson, 2003). Relationships within internal social networks (Borgatti & Cross, 2003; Thomas-Hunt, Ogden, & Neale, 2003) as well as networks to other firms (Uzzi & Lancaster, 2003) affect learning and knowledge transfer. Informal networks can help to make knowledge more proximate; and the informal ties involved can promote vicarious learning, with staff benefiting from the knowledge accumulated by close contacts and associates (Reagans & Zuckerman, 2001; Uzzi & Lancaster, 2003). Finally, the structural effect can extend to relationships embedded in transactive memory systems that facilitate knowledge retention and transfer (Borgatti & Cross, 2003; Liang, Moreland, & Argote, 1995) or where group members share a short-hand language (Weber & Camerer, 2003). Culture, including a firm's idiosyncratic conventions and specialist homemade language (Weber & Camerer, 2003) and its learning orientation and value (Bunderson & Sutcliffe, 2001; Edmonson, 1999), can also affect learning outcomes.

Teams

In spite of the popularity of teams in all kinds of organizations and their implied importance for both organizational learning and knowledge management, relatively little is known about how teams actually acquire and transfer knowledge (Argote, 1999; Edmondson, 1999; Zellmer-Bruhn, 2003). Organizations often employ multiple teams on the same or similar tasks, with innovative routines developed by one team transferring to others. The timing of team creation and the make-up of team membership are matters of critical importance, with an appropriate balance drawn between levels of experience and functional representation, the roles of participants, and allowance for membership from outside the organization all contributing to processes of self-organization and the building of trust and common perspectives (Nonaka, 2002). The use of cross-functional teams from different intellectual and occupational backgrounds has been found to increase the likelihood of combining knowledge in new or creative ways by bringing diverse skills, abilities, knowledge, and cognitive styles to bear on issues (Brown & Eisenhardt, 1995; Leonard, 1995; Madhavan & Grover, 1998). This includes teams that are geographically dispersed and often virtual (Boutellier, Gassmann, Macho, & Roux, 1998; Leonard, Brands, Edmondson, & Fenwick, 1998; Prokesch, 1997; Townsend, DeMarie, & Hendrickson, 1998). On the other hand, there is evidence of a negative influence of knowledge diversity with failures in synthesizing and leveraging expertise (Bechky, 2003; Dougherty, 1992) or in sharing knowledge from different contexts (Ancona & Caldwell, 1992; Lam, 1997; Williams & O'Reilly, 1998). Clearly, success in these matters can often depend upon task and contextual factors, but with this caveat, there are reasonable grounds for arguing that the operation of dispersed, cross-functional teams can help promote organizational learning, both as vehicles for the development of innovative products and processes and as sources of residual gains through the dispersion of knowledge in the organization (Sole & Edmondson, 2002).

After Action Reviews and Lessons Learned

The use of *After Action Reviews* and *Lessons Learned* from projects and engagements has become increasingly popular in the knowledge management field, initially through pioneering work by the U.S. Army (Botkin, 1999), but also at corporations such as General Motors, Mobil Oil, and BP Amoco (Collison & Parcell, 2004; Koenig & Srikantaiah, 2004). The essence of After Action Reviews is a *learning-by-doing* philosophy, where everybody involved in an action or a business project comes together as soon as possible after the event to conduct a dialogue that explains what happened and captures learning. These events are clearly not without risks, and a culture of risk-taking as well as of learning is necessary; but they can be powerful vehicles for organizational learning (Botkin, 1999; Collison & Parcell, 2004). They are an important explicit link between organizational learning and knowledge and are essential for expediting the process whereby one part of the firm, when it learns something of value, then makes this knowledge widely available (Garud & Kumaraswamy, 2005). The collection and compilation of lessons requires the right combination of infrastructure, technological and structural, and of staff skilled in eliciting and reporting the information (Botkin, 1999). Although not quite the same thing, there is also considerable value in learning from failure, although not unexpectedly, much less is heard about this than about successful projects. There is, however, some evidence for the value of such lessons (Starbuck & Milliken, 1988), not least in serving to counter deep-seated perceptions and foster innovative thinking (Lant & Montgomery, 1987).

Learning-by-Hiring

There remain conflicting views on the relative merits and efficiencies of learning from internal versus external sources. Thus it is claimed that valuable knowledge is much more likely to be diffused within the organization than outside it (Darr et al., 1995; Kane, Crawford, & Grant, 1999; Zucker, Darby, Brewer, & Peng, 1996), with, for example, evidence that knowledge is more likely to transfer across units that are part of the same organization (Ingram & Simons, 2002) and that *Best Practice* transfers are more likely within an organization than to units outside it

(Zellmer-Bruhn, 2003). However, even within a firm, tacit knowledge is *sticky* and does not necessarily flow easily unless the individuals possessing it also move (Szulanski, 1996). On the other hand, human mobility, notably involving the movement of experts between firms, is a key mechanism for knowledge transfer and interfirm learning (Almeida & Kogut, 1999; Menon & Pfeffer, 2003; Song et al., 2003). It is also argued that organizational members are more likely to value knowledge from external than internal sources because they are less familiar with its limitations and because valuing external knowledge would not reduce their own status.

Because knowledge may sometimes be difficult to separate from those who possess it, Dosi (1988) suggested that hiring people away from a rival is a way of transferring otherwise immobile knowledge. The mobility of experienced experts does not simply provide a one-time transfer of information, as is often the case with technology licensing, but may also facilitate the transfer of capabilities, permitting further knowledge building (Kim, 1997). Although hiring can result in new knowledge, the extent to which experts can leverage their former firm's knowledge bases may vary substantially with the attributes of both the hiring firm and the mobile experts. For example, it can be costly to change standardized routines in order to integrate knowledge and capabilities from elsewhere. The search for new knowledge is often localized or path-dependent, that is, it is influenced by a firm's past experiences (Nelson & Winter, 1982) and this can impede a firm's receptivity to external knowledge. Path-dependent firms will value knowledge close to existing technological and market conditions and myopically devalue more distant knowledge from outside the firm (Song et al., 2003). This can also result in firms that are satisfied with current levels of innovation being less motivated to access the expertise of others (Sorenson & Stuart, 2000). The hiring of outside experts could mitigate this tendency toward local search by exposing the firm to new ideas, practices, and areas of expertise and can be seen to comprise a form of *research by borrowing*, which can be extremely cost-effective (Ahuja, 2000; Keeble & Wilkinson, 2000). Other mechanisms for effecting knowledge transfer include the formation of alliances (Almeida, 1996; Mowery et al., 1996), co-location in technology-intensive regions, a search for Foreign Direct Investment (FDI), and the use of licensing agreements (Shan & Song, 1997), although firms with state-of-the-art knowledge are often reluctant to participate in this latter activity.

It might be thought that the link between organizational learning and successful business outcomes was so obvious as to be beyond debate but, as it happens, things are more complicated. First, Crossan et al. (1999) state that unlearning should be considered as a sub-dimension of organizational performance. Understanding involves both learning new knowledge and discarding obsolete and misleading knowledge, perhaps leading to the adoption of new practices or new work processes (Bellini & Lo Storto, 2006); a slow pace of unlearning is a crucial weakness of many organizations (Hedburg, 1981). Second, good performance is not necessarily a sign that learning has occurred. Other factors external to the organization—such as the failure of a competitor to service customers, changing government regulations that favor one company over another, or changes in the cost of producing or delivering a product or service as a result of favorable macroeconomic shifts, may enhance performance. Finally, there is no learning without risk and the kinds of knowledge with the highest value are often the most difficult to create (Cavalieri & Seivert, 2005). In addressing such challenges, it is important to understand the complicated relationship that obtains between data, information, and knowledge.

Data, Information, and Knowledge

Critics of knowledge management have dismissed it as being nothing more than an alternative term for information management. Although one would regard this description as an oversimplification, it is clear that information management is nonetheless an essential element of knowledge management. The nature of information and data and the relationships between these concepts on one hand and knowledge on the other (Ackoff, 1997; Bellinger, Castro, & Mills, 1997; Choo, Detlor, & Turnbull, 2000; Davenport & Prusak, 1998) have been described as the cornerstone for understanding knowledge management theory and practice in organizations (Alavi & Leidner, 2001).

At the most fundamental level, the relationships between these concepts have been modelled in hierarchical fashion, often as a pyramid with data (at the base) seen as facts, which can be structured purposefully to become information (in the middle), becoming knowledge (at the apex) when it is interpreted or put into context or when meaning is added to it (Alavi & Leidner, 2001). This hierarchical structure can be misleading, implying that one component of the model is superior to another, whereas each can be potentially valuable in appropriate circumstances (Stenmark, 2001). The model also overlooks the potential for alternative flows and transformations, most notably in a reversed hierarchy model where knowledge, when articulated, verbalized, and structured, becomes information which, when assigned a fixed representation and standard interpretation, becomes data (Tuomi, 2000). Both data and information require knowledge in order to be interpretable, but at the same time, data and information are useful tools for constructing new knowledge. In these processes knowledge embedded in human minds is a prerequisite and is significantly different from either data or information, which are not only similar in the roles they play, but in some circles are regarded as being essentially the same thing (Stenmark, 2001).

Other critics of the traditional hierarchical model contend that all these elements are in fact types of information. Information is not made from data. New data and knowledge are instead made through the

Knowledge Life Cycle (KLC) from pre-existing information, data, knowledge, and problems (Firestone & McElroy, 2003).

Knowledge today tends to be seen as emergent and resident in people, practices, artifacts, and symbols (Nidumolu et al., 2001) and as meaning that is continuously reproduced and potentially transformed in communicative interactions between people (Stacey, 2001). It is viewed alternately as a *stock*, and in some senses, a *thing* (Firestone & McElroy, 2003) and as a *flow*. In dynamic knowledge management contexts involving human actors, these seemingly incompatible perspectives will often be complementary, the major concern being which works in the circumstances (Demarest, 1997).

Intellectual Capital

From an organizational and managerial point of view, there are merits in subsuming the various forms and manifestations of knowledge—the insights, understandings, and practical know-how involved—under the rubric of *intellectual capital*. This is in spite of continuing confusion over terminology, with occasions when the term *intangibles* is being used interchangeably with *intellectual capital*, but more important with the continued tendency in accountancy circles to interpret *intangibles* as referring to non-fixed financial assets that have no physical substance but that are subject to control in accounting terms (Brennan & Connell, 2000; Marr, 2005). Although understandable in terms of context and purpose, this fails to do justice to intangibles such as brand recognition, business processes, customer loyalty, and employee expertise (Brennan & Connell, 2000; Marr, 2005; St. Onge & Wallace, 2003).

Whether described in terms of knowledge or of intellectual capital, these concepts sit at the core of knowledge management. Subsumed within them are all those competencies; networks and relationships; and learning and knowledge-creation activities, structures, strategies, and measurement methods that enable organizations to attend to the critical business of knowledge management. An organization's ability to develop and compete is clearly connected with its ability to learn and to exploit the capacity of individual employees to transform knowledge and experience, that is to say, intellectual capital into new or improved products and processes (Amo, 2006; Christensen, 2004; Hayton, 2005; Hejis, 2004; Mouritsen & Flagstad, 2004; Preiss & Spooner, 2003; Vedovello & Godinho, 2003). This portfolio of intangible resources has been conceptualized in various ways, including through variations on the themes of human, structural, and relational capital (Bontis, 2002; Roos, Roos, Dragonetti, & Edvinsson, 1998; St. Onge & Armstrong, 2004; Sveiby, 1997, 2002). However, although useful in itself, much more than recognition and identification of the nature and range of intellectual capital is needed if it is to be managed effectively.

The Management of Intellectual Capital

The management of intellectual capital poses major challenges owing to the elusive and dynamic nature of the core construct. It can often be difficult in practice to differentiate clearly between tangibles and intangibles. Intangibles are frequently embedded in physical assets (for example, technology in an aircraft) and in labor (the tacit knowledge of employees), leading to considerable interaction between tangible and intangible assets in the creation of value (Lev, 2001). For management, the response to such challenges is spread across a range of activities to do with management of the people, systems, and processes in whom intangible value frequently resides, including the design of systems to measure their impact and value. In spite of a proliferation of systems, much remains to be done before metrics for intangibles go beyond their current organization-specific and imperfect stage (Danish Ministry of Trade and Industry, 2000; Marr, 2005; MERITUM, 2002; Mouritsen, Bukh, Larsen, & Johansen, 2002). As in the case of frameworks, moreover, these are simply instruments, categorizations of resources, and in themselves they are redundant without direct links to organizational strategy and the markets in which the organization operates.

Knowledge Management

This chapter is grounded firmly in an interdisciplinary and organizational perspective on knowledge management. Although open to the argument that there are many knowledge managements rather than a single unified or unitary approach (Despres & Chauvel, 2000), it is heavily influenced by developments in the organizational and management sphere and less, for example, by those in, say, information science or computer science, which are regarded as playing supportive and enabling roles rather than constituting specific paradigms. This interdisciplinary approach is reflected in perceived similarities with the field of organizational learning. Perceived similarities include the same potential for lack of coherence in research and the existence of both prescriptive and descriptive approaches to the subjects (Argote, McEvily, & Reagans, 2003; Vera & Crossan, 2003). Indeed, it has been argued that there is no essential difference between knowledge management and organizational learning, and that it is pointless to differentiate between them (Stacey, 2000). In the theoretically eclectic context of knowledge management, the ability to understand the range of existing assumptions and paradigms is particularly important (Brusoni, Prencipe, & Pavitt, 2001; Cabrera & Cabrera, 2002; Davenport & Hall, 2002; Garcia-Lorenzo, Mitleton-Kelly, & Galliers, 2003; Land, Nolas, & Amjad, 2004, 2006a, 2006b; Tsoukas & Vladimirou, 2001). Efforts to clarify the paradigmatic status of knowledge management have identified a number of different, often conflicting, paradigms (Lam, 2000; Swann & Scarborough, 2001) and resulted in calls for a new and deeper focus on ontological and epistemological fundamentals (Brusoni et al., 2001; Day,

2005; Lam, 2000; Lanzara & Patriotta, 2001; McInerney & Day, 2007; Moffett, McAdam, & Parkinson, 2002). One group of management researchers, having applied a Kuhnian framework (Kuhn, 1970, 1977) for the identification of elements of the disciplinary matrix of knowledge management, concluded that knowledge management is at a prescientific state of development, in that a number of competing schools are claiming competence in the field but approaching it in different ways. They also concluded that at the moment, knowledge management, although showing signs of consensus and convergence, could not be regarded as possessing a clear and distinct paradigm (Hazlett, McAdam, & Gallagher, 2005).

This diversity of perception is clearly reflected in disagreement over certain proposed schools, ages, stages, or generations of knowledge management (Earl, 2001; Firestone & McElroy, 2003; Koenig, 2002; Snowden, 2002a; Wiig, 2004). Earl (2001) identified three broad schools of knowledge management: technocratic, economic, and behavioral, each with sub-types, but broadly representing information systems, commercial, and behavioral approaches, respectively. According to Koenig, the first age of knowledge management saw the application of technology to knowledge sharing and coordination across the enterprise; and the second moved beyond technology to recognition of the human and cultural factors in knowledge management. The third is basically focused on content management (Koenig, 2002). Snowden's stages began with a focus on the use of information for decision support, moving to a second stage launched basically through popularization of Nonaka and Takeuchi's SECI model of knowledge conversion. The third stage of knowledge management, which is now underway, involves a focus not on the management of knowledge as a thing, but on management of the ecology of knowledge (Snowden, 2002b). Both these approaches have been criticized in respect of the vagueness and inaccuracy of the stage timelines identified and for ignoring the large body of knowledge management activity that in many cases predated them (Firestone, 2001; Firestone & McElroy, 2003).

Most critically both the *ages* and *stages* approaches have been criticized for their conceptual and theoretical failings, notably by researchers from the so-called New or Second Generation Knowledge Management school (SGKM), which perceives the phenomenon in generational terms. Accordingly, first generation (or supply-side) knowledge management has been the majority view that operates around capture, codification, and re-use, with knowledge management perceived as comprising efforts at sharing already existing knowledge. Second generation (demand-side) knowledge management entails a focus on the creation of new knowledge through enhancing the conditions in which innovation and organizational creativity can flourish (Firestone & McElroy, 2003). In practice, both the demand- and supply-side approaches are necessary, but the significance of the New Knowledge Management lies not in its preference for two generations rather than three ages or stages but in its holistic nature. It is based on a knowledge life-cycle framework that not only emphasizes both knowledge production and knowledge integration, but also accounts for the existence of human social systems in which knowledge, organizational learning, innovation, and complexity all have roles to play. Critical to this approach is a core distinction between *knowledge processing*, which is a social process by which organizations produce and integrate knowledge, and *knowledge management*, or the activities performed by managers in their attempts to enhance knowledge processing (Firestone & McElroy, 2003).

Karl Wiig (2004), one of knowledge management's pioneers, has also adopted the supply-demand approach to what he describes as Next Generation Knowledge Management. The next generation will combine a *demand-pull* element of management philosophies and practice developments with an intellectual capital focus, with a *supply push* of new science and technology developments. The emphasis will lie on creating the kind of corporate environment in which people can make personal contributions to the overall enterprise, with a much deeper understanding both of how individuals acquire, use, and share knowledge and of how corporations can plan and organize to use this knowledge effectively in pursuit of corporate goals. The overall combination of a people focus, an intellectual asset focus, a technology focus, and an enterprise focus will lead to a comprehensive and strategic perspective on knowledge management (Wiig, 2004). In such a dynamic and interdisciplinary field, further enriched by ongoing exchanges between the workplace and the academy, one must be careful not to make too much of specific theories or sets of theories. However, the Second Generation approach probably represents the state of the art in terms of anything currently approaching a coherent theoretical framework for knowledge management.

Knowledge Management Practice

In what must necessarily be a limited treatment of knowledge management practice, the focus here will be on certain key elements. These include: frameworks for knowledge management, knowledge management processes, models for knowledge management, technologies for knowledge management, and strategies and cultures for knowledge management.

Frameworks for Knowledge Management

Over the years a number of frameworks have emerged, both generic and specific in scope (Davenport & Prusak, 1998; Demarest, 1997; Holsapple & Joshi, 1999, 2000, 2002; Leonard-Barton, 1995; van der Spek & Spijkervet, 1997; Wiig, 1997). Frameworks can be descriptive in nature, identifying key knowledge management phenomena, or prescriptive in that they prescribe methodologies for the conduct of knowledge management (Beckman, 1997). They can also be compared on both context and content dimensions. The context dimension refers to the focus or primary intent of the framework; the content dimension considers knowledge resources and those activities and factors that facilitate its management. Typically contained within these frameworks are the most important knowledge management processes and sub-processes to do with the creation or acquisition of knowledge, its organization, storage, transfer, and use. These frameworks have, however, been subject to criticism on the grounds that they have paid insufficient attention to knowledge resources and their interrelationships and manipulation (Holsapple & Joshi, 2002). More sophisticated examples are those that take a life-cycle approach that addresses knowledge management issues in a problem-solving context (Holsapple & Joshi, 2002; van der Spek & Spijkervet, 1997) or that distinguish between knowledge processing and knowledge management in the cyclical processes of knowledge production, evaluation, integration, and use (Cavalieri & Reed, 2000; Cavalieri & Seivert, 2005; Firestone, 2001; Firestone & McElroy, 2003; McElroy, 2000, 2002).

Processes in the Knowledge Management Cycle

All frameworks depict key knowledge management processes that, although often sequential, are not linear, emphasizing that knowledge processes are rarely a discrete linear set of events. These processes, which never really *stop* or *start* and may actually run in parallel include: acquiring and creating; codifying and locating; internalizing; storing; and using knowledge (van der Spek & de Hoog, 1994; Wiig, de Hoog, & van der Spek, 1997). Failure to appreciate their non-linear relationships can lead to their misuse as *recipes* for successful knowledge management, something that largely ignores the resource characteristics of knowledge and more significantly the need to manage these processes and resources (Holsapple & Joshi, 2002).

The need for broader frameworks that go beyond the identification of processes can be illustrated with examples from the core areas of knowledge sharing and transfer. At one level, the meaning of these terms is obvious, certainly at the level of categorizing knowledge management processes within frameworks. At the management level, matters are not so clear, with much of the underlying motivation and the mechanisms that enable sharing and transfer far from being understood.

Hence, in spite of its centrality to the overall knowledge management process, extensive knowledge sharing within organizations still appears to be the exception rather than the rule. Apart from a continuing tendency to hoard knowledge on the part of individuals, many firms actively limit knowledge sharing because of the threat of industrial espionage, as well as concerns about diverting or overloading the work-related attention of employees (Constant, Kiesler, & Sproull, 1996). Also, organizational incentive structures, such as *pay-for-performance* compensation schemes, can serve to discourage knowledge sharing if employees believe that sharing will hinder their personal efforts to distinguish themselves from their co-workers (Huber, 2001). Knowledge sharing concerns the willingness of individuals in an organization to share with others the knowledge they have acquired or created (Gibbert & Krause, 2002). This can be done directly via communication or indirectly via a knowledge archive; the key is willingness to share. Even with the codification of knowledge, many knowledge objects remain unexposed to, and hence unrecognizable by, others until the knowledge owner makes them available. In a practical sense, knowledge sharing cannot be forced, but can only be encouraged and facilitated (Gibbert & Krause, 2002). Sharing can be induced where there are perceived benefits to individuals, groups, or the organization. The organizational climate is very important here, including such elements as trust, an open exchange of information, tolerance of failure, and infusion of the organization with pro-social norms (Bock, Zmud, Kim, & Lee, 2005).

Researchers have tended to treat knowledge sharing and transfer as the same thing (Huber, 1991). Current practice revolves around a generic *source and recipient* model in which knowledge transfer is defined as exchanges of organizational knowledge between a source and a recipient unit in which the identity of the recipient matters (Szulanski, 1996), the process through which one unit (group, department, or division) is affected by the experience of another (Argote & Ingram, 2000), where a contributor shares knowledge that is used by an adopter (Darr & Kurtzberg, 2000), or where knowledge communicated from a source is learned and applied by a recipient (Ko, Kirsch, & King, 2005). The variables affecting knowledge transfer include: characteristics of the relationships between organizations or organizational units, communication and motivational factors, and knowledge and communication barriers (Argote, 1999; Szulanski, 2000; Ko et al., 2005). Because much new knowledge is created outside corporate boundaries, firms must develop the *absorptive capacity* to access and assimilate new knowledge from external sources. Also critical are those informal relationships that affect knowledge transfer and learning across organizational boundaries (Granovetter, 1985; Uzzi, 1996, 1997; Uzzi & Lancaster, 2003).

Knowledge Management Models

As knowledge management has become established there has been considerable activity in the area of model building, whether the modelling of knowledge management activities as a whole or of elements within knowledge management practice (Al-Ali, 2002; Bontis, 2001; Skyrme, 2003). However, in spite of claims for accuracy and *truthfulness*, it has to be remembered that models can be prescriptive and contextual and in any case are based on the perceptions of individuals at certain times. McAdam and McCreedy's (1999) classification of knowledge management models is still useful, with classes for knowledge category, intellectual capital, and social construction. Boisot (1987) provided an early *knowledge category model*, but the best known is Nonaka and Takeuchi's SECI model, wherein four kinds of knowledge conversion—socialization, externalization, internalization, and combination—drive knowledge creation (Holsapple & Joshi, 2002; McAdam & McCreedy, 1999; Nonaka & Takeuchi, 1995; Nonaka, Toyama, & Kono, 2001). Once all-powerful, this model is now regarded as presenting an over-simplified and somewhat mechanistic perspective on knowledge creation, but it remains extremely popular.

Among *intellectual capital models*, that created by Skandia Financial Services in Sweden (Edvinsson & Malone, 1997; Sveiby, 1997) is perhaps best known. Others include that devised at the Canadian Imperial Bank of Commerce in the 1990s (Stewart, 1997; Sullivan, 2000), the Intellectual Capital (IC) model (Al-Ali, 2002; Bukowitz & Williams, 1999), and more recently the model employed at Clarica Life Insurance in Canada (St. Onge & Wallace, 2003). Generally, all such models divide intellectual capital into categories such as human and structural. The models tend to take a broadly scientific approach that assumes knowledge can be commoditized, even as they largely ignore the socio-political aspects of knowledge management (McAdam & McCreedy, 1999).

These latter aspects are addressed in *socially constructed models* of knowledge management that link knowledge intrinsically with the social and learning processes within organizations, typically on the basis of the processes of knowledge construction, embodiment, dissemination, and use (Demarest, 1997; Despres & Chauvel, 2000; Jordan & Jones, 1997; Kruizinga, Heijst, & Spek, 1997; McAdam & McCreedy, 1999). Major influences on the development of models for knowledge management have been chaos and complexity theories, particularly in the case of Second Generation Knowledge Management (Cavalieri & Seivert, 2005). Prominent among such complexity-influenced approaches is Snowden's *Cynefin Model of Organisational Sensemaking*. Cynefin originated as a way of distinguishing between formal and informal communities and as a means of talking about the interaction of both with structured processes and uncertain conditions. It treats organizations as ecologies of communities and maps their attempts at knowledge creation and sense-making across four domains: the known, the knowable, the complex, and the chaotic (Kurtz & Snowden, 2003; Snowden, 2000, 2002a, 2002b). Originally linked with IBM, the sense-making model has attracted great interest around the world, not least in the corporate sector. In all likelihood this will continue, owing to the model's more recent application to interactions between structured and unstructured organizational processes in fields beyond that of knowledge management. However, the model has attracted its share of criticism, not least in its choice of domains and as regards its basic terminology (Firestone & McElroy, 2003). Although it seems unlikely that this criticism will seriously affect the popularity of the Cynefin approach, it serves as a reminder of the contextual and subjective nature of all such models and the need to treat them with care.

Technologies for Knowledge Management

A major challenge to any meaningful understanding of the subject of knowledge management remains the continuing tendency to equate it with developments in, for example, decision support or artificial intelligence. To this can be added ongoing difficulties over distinguishing between knowledge technologies and more familiar information management technologies, for example, between tools that enable workflows and communication, which although often embodying explicit knowledge, at best point to sources of tacit knowledge (Nissen, 2006). These are largely information management technologies and the search for a clear knowledge dimension is far from complete. Indeed, the management of tacit knowledge, although to an extent facilitated by communications technologies, happens best through face-to-face meetings, socialization, and mentoring activities. Put differently, information technology plays a supportive role in most knowledge management programs and people play the performative role (Alavi & Leidner, 2001; Alavi & Tiwana, 2003; Davenport, de Long, & Beers, 1998; Holsapple, 2005; McDermott, 1999; Nissen, 2006; Nissen, Kamel, & Sengupta, 2000; Purvis, Sambamurthy, & Zmud, 2005; Sambamurthy & Subramani, 2005).

It remains the case that technologies turn out to be most appropriate when knowledge management decisions are based on questions to do with *who* (people), *what* (knowledge), and *why* (business objectives). The choice of technology should be saved to the last *(Darwin Magazine*, 2002). Accordingly, whatever the technologies are called, before any decisions are taken with regard to technology purchases, organizations need to understand the uses to which these will be put, something that must occur within the wider context of organizational business practices and culture (Calabrese, 2005; Giraldo, 2005; Mitev, 1994; O'Sullivan, 2005; Park, 2005; Skyrme, 2003). The uses of technology can be couched in terms of internal and external knowledge flows involving the generation, creation, or acquisition of knowledge, its validation and codification, analysis and mining, transfer, sharing, and dissemination. In terms of purpose, this includes automation of aspects of the knowledge management cycle, the connection of people with common interests, removing obstacles to knowledge sharing, shaping the organization by automating routine work, and facilitating intelligent problem solving (Azar & Souter, 2001; Gray & Tehrani, 2003; Liebowitz & Wilcox, 1997; Malafsky, 2003; Marquardt & Kearsley, 1999; Marwick, 2001; O'Leary, 2003; Ruggles, 1997).

With regard to the selection of technologies to match such needs, surveys have identified the most common applications as including: groupware (messaging and e-mail), document management, workflow, data warehousing, multi-media repositories, intranets and portals, information retrieval technologies and search engines, business modelling, and intelligent agents (Calabrese, 2000, 2005). These and other technologies can be grouped by category such as: content management, knowledge transfer/retrieval and collaboration, or as distributive and collaborative technologies (Mack, Ravin, & Byrd, 2001; Nissen, 2006; Park, 2005; Pohs, Pinder, Dougherty, & White, 2001).

The trend in current knowledge management technologies is toward technologies that are more end-user focused and *intelligent* (Jackson, 2001; Smith & Farquhar, 2000). There may also be advances emanating from developments in the Semantic Web and related technologies (Berners-Lee, Hendler, & Lassila, 2001; Hunter, Falkovych, & Little, 2004; Miltiadis, Sicilia, Davies, & Kashyap, 2005). However, issues of context, need, purpose, suitability, and not least, organizational culture remain paramount (Ruggles, 1997; Mohamed, Stankowsky, & Murray, 2006).

Knowledge Management Strategy

The attention paid to knowledge management strategies in the various literatures has increased consonant with the overall development of interest in knowledge management. This includes work on knowledge management and knowledge-based strategies at the enterprise, group, and individual level (Bhatt, 2002; Maier & Remus, 2002; Russ, Jones, & Fineman, 2005), and on knowledge management as an element in or support for various business strategies. Under the influence of resource and knowledge-based theory, the emphasis in strategy has shifted from a product/market positioning perspective to one based on resources and capabilities that can be leveraged across a range of products and markets (Allee, 2000; Barney, 1996; Carlisle, 2000; Collis & Montgomery, 1995; Grant, 1991; Prahalad & Hamel, 1990; Zack, 1999, 2002). The knowledge-based view sees the primary rationale for the firm as the creation and application of knowledge (Bierly & Chakrabarty, 1996; Ordonez de Pablos, 2002; Spender, 1996b). Knowledge that is embedded in organizational routines and professional competence, and is unique and difficult to imitate, has become the most important strategic resource and capability for building competitive advantage, particularly within networks. Strategic knowledge management is a process that links organizational knowledge with the design of organizational structures that foster knowledge, business strategy and the development of knowledge workers (Ordonez de Pablos, 2002). A firm is likely to have a competitive advantage when, based on its strategic architecture (its resources and combinations of resources that together produce a greater return than they would alone) it can implement a knowledge strategy that generates returns and benefits in excess of those of current competitors (April, 2002; Barney, 1991; Ordonez de Pablos, 2002; Teece, 2001).

Knowledge-based strategy formulation should start with the primary intangible resource, the competence of people. People are seen as the only true agents in business; all tangible physical products and assets, as well as intangible relations, are results of human action and depend ultimately on people for their continued existence. People can use their competence to create value in two directions: by transferring and converting knowledge externally or internally to the organization to which they belong (Sveiby, 2002). It can also be helpful to distinguish between *strategy* and *knowledge* as something people *have*, and instead, to focus on the process of *strategizing and knowing* as something that people *do*. This reflects strategy formulation as emanating from the flow of micro-practices, processes, and negotiations constituting everyday organizational life (Cavalieri & Seivert, 2005; DeTiene & Jackson, 2001; Grant, 1991; Jarzabkowski, 2003; Johnson, Melin, & Whittington, 2003; Santos & Eisenhardt, 2005; Whittington, 2003).

However, knowledge is neither homogeneous nor one-dimensional, assuming different shapes and consistency in an organization, and being linked to resources inside and outside the firm and the context in which it operates. At any given time, the stock of knowledge in a firm is both the result of events, partially random and not controllable by the firm, and of chosen and planned decisions by its management (Bellini & Lo Storto, 2006). Hence it is necessary to focus attention on how knowledge has been accumulated over time, *layer by layer*, on *the structure of* knowledge. This is the outcome of a process of knowledge and competence accumulation aimed at achieving the strategic goals of the firm and based, therefore, on intentional decisions relative to the type of knowledge to accumulate, sources of external knowledge, and modality of acquisition (Bellini & Lo Storto, 2006). The resultant issues in terms of strategy formulation relate to leveraging a series of knowledge transfers involving internal structures (from concepts and models to administrative and computer systems to organizational cultures), external structures (such as relationships with customers and suppliers, and the firm's image), and the competencies of individual staff for value creation (Sveiby, 2002).

When it comes to the actual formulation of knowledge strategies, in many cases information systems planning methods have been applied (Alavi & Leidner, 2001; Earl, 2001; Kim, Yu, & Lee, 2003). Inevitably these have had their limitations, not least owing to the inherent differences between information and knowledge (Bohn, 1994, Edvinsson, 1997; Glazer, 1998) and the fact that knowledge management initiatives require a more integrated and comprehensive approach that embraces the administrative, cultural, and technical aspects of organizations (Garvin, 1993; Junnarkar, 1997; Lee & Kim, 2001; Wielinga, Sandberg, & Schreiber, 1997). It is important that the approach to knowledge strategy planning take account of both an enterprise-wide perspective focused on organizational performance and a process-level perspective aimed at the provision of task- or process-related knowledge (Bohn, 1994; Fernandez & Sabherwal, 2001; Kim et al., 2003; Maier & Remus, 2001, 2002). Process-oriented strategies that guide the design and implementation of business and knowledge processes have been presented as closing the gap between knowledge management and business strategy (Davenport, Jarvenpaa, & Beers, 1996; Kim et al., 2003; Maier

& Remus, 2002). Perhaps the most coherent taxonomy of strategies for knowledge management remains that of Earl (2001), which combined systems, behavioral, and strategic approaches with a six-step implementation method.

However, there are many possible strategic routes toward knowledge management including: building a technical infrastructure (Alavi & Leidner, 2001, Davenport & Prusak, 1998; Weilinga et al., 1997) structuring or restructuring a learning organization (Kogut & Zander, 1996; Nevis et al., 1995; Quintas, Lefrere, & Jones, 1997); fostering a knowledge-friendly culture (Garvin, 1993; Lee & Kim, 2001); establishing knowledge management processes (Demarest, 1997; Fernandez & Sabherwal, 2001; Gold, Malhotra, & Segars, 2001); measuring or leveraging intellectual capital (Edvinsson, 1997; Ulrich, 1998); and executing a variety of related policies or programs (Lee & Kim, 2001; Teece, 2001). Within this provenance are knowledge strategies that can be categorized in various ways; for example, by organizational level (enterprise-wide or department-level strategies), or by the type of knowledge involved (internal or external, tacit or explicit, best practices or intellectual Capital). Another common approach to categorization is in terms of opposites, for example: exploitative and explorative strategies, survival and advancement strategies, codification and personalization strategies, external acquisition–internal development, product–process, and brilliant design and master craftsman strategy (Benner & Tushman, 2003; Cavalieri & Seivert, 2005; Hansen, Nohria, & Tierney, 1999; Holden, 2001; Jones, 2000, 2002; Kluge, Wolfram, & Licht, 2000; Lane, Salk, & Lyles, 2001; Menor, Tatikonda, & Sampson, 2002; Parikh, 2001; Parise & Henderson, 2001; Sakkab, 2002; Schultz, 2001; Schultz & Jobe, 2001; Zack, 1999).

Over time, firms tend to cycle through a range of strategies, each with potential benefits and disadvantages. Hence, at one stage in its operation a firm may decide to follow an exploitation approach, described elsewhere as *performance-harvesting-utilizing*, and later turn to an exploration or advancement strategy that can be perceived in terms of *innovating-planting* (Cavalieri & Seivert, 2005). Other variants of the strategies already identified include those of *complementary-destroying* (Fleming, 2001; Hill & Rothaermel, 2003) and *concealment-transparent* (Inkpen, 1998; Bloodgood & Salisbury, 2001; Fjelstad & Haanaes, 2000; Lamming, Caldwell, Harrison, & Phillips, 2001; McGrath, 2001; von Furstenberg, 2001; Russ, Jones, & Fineman, 2006).

In spite of the continued focus on knowledge management, the evidence still tends to show that relatively few organizations have explicit knowledge management strategies. In many organizations, the knowledge management strategy formation process tends to be emergent rather than the subject of formal long-term planning. This is in line with identified trends in business strategy formation, where a shift in emphasis has occurred from highly prescriptive models to those that emerge as a result of a flexible approach driven by organizational learning.

Mintzberg and Lampel (1999) identified up to 10 different schools of strategy formation and concluded that dealing with the complexity of the different approaches in a single process might seem overwhelming. A further problem in examining the effectiveness of any strategy is the dependence of the outcome on the manner in which the strategy has been implemented. No matter how brilliant or well aligned a strategy may be, it will still be unlikely to lead to a successful outcome if it has been poorly implemented (Gamble & Blackwell, 2001; Massingham, 2004; Mintzberg & Lampel, 1999; St. Onge & Wallace, 2002; Subramanian & Venkratamen, 2000).

Culture and Knowledge Management

Organizational culture is widely regarded as a key influence on the success of knowledge management, relating directly and indirectly to attitudes, behaviors, practices, and outcomes (Alavi et al., 2006; Alzami & Zairi, 2003; De Long & Fahey, 2000; Fahey & Prusak, 1998; Gold et al., 2001; Gupta & Govindarajan, 2000; Harzing & Hofstede, 1996; Hofstede, 1993; Janz & Prasarnphanich, 2003; Karlsen & Gottschalk, 2004; Kayworth & Leidner, 2003; Knapp & Yu, 1999; Lee & Choi, 2003; Lopez, Peon, & Ordas, 2004). Although concerns have been raised from time to time about aspects of knowledge management culture and its relationship to organizational climate, structures, and practices (Cameron & Quinn, 1999; Denison, 1996; Firestone & McElroy, 2003; Holden, 2001; McDermott & O'Dell, 2001; Reichers & Schneider, 1990), this seems, if anything, to have merely reinforced the perceived significance of culture within the organization (Eisner, 2000; Gerstner, 2002; Goffee & Jones, 1996; Harzing & Hofstede, 1996; House, Hanges, Ruiz-Quintanilla, Dorfman, Javidan, Dickson, et al., 1999; Schein, 1992, 1996). Nevertheless, there is considerable variation in the more specific perceptions of organizational culture, whether in terms of assumptions, beliefs and ideologies, artifacts, symbols, and practices (Deal & Kennedy, 1982, 2004; Hatch, 1993; Pettigrew, 1979; Schein, 1985; Smircich, 1983), or the extent to which organizational cultures should be regarded as being homogeneous or diverse (Deal & Kennedy, 1982; Denison & Mishra, 1995; Jermier, Slocum, Fry, & Gaines, 1995; Kotter & Heskett, 1992; Martin & Siehl, 1983; Meyerson & Martin, 1987; Hofstede, 1998; Rose, 1988; Sackmann, 1992).

Organizations make choices about culture in the context of the philosophy and values of top management and the assumptions of founding principals and succeeding generations of organizational leaders, with the ability to shape organizational culture regarded as central to the successful conduct of knowledge management (Balthazard & Cooke, 2004; Hurley & Green, 2005; Karlsen & Gottschalk, 2004). Organizational culture emerges from the social construction of reality by individuals within organizations, often with a focus on the assumptions, values, behaviors, and interpersonal styles that are expected and rewarded by the organization, some of which are external and visible and others internal and invisible (Weick, Erez, & Gati, 2004). Hence, it represents qualities of human groups transmitted as a common world view from one generation to the next, an enduring set of values, beliefs, and assumptions that characterize organizations and their members (Alavi, Kayworth, & Leidner, 2006; Cameron & Quinn, 1999; McDermott & O'Dell, 2001; Schein, 1992, 1999; Van Maanen & Barley, 1985). However, these coherent interpretations of organizational culture have been challenged by, among other things, the rise of knowledge work, the growth of diversity in organizational form, and the ethnic make-up of workforces. One result is the need for coexistence between high level organizational cultures that represent generalized world views, which are acknowledged but not necessarily shared by everybody in the organization, and internal sub-cultures, including those formed on the basis of ethnicity and national origin, professional background, and organizational structures (Ardichvili, Maurer, Li, Wentling, & Stuedemann, 2006; Bhagat, Kedia, Harveston, & Triandis, 2002; Bloor & Dawson, 1994; Erez & Gati, 2004; Firestone & McElroy, 2003; Ford & Chan, 2003; Hofstede, 1998; Holden, 2001; Jermier et al., 1991).

Organizational cultures can be categorized in various ways. These include: *clan cultures*—characterized by loyalty, commitment, teamwork, and consensus; *ad hocracy cultures*—characterized by entrepreneurialism, innovation, and freedom; *hierarchical cultures*—characterized by formalism, structure, and stability; and *market cultures*, which are goal- and results-oriented and competitive (Cameron & Quinn, 1999). There are also cultures of: *control*—where certainty and control set the framework for knowledge; *collaboration*—where stakeholder synergies are linked to knowledge acquisition and use; *competence*—where distinctiveness in terms of competencies forms the setting for knowledge; and *cultivation*—where cultural enrichment is sought through the attainment of knowledge-based goals (Schneider, Brief, & Guzzo, 1996).

A recurring theme in the literature is the relationship between cultural strength and organizational performance (Denison & Mishra, 1995; Gordon & Tomaso, 1992; Kotter & Heskett, 1992; Lee & Yu, 2004; Miroshnik, 2002), with the assumption that unless there is room for cultures to adapt and learn they can run the risk of stagnation and lack of creativity (Beinhocker, 1999; Kaplan & Beinhocker, 2003; Lopez et al., 2004; Nemeth, 1997; Saffold, 1988; Schein, 1985). The assessment and measurement of cultures of varying strengths has been pursued on both a qualitative and quantitative basis (Ashkanasy, Trevor-Roberts, & Kennedy, 2000; Hofstede, 2001; Hofstede, Neuijen, Ohayv, & Sanders, 1990; O'Reilly, Chatman, & Caldwell, 1991; Rousseau, 1990; Siehl & Martin, 1988; Roman Valasquez, 2005). Although there is little consensus as to the validity of such approaches, other than the importance of using multiple methods, the importance of having reliable methods of assessment is linked closely to the value of unique and hard-to-imitate cultures for both short- and long-term competitive positions. In an environment of constant turbulence, norms and values too must change, and this in itself requires the kinds of cultures that are capable of self-adjustment and are still sufficiently rare to be imperfectly imitable (Lopez et al., 2004).

Cultural change is not something that happens overnight, although the transition period can be truncated with the appointment of new chief executive officers (CEOs) and management teams, not always with the desired results. It is clear, moreover, that where this involves the introduction of knowledge management initiatives it works best when these are adapted to fit the organizational culture rather than the other way around (Firestone & McElroy, 2003; McDermott & O'Dell, 2001). In the specific context of knowledge management, culture is central to the shaping of assumptions about what knowledge is worth exchanging (or converting from tacit to explicit, or from individual to corporate levels). Culture also defines relationships between individual and corporate knowledge, creates the context for the social interaction between individuals and groups that determines how knowledge will be shared in particular situations, and shapes the processes by which new knowledge is created, legitimized, and distributed in organizations (Bartol & Abhishek, 2002; Becerra-Fernandez & Sabherwal, 2001; Gold et al., 2001; Grant, 2001; Hurley & Green, 2005; Karlsen & Gottschalk, 2004; Meso & Smith, 2000). More succinctly, culture influences behaviors and the role of leaders, the selection of technology, the evolution of knowledge management, and its expected outcomes (Alavi et al., 2006). Consequently, organizations with more open and supportive features, such as those of trust, collaboration, and learning, are more likely to engage in effective knowledge creation and sharing practices, as well as to be more innovative and more flexible in responding rapidly to the needs of changing markets (Alavi et al., 2006; Allee, 1997; Barrett et al., 2004; Davenport et al., 1998; DeTiene & Jackson, 2001). Research supports the contention that successful knowledge management projects tend to recur within companies that have cultures that are collaborative and informal, which offer support at both senior and line management levels, and embody core values of teamwork, a bias toward action, and learning and informal communication channels, including the use of stories (Albert & Picq, 2004; Bierly et al., 2000; McDermott, 1999; Pfeffer & Sutton, 2000). Apart from matters of academic interest, moreover, there are sound business reasons for increasing understanding of those values and behaviors that lead to knowledge sharing and collaboration at the expense of knowledge hoarding and competition within organizations. Not only is it clear that cultural misalignments can lead directly to inappropriate behaviors, and to the failure of knowledge management initiatives, but also that unless there is a clear connection between knowledge capture and sharing projects and business goals and problems, these exercises are likely to prove pointless (De Long & Fahey, 2000; Dyer & Nobeoka, 2000; McDermott & O'Dell, 2001; Terra & Gordon, 2002).

Finally, as regards attempts to manage organizational culture, it seems clear that these must reflect the principles of leadership rather than control, and aim for the promotion and inculcation of an organizational ethos that embodies trust, sharing, collaboration, and learning (Drucker, 1994; Handy, 1995; Prokesch, 1997). For management this not only means leading by example, through personal behavior and support for and mentoring of staff, but also creation of the kinds of policies and structures that are likely to promote the desired behaviors (Terra & Gordon, 2002). Given that trust and the sharing of knowledge have to be earned rather than mandated or commanded, the literature exhibits ample treatment of the issue of rewards and sanctions for desired knowledge behaviors. This is clearly an area where management can take a lead, but it remains controversial among professionals and other knowledge workers (Bock & Kim, 2002; Hall, 2001). Where incentives are adopted, there is considerable variety in range and type and, increasingly, recognition of the need to couch these in terms of teams rather than simply as rewards for individual effort. There remains some doubt as to the efficacy of incentive systems, with for example, the search for predictability in behavior being seen as potentially contradictory to the levels of autonomy associated with knowledge workers. Nor would this by any means represent an assured path to innovation and creativity (Newell et al., 2002).

This review of developments in knowledge management has of necessity been selective, providing a broad overview of theory and the major impacts of research on management practice. In striving to capture the essential nature as well as the scope of knowledge management, it has avoided existential issues, seeking to demonstrate by its coverage that knowledge management is, indeed, a fact of organizational life. In terms of research directions and the academic status of the subject, perhaps the most exciting aspect of recent developments has been the prominence of knowledge management in journals of genuine substance and international standing, journals catering to positivist and structuralist audiences alike. The treatment of knowledge management in these sources is what would be expected for an area that has moved beyond the stage of definitions and boundary setting, and which embraces all aspects of the knowledge life cycle, the relationships between knowledge management and organizational learning, the strategic, cultural and behavioral dimensions (including knowledge work and knowledge workers), and the complex relationships between knowledge and emerging information and communication technologies (Alavi & Leidner, 2001; Alavi et al., 2006; Argote et al., 2003; Despres & Chauvel, 2000; Nidomolu, Subramani, & Aldrich, 2001; Vera & Crossan, 2003; Tsoukas & Mylonopoulos, 2004). Hence the management of knowledge is manifest, not in grand paradigmatic terms, but through the pervasive infiltration of knowledge-based principles and practices into every area of organizational management. It would be wrong to conclude, however, without acknowledgment of the potential downside to knowledge management, of the associated risks and of those failures that, although less prominent in the literature, are nonetheless present (Braganza & Möllenkramer, 2002; Chua & Lam, 2005; Lucier & Torsiliera, 1997; McKinley, 2002; Storey & Barnett, 2000). Overall, however, the story of knowledge management is a positive one and in view of its prominence across a wide range of literatures, including recognition by leading journals and its accession to the main body of management praxis, its prospects for the foreseeable future would appear to be encouraging.

References

Ackoff, R. (1997). Management misinformation systems. *Management Science, 14*, 147–156.

Adam, F., & Roncevic, B. (2003). Social capital: Recent debates and research trends. *Social Science Information, 42*(2), 155–183.

Ahuja, G. (2000). Collaborative networks, structural holes and innovation: A longitudinal study. *Administrative Science Quarterly, 45*, 425–455.

Al-Ali, N. (2002). *Comprehensive intellectual capital management: Step-by-step.* New York: Wiley.

Alavi, M., Kayworth, T. R., & Leidner, D. E. (2006). An empirical examination of the influence of organizational culture on knowledge management practices. *Journal of Management Information Systems, 22*(3), 191–224.

Alavi, M., & Leidner, D. (2001). Review: Knowledge management systems: Conceptual foundations and research issues. *MIS Quarterly, 25*(1), 107–136.

Alavi, M., & Tiwana, A. (2003). Knowledge management: The information technology dimension. In M. Easterby-Smith & M. Lyles (Eds.), *The Blackwell handbook of organisational learning and knowledge management* (pp. 104–121). Oxford, UK: Blackwell.

Alazmi, M., & Zairi, M. (2003). Knowledge management critical success factors. *Total Quality Management, 14*(2), 6–14.

Albert, M., & Picq, T. (2004). Knowledge-based organisations: Perspectives from San Francisco Bay area companies. *European Journal of Innovation Management, 7*(3), 169–177.

Allee, V. (2000). Reconfiguring the value network. *Journal of Business Strategy, 21*(4), 36–39.

Almeida, P. (1996). Knowledge sourcing by foreign multinationals: Patent citation analysis in the U. S. semiconductor industry. *Strategic Management Journal, 18*(2), 155–166.

Almeida, P., & Kogut, B. (1999). Localization of knowledge and the mobility of engineers in regional networks. *Management Science, 45*(7), 905–917.

Amo, B. W. (2006). What motivates knowledge workers to involve themselves in employee innovation behaviour? *International Journal of Knowledge Management Studies, 1*(1/2), 160–177.

Ancona, D., & Caldwell, D. (1992). Demography and design: Predictors of new product team performance. *Organization Science, 3*(3), 21–41.

April, K. A. (2002). Guidelines for developing a K-strategy. *Journal of Knowledge Management, 6*(5), 445–456.

Ardichvili, A., Maurer, M., Li, W., Wentling, T., & Stuedemann, R. (2006). Cultural influences on knowledge sharing through online communities of practice. *Journal of Knowledge Management, 10*(1), 94–107.

Argote, L. (1999). *Organizational learning: Creating, retaining and transferring knowledge*. Boston MA: Kluwer.

Argote, L., & Ingram, P. (2000). Knowledge transfer: A basis for competitive advantage in firms. *Organizational Behaviour and Human Decision Processes, 82*(1), 150–169.

Argote, L., McEvily, B., & Reagans, R. (2003, April). Managing knowledge in organizations: An integrative framework and review of emerging themes. *Management Science, 49*, 571–586.

Argyris, C. (2004). Double-loop learning and implementable validity. In H. Tsoukas & N. Mylonopoulos (Eds.), *Organizations and knowledge systems: Knowledge, learning and dynamic capabilities* (pp. 29–45). Basingstoke, UK: Palgrave Macmillan.

Argyris, C., & Schon, D. (1978). *Organizational learning: A theory of action*. Reading, MA: Addison-Wesley.

Armstrong, A., & Foley, P. (2003). Foundations for a learning organization: Organization learning mechanisms. *The Learning Organization, 10*(2), 74–103.

Arrow, K. (1962). The economic implications of learning by doing. *Review of Economic Studies, 29*, 155–173.

Arrow, K. J., & Hahn, F. H. (1971). *General competitive analysis*. San Francisco: Holden-Day.

Arthur, W. B. (1990, February). Positive feedbacks in the economy. *Scientific American, 262*(2), 92–99.

Arthur, W. B. (1994). *Increasing returns and path dependency in the economy*. Ann Arbor: University of Michigan Press.

Arthur, W. B. (1996). Increasing returns and the new world of business. *Harvard Business Review, 74*(4), 100–109.

Ásgeirsdóttir, B. (2005, January). *OECD work on knowledge and the knowledge economy*. Paper presented at the OECD/NSF Conference on Advancing Knowledge and the Knowledge Economy, Washington, DC.

Ashkanasy, N., Trevor-Roberts, E., & Kennedy, J. (2000). Leadership attributes and cultural values in Australia and New Zealand compared: An initial report based on GLOBE data. *International Journal of Organizational Behaviour, 1*(3), 37–44.

Assudani, R. (2005). Catching the chameleon: Understanding the elusive term knowledge. *Journal of Knowledge Management, 9*(2), 31–44.

Audia, P. G., Sorenson, O., & Hage, J. (2001). Tradeoffs in the organization of production: Multiunit firms, geographic dispersion and organizational learning. In J. A. C. Baum & H. R. Greve (Eds.), *Multiunit organization and multimarket strategy* (pp. 75–105). Oxford: Elsevier Science.

Azar, A., & Souter, J. (2001). The state of the art: Putting knowledge management technologies in context. *Knowledge Management, 5*(2). Retrieved November 21, 2007, from www.nelh.nhs.uk/knowledge_management/KM2/technology.asp

Bahra, N. (2001). *Competitive knowledge management*. London: Palgrave.

Balthazard, P., & Cooke, R. (2004). Organizational culture and knowledge management success: Assessing the behavior-performance continuum. *Proceedings of the 37th Hawaii International Conference on System Sciences*. Retrieved September 23, 2006, from ieeexplore.ieee.org/xpls/abs_all.jsp?arnumber=1265577

Barney, J. B. (1991). Firm resources and sustained competitive advantage. *Journal of Management, 17*(1), 99–120.

Barney, J. B. (1996). *Gaining and sustaining competitive advantage.* New York: Addison Wesley.

Barr, A. (1998). *Enterprise performance and the functional diversity of social capital* (Working Paper Series 98–1). Oxford, UK: University of Oxford, Institute of Economics and Statistics.

Barrett, M., Capplemann, S., Shoib, G., & Walsham, G. (2004). Learning in knowledge communities. *European Management Journal, 22*(1), 1–11.

Bartol, K. M., & Abhishek, S. (2002). Encouraging knowledge sharing: The role of organizational reward systems. *Journal of Leadership and Organizational Studies, 9*(1), 64–76.

Becerra-Fernandez, I., & Sabherwal, R. (2001). Organizational knowledge management: A contingency perspective. *Journal of Information Systems, 18*(1), 64–76.

Bechky, B. A. (2003). Shared meaning across occupational communities: The transformation of knowledge on a production floor. *Organization Science, 14,* 312–330.

Beckman, T. (1997). A methodology for knowledge management. *Proceedings of the IASTED International Conference on AI and Soft Computing,* 29–32.

Beinhocker, E. (1999). Robust adaptive strategies. *Sloan Management Review, 40*(3), 95–106.

Bellinger, G., Castro, D., & Mills, A. (1997). *Data, information, knowledge and wisdom.* Retrieved January 23, 2007, from www.outsights.com/systems/diko/diko.htm

Bellini, E., & Lo Storto, C. (2006). Growth strategy as practice in small firms as knowledge structure. *International Journal of Knowledge Management Studies, 1*(1/2), 133–159.

Benner, M., & Tushman, M. (2003). Exploitation, exploration and process management: The productivity dilemma revisited. *Academy of Management Review, 28,* 238–256.

Berners-Lee, T., Hendler, J., & Lassila, O. (2001). The semantic Web. *Scientific American, 284*(5), 34–43.

Bhagat, R., Kedia, B., Harveston, P., & Triandis, H. (2002). Cultural variations in the cross-border transfer of organizational knowledge: An integrative framework. *Academy of Management Review, 27*(2), 204–221.

Bhatt, G. D. (2002). Management strategies for individual and organizational knowledge. *Journal of Knowledge Management, 6*(1), 31–39.

Bierly, P., & Chakrabarty, A. (1996). Generic knowledge strategies in the U.S. pharmaceutical industry. *Strategic Management Journal, 17,* 123–135.

Bierly, P., Kessler, E., & Christensen, E. (2000). Organization, learning, knowledge and wisdom. *Journal of Organizational Change Management, 13*(6), 595–618.

Blackler, F. (1995). Knowledge, knowledge work and organizations: An overview and interpretation. *Organization Studies, 16*(6), 1021–1046.

Bloodgood, J., & Salisbury, W. (2001). Understanding the influence of organizational change strategies on information technology and knowledge management strategies. *Decision Support Systems, 31,* 55–69.

Bloor, G., & Dawson, P. (1994). Understanding professional culture in an organizational context. *Organization Studies, 15*(2), 275–296.

Bock, G. W., & Kim, Y. G. (2002). Breaking the myths of rewards: An exploratory study of attitudes about knowledge sharing. *Information Resources Management Journal, 15*(2), 14–21.

Bock, G. W., Zmud, R., Kim, Y. G., & Lee, J. N. (2005). Behavioral intention formation in knowledge sharing: Examining the roles of extrinsic motivators, social-psychological forces and organizational climate. *MIS Quarterly, 29*(1), 87–111.

Bogenrieder, I., & Nooteboom, B. (2004). The emergence of learning communities: A theoretical analysis. In H. Tsoukas & N. Mylonopoulos (Eds.), *Organizations and knowledge systems: Knowledge, learning and dynamic capabilities* (pp. 46–66). Basingstoke, UK: Palgrave Macmillan.

Bohn, R. E. (1994). Measuring and managing technological knowledge. *Sloan Management Review, 36*(1), 61–73.

Boisot, M. H. (1987). *Information and organizations: The manager as anthropologist*. London: Fontana/Collins.

Boisot, M. H. (1995). *Information space: A framework for learning in organizations, institutions and culture*. London: Routledge.

Boland, R. J., & Tenkasi, R. V. (1995). Perspective making and perspective taking in communities of knowing. *Organization Science, 6*(4), 360–372.

Bontis, N. (2001). Assessing knowledge assets: A review of the models used to measure intellectual capital. *International Journal of Management Reviews, 3*(1), 41–60.

Bontis, N. (2002). Managing organizational knowledge by diagnosing intellectual capital: Framing and advancing the state of the field. In C. Choo & N. Bontis (Eds.), *The strategic management of intellectual capital and organizational knowledge* (pp. 621–642). Oxford, UK: Oxford University Press.

Botkin, J. (1999). *Smart business: How knowledge communities can revolutionize your company*. New York: Free Press.

Borgatti, S. P., & Cross, R. (2003). A relational view of information seeking and learning in social networks. *Management Science, 49*, 432–446.

Boulding, K. E. (1955). Notes on the information concept. *Explorations, 6*, 103–112.

Bourdieu, P. (1986). Forms of capital. In J. C. Richards (Ed.), *Handbook of theory and research for the sociology of education* (pp. 241–258). New York: Greenwood Press.

Boutellier, R., Gassmann, O., Macho, H., & Roux, M. (1998). Management of dispersed product development teams: The role of information technologies. *R & D Management, 28*(1), 13–26.

Braganza, A., & Möllenkramer, G. (2002). Anatomy of a failed knowledge management initiative: Lessons from PharmaCorp's experiences. *Knowledge and Process Management, 9*(1), 23–33.

Brennan, N., & Connell, B. (2000). Intellectual capital: Current issues and policy implications. *Journal of Intellectual Capital, 1*(3), 206–240.

Brown, J. S., & Duguid, P. (2001). Knowledge and organization: A social-practice perspective. *Organization Science, 12*(2), 198–213.

Brown, S., & Eisenhardt, K. (1995). Product development: Past research, present findings and future directions. *Academy of Management Review, 20*(2), 343–378.

Brusoni, S., Prencipe, A., & Pavitt, K. (2001). Knowledge specialisation and organisational coupling and the boundaries of the firm: Why do firms know more than they make? *Administrative Science Quarterly, 46*(3), 597–625.

Buckland, J. (1998). Social capital and the sustainability of NGO-intermediated development projects in Bangladesh. *Community Development Journal, 33*(3), 236–248.

Buckley, P. J., & Carter, M. J. (1996). The economics of business process design: Motivation, information and coordination within the firm. *International Journal of the Economics of Business, 3*, 5–24.

Bukowitz, W. R., & Williams, R. L. (1999). *The knowledge management fieldbook.* London: Pearson Education.

Bunderson, J., & Sutcliffe, K. (2001). Comparing alternative conceptualizations of functional diversity in management teams: Process and performance effects (Ross School of Business, Working Paper 01–004). Ann Arbor: University of Michigan.

Burt, R. (1992). *Structural holes: The social structure of competition.* Cambridge, MA: Harvard University Press.

Cabrera, A., & Cabrera, E. (2002). Knowledge-sharing dilemmas. *Organizational Studies, 23*(4), 687–712.

Calabrese, F. A. (2000). *A suggested framework of key elements defining effective enterprise knowledge management programs.* Unpublished doctoral dissertation, George Washington University.

Calabrese, F. A. (2005). The early pathways: Theory to practice—A continuum. In M. Stankosky (Ed.), *Creating the discipline of knowledge management: The latest in university research* (pp. 15–50). Oxford, UK: Elsevier Butterworth-Heinemann.

Caldwell, B. (1997). Hayek and socialism. *Journal of Economic Literature, 35*(4), 1856–1890.

Caldwell, B. (2005). Information, the tip of the tacit iceberg. *Econ Journal Watch, 2*(1), 70–74.

Cameron, K., & Quinn, R. (1999). Successful knowledge management projects. *Sloan Management Review, 39*(2), 43–57.

Carlisle, Y. (2000). Strategic thinking and knowledge management. In S. Little, P. Quintas, & T. Ray (Eds.), *Managing knowledge: An essential reader* (pp. 122–138). London: Sage.

Casey, C. (2000). *Sociology sensing the body: Revitalising a dissociative discourse.* In J. Hassard, R. Holiday, & H. Wilmott (Eds.), *Body and organization* (pp. 52–70). London, Sage.

Cavalieri, S., & Reed, F. (2000). Designing knowledge generating processes. *Knowledge and Innovation, 1*(1), 109–131.

Cavalieri, S., & Seivert, S. (2005). *Knowledge leadership: The art and science of knowledge-based organization.* Burlington, MA: Elsevier Butterworth-Heinemann.

Chang, M. Y., & Harrington, J. (2003). Multi-market competition, consumer search and the organizational structure and multi-unit firms. *Management Science, 49*, 541–552.

Choo, C. W. (1998). *The knowing organization: How organizations use information to construct meaning.* Oxford, UK: Oxford University Press.

Choo, C. W., Detlor, B., & Turnbull, D. (2000). *Web work: Information searching and knowledge work on the World Wide Web.* Dordrecht, The Netherlands: Kluwer.

Chua, A., & Lam, W. (2005). Why KM projects fail: A multi-case analysis. *Journal of Knowledge Management, 9*(3), 6–17.

Christensen, K. (2004). A classification of the corporate entrepreneurship umbrella: Labels and perspectives. *International Journal of Management and Enterprise Development, 1*(4), 301–315.

Coase, R. H. (1988). *The firm, the market and the law.* Chicago: University of Chicago Press.

Cohen, D., & Prusak, L. (2001). *In good company: How social capital makes organizations work*. Boston: Harvard Business School Press.

Cohendet, P., & Steinmuller, W. E. (2000). The codification of knowledge: A conceptual and empirical exploration. *Industrial and Corporate Change, 92*(2), 95–120.

Coleman, J. C. (1988). Social capital in the creation of human capital. *American Journal of Sociology, 94*(Suppl.), S95–S120.

Coleman, J. S. (1990). *Foundations of social theory*. Cambridge, MA: Harvard University Press.

Collis, D., & Montgomery, C. (1995). Competing on resources: Strategy in the 1990s. *Harvard Business Review, 73*(4), 118–128.

Collison, C., & Parcell, G. (2004). *Learning to fly: Practical lessons from one of the world's leading knowledge companies*. London: Capstone.

Constant, D., Kiesler, S., & Sproull, L. (1996). What's mine is ours, or is it?: A study of attitudes about information sharing. *Information Systems Research, 5*(4), 400–421.

Cook, S. N., & Brown, J. S. (1999). Bridging epistemologies: The generative dance between organizational knowledge and organizational knowing. *Organization Science, 10*(4), 382–400.

Cowan, R., David, P., & Foray, D. (2000). The explicit economics of knowledge: Codification and tacitness. *Industrial and Corporate Change, 9*(2), 211–253.

Crossan, M., Lane, H., & White, R. (1999). An organizational learning framework: From institution to institution. *Academy of Management Review, 24*(3), 522–538.

Cyert, R., & March, J. (1963). *A behavioural theory of the firm* (2nd ed.). Malden, MA: Blackwell.

Daft, R., & Weick, K. (1984). Towards a model of organizations as interpretation systems. *Academy of Management Review, 9*(2), 284–295.

Danermark, B. (2002). Interdisciplinary research and critical realism: The example of disability research. *Alethia, 5*(1), 56–64.

Danish Ministry of Trade and Industry. (2000). *A guideline for intellectual capital statements: A key to knowledge management*. Copenhagen, Denmark: Ministry of Trade and Industry.

Darr, E. D., Argote, L., & Epple, D. The acquisition, transfer, and depreciation of knowledge in service organizations: Productivity in franchises. *Management Science, 4*(11), 1750–1762.

Darr, E., & Kurtzberg, T. (2000). An investigation of partner similarity dimensions on knowledge transfer. *Organizational Behaviour and Human Decision Processes, 82*(1), 28–44.

Darwin Magazine. (2002). Executive guides: Knowledge management. Retrieved June 20, 2006, from guide.darwinmag.com/technology/enterprise/knowledge/index.html

Dasgupta, P. (2000). Economic progress and the idea of social capital. In P. Dasgupta & L. Serageldin (Eds.), *Social capital: A multifaceted perspective* (pp. 325–424). Washington, DC: World Bank.

Davenport, E., & Hall, H. (2002). Organizational learning and communities of practice. *Annual Review of Information Science and Technology, 36*, 171–227.

Davenport, E., & Snyder, H. (2005). Managing social capital. *Annual Review of Information Science and Technology, 39*, 515–550.

Davenport, T. H., de Long, D. D., & Beers, M. C. (1998). Successful knowledge management projects. *Sloan Management Review, 39*(2), 43–57.

Davenport, T. H., Jarvenpaa, S. L., & Beers, M. C. (1996). Improving knowledge work processes. *Sloan Management Review, 37*(4), 53–65.

Davenport, T. H., & Prusak, L. (1998). *Working knowledge: How organizations manage what they know.* Cambridge, MA: Harvard Business School Press.

Day, G. S., & Schoemaker, P. J. H. (2000). *Wharton on managing emerging technologies.* New York: Wiley.

Day, R. E. (2005). Clearing up "implicit knowledge:" Implications for knowledge management, information science, psychology and social epistemology. *Journal of the American Society for Information Science and Technology, 56*(6), 630–635.

De Long, D. W., & Fahey, L. (2000). Diagnosing cultural barriers to knowledge management. *Academy of Management Executive, 14*(4), 113–127.

Deal, T. E., & Kennedy, A. A. (1982). *Corporate cultures: The rites and rituals of corporate life.* Reading, MA: Addison-Wesley.

Deal, T. E., & Kennedy, A. A. (1999). *The new corporate cultures: Revitalising the workplace after downsizing, mergers and reengineering.* Cambridge, MA: Perseus.

Demarest, M. (1997). Understanding knowledge management. *Long Range Planning, 30*(3), 374–384.

Denison, D. (1996). What is the difference between organizational culture and organizational climate?: A native's point of view in a decade of paradigm wars. *Academy of Management Review, 21*(3), 619–654.

Denison, D., & Mishra, A. (1995). Toward a theory of organizational culture and effectiveness. *Organization Science, 6*(2), 204–223.

Despres, C., & Chauvel, D. (2000). *Knowledge horizons: The present and the promise of knowledge management.* Boston: Butterworth Heinemann.

DeTiene, K., & Jackson, L. (2001). Knowledge management: Understanding theory and developing strategy. *Competitiveness Review, 11*(1), 1–11.

Dosi, G. (1988). Source, procedures, and microeconomic effects of innovation. *Journal of Economic Literature, 26*(3), 1120–1171.

Dougherty, D. (1992). Interpretive barriers to successful product innovation in large firms. *Organization Science, 3*(2), 179–202.

Drucker, P. (1994). *Knowledge work and knowledge society: The social transformation of this century.* Boston: Harvard University, John F. Kennedy School of Government.

Duguid, P. (2005). The art of knowing: Social and tacit dimensions of knowledge and the limits of the community of practice. *The Information Society, 21*, 109–118.

Durlauf, S. (2002). *The empirics of social capital: Some sceptical thoughts.* Washington, DC: World Bank.

Dyer, J. H., & Nobeoka, K. (2000). Creating and managing a high-performance knowledge-sharing network: The Toyota case. *Strategic Management Journal, 21*(3), 35–55.

Earl, M. J. (2001). Knowledge management strategies: Towards a taxonomy. *Journal of Management Information Systems, 18*(1), 215–233.

Edmonson, A. (1999). Psychological safety and learning behaviour in work teams. *Administrative Science Quarterly, 44*(4), 350–383.

Edvinsson, L. (1997). Developing intellectual capital at Skandia. *Long Range Planning, 30*(3), 366–373.

Edvinsson, L., & Malone, M. S. (1997). *Intellectual capital: The proven way to establish your company's real value by measuring its hidden values.* London: Piatkus.

Edwards, B., & Foley, M. (1988). Civil society and social capital beyond Putnam. *American Behavioral Scientist, 42*(1),124–140.

Eisner, M. (2000). *Work in progress: Risking failure, surviving success.* New York: Eisner Foundation.

Ekbia, H. R. (2004). How IT mediates organizations: Enron and the California energy crisis. *Journal of Digital Information, 5*(4). Retrieved February 1, 2007, from jodi.tamu.edu/Articles/v05/i04/Ekbia

Erez, M., & Gati, E. (2004). A dynamic, multi-level model of culture: From the micro level of the individual to the macro level of a global culture. *Applied Psychology, 53*(4), 583–598.

Fahey, L., & Prusak, L. (1998). The eleven deadliest sins of knowledge management. *California Management Review, 40*(3), 265–276.

Farr, J. (2003). Social capital: A conceptual history. *Political Theory, 31*(10), 1–28.

Fernandez, I. B., & Sabherwal, R. (2001). Organizational knowledge management: A contingency perspective. *Journal of Management Information Systems, 18*(1), 23–55.

Fine, B. (1999). The developmental state is dead—long live social capital. *Development and Change, 30*(1), 1–19.

Fine, B. (2001). *Social capital versus social theory: Political economy and social science at the turn of the millennium.* London: Routledge.

Firestone, J. M. (2001). Key issues in knowledge management. *Knowledge and Innovation, 1*(3), 8–38.

Firestone, J., & McElroy, M. (2003). *Key issues in the new knowledge management.* Boston: Butterworth Heinemann.

Fjelstad, O., & Haanaes, K. (2000). Strategy tradeoff in the knowledge and network economy. *Business Strategy Review, 12*(1), 1–10.

Flanagan, O. (1991). *Epistemology and cognition.* Boston: Harvard University Press.

Fleming, L. (2001). Recombinant uncertainty in technological research. *Management Science, 47,* 117–132.

Foote, N., Matson, E., Weiss, L., & Wenger, E. (2002). Leveraging group knowledge for high performance decision making. *Organizational Dynamics, 31*(3), 280–295.

Ford, D., & Chan, Y. (2003). Knowledge sharing in a multi-cultural setting: A case study. *Knowledge Management Research and Practice, 1*(1), 11–27.

Foss, N. J., Knudsen, C., & Montgomery, C. A. (1995). An exploration of common ground: Integrating evolutionary and strategic theories of the firm. In C. A. Montgomery (Ed.), *Resource-based and evolutionary theories of the firm* (pp. 1–18). Boston: Kluwer.

Fukuyama, F., (1995). *Trust: The social values and the creation of prosperity.* New York: Free Press.

Gamble, P. R., & Blackwell, J. (2001). *Knowledge management: A state of the art guide.* London: Kogan Page.

Garud, R., & Kumaraswamy, A. (2005). Vicious and virtuous cycles in the management of knowledge: The case of Infosys Technologies. *MIS Quarterly, 29*(1), 9–33.

Gerstner, L. V. (2002). *Who says elephants can't dance?* New York: Harper Collins.

Gibbert, M., & Krause, H. (2002). Practice exchange in a best practice marketplace. In T. Davenport & G. Probst (Eds.), *Knowledge management casebook: Best practices* (pp. 68–84). Berlin: Publicis MCD.

Giraldo, J. P. (2005). Relationship between knowledge management technologies and learning actions of global organisations. In M. Stankosky (Ed.), *Creating the discipline of knowledge management: The latest in university research* (pp. 118–133). Oxford, UK: Elsevier Butterworth-Heinemann.

Gittell, R., & Vidal, A. (1998). *Community organizing: Building social capital as a development strategy*. Thousand Oaks, CA: Sage.

Glazer, R. (1998). Measuring the knower: Towards a theory of knowledge equity. *California Management Review, 40*(3), 175–194.

Goffee, R., & Jones, G. (1996). What holds the modern company together? *Harvard Business Review, 74*(6), 133–148.

Gold, A. H., Malhotra, A., & Segars, A. (2001). Knowledge management: An organizational capabilities perspective. *Journal of Management Information Systems, 18*(1), 185–214.

Goldman, A. (1986). *Liaisons: Philosophy meets cognitive science*. Cambridge, MA: MIT Press.

Gordon, G., & Tomaso, N. (1992). Predicting corporate performance from organization culture. *Journal of Management Studies, 29*(6), 783–798.

Granovetter, M. (1973). The strength of weak ties. *American Journal of Sociology, 91*(3), 481–510.

Granovetter, M. (1985). Economic action and social structure: The problem of embeddedness. *American Journal of Sociology, 91*(3), 481–510.

Grant, R. M. (1991). The resource-based theory of competitive advantage: Implications for strategy formulation. *California Management Review, 33*(3), 114–135.

Grant, R. M. (1996a). Prospecting in dynamically competitive environments: Organizational capability as knowledge integration. *Organization Science, 7*(4), 375–387.

Grant, R. M. (1996b). Towards a knowledge-based theory of the firm. *Strategic Management Journal, 17*(4), 109–122.

Grant, R. M. (1997). The knowledge-based view of the firm: Implications for management practice. *Long Range Planning, 30*(3), 450–454.

Grant, R. M. (2001). Knowledge and organization. In I. Nonaka & D. Teece (Eds.), *Managing industrial knowledge: Creation, transfer and utilisation* (pp. 145–169). London: Sage.

Gray, P., & Tehrani, S. (2003). Technologies for disseminating knowledge. In C. W. Holsapple (Ed.), *Handbook on knowledge management* (Vol. 2, pp. 109–128). Heidelberg, Germany: Springer.

Guglielmino, P. J., & Guglielmino, L. M. (2001). Moving toward a distributed learning model based on self-managed learning. *SAM Advanced Management Journal, 66*(3), 36–43.

Gupta, A. K., & Govindarajan, V. (2000). Knowledge management's social dimension: Lessons from Nucor Steel. *Sloan Management Review, 42*(1), 71–80.

Hall, H. (2001). Input-friendliness: Motivating knowledge sharing across intranets. *Journal of Information Science, 27*(2), 139–146.

Hall, R. (1993). A framework linking intangible resources and capabilities to sustain competitive advantage. *Strategic Management Journal, 14*(8), 607–618.

Hallwood, C. P. (1997). An efficient capital asset pricing theory of the firm. *Journal of Institutional and Theoretical Economics, 153*(3), 532–544.

Hamel, G. (2000). *Leading the revolution*. Cambridge, MA: Harvard Business School Press.

Hamel, G., & Prahalad, C. K. (1989). Strategic intent. *Harvard Business Review, 67*, 63–76.

Handy, C. (1995). Trust and the virtual organization. *Harvard Business Review, 73*(3), 40–50.

Hansen, M., Nohria, N., & Tierney, T. (1999). What's your strategy for managing knowledge? *Harvard Business Review*, *77*(2), 106–116.

Harriss, J., & De Renzio, P. (1997). Policy arena: Missing link or analytically missing? The concept of social capital. *Journal of International Development*, *9*(7), 919–937.

Harzing, A. W., & Hofstede, G. (1996). Planned change in organizations: The influence of national culture. *Research in the Sociology of Organizations*, *14*, 297–340.

Hatch, M. J. (1993). The dynamics of organizational culture. *Academy of Management Review*, *18*(4), 657–693.

Hayton, J. (2005). Competing in the new economy: The effects of intellectual capital on corporate entrepreneurship in high technology, new ventures. *R & D Management*, *35*(2), 137–155.

Hazlett, S.-A., McAdam, R., & Gallagher, S. (2005). Theory building in knowledge management: In search of paradigms. *Journal of Knowledge Management Inquiry*, *14*(1), 31–43.

Hedburg, B. (1981). How organizations learn and unlearn. In P. Nystrom & W. Starbuck (Eds.), *Handbook of organizational design* (pp. 3–27). New York: Oxford University Press.

Hejis, J. (2004). Innovation capabilities and learning: A vicious circle. *International Journal of Innovation and Learning*, *1*(3), 263–278.

Helfat, C. E., & Raubitschek, R. S. (2002). Product sequencing: Coevolution of knowledge, capabilities and products. In C. W. Choo & N. Bontis (Eds.), *The strategic management of intellectual capital and organizational knowledge* (pp. 317–337). Oxford, UK: Oxford University Press.

Hildreth, P., Kimble, C., & Wright, P. (2000). Communities of practice in the distributed international environment. *Journal of Knowledge Management*, *4*(1), 27–38.

Hill, C., & Rothermael, F. (2003). The performance of incumbent firms in the face of radical technological innovation. *Academy of Management Review*, *8*, 257–274.

Hodgson, G. (1994). Critique of neoclassical microeconomic theory. In G. Hodgson, W. J. Samuels, & M. R. Tool (Eds.), *The Elgar companion to institutional and evolutionary economics* (pp. 128–134). Brookfield, VT: Edward Elgar.

Hofstede, G. (1993). Cultural constraints in management theories. *Academy of Management Executive*, *7*(1), 81–94.

Hofstede, G. (1998). Identifying organizational sub-cultures: An empirical approach. *Journal of Management Studies*, *35*(1), 1–12.

Hofstede, G. (2001). *Culture's consequences: Comparing values, behaviors, institutions and organizations across nations*. Thousand Oaks, CA: Sage.

Hofstede, G., Neuijen, B., Ohayv, D., & Sanders, G. (1990). Measuring organizational cultures: A qualitative and quantitative study across 20 cases. *Administrative Science Quarterly*, *35*, 286–316.

Holden, N. (2001). Facilitating knowledge sharing in Russian and Chinese subsidiaries: The role of personal networks and group membership. *Journal of Knowledge Management*, *8*(3), 155–163.

Holsapple, C. W. (2005). The inseparability of modern knowledge management and computer-based technology. *Journal of Knowledge Management*, *9*(1), 42–52.

Holsapple, C. W., & Joshi, K. D. (1999). Description and analysis of existing knowledge management frameworks. *Proceedings of the 32nd Hawaii International Conference on System Sciences*, 1072–1087.

Holsapple, C. W., & Joshi, K. D. (2000). An investigation of factors that influence the management of knowledge in organizations. *Journal of Strategic Information Systems*, 7(4), 75–91.

Holsapple, C. W., & Joshi, K. D. (2002). Understanding knowledge management solutions: The evolution of frameworks in theory and practice. In S. Barnes (Ed.), *Knowledge management systems: Theory and practice* (pp. 222–241). London: Thomson Learning.

Hornburg, S., & Lang, R. (1998). What is social capital and why is it important to public policy? *Housing Policy Debate*, 9(1), 1–16.

House, R., Hanges, P., Ruiz-Quintanilla, S., Dorfman, P., Javidan, M., & Dickson, M. (1999). Cultural influences on leadership and organisation: Project GLOBE. In W. H. Mobley, M. J. Gessner, & V. Arnold (Eds.), *Advances in global leadership* (pp. 171–233). Stamford, CT: JAI Press.

Huber, G. (1991). Organizational learning: The contributing processes and the literature. *Organization Science*, 2(1), 88–115.

Huber, G. (2001). The transfer of knowledge in knowledge management systems: Unexplored issues and suggested studies. *European Journal of Information Systems*, 10, 72–79.

Hunter, J., Falkovych, K., & Little, S. (2004). Next generation search interfaces. *Proceedings of the European Conference on Digital Libraries*, 86–98.

Hurley, T., & Green, C. (2005). Knowledge management and the non-profit industry: A within and between approach. *Journal of Knowledge Management Practice*, 6. Retrieved November 21, 2006, from www.tlainc.com/articl79.htm

Ingram P., & Braun, J. A. C. (1997). Opportunity and constraint: Organizations' learning from the operating and competitive experience of industries. *Strategic Management Journal*, 18, 75–98.

Ingram P., & Simons, T. (2002). The transfer of experience in groups of organizations: Implications for performance and competition. *Management Science*, 48(12), 1517–1534.

Inkpen, A. (1998). Learning and knowledge acquisition through international strategic alliances. *Academy of Management Executive*, 12(4), 69–80.

Jackson, C. (2001). *Process to product: Creating tools for knowledge management*. Retrieved June 14, 2006, from www.brint.com/members/online/120305/jackson/secn1.htm

Janz, B. D., & Prasarnphanich, P. (2003). Understanding the antecedents of effective knowledge management: The importance of a knowledge-centred culture. *Decision Sciences*, 34(2), 351–384.

Jarzabkowski, P. (2003). Strategic practices: An activity theory perspective on continuity and change. *Journal of Management Studies*, 40(1), 23–55.

Jensen, M. C., & Meckling, W. H. (1992). Specific and general knowledge and organizational structure. In L. Werin & H. Wijkander (Eds.), *Contract economics* (pp. 251–274). Oxford, UK: Blackwell.

Jermier, J. M., Slocum, J. W., Fry, L. W., & Gaines, J. (1991). Organizational subcultures in a soft bureaucracy: Resistance behind the myth and façade of an official culture. *Organization Science*, 2(2), 170–194.

Johnson, G., Melin, L., & Whittington, R. (2003). Introduction: Micro-strategy and strategizing: Toward an activity-based view. *Journal of Management Studies*, 40(1), 3–21.

Johnson, P., & Duberley, J. (2000). *Understanding management research.* London: Sage.

Jones, P. (2000, September). Knowledge strategy: Aligning knowledge programs to business strategy. Paper presented at Knowledge Management World 2000, Santa Clara, CA. Retrieved March 21, 2007, from redesignresearch.com/ks-kmw2000.htm

Jones, P. (2002). When successful products prevent strategic innovation. *Design Management Journal, 13*(2), 30–37.

Jordan, J., & Jones, P. (1997). Assessing your company's knowledge management style. *Journal of Long Range Planning, 30*(3), 392–398.

Junnarkar, B. (1997). Leveraging collective intellect by building organisational capabilities. *Expert Systems with Applications, 13*(1), 29–40.

Kakabadse, N., Kakabadse, A., & Kouzmin, A. (2003). Reviewing the knowledge management literature: Towards a taxonomy. *Journal of Knowledge Management, 7*(4), 75–91.

Kaldor, N., & Mirrlees, J. (1962). A new model of economic growth. *Review of Economic Studies, 29*(3), 174–192.

Kane, B., Crawford, J., & Grant, D. (1999). Barriers to effective HRM. *International Journal of Manpower, 20*, 494–515.

Kaplan, S., & Beinhocker, E. (2003). The real value of strategic planning. *Sloan Management Review, 44*(2), 71–76.

Karlsen, J. T., & Gottschalk, P. (2004). Factors affecting knowledge transfer in IT projects. *Engineering Management Journal, 16*(1), 3–10.

Kayworth, T., & Leidner, D. (2003). Organizational culture as a knowledge resource. In C. W. Holsapple (Ed.), *Handbook on knowledge management* (Vol. 1, pp. 235–252). Heidelberg, Germany: Springer.

Keeble, D., & Wilkinson, F. (Eds.). (2000). *High-technology clusters: Networking and collective learning in Europe.* Aldershot, UK: Ashgate.

Kim, D. H. (1993). The link between individual and organizational learning. *Sloan Management Review, 35*(1), 37–50.

Kim, L. (1997). The dynamics of Samsung's technological learning in semiconductors. *California Management Review, 39*(3), 86–100.

Kim, Y.-G., Yu, S. H., & Lee, J. H. (2003). Knowledge strategy planning: Methodology and case. *Expert Systems with Applications, 24*(3), 295–307.

Kluge, J., Wolfram, S., & Licht, T. (2000). *Knowledge unplugged: The McKinsey & Company global survey on knowledge management.* Houndsmills, UK: Palgrave.

Knapp, E., & Yu, D. (1999). How culture helps or hinders the flow of knowledge. *Knowledge Management Review, 2*(1), 16–21.

Ko, D. G., Kirsch, L., & King, W. R. (2005). Antecedents of knowledge transfer from consultants to clients in enterprise system implementations. *MIS Quarterly, 29*(1), 59–85.

Koenig, M. E. D. (2002). The third stage of KM emerges. *KM World, 11*(3). Retrieved April 2, 2007, from www.kmworld.com/Articles/ReadArticle.aspx?ArticleID=9327

Koenig, M. E. D., & Srikantaiah, T. K. (Eds.). (2004). *Knowledge management lessons learned: What works and what doesn't.* Medford, NJ: Information Today.

Kogut, B., & Zander, U. (1996). What do firms do?: Coordination, identity and learning. *Organization Science, 7*(5), 502–518.

Kotter, J., & Heskett, J. (1992). *Corporate culture and performance.* New York: Free Press.

Kruizinga, E., Heijst, G., & Spek, R. (1997). Knowledge infrastructures and intranets. *Journal of Knowledge Management, 1*(1), 27–32.

Kuhn, T. S. (1970). *The structure of scientific revolutions.* Chicago: University of Chicago Press.

Kuhn, T. S. (1977). Second thoughts on paradigms. In T. S. Kuhn (Ed.), *The essential tension* (pp. 293–319). Chicago: University of Chicago Press.

Küpers, W. (2005). Phenomenology of embodied implicit and narrative knowing. *Journal of Knowledge Management, 9*(6), 114–133.

Kurtz, C. F., & Snowden, D. J. (2003). The new dynamics of strategy: Sensemaking in a complex and complicated world. *IBM Systems Journal, 42*(3), 462–483.

Lam, A. (1997). Embedded firms, embedded knowledge: Problems of collaboration and knowledge transfer in global cooperative ventures. *Organization Studies, 18*(6), 973–996.

Lam, A. (2000). Tacit knowledge, organizational learning and societal institutions: An integrated framework. *Organizational Studies, 22*(2), 487–511.

Lamming, R., Caldwell, N., Harrison, D., & Phillips, W. (2001). Transparency in supply relationships: Concepts and practice. *Journal of Supply Chain Management, 37*(4), 4–10.

Land, F., Nolas, S., & Amjad, U. (2004). Knowledge management: The dark side of KM. *Proceedings of the 7th International Conference on the Social and Ethical Impacts of Information and Communication Technologies,* Vol. 2. Retrieved September 23, 2006, from www.ccsr.cmc.dmu.ac.uk. conferences/ethicomp2004

Land, F., Nolas, S., & Amjad, U. (2006a). Knowledge management processes. In D. G. Swartz (Ed.), *Encyclopaedia of knowledge management* (pp. 403–409). Hershey, PA: Idea Group Reference.

Land, F., Nolas, S., & Amjad, U. (2006b). Theoretical and practical aspects of knowledge management. In D. G. Swartz (Ed.), *Encyclopaedia of knowledge management* (pp. 855–861). Hershey, PA: Idea Group Reference.

Lane, P., Salk, J., & Lyles, M. (2001). Absorptive capacity, learning and performance in international joint ventures. *Strategic Management Journal, 22,* 1139–1161.

Langlois, R. N. (1999a). The coevolutions of technology and organization in the transition to the factory system. In P. L. Robertson (Ed.), *Authority and control in modern industry* (pp. 45–72). London: Routledge.

Langlois, R. N. (1999b). Scale, scope and the reuse of knowledge. In *Economic organization and economic knowledge: Essays in honour of Brian J. Loseby* (Vol.1, pp. 239–254). Cheltenham, UK: Edward Elgar.

Langlois, R. N. (2001). Knowledge, consumption and endogenous growth. *Journal of Evolutionary Economics, 11*(1), 77–93.

Lant, T. K., & Montgomery, D. B. (1987). Learning from strategic success and failure. *Journal of Business Research, 15*(6), 503–518.

Lanzara, G., & Patriotta, G. (2001). Technology and the courtroom: An inquiry into knowledge making in organizations. *Journal of Management Studies, 38*(7), 943–972.

Lave, J., & Wenger, E. (1991). *Situated learning: Legitimate peripheral participation.* Cambridge, UK: Cambridge University Press.

Lee, H., & Choi, B. (2003). Knowledge management enablers, processes and organizational performance: An integrative view and empirical example. *Journal of Management Information Systems, 20*(1), 179–228.

Lee, J. H., & Kim, Y. G. (2001). A stage model of organizational knowledge management: A latent content analysis. *Expert Systems with Applications, 20*(4), 299–311.

Lee, K. J., & Yu, K. (2004). Corporate culture and organizational performance. *Journal of Managerial Psychology, 19*(4), 340–359.

Leonard, D., Brands, P., Edmondson, A., & Fenwick, J. (1998). Virtual teams: Using communications technology to manage geographically dispersed development groups. In S. P. Bradley & R. L. Nolan (Eds.), *Sense and respond: Capturing value in the network era* (pp. 285–298). Boston: Harvard Business School Press.

Leonard-Barton, D. (1992). Core capabilities and core rigidities: A paradox in managing new product development. *Strategic Management Journal, 13*, 111–125.

Leonard-Barton, D. (1995). *Wellsprings of knowledge*. Boston: Harvard Business School Press.

Lev, B. (2001). *Intangibles: Management, measurement and reporting*. Washington, DC: The Brookings Institution.

Levitt, B., & March, J. G. (1988). Organizational learning. *Annual Review of Sociology, 14*, 319–340.

Liang, D., Moreland, R., & Argote, L. (1995). Group versus individual training and groups performance: The mediating role of transactive memory. *Personality and Social Psychology Bulletin, 21*(4), 384–393.

Liebowitz, J., & Wilcox, L. (Eds.). (1997). *Knowledge management and its integrative elements*. New York: CRC Press.

Loermans, J. (2002). Synergizing the learning organization and knowledge management. *Journal of Knowledge Management, 6*(3), 285–294.

Lopez, S., Peon, J., & Ordas, C. (2004). Managing knowledge: The link between culture and organizational learning. *Journal of Knowledge Management, 8*(6), 93–104.

Lucier, C., & Torsiliera, J. (1997). Why knowledge programs fail. *Strategy and Business, 4th Quarter*, 14–28.

Mack, R., Ravin, Y., & Byrd, R. (2001). Knowledge portals and the emerging digital knowledge workplace. *IBM Systems Journal, 40*(4), 925–953.

MacKay, D. M. (1969). *Information, mechanism and meaning*. Cambridge, MA: MIT Press.

MacMorrow, N. (2001). Knowledge management: An introduction. *Annual Review of Information Science and Technology, 35*, 381–421.

Madhavan, R., & Grover, R. (1998). From embedded knowledge to embodied knowledge: New product development as knowledge management. *Journal of Marketing, 62*(4), 1–12.

Maier, R., & Remus, U. (2001). Towards a framework for knowledge management strategies: Process orientation as a strategic starting point. Paper presented at the 34th Annual Hawaii International Conference on System Sciences. Retrieved March 21, 2007, from www.hicss.hawaii.edu/HICSS_34/PDFs/DD OML04.pdf

Maier, R., & Remus, U. (2002). Defining process-oriented knowledge management strategies. *Knowledge and Process Management, 9*(2), 103–118.

Malafsky, G. P. (2003). Technology for acquiring and sharing knowledge assets. In C. W. Holsapple (Ed.), *Handbook on knowledge management* (Vol. 2, pp. 85–108). Heidelberg, Germany: Springer.

Maluccio, J., Haddad, L., & May, J. (2000). Social capital and household welfare in South Africa, 1993–1998. *Journal of Development Studies, 36*(6), 54–81.

March, J. G. (1991). Exploration and exploitation in organizational learning. *Organization Science, 2*(1), 71–87.

Marquardt, M. J., & Kearsley, G. (1999). *Technology-based learning.* Boca Raton, FL: St. Lucie Press.

Marr, B., Schiuma, G., & Neely, A. (2004). Intellectual capital: Defining key performance indicators for organizational knowledge assets. *Business Process Management Journal, 10*(5), 551–569.

Marshall, A. (1890). *Principles of economics.* London: Macmillan.

Martin, J., & Siehl, C. (1983). Organizational culture and counter-culture: An uneasy symbiosis. *Organizational Dynamics, 12*(2), 52–64.

Marwick, A. D. (2001). Knowledge management technology. *IBM Systems Journal, 40*(4), 814–830.

Massingham, P. (2004). Linking business level strategy with activities and knowledge resources. *Journal of Knowledge Management, 8*(6), 50–62.

Mayer, T. (2005). Information, knowledge, understanding and wisdom. *Econ Journal Watch, 2*(1), 66–69.

McAdam, R., & McCreedy, S. (1999). A critical review of knowledge management models. *The Learning Organization, 6*(3), 91–100.

McCarthy, E. D. (1996). *Knowledge as culture: The new sociology of knowledge.* London: Routledge.

McDermott, R. (1999). Why information technology inspired but cannot deliver knowledge management. *California Management Review, 41*(4), 103–117.

McDermott, R., & O'Dell, C. (2001). Overcoming cultural barriers to sharing knowledge. *Journal of Knowledge Management, 5*(1), 76–85.

McElroy, M. W. (2000). The new knowledge management. *Knowledge and Innovation, 1*(1), 43–67.

McElroy, M. W. (2002). A framework for knowledge management. *Cutter IT Journal, 15*(3), 12–17.

McGrath, R. (2001). Exploiting learning, innovative capacity and managerial oversight. *Academy of Management Journal, 44*, 118–131.

McInerney, C. R., & Day, R. E. (Eds.). (2007). *Rethinking knowledge management: From knowledge management to knowledge processes.* Berlin, Germany: Springer.

Menon, T., & Pfeffer, J. (2003). Valuing internal vs external knowledge: Explaining the preference for outsiders. *Management Science, 49*(4), 497–516.

Menor, L., Tatikonda, M., & Sampson, S. (2002). New service development: Areas for exploitation and exploration. *Journal of Operations Management, 20*, 135–157.

MERITUM. (2002). *Guidelines for managing and reporting on intangibles.* Madrid, Spain: Airtel-Vodafone Foundation.

Meso, P., & Smith, R. (2000). A resource-based view of organizational knowledge management systems. *Journal of Knowledge Management, 4*(3), 224–234.

Meyerson, D., & Martin, J. (1987). Cultural change: An integration of three different views. *Journal of Management Studies, 24*(6), 623–647.

Miltiadis, L., Sicilia, M., Davies, J., & Kashyap, V. (2005). Digital libraries in the knowledge era: Knowledge management and semantic Web technologies. *Library Management, 26*(4/5), 170–175.

Mintzberg, H., & Lampel, J. (1999). Reflecting on the strategy process. *Sloan Management Review, 40*(3), 21–30.

Miroshnik, V. (2002). Culture and international management: A review. *Journal of Management Development, 21*(7), 521–544.

Mitev, N. N. (1994). The business failure of knowledge-based systems: Linking knowledge-based systems and information systems methodologies for strategic planning. *Journal of Information Technology, 9*, 173–184.

Moffett, S., McAdam, R., & Parkinson, S. (2002). Developing a model for technology and cultural factors in knowledge management: A factor analysis. *Knowledge Process and Management Journal, 9*(4), 237–255.

Mohamed, M., Stankowsky, M., & Murray, A. (2006). Knowledge management and information technology: Can they work in perfect harmony? *Journal of Knowledge Management, 10*(3), 103–116.

Montgomery, C. A. (1995). *Resource-based and evolutionary theories of the firm.* Norwell, MA: Kluwer.

Mouritsen, J., Bukh, P., Larsen, H., & Johansen, M. (2002). Developing and managing knowledge through intellectual capital statements. *Journal of Intellectual Capital, 3*(1), 10–29.

Mouritsen, J., & Flagstad, K. (2004). Managing organizational learning and intellectual capital. *International Journal of Learning and Intellectual Capital, 1*(1), 72–90.

Murray, P., & Donegan, K. (2003). Empirical linkages between firm competencies and organizational learning. *The Learning Organization, 10*(1), 51–62.

Nadler, D., Shaw, R., & Walton, A. (1995). *Discontinuous change: Leading organizational transformations.* San Francisco: Josey-Bass.

Nahapiet, J., & Ghosal, S. (1998). Social capital, intellectual capital and the organizational advantage. *Academy of Management Review, 23*(2), 242–266.

Neef, D. (1999). *A little knowledge is a dangerous thing: Understanding our global knowledge economy.* Boston: Butterworth-Heinemann.

Nelson, R. R. (1991). Why do firms differ and how does it matter? *Strategic Management Journal, 12*, 61–74.

Nelson, R. R. (1992). What is *commercial* and what is *public* about technology, and what should be. In N. Rosenberg, R. Landau, & D. C. Mowery (Eds.), *Technology and the wealth of nations* (pp. 57–72). Stanford, CA: Stanford University Press.

Nelson, R. R., & Winter, S. G. (1982). *An evolutionary theory of economic change.* Cambridge, MA: Harvard University Press.

Nemeth, C. (1997). Managing innovation: When less is more. *California Management Review, 40*(1), 59–74.

Nevis, E., DiBella, A., & Gould, J. (1995, Winter). Understanding organizations as learning systems. *Sloan Management Review*, 73–85.

Newell, S., Robertson, M., Scarborough, H., & Swan, J. (2002). *Managing knowledge work.* London: Palgrave.

Nidumolu, S., Subramani, M., & Aldrich, A. (2001). Situated learning and the situated knowledge web: Exploring the ground beneath knowledge management. *Journal of Management Information Systems, 118*, 115–150.

Nissen, M. (2006). *Harnessing knowledge dynamics.* Hershey, PA: IRM Press.

Nissen, M., Kamel, N., & Sengupta, K. (2000). Integrated analysis and design of knowledge systems and processes. *Information Resources Management Journal, 13*(1), 24–43.

Nohria, N., & Eccles, R. (1992). Face-to-face: Making network organizations work. In N. Nohria & E. Eccles (Eds.), *Networks and organizations: Structure, form and action* (pp. 288–308). Boston: Harvard Business School Press.

Nonaka, I. (1994). A dynamic theory of organizational knowledge creation. *Organization Science, 5*(1), 14–37.

Nonaka, I. (2002). A dynamic theory of organizational knowledge creation. In C. W. Choo & N. Bontis (Eds.), *The strategic management of intellectual capital and organizational knowledge* (pp. 437–462). Oxford, UK: Oxford University Press.

Nonaka, I., & Takeuchi, H. (1995). *The knowledge-creating company.* New York: Oxford University Press.

Nonaka, I., Toyama, R., & Kono, N. (2001). SECI, Ba and leadership: A unified model of dynamic knowledge creation. In I. Nonaka & D. Teece (Eds.), *Managing industrial knowledge: Creation, transfer and utilisation* (pp. 13–43). London, Sage.

North, D. C. (1981). *Structure and change in economic history.* New York: Norton.

Okhuyzen, G. A., & Eisenhardt, K. M. (2002). Integrating knowledge in groups. *Organization Science, 13*(4), 370–386.

O'Leary, D. E. (2003). Technologies for knowledge storage and assimilation. In C. W. Holsapple (Ed.), *Handbook on knowledge management* (Vol. 2, pp. 29–46). Heidelberg, Germany: Springer.

Ordonez de Pablos, P. (2002). Knowledge management and organizational learning: Typologies of knowledge strategies in the Spanish manufacturing industry from 1995 to 1999. *Journal of Knowledge Management, 6*(1), 52–62.

O'Reilly, C., Chatman, J., & Caldwell, D. (1991). People and organizational culture: A profile comparison approach to assessing person-organization fit. *Academy of Management Journal, 34*(3), 487–516.

Organisation for Economic Co-operation and Development. (1996). *The knowledge-based economy.* Paris: The Organisation.

Orlikowski, W. J. (2002). Knowing in practice: Enacting a collective capability in distributed organizing. *Organization Science, 13*(3), 249–273.

Osterloh, M., & Frey, B. (2000). Motivation, knowledge transfer and organizational form. *Organization Science, 11*(5), 538–550.

O'Sullivan, K. (2005). Leveraging knowledge management technologies to manage intellectual capital. In M. Stankosky (Ed.), *Creating the discipline of knowledge management: The latest in university research* (pp. 134–140). Oxford, UK: Elsevier Butterworth-Heinemann.

Paldam, M., & Svendsen, G. (2000). An essay on social capital: Looking for the fire behind the smoke. *The European Journal of Political Economy, 16,* 339–366.

Parikh, M. (2001). A knowledge management framework for high-tech research and development. *Engineering Management Journal, 13*(1), 27–33.

Parise, S., & Henderson, J. (2001). Knowledge resource exchange in strategic alliances. *IBM Systems Journal, 40*(4), 908–924.

Park, H. (2005). Knowledge management technology and organizational culture. In M. Stankosky (Ed.), *Creating the discipline of knowledge management: The latest in university research* (pp. 141–156). Oxford, UK: Elsevier Butterworth-Heinemann.

Patriotta, G. (2003). Sense-making on the shopfloor: Narratives of knowledge in organizations. *Journal of Management Studies, 40*(2), 349–375.

Patriotta, G. (2004). On studying organizational knowledge. *Knowledge Management Research and Practice, 2*(1), 3–12.

Penrose, E. T. (1959). *The theory of the growth of the firm.* New York: Wiley.

Pettigrew, A. M. (1979). On studying organizational cultures. *Administrative Science Quarterly, 24*(4), 570–581.

Pfeffer, J., & Sutton, R. (2000). *The knowing-doing gap: How smart companies turn knowledge into action.* Cambridge, MA: Harvard Business School Press.

Pohs, W., Pinder, G., Dougherty, C., & White, M. (2001). The Lotus Knowledge Discovery System: Tools and experiences. *IBM Systems Journal, 40*(4), 956–966.

Polanyi, M. (1957). *The great transformation.* Boston: Beacon Press.

Polanyi, M. (1966). *The tacit dimension.* New York: Doubleday.

Porter, M. E. (1991). Towards a dynamic theory of strategy. *Strategic Management Journal, 12,* 95–117.

Portes, A. (1998). Social capital: Its origins and applications in modern sociology. *Annual Review of Sociology, 24,* 1–24.

Prahalad, C. K., & Hamel, G. (1990). The core competence of the corporation. *Harvard Business Review, 68*(3), 79–93.

Preiss, K., & Spooner, K. (2003). Innovation creation and diffusion in the Australian economy. *International Journal of Entrepreneurship and Innovation Management, 3*(3), 197–210.

Prokesch, S. (1997). Unleashing the power of learning: An interview with British Petroleum's John Browne. *Harvard Business Review, 75*(5), 147–168.

Purvis, R. L., Sambamurthy, V., & Zmud, R. W. (2001). The assimilation of knowledge platforms in organizations: An empirical investigation. *Organization Science, 12*(2), 117–135.

Putnam, R. D. (1993). *Making democracy work: Civic traditions in modern Italy.* Princeton, NJ: Princeton University Press.

Putnam, R. D. (2000). *Bowling alone: The collapse and revival of American community.* New York: Simon and Schuster.

Quintas, P., Lefrere, P., & Jones, G. J. (1997). Knowledge management: A strategic agenda. *Long Range Planning, 30*(3), 385–391.

Reagans, R., & Zuckerman, E. (2001). Networks, diversity and productivity: The social capital of corporate R&D teams. *Organization Science, 12*(4), 503–517.

Reichers, A., & Schneider, B. (1990). Climate and culture: An evolution of constructs. In B. Schneider (Ed.), *Organizational climate and culture* (pp. 5–39). San Francisco: Jossey-Bass.

Rivkin, J. (2000). Imitation of complex strategies. *Management Science, 46,* 824–844.

Roman Valasquez, J. (2005). An empiric study of organizational culture types and their relationship with the success of a knowledge management system and the flow of knowledge in the U.S. government and nonprofit sectors. In M. Stankosky (Ed.), *Creating the discipline of knowledge management: The latest in university research* (pp. 66–91). Boston: Elsevier Butterworth-Heinemann.

Romer, P. M. (1986). Increasing returns and long-run growth. *Journal of Political Economy, 94*(5), 1002–1037.

Romer, P. M. (1990). Endogenous technological change. *Journal of Political Economy, 98*(5), S71–S102.

Romer, P. M. (1996). Why indeed in America? Theory, history and the origins of modern economic growth. *American Economic Review, 86,* 202–206.

Roos, J., Roos, G., Dragonetti, N., & Edvinsson, L. (1998). *Intellectual capital: Navigating in the new business landscape.* New York: New York University Press.

Rose, R. A. (1988). Organizations as multiple cultures: A rules theory analysis. *Human Relations, 41*(2), 139–170.

Rosenau, P. M. (1992). *Post-modernism and the social sciences.* Princeton, NJ: Princeton University Press.

Rousseau, D. M. (1990). Assessing organizational culture: The case for multiple methods. In B. Schneider (Ed.), *Organizational climate and culture* (pp. 153–192). San Francisco: Jossey-Bass.

Ruggles, R. (1997). Tools for knowledge management: An introduction. In R. Ruggles (Ed.), *Knowledge management tools* (pp. 1–8). Boston: Butterworth Heinemann.

Russ, M., Jones, J., & Fineman, R. (2005). Knowledge-based strategies: A foundation of a typology. *International Journal of Knowledge and Learning, 4*(2), 138–165.

Russ, M., Jones, J., & Fineman, R. (2006). Towards a taxonomy of knowledge-based strategies: Early findings. *International Journal of Knowledge and Learning, 2*(1/2), 1–40.

Sackmann, S. A. (1992). Culture and sub-cultures: An analysis of organizational knowledge. *Administrative Science Quarterly, 37*(1), 140–161.

Saffold, G. (1988). Culture traits, strengths and organizational performance: Moving beyond strong culture. *Academy of Management Review, 13*(4), 546–558.

Sakkab, N. (2002). Connect and develop complements research and development at P & G. *Research Technology Management, 3*(1), 38–45.

Sambamurthy, V., & Subramani, M. (2005). Introduction: Special issue on information technology and knowledge management. *MIS Quarterly, 29*(1), 1–7.

Santos, F., & Eisenhardt, K. (2005). Organizational boundaries and theories of organization. *Organization Science, 16*(5), 491–508.

Saviotti, P. P. (1998). On the dynamics of appropriability of tacit and codified knowledge. *Research Policy, 26*(7/8), 843–856.

Schein, E. H. (1985). How culture forms, develops and changes. In R. H. Kilmann, M. J. Saxton, & R. Serpa (Eds.), *Gaining control of the corporate culture* (pp. 17–43). San Francisco: Jossey-Bass.

Schein, E. H. (1992). *Organizational culture and leadership*. San Francisco: Jossey-Bass.

Schein, E. H. (1996). Culture: The missing concept in organization studies. *Administrative Sciences Quarterly, 41*, 483–503.

Schein, E. H. (1999). *The corporate culture survival guide*. San Francisco: Jossey-Bass.

Schneider, B., Brief, B., & Guzzo, R. (1996). Creating a climate and culture for sustainable organizational change. *Organizational Dynamics, 24*(4), 7–19.

Schulgasser, D. (1999). Making something out of nothing: Social capital development in Newark New Jersey's Enterprise Community. *National Civic Review, 88*(4), 341–350.

Schultz, M. (2001). The uncertain relevance of newness: Organizational learning and knowledge flows. *Academy of Management Journal, 44*(4), 661–681.

Schultz, M., & Jobe, L. (2001). Codification and tacitness as knowledge management strategies: An empirical exploration. *Journal of High Technology Management Research, 12*(1), 139–165.

Shan, N., & Song, J. (1997). Foreign direct investment and the sourcing of technological advantage: Evidence from the biotechnology industry. *Journal of International Business Studies, 28*(2), 267–284.

Siehl, C., & Martin, J. (1988). Measuring organization culture: Mixing qualitative and quantitative methods. In M. O. Jones, M. D. Moore, & R. C. Snyder (Eds.), *Inside organizations: Understanding the human dimension* (pp. 79–103). Newbury Park, CA: Sage.

Skyrme, D. (1999). *Knowledge networking: Creating the collaborative company.* Boston: Butterworth-Heinemann.

Smircich, L. (1983). Concepts of culture and organizational analysis. *Administrative Science Quarterly, 28*(3), 339–358.

Smith, A. (1861). *An inquiry into the nature and causes of the wealth of nations* (5th ed.). Edinburgh, Scotland: Adam and Charles Black. (Original work published in 1776.)

Smith, R. G., & Farquhar, A. (2000). The road ahead for knowledge management. *AI Magazine, 21*(4), 17–40.

Snowden, D. J. (1999). The paradox of story: Simplicity and complexity in strategy. *Scenario and Strategy Planning, 1*(5), 16–20.

Snowden, D. J. (2000). The social ecology of knowledge management. In C. Despres & D. Chauvel (Eds.), *Knowledge horizons: The present and the promise of knowledge management* (pp. 237–265). Boston: Butterworth-Heinemann.

Snowden, D. J. (2002a). Complex acts of knowing: Paradox and descriptive self-awareness. *Journal of Knowledge Management, 6*(2), 1–14.

Snowden, D. J. (2002b). Narrative patterns: Uses of story in the third age of knowledge management. *Journal of Information and Knowledge Management, 1*(1), 1–6.

Sole, D., & Edmonson, A. (2002). Bridging knowledge gaps: Learning in geographically-dispersed cross-functional development teams. In C. W. Choo & N. Bontis (Eds.), *The strategic management of intellectual capital and organizational knowledge* (pp. 587–604). Oxford, UK: Oxford University Press.

Song, J., Almeida, P., & Wu, G. (2003). Learning-by-hiring: When is mobility more likely to facilitate interfirm knowledge transfer? *Management Science, 49*(4), 351–366.

Sorenson, O. (2003). Interdependence and adaptability: Organizational learning and the long-term effect of integration. *Management Science, 49*(4), 446–464.

Sorenson, J., & Stuart, T. (2000). Aging, obsolescence and organizational innovation. *Administrative Science Quarterly, 45*(1), 81–113.

Spender, J. C. (1996a). Making knowledge the basis of a dynamic theory of the firm. *Strategic Management Journal, 17*(4), 45–62.

Spender, J. C. (1996b). Organizational knowledge, learning and memory: Three concepts in search of a theory. *Journal of Organizational Change Management, 9*(1), 63–79.

St. Onge, H., & Armstrong, C. (2004). *The conducive organization: Building beyond sustainability.* Boston: Butterworth-Heinemann.

St. Onge, H., & Wallace, D. (2003). *Leveraging communities of practice for strategic advantage.* Boston: Butterworth-Heinemann.

Stacey, R. (2000). The emergence of knowledge in organizations. *Emergence, 2*(4), 23–29.

Stacey, R. (2001). *Complex responsive processes in organizations: Learning and knowledge creation.* London: Routledge.

Starbuck, W. H., & Milliken, F. J. (1988). Challenger: Fine-tuning the odds until something breaks. *Journal of Management Studies, 25*(4), 319–340.

Stenmark, D. (2001). Leveraging tacit organizational knowledge. *Journal of Management Information Systems, 17*(3), 9–24.

Stewart, T. A. (1997). *Intellectual capital: The new wealth of nations.* New York: Doubleday/Currency.

Styhre, A. (2003). *Understanding knowledge management: Critical and postmodern perspectives.* Copenhagen, Denmark: Copenhagen Business School Press.

Styhre, A. (2004). Rethinking knowledge: A Bergsonian critique of the notion of tacit knowledge. *British Journal of Management, 15*(2), 177–188.

Stiglitz, J. E. (1985). Information and economic analysis: A perspective. *The Economic Journal, 95*(Suppl.), 21–41.

Storey, J., & Barnett, E. (2000). Knowledge management initiatives: Learning from failure. *Journal of Knowledge Management, 4*(2), 145–156.

Subramanian, M., & Venkrataman, N. (2000). Determinants of transnational new product development capacity: Testing the influence of transferring and deploying tacit overseas knowledge. *Strategic Management Journal, 20*, 359–378.

Sullivan, P. (2000). *Value-driven intellectual capital: How to convert intangible corporate assets into market value.* New York: Wiley.

Sveiby, K.-E. (1997). *The new organizational wealth: Managing and measuring knowledge-based assets.* San Francisco: Berrett-Koehler.

Sveiby, K.-E. (2002). A knowledge-based theory of the firm to guide strategy formulation. *Journal of Intellectual Capital, 2*(4), 344–359.

Swann, J., & Scarborough, H. (2001). Knowledge management: Concepts and controversies. *Journal of Management Studies, 38*(7), 913–922.

Szulanski, G. (1996). Exploring internal stickiness: Impediments to the transfer of best practice within the firm. *Strategic Management Journal, 17*(4), 27–43.

Szulanski, G. (2000). The process of knowledge transfer: A diachronic analysis of stickiness. *Organizational Behaviour and Human Decision Processes, 82*(1), 9–27.

Teece, D. J. (1977). Technology transfer by multinational firms: The resource cost of transferring technical know-how. *The Economic Journal, 87*, 242–261.

Teece, D. J. (1998). Capturing value from knowledge assets: The new economy, markets for know-how and intangible assets. *California Management Review, 40*(3), 55–79.

Teece, D. J. (2001). Strategies for managing knowledge assets: The role of firm structure and industrial context. In I. Nonaka & D. Teece (Eds.), *Managing industrial knowledge: Creation, transfer and utilisation* (pp. 125–144). London, Sage.

Teece, D. J., & Pisano, G. (1994). The dynamic capabilities of firms: An introduction. *Industrial and Corporate Change, 3*(3), 537–556.

Terra, J. C., & Gordon, C. (2002). *Realizing the promise of corporate portals: Leveraging knowledge for business success.* Boston: Butterworth-Heinemann.

Thomas-Hunt, M., Ogden, T., & Neale, M. (2003). Who's really sharing?: Effects of social and expert status on knowledge exchange within groups. *Management Science, 49*(4), 464–478.

Townsend, A., DeMarie, S., & Hendrickson, A. (1998). Virtual teams: Technology and the workplace of the future. *Academy of Management Executive, 12*(3), 17–29.

Tsoukas, H. (1997). The tyranny of light: The temptations and the paradoxes of the information society. *Futures, 29*, 827–844.

Tsoukas, H., & Mylonopoulos, N. (Eds.). (2004). *Organizations as knowledge systems: Knowledge, learning and dynamic capabilities.* Basingstoke, UK: Palgrave Macmillan.

Tsoukas, H., & Vladimirou, E. (2001). What is organizational knowledge? *Journal of Management Studies, 38*(7), 973–994.

Tuomi, I. (2000). Data is more than knowledge: Implications of the reversed knowledge hierarchy for knowledge management and organizational memory. *Journal of Management Information Systems, 16*(3), 103–117.

Ulrich, D. (1998). Intellectual capital = competence x commitment. *Sloan Management Review*, *39*(2), 15–26.

Uzzi, B. (1996). The sources and consequences of embeddedness for the economic performance of organizations. *American Sociological Review*, *61*, 674–698.

Uzzi, B. (1997). Social structure and competition in interfirm networks: The paradox of embeddedness. *Administrative Science Quarterly*, *42*, 35–67.

Uzzi, B., & Lancaster, R. (2003). Relational embeddedness and learning: The case of bank loan managers and their clients. *Management Science*, *49*(4), 383–400.

van der Spek, R., & de Hoog, R. (1994). Towards a methodology for knowledge management. *Proceedings of International Symposium on the Management of Industrial and Corporate Knowledge*, 93–102.

van der Spek, R., & Spijkervet, A. (1997). Knowledge management: Dealing intelligently with knowledge. In J. Liebowitz & L. Wilcox (Eds.), *Knowledge management and its integrative elements* (pp. 93–102). New York: CRC Press.

van Maanen, J., & Barley, S. R. (1985). Cultural organization: Fragments of a theory. In P. J. Frost, L. F. More, M. R. Louise, C. C. Lundberg, & J. Martin (Eds.), *Organizational culture* (pp. 31–54). Beverly Hills, CA: Sage.

Vedovello, C., & Godinho, M. (2003). Business incubators as a technological infrastructure for supporting small innovative firms' activities. *International Journal of Entrepreneurship and Innovation Management*, *3*(1/2), 4–21.

Venzin, M., von Krogh, G., & Roos, J. (1998). Future research into knowledge management. In G. von Krogh, J. Roos, & D. Kleine (Eds.), *Knowing in firms: Understanding, managing and measuring knowledge* (pp. 26–66). London: Sage.

Vera, D., & Crossan, M. (2003). Organizational learning and knowledge management: Toward an integrative framework. In M. Easterby-Smith & M. A. Lyles (Eds.), *The Blackwell handbook of organizational learning and knowledge management* (pp. 122–141). Oxford, UK: Blackwell.

von Furstenburg, G. (2001). Hopes and delusions of transparency. *North American Journal of Economics and Finance*, *12*, 105–120.

von Hayek, F. A. (1937), Economics and knowledge. *Economica*, *4*(13), 33–54.

von Hayek, F. A. (1945). The use of knowledge in society. *American Economic Review*, *35*(4), 519–530.

von Krogh, G., & Grand, S. (2002). From economic theory toward a knowledge-based theory of the firm: Conceptual building blocks. In C. W. Choo & N. Bontis (Eds.), *The strategic management of intellectual capital and organizational knowledge* (pp. 163–184). Oxford, UK: Oxford University Press.

von Krogh, G., Ichijo, K., & Nonaka, I. (2000). *Enabling knowledge creation: How to unlock the mystery of tacit knowledge and release the power of innovation.* New York: Oxford University Press.

von Krogh, G., & Roos, J. (1996). Five claims of knowing. *European Management Journal*, *14*(4), 423–426.

Wang, C. L., & Ahmed, P. L. (2003). Organizational learning: A critical review. *The Learning Organization*, *10*(1), 8–17.

Weber, R. A., & Camerer, C. F. (2003). Cultural conflict and merger failure: An experimental approach. *Management Science*, *49*(4), 400–416.

Weilinga, B., Sandberg, J., & Schreiber, G. (1997). Methods and techniques for knowledge management: What has knowledge engineering to offer? *Expert Systems with Applications*, *13*(1), 73–84.

Whiteley, P. (2000). Economic growth and social capital. *Political Studies*, *48*(3), 443–466.

Whittington, R. (2003). The work of strategizing and organizing: For a practice perspective. *Strategic Organization, 1*(1), 117–126.

Wiig, K. M. (1997). Knowledge management: An introduction and perspective. *Journal of Knowledge Management, 1*(1), 6–14.

Wiig, K. M. (2004). *People-focused knowledge management.* Boston: Butterworth-Heinemann.

Wiig, K. M., de Hoog, R., & van der Spek, R. (1997). Supporting knowledge management: A selection of methods and techniques. *Expert Systems with Applications, 13*(1), 15–27.

Williams, K., & O'Reilly, C. (1998). Demography and diversity in organizations. In B. Straw & R. Sutton (Eds.), *Research in organizational behavior* (pp. 77–140). Stamford, CT: JAI Press.

Williamson, O. E. (1985). *The economic institutions of capitalism.* New York: Free Press.

Williamson, O. E. (1991). Strategizing, economizing and economic organization. *Strategic Management Journal, 12*(8), 75–94.

Williamson, O. E. (1999). Strategy research: Governance and competence perspectives. *Strategic Management Journal, 29*(12), 1087–1108.

Winter, S. G. (1995). Four Rs of profitability: Rents, resources, routines and replication. In C. A. Montgomery (Ed.), *Resource-based and evolutionary theories of the firm* (pp. 147–178). Norwell, MA: Kluwer.

Woolcock, M., & Narayan, D. (2000). Social capital: Implications for development theory, research and policy. *World Bank Research Observer, 15*(2), 225–249.

World Bank (1999). What is social capital? *PovertyNet.* Retrieved March 12, 2006, from www.worldbank.org/poverty/scapital/whatsc.htm

Yeager, L. B. (2005). Why distinguish between information and knowledge? *Econ Journal Watch, 2*(1), 82–87.

Zack, M. H. (1999). Managing codified knowledge. *Sloan Management Review, 40*(4), 45–58.

Zack, M. H. (2002). Developing a knowledge strategy. In C. W. Choo & N. Bontis (Eds.), *The strategic management of intellectual capital and organizational knowledge* (pp. 255–276). Oxford, UK: Oxford University Press.

Zellmer-Bruhn, M. E. (2003). Interruptive events and team knowledge acquisition. *Management Science, 49*(4), 514–529.

Zucker, L., Darby, M., Brewer, M., & Peng, Y. (1996). Collaboration structure and information dilemma in biotechnology: Organizational boundaries as trust production. In R. Kramer & T. Tyler (Eds.), *Trust in organizations* (pp. 90–113). Thousand Oaks, CA: Sage.

CHAPTER 10

Syndromic Surveillance Systems

Ping Yan
Hsinchun Chen
Daniel Zeng
University of Arizona

Introduction

Syndromic surveillance is concerned with continuous monitoring of public health-related information sources and early detection of adverse disease events. Syndromic surveillance research is by nature multidisciplinary and has attracted significant attention in recent years. Syndromic surveillance systems are also being adopted to meet the critical need of effective prevention, detection, and management of infectious disease outbreaks, either naturally occurring or caused by bioterrorism attacks. This chapter presents a comprehensive survey of state-of-the-art syndromic surveillance research and system development efforts from the perspective of information science and technology. Based on a detailed analysis of fifty local, state, national, and international syndromic surveillance systems and a review of about 200 academic publications, we discuss the technical challenges, applicable approaches or solutions, and the current state of system implementation and adoption for various components of syndromic surveillance systems, covering system architecture, data collection and sharing, data analysis, and data access and visualization. A case study comparing three state-of-the-art syndromic surveillance systems is presented to illustrate the technical discussions in an integrated, real-world context. Critical non-technical issues including data sharing policies and system evaluation and adoption are also discussed.

Background and Motivation

In this time of increasing concern over the potentially deadly and costly threats of infectious diseases caused by natural disasters or bioterrorism attacks, preparation for, early detection of, and timely response to infectious diseases and epidemic outbreaks are a key public health priority and are driving an emerging field of multidisciplinary research. Recent disastrous events that have threatened the public health of large populations around the world include Severe Acute Respiratory Syndrome (SARS) epidemics in Asia (Li, Yu, Xu, Lee, Wong, Ooi, et al., 2004), the outbreak of Avian flu in East Asian countries (National Biological Information Infrastructure, 2006; U.S. Department of Agriculture, 2006), and the catastrophic aftereffects of Hurricane Katrina in New Orleans, Louisiana, as well as the looming threats of bioterrorism since the anthrax attacks in October 2001 (Buehler, Berkelman, Hartley, & Peters, 2003; Cronin, 2005; Siegrist, 1999).

Public health surveillance has been practiced for decades and continues to be an indispensable approach for detecting emerging disease outbreaks and epidemics. Early knowledge of a disease outbreak plays an important role in improving response effectiveness (Pinner, Rebmann, Schuchat, & Hughes, 2003). Traditional disease surveillance often relies on time-consuming laboratory diagnosis and the reporting of notifiable diseases is often slow and incomplete, but a new breed of public health surveillance systems has the potential to accelerate detection of disease outbreaks significantly. These new, computer-based surveillance systems offer valuable and timely information to hospitals as well as to state, local, and federal health officials (Dembek, Carley, & Hadler, 2005; Pavlin, 2003). They are capable of real-time or near-real-time detection of serious illnesses and potential bioterrorism agent exposures, allowing for rapid public health response. This public health surveillance approach is generally called syndromic surveillance, which is defined as an ongoing, systematic collection, analysis, and interpretation of "syndrome"-specific data for early detection of public health aberrations.

The rationale behind syndromic surveillance lies in the fact that specific diseases of interest can be monitored by syndromic presentations that can be shown in a timely manner, such as nurse calls, medication purchases, and school or work absenteeism. In addition to early detection and reporting of monitored diseases, syndromic surveillance also provides a rich data repository and highly active communication system for situation awareness and event characterization. Multiple participants provide interconnectivity among disparate and geographically separated sources of information to facilitate a clear understanding of the evolving situation. This is of importance for event reporting, strategic response planning, and disaster victim tracking. Information gained from syndromic surveillance data can also guide the planning, implementation, and evaluation of long-term programs to prevent and control diseases, including distribution of medication, vaccination plans, and allocation of resources (Mostashari & Hartman, 2003).

In recent years, several syndromic surveillance approaches have been proposed. According to a study conducted by the U.S. Centers for Disease Control and Prevention (CDC) in 2003 (Buehler et al., 2003), roughly 100 sites throughout the country have implemented and deployed syndromic surveillance systems. These systems, although sharing similar objectives, vary in system architecture, information processing and management techniques, and algorithms for anomaly detection; they also have different geographic coverage and disease foci. We see a critical need for an in-depth survey that analyzes and evaluates existing systems and related outbreak modeling and detection work under a unified framework. Such a survey will be useful for researchers who are working or have an interest in public health surveillance. It will also provide a much-needed comparative study for public health practitioners and offer concrete insights that could help future syndromic surveillance system development and implementation.

Significance of the Survey

This survey is designed to investigate the surveillance capacity and effectiveness of existing syndromic surveillance systems in order to present a synthesized review of state-of-the-art syndromic surveillance research and practice and provide insights and guidelines for future research and system implementation. In comparison with several review articles that have been published in this area (Bravata, McDonald, Smith, Rydzak, Szeto, Buckeridge, et al., 2004; Lober, Karras, & Wagner, 2002; Mandl, Overhage, Wagner, Lober, Sebastiani, Mostashari, et al., 2004; Yan, Zeng, & Chen, 2006), this review focuses on an in-depth description of the technical components of syndromic surveillance systems and frames the related research questions from an information technology (IT) and informatics perspective.

More specifically, this survey seeks to: 1) provide an updated review of existing system development efforts and emerging syndromic surveillance techniques; 2) identify emerging needs and challenges; 3) present in a synthesized manner the research and development efforts of public health agencies, research institutions, and industry from an IT perspective; and 4) serve as a tutorial for IT researchers interested in the emerging field of syndromic surveillance and infectious disease informatics. The survey aims to answer the following questions:

- Is syndromic surveillance an effective approach to the public health surveillance problem?
- To what extent are existing systems already serving the purpose of early event detection, situation awareness, and response facilitation? How can their usability and effectiveness be validated?
- What information sharing, outbreak detection, and information access and visualization techniques have been implemented and how well do these techniques perform?
- Are there any technical barriers to the design and implementation of these approaches in public health?
- What is the deployment status of existing syndromic surveillance systems in the United States and other parts of the world?
- Are there any legal or administrative challenges hindering their widespread adoption?

Review Scope and Methods

This survey investigates a number of public health syndromic surveillance systems and related outbreak modeling and detection research, with the specific emphasis on the most promising practices in applying advanced information technologies to public health surveillance. It focuses primarily on major efforts from the public health agencies, research institutions, and industry in the U.S. Some other countries with major syndromic surveillance practices, including Canada, the U.K., Australia, Japan, and Korea, are also included in the survey.

We reviewed about 200 publications from 1997–2006. To identify related work, we searched archival journals including but not limited to the *Journal of Biomedical Informatics*, *Journal of the American Medical Informatics Association*, *Journal of Urban Health*, *Artificial Intelligence in Medicine*, and *Annual Review of Information Science and Technology*. Journal articles were mainly retrieved from online bibliographical databases including PubMed, ScienceDirect, and SpringerLink. Our literature search used both general keywords such as "syndromic surveillance" and "biosurveillance," and keywords pertaining to various technical aspects of syndromic surveillance such as "outbreak detection," "spatial surveillance," and "bioterrorism preparedness." In addition, we investigated other research outlets, including proceedings and presentation material from various workshops (e.g., Arizona Spring Biosurveillance Workshop [ai.arizona.edu/BIO2006] and Rutgers's DIMACS Working Group on BioSurveillance Data Monitoring and Information Exchange). User manuals and system brochures that are available electronically (e.g., from state/national health department Web sites) were also studied.

Our survey aims to be comprehensive and is based on a systematic study of fifty unique syndromic surveillance systems. (We do not count implementations of one system in multiple sites.) We believe these represent most of the known syndromic surveillance systems for which technical descriptions in varying degrees of detail are available from public sources. Technical approaches or solutions from each system are carefully cataloged and analyzed based on their purpose, input assumed, and output produced. The similarities and differences of these approaches are identified and their relative strengths and weaknesses summarized. In addition, an attempt has been made to perform a post analysis, cutting across all these systems with the objective of assessing the extent to which a particular technical approach has been used to meet a specific functional requirement of syndromic surveillance.

Chapter Structure

The chapter is structured as follows. We present a conceptual framework to analyze syndromic surveillance systems, supplemented by a comprehensive summary of all the systems surveyed, in a tabular format. We then devote sections to data collection, data analysis and outbreak detection, and data visualization and information dissemination. System assessment and other policy issues are reviewed subsequently. The penultimate section reports a case study, summarizing and comparing three critical and unique syndromic surveillance systems: BioSense, RODS, and BioPortal. The chapter concludes with a discussion of critical issues and challenges to syndromic surveillance research and system development, and future directions.

Analysis Framework and a Summary of Surveyed Public Health Syndromic Surveillance Systems

Our discussion of public health syndromic surveillance systems is based on a conceptual framework that views syndromic surveillance as composed of three principal functional areas: data sources and collection strategies; data analysis and outbreak detection; and data visualization, information dissemination, and reporting.

The first is concerned primarily with where and how to collect data. Related issues include data entry approaches, data sharing protocols, and transmission techniques. The second area involves modeling, analysis, and data mining approaches to monitor for data anomalies and to discover whether the aberrant data condition is caused by a real change in disease occurrence. The syndrome classification process, a critical step that occurs between data collection and anomaly detection, focuses on classifying the raw, observational data into syndrome groups to provide evidence to detect aberrations in any monitored illness. The third area involves data visualization, user interface, and information dissemination functionalities. Public health officials, epidemiologists, and, if needed, emergency responders and homeland security personnel interact with the syndromic surveillance systems through these components to access detailed information for further investigation, gain situational awareness, make decisions about alert generation and dissemination, and collect information needed for response planning and event management.

In the remainder of this section, we summarize the key local, state, national, and international syndromic surveillance systems and related ongoing research programs of interest. This summary provides the needed background information and application contexts. It also offers a snapshot of current syndromic surveillance practice in general. Because our primary focus is public health surveillance, closely related issues such as response planning and resource allocation strategies after an event is confirmed (e.g., Carley, Fridsma, Casman, Altman, Chang, Kaminsky, et al., 2003) are beyond the scope of this study.

For each system surveyed, we list its main contributors and stakeholders. We also include an overall system/project description, relevant data sources, syndromes monitored, data analysis and outbreak detection methods implemented, frequency of data collection and analysis, whether a geographic information system (GIS) component is used, and its deployment strategy and status.

Although the review is intended to be detailed and comprehensive, our effort has been hampered by the unavailability of the technical details of many syndromic surveillance systems from either the published literature or the publicly available sources such as project Web sites. Furthermore, in spite of our best efforts, the literature review is unlikely to be exhaustive; we may have missed some interesting and emerging local and/or international syndromic surveillance system implementations. Nonetheless, our review offers a fairly detailed and up-to-date snapshot of research into, and successful implementations of, syndromic surveillance systems for public health and biodefense.

Summary of Nationwide Syndromic Surveillance Systems

Twelve nationwide syndromic surveillance systems have been identified in our study. Table 10.1 presents a summary of these systems. We provide additional information for each of these systems in the remainder of this chapter.

CDC's BioSense system is a national initiative to support early outbreak detection by providing technologies for timely data acquisition, near real-time reporting, automated outbreak identification, and related analytics (Bradley, Rolka, Walker, & Loonsk, 2005; Ma, Rolka, Mandl, Buckeridge, Fleischauer, & Pavlin, 2005; Sokolow, Grady, Rolka, Walker, McMurray, English-Bullard, et al., 2005). BioSense collects ambulatory care data, emergency room diagnostic and procedural information from military and veteran medical facilities, and clinical laboratory test orders and results from LabCorp. BioSense also monitors over-the-counter (OTC) drug sales and laboratory test results for environmental samples collected through the BioWatch effort. In its most recent implementation, BioSense aims to monitor eleven syndromes.

The Real-time Outbreak Detection System (RODS) is grounded in public health practice and focuses on collecting surveillance data for algorithm validation and investigating different types of novel data for outbreak detection (Espino, Wagner, Szczepaniak, Tsui, Su, Olszewski, et al., 2004; Tsui et al., 2003). It has been connected to more than 500 hospitals' emergency departments nationwide for syndromic surveillance purposes. RODS collects chief complaints from emergency rooms, admission records from hospitals, and OTC drug sales data in real time. Syndrome categories are monitored with a variety of data analysis methods.

In 1999, the Walter Reed Army Institute of Research (WRAIR) created the Electronic Surveillance System for the Early Notification of Community-Based Epidemics (ESSENCE) (Lombardo, Burkom, & Pavlin, 2004). ESSENCE has been used to monitor the health status of military healthcare beneficiaries worldwide, relying on outpatient ICD-9 diagnostic codes for outbreak detection (Burkom, Elbert, Feldman, & Lin, 2004; Lombardo et al., 2003; Lombardo, Burkom, Elbert, Magruder, Lewis, Loschen, et al., 2004). The system uses military and civilian ambulatory visits, civilian emergency department chief-complaint records, school-absenteeism data, OTC and prescription medication sales, veterinary health records, and requests for influenza testing to evaluate health status with a focus on cases of death, GI, neurological, rash, respiratory, sepsis, unspecified infection, and other illnesses. By 2003 ESSENCE had been deployed in the National Capital Area, and 300 military clinics worldwide (Lombardo et al., 2003).

The Rapid Syndrome Validation Project (RSVP) is an Internet-based population health surveillance tool designed to facilitate rapid communications between epidemiologists and healthcare providers (Zelicoff, 2002; Zelicoff, Brillman, & Forslund, 2001). Through RSVP, patient encounters labeled with syndrome categories (including flu-like illness, fever with skin findings, fever with altered mental status, acute bloody diarrhea, acute hepatitis, and acute respiratory distress) and clinicians' judgments regarding the severity of illness are reported to facilitate timely geographic and temporal analysis (Zelicoff, 2002).

The Early Aberration Reporting System (EARS) (www.bt.cdc.gov/ surveillance/ears) is used to monitor bioterrorism activities during large-scale events. Its evolution to a standard surveillance tool began in New York City and the national capitol region following the terrorist attacks of September 11, 2001 (Hutwagner, Thompson, Seeman, & Treadwell, 2003). Emergency department visits, 911 calls, physician office data, school and work absenteeism, and OTC drug sales are monitored for forty-two syndrome categories (Hutwagner et al., 2003). EARS has been implemented in emergency departments in the state of New Mexico. It was also used for syndromic surveillance purposes at the 2000 Democratic National Convention, the 2001 Super Bowl, and the 2001 World Series.

The National Bioterrorism Syndromic Surveillance Demonstration Program covers a population of more than 20 million people. This program monitors and analyzes disease cases for neurologic, upper/lower gastrointestinal (GI), upper/lower respiratory, dermatologic, sepsis/fever, bioterrorism category A agents (anthrax, botulism, plague, smallpox, tularemia, and hemorrhagic fever), and influenza-like illness (ILI). The data utilized are derived from electronic patient-encounter records from participating healthcare organizations including ambulatory-care and urgent-care encounters (Lazarus, Kleinman, Dashevsky, Adams, Kludt, DeMaria et al., 2002; Lazarus, Kleinman, Dashevsky, DeMaria, & Platt, 2001; Platt, Bocchino, Caldwell, Harmon, Kleinman, Lazarus, et al., 2003; Yih, Caldwell, & Harmon, 2004). This project provides a testbed for analyzing various outbreak detection algorithms and implements a model-adjusted SaTScan approach and the SMART (small area regression and testing) algorithm (Kleinman, Lazarus, & Platt, 2004).

The Bio-event Advanced Leading Indicator Recognition Technology (BioALIRT) program examines the use of spatial and other covariate information from disparate sources to improve the timeliness of outbreak detection in response to possible bioterrorism attacks (Buckeridge, Burkom, Campbell, Hogan, & Moore, 2005; Siegrist, McClellan, Campbell, Foster, Burkom, Hogan, et al., 2004). In a number of regions including Norfolk, Virginia; Pensacola, Florida; Charleston, South Carolina; Seattle, Washington; and Louisville, Kentucky, the BioALIRT system monitors military and civilian outpatient-visit records with ICD-9 codes and military outpatient prescription records for unusual ILI and GI occurrences.

BioDefend is another program that aims to develop an effective and practical approach for rapid detection of outbreaks (BioDefend, 2006; Uhde, Farrell, Geddie, Leon, & Cattani, 2005). Patient encounter information is collected automatically or manually from clinics, emergency departments, and first-aid stations at the first point of patient contact. Syndrome categories monitored include respiratory tract infection with fever, botulism-like illness, ILI, death with fever, GI, encephalitis/meningitis-like illness, febrile, rash with fever, fever of unknown origin, sepsis, contact dermatitis, and non-traumatic shock.

Biological Spatio-Temporal Outbreak Reasoning Module (BioStorm) aims to integrate disparate data sources and deploys various analytic problem solvers to support public health surveillance. The framework is ontology-based and consists of a data broker, a data mapper, a control structure, and a library of statistical and spatial problem solvers (Buckeridge, Graham, O'Connor, Choy, Tu, & Musen, 2002; Crubézy, O'Connor, Pincus, & Musen, 2005). It monitors and analyzes data such as 911 emergency calls collected from San Francisco, emergency department dispatch data from the Palo Alto Veteran's Administration Medical Center, and emergency department respiratory records from hospitals in Norfolk, Virginia. Based on a customized knowledge base, BioStorm has implemented a library of statistical methods analyzing data as single or multiple time series and knowledge-based methods that relate detected abnormalities to knowledge about reportable diseases.

BioPortal is another biosurveillance system that provides a flexible and scalable infectious disease information sharing (across species and jurisdictions), alerting, analysis, and visualization platform (Chen & Xu, 2006; Zeng, Chen, Tseng, Larson, Eidson, Gotham, et al., 2005). The system supports interactive, dynamic spatial-temporal analysis of epidemiological, textual, and sequence data (Chen & Xu, 2006; Thurmond, 2006; Zeng, Chen, Tseng, Chang, Eidson, Gotham, et al., 2005). BioPortal makes available a sophisticated spatial-temporal visualization environment to help present public health case reports and analysis results. Similar to EARS, BioPortal uses customized syndrome categories, which were developed by the State of Arizona Department of Health Services and hospitals in Taiwan. A number of retrospective and prospective spatial-temporal clustering approaches (hotspot analysis) are developed and implemented in BioPortal for outbreak detection purposes. They are Risk-adjusted Support Vector Clustering (RSVC) (Zeng, Chang, & Chen, 2004), Prospective Support Vector Clustering (Chang, Zeng, & Chen, 2005), and space-time correlation analysis (Ma, Zeng, & Chen, 2006).

Bio-Surveillance Analysis, Feedback, Evaluation and Response (B-SAFER) is a Web-based infectious disease monitoring system that is part of the open source OpenEMed project (openemed.org) for use in urgent care settings (Umland, Brillman, Koster, Joyce, Forslund, Picard, et al., 2003). It collects chief complaints, discharge diagnoses, and disposition data for detection analysis concerning a group of syndromes including respiratory, GI, undifferentiated infection, lymphatic, skin, and neurological. The collected data are analyzed daily by a first-order model that uses regression to fit trends, seasonal effects, and day-of-week effects (Brillman, Burr, Forslund, Joyce, Picard, & Umland, 2005).

INtegrated Forecasts and EaRly eNteric Outbreak (INFERNO) incorporates infectious disease epidemiology into adaptive forecasting and uses the concept of an outbreak signature as a composite of disease epidemic curves (Naumova, O'Neil, & MacNeill, 2005). The system has been tested with a dataset of emergency department records associated with a substantial waterborne outbreak of cryptosporidiosis that occurred in Milwaukee, Wisconsin, in 1993.

Table 10.1 Twelve nationwide syndromic surveillance systems

System	Stakeholders	Monitored datasets	Syndrome categories	Data analysis methods	Frequency	GIS
BioSense	CDC	Multiple	11	CUSUM (Cumulative Sums), EWMA (Exponentially Weighted Moving Average), and SMART	Daily	Y
RODS	University of Pittsburgh and Carnegie Mellon University	Multiple	8	Autoregressive modeling, CUSUM, scan statistics, WSARE (What is Strange About Recent Events), PANDA (Population-wide Anomaly Detection and Assessment) and others	Every 8 hours	Y
ESSENCE	DoD-GEIS (DoD-Global Emerging Infections	Multiple	8	CUSUM, EWMA, WSARE,	Daily	Y

Table 10.1 *(cont.)*

	Surveillance and Response System) and Johns Hopkins University			SMART (Small Area Regression and Testing), and scan statistics		
RSVP	Sandia National Lab and State of New Mexico Dept. of Health and clinicians, Los Alamos National Lab (LANL), University of New Mexico	Multiple	6	CUSUM, EWMA and wavelet algorithms	Daily	Y
EARS	CDC	Multiple	About 42	Shewhart chart, moving average, and variations of CUSUM (C1-MILD, C2-MEDIUM, and C3-ULTRA)	Daily	N
National Bioterrorism Syndromic Surveillance Demonstration Program	Harvard Medical School's Channing Lab	Multiple	12	Model-adjusted SaTScan™ approach and SMART	Daily	N
BioALIRT	DARPA, Johns Hopkins U., Walter Reed Army Institute of Research; U. of Pittsburgh/Carnegie Mellon U.; etc.	Multiple	ILI, GI	Algorithms developed by RODS, CDC, ESSENCE, and IBM	Daily	N
BioDefend	U. of South Florida's Center for Biological Defense and Datasphere, LLC	Multiple	12	Time series pattern deviation detection, based on a 30-day rolling mean as threshold	Daily	N
BioStorm	Stanford U.	Multiple	Based on a customized knowledge base	A library of statistical methods and knowledge-based methods	N/A	N
BioPortal	U. of Arizona, U. of California, Davis, Kansas State U., National Taiwan U., Arizona/California Dept. of Public	Multiple	More than 40	RSVC, Prospective SVC, and correlation analysis	N/A	Y

Table 10.1 (*cont.*)

	Health Services, New York State Dept. of Health					
B-SAFER	DoD's National Biodefense Initiative and Dept. of Energy, in collaboration with the Los Alamos National Lab, U. of New Mexico Health Sciences Center, and the New Mexico Dept. of Health	Multiple	7	First-order model	Daily	N
INFERNO	Sponsored by National Institutes of Health	Multiple	GI	Retrospective daily time series	N/A	N

Summary of Syndromic Surveillance Systems at the Local, County, and State Levels

Eighteen syndromic surveillance systems implemented at the local, county, and state levels have been identified in our study. Table 10.2 presents a summary of these systems. Note that technical information about these systems is often much more difficult to locate (in many cases unavailable publicly) when compared with nationwide systems.

The syndromic surveillance system implemented in New York City uses ETL (extract, transform, and load) middleware technology from iWay Software over secure, Web-based reporting channels to receive and process a high volume of daily reports at a central data repository. A custom analytical application based on spatial data analysis software SaTScan and ArcView desktop GIS and mapping software from ESRI is used to perform statistical analysis and related visualization functions (Heffernan, Mostashari, Das, Besculides, Rodriguez, Greenko, et al., 2004; Heffernan, Mostashari, Das, Karpati, Kulldorf, & Weiss, 2004).

Syndromic Surveillance Information Collection (SSIC) is a complex, heterogeneous database system intended to facilitate the early detection of possible bioterrorism attacks (with such agents as anthrax, brucellosis, plague, Q-fever, tularemia, smallpox, viralencephalitides, hemorrhagic fever, botulism toxins, and staphylococcal enterotoxin-B) as well as naturally occurring disease outbreaks including large food-borne disease outbreaks, emerging infections, and pandemic influenza (Karras, 2005).

Table 10.2 Syndromic surveillance system implementation at local or state levels

System	Stakeholders
Syndromic Surveillance Project in New York City	New York City Dept. of Health and Mental Hygiene (NYCDOHMH)
SSIC	U. Washington
Syndromal Surveillance Tally Sheet	EDs of Santa Clara County, California
Syndromic Surveillance Using Automated Medical Records	Greater Boston
New Hampshire (NH) Syndromic Surveillance System	Division of Public Health Services, NH Dept. of Health and Human Services (NH DHHS)
Connecticut Hospital Admissions Syndromic Surveillance	Connecticut Dept. of Public Health (CDPH)
Catalis Health System for syndromic surveillance in a rural outpatient clinic in Texas	Texas Dept. of State Health Services (DSHS)
NC DETECT	North Carolina Division of Public Health (NC DPH)
SENDSS	Georgia Division of Public Health
Syndromic surveillance system in Miami-Dade County	Office of Epidemiology & Disease Control, Miami-Dade County Health Department
Early Event Detection in San Diego	San Diego County
Syndromic Surveillance In New Jersey (NJ)	NJ Dept. of Health and Senior Services (NJDHSS)
EED in South Carolina	South Carolina Dept. of Health and Environmental Control
Indiana's pilot program for syndromic surveillance	Indiana State Dept. of Health
National Capitol Region's ED syndromic surveillance system	Maryland, the District of Columbia, and Virginia
Michigan Disease Surveillance System Syndromic Surveillance Project	Michigan Dept. of Community Health (MDCH)
HESS and HASS	Missouri Dept. of Health and Senior Services
North Dakota Department of Health Syndromic Surveillance Program	North Dakota Dept. of Health

The Syndromal Surveillance Tally Sheet program is based on the triage nurses' counts of the numbers of patients presenting the syndromes of interest collected from emergency departments of Santa Clara County, California (Bravata et al., 2002). (This manual system proved to be staff and resource intensive and was replaced by an ESSENCE implementation in 2005.)

The system used in the greater Boston area is for rapid identification of illness syndromes using automated records from 1996 through 1999 of approximately 250,000 health plan members in the area (Lazarus et al., 2001).

New Hampshire Syndromic Surveillance System collects information from multiple sites in New Hampshire including emergency departments, twenty-three city schools, five workplaces, participating pharmacies, as well as military and veteran medical facilities, and LabCorp through the BioSense program. Data are either key punched or electronically transferred into the Syndromic Tracking Encounter Management System (STEMS) for analysis and geo-coding (Miller, Fallon, & Anderson, 2003).

In the state of Connecticut, a Hospital Admissions Syndromic Surveillance system is implemented by the Connecticut Department of Public Health. This system monitors hospital admissions from the previous day rather than outpatient visits as most other syndromic systems do (Dembek et al., 2005; Dembek, Carley, Siniscalchi, & Hadler, 2004).

Catalis Health System for syndromic surveillance in Texas uses available clinic practice management systems to produce a standardized dataset via a point-of-care Electronic Medical Record (EMR). This system supports data flows directly from clinic providers to the health department for syndromic surveillance. Rural counties with limited epidemiological resources have benefited from this approach (Nekomoto, Riggins, & Franklin, 2003).

North Carolina Disease Event Tracking and Epidemiologic Collection Tool (NC DETECT), formerly known as the North Carolina Bioterrorism and Emerging Infection Prevention System, analyzes a variety of data sources including the North Carolina Emergency Department Database (NCEDD) and the Carolinas Poison Center with the EARS software tool (North Carolina Public Health Information Network, 2006).

The Georgia Division of Public Health takes a centralized approach by comparing local data to those from other districts and state totals. The clinical and non-clinical data are collected and the results of the analysis are displayed through a Web-based program called the State Electronic Notifiable Disease Surveillance System (SENDSS) (health.state.ga.us/epi/sendss.asp).

The syndromic surveillance system in Miami-Dade County, Florida (www.dadehealth.org/discontrol/DISCONTROLflucontainment.asp), is a Web-based system where syndromic data are transferred from emergency departments to an ESSENCE server for data analysis and anomaly detection.

The Early Event Detection system in San Diego constantly monitors emergency room visits, paramedic transports, 911 calls, school absenteeism data, and OTC sales for early event detection. It supports interoperability with local SAS/Minitab installations, ESSENCE, and BioSense (Johnson, 2006).

The New Jersey syndromic system includes four components: emergency department-based surveillance using visit and admission data from participating hospitals statewide and a modified CUSUM (cumulative sums) method to detect aberrations, OTC pharmacy sales surveillance from RODS, an ILI surveillance module, and a Web-based Communicable Disease Reporting System (CDRS) for real time data transmission and reporting (Hamby, 2006).

The Early Event Detection (EED) system in South Carolina provides syndromic surveillance capabilities at the state/local level using data from BioSense, OTC sales, and Palmetto Poison Center (Drociuk, Gibson, & Hodge, 2004). The EED system is among a number of disease surveillance systems in South Carolina, including ESSENCE, BioSense, and Sentinel Providers Network with ILI reporting. As of February 2006, there were 536 distinct sources providing OTC drug sales data.

Indiana's pilot program for syndromic surveillance is currently taking in data from seventeen hospitals, most of them in Indianapolis. Indiana's system is expected to include a variety of sources: coroners' reports, calls to the Indiana Poison Control Center, school absenteeism counts, lab test orders, veterinary lab results, and reports from day care centers (Lober et al., 2002).

The National Capitol Region's Emergency Department syndromic surveillance system is a cooperative effort between Maryland, the District of Columbia, and Virginia that uses chief complaints for syndromic assignment. Using a syndrome assignment matrix (Begier, Sockwell, Branch, Davies-Cole, Jones, Edwards, et al., 2003), the emergency department visits are coded into one of eight mutually exclusive syndromes: "death," "sepsis," "rash," "respiratory" illness, "gastrointestinal" illness, "unspecified infection," "neurologic" illness, and "other."

The Michigan Syndromic Surveillance Project (www.michigan.gov/mdch) tracks chief complaints using RODS. Detection algorithms run every hour and send e-mail alerts to public health officials when deviations are found. State and regional epidemiologists are provided with Web access to the charts and maps of the data analytical results.

The Hospital Electronic Syndromic Surveillance (HESS) and Hospital Admission Syndromic Surveillance (HASS) systems, implemented in the State of Missouri, are designed to provide early warning of public health emergencies including bioterrorism events and offer outbreak detection and epidemiologic monitoring functions. HESS collects data electronically from existing electronic systems and requires all hospitals to participate; HASS receives data on a paper form from selected sentinel hospitals (Missouri Department of Health and Senior Services, 2006).

The North Dakota Department of Health (2006) Syndromic Surveillance Program is based on chief complaint data received electronically from seven large hospital emergency departments located in North Dakota's four largest cities. In addition, data from a call center in North Dakota's largest city are received and reviewed daily. Data analysis functions are provided by commercial software called RedBat. More than 50 percent of the state's population is currently involved in this program.

Summary of Industrial Solutions for Syndromic Surveillance

We now discuss seven representative industrial solutions for syndromic surveillance, as summarized in Table 10.3.

Table 10.3 Industrial solutions for syndromic surveillance

System	Company
LEADERS	Idaho Technology, Inc., Salt Lake City, Utah
FirstWatch Real-Time Early Warning System	Stout Solutions, LLC., Encinitas, California
STC syndromic surveillance product	Scientific Technologies Corporation (STC), Tucson, Arizona
RedBat (Multi-use syndromic surveillance system for hospitals and public health agencies)	ICPA, Inc., Austin, Texas
EDIS (Emergisoft's Emergency Department Information System)	Emergisoft Corporate, Arlington, Texas
Spatiotemporal Epidemiological Modeler (STEM) tool	IBM, Almaden Research Center, California
Emergint Data Collection and Transformation System (DCTS)	Emergint, Inc., Louisville, Kentucky

The Lightweight Epidemiology Advanced Detection and Emergency Response System (LEADERS) is an Internet-based integrated medical surveillance system for collecting, storing, analyzing, and viewing critical medical incidents. LEADERS was deployed at the 1999 World Trade Organization Summit, both the 2000 Republican and Democratic National Conventions, the Presidential Inaugural Activities, and the Super Bowl. Portions of LEADERS have been deployed by U.S. military forces worldwide since 1998 (Ritter, 2002).

FirstWatch integrates data from 911 calling systems, emergency departments, lab tests, pharmacies, poison control centers, and paramedic practice, all of which are monitored in real time. Real-time alerting and reporting are also supported (First Watch, 2006).

The Web-based STC syndromic surveillance product (www.stchome.com) is compatible with the CDC NEDSS Logical Data Module (LDM). Its current clients include public health departments in Connecticut, Louisiana, New York City, and Washington, D.C. The analysis and alerting algorithms implemented in the system, such as CUSUM, 3rd Sigma, and STC's Zhang Methodology, are applied to a variety of data sources that include OTC sales, school nurse visits, and emergency rooms.

RedBat automatically imports existing data from hospitals and public health agencies. In addition to outbreak detection, it is also capable of tracking injuries, reportable diseases, asthma, and disaster victims (ICPA, Inc., 2006). Emergisoft is a software solution for syndromic surveillance that has been employed in the 1996 Olympics in Atlanta and in the metropolitan areas of New York City and Los Angeles (Emergisoft, 2006).

A Spatiotemporal Epidemiological Modeler (STEM) tool, developed at the IBM Almaden Research Center, can be used to develop spatial and temporal models of emerging infectious diseases. These models can involve multiple populations/species and interactions among diseases.

GIS data for every county in the U.S. have been integrated into the STEM application (Ford, Kaufman, Thomas, Eiron, & Hammer, 2005).

Emergint provides a syndromic surveillance system for data collection and processing. It can interface with care providers, laboratories, research organizations, and federal and state health departments. Emergint (2004) also provides data aggregation analysis as well as visualization functions.

Summary of International Syndromic Surveillance Projects and Syndromic Surveillance for Special Events

Table 10.4 summarizes seven international syndromic surveillance efforts.

Table 10.4 International syndromic surveillance systems

System	Agency
National Health Service (NHS) Direct Syndromic Surveillance	Operated by NHS of UK
Early Warning Outbreak Recognition System (EWORS)	Association of South East Asian Nations
Alternative Surveillance Alert Program (ASAP)	Health Canada
Emergency Department Information System in Korea	Korea
Experimental Three Syndromic Surveillances in Japan	National Institute of Infectious Diseases, Japan
Australian Sentinel Practice Research Network (ASPREN)	The Royal Australian College of General Practitioners; the Dept. of General Practice, U. of Adelaide; Australian Government Dept. of Health and Ageing
ILI surveillance in France	France

The National Health Service (NHS) in the U.K. operates an NHS Direct Syndromic Surveillance system that monitors the nurse-led telephone helpline data collected electronically by the Health Protection Agency from all twenty-three NHS Direct sites in England and Wales (Doroshenko, Cooper, Smith, Gerard, Chinemana, Verlander, et al., 2005). Syndromes monitored include cold/influenza, cough, diarrhea, difficulty breathing, double vision, eye problems, lumps, fever, rash, and vomiting. Data streams are analyzed every two hours by statistical methods such as confidence intervals and control chart methods (Cooper, Dash, Levander, Wong, Hogan, & Wagner, 2004).

The Association of South East Asian Nations (ASEAN) has developed the Early Warning Outbreak Recognition System (EWORS) for disease surveillance. EWORS (www.namru2.med.navy.mil/ewors.htm) collects data from a network of hospitals and provides technical approaches to distinguish epidemic from endemic diseases. Free-text or ICD-9 coded symptom reports can be collected through EWORS to monitor a number of infectious diseases, including malaria and hemorrhagic fever due to Hantaan virus infection. Statistical analysis methods are used for daily data analysis and visualization. The system is currently implemented by the public health departments of Indonesia, Cambodia, Vietnam, and Laos.

The Alternative Surveillance Alert Program (ASAP), initiated by Health Canada, currently monitors gastrointestinal disease trends by analyzing OTC anti-diarrheal and anti-nausea sales data and calls to Telehealth lines (Edge, Lim, Aramini, Sockett, & Pollari, 2003). The system is planned to be deployed at the community, provincial, and national levels.

In Korea, 120 emergency departments from sixteen provinces and cities are now connected to the Korea Emergency Department Information System for daily analysis of acute respiratory syndrome. The system was initially developed for the 2002 Korea-Japan FIFA (Fédération Internationale de Football Association) World Cup Games (Cho, Kim, Yoo, Ahn, Wang, Hur, et al., 2003).

The National Institute of Infectious Diseases (NIID) has developed a syndromic surveillance system based on EARS syndrome categories and EARS software to analyze OTC sales data, outpatient visits, and ambulance transfer data in Tokyo (Ohkusa, Shigematsu, Taniguchi, & Okabe, 2005; Ohkusa, Sugawara, Hiroaki, Kawaguchi, Taniguchi, & Okabe, 2005). Approximately 5,000 sites nationwide in Japan are now connected to this system. The system was used for the 2000 G8 Summit and 2002 FIFA World Cup Games.

The Australian Sentinel Practice Research Network (ASPREN) is a national network of general practitioners who collect and report data on selected conditions such as ILI for weekly statistical analysis (Clothier, Fielding, & Kelly, 2006). It is now being used by about fifty general practitioners throughout Australia.

ILI surveillance is practiced in 11,000 pharmacies throughout France (about 50 percent of all pharmacies in the country) in 21 regions. This ILI surveillance system is a Web-based system that collects medication sales and weekly office visit data to provide forecasts of influenza outbreaks using a Poisson regression model (Vergu, Grais, Sarter, Fagot, Lambert, Valleron, et al., 2006).

The last category of syndromic surveillance practice surveyed in this chapter is concerned with syndromic surveillance for special and large-scale events. Teams of public health officials often need to work together to monitor public health status for such events (e.g., the 2002 World Series in Phoenix [Das, Weiss, & Mostashari, 2003] and the wildfire outbreak in San Diego, 2003 [Johnson, Hicks, McClean, & Ginsberg, 2005]). During the Korea-Japan FIFA World Cup 2002 in Japan (Suzuki, Ohyama, Taniguchi, Kimura, Kobayashi, Okabe, et al., 2003) and Korea (Cho et al., 2003), syndromic surveillance systems also played a role in public health status monitoring. Two other examples are the syndromic surveillance systems implemented for the 2002 Kentucky Derby (Goss, Carrico, Hall, & Humbaugh, 2003) and G8 Summit in Gleneagles,

Auchterarder, Scotland in 2005 (G8 Gleneagles 2005 statement on counter-terrorism, 2005). Typically, data from regional emergency departments will be collected during the events. Information concerning a pre-defined list of symptoms and probable diagnoses will also be collected manually using special-purpose forms or via a Web-based interface. Table 10.5 summarizes six representative efforts in this category.

Table 10.5 Syndromic surveillance efforts for special events

Syndromic surveillance systems for special events	Stakeholders/Location
Syndromic surveillance for Korea-Japan FIFA World Cup 2002 in Japan	National Institute of Infectious Diseases, Japan
Communitywide syndromic surveillance for 2002 Kentucky Derby	University of Louisville Hospital and Jefferson County Health Dept., Kentucky
Syndromic surveillance for Korea-Japan FIFA World Cup 2002 in Korea	Korea
Drop-in bioterrorism surveillance system for World Series 2002 in Phoenix, Arizona	Phoenix, Arizona
Syndromic surveillance during the wildfires outbreak in San Diego, 2003	San Diego County, California
Syndromic surveillance for G8 Summit in Gleneagles, Auchterarder, Scotland, July 2005	Scotland, UK

In addition to the surveillance efforts of varying dimensions summarized here, there has been increasing need for the development of syndromic surveillance systems at the global scale. The World Health Organization's (WHO) Epidemic and Pandemic Alert and Response program (www.who.int/csr/en) represents one such effort at global syndromic surveillance. It should be noted that the challenge of implementing a global surveillance system is more of a policy and administration than a technical issue.

In the next sections we discuss syndromic data collection strategies; summarize analytical approaches employed; and evaluate the security, efficiency, scalability, and capacity of existing systems.

Data Sources and Collection Strategies

Data collection is a critical early step when developing a syndromic surveillance system. It involves the selection of data sources, choices of vocabulary to be used, data entry approaches, and data transmission strategies and protocols. Related technical issues will be discussed in the following subsections. Toward the end of this section, we briefly summarize additional policy-related considerations that may affect data collection.

Data Sources for Public Health Syndromic Surveillance

Syndromic surveillance is largely a data-driven public health surveillance approach. Data sources used in syndromic surveillance systems are expected to provide timely, pre-diagnosis health indicators and are typically electronically stored and transmitted. Most syndromic surveillance data were originally collected and used for other purposes and such data now serve dual-purposes. In their empirical study, Platt et al. (2003) found that most data collected for syndromic surveillance purposes include similar elements: demographic data such as gender, age, area of residence; and data relevant to patient visits such as hospital name, date of visit, and symptom set (chief complaints or admission status).

In this survey, we identify the range of syndromic data sources and briefly summarize how they are used. Healthcare providers, schools, pharmacies, laboratories, and military medical facilities are all data contributors for syndromic surveillance. Specifically, data used for syndromic surveillance include emergency department (ED) visit chief complaints, ambulatory visit records, hospital admissions, OTC drug sales from pharmacy stores, triage nurse calls, 911 calls, work or school absenteeism data, veterinary health records, laboratory test orders, and health department requests for influenza testing (Ma et al., 2005).

A quantitative compilation of our research results shows that most of the syndromic surveillance systems monitor a combination of data sources from multiple sites instead of relying on a single data indicator. Of the 50 systems numerated in Tables 10.1 through 10.5, for which the details are known, 60 percent use ED chief complaints (both free text and ICD-9 coded chief complaints) as a timely public health indicator. Fifty percent of the systems monitor OTC drug sales. Thirty percent of the systems use hospital admission data as one of the inputs. Thirty of the systems also collect school/work absenteeism data. However, absenteeism or drug sales are never used alone. A few systems also connect to poison control centers or laboratories for test orders, or monitor 911 calls. Figure 10.1 shows the usage of the six primary syndromic surveillance data sources. Additionally, chief complaints from patient encounters are collected more often as free text (70 percent) than in ICD-9 coded formats (30 percent), which may suggest the importance of natural language processing techniques for medical information processing in this area.

A major question about the data used in surveillance activities concerns their effectiveness and validity for illness pattern detection. To be valid in the context of syndromic surveillance, evidence is needed that a data source may have value in identifying an outbreak or biological attack. A number of studies have examined to some degree whether and how effective the data sources are, as well as a possible time lead compared with diagnosis. Magruder's (2003) study of OTC data/sales as a possible early warning indicator of human diseases revealed about a 90 percent correlation between flu-remedy sales and physician diagnoses of acute respiratory conditions together with a 3-day lead time reported. Another study (Doroshenko et al., 2005) shows that nurse-led helpline calls can also be used for early event detection. The SSIC (Syndromic Surveillance Information Collection) program tested the use of visit-level

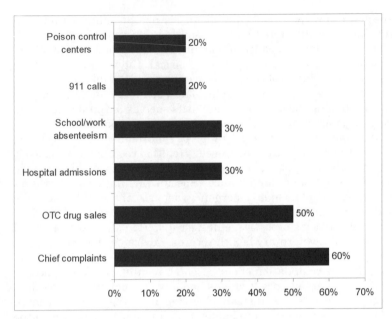

Figure 10.1 Primary data sources monitored.

discharge diagnoses from several clinical information systems as a syndromic data source (Duchin, Karras, Trigg, Bliss, Vo, Ciliberti, et al., 2001; Lober, Trigg, Karras, Bliss, Ciliberti, Stewart, et al., 2003). One limitation of using chief complaints as syndromic data is that they provide different predictive values from discharge diagnosis. Generally, chief complaints best capture illnesses mainly characterized by nonspecific symptoms like fever, while discharge diagnoses appear better at tracking illnesses requiring brief ED clinical evaluation and testing, such as sepsis and possibly meningitis (Begier et al., 2003).

Most syndromic surveillance systems use multiple data sources, so it is important to establish whether the different data are telling the same story, that is, flagging possible outbreaks for certain illness with consistency. Edge, Pollari, and Lim (2004) reported correlations between OTC anti-nausea and anti-diarrhea medication sales and ED admissions. However, a study conducted by the Infectious Disease Surveillance Center, Japan (Ohkusa, Shigematsu, et al., 2005), found no evidence that sales of OTC medications used to treat the common cold correlated with influenza activities.

Preliminary investigations have evaluated the effectiveness of various data sources in syndromic surveillance and studied the differences among them in terms of information timeliness and characterization ability for outbreak detection, as they represent various aspects of patient healthcare-seeking behavior (Ma et al., 2005). For example, school/work absenteeism comes to notice relatively early as individuals take leave before seeking healthcare in hospitals or clinics, but specific disease evidence provided by the absenteeism data is limited. Table 10.6 provides a classification of different data sources used for syndromic surveillance organized by their timeliness and capability to characterize epidemic events.

Table 10.6 Data sources and their timeliness and disease characterization capability

Data source	Description	Specificity*	Timeliness**	Advantages	Weaknesses
Chief complaints from ED visits or ambulatory visits	Patient-reported signs and symptoms of their illness (e.g., coughing, headache, etc.) (Bradley et al., 2005; Espino & Wagner, 2001; Lombardo et al., 2004)	High	Medium-High	Routinely generated; available typically on the same day the patient is seen; and often available in electronic format	Available in short free-text phrases that contain misspellings and abbreviations; need to be cleaned; vocabulary differences across hospitals
OTC medication sales, prescription medication data	Medication sales data indicative of certain illness (e.g., influenza) as patients seek remedies (Besculides, Heffernan, Mostashari, & Weiss, 2004; Thomas, Arouh, Carley, Kraiman, & Davis, 2005)	Medium-High	High	Providing early signs and indications more timely than patient visits; data routinely generated and available in electronic format	Additional information about medication purchasers unknown
School or work absenteeism	Collected from school or workplace (Besculides et al., 2004; Thomas et al., 2005)	Low-Medium	High	Timely	Lack of disease characterization (Quenel, Dab, Hannoun, & Cohen, 1994)
Hospital admission	Data is recorded when hospitalization takes place (Dembek et al., 2004; Dembek et al., 2005)	High	Medium	Highly reliable disease diagnosis	Generally an interval (1–3 days) exists between the first health care visit and admission. (Buehler et al., 2003)

Table 10.6 (*cont.*)

Triage nurse calls, 911 calls	Symptoms of signs recorded during patient calls consulting health care nurses (Crubézy et al., 2005)	High	Relatively timely, as patients usually make phone calls before office visit	Need to be cleaned	
ICD-9 (International Classification of Diseases, 9th edition) coded billing info	Preliminary diagnosis for billing (Begier et al., 2003; Espino & Wagner, 2001; Tsui, Wagner, Dato, & Chang, 2002)	High	Medium	May provide a better positive predictive value than chief complaints. Available in most electronic medical systems	Often available after a relatively brief ED evaluation (days or weeks after an encounter)
ICD-9-CM (International Classification of Diseases, 9th edition, Clinical Modification)	Allow assignment of codes to diagnoses and procedures; often used for third-party insurance reimbursement purposes	High	Medium	Relatively timely and specific regarding illness characterization	Often assigned to patient visit days or even weeks after patient encounter
Laboratory test orders	Orders for laboratory tests (Wagner, Tsui, Espino, Dato, Sittig, Caruana, et al., 2001)	Medium	Medium-High	Relatively timely and specific regarding illness characterization	
Laboratory test results	Results of laboratory tests	High	Low	Disease cases can be reported with high reliability	Lack of timeliness (test results may take more than a week)
Public sources (local or regional events)	News reports or bulletin notification	Low	Information reference	May not be available when needed	

* Disease characterization capability
** Time lead advancing the confirmed diagnosis

Standardized Vocabularies

Significance of Standard Development

Data standard development, or more generally interoperability, is a key to successful, cross-jurisdictional syndromic surveillance. A standardized syndromic data representation would have a number of implications. First, a specialized vocabulary enables accurate representation for communicating information and events. Data formats and coding conventions that are inconsistent across different sites (e.g., laboratory tests and results can be reported in multiple ways) could be an obstacle in capturing illness cases.

More importantly, streamlining the delivery of electronic data across multiple sites saves time and eventually enables real-time reporting and alerting. Real-time data transmission and event reporting with a universal data format standard and messaging protocol are primary motivators in the development of syndromic surveillance systems. Due to differences in internal data structures and database schema among various healthcare information systems, it takes a significant amount of time and processing resources for data conversion and normalization. According to a 2004 estimate, the use of data exchange standards in healthcare could save up to $78 billion annually (Pan, 2004).

In addition, syndromic surveillance systems that are complex and geographically distributed need to be interoperable to enhance jurisdictional collaboration for timely event detection and response. Therefore, developing and imposing standards from programmatic, constructive, architectural, and managerial perspectives is a major focus of CDC-led syndromic surveillance initiatives. These are collaborative efforts involving the Public Health Information Network (PHIN) framework (www.cdc.gov/phin/index.html), the National Electronic Disease Surveillance System (NEDSS) (Centers for Disease Control and Prevention, 2004), the National Center for Vital Health Statistics, Department of Defense, Department of Veterans Affairs, and all National Institutes of Health.

This section discusses the development, adoption, and implementation of standard vocabularies for electronic emergency room records, laboratory testing, clinical observations, and prescriptions, along with the messaging standard to transport these records. Many available code standards currently used in syndromic surveillance have been borrowed from public health systems (Wurtz, 2004). Current efforts to standardize vocabulary are based on Logical Observation Identifiers Names and Codes (LOINC), Systematized Nomenclature of Medicine (SNOMED), International Classification of Diseases, Ninth Revision (ICD-9), and Current Procedural Terminology (CPT) as core vocabularies. In addition, the Unified Medical Language System (UMLS) has been used as a cross-reference ontology among these coding systems. Health Level Seven (HL7) is used as a messaging standard in public health.

Existing Data Standards in Syndromic Surveillance

Here we provide a brief summary of each coding system to illustrate their scope and target medical domain (see Table 10.7).

UMLS: The Unified Medical Language System (UMLS) (www.nlm.nih.gov/research/umls) provides a cross-reference ontology among a number of different biomedical coding systems and standards, and a semantic structure defining relationships among different clinical entities. Its Semantic Network and Metathesaurus help system

Table 10.7 Adopted healthcare information standards in syndromic surveillance

Clinical vocabulary	Main contents	Advantages	Limitations
UMLS	The UMLS Metathesaurus is a collection of different source vocabularies, organized according to meaning and lexical characteristics of terms. The Semantic Network contains explicit biomedical concepts and relationships.	Provides the cross-referencing between multiple vocabularies	Lacking granularity for medical diagnosis and syndromic surveillance (Lu, Zeng, & Chen, 2006)
LOINC	Laboratory results and observations. Could refer to a laboratory value (e.g., potassium, white blood cell count) or a clinical finding (e.g., blood pressure, EKG pattern)	Contains many genetic tests. It is mapped to UMLS and SNOMED RT and CT	Not suitable to capture the purpose or results of the test.
SNOMED-CT (SNOMED-Clinical Terminology)	Used to distinguish concepts for the condition (e.g., pertussis) and the causative organism (e.g., bordetella pertussis), suitable to code laboratory results, non-laboratory interventions and procedures, and anatomy and diagnosis	Combines SNOMED RT and Clinical Terms Version 3	Proprietary
SNOMED-RT (SNOMED-Reference Terminology)	Includes concepts and terms for findings (disorders and clinical findings by site, method, and function), normal structures (anatomy/topography) and abnormal structures (pathology/morphology)	Well-tested and have been used in the field for decades	Proprietary
ICD-9-CM	Used to code morbidity data, final diagnosis, procedures, and reimbursement	Widely used (state-mandated)	Not suitable for clinical documentation of diagnoses, symptoms, signs and problem lists. (Hogan, Wagner, & Tsui, 2002)

developers build or enhance electronic information systems that integrate and/or aggregate biomedical and health data and knowledge.

LOINC: LOINC (www.regenstrief.org/loinc) codes are universal identifiers for laboratory and other clinical observations. Distinct LOINC codes are assigned based on specimen types (e.g., "ser" = serum) and methods of the test (e.g., immune fluorescence), with specific descriptions for different conditions. Because LOINC codes were originally developed for billing purposes, they do not convey information about the purpose or results of the test (Wurtz, 2004). The CDC has developed Nationally Notifiable Conditions Mapping Tables (www.cdc.gov/PHIN/data_ models), which provide mappings from LOINC codes to nationally notifiable (and some state-notifiable) diseases or conditions.

SNOMED: SNOMED (www.snomed.org) is a nomenclature classification scheme for indexing medical vocabulary, including signs, symptoms, diagnoses, and procedures. It defines code standards in a variety of clinical areas, called coding axes. It can identify procedures and possible answers to clinical questions that are coded through LOINC.

ICD-9-CM: ICD-9-CM was developed to allow assignment of codes to diagnoses and procedures associated with hospital utilization in the United States and is often used for third-party insurance reimbursement purposes.

HL7: HL7 (www.HL7.org) (Hooda, Dogdu, & Sunderraman, 2004; Thomas & Mead, 2005) is the American National Standards Institute (ANSI)-accredited healthcare standard messaging format, used for transmitting information across a variety of clinical and administrative healthcare information systems. It specifies the syntax that describes where a computer algorithm can find various data elements in a transmitted message, enabling it to parse the message and reliably extract the data elements contained therein. HL7 Version 2.3 provides a protocol that enables the flow of data between systems. HL7 Version 3.0 (Beeler, 1998) is being developed through the use of a formalized methodology involving the creation of a Reference Information Model to encompass the ability not only to move data, but also to use them once they have been moved.

Development and adaptation of coding standards and standardized messaging formats are essential for information exchange and sharing, a prerequisite for public health surveillance. However, different standards and implementations exist for operational clinical, laboratory, and hospital information systems, which causes significant obstacles for information sharing. Nonetheless, standards are being developed, improved, and adopted increasingly widely.

In addition to leveraging existing healthcare standards, some groups have proposed additional coding and messaging standards tailored specifically for syndromic surveillance. For example, the Frontlines group (Barthell, Aronsky, Cochrane, Cable, & Stair, 2004; Barthell, Cordell, Moorhead, Handler, Feied, Smith, et al., 2002) is focusing on the development of standard reporting and coding structures specific to syndromic data. They have defined the data elements in triage surveillance reports and a set of codified values for chief complaints. They have also proposed a system to facilitate continuous flow of XML (eXtensible

Mark-up Language)-based triage report data among hospital EDs, and state and local health agencies.

In addition to technical considerations, regulatory and compliance issues also need to be examined carefully in the context of data standardization challenges. For instance, the U.S. has implemented laws, such as HIPAA's (Health Insurance Portability and Accountability Act) Administrative Simplification, to enforce standardization in healthcare information through such mandates as requiring health plans, healthcare clearinghouses, and providers that conduct certain transactions electronically to comply with the HIPAA transaction standards (mass.gov/dph/comm/hipaa/background.htm).

Data Entry and Data Transmission

Syndromic data are being collected through various kinds of healthcare and public health information systems. This section discusses related data entry and transmission techniques.

Data Entry Approaches

Data entry approaches for syndromic surveillance fall into four categories: paper-based forms, Web-based interfaces, local data input software applications, and hand-held devices (Zelicoff et al., 2001). Many systems support multiple data entry approaches because they involve multiple sites with possibly different IT infrastructure support (Espino et al., 2004; Lombardo et al., 2003). In general, the manual approach using paper-based forms can lead to unwanted delays as the records must be converted to an electronic format.

Secure Data Transmission

Secure data transmission is critical to data integrity and confidentiality. The specific challenges are: How can a syndromic surveillance system retrieve syndromic data from data providers (e.g., hospitals and pharmacies)? How can data transfers be done securely over communication channels such as the Internet?

Existing transmission approaches are either automated or manual. *Automated* transmission refers to transferring of data over a communication media where human intervention (e.g., to initiate each transmission transaction) is not required. Manual transmission entails significant human intervention. Figure 10.2 shows commonly used data transmission techniques.

About 33 percent of the 50 systems surveyed rely primarily on automated data transmission. The remainder requires human intervention for both data requesting and receiving. E-mail messages with text reports or data files as attachments, in spite of the security and data exposure risks, are still widely used to transfer syndromic data from clinical systems to syndromic surveillance systems.

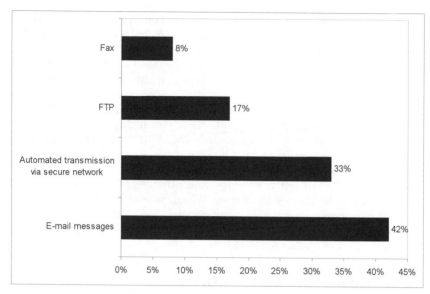

Figure 10.2 **Data transmission techniques for syndromic surveillance data.**

The XML-based HL7 messaging standards play an important role in automated data transmission because a significant portion of health systems support HL7. Among the systems surveyed, those capable of automated data transmission all use HL7 in one form or another. For example, the RODS system and the BioPortal system use HL7 messaging protocols for automatic syndromic data transmission. In RODS, an HL7 listener implemented as Enterprise JavaBean (EJB) receives HL7 messages from each underlying health system. The messages transmitted are first parsed by an HL7 parser bean before being loaded into the database. A configuration file written in XML specifies the hierarchical structure of the data elements in each HL7 message (Tsui, Espino, Dato, Gesteland, Hutman, & Wagner, 2003). BioPortal also replies on an HL7-based approach to transmit data as HL7-compliant XML messages. This allows for dynamic changes in the message structure (Hu, Zeng, Chen, Larson, Chang, & Tseng, 2005; Zeng, Chen, Tseng, Larson, Eidson, Gotham, et al., 2004).

Compared with other approaches that support file-based transmissions in a batch mode, HL7-based approaches are more efficient and effective. According to a RODS study (Tsui, Espino, & Wagner, 2005), they could reduce reporting latency by twenty hours. Secure networking techniques such as VPNs (Virtual Private Networks), SSL (secure socket layer), HTTPS, and SFTP (secure file transfer protocol) are being increasingly utilized (Rhodes & Kailar, 2005).

Is there a best approach to transmit data from data providers to syndromic surveillance systems and the relevant public health agencies?

There is no simple answer to this question. Typically the IT infrastructure of the data providers (e.g., hospitals) needs to be upgraded to enable timely, reliable, and secure data collection.

Many practical challenges hindering the data collection effort also need to be addressed: 1) providing and transmitting data either requires staff intervention or dedicated network infrastructure, which often require extra costs; 2) data sharing and transmission must comply with HIPAA and other privacy regulations; 3) reducing data acquisition latency has important implications for syndromic surveillance yet is difficult and can be costly; 4) data quality concerns (e.g., incompleteness and duplication) often pose additional challenges. In particular, data ownership, confidentiality, security, and other legal and policy-related issues need to be closely examined. When infectious disease data sets are shared across jurisdictions, important access control and security issues should be resolved in advance among the various data providers and users (Hu et al., 2005).

Data Analysis and Outbreak Detection

The analysis components of a syndromic surveillance system focus on detecting changes in public health status that may be indicative of disease outbreaks. At the core of these components is the automated process of detecting aberration or anomalies in public health surveillance data, which often have prominent temporal and spatial data elements, by statistical analysis or data mining techniques.

When processing public health surveillance data streams, it is often necessary to map the syndromic data into a small set of syndrome categories to facilitate follow-up analysis and outbreak detection. The first subsection discusses related syndrome classification approaches. In the next subsection, we provide a taxonomy of anomaly analysis and outbreak detection methods used in biosurveillance. The remaining subsections summarize specific detection methods spanning classic statistical methods to data mining approaches, which quantify the possibility of an outbreak based on surveillance data.

Syndrome Classification

The onset of a number of syndromes can indicate certain diseases threatening public health. For example, the influenza-like syndrome could be due to an anthrax attack, which is of particular interest to biodefense. Syndrome classification thus is one of the first and most important steps in syndromic data processing and analysis.

A substantial amount of research effort has been expended to classify free-text chief complaints into syndromes. This classification task is difficult because different expressions, acronyms, abbreviations, and truncations are often found in free-text chief complaints (Sniegoski, 2004). For example, "chst pn," "CP," "c/p," "chest pai," "chert pain," "chest/abd pain," and "chest discomfort" can all mean "chest pain." Based on our summary findings reported in the section on data entry approaches, a majority of syndromic surveillance systems use chief complaints as a major source of data. Therefore, the problem of mapping each chief complaint record to a syndrome category, referred to as syndrome classification, is an important practical challenge needing a solution. Another syndromic data type often used for syndromic surveillance purposes, such as ICD-9 or ICD-9-CM codes, also needs to be grouped into syndrome categories. Processing such information is somewhat easier because the data records are structured. A syndrome category is defined as a set of symptoms that is an indicator of some specific diseases. For example, a short-phrase chief complaint "coughing with high fever" can be classified as the "upper respiratory" syndrome. Table 10.8 summarizes some of the most commonly monitored syndrome categories. Note that different syndromic surveillance systems may monitor different categories. For example, in the RODS system there are seven syndrome groups of interest for bio-surveillance purposes; EARS defines a more detailed list of forty-three syndromes. Some syndromes (e.g., respiratory or gastrointestinal) are of common interest across different systems.

Table 10.8 Diseases and syndrome categories commonly monitored

Influenza-like	Respiratory	Dermatological
Fever	Neurologic	Cold
Gastrointestinal	Rash	Diarrhea
Hemorrhagic illness	Severe illness and death	Asthma
Localized cutaneous lesion	Specific infection	Vomit
Lymphadenitis	Sepsis	Other/none of the above
Constitutional		
Bioterrorism agent-related diseases		
Anthrax	Botulism-like/botulism	Plague
Tularemia	Smallpox	SARS (Severe Acute Respiratory Syndrome)

Syndrome Classification Approaches

Syndrome classification can be undertaken either as a manual process or through an automated system. The BioSense system, developed by CDC (Ma et al., 2005), for instance, relies on a working group that develops syndrome mapping using CDC definitions. However, automated, computerized syndrome classification is essential to real-time syndromic surveillance. The software application that evaluates the patient's chief complaints or ICD-9 codes and then determines a syndrome category is often known as a syndrome classifier.

Classification methods that have been studied and employed can be fitted into three groups: 1) rule-based classification, such as text string searching methods employed by EARS and ESSENCE (Hutwagner et al., 2003); 2) natural language processing, such as the Bayesian classifiers proposed by RODS (Ivanov, Wagner, Chapman, & Olszewski, 2002; Sniegoski, 2004); and 3) ontology-based classification methods (Leroy & Chen, 2001) that include UMLS vocabularies and semantics, as proposed in the BioPortal project (Lu, Zeng, & Chen, 2006). We summarize representative syndrome classification methods in Table 10.9.

Performance of Syndrome Classification Approaches

Based on our survey, about 40 percent of syndromic surveillance systems use automated syndrome classification, with another 40 percent relying on a manual approach (details are unknown for the remaining 20 percent). There appears to be a lot of room for improvement and the adoption of automated methods.

Evaluation studies have been conducted to compare various classifiers' performance for selected syndrome types (Travers & Haas, 2004). For instance, experiments comparing two Bayesian classifiers for the acute gastrointestinal syndrome showed a 68 percent mapping success against expert classification of ED reports (Ivanov et al., 2002). In general, however, it is difficult to paint a general picture of how well syndromic classifiers perform and how they fare against each other, as many of these systems have not been evaluated on classification accuracy. In addition, the performance of these classifiers varies with different syndrome categories, further complicating the evaluation task.

Many prior studies show that a considerable portion (30 to 40 percent) of the chief complaints data are not classifiable because they are so noisy. However, combining chief complaints with the diagnostic codes (such as ICD-9) during the same visit can result in more accurate classification (Reis & Mandl, 2004).

Another challenge facing syndrome classification is that there are no universally accepted, standardized syndrome definitions. As a result, significant rewriting/fine-tuning efforts are needed when applying a classification approach in particular application contexts. One possible approach to deal with these difficulties is to create intermediary representations (such as symptom groups) and create explicit rules that map these intermediary representations onto customized syndrome categories (Lu et al., 2006).

A Taxonomy of Outbreak Detection Methods

Syndromic surveillance systems typically offer multiple outbreak detection algorithms because no single method can deliver superior performance across a wide range of scenarios or meet different surveillance objectives (Buckeridge, Musen, Switzer, & Crubézy, 2003).

Many statistical and data mining techniques for syndromic surveillance have been proposed in the literature. These can be divided into retrospective and prospective approaches. If we consider instead the characteristics of the surveillance data analyzed, another orthogonal classification scheme is possible, dividing the outbreak detection methods

Table 10.9 Representative syndrome classification approaches

Category	Example Approaches	Application
Manual grouping	Medical experts in syndromic surveillance, infectious diseases, and medical informatics perform the mapping of laboratory test orders into syndrome categories (Ma et al., 2005).	The BioSense system (Bradley et al., 2005; Sokolow et al., 2005) and Syndromal Surveillance Tally Sheet program used in EDs of Santa Clara County, California.
Natural language processing (NLP)	NLP-based approaches classify free-text CCs with simplified grammar containing rules for nouns, adjectives, prepositional phrases, and conjunctions. Critiques of NLP-based methods include lack of semantic markings in chief complaints and the amount of training needed.	As part of RODS, Chapman et al. adapted the MPLUS, a Bayesian network-based NLP system, to classify the free-text chief complaints (Chapman et al., 2005; Wagner, Espino, Tsui, Gesteland, Chapman, Ivanov, et al., 2004).
Bayesian classifiers	Bayesian classifiers, including naïve Bayesian classifiers, bigram Bayes, and their variations, can classify CCs learned from the training data consisting of labeled CCs.	The CoCo Bayesian classifier from the RODS project (Chapman, Cooper, Hanbury, Chapman, Harrison, & Wagner, 2003).
Text string searching	A rule-based method that first uses keyword matching and synonym lists to standardize CCs. Predefined rules are then used to classify CCs or ICD-9 codes into syndrome categories.	EARS (Yih, Abrams, Danila, Green, Kleinman, Kulldorf, et al., 2005), ESSENCE (Centers for Disease Control and Prevention, 2003b), and the National Bioterrorism Syndromic Surveillance Demonstration Program (Yih et al., 2005).
Vocabulary abstraction	This approach creates a series of intermediate abstractions up to a syndrome category from the individual data (e.g., signs, lab tests) for syndromes indicative of illness due to an agent of bioterrorism.	The BioStorm system (Buckeridge et al., 2002; Crubézy, O'Connor, Pincus, & Musen, 2005; Shahar & Musen, 1996).
Ontology-based classification	A rule-based system that can generalize symptoms grouping rules based on UMLS-derived vocabularies and semantics. It provides a flexible architecture for changing or adapting new syndromic categories.	The syndromic mapping component of the BioPortal system (Lu et al., 2006).

into temporal analysis, spatial analysis, and spatial-temporal analysis approaches. This subsection focuses on both schemes.

Interested readers are referred to StatPages.net (statpages.org), which provides tutorials for various kinds of parametric and non-parametric statistical tests that form the statistical foundation of outbreak detection, and Statistical Data Mining Tutorials (www.autonlab.

org/tutorials), which include statistical data mining and machine learning tutorials. Review articles on data mining and its application in health and medical information (Bath, 2004; Benoît, 2002) also provide in-depth background for the material presented in this section.

Retrospective vs. Prospective Syndromic Surveillance

Several surveillance approaches fall under the general umbrella of *retrospective* models, which aim at testing statistically whether events are randomly distributed over space and time for a predefined geographical region during a predetermined time period (Kulldorff, 2001). Examples of retrospective methods include space scan statistic (www.satscan.org) (Kulldorff, 1997), Nearest Neighbor Hierarchical Clustering (NNH) (Levine, 2002), and Risk-adjusted Support Vector Clustering (RSVC) (Zeng, Chang, et al., 2004). When applying retrospective methods, there is usually a clear distinction between the baseline data points and the observations of interest, where the baseline data correspond to known "normal" health status and the observations of interest are case reports to be examined for surveillance purposes. In applications where the separation between the baseline data and observations of interest can be cleanly and meaningfully done, retrospective methods can be applied effectively.

One major limitation of retrospective methods is that they are slow in detecting emerging clusters when the separation between the baseline data and observations of interest is not obvious. The resulting manual trial-and-error interventions severely limit the applicability of retrospective methods.

Prospective surveillance often entails repeated analyses performed periodically on incoming surveillance data streams to identify statistically significant changes (Chang et al., 2005). Using such a method, the separation of the baseline data and observations of interest is no longer needed because the system automatically tries various combinations of time windows for the baseline and periods after them as the time of interest.

Prospective analysis has long been used in disease surveillance applications. The CUSUM method is one of the most established methods. Other examples include Rogerson's approaches (Rogerson, 1997), Kulldorff's (2001) prospective version of time-space scan statistics, and the Prospective Support Vector Clustering (PSVC) method (Chang et al., 2005).

Temporal, Spatial, and Spatial-Temporal Outbreak Detection Methods

Table 10.10 summarizes a wide range of outbreak detection methods, all of them implemented in one or more of the syndromic surveillance systems we surveyed. They are divided into three groups: temporal, spatial, and spatial-temporal (Buckeridge, Switzer, Owens, Siegrist, Pavlin,

& Musen, 2005; Mandl et al., 2004). This table does not attempt to list every detection algorithm proposed in the literature. Interested readers can refer to the work of Brookmeyer and Stroup (2004) and Lawson and Kleinman (2005) for recent in-depth reviews of a more comprehensive set of algorithms. The methods listed in Table 10.10 are chosen because of their connection with the syndromic surveillance systems surveyed. Although not exhaustive, Table 10.10 covers most of the detection method types and provides a useful picture of current practice.

Because of the importance of outbreak detection algorithms for syndromic surveillance, we shall review some of the critical methods adopted in more detail.

Temporal Data Analysis

This section discusses representative temporal anomaly detection methods.

Statistical Process Control (SPC)-Based Anomaly Detection

A majority of the systems surveyed employ statistical process control (SPC)-based algorithms. These algorithms were originally developed to monitor a process and its mean in industrial settings. The

Table 10.10 Outbreak detection algorithms

Algorithm	Short Description	Availability and Applications	Features and Problems
Temporal Analysis			
Serfling method	A static cyclic regression model with predefined parameters optimized through the training data.	Available from RODS (Tsui et al., 2002); used by CDC for flu detection; Costagliola et al. (1991) applied Serfling's method to the French influenza-like illness surveillance.	The model fits data poorly during epidemic periods. To use this method, the epidemic period has to be predefined.
Autoregressive Integrated Moving Average (ARIMA)	A linear function learns parameters from historical data. Seasonal effect can be adjusted.	Available from RODS.	Suitable for stationary environments.
Recursive Least Square (RLS)	A dynamic autoregressive linear model that predicts the current count of each syndrome within a region based on the historical data; it continuously adjusts	Available from RODS.	Suitable for dynamic environments.

Table 10.10 (*cont.*)

	model coefficients based on prediction errors.		
Exponentially Weighted Moving Average (EWMA)	Predictions based on exponential smoothing of previous several weeks of data with recent days having the highest weight (Neubauer, 1997).	Available from ESSENCE.	Allowing the adjustment of shift sensitivity by applying different weighting factors.
Cumulative Sums (CUSUM)	A control chart-based method to monitor for the departure of the mean of the observations from the estimated mean (Das et al., 2003; Grigoryan, Wagner, Waller, Wallstrom, & Hogan, 2005). It allows for limited baseline data.	Widely used in current surveillance systems including BioSense, EARS (Hutwagner, Thompson, Seeman, & Treadwell, 2003), and ESSENCE, among others.	This method performs well for quick detection of subtle changes in the mean (Rogerson, 2005); it is criticized for its lack of adjustability for seasonal or day-of-week effects.
Hidden Markov Models (HMM)	HMM-based methods use a hidden state to capture the presence or absence of an epidemic of a particular disease and learn probabilistic models of observations conditioned on the epidemic status.	Discussed by Rath, Carreras, and Sebastiani (2003).	A flexible model that can adapt automatically to trends, seasonality, covariates (e.g., gender and age), and different distributions (normal, Poisson, etc.).
Wavelet algorithms	Local frequency-based data analysis methods; they can automatically adjust to weekly, monthly, and seasonal data fluctuations.	Used in NRDM to indicate zip-code areas in which OTC medication sales are substantially increased (Espino & Wagner, 2001; Zhang, Tsui, Wagner, & Hogan, 2003).	Account for both long-term (e.g., seasonal effects) and short-term trends (e.g., day-of-week effects) (Wagner, Tsui et al., 2004).
Spatial Analysis			
Generalized Linear Mixed Modeling (GLMM)	Evaluating whether observed counts in relatively small areas are larger than expected on the basis of the history of naturally occurring diseases) (Kleinman, Abrams, Kulldorff, & Platt, 2005; Kleinman et al., 2004).	Used in Minnesota (Yih et al., 2005).	Sensitive to a small number of spatially focused cases; poor in detecting elevated counts over contiguous areas when compared with scan statistic and spatial CUSUM approaches (Kleinman et al., 2004).
SMall Area Regression and Testing (SMART)	An adaptation of GLMM that takes into account multiple comparisons and includes parameters	Available from BioSense and National Bioterrorism Syndromic	Seasonal, weekly effects, and other parameters under consideration can be adjusted during the

Table 10.10 (*cont.*)

	for ZIP code, day of the week, holiday, and seasonal cyclic variation.	Surveillance Demonstration Program (Yih et al., 2005).	regression process.
Spatial scan statistics and variations	The basic model relies on using simply shaped areas to scan the entire region of interest based on well-defined likelihood ratios. Its variation takes into account factors such as people mobility.	Widely adopted by many syndromic surveillance systems; a variation proposed by Duczmal and Buckeridge (2005); visualization available from BioPortal (Zeng, Chang et al., 2004).	Well-tested for various outbreak scenarios with positive results; the geometric shape of the hotspots identified is limited.
Bayesian spatial scan statistics	Combining Bayesian modeling techniques with the spatial scan statistics method; outputting the posterior probability that an outbreak has occurred, and the distribution of this probability over possible outbreak regions.	Available from RODS (Neill, Moore, & Cooper, 2005).	Computationally efficient; can easily incorporate prior knowledge such as the size and shape of outbreak or the impact on the disease infection rate.
Spatial-Temporal Analysis			
Space-time scan statistic	An extension of the space scan statistic that searches all the sub-regions for likely clusters in space and time with multiple likelihood ratio testing (Kulldorff, 2001).	Widely used in many community surveillance systems including the National Bioterrorism Syndromic Surveillance Demonstration Program (Yih et al., 2004).	Regions identified may be too large in coverage.
What is Strange About Recent Event (WSARE)	Searching for groups with specific characteristics (e.g., a recent pattern of place, age, and diagnosis associated with illness that is anomalous when compared with historic patterns) (Kaufman et al., 2005).	Available from RODS. Implemented in ESSENCE.	In contrast to traditional approaches, this method allows for use of representative features for monitoring (Wong, Moore, Cooper, & Wagner, 2002, 2003). To use it, however, the baseline distribution must be known.
Population-wide ANomaly Detection and Assessment (PANDA)	A causal Bayesian network approach to model a population and infer the spatial-temporal probability distribution of disease for the entire	Available from RODS (Cooper et al., 2004; Moore, Cooper, Tsui, & Wagner, 2002).	Extensive computational effort.

Table 10.10 (cont.)

	population or individual patients.		
Prospective Support Vector Clustering (PSVC)	This method uses the Support Vector Clustering method with risk adjustment as a hotspot clustering engine and a CUSUM-type design to keep track of incremental changes in spatial distribution patterns over time.	Developed in BioPortal (Chang et al., 2005; Zeng, Chang, et al., 2004).	This method can identify hotspots with irregular shapes in an online context.

ability to differentiate the "out-of-control" mean from the "in-control" mean makes these methods readily applicable for anomaly detection.

The basic idea behind SPC-based algorithms is as follows. A small random sample $x=(x_1,...x_p,...)$ is drawn repeatedly at certain time intervals. The sample mean is compared against given thresholds; alarms are triggered at $t_A = min\{s;\ sample\_mean\ x_s > G(s)\}$, if the sample mean exceeds the control limit $G(s)$.

The most widely used SPC method is the statistical cumulative sums (CUSUM). CUSUM keeps track of the accumulated deviation between observed and expected values. Formally, the accumulated deviation is defined as $S_t = max(0, S_{t-1} + z_t - k)$, where k is a control parameter and z_t models the distribution of the variable of interest (e.g., $z_t = \frac{x_t - \mu_t}{\sigma_t}$, if the variable is normally distributed) (Rogerson, 2005).

Different forms of CUSUM have been developed, which assume that the underlying distribution could be Poisson or exponential (Rogerson, 2005). Nonparametric models have also been developed, removing the need for knowledge of the underlying distribution.

Another popular SPC-based algorithm, EWMA, monitors the weighted sum of multiple deviations as opposed to a single deviation at the current time (Neubauer, 1997).

Serfling Statistic

The Serfling statistic, originally proposed by Serfling (1963) for statistical analysis of weekly pneumonia and influenza deaths in 108 U.S. cities in 1963, has been applied to a number of disease surveillance practices such as the French influenza-like syndrome data (Costagliola, Flahault, Galinec, Garnerin, Menares, & Valleron, 1991). It is also implemented in the RODS system.

Autoregressive Model-Based Anomaly Detection

Time series-based autoregressive integrated moving average (ARIMA) models have been applied to pneumonia and influenza deaths for detection of outbreaks (Reis & Mandl, 2003). These models are available in many common statistical software packages (e.g., SAS Time Series Forecasting module). One drawback of the ARIMA models is that there is no systematic way to update model parameters when new data points arrive.

Recursive Least Square (RLS) is another method based on autoregressive linear models and is implemented as part of RODS (Wong et al., 2003; Wong, Moore, Cooper, & Wagner, 2002). It learns from the time series but does not need a large learning sample. Unlike ARIMA or the Serfling method, RLS continuously updates its parameters.

Hidden Markov Model (HMM)-Based Models

The basic idea behind HMM-based models is to add another layer of random signal generation process conditioned on the state of a hidden Markov process to determine the conditional distribution of each observed data point. The sequence of state transitions is reconstructed using statistical methods to calculate the most likely trends in the surveillance data. HMM-based models are sufficiently flexible to be easily adapted automatically to trends, seasonality, covariates (e.g., gender and age), and different distributions (normal, Poisson, etc.). HMM-based models have been applied in a number of surveillance data time series analysis studies (e.g., ILI surveillance in France, Le & Carrat, 1999).

Spatial Data Analysis

Spatial analysis techniques are used to find the extent of clustering of cases across a map and have long been an important component of the surveillance analysis toolset. More specifically, spatial clustering analysis aims to detect and locate the anomalies in disease occurrences or outbreaks by examining the surveillance data's spatial distribution. It also provides the capability of tracking the progression of disease outbreaks and identifying the population at risk.

The rationale behind spatial surveillance is that natural disease outbreaks or biological attacks are typically localized at some spatial scale. Spatial analysis in syndromic surveillance uses spatial information residing in the data, such as the patient's home residence and the location of the hospital where the illness is reported.

Investigations of clusters in space often associate the varying population density with the null hypothesis. Denote the intensity of the disease cases (the number of expected events per unit area) by $\lambda_0(s)$, where s represents a location in the study area. Also denote by $\lambda_1(s)$ the intensity function of the population at risk. The null hypothesis of normal spatial distribution is in fact a proportional intensity function, $H0: \lambda_0(s) = \rho \, \lambda_1(s)$, where ρ is the expected number of cases divided by the expected number at risk.

One widely used spatial analysis algorithm is SMART, made available through the BioSense system and the National Bioterrorism Syndromic Surveillance Demonstration Program. Other popular methods include the GLMM (generalized linear mixed models) algorithm (Kleinman et al., 2004), spatial scan statistics (Kulldorff, 1999), and a number of its variations such as modified spatial scan statistics (Duczmal & Buckeridge, 2005) and the Risk-adjusted Support Vector Clustering (RSVC) method (Zeng, Chang, et al., 2004).

Temporal analysis methods such as CUSUM can also be adapted to analyze spatial information by maintaining CUSUM charts for the surrounding neighborhood of each individual region as local spatial statistic or by maintaining multivariate CUSUM charts for all regions in a global setting (Lawson & Kleinman, 2005).

GLMM Model and SMART Algorithm

Kleinman et al. proposed the use of GLMM statistics based on a logistic regression model to estimate the probability that each subject under surveillance is a case, in each area, on a given day (Kleinman, Abrams, Kulldorff, & Platt, 2005). The simple logistic regression model introduces shrinkage estimators showing the density of population in each area because the size of the population under surveillance in each area often varies.

SMART is an adaptation of the GLMM method, taking additional parameters into account to adjust for seasonal, weekly, social trends, and holiday status (Bradley et al., 2005). In such an approach, generalized linear models are used to establish the expected count per ZIP code per day based on regressing historical series of counts in each small area. The established distribution of case counts is then refined to account for multiple ZIP codes through multiple testing. One experimental study suggested that SMART delivered slightly inferior results to the spatial scan statistic method. However, both methods achieved good performances (Kleinman, Abrams, Kulldorff, et al., 2005).

Spatial Scan Statistic and Its Variations

Most syndromic surveillance systems make use of the spatial scan statistic and its variations. Using such methods for spatial analysis, many circular windows of varying sizes are imposed on the map in different locations to search for clusters over the entire region. Because the cluster size is unknown a priori, the scan statistic method uses a likelihood-ratio test where the alternative hypothesis is that there is an elevated rate within the scanning window as compared to outside. The most likely clusters can then be identified based on the likelihood-ratio test if the null hypothesis is rejected. For each distinct window, the likelihood ratio is proportional to: $(\frac{n}{\mu})^n (\frac{N-n}{N-\mu})^{N-n}$ where n is the number of cases inside the circle, N is the total number of cases, and μ is the expected number of cases inside the circle (Kulldorff, 1997).

There are several advantages to using the scan statistic method. First, it avoids pre-selection bias regarding the size or location of clusters. Second, it can be adjusted easily for non-uniform population density as well as other factors such as age.

The spatial-temporal version of the scan statistic uses cylinders instead of circles, where the height of the cylinder represents time. The remainder of the process is unchanged. A moving cylindrical window with variable sizes in both space and time visits all spatial-temporal locations to identify a significant excess of cases within it, until it reaches a predetermined size limit (Kulldorff, 1999, 2001).

SaTScan is a freely available software package that implements various types of spatial and space-time scan statistics (www.satscan.org). It has been used in more than ten syndromic surveillance systems, according to our survey. Two commercial products, WpiAnalyst extension for ArcView GIS from the Public Health Research Laboratories (www.phrl.org), and ClusterSeer developed by TerraSeer (www.terra seer.com) contain both spatial and spatial-temporal scan statistics together with many other statistical clustering methods.

A modified spatial scan statistic proposed by Duczmal and Buckeridge (2005) considers work-related factors. A factor reflecting the number of "contaminations" from workers at the nearest neighbors is added to the observed cases in the residential zones (p. 187). Their simulation shows that the approach can achieve greater detection power than the scan statistics that do not consider the movement of people. Their approach requires workplace location information, which unfortunately is not commonly available in surveillance data sources.

There are a few known problems with spatial scan methods. First, they can identify only clusters in simple regular shapes. Second, it is difficult to incorporate prior knowledge, such as the size or shape of the outbreaks or the impact on disease infection rate. Third, exhaustive search over a large region to perform statistical tests could be computationally expensive.

The method summarized in the next subsection deals with the first problem. To address the second and third problems, Neill, Moore, and Cooper (2005) proposed a Bayesian spatial scan statistic that is computationally more efficient and capable of combining the a priori knowledge of the investigated outbreak. A conjugate Gamma-Poisson model, as opposed to the Poisson model in Kulldorff's original spatial scan statistic, is used to produce a spatially smoothed map of disease rates, with a focus on computing the posterior probabilities to determine the outbreak likelihood and to estimate the location and size of potential outbreaks.

Risk-Adjusted Support Vector Clustering (RSVC) Algorithm

Zeng, Chen, et al. (2004) developed an approach called RSVC that combined the risk adjustment idea with a robust Support Vector Clustering (SVC) method to improve the quality of retrospective spatial-temporal analysis. For regions with prior dense baseline data distribution, data points are less likely to be grouped to form anomaly clusters. Several steps are involved in the clustering process. First, the input data are implicitly mapped to a high-dimensional feature space defined by a kernel function (typically the Gaussian kernel). Second, the algorithm finds a hypersphere in the feature space with a minimal radius to contain most of the data. The problem of finding this hypersphere can be formulated as a quadratic or linear programming problem depending on the distance function used. Third, the function estimating the support of the underlying data distribution is constructed using the kernel function and the parameters learned in the second step. The width parameter in the Gaussian kernel function is dynamically adjusted based on kernel density computed using background data. When mapped back to the original space, the hypersphere splits into several clusters that indicate high risk outbreak areas.

Spatial-Temporal Data Analysis

Rule-Based Anomaly Detection with Bayesian Network Modeling (WSARE)

WSARE (What's Strange About Recent Events) performs a heuristic search over combinations of temporal and spatial features to detect irregularities in space and time. The case features analyzed by WSARE include syndrome category, age, gender, and geographical information. Environmental attributes such as season and day of week can be incorporated in the model as conditional probability. Historic data (e.g., recent weeks before the day of analysis) is fed to a Bayesian network to create a baseline distribution and hypothesis testing is conducted for each feature combination against the baseline distribution to generate the scores. The network structure is rebuilt every month, with the parameters updated daily. Compared with several other algorithms that do not examine covariate information, WSARE performed better as measured by timeliness but with a slightly higher false-positive rate (Wong, Moore, Cooper, & Wagner, 2002).

Population-Wide Anomaly Detection and Assessment (PANDA)

PANDA is a causal Bayesian network-based model constructing and inferring the spatial-temporal probability distribution of disease in a population as a whole. The causal Bayesian network consists of a large set of inter-linked, patient-specific, probabilistic causal models, each of which includes variables that represent risk factors (e.g., infectious disease exposures of various types), disease states, and patient symptoms (Cooper et al., 2004). Simulation conducted by the RODS team showed that the model can handle a population size of 1.4 million (Cooper et al., 2004).

Monitoring Multiple Data Streams

In this subsection and the next, we discuss two specific sets of issues concerning outbreak detection that are worth separate treatments.

One potentially fruitful detection approach is data fusion, using multiple sources of data (e.g., ED visits and OTC sales data) to perform outbreak detection. For example, MCUSUM and MEWMA (Yeh, Huang, & Wu, 2004; Yeh, Lin, Zhou, & Venkataramani, 2003) were developed to increase detection sensitivity while limiting the number of false alarms. Another approach is to monitor stratified data (e.g., based on syndrome type or age group, counties or treatment facilities) in parallel.

The majority of implemented detection algorithms monitor individual data sources and do not cross reference between them. In a study by the BioStorm research group, different analytical methods are assigned to different types of surveillance data in different settings (Buckeridge et al., 2002; Crubézy et al., 2005). Multiple univariate statistical techniques and multivariate methods have also been used in prior studies based on different independence assumptions among the data streams. Multiple univariate methods assume independence among the data; multivariate methods establish the covariance matrix typically estimated from a baseline period (Buckeridge, Burkom, et al., 2005). However, to model the multiple univariate signals from different data streams, an in-depth investigation and characterization of healthcare-seeking behavior is necessary. In the ESSENCE II project, chief complaints data and sales of OTC medications are treated as covariates (Lombardo et al., 2004). Rigorous comparative evaluations to quantify the gain of using covariates from multiple data sources in surveillance are needed.

Special Events Surveillance

Another challenging issue for real-time outbreak detection is that the surveillance algorithms often rely on historic datasets that span a considerable length of time. Few methods demonstrate reliable detection capability with short-term baseline data. This is a particular concern for surveillance systems for special events (also referred to as drop-in models) that are implemented against bioterrorism attacks or natural disease outbreaks in settings such as international or national sporting events or meetings that involve many participants in a compressed time frame.

EARS was used for syndromic surveillance at several large public events in the United States, including the Democratic National Convention of 2000, the 2001 Super Bowl, and the 2001 World Series (Hutwagner et al., 2003). The RODS system was used during the 2002 Winter Olympic Games (Gesteland, Wagner, Chapman, Espino, Tsui,

Gardner, et al., 2002). The LEADERS system often serves as a drop-in surveillance system intended to facilitate communication and coordination within and among public health facilities (Ritter, 2002).

Data Visualization, Information Dissemination, and Reporting

In this section we summarize various data visualization techniques as applied in biosurveillance systems. We also provide a brief review of information dissemination and reporting mechanisms for real-time alerting and response triggering.

Data Visualization

Epidemiologists and public health officials, as the users of syndromic surveillance systems, need to analyze and summarize collected syndromic surveillance information. Data visualization can facilitate such tasks by providing easy-to-understand visual representations of (typically) voluminous surveillance data. There are two main types of visualization in syndromic surveillance: visual information display and interactive visual data exploration. We discuss these two types in turn.

Visual Information Display

Visual information display techniques aim to present visually either raw surveillance data or analysis results (e.g., from the data anomaly detection algorithms) (Zhu & Chen, 2005). Color-coded maps are often used to represent disease cases and clusters with case locations. Other widely used methods that can help enhance understanding of the data include various static statistical graphics, such as line graphs, scatter plots, bar charts, and pie charts.

Line charts are a popular way to visualize time-series data because they can help identify spikes or clusters. Line charts and other plotting methods for time-series analysis are supported by most statistical analysis packages (e.g., SAS and SPSS). Figure 10.3, on the left, shows a screenshot from the EARS system (Hutwagner et al., 2003), visualizing daily data feed from a hospital and the results of applying the CUSUM algorithm. Other types of plottings, such as candlestick plots and density ratio maps, are also seen in syndromic surveillance applications. Figure 10.3(b) shows a density-ratio map visualizing data aggregated by patient age in several influenza seasons (Center for Discrete Mathematics and Computer Science, 2006).

Several techniques are available for displaying spatial information contained in syndromic data. Printed maps are often used to identify geographic clusters or hotspots. CDC and the National Center for Health Statistics support research into design and display for disease atlases (Lawson & Kleinman, 2005). Geographical display of disease statistics in

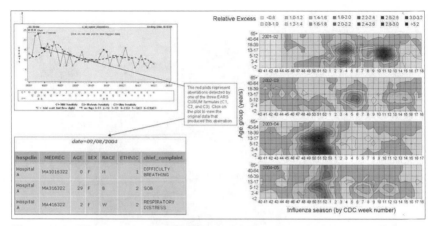

Figure 10.3 Time-series analysis plottings. (a) Line chart plotting temporal pattern of disease cases (the figure on the left side). (b) Density ratio map visualizing data aggregated by patient age (the figure on the right side). (Figure available in color at www.asis.org/Publications/ARIST/vol42/YanFigures.html)

real time is widely used for situation awareness and incident response (Kulldorff, 2001).

Techniques also exist to smooth the borders of identified regions of interest and display overlapping clusters. Boscoe, McLaughlin, Schymurab, and Kielb (2003) proposed an approach for visualizing spatial scan statistic analysis results using nested circles; this displays both the relative risk and statistical significance of identified hotspots. They show that the mapped clusters typically do not have precise boundaries: They consist of relatively well-defined cores with fuzzy edges.

Another study presents the health statistics on a map with both geographical information and the reliability of the displayed data indicated by a texture overlay (MacEachren, Brewer, & Pickle, 1998). A screenshot from their work is shown in Figure 10.4.

Color coding is a traditional visualization technique to display indirectly standard deviations by which the observed data (e.g., the number of cases of a particular syndrome category in a ZIP code) deviate from the expected counts. The idea is to use different colors or shadings to illustrate clusters of high or low rates of disease incidence. The screenshot in Figure 10.4 employs such a color encoding technique.

Geographic information systems (GIS) are powerful spatial information visualization tools with important applications in public health surveillance (Centers for Disease Control and Prevention, 2007; Hurt-Mullen & Coberly, 2005; Lombardo et al., 2003). In GIS applications, disease cases can be visualized in multiple layers along with background and environmental information such as population estimates, major roads, lakes, census tracts, county, and climate data.

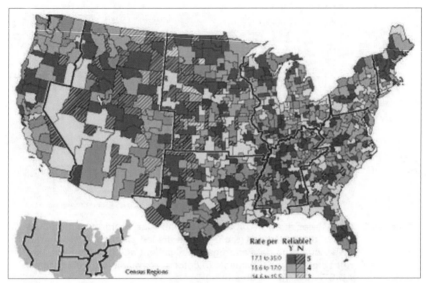

Figure 10.4   A screenshot from MacEachren, Brewer, and Pickle (1998) showing
both geographical information and data reliability. (Figure available
in color at www.asis.org/Publications/ARIST/vol42/YanFigures.html)

GIS techniques have been applied in public health situation awareness
and response planning.

One popular GIS deployment platform is ESRI's ArcView
(www.esri.com) that supports dynamically generated views, zooming,
brushing, and animation. It also integrates various kinds of visual and
analytical methods to find spatial clusters.

Interactive Visual Data Exploration

User interfaces enable effective navigation on computer screens, facilitating the process of information query and, if needed, close examination
of individual cases or patterns (Shneiderman, 1998). Interfaces are
expected to provide support for interactive data exploration.

There are six types of interface functionality in syndromic surveillance applications: overview, zoom, filtering, details on demand, relate,
and history (MacEachren et al., 1998). The interactive visual data exploration environment from the BioPortal project, called the Spatial-
Temporal Visualizer, supports all six elements to display disease
hotspots (see Figure 10.5). This environment consists of a GIS display, a
Gantt-chart temporal display, statistical plottings, and a time-range filter, all user controllable and synchronized.

In summary, we found that very few systems (e.g., BioPortal) support
dynamic GIS functions or a full-blown interactive visual data exploration environment. Systems such as RODS, ESSENCE, and BioSense
provide limited support for interactive data exploration. Most syndromic

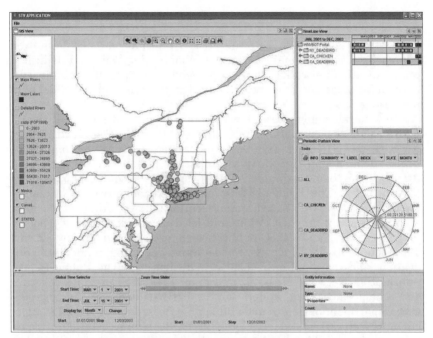

Figure 10.5 A screenshot of BioPortal's spatial-temporal visualizer (Arizona
Spring Biosurveillance Workshop, 2006).

surveillance systems support geographic displays of a local region with
vector maps. All systems offer time-series plottings, arranged or aggregated by syndrome categories, ages, and other covariates.

Several challenges are associated with data visualization in syndromic surveillance. First, the number of maps generated daily for
review is often large (Wagner, Tsui, Espino, Hogan, Hutman, Hersh, et
al., 2004). For example, if there are eight syndrome categories and ten
geographical regions, at least eighty maps must be generated for daily
review. If other parameters such as age and gender are also included in
the analysis, the number of maps quickly becomes unmanageable.
Therefore, automatic screening of the maps (e.g., based on anomaly
detection algorithms) is critical. In general, we note that interactive,
user-controlled data visualization can be leveraged to enable effective
surveillance and decision support; this represents an important research
direction.

Information Dissemination and Alerting

Information dissemination and alerting are concerned with managing and distributing daily or weekly public health updates and outbreak alerts for involved parties such as public health officials,

analysts, primary care providers, and possibly public safety and homeland security officials.

Existing syndromic surveillance information dissemination approaches include e-mail, fax, pager, phone calls, Web, and dedicated communication networks. These approaches differ greatly in their level of security, labor and resources involved in the procedure, and delay in processing time.

A few nationwide secure networks have been built for public health information dissemination and alerting. The CDC's Health Alert Network (HAN) serves as a communication backbone, linking public health departments in thirty-seven states to CDC headquarters in Atlanta; it is being expanded nationwide (Minnesota Department of Health, 2004). The Epidemic Information Exchange (Epi-X) system is the CDC's secure, Web-based communications network that serves as an exchange among the CDC, state and local health departments, poison control centers, and other public health professionals (www.cdc.gov/mmwr/epix/epix.html). Epi-X provides rapid reporting, immediate notification, and coordination of health investigations. The Public Health Information Network Messaging System (PHINMS) provides a secure and reliable messaging system for the PHIN (Rhodes & Kailar, 2005; U.S. Department of Health and Human Services, 2003). PHINMS implements the ebXML standard (Kotok, 2003) for bidirectional data transport, which offers high-quality encryption and authentication. Daniel et al. (2005) describe an implementation of HAN- and PHINMS-based syndromic surveillance.

As shown in Figure 10.6, most syndromic surveillance systems support multiple dissemination channels. The most commonly used methods, such as e-mail notification and voice communications, are relatively fast. Web-based messages and alerting networks are used less frequently. Secure network alerting with automatic role-based personnel directory access can be very useful in real-time alert distribution and is gaining increasing acceptance.

Syndromic Surveillance System Assessment

Substantial costs can be incurred when developing or managing syndromic surveillance systems and investigating possible outbreaks (Reingold, 2003). As Doroshenko et al. (2005) report, the annual cost of the NHS Direct Syndromic Surveillance System is about $280,000 and the usefulness of surveillance systems for early detection and response has yet to be established. Therefore, assessing the performance of these surveillance systems is of great importance for improving the efficacy of the investment in system development and management (Buehler, Hopkins, Overhage, Sosin, & Tong, 2004).

Several aspects of syndromic surveillance systems need to be evaluated using various criteria. These include the measurement of data quality (e.g., simplicity, flexibility, acceptability, sensitivity, predictive

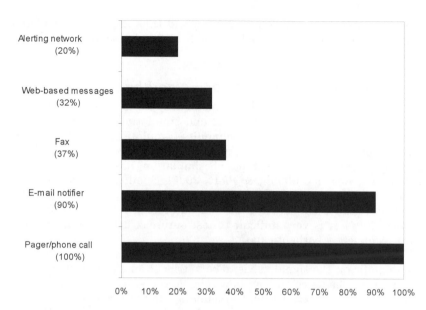

Figure 10.6 **Information dissemination channels used in syndromic surveillance.**

value positive, timeliness, and stability). These criteria are in line with the CDC evaluation guidelines (Publication of updated guidelines, 2001) and the prior literature (Buehler et al., 2004; Romaguera, German, & Klaucke, 2000).

Evaluation of Data Collection and Information Dissemination Components

The system components for data collection and information dissemination need to be evaluated in terms of HIPAA compliance, scalability, and flexibility. HIPAA privacy rules govern the obligations and reporting requirements of healthcare data (Centers for Disease Control and Prevention, 2003a). HIPAA security regulations require methods that protect data from disclosure in transport. To be HIPAA compliant, the data collection and dissemination components of syndromic surveillance systems need to provide security measures such as data encryption, secure sockets, secure shell tunneling, or the use of a virtual private network.

System scalability and flexibility indicate how scalable a syndromic surveillance system is in monitoring new diseases, accommodating new syndrome categories, or incorporating new types of data. Geographic coverage should be able to be expanded with small costs as additional healthcare facilities and jurisdictions participate. In addition, systems that use standard data formats (e.g., in electronic data interchange) can easily interoperate with other systems and thus might be considered more flexible and more scalable (Publication of updated guidelines, 2001).

Evaluation of Outbreak Detection Algorithms

There are many well-developed methodologies to evaluate detection algorithms. Surveys, chart reviews, and simulations are employed to test the algorithms' validity and reliability. Simulations often specify different types of signals, duration, and case distributions. Without actual data and outbreaks, this type of simulation has limited validity (Kleinman, Abrams, Mandl, & Platt, 2005). Simulated outbreaks can also be superimposed on real data to provide additional tests for model validity. Because the number of real outbreaks is small (Siegrist & Pavlin, 2004), it is very difficult to test outbreak detection algorithms using completely authentic data.

The main concerns regarding anomaly detection algorithms include how significant the signal needs to be to trigger an alarm, how early an outbreak can be detected, and how reliable the alarms are. Three metrics: sensitivity, specificity, and timeliness, are most commonly seen in the literature (Buckeridge, Burkom, Moore, Pavlin, Cutchis, & Hogan, 2004; Sonesson & Bock, 2003). Sensitivity measures the probability that an alarm is correctly triggered when an outbreak indeed occurs. Specificity measures the probability that an alarm is not triggered if there is no outbreak. There is a tradeoff when achieving optimality (Buckeridge et al., 2004; Siegrist & Pavlin, 2004). The Receiver Operating Characteristics (ROC) curve and the area beneath it are further evaluation metrics that plot sensitivity against specificity (Reis & Mandl, 2003).

Timeliness measures both the delay in reporting and the time required for the identification of outbreaks. As a means to measure the efficiency of detection algorithms, it refers to how fast an abberration is signaled. The activity monitoring operating characteristic (AMOC) is also used to associate a timeliness score with each false alarm. Buckeridge, Switzer, et al. (2005) provide a summary of detection algorithm evaluation metrics.

Assessment of Interface Features

Interface features are concerned with usability and user satisfaction. The evaluation study by Hu et al. (2005) is representative of research examining syndromic surveillance system usability issues, such as readability, learning curve, and decision making assistance. They used the Questionnaire for User Interaction Satisfaction (QUIS) developed by Chin, Diehl, and Norman (1988) to evaluate the usability of the BioPortal system, based on the Object-Action Interface model developed by Shneiderman (1998). They examined overall reactions to the system, screen layout and sequence, system capability, terminology/information used, and subjects' ease of learning, based on a nine-point Likert scale (Hu et al., 2005).

Summary

Our survey revealed that rigorous evaluation efforts are critically needed in syndromic surveillance research. Of 65 publications that claim to evaluate syndromic surveillance systems, 23 reported evaluation results or system experiences with varying degrees of detail. Two systems were compared with a reference detection system. Timeliness versus false positives plotting was provided in 19 quantitative evaluations of algorithms' detection delay (e.g., WSARE, SaTScan, and RSVC). Twelve systems reported detection sensitivity and specificity through the ROC curve. The ability of an algorithm to identify the geographic location of an outbreak was rarely measured and reported. The simulation models and datasets used for evaluating each algorithm differ, so a conclusive performance report is not feasible.

Evaluation of syndromic surveillance systems is confounded by a number of factors. First, few real-world datasets are available for evaluation and comparison purposes because of the low frequency or absence of outbreaks of most diseases. Second, timeliness of detection is closely related to the timing of patient visits or medication purchases, determined by a patient's behavior. Third, data quality and availability are seldom considered in algorithm evaluations. Incomplete data from various healthcare participants can potentially impair an algorithm's detection power. Lastly, the criteria for optimized detection performance may vary for different illnesses. Different bioterrorism agents display different temporal and spatial patterns. Botulism and toxic shock syndrome are readily detected in relatively smaller clusters; detection of SARS presents a greater challenge because the syndrome is less specific and the impact may be more widely spread. The incubation time and the time between exposure and symptom onset could be longer or shorter depending on the type of biologic agent. The detection power of the algorithms for rare diseases (e.g., botulism-like illness or smallpox) is yet to be reported.

Syndromic Surveillance System Case Studies

To illustrate the earlier discussion of the data sources used, technical components of syndromic surveillance systems, and related implementation issues, we present three case studies in this section. In each case study, we describe the system in detail, employing the data collection, data analysis, and data visualization/information dissemination structure used in previous discussions.

The first case study focuses on the BioSense system, a nationwide "safety net" for early detection in major cities, initiated and administrated by the U.S. CDC. BioSense represents a major effort at infrastructure building targeted at near-real-time data collection at local, state, and national levels. The second case study examines the RODS system, which has been deployed across the nation. The RODS project is a collaborative effort between the University of Pittsburgh and Carnegie Mellon University. It provides a computing platform for the implementation and evaluation of different analytic approaches for outbreak detection, among other data collection and reporting functions. The third case study examines the BioPortal system. Funded by the U.S. National Science Foundation (NSF) and U.S. Department of Homeland Security (DHS), the BioPortal project was initiated in 2003. This system is unique for its Web-based, highly interactive, and customizable spatial-temporal data visualization and analysis. This environment provides integrated support for sequence-based phylogenetic tree visualization when sequence information is available. BioPortal enables epidemiological data sharing across jurisdictions. It also provides support for syndromic surveillance based on free-text chief complaints (in both English and Chinese). In addition to human infectious diseases, BioPortal has been applied to animal diseases such as foot-and-mouth.

BioSense

BioSense is part of the CDC's Public Health Information Network (PHIN) framework managed through the CDC BioIntelligence Center. It supports early outbreak detection at the local, state, and national levels. In March 2005, BioSense had more than 340 state and local health department user accounts, representing 49 states. Its user base continues to expand. The system has also been used in several high-profile events (e.g., the G8 meeting in 2004) (Bradley et al., 2005; Ma et al., 2005; Sokolow et al., 2005).

BioSense Data Collection

Figure 10.7 shows the BioSense system architecture. BioSense data providers include Department of Defense (DoD)-Military Treatment Facilities (MTF), the Department of Veterans Affairs (VA), the Laboratory Response Network (LRN), and Electronic Laboratory Results (ELR) reporting systems.

The system accepts, receives, and collects up to four IDC-9-CM diagnosis codes identifying the reason for every ambulatory care (including ER) visit and procedure-encoded CPT ordered for every ambulatory care visit from DoD-MTF and VA. Clinical laboratory tests orders are collected nationally through the commercial lab operator LabCorp (Laboratory Corporation of America). It also receives lab results from BioWatch environmental sensors (Sokolow et al., 2005). BioSense monitors 11 syndrome categories:

Fever
Gastrointestinal
Hemorrhagic illness

Localized cutaneous lesion
Lymphadenitis
Botulism-like/botulism
Neurologic
Rash
Severe illness and death
Specific infection
Respiratory

The BioSense system supports automated messaging through HL7 protocols in either a batch mode or a near real-time mode.

BioSense Data Analysis

BioSense employs the Bayesian classifier—CoCo from the RODS laboratory (see the next subsection)—for syndrome classification. (In a previous version of BioSense, domain experts from different agencies were invited to map the syndromic data manually into syndrome categories.)

The CUSUM algorithm is used as a short-term surveillance technique to indicate recent data changes through the comparison of moving averages (Bradley et al., 2005). Because of the high variability within the data, CUSUM values are computed for each date-source-syndrome combination at the state or MRA (Metropolitan Reporting Area) level rather than for individual ZIP codes (Bradley et al., 2005). EWMA and SMART algorithms are also used to predict the day-source-syndrome counts at the ZIP code level, with seasonality and day-of-week effects considered. The calculations are conducted on a daily basis. Application of spatial-temporal clustering methods such as various scan statistics is also planned for the BioSense system.

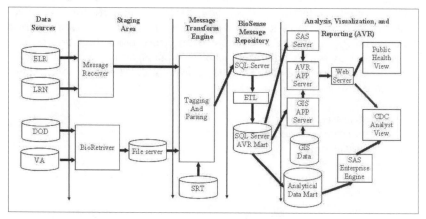

Figure 10.7   BioSense system architecture (Rolka, 2005).

BioSense Data Visualization, Information Dissemination, and Reporting

BioSense is an Internet-accessible, secure system. It displays data in multiple formats including line graphs, maps, tabular summaries, and case details. Graph plotting for individual data source, individual syndrome category, and different level of geographical regions is also available. CDC BioIntelligence Center is the agency responsible for monitoring anomalies detected by BioSense. The lightweight directory access protocol (LDAP) is employed for information reporting.

RODS

The Realtime Outbreak and Disease Surveillance system was initiated by the RODS Laboratory at the University of Pittsburgh, in 1999. The system is now an open source project under the GNU license. The RODS development effort has been organized into seven functional areas: overall design, data collection, syndrome classification, database and data warehousing, outbreak detection algorithms, data access, and user interfaces. Each functional area has a coordinator for the open source project and there is an overall coordinator responsible for the architecture, overall integration of components, and overall quality of the JAVA source code. Figure 10.8 illustrates the RODS system architecture.

The RODS system as a syndromic surveillance application was originally deployed in Pennsylvania, Utah, and Ohio. It is currently deployed in New Jersey, Michigan, and several other states. By June 2006, about 20 regions with more than 200 healthcare facilities were connected to RODS in real time. It was also deployed during the 2002 Winter Olympics (Espino et al., 2004).

RODS Data Collection

The National Retail Data Monitor (NRDM) is a component of the RODS system, collecting and analyzing daily sales data for OTC medication sales. It also collects and analyzes chief complaints data from various hospitals. There are plans to integrate laboratory orders, dictated radiology reports, dictated hospital reports, and poison control center calls in future versions. The RODS system currently monitors eight syndrome categories:

> Gastrointestinal
> Hemorrhagic illness
> Constitutional
> Neurologic
> Rash
> Respiratory
> Botulism-like/botulism
> Others

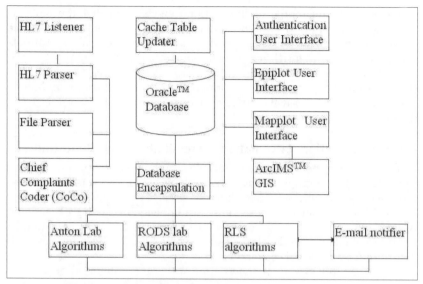

Figure 10.8   RODS system architecture (Espino et al., 2004).

The RODS data are collected in real time through HL7 messages from other computer systems such as registration systems and laboratory information systems over a Secure Shell-protected Internet connection in an automated mode.

RODS Data Analysis

One of RODS's major strengths lies in data analysis. A number of syndrome classification approaches have been tested and implemented in the RODS system. It applies a keyword classifier and an ICD-9 classifier to chief complaint data. The CoCo module, a syndrome mapping component, has been tested in multiple settings (Olszewski, 2003). For the respiratory syndrome, based on manually classified results, CoCo's sensitivity level achieves 77 percent and specificity level 90 percent (Wagner, Tsui, et al., 2004). Wagner, Tsui, et al. (2004) describe the classifier's performance for other syndrome categories. Chapman, Christensen, Wagner, Haug, Ivanov, Dowling, et al. (2005) proposed a Bayesian network-based semantic model that has been shown to classify free-text chief complaints effectively at the expense of added system complexity and computational overhead. The performance of the classifier represented by the ROC curve for each syndrome category varied between 0.95 and 0.99.

The RODS laboratory, in collaboration with the Auton Lab at Carnegie Mellon University, continues to develop additional algorithms to model both the temporal fluctuations and spatial distribution patterns in syndromic surveillance datasets. The current open source release of the RODS system includes implementations of several outbreak detection algorithms: wavelet-detection algorithms, CUSUM, SMART, scan statistics, RLS, and WSARE. A future release will allow the import and export of data as common text files such that stand-alone algorithms and statistical software packages can be used to analyze the data.

RODS Visualization, Information Dissemination, and Reporting

The RODS system provides multiple graphing techniques with both time-series and geographical displays available via an encrypted, password-protected Web interface. Three different data views—Main, Epiplot, and Mapplot—are supported. These views are implemented using JFreeChart (www.jfree.org/jfreechart, an open-source graphing package) and ArcIMS (an Internet GIS server developed by the Environmental Systems Research Institute, Inc., www.esri.com/arcims).

The main RODS screen shows time-series plots updated on a daily basis for each syndrome. The user can also view these graphs by county or for the whole state. The Epiplot screen is highly interactive; the user can specify the syndrome, region, start dates, and end dates to generate customized time-series plots. A "get cases" button allows users to view case-level detail for encounters making up the specific time-series. The Mapplot screen provides an interface to the ArcIMS package, to display disease cases' spatial distribution using patients' ZIP code information.

BioPortal

The BioPortal project was initiated in 2003 by the University of Arizona Artificial Intelligence Lab and its collaborators in the New York State Department of Health and the California Department of Health Services to develop an infectious disease surveillance system. The project has been sponsored by NSF, DHS, DoD, Arizona Department of Health Services, and Kansas State University's BioSecurity Center, under the guidance of a federal inter-agency working group named the Infectious Disease Informatics Working Committee (IDIWC). Its partners include all the original collaborators as well as the U.S. Geological Survey; University of California, Davis; University of Utah; the Arizona Department of Health Services; Kansas State University; and the National Taiwan University. The BioPortal research prototype provides distributed, cross-jurisdictional access to datasets concerning several major infectious diseases, including Botulism, West Nile Virus, foot-and-mouth disease, livestock syndromes, and chief complaints (in both English and Chinese). It features advanced spatial-temporal data analysis methods and visualization capabilities. BioPortal supports syndromic surveillance of epidemiological data and free-text chief complaints. It also supports analysis and visualization of lab-generated gene sequence information. Figurea 10.9a and 10.9b show the BioPortal system architecture.

BioPortal Data Collection

ED chief complaint data in the free-text format are provided by the Arizona Department of Health Services and several hospitals in a batch mode for syndrome classification. Various disease-specific case reports for both human and animal diseases are another source of data for BioPortal. It also makes use of surveillance datasets such as dead bird sightings and mosquito control information. The system's communication backbones, initially for data acquisition from New York or California disease datasets, consist of several messaging adaptors that can be customized to interoperate with various messaging systems. Participating syndromic data providers can link to the BioPortal data repository via the PHINMS and an XML/HL7 compatible network.

BioPortal Data Analysis

BioPortal provides automatic syndrome classification capabilities based on free-text chief complaints. One method recently developed uses a concept ontology derived from the UMLS (Lu et al., 2006). For each chief complaint (CC), the method first standardizes the CC into one or more medical concepts in the UMLS. These concepts are then clustered into existing symptom groups using a set of rules constructed from a symptom grouping table. For symptoms not in the table, a Weighted Semantic Similarity Score algorithm, which measures the semantic similarity between the target symptoms and existing symptom groups, is used to determine the best symptom group for the target symptom. The ontology-enhanced CC classification method has also been extended to handle CCs in Chinese.

BioPortal supports hotspot analysis using various methods for detecting unusual spatial and temporal clusters of events. Hotspot analysis facilitates disease outbreak detection and predictive modeling. BioPortal supports various scan statistics using SaTScan, the Nearest Neighbor Hierarchical Clustering method, and two new methods (Risk-Adjusted Support Vector Clustering, and Prospective Support Vector Clustering) developed in-house (discussed in the section on the RSVC algorithm) (Chang et al., 2005; Zeng, Chang, et al., 2004).

BioPortal Visualization, Information Dissemination, and Reporting

BioPortal offers a visualization environment called the Spatial-Temporal Visualizer (STV), which allows users to interactively explore spatial and temporal patterns, based on an integrated toolset consisting of a GIS view, a timeline tool, and a periodic pattern tool (Hu et al., 2005).

Figure 10.5 in the section on interactive visual data exploration illustrates how these three views can be used to explore an infectious disease

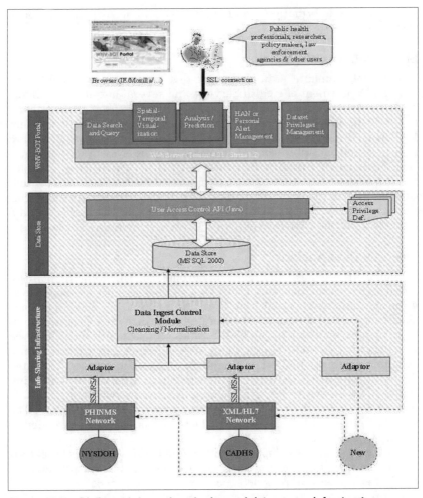

Figure 10.9a   BioPortal information sharing and data access infrastructure.

dataset. The GIS view displays cases and sightings on a map. The user can select multiple datasets to be shown on the map in different layers using the checkboxes (e.g., disease cases, natural land features, and land-use elements). Through the periodic view the user can identify temporal patterns (e.g., which months or weeks have an unusually high number of cases). The unit of time for aggregation can also be set as days or hours. The timeline view incorporates a hierarchical display of the data elements, organized as a tree. A sequence-based phylogenetic tree visualizer has been developed for diseases such as foot-and-mouth disease, for which gene sequence information is available. This allows BioPortal users to explore geospatial and sequence data concurrently.

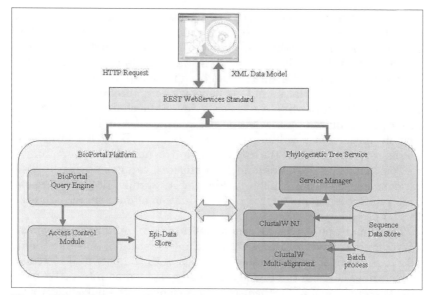

Figure 10.9b   BioPortal enhanced system architecture with epidemiological data and gene sequence data surveillance.

Data confidentiality, security, and access control are among the key research and development issues for the BioPortal project. An access control mechanism is implemented based on data confidentiality and user access privilege. For example, access privilege to the ZIP code and county level of individual patient records may be granted to selected public health epidemiologists. The project also developed various Memoranda of Understanding (MOUs) for data sharing among different local and state agencies.

Challenges and Future Directions

We conclude this review by discussing key challenges facing syndromic surveillance research and summarizing future directions.

Challenges for Syndromic Surveillance Research

Although syndromic surveillance has gained wide acceptance as a response to disease outbreaks and bioterrorism attacks, many research challenges remain.

First, there are circumstances in which syndromic surveillance may not be effective or necessary. The potential benefit of syndromic surveillance in terms of timeliness of detection could not be realized if there were hundreds or thousands of people infected simultaneously. In extreme cases, modern biological weapons could easily lead to mass infection via airborne or waterborne agents. In another scenario, syndromic surveillance could be rendered ineffective if the cases involved only a few people (e.g., the anthrax outbreak in 2001) and thus could go undetected (DrugRehabs.org, 2005). In this situation, a single positive diagnosis of a spore of anthrax could be sufficient to confirm the event.

Second, disease data tend to be noisy and incomplete. Although reporting of most notifiable diseases through the chain of public health agencies is required by law, hospitals, laboratories, and clinicians participate largely on a voluntary basis. Patients making ER visits may not be representative of the population in the neighboring community; the participating hospitals and laboratories are not necessarily good random samples from which reliable statistical inference can be made. This reinforces the need for careful evaluation of data sources and collection procedures.

Third, many public health practitioners are unfamiliar with advanced surveillance analytics. Model selection, interpretation, and fine-tuning all require proper training. One approach with the potential to reduce the learning curve is to provide a carefully engineered interactive visualization environment for the user to experiment with analysis methods, explore results, and validate hypotheses in an intuitive and visually informative environment.

Fourth, many false alarms are being generated by syndromic surveillance systems daily or weekly because it is difficult to distinguish natural data variations from real outbreaks. Human reviews and follow-up investigations are necessary for the signaled outbreak, which is costly in time and labor. A typical investigation requires a group of epidemiologists, public health officials, healthcare providers, and their support staff to go through a multi-step procedure for alert review and event evaluation.

Fifth, there is a critical need to develop computational and mathematical methods to facilitate response planning and related policy and decision making. Such methods should rely on an understanding of specific disease-spreading patterns. They can be used to evaluate alternative policies and interventions and provide guidelines for scenario development, risk assessment, and trend prediction (Roberts, 2002).

Summary and Future Directions

We first summarize our post-analysis findings.

Existing systems differ significantly in scope and purpose (e.g., geographical coverage as well as types of data and diseases monitored). For instance, a majority of the systems surveyed focus on biodefense and detecting bioterrorism attacks; others target outbreak detection for specific diseases such as influenza (Hyman & LaForce, 2004).

The absence of standard vocabularies and messaging protocols leads to interoperability problems among syndromic surveillance systems and underlying data sources. The HL7 standards and XML-based messaging protocols represent a potential solution for addressing these problems.

Each syndromic surveillance system implements a set of outbreak detection algorithms. There is an urgent need for a better understanding of the strengths and limitations of various detection techniques and their applicability. Also, implemented algorithms could be reused across systems as sharable resources.

System evaluation and comparison are confounded by a number of practical issues. Systematic, field-based, objective, comparative studies of systems are needed.

With regard to promising future research directions in syndromic surveillance, we see many opportunities for informatics studies on a wide range of topics: (a) Data visualization techniques, especially interactive visual data exploration techniques, need to be further developed to meet the specific analysis needs of syndromic surveillance. (b) Outbreak detection algorithms need to be improved in terms of sensitivity, specificity, and timeliness, specifically, how to deal with incomplete data records, how to perform privacy-conscious data mining, how to leverage multiple data streams. Furthermore, thorough evaluation of outbreak detection algorithms using synthetic or real data is critically needed. (c) System interoperability research and event management models are worth studying. (d) In the context of bioterrorism preparation, research on predicting and responding to bio-attacks is critically needed. Work reported by Harmon (2003) points to an interesting direction in this area of study: by examining antecedent events, using, for example, historical data on terrorism attacks, the culminating event can be predicted to occur within a certain time window. (e) The present survey is focused on human diseases. Agricultural bio-attacks and certain animal diseases (e.g., mad cow, foot-and-mouth, and avian flu) are gaining increasing attention in biosurveillance practice. For example, the U.S. Department of Agriculture and the U.S. Geological Survey, through its National Wildlife Health Center and other partners, administer and manage databases for wildlife diseases (www.usda.gov). How to detect and respond to agricultural bio-attacks and disease events pose interesting technical challenges (e.g., the importance of environmental data on air, water, or weather). Developing cross-species syndromic surveillance approaches and cross-fertilizing methods from human and animal syndromic surveillance research hold considerable potential.

In closing, we briefly note the expanding scope of syndromic surveillance systems. Although syndromic surveillance systems have been developed and deployed in many state public health departments, there is an urgent need to create a cross-jurisdictional data sharing infrastructure to maximize the potential benefit and practical impact of syndromic surveillance. In a broader context, public health surveillance should be a truly global effort for pandemic diseases such as SARS. There is a need to address issues concerning global data sharing (including multilingual information processing) and development of models that work internationally. International politics, global commerce, and cultural factors are some of the issues that need to be considered in global syndromic surveillance.

Acknowledgments

The research reported here is supported in part by the National Science Foundation through Digital Government Grant #EIA-9983304, Information Technology Research Grant #IIS-0428241, Department of Homeland Security/United States Department of Agriculture, FMD BioPortal, USDA Grant # 2006-39546-17579, and Arizona Department of Health Services, Syndromic Surveillance for the State of Arizona grant. This chapter is the collective effort of the following partners and contributors: Ken Komatsu and Lea Trujillo from Arizona Department of Health Services; Marty Vavier at Kansas State University; Mark Thurmond, Foot-and-Mouth Disease Lab, University of California, Davis; Paul Hu, University of Utah; Millicent Eidson and Ivan Gotham, New York State Department of Health and SUNY, Albany; Cecil Lynch from the California Department of Health Services, U.C. Davis; and Michael Ascher from the Lawrence Livermore National Laboratory, among others. The third author is an affiliated professor at the Institute of Automation, the Chinese Academy of Sciences, and wishes to acknowledge support from a research grant (60573078) from the National Natural Science Foundation of China, an international collaboration grant (2F05N01) from the Chinese Academy of Sciences, and a National Basic Research Program of China (973) grant (2006CB705500) from the Ministry of Science and Technology.

References

Arizona Spring Biosurveillance Workshop. (2006, March 7–8). Retrieved April 1, 2006, from ai.arizona.edu/BIO2006

Barthell, E., Aronsky, D., Cochrane, D., Cable, G., & Stair, T. (2004). The Frontlines of Medicine Project progress report: Standardized communication of emergency department triage data for syndromic surveillance. *Annals of Emergency Medicine, 44*(3), 247–252.

Barthell, E., Cordell, W., Moorhead, J., Handler, J., Feied, C., Smith, M., et al. (2002). The Frontlines of Medicine Project: A proposal for the standardized communication of emergency department data for public health uses including syndromic surveillance for biological and chemical terrorism. *Annals of Emergency Medicine, 39*(4), 422–429.

Bath, P. A. (2004). Data mining in health and medical information. *Annual Review of Information Science and Technology, 38,* 331–369.

Beeler, G. (1998). HL7 Version 3: An object-oriented methodology for collaborative standards development. *International Journal of Medical Informatics, 48,* 151–161.

Begier, E. M., Sockwell, D., Branch, L. M., Davies-Cole, J. O., Jones, L. H., Edwards, L., et al. (2003). The National Capitol Region's Emergency Department Syndromic Surveillance System: Do chief complaint and discharge diagnosis yield different results? *Emerging Infectious Diseases, 9*(3). Retrieved February 17, 2007, from www.cdc.gov/ncidod/eid/vol9no3/02-0363.htm

Benoît, G. (2002). Data mining. *Annual Review of Information Science and Technology, 36,* 265–310.

Besculides, M., Heffernan, R., Mostashari, F., & Weiss, D. (2004). Evaluation of school absenteeism data for early outbreak detection: New York City, 2001–2002. *Morbidity and Mortality Weekly Report, 53*(Suppl.), 230. Retrieved February 17, 2007, from www.cdc.gov/mmwr/preview/mmwrhtml/su5301a42.htm

BioDefend™. (2006). Tampa: University of South Florida. Center for Biological Defense. Retrieved March 01, 2006, from www.bt.usf.edu

Boscoe, F. P., McLaughlin, C., Schymurab, M. J., & Kielb, C. L. (2003). Visualization of the spatial scan statistic using nested circles. *Health & Place, 9,* 273–277.

Bradley, C. A., Rolka, H., Walker, D., & Loonsk, J. (2005). BioSense: Implementation of a national early event detection and situational awareness system. *Morbidity and Mortality Weekly Report, 54*(Suppl.), 11–20.

Bravata, D. M., McDonald, K., Owens, D. K., Buckeridge, D., Haberland, C., & Rydzak, C. (2002). *Bioterrorism preparedness and response: Use of information technologies and decision support systems* (Evidence Report/Technology Assessment No, 59). Rockville, MD: Agency for Healthcare Research and Quality.

Bravata, D. M., McDonald, K., Smith, W., Rydzak, C., Szeto, H., Buckeridge, D., et al. (2004). Systematic review: Surveillance systems for early detection of bioterrorism-related diseases. *Annals of Internal Medicine, 140,* 910–922.

Brillman, J. C., Burr, T., Forslund, D., Joyce, E., Picard, R., & Umland, E. (2005). Modeling emergency department visit patterns for infectious disease complaints: Results and application to disease surveillance. *BMC Medical Informatics and Decision Making, 5*(4). Retrieved February 17, 2007, from www.biomedcentral.com/1472-6947/5/4

Brookmeyer, R., & Stroup, D. (2004). *Monitoring the health of populations: Statistical surveillance in public health.* New York: Oxford University Press.

Buckeridge, D., Burkom, H., Campbell, M., Hogan, W., & Moore, A. (2005). Algorithms for rapid outbreak detection: A research synthesis. *Journal of Biomedical Informatics, 38,* 99–113.

Buckeridge, D., Burkom, H., Moore, A., Pavlin, J., Cutchis, P., & Hogan, W. (2004). Evaluation of syndromic surveillance systems: Development of an epidemic simulation model. *Morbidity and Mortality Weekly Report, 53*(Suppl.), 137–143.

Buckeridge, D., Graham, J., O'Connor, J., Choy, M. K., Tu, S. W., & Musen, M. (2002). Knowledge-based bioterrorism surveillance. *Proceedings of the American Medical Informatics Association Symposium,* 76–80. Retrieved February 17, 2007, from smi.stanford.edu/smi-web/reports/SMI-2002-0946.pdf

Buckeridge, D., Musen, M., Switzer, P., & Crubézy, M. (2003). An analytic framework for space-time aberrancy detection in public health surveillance data. *Proceedings of the American Medical Informatics Association Symposium,* 120–124.

Buckeridge, D., Switzer, P., Owens, D., Siegrist, D., Pavlin, J., & Musen, M. (2005). An evaluation model for syndromic surveillance: Assessing the performance of a temporal algorithm. *Morbidity and Mortality Weekly Report, 54*(Suppl.), 109–115.

Buehler, J., Berkelman, R., Hartley, D., & Peters, C. (2003). Syndromic surveillance and bioterrorism-related epidemics. *Emerging Infectious Diseases, 9*(1), 197–204.

Buehler, J., Hopkins, R., Overhage, J., Sosin, D., & Tong, V. (2004). Framework for evaluating public health surveillance systems for early detection of outbreaks: Recommendations from the CDC working group. *Morbidity and Mortality Weekly Report, 53(RR-5)*, 1–13.

Burkom, H., Elbert, E., Feldman, A., & Lin, J. (2004). Role of data aggregation in biosurveillance detection strategies with applications from ESSENCE. *Morbidity and Mortality Weekly Report, 53*(Suppl.), 67–73.

Carley, K., Fridsma, D., Casman, E., Altman, N., Chang, J., Kaminsky, B., et al. (2003). BioWar: Scalable Multi-Agent Social and Epidemiological Simulation of Bioterrorism Events. Retrieved July 6, 2006 from www.savannah-simulations.com/about_simulation/agent_based/Carley_2003.pdf.

Center for Discrete Mathematics and Computer Science. (2006). *DIMACS Working Group on BioSurveillance Data Monitoring and Information Exchange.* New Brunswick, NJ: Rutgers University. Retrieved April 1, 2006, from dimacs.rutgers.edu/Workshops/Surveillance

Centers for Disease Control and Prevention. (2003a). HIPAA Privacy Rule and public health: Guidance from CDC and the US Department of Health and Human Services. *Morbidity and Mortality Weekly Report, 52*(Suppl.), 1–20.

Centers for Disease Control and Prevention. (2003b). *Syndrome definitions for diseases associated with critical bioterrorism-associated agents.* Atlanta, GA: U.S. Department of Health and Human Services. Retrieved February 17, 2007, from www.bt.cdc.gov/surveillance/syndromedef/index.asp

Centers for Disease Control and Prevention. (2004). *National electronic disease surveillance system: The surveillance and monitoring component of the Public Health Information Network.* Atlanta, GA: U.S. Department of Health and Human Services. Retrieved February 17, 2007, from www.cdc.gov/nedss

Centers for Disease Control and Prevention. (2007). *Public health GIS news and information.* Retrieved February 17, 2007, from www.cdc.gov/nchs/about/otheract/gis/gis_publichealthinfo.htm

Chang, W., Zeng, D., & Chen, H. (2005, September). Prospective spatio-temporal data analysis for security informatics. *Proceedings of the 8th IEEE International Conference on Intelligent Transportation Systems*, 1120–1124.

Chapman, W. W., Christensen, L., Wagner, M. M., Haug, P., Ivanov, O., Dowling, J., et al. (2005). Classifying free-text triage chief complaints into syndromic categories with natural language processing. *Artificial Intelligence in Medicine, 33*(1), 31–40.

Chapman, W. W., Cooper, G. F., Hanbury, P., Chapman, B. E., Harrison, L. H., & Wagner, M. M. (2003). Creating a text classifier to detect radiology reports describing mediastinal findings associated with inhalational anthrax and other disorders. *Journal of the American Medical Informatics Association, 10*(5), 494–503.

Chen, H., & Xu, J. (2006). Intelligence and security informatics. *Annual Review of Information Science and Technology, 40*, 229–299.

Chin, J. P., Diehl, V. A., & Norman, K. L. (1988). Development of an instrument measuring user satisfaction of the human–computer interface. *Proceedings of the SIGCHI Conference on Human Factors in Computing Systems*, 213–218.

Cho, J., Kim, J., Yoo, I., Ahn, M., Wang, S., Hur, T., et al. (2003). Syndromic surveillance based on the emergency department in Korea. *Journal of Urban Health, 80*(2), 124.

Clothier, H. J., Fielding, J. E., & Kelly, H. A. (2006). *An evaluation of the Australian Sentinel Practice Research Network (ASPREN) surveillance for influenza-like illness.* Retrieved May 11, 2006, from www.health.gov.au/internet/wcms/publishing.nsf/content/cda-cdi2903a.htm#data

Cooper, G. F., Dash, D. H., Levander, J. D., Wong, W. K., Hogan, W. R., & Wagner, M. M. (2004). Bayesian biosurveillance of disease outbreaks. *Proceedings of the Twentieth Conference on Uncertainty in Artificial Intelligence,* 94–103.

Costagliola, D., Flahault, A., Galinec, D., Garnerin, P., Menares, J., & Valleron, A. (1991). A routine tool for detection and assessment of epidemics of influenza-like syndromes in France. *American Journal of Public Health, 81*(1), 97–99.

Cronin, B. (2005). Intelligence, terrorism, and national security. *Annual Review of Information Science and Technology, 39,* 395–432.

Crubézy, M., O'Connor, M., Pincus, Z., & Musen, M. A. (2005). Ontology-centered syndromic surveillance for bioterrorism. *IEEE Intelligent Systems, 20*(5), 26–35.

Daniel, J. B., Heisey-Grove, D., Gadam, P., Yih, W., Mandl, K., DeMaria, A. J., et al. (2005). Connecting health departments and providers: Syndromic surveillance's last mile. *Morbidity and Mortality Weekly Report, 54*(Suppl.), 147–151.

Das, D., Weiss, D., & Mostashari, F. (2003). Enhanced drop-in syndromic surveillance in New York City following September 11, 2001. *Journal of Urban Health, 80*(1, Suppl.), 176–188.

Dembek, Z., Carley, K., & Hadler, J. (2005). Guidelines for constructing a statewide hospital syndromic surveillance network. *Morbidity and Mortality Weekly Report, 54*(Suppl.), 21–26.

Dembek, Z., Carley, K., Siniscalchi, A., & Hadler, J. (2004). Hospital admissions syndromic surveillance: Connecticut, September 2001–November 2003. *Morbidity and Mortality Weekly Report, 53*(Suppl.), 50–52.

Doroshenko, A., Cooper, D., Smith, G., Gerard, E., Chinemana, F., Verlander, N., et al. (2005). Evaluation of syndromic surveillance based on National Health Service Direct derived data: England and Wales. *Morbidity and Mortality Weekly Report, 54*(Suppl.), 117–122.

Drociuk, D., Gibson, J., & Hodge, J. J. (2004). Health information privacy and syndromic surveillance systems. *Morbidity and Mortality Weekly Report, 53*(Suppl.), 221–225.

DrugRehabs.org. (2005). *Indiana: Syndromic surveillance.* Retrieved July 27, 2006, from www.drug-rehabs.org/content.php?cid=1504&state=Indiana

Duchin, J., Karras, B., Trigg, L., Bliss, D., Vo, D., Ciliberti, J. S. L., et al. (2001). Syndromic surveillance for bioterrorism using computerized discharge diagnosis databases. *Proceedings of the American Medical Informatics Association Symposium,* 897.

Duczmal, L., & Buckeridge, D. (2005). Using modified spatial scan statistic to improve detection of disease outbreak when exposure occurs in workplace: Virginia, 2004. *Morbidity and Mortality Weekly Report, 54*(Suppl.), 187.

Edge, V. L., Lim, G. H., Aramini, J. J., Sockett, P., & Pollari, F. L. (2003). Development of an Alternative Surveillance Alert Program (ASAP): Syndromic surveillance of gastrointestinal illness using pharmacy over-the-counter sales. *Journal of Urban Health, 80*(2), i138.

Edge, V. L., Pollari, F., & Lim, G. (2004). Syndromic surveillance of gastrointestinal illness using pharmacy over-the-counter sales: A retrospective report of waterborne outbreaks in Saskatchewan and Ontario. *Canada Journal of Public Health*, *95*, 446–450.

Emergint. (2004). Emergint Data Collection and Transformation System. Louisville, KY: Emergint. Retrieved March 23, 2006, from www.emergint. com/jsp/datasheet.pdf

Emergisoft. (2006). Emergisoft's ED syndromic surveillance solutions. Arlington, TX: Emergisoft. Retrieved June 12, 2006, from www.emergisoft.com/product info/syndromic_surveillance/

Espino, J. U., & Wagner, M. M. (2001). The accuracy of ICD-9 coded chief complaints for detection of acute respiratory illness. *Proceedings of the American Medical Informatics Association Symposium*, 164–168.

Espino, J. U., Wagner, M. M., Szczepaniak, C., Tsui, F.-C., Su, H., Olszewski, R., et al. (2004). Removing a barrier to computer-based outbreak and disease surveillance: The RODS open source project. *Morbidity and Mortality Weekly Report*, *53*(Suppl.), 34–41.

First Watch. (2006). *Early event detection & syndromic surveillance*. Retrieved June 23, 2006, from www.firstwatch.net

Ford, D., Kaufman, J. H., Thomas, J., Eiron, I., & Hammer, M. (2005). *Spatiotemporal Epidemiological Modeler: A tool for spatiotemporal modeling of infectious agents across the United States*. Retrieved Oct 10, 2006, from www.alphaworks.ibm.com/tech/stem

G8 Gleneagles 2005 statement on counter-terrorism. (2005). Retrieved July 31, 2006, from www.privacyinternational.org/article.shtml?cmd%5B347%5D=x-347-260977

Gesteland, P. H., Wagner, M. M., Chapman, W. W., Espino, J. U., Tsui, F.-C., Gardner, R. M., et al. (2002). Rapid deployment of an electronic disease surveillance system in the state of Utah for the 2002 Olympic winter games. *Proceedings of the American Medical Informatics Association Symposium*, 285–289.

Goss, L., Carrico, R., Hall, C., & Humbaugh, K. (2003). A day at the races: Communitywide syndromic surveillance during the 2002 Kentucky Derby Festival. *Journal of Urban Health*, *80*(2), i124.

Grigoryan, V. V., Wagner, M. M., Waller, K., Wallstrom, G. L., & Hogan, W. R. (2005). *The effect of spatial granularity of data on reference dates for influenza outbreaks* (RODS Laboratory Technical Report). Pittsburgh, PA: University of Pittsburgh, RODS Laboratory. Retrieved February 17, 2007, from rods.health.pitt.edu/LIBRARY/2005%20AMIA-Grigoryan-Reference%20 dates%20for%20flu-submitted.pdf

Hamby, T. (2006). *New Jersey experience and protocol development*. New Brunswick, NJ: Rutgers University, DIMACS Working Group on Biosurveillance Data Monitoring and Information Exchange.

Harmon, G. (2003). Predicting major terrorist attacks: An exploratory analysis of predecessor event intervals in timelines. *Proceedings of the Biological Terrorism Response*, 78–80.

Heffernan, R., Mostashari, F., Das, D., Besculides, M., Rodriguez, C., Greenko, J., et al. (2004). New York City syndromic surveillance systems. *Morbidity and Mortality Weekly Report*, *53*(Suppl.), 23–27.

Heffernan, R., Mostashari, F., Das, D., Karpati, A., Kulldorff, M., & Weiss, D. (2004). Syndromic surveillance in public health practice, New York City.

Emerging Infectious Diseases, *10*(5). Retrieved February 17, 2007, from www.cdc.gov/ncidod/EID/vol10no5/03-0646.htm

Hogan, W. R., Wagner, M. M., & Tsui, F.-C. (2002, November). *Experience with message format and code set standards for early warning public health surveillance systems*. Poster presented at the Annual Fall Symposium of the American Medical Informatics Association, San Antonio, TX. Retrieved March 5, 2007, from rods.health.pitt.edu/Technical%20Reports/Hogan-AMIA-2002-poster1.pdf

Hooda, J., Dogdu, E., & Sunderraman, R. (2004). Health Level-7 compliant clinical patient records system. *Proceedings of the 2004 ACM Symposium on Applied Computing*, 259–263.

Hu, P. J.-H., Zeng, D., Chen, H., Larson, C. A., Chang, W., & Tseng, C. (2005). Evaluating an infectious disease information sharing and analysis system. Proceedings *of the IEEE International Conference on Intelligence and Security Informatics*, 412–417.

Hurt-Mullen, K., & Coberly, J. (2005). Syndromic surveillance on the epidemiologist's desktop: Making sense of much data. *Morbidity and Mortality Weekly Report*, *54*(Suppl.), 141–147.

Hutwagner, L., Thompson, W., Seeman, G. M., & Treadwell, T. (2003). The bioterrorism preparedness and response. Early Aberration Reporting System (EARS). *Journal of Urban Health*, *80*(2, Suppl. 1), 89–96.

Hyman, J., & LaForce, T. (2004). Modeling the spread of influenza among cities. In H. Banks & C. Castillo-Chàvez (Eds.), *Bioterrorism: Mathematical modeling applications in homeland security* (pp. 211–236). Philadelphia: Society for Industrial and Applied Mathematics.

ICPA, Inc. (2006). *Redbat features & benefits*. Austin, TX: ICPA, Inc. Retrieved May 23, 2006, from www.icpa.net/redbat-features.html

Ivanov, O., Wagner, M. M., Chapman, W. W., & Olszewski, R. T. (2002). Accuracy of three classifiers of acute gastrointestinal syndrome for syndromic surveillance. *Proceedings of the American Medical Informatics Association Symposium*, 345–349.

Johnson, J. M. (2006). *To ignore or not to ignore: Follow-up to statistically significant signals*. New Brunswick, NJ: Rutgers University, DIMACS Working Group on Biosurveillance Data Monitoring and Information Exchange.

Johnson, J. M., Hicks, L., McClean, C., & Ginsberg, M. (2005). Leveraging syndromic surveillance during the San Diego wildfires, 2003. *Morbidity and Mortality Weekly Report*, *54*(Suppl.), 190.

Karras, B. T. (2005). *Syndromic surveillance information collection: King County (SSIC-KC) for bioterrorism detection*. Retrieved July 10, 2006, from www.phig.washington.edu/projectform_show.php?id=6

Kaufman, Z., Cohen, E., Peled-Leviatan, T., Lavi, C., Aharonowitz, G., Dichtiar, R., et al. (2005). Using data on an influenza B outbreak to evaluate a syndromic surveillance system: Israel, June 2004 [abstract]. *Morbidity and Mortality Weekly Report*, *54*(Suppl.), 191.

Kleinman, K., Abrams, A., Kulldorff, M., & Platt, R. (2005). A model-adjusted spacetime scan statistic with an application to syndromic surveillance. *Epidemiology and Infection*, *119*, 409–419.

Kleinman, K., Abrams, A., Mandl, K., & Platt, R. (2005). Simulation for assessing statistical methods of biologic terrorism surveillance. *Morbidity and Mortality Weekly Report*, *54*(Suppl.), 103–110.

Kleinman, K., Lazarus, R., & Platt, R. (2004). A generalized linear mixed models approach for detecting incident cluster/signals of disease in small areas, with an application to biological terrorism (with invited commentary). *American Journal of Epidemiology, 159*, 217–224.

Kotok, A. (2003). *ebXML case study: Centers for Disease Control and Prevention, Public Health Information Network Messaging System (PHINMS).* Retrieved Aug 11, 2006, from www.ebxml.org/case_studies/documents/casestudy_cdc_phinms.pdf

Kulldorff, M. (1997). A spatial scan statistic. *Communications in statistics: Theory and Methods, 26*, 1481–1496.

Kulldorff, M. (1999). Spatial scan statistics: Models, calculations, and applications. In J. B. Glaz (Ed.), *Scan statistics and applications* (pp. 303–322). Boston: Birkhauser.

Kulldorff, M. (2001). Prospective time periodic geographical disease surveillance using a scan statistic. *Journal of the Royal Statistical Society, Series A, 164*, 61–72.

Lawson, A. B., & Kleinman, K. (Eds.). (2005). *Spatial and syndromic surveillance for public health*. Chichester, UK: Wiley.

Lazarus, R., Kleinman, K., Dashevsky, I., Adams, C., Kludt, P., DeMaria, A. J., et al. (2002). Use of automated ambulatory-care encounter records for detection of acute illness clusters, including potential bioterrorism events. *Emerging Infectious Diseases, 18*(8). Retrieved February 17, 2007, from www.cdc.gov/ncidod/EID/vol8no8/02-0239.htm

Lazarus, R., Kleinman, K., Dashevsky, I., DeMaria, A., & Platt, R. (2001). Using automated medical records for rapid identification of illness syndromes (syndromic surveillance): The example of lower respiratory infection. *BMC Public Health, 1*(9). Retrieved March 5, 2007, from www.biomedcentral.com/1471-2458/1/9

Le, S. Y., & Carrat, F. (1999). Monitoring epidemiologic surveillance data using hidden Markov models. *Statistics in Medicine, 18*(24), 3463–3478.

Leroy, G., & Chen, H. (2001). Meeting medical terminology needs: The ontology-enhanced medical concept mapper. *IEEE Transactions on Information Technology in Biomedicine, 5*, 261–270.

Levine, N. (2002). *CrimeStat III: A spatial statistics program for the analysis of crime incident locations*. Washington, DC: National Institute of Justice.

Li, Y., Yu, L., Xu, P., Lee, J., Wong, T., Ooi, P., et al. (2004). Predicting super spreading events during the 2003 Severe Acute Respiratory Syndrome epidemics in Hong Kong and Singapore. *American Journal of Epidemiology, 160*, 719–728.

Lober, W. B., Karras, B. T., & Wagner, M. M. (2002). Roundtable on bioterrorism detection: Information system-based surveillance. *Journal of the American Medical Informatics Association, 9*, 105–115.

Lober, W. B., Trigg, L. J., Karras, B. T., Bliss, D., Ciliberti, J., Stewart, L., et al. (2003). Syndromic surveillance using automated collection of computerized discharge diagnoses. *Journal of Urban Health, 80*(2), 97–106.

Lombardo, J., Burkom, H., Elbert, E., Magruder, S. F., Lewis, S. H., Loschen, W., et al. (2004). A systems overview of the Electronic Surveillance System for the Early Notification of Community-based Epidemics (ESSENCE II). *Journal of Urban Health, 80*(2), 32–42.

Lombardo, J., Burkom, H., & Pavlin, J. (2004). Electronic Surveillance System for the Early Notification of Community-Based Epidemics (ESSENCE II) framework for evaluating syndromic surveillance systems. Syndromic surveillance: Report from a national conference, 2003. *Morbidity and Mortality Weekly Report, 53*(Suppl.), 159–165.

Lu, H.-M., Zeng, D., & Chen, H. (2006). *Ontology-based automatic chief complaints classification for syndromic surveillance.* Tucson: University of Arizona, AI Lab.

Ma, H., Rolka, H., Mandl, K., Buckeridge, D., Fleischauer, A., & Pavlin, J. (2005). Implementation of laboratory order data in BioSense Early Event Detection and Situation Awareness System. *Morbidity and Mortality Weekly Report, 54*(Suppl.), 27–30.

Ma, J., Zeng, D., & Chen, H. (2006). Spatial-temporal cross-correlation analysis: A new measure and a case study in infectious disease informatics. *Proceedings of the IEEE Intelligence and Security Informatics Conference* (Lecture Notes in Computer Science, 3975), 542–547.

MacEachren, A., Brewer, C., & Pickle, L. (1998). Visualizing georeferenced data: Representing reliability of health statistics. *Environment and Planning A, 30*(9), 1547–1561.

Magruder, S. F. (2003). Evaluation of over-the-counter pharmaceutical sales as a possible early warning indicator of human disease. *Johns Hopkins APL Technical Digest, 24*(4). Retrieved March 5, 2007, from techdigest.jhuapl.edu/td2404/Magruder.pdf

Mandl, K. D., Overhage, J. M., Wagner, M. M., Lober, W. B., Sebastiani, P., Mostashari, F., et al. (2004). Implementing syndromic surveillance: A practical guide informed by the early experience. *Journal of the American Medical Informatics Association, 11*(2), 141–150.

Miller, S., Fallon, K., & Anderson, L. (2003). New Hampshire emergency department syndromic surveillance system. *Journal of Urban Health, 80*(2, Suppl. 1), i118.

Minnesota Department of Health. (2004). Health Alert Network (HAN). St. Paul: The Department. Retrieved June 15, 2006, from www.health.state.mn.us/han/lopubhlth/2004AboutHan.pdf

Missouri Department of Health and Senior Services. (2006). Hospital electronic syndromic surveillance. Jefferson City, MO: The Department. Retrieved April 21, 2006, from www.dhss.mo.gov/HESS

Moore, A. W., Cooper, G., Tsui, F.-C., & Wagner, M. M. (2002). *Summary of biosurveillance-relevant statistical and data mining techniques* (RODS Laboratory Technical Report). Pittsburgh, PA: University of Pittsburgh, RODS Laboratory. Retrieved February 17, 2007, from rods.health.pitt.edu/published%20articles.htm

Mostashari, F., & Hartman, J. (2003). Syndromic surveillance: A local perspective. *Journal of Urban Health, 80*(2), i1–i17.

National Biological Information Infrastructure. (2006). *Highly pathogenic Avian Influenza early detection data system.* Retrieved June 14, 2006, from wildlifedisease.nbii.gov

Naumova, E. N., O'Neil, E., & MacNeill, I. (2005). INFERNO: A system for early outbreak detection and signature forecasting. *Morbidity and Mortality Weekly Report, 54*(Suppl.), 77–83.

Neill, D., Moore, A., & Cooper, G. (2005). A Bayesian spatial scan statistic. *Advances in Neural Information Processing Systems, 16*, 651–658.

Nekomoto, T. S., Riggins, W. S., & Franklin, M. (2003). *Pilot results: Syndromic surveillance utilizing Catalis Health Point-of-Care Technology in a rural Texas outpatient clinic.* Retrieved June 23, 2006, from www.thecatalis.com/syndromic/SyndromicSurveillanceusingCatalis.pdf

Neubauer, A. (1997). The EWMA control chart: Properties and comparison with other quality-control procedures by computer simulation. *Clinical Chemistry, 43*(4), 594–601.

North Carolina Public Health Information Network. (2006). *Disease Event Tracking and Epidemiologic Collection Tool.* Chapel Hill, NC: The Network. Retrieved June 13, 2006, from www.ncdetect.org

North Dakota Department of Health. (2006). *Syndromic surveillance.* Bismarck, ND: The Department. Retrieved May 12, 2006, from www.health.state.nd.us/disease/Surveillance/syndromicsurveillance.htm

Ohkusa, Y., Shigematsu, M., Taniguchi, K., & Okabe, N. (2005). Experimental surveillance using data on sales of over-the-counter medications: Japan, November 2003–April 2004. *Morbidity and Mortality Weekly Report, 54*(Suppl.), 47–52.

Ohkusa, Y., Sugawara, T., Hiroaki, S., Kawaguchi, Y., Taniguchi, K., & Okabe, N. (2005). Experimental three syndromic surveillances in Japan: OTC, outpatient visits and ambulance transfer [Poster]. *Proceedings of the Syndromic Surveillance Conference*, Seattle, WA.

Olszewski, R. T. (2003). Bayesian classification of triage diagnoses for the early detection of epidemics. *Proceedings of the 16th International Conference of the Florida Artificial Intelligence Research Society*, 412–416.

Pan, E. (2004). *The value of healthcare information exchange and interoperability.* Boston: Center for Information Technology Leadership.

Pavlin, J. A. (2003). Investigation of disease outbreaks detected by "syndromic" surveillance systems. *Journal of Urban Health, 80*(2), 107–114.

Pinner, R., Rebmann, C., Schuchat, A., & Hughes, J. (2003). Disease surveillance and the academic, clinical, and public health communities. *Emerging Infectious Diseases, 9*, 781–787.

Platt, R., Bocchino, C., Caldwell, B., Harmon, R., Kleinman, K., Lazarus, R., et al. (2003). Syndromic surveillance using minimum transfer of identifiable data: The example of the National Bioterrorism Syndromic Surveillance Demonstration Program. *Journal of Urban Health, 80*(2), i25–i31.

Publication of updated guidelines for evaluating public health surveillance systems. (2001). *Journal of the American Medical Association, 286*(12), 1446.

Quenel, P., Dab, W., Hannoun, C., & Cohen, J. (1994). Sensitivity, specificity and predictive values of health service based indicators for the surveillance of Influenza A epidemics. *International Journal of Epidemiology, 23*, 849–855.

Rath, T. M., Carreras, M., & Sebastiani, P. (2003). Automated detection of influenza epidemics with hidden Markov models. *Proceedings of the 5th International Symposium on Intelligent Data Analysis* (Lecture Notes in Computer Science 2810), 521–532.

Reingold, A. (2003). If syndromic surveillance is the answer, what is the question? *Biosecurity and Bioterrorism, 1*, 1–5.

Reis, B., & Mandl, K. (2003). Time series modeling for syndromic surveillance. *BMC Medical Informatics and Decision Making, 3*. Retrieved February 17, 2007, from www.biomedcentral.com/content/pdf/1472-6947-3-2.pdf

Reis, B., & Mandl, K. (2004). Syndromic surveillance: The effects of syndrome grouping on model accuracy and outbreak detection. *Annals of Emergency Medicine, 44*(3), 235–241.

Rhodes, B., & Kailar, R. (2005). *On securing the Public Health Information Network Messaging System.* Retrieved July 9, 2006, from middleware.internet 2.edu/pki05/proceedings/kailar-phinms.pdf

Ritter, T. (2002). LEADERS: Lightweight Epidemiology Advanced Detection and Emergency Response System. Chemical and Biological Sensing III (Proceedings of SPIE, vol. 4722), 110–120.

Roberts, F. S. (2002). *Challenges for discrete mathematics and theoretical computer science in the defense against bioterrorism.* New Brunswick, NJ: Rutgers University, Center for Discrete Mathematics and Computer Science.

Rogerson, P. A. (1997). Surveillance systems for monitoring the development of spatial patterns. *Statistics in Medicine, 16*(18), 2081–2093.

Rogerson, P. A. (2005). Spatial surveillance and cumulative sum methods. In A. B. Lawson & K. Kleinman (Eds.), *Spatial and syndromic surveillance for public health* (pp. 95–113). Chichester, UK: Wiley.

Rolka, H. (2005). *National Academy of Sciences Workshop, Toward Improved Visualization of Uncertain Information.* Washington, DC: The Academy.

Romaguera, R. A., German, R. R., & Klaucke, D. N. (2000). Evaluating public health surveillance. In S. M. Teutsch & R. E. Churchill (Eds.), *Principles and practice of public health surveillance* (2nd ed.). New York: Oxford University Press.

Serfling, R. E. (1963). Methods for current statistical analysis of excess pneumonia influenza deaths. *Public Health Reports, 78*, 494–506.

Shahar, Y., & Musen, M. (1996). Knowledge-based temporal abstraction in clinical domains. *Artificial Intelligence in Medicine, 8*, 267–298.

Shneiderman, B. (1998). *Designing the user interface: Strategies for effective human–computer interaction* (3rd ed.). Reading, MA: Addison-Wesley.

Siegrist, D. (1999). The threat of biological attack: Why concern now? *Emerging Infectious Diseases, 5*, 505–508.

Siegrist, D., McClellan, G., Campbell, M., Foster, V., Burkom, H., Hogan, W., et al. (2004). *Evaluation of algorithms for outbreak detection using clinical data from five U.S. cities* (Technical Report, DARPA Bio-ALIRT Program). Retrieved March 5, 2007, from www.syndromic.org/publications/5_cities_eval_final.pdf

Siegrist, D., & Pavlin, J. (2004). Bio-ALIRT biosurveillance detection algorithm evaluation. *Morbidity and Mortality Weekly Report, 53*(Suppl.), 152–158.

Sniegoski, C. A. (2004). Automated syndromic classification of chief complaint records. *Johns Hopkins APL Technical Digest, 25*(1), 68–75.

Sokolow, L. Z., Grady, N., Rolka, H., Walker, D., McMurray, P., English-Bullard, R., et al. (2005). Deciphering data anomalies in BioSense. *Morbidity and Mortality Weekly Report, 54*(Suppl.), 133–140.

Sonesson, C., & Bock, D. (2003). A review and discussion of prospective statistical surveillance in public health. *Journal of the Royal Statistical Society Series A, 166*(1), 5–21.

Suzuki, S., Ohyama, T., Taniguchi, K., Kimura, M., Kobayashi, J., Okabe, N., et al. (2003). Web-based Japanese syndromic surveillance for FIFA World Cup 2002. *Journal of Urban Health, 80*(2), i123.

Thomas, D., Arouh, S., Carley, K., Kraiman, J., & Davis, J. (2005). Automated anomaly detection processor for biologic terrorism early detection: Hampton, Virginia. *Morbidity and Mortality Weekly Report, 54*(Suppl.), 203.

Thomas, M., & Mead, C. (2005). The architecture of sharing: An HL7 version 3 framework offers semantically interoperable healthcare information. *Healthcare Informatics.* Retrieved June 23 from www.healthcare-informatics.com/issues/2005/11_05/jones.htm

Thurmond, M. (2006, March). *Global foot-and-mouth disease modeling and surveillance*. Paper presented at the Arizona Biosurveillance Workshop, Tucson, AZ.

Travers, D. A., & Haas, S. W. (2004). Evaluation of emergency medical text processor, a system for cleaning chief complaint textual data. *Academic Emergency Medicine, 11*, 1170–1176.

Tsui, F.-C., Espino, J. U., Dato, V. M., Gesteland, P. H., Hutman, J., & Wagner, M. M. (2003). Technical description of RODS: A real-time public health surveillance system. *Journal of the American Medical Informatics Association, 10*, 399–408.

Tsui, F.-C., Espino, J. U., & Wagner, M. M. (2005). *The timeliness, reliability, and cost of real-time and batch chief complaint data*. Retrieved July 9, 2006, from rods.health.pitt.edu/LIBRARY/2005%20Tsui-Real-time%20&%20Batch% 20Chief%20ComplaintData-FINAL.pdf

Tsui, F.-C., Wagner, M. M., Dato, V. M., & Chang, C. C. H. (2002). Value of ICD-9–coded chief complaints for detection of epidemics. *Journal of American Medical Informatics Association, 9*(6 Suppl 1), s41–s47.

Uhde, K. B., Farrell, C., Geddie, Y., Leon, M., & Cattani, J. (2005). Early detection of outbreaks using the BioDefend™ syndromic surveillance system: Florida, May 2002-July 2004. *Morbidity and Mortality Weekly Report, 54*(Suppl.), 204.

Umland, E., Brillman, J., Koster, F., Joyce, E., Forslund, D., Picard, R., et al. (2003). Fielding the bio-surveillance analysis, feedback, evaluation and response (B-SAFER) System. *Proceedings of the 3rd Annual Biological Threat Reduction Conference*, 185–190.

U.S. Department of Agriculture. (2006). *An early detection system for highly pathogenic H5N1 avian influenza in wild migratory birds: U.S. interagency strategic plan*. Retrieved July 13, 2006, from www.usda.gov/documents/wild birdstrategicplanpdf.pdf

U.S. Department of Health and Human Services. (2003). *An overview of PHINMS*. Retrieved July 9, 2006, from www.nyc.gov/html/doh/downloads/ pdf/acco/2004/acco-rfp-fund-20041122-PHINMS.pdf

Vergu, E., Grais, R. F., Sarter, H., Fagot, J.-P., Lambert, B., Valleron, A.-J., et al. (2006). Medication sales and syndromic surveillance: France. *Emerging Infectious Diseases, 12*, 416–421.

Wagner, M. M., Espino, J., Tsui, F. C., Gesteland, P., Chapman, W. W., Ivanov, O., et al. (2004). Syndrome and outbreak detection using chief-complaint data: Experience of the real-time outbreak and disease surveillance project. *Morbidity and Mortality Weekly Report, 53*(Suppl.), 28–32.

Wagner, M. M., Tsui, F.-C., Espino, J. U., Dato, V. M., Sittig, D. F., Caruana, R. A., et al. (2001). The emerging science of very early detection of disease outbreaks. *Journal of Public Health Management Practice, 7*(6), 51–59.

Wagner, M. M., Tsui, F.-C., Espino, J. U., Hogan, W., Hutman, J., Hersh, J., et al. (2004). National retail data monitor for public health surveillance. *Morbidity and Mortality Weekly Report, 53*(Suppl.), 40–42.

Wong, W. K., Moore, A., Cooper, G. F., & Wagner, M. (2002). Rule-based anomaly pattern detection for detecting disease outbreaks. *Proceedings of the American Association for Artificial Intelligence*, 217–223.

Wong, W. K., Moore, A., Cooper, G. F., & Wagner, M. (2003). WSARE: What's Strange About Recent Events? *Journal of Urban Health, 80*(2, Suppl. 1), 66–75.

Wurtz, R. (2004). *White paper: ELR, LOINC, SNOMED, and limitations in public health*. Retrieved July 01 from www.stchome.com/White_Papers/ WHP042%20Limitations%20in%20PH.pdf

Yan, P., Zeng, D., & Chen, H. (2006). A review of public health syndromic surveillance systems. *Proceedings of the IEEE International Conference on Intelligence and Security Informatics*, 249–260.

Yeh, A. B., Huang, L., & Wu, Y.-F. (2004). A likelihood-ratio-based EWMA control chart for monitoring variability of multivariate normal processes. *IIE Transactions, 36*(9), 865–879.

Yeh, A. B., Lin, D. K. J., Zhou, H., & Venkataramani, C. (2003). A multivariate exponentially weighted moving average control chart for monitoring process variability. *Journal of Applied Statistics, 30*(5), 507–536.

Yih, W., Caldwell, B., & Harmon, R. (2004). The National Bioterrorism Syndromic Surveillance Demonstration Program. *Morbidity and Mortality Weekly Report, 53*(Suppl.), 43–46.

Yih, W. K., Abrams, A., Danila, R., Green, K., Kleinman, K., Kulldorff, M., et al. (2005). Ambulatory-care diagnoses as potential indicators of outbreaks of gastrointestinal illness: Minnesota. *Morbidity and Mortality Weekly Report, 54*(Suppl.), 157–162.

Zelicoff, A. (2002). *The Rapid Syndrome Validation Project (RSVP) ™ Users' Manual and Description*. Albuquerque, NM: Sandia National Laboratories.

Zelicoff, A., Brillman, J., & Forslund, D. (2001). The Rapid Syndrome Validation Project (RSVP). *Proceedings of the American Medical Informatics Association Symposium*, 771–775.

Zeng, D., Chang, W., & Chen, H. (2004). A comparative study of spatio-temporal hotspot analysis techniques in security informatics. *Proceedings of the 7th IEEE International Conference on Intelligent Transportation Systems*, 106–111.

Zeng, D., Chen, H., Tseng, C., Chang, W., Eidson, M., Gotham, I., et al. (2005). BioPortal: A case study in infectious disease informatics. *Proceedings of the Joint Conference on Digital Libraries*, 418.

Zeng, D., Chen, H., Tseng, C., Larson, C. A., Eidson, M., Gotham, I., et al. (2004). West Nile virus and botulism portal: A case study in infectious disease informatics. *Proceedings of the IEEE International Conference on Intelligence and Security Informatics* (Lecture Notes in Computer Science 3073), 28–41.

Zeng, D., Chen, H., Tseng, C., Larson, C. A., Eidson, M., Gotham, I., et al. (2005). BioPortal: An integrated infectious disease information sharing and analysis environment. *Proceedings of the Digital Government Conference, DG.O*, 235–236.

Zhang, J., Tsui, F., Wagner, M., & Hogan, W. (2003). Detection of outbreaks from time series data using wavelet transform. *Proceedings of the American Medical Informatics Association Symposium*, 748–752.

Zhu, B., & Chen, H. (2005). Information visualization. *Annual Review of Information Science and Technology, 39*, 139–177.

CHAPTER 11

Educational Informatics

Nigel Ford
University of Sheffield

Introduction

Educational informatics is a relatively new area of research, representing the convergence of aspects of information science, computing, education, instructional systems technology, and learning sciences; and building on, integrating, and extending these areas of endeavor. Its development represents a response to the question: How can we bring together educational computing and information science to better harness the increasing wealth of resources accessible via the Internet for the purposes of learning? Learning may be formal, entailing teacher-led activities that take place in educational institutions such as schools and universities. However, it may also take the form of self-directed lifelong learning. The former emphasizes "mediation"—used here to refer to intervention on the part of teachers and learning designers in the learning process, typically to select and present information to learners. The latter entails autonomous information seeking on the part of the learner. These two strands may, of course, blend and intersect to a degree, in that aspects of autonomy and self-direction are increasingly incorporated into formal education, for example in the move toward inquiry-based learning, and lifelong autonomous learners may at any stage opt to partake in mediated learning activity.

Developments in educational computing have attempted to bring increasing levels of individualization to learning by making use of pedagogical[1] knowledge to enable systems to select and present information in response to the needs and preferences of individual learners. Typically, such systems have been characterized by relatively sophisticated pedagogical mediation and relatively small volumes of closed corpus information—relative, that is, to systems developed within information science. Conversely, information science has been particularly concerned with the development of systems that access relatively large volumes of diverse information sources without attempting to provide a high level of pedagogical mediation.

By combining key aspects of both of these fields of endeavor, educational informatics seeks to:

(a) Furnish information seeking tools with the capacity to offer a degree of pedagogical mediation (i.e., make use of some representation of pedagogical knowledge) designed to help autonomous learners access large volumes of diverse information sources more effectively in terms of their learning

(b) Furnish highly pedagogically mediated, computer-assisted learning systems with the capacity to find, access, and make use of large volumes of diverse information sources for learning purposes

Educational informatics systems may be useful to both teachers and learners. Clearly, teachers may benefit from any enhanced capability to discover potentially useful learning resources available, for example, over the Internet. However, learners engaged in relatively autonomous information seeking—whether in the context of formal education or of self-directed lifelong learning—may benefit from the availability of pedagogical assistance in the discovery of appropriate information sources.

Educational informatics may be defined with different levels of breadth. Levy, Ford, Foster, Madden, Miller, Nunes, et al. (2003, p. 299) apply a relatively broad definition when they describe educational informatics as the study of:

> the application of digital technologies and techniques to the use and communication of information in learning and education.

The present review applies a somewhat narrower definition, as the study of:

> the development and application of digital technologies and techniques that use pedagogical knowledge representations in order to facilitate or engage in educational resource discovery for learning.

The principal purpose of taking this narrower view is to differentiate educational informatics from the more general field of educational computing. Including *resource discovery*[2] as a defining criterion enables differentiation of educational informatics systems from the type of computer-assisted learning systems that have existed since the 1960s. It also excludes the application of information and communication technologies (ICT) in general to education, meaning that the use of, for example, newer technologies such as Web 2.0 technologies, gaming, and m-learning do not per se come within the remit of educational informatics as defined here.

The inclusion of the use of *pedagogical knowledge representations* serves to differentiate educational informatics systems from, say, the use of an information retrieval system such as a Web search engine to locate educational materials. It also excludes more general information systems that may be used within education—for example, educational administrative systems not directly dealing with teaching and learning. However, it is acknowledged that a less restrictive definition of educational informatics is found useful by many working in the field.[3.]

The next section begins by exploring the foundations on which educational informatics is being built. Particularly important are developing standards relating to interoperability and the sharing of educational resources, and to metadata standards to support resource discovery. The following section then introduces a selection of developments in educational informatics that illustrate key themes relating to both what educational informatics researchers are trying to achieve and how they are going about it. These content- and process-based themes are elaborated in the final section, which goes on to propose that they echo tensions arguably characterizing research more generally and to suggest the potential usefulness of a dialectical approach, focusing more explicitly upon the nature of conflicts and tensions.

Foundations

Educational informatics has its roots in a number of developments in computing, education, and information science. From the development of the first computer-assisted instructional (CAI) systems in the 1960s, educational technologists have been keen to exploit the potential of the computer to enable a level of *individualization* in learning. The mid-1980s saw the development of Intelligent Tutoring Systems (ITS) as artificial intelligence techniques came on stream and were applied to education, and increasingly sophisticated models of the learner were incorporated into the systems. The 1990s saw a shift on the part of ITS developers away from an exclusive concern with individualist objectivist views of learning, to embrace social constructivist perspectives. The early 1990s saw the development of Internet-based training, with the emergence in the late 1990s of the concept of *e-learning*. This period also saw the rapid development of learning management systems (LMS) and of standards to support interoperability between such systems.

Another key theme has been increasing interest in the role of various types and levels of *autonomy* in learning. There was great interest in the 1970s in the notion of independence in learning; the 1980s witnessed a shift to resource-based and project work in schools, and independent study and inquiry-based learning in higher education. At the same time, interest grew in the notion of lifelong, self-directed learning. The notion of *information seeking* on the part of the learner is a key element of such forms of study. Concern to promote autonomy and the development of "learning to learn" meta-cognitive skills—essentially a movement from learning content to learning processes—have increased from the 1990s to the present time.

During this period there has been growing interest in increasing the synergy between well established *resource discovery* systems and standards developed in the library and information science world—including classification schemes, thesauri, cataloging codes, and cross-search client-server protocols—and the more sophisticated forms of resource discovery facilities for Web-based information sources.

It is on these foundations that the developments described in educational informatics are based. This section briefly summarizes key historical developments in educational computing and information science that support educational informatics.

Interoperability and the Sharing of Learning Resources

Early computer-assisted learning (CAL) systems, although they made use of pedagogic knowledge in their functioning, did not engage in resource discovery. Early systems were content-bound in the sense that content and control were inextricably linked. The advent of intelligent tutoring systems did not bring with it any easy ability to slot in alternative content. Later knowledge-based tutoring systems (KBTS) and the availability of software such as expert system shells with which they could be built, on the other hand, were characterized by a separation of content from control in that knowledge representations were explicit and editable independently from the inference and other control (e.g., explanation) facilities. Content was represented in agreed formalisms that were supported by standard inference techniques such as backward and forward chaining rule systems. Work on intelligent educational systems continues and, with an increasing focus on the integration of resource discovery using educational metadata, it constitutes an important strand in the development of educational informatics.

At the level of educational course management there has been an increasing take-up, by organizations delivering education and training, of virtual learning environments (VLEs) and learning management systems (LMSs). Basically, LMSs act as a shell into which different subject content can be slotted. Early VLEs and LMSs were not characterized by interoperability. Courses developed for one system could not necessarily be imported by another. Recent years, however, have seen the development of standards designed to support the sharing and reuse of learning resources, and to promote interoperability between different delivery systems.

These developments have brought into prominence the role of resource discovery. As discussed in the section on adaptive systems for personalized resource discovery, an important strand of educational informatics is represented by work integrating course construction with metadata-based resource discovery to provide personalized learning experiences. These developments are closely related to the emergence of the concept of re-usable learning objects in which there has been much interest, along with standards for describing, structuring, and utilizing them.

The Shareable Content Object Reference Model (SCORM), developed by the Advanced Distributed Learning (ADL) initiative of the U. S. Department of Defense and the White House Science and Technology Bureau (Advanced Distributed Learning, 2006), details how learning objects should be structured and packaged in order to facilitate reuse and incorporation within different learning environments (Bohl, Schellhase, Sengler, & Winand, 2002). According to Wiley and Edwards (2002, p. 33), a learning object is "any digital resource that can be reused to mediate learning." SCORM uses the term "sharable content object" to describe "a learning object that has the appropriate metadata, and is packaged according to the SCORM" (Ploetz, 2004, online). To quote Bohl et al. (2002, p. 950):

> SCORM denominates the smallest unit which can be administered by an LMS as a Sharable Content Object (SCO). An SCO represents one or more assets which use the SCORM run-time environment to communicate with different LMSs. An SCO represents the lowest level of content granularity which can be tracked by an LMS. An SCO should be independent of learning context to be reusable in different learning situations. Moreover, several SCOs can be assembled to form learning or exercise units on a superordinate level. To make a potential reuse practicable, SCOs should be small units. They can be the basis for sharable content repositories which facilitate their exchange.

SCORM also provides guidelines, in the form of the SCORM CAM (Content Aggregation Model), for the aggregation of SCOs to form learning objects of larger granularity (Advanced Distributed Learning, 2004). Other content aggregation schemes include the IMS (Instructional Management System) Simple Sequencing Specification (IMS Global Learning Consortium, 2003b).

Interoperability standards also exist relating to the assessment of learning. The IMS QTI (Question and Test Interoperability) standard (IMS Global Learning Consortium, 2006), for example, describes how assessment procedures—whether individual test questions or aggregations of them relating to particular learning objects—and procedures for processing the results should be specified so that they and the learner data they generate can be exchanged and used in different LMS. The IMS Global Learning Consortium (www.imsproject.org) has also developed standards relating to the tracking of learner progress and the exchange of student records between systems.

Resource Discovery via Educational Metadata

Educational computing and information science profitably combine insofar as the widespread sharing and reuse of learning objects and other learning resources require facilities that enable the discovery of resources, whether these reside in specialist learning object repositories or as open corpus material on the Web. Indeed, the very nature of shareability and reusability means that they are essentially linked to the concept of resource discovery.

Such discovery is one of the key functions of metadata. The IEEE (Institute of Electrical and Electronics Engineers) Learning Technology Standards Committee's (2002) Draft Standard for Learning Object Metadata (LOM) is a leading contender as a worldwide standard for learning object metadata. Godby (2004, online) describes its importance:

> As learning objects grow in number and importance, institutions are faced with the daunting task of managing them. Like familiar items in library collections, learning objects need to be organised by subject and registered in searchable repositories. But they also introduce special problems. As computer files, they are dependent on a particular hardware and software environment. And as materials with a pedagogical intent, they are associated with metrics such as learning objectives, reading levels and methods for evaluating student performance. The conventional wisdom is that a learning object should be accompanied by a metadata record, whose minimal form would contain the information typically found in the description of a book or journal article, such as *title, author, subject*, and a unique identifier. But a more complete record would describe the technical and educational context required to activate the learning object and connect it with others to create a rich educational experience for an appropriate audience.

LOM descriptions include pedagogic knowledge in the form of specifications of a range of learning object characteristics, including level of difficulty, interactivity type and level, semantic density, intended end-user role, typical learning time, and educational context. Other standards include Dublin Core Education (DC-Ed) from the Dublin Core Metadata Initiative (DCMI) Education Working Group (DCMI Education Working Group, 2004), and the IMS Global Learning consortium's metadata specification (IMS Global Learning Consortium, 2002).

Different communities engaged in the creation and use of metadata have different needs and, for this reason, make use of different "application profiles." For example the SCORM, the Education Network Australia, ARIADNE, and the Gateway to Educational Materials application profiles are based on Dublin Core, and those of UK LOM Core and

CanCore are based on IEEE LOM. These entail potentially different selections, uses, and interpretations of metadata elements from one or more metadata standards, and are thus not necessarily interoperable. Such application profiles may diverge from—and thus be incompatible with—the generic standards from which they derive elements in that they may interpret existing elements differently, and/or develop their own new elements, to reflect local needs. As Godby (2004, online) points out:

> two application profiles might use *LOM.Classification. Purpose* and still fail to interoperate because this element could be used to annotate different facets of the resource, such as pedagogical intent and position within a knowledge hierarchy.

Godby goes on to note that agreed controlled vocabularies and tools to enforce consistent interpretation are not yet widely available. She reports a comparative survey designed to investigate the degree of overlap among thirty-five application profiles developed by a range of organizations engaged in the creation and use of learning object metadata. She concludes that there is a trade-off between breadth of interoperability and depth of exposure of technical and pedagogic features of the resources addressed by the metadata. She describes the possibility of deriving an interoperable composite metadata record thus:

> A viable record can be assembled from the most highly recommended LOM elements. It is descriptively similar to an unqualified Dublin Core record and exhibits regional variation. Such a record lacks the elements for describing the educational, social, and technical contexts required for a successful interaction with a learning object. But application profiles designed primarily for the management of locally produced records, such as ENC, include most of these elements and support a rich description. By contrast, meta-profiles such as CanCore, RDN, and UK LOM Core, which are designed to promote interoperability among similar projects, have far fewer recommended fields. (Godby, 2004, online)

After observing that organizations tend either to adopt an abbreviated form of a complete scheme or to mix elements from different schemes, Sun and Fu (2005, p. 402) propose a LOM-based application profile that they argue provides sufficient educational and technical context detail to enable successful learning interactions, including "personalised content configuration"—a prime feature of current educational informatics developments. Qin and Hernandez (2006) see an urgent need to develop an agreed controlled vocabulary for learning objects at a level of detail not catered for in existing metadata schemes. They propose a learning objects ontology, which they argue is desirable in order to overcome the limitations of metadata standards to express structural components of learning objects.

Standards are also being developed to describe learning competencies, and learners themselves, in terms of, for example, their learning goals, existing levels of knowledge and attainment, and learning styles and preferences. Standards developed for the specification of learning competencies include the IEEE Learning Technology Standards Committee's (2005) Draft Standard for Competency Definition Data Objects. Specifications also exist for educational levels, such as those of the Metadata for Education Group (www.ukoln.ac.uk/metadata/education/documents/ed-level.html). Learners themselves may be described using schemes such as IMS LIP (Learner Information Package) (IMS Global Learning Consortium, 2001) and the IEEE Learning Technology Standards Committee's (2001, online) PAPI (Public and Private Information) draft scheme, which:

> defines and/or references elements for recording descriptive information about: knowledge acquisition, skills, abilities, personal contact information, learner relationships, security parameters, learner preferences and styles, learner performance, learner-created portfolios, and similar types of information. This standard permits different views of the learner information (perspectives: learner, teacher, parent, school, employer, etc.) and substantially addresses issues of privacy and security.

Metadata terms used to describe learners and learning resources are underpinned by ontologies specifying concepts, and relationships among them, that make up the particular domains they represent. To this extent ontologies may be considered models of their domain. However, as well as enabling metadata to be derived from them, ontologies may also be used to infer—from the hierarchical subordination of certain concepts within an ontology—pedagogic knowledge such as which concepts are prerequisites for the learning of others. Ontologies may also underpin standards for the specification of pedagogical designs, such as the IMS Global Learning Consortium's (2003a) Learning Design Specification (IMS LD) and the Educational Modelling Language (EML) on which it is based. Koper and Manderveld (2004, p. 537) define the EML as "a semantically rich information model and binding, describing the content and process within units of learning from a pedagogical perspective in order to support reuse and interoperability."

Developmental Strands in Educational Informatics

The simplest form of educational informatics system is a retrieval system that enables resource discovery via some pedagogic knowledge representation, for example in the form of pedagogical metadata. A number of educational repositories (Sampson & Karampiperis, 2006) enable users to search for learning resources via metadata that specifies various pedagogical features of those resources. Examples include ARIADNE (www.ariadne-eu.org), CANCORE (www.cancore.ca/en), EducaNext (www.educanext.org), the Educational Network Australia (www.edna.edu.au), the Gateway to Educational Materials (www.thegateway.org), the Globewide Network Academy (www.gnacademy.org), the LearnAlberta Portal (www.learnalberta.ca/Main.aspx), the Multimedia Educational Resource for Learning and Online Teaching (www.merlot.org), the Science, Mathematics, Engineering and Technology Education Digital Library (www.smete.org), the Scottish electronic Staff Development Library (www.sesdl.scotcit.ac.uk), and the World Lecture Hall (www.utexas.edu/world/lecture).

The following sections introduce a number of more complex educational informatics systems, which form the main focus of this review. The first three sections relate predominantly to views of learning in terms of *individual* activity. The three following sections relate to alternative pedagogies that focus more on *social and community* aspects of learning.

We begin with the description of a relatively simple form of educational informatics system that enables users to browse using pedagogical knowledge representations, as well as the representation of subject domain knowledge, in the form of ontologies. The second system described (TM4L) also utilizes pedagogical as well as subject domain knowledge in the form of *themes* that enable individualized browsing of learning resources based on topic maps.

In the systems described in the section on ontology-based learning resource repositories, these pedagogical knowledge representations were used, in conjunction with subject domain representations, essentially as navigation tools for learning resource repositories, enabling users to browse and filter their searches. The section on systems to empower learners explores attempts to build systems that use pedagogic knowledge to place learners in control, and to suggest to them information seeking strategies that are appropriate to particular educational tasks. In this case, the pedagogical knowledge is used to enhance the information seeker's abilities and level of control, rather than the navigation tools available to him or her. Pedagogical knowledge is used here to enhance information seekers' *meta-cognition*—awareness and management of their own learning processes.

The section on adaptive systems for personalized resource discovery introduces systems that themselves directly process pedagogical knowledge representations in order to search for, retrieve, process, and present information *for* the learner. They are designed to perform on behalf of the learner—or *supplant*—some of the intellectual processes that otherwise would be required of him or her. In view of the amount of work in this area, this section is divided into subsections outlining the basic approach, reflecting moves to provide access to increasingly heterogeneous sources of information sources and addressing open corpus information sources.

The next three sections discuss the need to address pedagogies that focus on social and community aspects of learning. An "ecological" approach to supporting learning is introduced in the section on harnessing knowledge of community learning activity, which relies on gathering, interpreting, and using data from communities of learners over time. The system learns via the analysis of these data in order to generate new pedagogic knowledge, which can be further used in the system. The final section also explores community-based learning, extending the notion of pedagogic knowledge representations to include academic argumentation in the form of *knowledge charts* for use in *knowledge neighborhoods*.

Ontology-Aware Learning Resource Repositories to Support Learners' Information Seeking

Shabajee, McBride, Steer, and Reynolds (2006, p. 464) report the development of a prototype "digital resource discovery portal," the objective of which was:

> to provide a usable and effective means for school teachers and students to access digital resources in support of their teaching and learning (linked to the local curriculum) from multimedia/interactive-media spread across multiple collections in Singapore.

The system uses a Content Exchange Metadata Exchange Standard (CEMS) metadata application profile especially constructed to reflect the specific topics, types of resource, and educational levels of the Singaporean school curriculum (National Computer Systems, 2004). The "subject" element of this profile was extended with a thesaurus providing a curriculum-specific controlled vocabulary.

The metadata application profile was converted using the Web Ontology Language (OWL) to form a richer ontological model of the curriculum structure including year groups, types of students, and courses. The linked curriculum thesaurus was also converted, based on the SKOS RDF (Resource Description Framework) thesaurus format (Miles & Brickley, 2005). However, the system is also able to link to more detailed subject-specific curriculum ontologies created externally to reflect the degree of detail required to support specific curricula. One such demonstrator ontology was produced for the project in the area of history; it enabled learning resources to be tagged with metadata relating to specific people, places, and events. The system is also able to link to external information such as topical news and local events tagged as relevant to particular curriculum topics.

Learners use a faceted search/browse approach whereby they can apply filters progressively to refine search results by facet, including curriculum subject, type of resource (for example, lesson plan), type of media, educational level, availability and licensing terms, and by text search. Metadata terms link to items in the subject ontologies, enabling resource discovery to take advantage of Semantic Web-based inferencing. Thus a text search that includes a particular term describing an ontology element could retrieve resources tagged by terms that are related to that ontology element—for example, instances of a more general concept. By the same token, the addition of a new property to an ontology element would render all resources tagged by metadata linked to that element retrievable by the new property—without requiring that each resource be tagged with the new property.

Ontology awareness is also a key feature of TM4L. This is an environment designed to support the building and accessing of ontology-aware learning resource repositories using topic maps (Park & Hunting, 2002; Tramullas & Garrido, 2005). Topic maps are standards-based conceptual graphs similar to semantic networks. Internal and external learning resources are tagged by metadata, including LOM elements, and linked to ontologies that can be created by topic map authors. Authors can also create filters, or themes, to provide views of the concept maps to reflect different perspectives. As Dicheva and Dichev (2006, p. 394) noted, the result is that:

> a user's access to the learning collection is mediated by a multilayered browsable conceptual map of the subject domain. Strictly speaking, access to the learning collection is mediated by a set of browsable maps corresponding to the set of contexts or perspectives defined on the learning collection. Exploiting the map metaphor, the set of contexts or perspectives on a learning collection are analogous to the different types of maps used in practice, e.g., physical, political, economic, climate and population maps.

By applying themes, personalized views can be made available for different classes of learner (for example, those new to and those more experienced in a particular subject domain). The aim is to facilitate learners' resource discovery by enabling them to browse and search within the constraints of particular contexts specified by topic map authors, thus removing the need for them to sift through large volumes of materials that may be irrelevant due to the imprecision of more traditional keyword searching and browsing systems. The TM4L environment also provides support for the merging of ontologies.

Systems to Empower Learners and Enhance Meta-Cognitive Skills

The educational informatics systems discussed in the subsections on adaptive systems for personalized resource discovery make intelligent use of pedagogic knowledge in order to engage in effective resource searching. In doing so, they take certain decisions on behalf of the learner—in other words, to an extent *supplant* certain of the learner's intellectual processes. However, a number of educational informatics systems adopt a different approach in that they seek to increase the degree of learners' control over their own learning processes and to enhance their meta-cognitive skills.

For example, Papanikolaou and Grigoriadou (2006) propose an instructional framework designed to give learners control over the level of autonomy with which they learn. After choosing a learning goal to work on, the learner is provided with choice in relation to learning approach and the level of guidance he or she would like to receive. If the learner chooses a prescriptive approach, the system generates a learning sequence. It selects learning objects according to each person's learning style and provides navigation advice tailored to each learner's level of competence in the topics being taught. It also gives learners the opportunity to take more control by changing their own profiles relating to competence and preferred style, and/or switching off the system's adaptive and advisory features.

If the learner chooses a constructivist approach, the system provides project-based tasks. This mode includes a *problem manipulation space* in which the learner can generate a hypothesis and search for appropriate information to support it. The system provides support by suggesting appropriate Web resources and peers who may be able to help. These suggestions are based on the system's information on each learner's existing level of knowledge and his/her learning style. The learner can switch to prescriptive mode if he or she wishes at any time. The system thus enables learners to take varying levels of control over certain aspects of their learning. The constructivist learning mode entails a looser degree of supplantation in that open corpus materials are recommended within the context of more learner-driven information seeking.

Czarkowski and Kay (2006) report the development of Tutor3, which is also designed to make its adaptivity transparent to and controllable by users. The authors note that this is desirable to the extent that it may engender more trust in the system on the part of users, compensate for any errors or limitations in the adaptations, and be useful in facilitating reflective learning. The authors note that transparency also addresses, to some extent, issues Kobsa (2002) raised relating to legal requirements for people to be able to access personal details stored about them, to understand the ways in which they are being used, and to modify them if necessary.

Learning content is marked up using the Adaptive Text Markup Language (ATML) designed by the authors. This enables descriptions of adaptive components of learning resources to be attached to the resources themselves as metadata. These data are then used to enable a matching between learner characteristics and required adaptations. A document may thus contain different content for display in response to different learner requirements, which are stored in the user profile. Learners are initially asked about their learning goals and preferences, and this information is stored in each learner's profile. Such knowledge relates, for example, to the person's learning objectives, interests, and preferences— for example, to learn new material or to revise; to engage in minimal levels of learning just enough to pass or to master the material thoroughly; or to work with abstract definitions or concrete examples.

ATML enables different sections of a document to be tagged with information specifying the learner profile features for which they are appropriate. Thus, for example, only appropriately tagged content will be presented to a learner who has expressed a preference for a minimalist approach to learning; or, if the learner's current learning objective is to revise, then he or she will be passed to a set of multiple choice revision questions. The approach is similar to but simpler than that used in the AHA system (De Bra & Ruiter, 2001). A wide range of adaptive methods and techniques is available to the designers of educational systems and the notion of transparency in adaptation is likely to receive increasing attention. Brusilovsky (2003), for example, based on empirical evidence that individuals with differing levels of domain knowledge may react differently to different adaptive approaches, makes the case for systems that are able to adapt the nature of adaptation to individual users.

Rather than enabling learners to control the type and level of supplantation they receive from the system in relation to the processes of resource discovery, the approach described here seeks to generate pedagogic activity within learners so that they can themselves more effectively engage in resource discovery. The system makes use of relatively generic pedagogic knowledge in order to bring about more specific learning-related activities in the learner appropriate to the particular learning task on which he or she is engaged. It does this by seeking to make explicit and accessible learners' own implicit pedagogic knowledge.

This approach to educational informatics is employed in work reported by Cole, Cantero, and Ungar (2000), designed to build what may be described as pedagogically facilitating expertise into an information retrieval system. This work is predicated on a recognition of the inherently imprecise nature of information needs, and builds on a range of information science-based theoretical perspectives including those of Kuhlthau, Taylor, Belkin, and Oddy. Taylor (1968) suggested that awareness of one's information needs may vary from unconscious to explicitly known and clearly expressible. Importantly, in the early stages of working on an assignment, although the overall problem or topic may be clear, the associated information needs may be far from so, and not explicitly known or expressible by the learner. Cole follows Belkin (Belkin, Oddy, & Brooks, 1982a, 1982b) in acknowledging the paradox whereby information seekers may be required to express clearly what they do not know. This is the case particularly where a learner is in the early exploratory stages of an assignment—for example, Kuhlthau's (2005) *focusing* stage—a stage at which, Cole argues, many university students approach an information retrieval system to help them in essay assignments.

Cole argues that the expressed information need (forming a query to an information retrieval system) may not correspond at all well with what may subsequently turn out to be much more appropriate at a more advanced stage of learning. He argues that the refinement and increased awareness of the learner's information need may emerge during, and as a result of, interaction with an "enabling" information retrieval system (Cole et al., 2000, p. 499).

The ultimate aim is of a tool that can be added to the front-end of an information retrieval system that:

> if administered to the undergraduate at the beginning of his or her interaction with the IR system, will allow the system to make this diagnosis, then select the "enabling" device that is most appropriate to that particular student at that particular time. The "enabling" device ... is also a query formulation device: it draws-out from the student the concepts most pertinent to the task of writing an undergraduate essay for the student's topic; it then sorts/weights the concepts into a truly "effective" query to the IR system. (Cole et al., 2000, p. 499)

Cole has developed models and associated prototypes relating to the notion of an enabling information retrieval system. This work is included here because the system entails the use of pedagogic knowledge in order to facilitate more effective resource discovery. The conceptual and prototype experiments have also been developed with reference to a specifically educational task. The system provides searchers with a degree of pedagogic stimulation in the form of a template task structure model relating specifically to a particular type of essay typically set for undergraduate social sciences/humanities courses.

This work is based *inter alia* on Brookes's (1977, 1980) conjecture that communication entails a two level process. The first involves an analysis of what the sender of a communication is intending to say. The second represents the receiver's integration of the author's message within the broader context of the task in which he or she is engaged (Cole & Mandelblatt, 2000).

The system prompts the learner to engage in Brookes's second level of analysis, providing a degree of support in the form of a Task

Intervention Device. This consists of specific instructions aimed at help-ing the searcher better align his or her query to the information system and the structural requirements of the essay task (Cole, 2000, p. 423):

> The IRS [information retrieval system] offers the device to the student when the student indicates the nature of his or her information task to the system. In summary, the device schematizes a type of essay structure commonly used in his-tory called the compare-and-contrast essay. Second, the device forces the student to think of the essay as an inte-grated whole, centered on an argument or thesis statement. … While filling in the device, … the student must cognitively integrate the structure of a compare-and-contrast essay into what he or she already knows about his or her essay topic. The result for the student of being stimulated by the IR device to assemble then task-focus his or her response to the IRS's informative message is the transformation of the stu-dent's cognitive state or way of thinking about the essay. The student's cognitive state is then ready to receive the informa-tion contained in the next IRS message in a more productive, application-focused manner.

The device has also been embedded in a more complex strategy elab-orated by Cole et al. (2000) and Cole, Beheshti, Leide, and Large (2005).

More recent work is reported by Cole and Leide (2006), exploring the pedagogic potential of *metaphor instantiation* as the basis for developing information retrieval systems capable of helping people new to a topic learn more effectively from interacting with an information retrieval system by developing more appropriate retrieval queries. This work also focuses on stimulating learners' own metacognition. They seek to address the problem that a topic novice must query an information retrieval system on the basis of his or her own existing knowledge about concepts of which he or she wishes to learn more, whether entering his or her own keywords or using concepts located in a system thesaurus. Citing Barsalou (1992), Cole and Leide (2006, p. 173) note:

> For domain novice users, these concepts are taken from what little they know about the domain—concepts users think they know a little about but primarily want to find out more about. The concept terms in the query, representing the user's infor-mation need, are the user's own, fluctuating conceptualiza-tions of categories of objects, events or subject topics, found in his/her own memory.

These concepts do not necessarily map accurately onto those used to describe relevant documents in an information retrieval system. Metaphor instantiation is "a memory device for facilitating unfamiliar information processing" (Cole & Leide, 2006, p. 172) and the authors report investigations seeking to explore its potential use as a component of an information retrieval system designed to provide a temporary scaffolding structure from a known to an unknown domain, sufficient to enhance information seeking until a more appropriate structure can be established as the result of learning.

The research is in its early stages and has concentrated on researchers in the area of history. Cole & Leide have made progress developing a methodology for eliciting both metaphoric descriptions of users' research problems and search terms derived from these metaphors. The resulting lists of search terms display interesting variations. Work is progressing to evaluate the effectiveness of search terms derived from different sources of metaphor, namely those derived from the user's perceptions of his or her research topic, research problem situation, and the problem situation of the people on whom the researcher's study is focusing.

This work falls within educational informatics in that it is geared to developing new information retrieval systems that utilize pedagogic principles derived from a review of research in cognitive science. The hypothesis is that stimulation of users, by an information retrieval system, to generate deeper understanding of the learning needs underlying their information needs can result in the generation of queries to the information retrieval system that are more appropriate and effective than they would be if generated without such a device.

The devices Cole used constitute what Allert, Richter, and Nejdl (2004, p. 701) term "second-order learning objects." They differentiate between first-order learning objects, which essentially support reproductive learning, and second-order learning objects, which support productive or generative learning. Reproductive learning entails adaptation on the part of learners to their environment; generative learning may entail changes in the environment as a result of learning processes. First-order learning objects are designed around the learner achieving some specific learning objective. Second-order learning objects are designed to empower the learner to engage in enquiry and innovation—the situated identification of problems and the generation of solutions. They support strategies such as reflection, planning, decision making, and problem solving and may result in the development and change of the learning objects themselves. This type of learning is particularly appropriate to the knowledge creation perspective described in the section on alternative pedagogies; it requires the accommodation of open-ended and ill-structured goals and activities that defy complete planning, control, and predetermination. Examples of second-order learning objects include meta-cognitive strategies, creativity techniques, strategic planning methods, and problem-solving strategies.

Adaptive Systems for Personalized Resource Discovery

Insofar as they facilitate or engage in resource discovery using pedagogic knowledge representations, many modern Web-based adaptive systems may also be considered to be firmly within the scope of educational informatics as defined here. Via metadata, they are capable of retrieving and integrating a wide range of remotely authored shareable learning resources into personalized learning experiences for individual learners.

Personalized Resource Discovery

An example of such a system is the Adaptive Personalized eLearning Service (APeLS) reported by Conlan, Hockemeyer, Wade, and Albert (2003). APeLS can take metadata describing an individual's learning needs, prior competencies, and personal characteristics and construct a personalized course by sequencing appropriate learning objects discovered within one or more distributed specialist repositories. Input to a rule-based adaptive engine includes metadata relating to the learner, content in the form of learning resources, and narratives. A narrative is a description of the required conceptual pathway for a particular learner; it is built prior to searching for particular learning resources, taking account, for example, of prerequisite concepts and their sequencing. Thus, the system's narrative model refers to concepts rather than specific resources.

The system builds a list of candidate alternative resources that have the capacity to teach a particular narrative. This candidacy approach addresses the criticism that metadata can be too fine-grained in that they relate to specific learning resources as opposed to more abstract concepts (Dagger, Conlan, & Wade, 2003, p. 50):

> This abstraction allows the course author and instructional designer to design the course in a more structured way without necessarily being concerned with the individual pieces of content that will be used to populate the final course.

Candidate content groups can be formed containing alternative resources that share a common learning objective or prerequisite set of concepts. Such resources may reside in distributed repositories. A specific resource may subsequently be selected using a candidate selector set of rules (described by its own metadata) on the basis of further decision making according to other rules that take as input learning style or preferred teaching approach.

> For example, a narrative that adds concepts based on the learner's prior knowledge would, through the rule engine, look at the learner model repository to access the current learner's model. It would then query the learned competencies of that

learner before adding the concept. If that concept was represented by a candidate content group with several learning resources the rule engine would execute a candidate selector to choose the appropriate learning resource. The candidate selector would use the rule engine to access the content model of each candidate pagelet before making its selection. (Dagger et al., 2003, p. 54)

The "pagelet" in the last line of this quotation refers to a unit of content that is more flexible than a page. The authors note that it is useful for the course designer to decide, prior to creating a narrative, on the granularity of the desired personalization, which may be at different levels—for example, paragraph, section, or page.

O'Keeffe, Brady, Conlan, and Wade (2006) note that although early adaptive hypermedia systems personalized learning according to learners' prior knowledge, goals, and preferences, they did not explicitly address pedagogy. They report the incorporation and further development of the APeLS system in iClass, which is a framework of services designed to support teachers and learners in providing personalized learning experiences. In terms of standards, OWL is used for domain ontologies; IMS Learning Design (IMS LD) for structuring learning activities; IMS LIP for learner profiles; and SCORM for learning object manifests.

Like APeLS, iClass separates the generation of personalized conceptual learning paths from specific resources that can instantiate such paths. However, an important way in which iClass differs from APeLS is that pedagogy is explicitly represented in a separate model distinct from domain knowledge. The representation of pedagogies in a separate model means that they can be reused. The iClass Selector service generates a personalized learning path of concepts by reconciling requirements specified by its models relating to learners, teachers, subject conceptual domain, and pedagogical strategy. In doing so it takes account of the learner's characteristics and the teacher's preferred pedagogical strategy (although teachers can, if they wish, request the system to select pedagogical strategies). Pedagogical strategies specify the type of learning object and relations among them that the strategies require. For example, a case study strategy entails an introduction to the concept to be learned, presentation of a problem, provision of appropriate learning resources, and an example solution.

The Learning Object Generator service finds and/or creates appropriate learning objects to teach the concepts specified in the conceptual personalized learning path. It has access to metadata describing SCORM-based SCOs. If an existing SCO is appropriate and sufficient to constitute a suitable learning object, it is selected. If it is not, the generator is able to attempt to modify it in such a way as to make it suitable. If this is not possible, the generator can create a new learning object by combining and sequencing SCOs. The selection and sequencing take account of pedagogy and learner characteristics. New or modified learning objects are stored and a metadata manifest describing them is created.

Castillo, Gama, and Breda (2006) report on GIAS, a system also designed to select from a repository learning resources that are appropriate to individual learners' current states of knowledge and their preferred learning styles. However, the system differs from others in that, from a baseline initial psychometric assessment of learning style, it fine-tunes its model of each learner's style in response to feedback from interactions between the learner and learning resources. This ongoing adaptation is necessary because of inherent uncertainty in any psychometric assessment of learning style, as well as possible drift in learners' preferences over time and as a result of interactions with resources.

Metadata includes descriptions of resources in terms of the type of learning activity they represent (e.g., conceptual map, summary, historical review, lesson objectives), their medium of expression (e.g., text, picture, animated picture, audio, video), and their level of difficulty. Learner descriptions include domain knowledge and learning style.

Learning resources in the repository are first filtered to exclude those unsuitable for the learner's current level of domain knowledge. Further filtering then takes place via the matching of features of the resource with learning style preferences. Prior to obtaining any feedback from learner interactions with resources, the system assesses each person's learning style using Felder and Soloman's Index of Learning Styles Questionnaire. The system has a model that predicts the features of learning resources learners will prefer, characterized by each particular style.

However, from an initial state of prediction based on descriptions of stereotypical learning style preferences derived from the literature, this model is able to fine-tune its predictions in relation to each particular individual learner using feedback from ongoing interactions between learner and resources. Data indicating which resource links are visited, and explicit ratings of resources by learners, are able to provide suitable input to an adaptive version of the Naïve Bayes probabilistic classifier—the Adaptive Bayes (Gama & Castillo, 2002), which takes account of new incoming data to update its current model.

Resource Discovery from Heterogeneous Repositories

Simon, Dolog, Miklós, Olmedilla, and Sintek (2004, online) also report the development of a personalized adaptive system. Their focus is providing unified intelligent access to the diversity of heterogeneous resources potentially accessible to support learning by employees in large organizations. These may include, for example, training materials developed in-house, locally available learning management systems, commercially available courses, in-house knowledge management systems, and online bookstores. The authors refer to such a range of resources as a "learning space," and report work to develop what they term "smart spaces for learning" entailing systems and approaches capable of providing not only a unified "view" of a learning space, but also the ability to generate personalized learning experiences via a "Personal Learning Assistant" that searches for appropriate resources using metadata describing potential learning resources, subject domains, and learners.

As part of the ELENA project (www.elena-project.org), a prototype system has been set up integrating a range of sources of learning resources including:

- Educanext (a portal supporting the exchange of learning resources)
- The ULI (Universitärer Lehrverbund Informatik) project (a university teaching network entailing the exchange of course materials, courses and certificates)
- IMC CLIX (a commercially produced Learning Management System)
- IteachYou (a multimedia learning environment designed for the Internet or intranets)
- Arel (a service for relatively large organizations offering live and on-demand broadcasts by experts to virtual classes)

The Personal Learning Assistant provides personalized access to the learning space, enabling learners to search for and select appropriate learning resources. The system is predicated on the existence of RDF-based metadata describing services, resources, and learners. These metadata can be used as input to reasoning mechanisms using, for example, the TRIPLE Semantic Web RDF querying language (Henze, Dolog, & Nejdl, 2004; Sintek & Decker, 2002) to engage in intelligent reasoning. Such reasoning can map diverse metadata schemes (used by different communities providing metadata) to that preferred by the Personal Learning Assistant. The Personal Learning Assistant can take as input an individual's learner profile, consisting of metadata relating to his or her learning needs and existing accredited competencies (for example, levels of knowledge of particular topics measured on a particular test) in relation to those needs, and can then search the metadata describing the distributed learning resources on the network in order to achieve a match, generating personalized learning experiences for learners.

The learner profile is coded using the IEEE PAPI standard. The IMS LIP standard enables learner preferences to be expressed as well (e.g., language, location, disability, communication device preference). Work is also reported, designed to incorporate metadata relating to learners' organizational roles and aspirations to which their employing organization may have input (Gunnarsdóttir, Heimerl, Kieslinger, Simon, & Tsiortou, 2004). Learning resources are described using the IEEE LOM standard that enables their description in terms of, for example, their educational level, objectives, and prerequisites in terms of other learning resources or competencies.

Melis, Goguadze, Homik, Libbrecht, Ullrich, and Winterstein (2006) also report the development of a system designed to provide intelligent access to learning objects stored in diverse repositories using different metadata schemes. The system is based on an open services-oriented architecture, its components and Web services can be used by different applications. The system is specific to the teaching of mathematics; it enables the use of learning objects that have been semantically marked up using the OMDoc standard (Caprotti, Carlisle, & Cohen, 2002). This allows the interpretation and validation of mathematical expressions (enabling, for example, feedback on exercises) and the use of various standard mathematical services.

Learning objects are tagged with metadata derived from Dublin Core and LOM. However, unsatisfied with the expressive power of LOM, the researchers developed an ontology of learning objects. This ontology is independent of any particular pedagogy and specifies, for example, types of interactivity (e.g., exercise, exploration, real world problem), evidence (proof, demonstration), and illustration (example, counter-example).

The "mediator" service (Melis et al., 2006, p. 409) can also search for content located in distributed repositories and tagged using different metadata schemes:

> A typical query to the ActiveMath mediator inquires about the existence of elements that fulfill given constraints. An answer consists of a list of identifiers of matching elements. For instance, the query *(getItems [class exercise] [property for derivation] [property difficulty low] [property field computer science])* returns all easy exercises for the mathematical concept derivation with a computer science context.

The mediator service translates a query from a client component, formulated in its own metadata schema, into the mediator's own schema. It then searches remote repositories, translating the query into the different metadata schemas used by these repositories before merging the results and passing them back to the client. This work complements other approaches to the mapping of different ontologies within an e-learning context such as that reported by Gašević and Hatala (2006).

The course generator assembles learning objects using a hierarchical task network planner. In selecting appropriate learning objects it takes account of each learner's existing knowledge stored in its learner model, in order to identify prerequisite concepts to be taught. The planner can generate different learning sequences to reflect different tutorial strategies. The authors give the example sequenced according to Merrill's (2002, p. 43) "first principles of instruction," which entails presentation of learning objects designed to provide motivation and basic familiarization with the concept to be taught, followed by presentation of the concept, elaborations, examples, exercises, and finally concluding comments.

Open Corpus Resource Discovery

Many educational informatics systems are designed to enable resource discovery of not only materials stored in specialized repositories, but also open corpus material available on the Web. Dolog, Henze, Nejdl, and Sintek (2004), for example, report development of the Personal Reader, which is also based on metadata-based reasoning mechanisms.

From the starting point of a learning resource being studied by a learner, the Personal Reader discovers resources that are related to the currently viewed resource. It can recommend resources that provide a different perspective on the topic—for example, a summary, more general or more specific material, or examples illustrating the concepts involved. It can do this at a local level utilizing closed corpus resources stored in a particular educational repository. However, at a global level it can also engage in the discovery of open corpus material available on the Web. The authors' aim is to work toward the vision of an adaptive Web capable of leveraging open corpus material (Brusilovsky, 2001; Brusilovsky & Maybury, 2002; Henze & Nejdl, 2001).

Metadata relating to resources, learners, learning activities, interactions, subject domains, and documents are represented as RDF triples. As in the case of the previously described Personal Learning Assistant, reasoning takes place using the TRIPLE RDF querying language. Metadata describing particular documents employ terms from a subject domain ontology, allowing prerequisite and other relationships among topics to be established. Users are also described using metadata relating to learning performance, competencies, and certification. Metadata describing a particular learner could indicate, for example, that he or she has obtained a particular score in a test after studying a concept.

The system uses adaptation reasoning rules (described more fully by Dolog, Henze, Nejdl, & Sintek, 2003) to discover and recommend additional resources conceptually and pedagogically linked to the resource currently being viewed by the learner—such as an instance of the concept under consideration. Examples can be recommended on the basis of what the learner has and has not already learned. Reasoning rules can use ontology relationships specifying, for example, that a particular concept is a sub-concept of another. This can be used to discover and recommend more general or more specific resources.

As has been noted, as well as operating within the context of a closed corpus repository of learning materials, the Personal Reader system is also able to access open corpus materials such as those available on the Web. A minimal requirement for Personal Reader to be able to utilize any such open corpus resource is that it is described by metadata in RDF format. However, problems may still arise because the quality, completeness, and extent of metadata describing those resources can vary, and the metadata schemes used may differ from source to source. Thus the system has a number of strategies to discover and utilize open corpus materials. As when operating with a closed corpus repository, the first task is to obtain metadata describing the resource currently being studied by the user. On the basis of this, a query is constructed and then run using Edutella (Nejdl, Wolf, Qu, Decker, Sintek, Naeve, et al., 2002), TAP Semantic Web search (Guha, McCool, & Miller, 2003) or Lixto (Baumgartner, Flesca, & Gottlob, 2001).

An ontology mapping function makes use of the TRIPLE language to map metadata expressed in different schemes to those used by the system (Miklos, Neumann, Zdun, & Sintek, 2003). However, even allowing for such a mapping, the variable nature of metadata describing open corpus resources means that any given resource may be only minimally or partially described compared to what the Personal Reader would optimally require. Thus if an insufficient number of resources is located, a query relaxation function can use the underlying ontology to find broader, sibling, or narrower concepts or drop a restriction such as resource type. The authors report that such heuristics enable successful query reformulation even when metadata quality is low. Where metadata describing a particular resource do not indicate prerequisite concepts, these can, to some extent, be inferred from ontologies relevant to the subject of the resource (Dolog et al., 2004).

Lawless, Wade, and Conlan (2005) also address the issue of enabling personalized adaptive systems to discover open corpus material. They report explorations designed to enable the previously described APeLS adaptive system use unstructured or inconsistently structured open corpus content, including that available on the Web and in other open source repositories. They propose an extension of the APeLS system to incorporate a search function for open corpus content to generate learning objects that can provide input to existing APeLS adaptive facilities. When the newly sourced content does not have structured metadata from a standard scheme recognized by the system, it must be analyzed in order to generate a new learning object. The learning object generator receives metadata relating to both the learner and the specification of the learning object that is required (for example, learning objectives and prerequisite knowledge). The generator uses this information to determine which parts of the newly sourced content to include and how to structure them to form the learning object. Once created, the learning object can be tagged with metadata and made available to the APeLS adaptive engine as it attempts to generate a personalized course.

Alternative Pedagogies

Several well rehearsed criticisms of educational systems are predicated on the use of learning objects and metadata as described thus far. Allert (2004) considers current educational metadata schemes to be severely limited in terms of the type and range of pedagogical knowledge they can express. Schemes such as LOM, although claiming to be neutral, in fact display epistemological and ontological assumptions that restrict them to particular pedagogic perspectives. They seek to describe features of a learning object created for use in a particular context, in such a way that it can be discovered and reused by others in other contexts. The intention is to encapsulate the *aboutness* of the object—and characteristics that may determine its potential educational usefulness and learnability—in its metadata. These metadata can then be used as input variables to an equation matching learners with learning resources that are "about" the topic of interest and that are suitably matched with variables such as learning style and prior knowledge. Learning object metadata describing the topic the learning object is designed to teach can be mapped onto ontologies that indicate, for example, prerequisite topics. The result of the equation is a personalized selection and sequence of learning objects designed effectively and efficiently to teach the learner the required knowledge.

As Allert (2004, online) notes, LOM:

> aims at an absolute description of an object and assumes de-contextualization. Meaning is completely deduced from the object itself, which means that the entire meaning lies within the object. LOM's concept of semantics is based on epistemological and ontological assumptions comparable to those of the acquisition metaphor of learning.

This is at odds with a view of learning in which the broader context affects the nature and effectiveness of that learning. The same learning resource may be differentially effective when used in different contexts. From this perspective, the notion of de-contextualization in relation to learning objects and their metadata is less than helpful. Rather than representing noise to be factored out so that the essential content of a learning object can be more accurately described, context is central to meaning.

Mwanza and Engeström (2005, p. 454) "considered the task of understanding and describing activities in context as an integral part of the metadata abstraction. This is due to the fact that acquired contextual insight is considered to be crucial to the appropriate categorization and description of education content." They argue that failing to take into account such context may result in a misunderstanding of learners' real needs. Within particular communities, socio-cultural and pedagogic norms that provide the context for searching for and using learning resources can be implicit, potentially causing ambiguities and misunderstandings where resources are used across contexts.

Indeed, the whole enterprise whereby personalized learning is delivered via matching de-contextualized learning object metadata with metadata describing learners and their needs is itself arguably based on epistemological and ontological assumptions that align it with a particular and limited perspective on teaching and learning. These assumptions map particularly well onto what has been termed an "acquisition"—as opposed to "participation" (Sfard, 1998, p. 4) or "knowledge-creation" (Paavola, Lipponen, & Hakkarainen, 2002, p. 24)— metaphor for learning.

Viewed from a participant perspective on learning, the prime goal of learning is not the individual's acquisition of knowledge and skills that can be applied in new contexts. Rather, it is building communities in which knowledge is communally constructed through participation in shared learning activities and social processes. The perspective is rooted in the notion of *situated* learning in which knowing is *located* in social interaction and participation. Allert (2004) quotes Hanks (1991, pp. 14–15):

> The individual learner is not gaining a discrete body of abstract knowledge which (s)he will then transport and reapply in later contexts. ... There is no necessary implication that a learner acquires mental representations that remain fixed thereafter, not that the "lesson" taught consists itself in a set of abstract representations.

Allert notes that Paavola, Lipponen, and Hakkarainen (2002) have extended Sfard's participation metaphor to what they term the *knowledge creation* metaphor, focusing on *innovation* and particularly applicable to modern communities characterized by constant change and transformation. From such a knowledge creation perspective (Paavola et al., 2002, p. 24):

> learning is seen as analogous to processes of inquiry, especially to innovative processes of inquiry where something new is created and the initial knowledge is either substantially enriched or significantly transformed during the process.

Such learning entails tackling poorly structured problems, with outcomes that cannot be accurately planned and predicted in detail. Learning is seen as too complex to be viewed via any simple predictable cause and effect relationship as the direct result of teaching.

Mwanza and Engeström consider it necessary to be able to express such pedagogical contexts in metadata. Although LOM can express certain pedagogical information about a learning object, this facility is underdeveloped. Indeed, others such as Huang, Webster, Wood, and Ishaya (2006, p. 354) have commented that: "In terms of standardisation, LOM ... and Sharable Content Object Reference Model (SCORM), ... the most popular e-learning standards, have not taken pedagogy support as one of their core issues in specification."

However, Mwanza and Engeström (2005, p. 460) note that LOM does enable its top level categories to be extended:

> A key advantage of using the LOM standard is evident in the provision for extending LOM top-level categories ... this implies that extensions can be created and added to LOM top-level categories so as to introduce theory-driven subcategories and elements drawn from specific theories of learning and social–cultural perspectives.

They have used this facility to propose extensions to LOM, based on Expansive Learning theory, which requires pedagogical and social context to be taken into account. This theory was developed by Engeström (1987), based on the more general Activity Theory, itself receiving increasing attention in both education (Collis & Margaryan, 2004) and information science (Wilson, 2006; see also the chapter by Wilson in this volume). As Activity Theory views human activities as developmental processes, so Expansive Learning views learning as emerging from the creation of new artifacts by learners and teachers engaged in real life problem solving.

Mwanza and Engeström (2005, p. 457) note that within Activity Theory,

> participants in an activity are portrayed as *subjects* interacting with *objects* to achieve desired *outcomes*. Meanwhile, human interactions are mediated with each other and with objects of the environment through the use of *tools*, *rules*, and *division of labor*. Mediators represent the nature of relationships that exist *within* and *between* participants of an activity in a given *community* of practices.

They thus add, as extensions to LOM's "educational" category, key concepts deriving from Expansive Learning including: *subjects*, *tools*, *objectives*, *rules*, *community*, *division of labor*, and *desired outcomes*.

The metadata standard's inability to accommodate situated learning is addressed by Specht (2006), who reports work developing adaptive systems to support situated learning as part of the European Union–funded Remotely Accessible Field Trips (RAFT) project. As with other systems, learners are described in terms of their knowledge, preferences, interests, and capabilities. However, metadata describing resources include not only LOM categories but also a series of environmental parameters appropriate to support learners engaged in field trip activities. As information is collected, metadata are attached relating to environmental factors such as location and position. The information is made available to the field trip participants. The prototype Situated Mobile Learning Support (SMILES) system enables the recording and accessing of such resources. Specht (2006, pp. 345–346) provides the following example of the use of such environmental metadata:

> learners could browse a database of pictures in a biology field trip filtered by the location and the time of the year. Using this approach students could explore and learn about simple questions like "Which flowers grow here at what time of the year?" Additionally, metadata such as the precise time when the picture was taken and the weather conditions on that day can give interesting materials for exploring and learning about important factors of flower growth.

This work represents the extension of metadata to include features specifically designed to support situated learning.

Limitations have also been noted in relation to standards such as the Educational Modelling Language (EML), on which the IMS Learning Design (IMS LD) is based, developed to enable the specification of learning designs, to the extent that they display inherent assumptions. EML represented an attempt to avoid the danger of building in a particular pedagogical perspective. Indeed, at the top level, EML offers a *pedagogical meta-model* that enables the modeling of different pedagogical approaches (Hummel, Manderveld, Tattersall, & Koper, 2004). This pedagogical meta-model was derived by mapping of commonalities from a wide range of learning and instructional theories and models covering behaviorist, cognitivist, constructivist, and situationalist perspectives.

Sicilia and Lytras (Sicilia, 2006; Sicilia & Lytras, 2005) investigate ontological structures for generic constructivist and socio-cultural learning. They criticize the EML approach (in the form of IMS LD) on the grounds that, although it is neutral to and can accommodate different pedagogical perspectives, it does not allow their explicit expression. There is no problem expressing a range of different learning designs, but the underlying rationale that led to a particular design—that is, the assumptions and theoretical perspective behind it—cannot be expressed. Such representations are crucial, they argue, for linking theories to practice and for evaluating the validity of theoretical assumptions. They report work developing ontologies that explicitly represent constructivist and socio-cultural learning frameworks and allow the expression of learning design rationales.

Allert (2004) has criticized EML's activity-based nature. The EML meta-model assumes that learners learn by engaging in goal-directed activities in some environment consisting of a set of objects, services, and/or people. Learning may be facilitated insofar as the learner is motivated, provided with an appropriate environment, and possesses the necessary prerequisites and abilities. Irrespective of pedagogical approach, people acquire *roles* and engage in learning and/or support *activities* (which may be aggregated into *activity structures*) within an *environment* in pursuit of particular *outcomes*. Determination of which activities are associated with which roles is made by a *method* created to achieve particular learning objectives. A method consists of one or more *plays*, which themselves are made of one or more sequential *acts*, and may include "if ... then ... else ..." rules.

Specifications such as the EML enable the description of strategic pedagogical procedures and processes designed to move learners from one state of knowledge to another. These descriptions can also be fed into the personalized learning equation, for example to sequence the selected learning materials to suit a preferred pedagogic strategy. They describe learning in terms of pedagogical means and ends, and the planning of educational activities in order to achieve pre-planned objectives via causal relationships. However, as Allert (2004, p. 16) notes: "innovative learning processes are contextualized, generative, ill-structured, and long lasting processes, which do not directly lead to a predetermined objective. ... A sufficient model therefore must be able to describe open systems, ill-structured non-deterministic processes of change." Thus, although able to accommodate a range of pedagogical perspectives, and to set learning objects within their broader pedagogical context, certain of what in the EML are considered basic assumptions do arguably resonate more with particular pedagogical positions than with others. This view is at odds with pedagogical perspectives that emphasize relatively open-ended knowledge creation as previously described.

Allert proposes a multi-layered, relativistic modeling approach which seeks to overcome the inherent limitation of activity-centered models. Within her proposed system, the same object (level 0) may be annotated with metadata describing (a) characteristics that can be de-contextualized, and that represent universal defining features of the object, and (b) different roles that object may play in different pedagogical contexts (both described at level 1). At a higher level (level 2), different pedagogical approaches are themselves explicitly represented. A given object (level 0) may be linked to different roles (level 1), each of which may be linked to a different pedagogical approach (level 2).

Harnessing Knowledge of Community Learning Activity to Support Learners

McCalla takes a bottom up approach to building shared knowledge entailing learning on the part of the system in his "ecological" paradigm for the development of educational systems (McCalla, 2004, online; see also Brooks & McCalla, 2006). This adaptive approach provides personalized learning that not only makes use of standard pedagogical metadata, but also dynamically collects and cumulates other metadata relating to resources, learners, and the interactions between the two, at the time of use. The approach also involves mining these data in order to generate new pedagogic knowledge as required for different purposes.

Metadata are gathered at the time a resource is used, as opposed to being pre-assigned by human experts. As a learner accesses a particular resource, metadata that relate to the learner, the resource and the interaction between the two are attached to that resource. *Learner* information may include, for example, cognitive and affective characteristics and learning goals. *Resource* information may include interpretations of what the resource is about as specified by the learner, and also as inferred by text-processing algorithms as well as descriptions assigned from recognized metadata schemata and ontologies. *Interaction* information may include recorded patterns of access, dwell time, the learner's evaluation of the usefulness of the resource in addressing his or her learning need, and the software and hardware used by the learner in accessing the resource.

More metadata will be attached to the resource as it is used by different learners, and/or by the same learner on different occasions. In other words, each time a learning resource is used, a *model* of the learner and the interaction is attached to it. The model represents a context- and time-bound snapshot. Next time the learner accesses the same resource, the model will have changed. The learner model has two main elements. The *characteristics* component records relatively enduring learner features including age, cognitive style, current learning goals, history of learning resources previously studied, and past learning assessments. The *episodic* component of the learner's model records aspects of the learner's interactions with the current learning resource, including, for example, his/her evaluation of the resource in terms of its perceived difficulty and data relating to any test the learner has completed in relation to the resource.

Over time, each learning resource will accumulate many models. These data can then be mined in order to discover patterns that are useful in achieving particular tasks. Such tasks may include information retrieval and personal recommendation; discovering resources (including people) most suited, across a range of parameters including pedagogic, to providing personalized assistance to learners; and even aspects of resource collection management such as weeding less useful resources as other more useful ones are added to the collection. McCalla (2004, online) notes that:

> The approach is ecological because over time the system is populated with more and more information, and something like natural selection based on purposes determines what information is useful and what is not. ... In a phrase, the approach involves attaching models of users to the information they interact with, and then mining these models for patterns that are useful for various purposes. The information and the data mining algorithms interact with one another in an ecosystem where the relevance and usefulness of information is always being adjusted to suit the changing needs of learners and teachers and to fit changes in the external environment and the system's perceptions.

Thus the system both generates pedagogic knowledge by mining data from learner interactions with resources and in turn uses this acquired knowledge in order to facilitate the discovery and selection of further resources.

Tang and McCalla (2003) report a system based on this approach, designed to search CITESEER and recommend relevant papers to research students. Each time a paper is read by a learner, an instance of the learner's model is attached to the paper's metadata. The system also enables the learner to annotate the resource, this information feeding into the model (recording the learner's interactions with resources). The retrieval of relevant papers in response to a request by a particular learner proceeds by matching that learner's model (in terms of both its *characteristics* and *episodic* components) with those of other learners who share relevant characteristics and who have evaluated the papers positively in relation to their own use of them. By examining appropriate aspects of the learner models (particularly their evaluations relating to usefulness) attached over time to particular papers, any ongoing changes in their perceived relevance can be mapped. As McCalla (2004, online) notes:

> More sophisticated and intelligent examination of the papers in the repository through the lens of the students' experiences with them could allow all manner of inferences to be drawn about papers, including what they are about, how they relate to each other, how the research discipline is changing, what papers appeal to what types of readers, etc.

Such facilities could, for example, enable the weeding of a resource collection, as the usefulness of certain papers is perceived to wane over time as new papers appear.

Work is reported (McCalla, Vassileva, Greer, & Bull, 2000; Niu, McCalla, & Vassileva, 2005; Vassileva, McCalla, & Greer, 2003) further developing approaches to the learner modeling that is a key feature of ecological systems. What these authors term the "active learner modeling" (McCalla et al., 2000, p. 53) paradigm entails the development and application of partial and context-bound learner models in which knowledge of any particular learner is fragmented among the various distributed agents that collect it. The agents can then use their particular knowledge to negotiate with other agents in order to fulfill whatever learning task is being worked on at the time. This involves analysis of raw data computed as required and specific to particular purposes and contexts of use.

Negotiation by distributed active agents in pursuit of particular goals is also the essence of the I-Help system (Brooks & McCalla, 2006; McCalla, Greer, Vassileva, Deters, Bull, & Kettel, 2001). This system supports learners by finding suitable people to help them with the particular learning problem they are experiencing. Each learner is represented by an agent, which maintains a model of its owner. When a learner issues a request for help, his or her agent negotiates with the agents of others to find the best match. After the help interaction, the consumer of the help provides feedback on the effectiveness of the help, and this information is fed into the user models of both the consumer and the provider of the help.

The metadata used in the matching process by each agent include (a) information provided by the learner, in the form of self-assessments of his or her level of knowledge in particular areas, and availability, (b) the feedback evaluations previously described, (c) knowledge at the system level of the frequency of both online availability and levels of past participation in the public discussion component of I-Help, of the agent owner. These multiple fragmented learner models are constantly updated and negotiate among themselves to find an optimal solution to a particular problem dynamically at the time it is required. This work has been further developed in the form of the Helper's Assistant framework (Kumar, Greer, & McCalla, 2005).

The LORNET project (McCalla, 2004) displays the application of the active learner modeling developed in the I-Help system to learning objects. This project seeks to enable such objects themselves to become active agents, able to negotiate with both other learning objects and agents representing learners.

Supporting Argumentation and Debate in Learning Communities

Learner control, as opposed to high levels of supplantation, is characteristic of a number of systems designed to facilitate community-based learning. Such systems act as intermediary tools that communities can use to assist in resource discovery and learning. They may entail more explicit and accessible pedagogic features of information sources.

Stutt and Motta (2004, online), for example, report a vision of—and early empirical work relating to—the development of semantic learning webs in which "semantic browsers" and "semantic constructors" allow community-based "knowledge neighborhoods" to engage in the creation of "knowledge charts" enabling "knowledge navigation." Learning is a prime function of knowledge neighborhoods: "A Knowledge Neighbourhood can be viewed as a location in cyberspace where learners can congregate into groups or larger communities with the goal of acquiring knowledge about some topic" (p. 20).

Indeed, the starting point for their work is focused on "learner needs:"

> It is possible to give an even more abstract account of learner needs which we can use to guide our thoughts about future learning environments. At a more cognitive level students need environments which are congruent with what goes on in learning. From what we have said already we can distinguish

between three types of learner needs: for *structure, relatedness* and *interpretation*. These correlate more or less with the first two items in Laurillard's (2002) characterization of learning as: *apprehending structure, integrating parts, acting on the world, using feedback, and reflecting on goals.* (p. 6)

This work entails a less *explicitly* pedagogical form of knowledge, in that it relates to forms of reasoning by which we learn—for example, argumentation structures by which particular information sources contribute to and interact with evolving idea generation and scholarly debate. Resource discovery is facilitated by knowledge representations geared to making explicit (and navigable) the ways in which we may come to understand or make sense of information (i.e., learn). Knowledge charts, to which information resources are linked via metadata, render the information sources discoverable in terms of how the knowledge fits into its broader context—for example, its role in an ongoing scientific debate. The learning-related features of *structure, relatedness,* and *interpretation* are precisely what knowledge charts are intended to help the learner develop. Stutt and Motta also envisage the addition of ontologies relating to specific pedagogic purposes attributed to particular knowledge charts via extension of the Education Modelling Language (EML).

Knowledge charts are ontology-based representations of agreed knowledge within particular communities. However, the ontologies on which they are based are not restricted to domain concepts and relationships. The types of ontology envisioned relate to types of knowledge in terms of their underlying reasoning structures, and as such represent a type of pedagogic knowledge—knowledge of how we may come to understand, or learn about, complex topics. Such types include, for example, *argumentation* and *debate*, reasoning by *analogy*, constructing *narratives* by which phenomena can be understood, *simulations*, and *cause/effect* models. At one level, an ontology would describe basic knowledge types; and each knowledge type, in turn, would have its own ontology. For example, an argumentation/debate ontology could include concepts such as claim, refutation, support, and confirmation, as well as "debate moves" linked by rhetorical relations.

Stutt and Motta (2004, online) describe knowledge charts as "the ontologically permeated representations of a community's knowledge or point of view." They propose that metadata describing information resources be extended so they could be linked to appropriate knowledge charts. Marking up may be done by humans and/or through the development of software such as that being developed to enable the extraction of argument and story structures from texts (e.g., Vargas-Vera & Celjuska, 2003; Vargas-Vera & Moreale, 2003). Knowledge charts thus represent reasoning structures found within (single or multiple) documents.

Semantic browsers are designed to use domain ontologies to identify and highlight important concepts in a document, so that the user can follow links from such concepts to related knowledge maps. The maps enable both navigation and interpretation, allowing the user not only to access explanations of the concepts entailed, but also to set the concepts within a broader context, for example by showing their role and relationships within an ongoing scholarly debate. By selecting elements of the knowledge chart, users can navigate to explore related or more detailed component arguments, or access original documents. Domingue and Dzbor (2004) and Dzbor, Domingue, and Motta (2003) report the development of such a semantic browser in the form of Magpie developed at the U.K.'s Open University's Knowledge Media Institute.

Knowledge charts would be created and used by members of particular knowledge neighborhoods. These are virtual knowledge generating and learning communities relating to particular areas of interest. Knowledge charts could be a means to enable such neighborhoods to communicate with each other insofar as they represent "boundary objects" (Arias & Fischer, 2000, online). Such boundary objects would facilitate the linking of ontologies envisaged by Berners-Lee (2004, quoted by Yli-Luoma & Naeve, 2006, p. 446):

> The Semantic Web will have to be as messy as the World Wide Web. Instead of common ontologies, local ontologies will be stitched together at the edges into a quilt of ontologies.

Such "stitching" would require a degree of semantic integration or mapping of different ontologies (e.g., Akahani, Hiramatsu, & Satoh, 2003; Gašević & Hatala, 2005, 2006; Silva & Rocha, 2003). But as well as the linking of discrete ontologies generated by different communities so that they can reference and communicate with each other, there will be an increasing need to come to terms with a diversity of competing ontological perspectives within communities requiring negotiation to establish, and record, parameters of agreement and disagreement.

Indeed, Sheth, Ramakrishnan, and Thomas (2005, p. 1) recognize the fundamental complexity inherent in the notion of "meaning" that underlies attempts to agree on common representations of what we "know" about domains, topics and objects:

> Semantics has been a part of several scientific disciplines, both in the realm of computer science and outside of it. ... Most of these areas have very different views of what "meaning" is, and these views all build on some metatheoretical and epistemological assumptions. These different views imply very different views of cognition, of concepts and of meaning. ... Ontologies for everything seem to be the new buzzword of our decade. However, this ontology mania requires a community consensus and agreement. In a recent interview with

Tom Gruber for *AIS SIGSEMIS Bulletin*—(Gruber, 2004)—
he emphasises that "Every ontology is a treaty—a social
agreement—among people with some common motive in
sharing."

Such negotiation is addressed by Naeve (2005, online), who proposes
the building of ontological bridges between different perspectives by
means of "conceptual calibration." Echoing Pask's (1976; see also Scott,
2001) work on Conversation Theory, this entails establishing agreement
on what is agreed, what is not agreed, and how such agreements and disagreements should be recorded.

The notion of alternative perspectives and disputed understandings
is central to the Scholarly Ontologies (or ScholOnto) project at the Open
University's Knowledge Media Institute. As part of this project, a number of tools have been developed, including "ClaiMapper," which enables
users to create "argument maps" relating to information sources and
their interconnections, and "ClaimFinder," which facilitates searching
across the claims mapped by ClaiMapper. The "ClaiMaker" server supports the representation, discovery, and navigation of scholarly discourse and argumentation (Uren, Buckingham Shum, Bachler, & Li,
2006).

"ClaimSpotter" (Buckingham Shum, Uren, Li, Sereno, & Mancini,
2007; Sereno, Buckingham Shum, & Motta, 2005) is an environment
designed to support the annotation of scholarly documents with metadata derived from an ontology of discourse. This discourse relates to naturalistic scholarly argumentation—that is, the way in which we make
sense of, discuss, and negotiate the type of complex ideas that are open
to debate and interpretation, as typically found in academic documents.
This work falls within the realm of educational informatics as defined
here in the same way as does the previously described work of Stutt and
Motta (2004), in that the ontology and metadata document annotations
represent a type of pedagogic knowledge, and as will be discussed, the
system uses this knowledge to enable resource discovery to support
learning.

The ontology of scholarly discourse includes relations such as the
extent to which an idea supports or challenges other ideas (proves,
refutes, is evidence for, is evidence against, agrees with, disagrees with,
is consistent with, is inconsistent with); how it relates to a particular
problem or issue (addresses, solves); how it affects other ideas (predicts,
envisages, causes, is capable of causing, is prerequisite for, prevents, is
unlikely to affect); is similar or dissimilar (is identical to, is similar to, is
different from, is the opposite of, shares issues with, has nothing to do
with, is analogous to, is not analogous to); is taxonomically related (part
of, example of, subclass of, not part of, not example of); or linked by more
general relationships (is about, uses/applies/is enabled by, improves on,
impairs).

Rather than relatively factual, static aspects of a document as described by standard metadata schemes, Sereno et al. (2005, p. 199) are interested in:

> the annotation of documents with knowledge resulting from a sensemaking process. Consider a scholarly document. What its salient points are, how it relates to previous works in a community, and how innovative it is might not appear immediately. Carefully reading the paper, identifying the themes of interest, arguing with the position defended, building on the previous papers we, as scholars, have read beforehand, understanding why a particular paper is cited ..., drawing our own connections to other papers which are (or not) cited ... all these steps, among others, are involved in an interpretation process, a sensemaking process. Not to mention that this interpretation might change over time as our research interests evolve, and of course that two readers might see different aspects in the same document.

Different users can annotate a document with potentially contradictory interpretations. The interpretations are accessible to other users of the system, which enables the discovery of documents that are related in terms of their perceived argumentation structures to a document being considered by a user. Documents unrelated formally may be discovered via relations solely existing in user interpretations. Not only can such relationships be discovered, but the nature of the relationship is made explicit. Users can also discover the various ways in which a particular issue has been addressed by a community, and/or identify other people supporting or contesting particular ideas.

The annotations are represented as triples linking a source concept and a destination concept via a relationship. The relationships must be selected from the discourse ontology. The concepts are unconstrained and can consist of a word or paragraph of free text. ClaimSpotter provides support for annotators by flagging examples of the ontology relationships where they exist in a document and identifying tentative potential concepts that the annotator may wish to consider. It does this by analyzing the text to find, for example, author-provided keywords, noun groups, and other specified sequences of words. Importantly, the system provides suggestions only to annotators, who are free to ignore or use them, and to generate their own concepts as they wish.

Themes and Research Issues

Emergent Themes

Like any complex field of endeavor, educational informatics is characterized by a rich diversity of perspectives and approaches. The dimensions of difference apparent in the research reviewed in this chapter are not restricted to educational informatics. They reflect relatively fundamental differences in the ways researchers approach an essential component of information science, namely, the description of intellectual content in order to enable its discovery.

From one perspective, complex intellectual content (information sources) can be productively analyzed into discrete components for use in contexts other than those in which, and for which, the content may have been originally created. The role of metadata is to provide an objective description of context-free aspects of content, such that others working in different contexts can assess their relevance and potential usefulness to them of these information sources. From another perspective, however, complex content cannot effectively be decomposed and the components de-contextualized because it is the Gestalt (the whole which is more than the sum of the parts) and the context of production and use that give them meaning and effectiveness. For this reason, an essential aspect of metadata is their capacity to provide rich contextual descriptions. Rather than being considered noise, context is an essential component of meaning.

The function of metadata may be considered to be the provision of an authoritative description of an information source, generated prior to, and anticipating, its discovery and use and remaining static (i.e., not subject to constant change). This may be contrasted with a view of metadata as more user-centric and divergent, in the sense that a given source may be described by different co-existing (possibly conflicting) metadata, generated by users at the time of the interaction. Such metadata may also be fluid—subject to constant change with every new interaction.

Metadata may derive from ontologies (and other knowledge representation formalisms) designed to establish a maximally authoritative consensual view of a domain agreed within and across different communities. However, this may be contrasted with a view of ontologies as representing diverse and divergent ontological knowledge possessed by individuals and groups, including multiple and potentially conflicting views, and supporting the social negotiation of agreements and disagreements in relation to them.

System-held knowledge (in the case of educational informatics systems, pedagogic knowledge) may be used to control and sequence certain intellectual processes in order to bring about specified outcomes—to do certain things and make certain decisions for the user—representing a degree of supplantation. Alternatively, the complexity of intellectual processing may be acknowledged and preserved in a system that does not attempt to control and sequence it for users; such a system may attempt to empower users—to stimulate their metacognitive awareness and powers.

The desired outcomes of an information system may be viewed primarily in terms of enhanced knowledge and/or performance on the part of the *individual*, or from the perspective of the individual as an active participant within a social network (group, organization, or community). Such outcomes may also be viewed primarily as convergent—in the sense of conforming with agreed, clearly pre-specified objectives—as opposed to divergent, in the sense of individualistic and open-ended, and therefore relatively uncertain and unpredictable.

These distinctions are summarized in Figure 11.1, arranged across two basic dimensions. The vertical arrow represents a dimension from one pole characterized by convergence to some authority-based consensus (for example, objective rules, standards, or procedures agreed within a particular community) to a pole characterized by relative idiosyncrasy (subjectivity and individuality that diverges from the consensual norm).

The horizontal arrow depicts an independent dimension representing the degree to which phenomena are considered, in system and/or research design, as a complex Gestalt in which complexity and context are preserved. One pole represents an orientation toward such a holistic perspective. The other pole represents more analytic thinking characteristic of classic scientific method in which complex phenomena are broken into their component parts, understanding (or development) of the parts being re-combined to form understanding (or development) of the whole.

The dotted diagonal arrow represents a further dimension arguably characterizing much research and development relating to the extent to which phenomena under study and/or the desired effects of systems

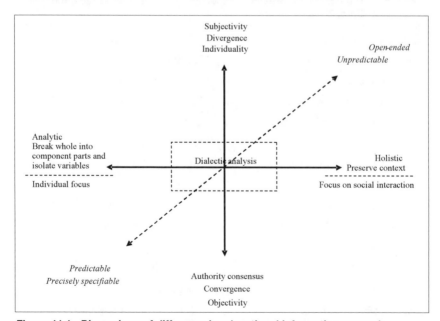

Figure 11.1 Dimensions of difference in educational informatics research.

being developed can be tightly controlled and predicted, as opposed to being relatively open-ended and less subject to control and prediction.

The horizontal dimension maps to some extent onto *research approach* and the vertical onto nature of *acceptable evidence*. The diagonal dimension maps onto *nature of the phenomena* that form the focus of the research.

Combining Evidential Forces

The themes that have emerged from this review of educational informatics research would appear to echo differences that arguably characterize perspectives on and approaches to research at a more fundamental level. Indeed, there is evidence in information science research of activity toward each of the poles of the dimensions—and of both synthesis and antithesis between the different poles. Table 11.1 summarizes commonly observed and reported differences in research perspective and approach generally within information science, not restricted to educational informatics (Ford, 2005). The differences between the left and right columns, although by no means representing a one-to-one mapping, nevertheless reflect the poles of the dimensions shown in Figure 11.1.

Several researchers emphasize a need to blend approaches, advocating methodological pluralism and triangulation; others, however, have

Table 11.1 Differences in research perspectives and approaches (adapted from Ford, 2005)

Quantitative/statistical	Qualitative/interpretative
Atomistic	Holistic
Sequential processing	Parallel processing
Isolate and control variables	Preserve complexity of "real-life"
Precise analytic definition and	situations
measurement	"Fuzzy" intuitive concepts
Study discrete relationships	Study complex interacting relationships
Logico-mathematical	Intuitive-social
Convergent processing	Divergent processing
Control	Lack of precise control
Predictability	Idiosyncrasy
Objectivity	Subjectivity
Mechanistic	Contructivist
Generalizable knowledge	Context-bound "transferable" insights

noted the apparent tensions between different perspectives, ranging from bias toward and preference for a particular approach, to partisan, not to say entrenched, positions on the part of different research camps—and even outright hostility in the form of paradigm wars (Ford, 2000; Kuhlthau, 2005).

Less prevalent have been calls to focus more specifically on the nature of the tensions between different perspectives. Thornley (2005, p. 197) introduces a dialectical model as "a way of understanding meaning as a dialectical conflict between the subjective and the objective," which "exist in a mutually antagonistic and dependent relationship" (p. vi). She argues (pp. 256-258) that:

> The dialectical model relies on the hypotheses that the subjective/objective divide is important, that it can be characterised as a mutually antagonistic and dependent relationship, and that this plays a central role in both meaning and information. ... The continuing dissatisfaction with theoretical development in IR, and also perhaps in IS, can now be interpreted as a frustration with attempts to create a stable synthesis in a subject matter which cannot contain such a synthesis. ... A dialectical understanding of the relationship between "what is" and "what is not" can help explain why stable synthesis is so difficult to achieve in IR. The nature of its subject matter, meaning and information is characterised by this relationship, which means that any position in IR which aims for synthesis will always be unstable. The aspects of meaning and information, which it either ignores or explicitly rejects, will also be essential to its position.

To take a visual analogy, Figure 11.2(a) shows a familiar optical illusion. However, understanding the nature of what is depicted is not advanced by intensive study of Figure 11.2(b) and Figure 11.2(c) in isolation. The "problem" cannot be solved by intensifying the level of scrutiny applied to (b) and (c). Only by thinking outside the boxes—that is, at Figure 11.2(a)—can the dialectic nature of the phenomenon be perceived and the nature of the incongruity tackled.

Such a broader perspective enables assumptions to be made explicit, questioned, and resolved via the application of a higher-level *integrating theme*. In this case, it is apparent that the incongruity stems from the assumption that Figure 11.2(a) represents some sort of physical object. Making the assumption explicit and applying a meta-analysis in which this assumption is only one component allows the emergence of the meta-interpretation that the figure is "about" the effect of assumptions on human perception rather than being "about" the depiction of a physical object.

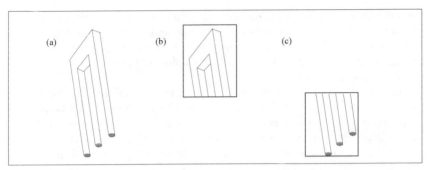

Figure 11.2 Levels of perspective.

Such an approach is inherent in the basic processes by which we build more sophisticated understanding. We may do this by realizing the limiting assumptions inherent in a particular frame of reference, and develop a more abstract one that takes account of, and attempts to overcome, such limitations. Indeed, this review of developments in educational informatics gives examples where increasingly "meta" abstractions (designed to represent and model ontological aspects of pedagogic knowledge) have been developed, each attempting to overcome limitations perceived in some previous abstraction.

The need to shift from a physical (object representation) to a psychological (perceptual illusion) frame of reference in the example shown in Figure 11.2 is quickly obvious in this simple case. However, the tensions between different research camps previously alluded to suggest that it may not always be easy to effect such shifts in the context of complex research phenomena. In this context, developing an appropriate meta-level frame of reference may require an explicit mapping of relationships between different evidential purposes—for example, to chart the possible or predict the probable, to build watertight theory or pragmatically influence practice, to describe the unique or explain the universal. Focusing more explicitly and directly on the precise nature of apparent incongruities is the only way to enable a degree of cumulative (and/or interactive) contribution to knowledge from heterogeneous types of evidence generated from different perspectives.

Endnotes

1. The term *pedagogic* is used here broadly. Strictly speaking, pedagogy does not embrace adult education and focuses essentially on teaching rather than learning activities. *Andragogy* relates specifically to adult education and the term *mathemagenic* (coined by Rothkopf in 1970, p. 325) refers to "those activities which give birth to learning." "Mathemagenic" would thus appear to be more appropriate than "pedagogic" in the context of this review because it embraces not only pedagogy and andragogy, but also autonomous and self-regulated learning outside any formal educational institutional context.

Pedagogy and andragogy entail the application of mathemagenic knowledge by educators in order to help others learn; autonomous self-regulated learning entails learners applying their own mathemagenic knowledge—metacognition—in order to self-teach. "Pedagogy" is used in this review to include all of these aspects; it has been used because it is a readily understood and commonly used term.

2. "Resource discovery" is used here in the sense given in the British Library's (2005, online) glossary: "Resource discovery involves the searching, locating and retrieving of information resources on computer-based networks, in response to queries of a human user or an automated mechanism."

3. A much broader definition is given in Wikipedia (Education Informatics, 2007): "Education Informatics is the intersection of informatics principles and practices and education, including teaching, learning, administration, logistics, planning, evaluation and research. ... Education Informatics covers any form of organized educational system that handles information as one of its core activities. More specifically it includes:

- Educational technologies such as MLEs, LMSs, VLEs, learning objects, e-portfolios, and digital repositories

- Education standards and specifications such as those developed by IMS, Advanced Distributed Learning and the IEEE

- Education workflows such as assessment, accreditation, curriculum development, evaluation, and audit

- Digital libraries

- Intersecting online services such as Facebook."

References

Advanced Distributed Learning. (2004). *SCORM XML controlling document: SCORM CAM* (Version 1.3); *Content packaging extensions XML XSD* (Version 1.0). Retrieved September 3, 2006, from www.adlnet.gov/downloads/58.cfm

Advanced Distributed Learning. (2006). *ADL releases SCORM 2004 3rd edition public draft*. Retrieved January 18, 2007, from www.adlnet.gov/news/articles/375.cfm

Akahani, J., Hiramatsu, K., & Satoh, T. (2003). Approximate query reformulation for ontology integration. *Proceedings of the Semantic Integration Workshop Collocated with the 2nd International Semantic Web Conference*, 3–8.

Allert, H. (2004). Coherent social systems for learning: An approach for contextualized and community-centred metadata. *Journal of Interactive Media in Education*, *2004*(2). Retrieved January 18, 2007, from www-jime.open.ac.uk/2004/2

Allert, H., Richter, C., & Nejdl, W. (2004). Lifelong learning and second-order learning objects. *British Journal of Educational Technology*, *35*(6), 701–715.

Arias, E., & Fischer, G. (2000). *Boundary objects: Their role in articulating the task at hand and making information relevant to it*. Paper presented at the International Computer Science Conventions Symposium on Interactive and Collaborative Computing. Retrieved January 18, 2007, from www.cs.colorado.edu/~gerhard/papers/icsc2000.pdf

Barsalou, L. W. (1992). *Cognitive psychology: An overview for cognitive scientists.* Hillsdale, NJ: Erlbaum.

Baumgartner, R., Flesca, S., & Gottlob, G. (2001). Declarative information extraction, Web crawling, and recursive wrapping with lixto. Paper presented at the 6th International Conference on Logic Programming and Nonmonotonic Reasoning, Vienna, Austria, 21–41.

Belkin, N. J., Oddy, R. N., & Brooks, H. M. (1982a). ASK for information retrieval: Part I. Background and theory. *Journal of Documentation, 38*(2), 61–71.

Belkin, N. J., Oddy, R. N., & Brooks, H. M. (1982b). ASK for information retrieval: Part II. Results of a design study. *Journal of Documentation, 38*(3), 145–164.

Berners-Lee, T. (2004, May). *Will the Semantic Web scale?* Keynote address presented to the Thirteenth Annual World Wide Web Conference, New York, NY.

Bohl, O., Schellhase, J., Sengler, R., & Winand, U. (2002). The Sharable Content Object Reference Model (SCORM): A critical review. *Proceedings of the International Conference on Computers in Education,* 950–951.

British Library. (2005). *Redefining the library: The British Library's strategy 2005–2008.* Retrieved January 18, 2007, from www.bl.uk/about/strategic/glossary.html

Brookes, B. C. (1977). The developing cognitive viewpoint in information science. *Journal of Informatics, 1,* 55–62.

Brookes, B. C. (1980). Measurement in information science: Objective and subjective metrical space. *Journal of the American Society for Information Science, 31,* 248–255.

Brooks, C., & McCalla, G. (2006). Towards flexible learning object metadata. *International Journal of Continuing Engineering Education and Life Long Learning, 16*(1–2), 50–63.

Brusilovsky, P. (2001). Adaptive hypermedia. *User Modeling and User-Adapted Interaction, 11*(1–2), 87–100.

Brusilovsky, P. (2003). Adaptive navigation support in educational hypermedia: The role of student knowledge level and the case for meta-adaptation. *British Journal of Educational Technology, 34*(4), 487–497.

Brusilovsky, P., & Maybury, M. (2002). From adaptive hypermedia to the adaptive Web. *Communications of the ACM, 45*(5), 30–33.

Buckingham Shum, S. J., Uren, V., Li, G., Sereno, B., & Mancini, C. (2007). Modelling naturalistic argumentation in research literatures: Representation and interaction design issues. *International Journal of Intelligent Systems, 22*(1), 17–47.

Caprotti, O., Carlisle, D., & Cohen, A. (2002). The OpenMath Standard. Kaiserslautern, Germany: The OpenMath Consortium. Retrieved January 18, 2007, from www.openmath.org/cocoon/openmath/standard/om11/index.html

Castillo, G., Gama, J., & Breda, A. M. (2006). An adaptive predictive model for student modelling. In G. D. Magoulas & S. Y. Chen (Eds.), *Advances in Web-based education: Personalized learning environments* (pp. 70–92). London: Information Science Publishing.

Cole, C. (2000). Interaction with an enabling information retrieval system: Modeling the user's decoding and encoding operations. *Journal of the American Society for Information Science, 51*(5), 417–426.

Cole, C., Beheshti, J., Leide, J. E., & Large, A. (2005). Interactive information retrieval: Bringing the user to a selection state. In A. Spink & C. Cole (Eds.),

New directions in cognitive information retrieval (pp. 13–41). Dordrecht, The Netherlands: Springer.

Cole, C., Cantero, P., & Ungar, A. (2000). The development of a diagnostic-prescriptive tool for undergraduates seeking information for a social science/humanities assignment: Part III. Enabling devices. *Information Processing & Management, 36,* 481–500.

Cole, C., & Leide, J. E. (2006). A cognitive framework for human information behaviour: The place of metaphor in human information organizing behaviour. In A. Spink & C. Cole (Eds.), *New directions in human behaviour* (pp. 171–202). Dordrecht, The Netherlands: Springer.

Cole, C., & Mandelblatt, B. (2000). Using Kintsch's discourse comprehension theory to model the user's coding of an informative message from an enabling information retrieval system. *Journal of the American Society for Information Science, 51*(11), 1033–1046.

Collis, B., & Margaryan, A. (2004). Applying Activity Theory to computer-supported collaborative learning and work-based activities in corporate settings. *Educational Technology Research & Development, 52*(4), 38–52.

Conlan, O., Hockemeyer, C., Wade, V., & Albert, D. (2003). Metadata driven approaches to facilitate adaptivity in personalized e-learning systems. *Journal of the Japanese Society for Information and Systems in Education.* Retrieved January 18, 2007, from www.cs.tcd.ie/Owen.Conlan/publications/JSISEv1.23_Conlan.pdf

Czarkowski, M., & Kay, J. (2006). Giving learners a real sense of control over adaptivity, even if they are not quite ready for it yet. In G. D. Magoulas & S. Y. Chen (Eds.), *Advances in Web-based education: Personalized learning environments* (pp. 93–125). London: Information Science Publishing.

Dagger, D., Conlan, O., & Wade, V. (2003). An architecture for candidacy in adaptive elearning systems to facilitate the reuse of learning resources. *Proceedings of the World Conference on E-Learning in Corporate, Government, Healthcare and Higher Education,* 49–56.

DCMI Education Working Group. (2004). *Education application profile.* Retrieved April 1, 2007, from projects.ischool.washington.edu/sasutton/dcmi/ed/04-05/DC-Education_AP_11-30-04.html

De Bra, P., & Ruiter, J. P. (2001). AHA! Adaptive hypermedia for all. *Proceedings of the Webnet Conference,* 262–268.

Dicheva, D., & Dichev, C. (2006). TM4L: Creating and browsing educational topic maps. *British Journal of Educational Technology, 37*(3), 391–404.

Dolog, P., Henze, N., Nejdl, W., & Sintek, M. (2003, December). *Towards an adaptive Semantic Web.* Paper presented at the Principles and Practice of Semantic Web Reasoning, Mumbai, India.

Dolog, P., Henze, N., Nejdl, W., & Sintek, M. (2004). The personal reader: Personalizing and enriching learning resources using semantic Web technologies. *Proceedings of the Third International Conference on Adaptive Hypermedia and Adaptive Web-Based Systems,* 85–94.

Domingue, J., & Dzbor, M. (2004). Magpie: Supporting browsing and navigation on the Semantic Web. *Proceedings of the 9th International Conference on Intelligent User Interface,* 191–197.

Dzbor, M., Domingue, J., & Motta, E. (2003). Magpie: Towards a Semantic Web browser. *Proceedings of the Second International Semantic Web Conference* (Lecture Notes in Computer Science, 2870), 738–753.

Education Informatics. (2007, January 4). In *Wikipedia: The free encyclopedia*. Retrieved January 7, 2007, from en.wikipedia.org/wiki/Education_Informatics

Engeström, Y. (1987). *Learning by expanding: An activity-theoretical approach to developmental research*. Helsinki, Finland: Orienta-Konsultit Oy.

Ford, N. (2000). Improving the 'darkness to light' ratio in user-related IR research. *Journal of Documentation, 56*(6), 624–643.

Ford, N. (2005). New cognitive directions. In A. Spink & C. Cole (Eds.), *New directions in cognitive information retrieval* (pp. 81–96). Dordrecht, The Netherlands: Springer.

Gama, J., & Castillo, G. (2002). Adaptive Bayes. In F. Garijo, J. Riquelme, & M. Toro (Eds.), *Advances in artificial intelligence* (Lecture Notes in Artificial Intelligence, 2527, pp. 765–774). Berlin, Germany: Springer.

Gašević, D., & Hatala, M. (2005). Searching context relevant learning resource using ontology mappings. *Proceedings of the SW-EL Workshop at the 3rd International Conference on Knowledge Capture*. Retrieved April 2, 2007, from www.win.tue.nl/SW-EL/2005/swel05-kcap05/proceedings/%235-Gasevic-Hatala.pdf

Gašević, D., & Hatala, M. (2006). Ontology mappings to improve learning resource search. *British Journal of Educational Technology, 37*(3), 375–389.

Godby, C. J. (2004). What do application profiles reveal about the learning object metadata standard? *Ariadne, 41*. Retrieved January 18, 2007, from www.ariadne.ac.uk/issue41/godby/intro.html

Gruber, T. (2004). Every ontology is a treaty—a social agreement—amongst people with some common motive in sharing: An interview with Tom Gruber. *AIS SIGSEMIS Bulletin, 1*(3), 4–8.

Guha, R., McCool, R., & Miller, E. (2003). Semantic search. *Proceedings of the 12th International Conference on World Wide Web*, 700–709.

Gunnarsdóttir, S., Heimerl, U., Kieslinger, B., Simon, B., & Tsiortou, S. (2004). *Current issues of training management in European entreprises: ELENA whitepaper*. Retrieved January 18, 2007, from www.zsi.at/attach/Training_Mgt.PDF

Hanks, W. F. (1991) Foreword. In J. Lave & E. Wenger, Situated learning: Legitimate peripheral participation (pp. 13–21). Cambridge, UK: Cambridge University Press.

Henze, N., Dolog, P., & Nejdl, W. (2004). Reasoning and ontologies for personalized e-learning in the Semantic Web. *Educational Technology and Society, 7*(4), 82–97.

Henze, N., & Nejdl, W. (2001). Adaptation in open corpus hypermedia. *International Journal of Artificial Intelligence in Education, 12*, 325–350.

Huang, W., Webster, D., Wood, D., & Ishaya, T. (2006). An intelligent semantic e-learning framework using context-aware Semantic Web technologies. *British Journal of Educational Technology, 37*(3), 351–373.

Hummel, H., Manderveld, J., Tattersall, C., & Koper, R. (2004). Educational modelling language and learning design: New opportunities for instructional reusability and personalised learning. *International Journal of Learning Technology, 1*(1), 111–126.

IEEE. Learning Technology Standards Committee. (2001). *IEEE P1484. Draft standard for learning technology: Public and private information (PAPI) for learners (PAPI Learner): Draft 8 specification core features*. Retrieved September 5, 2006, from edutool.com/papi

IEEE. Learning Technology Standards Committee. (2002). *Learning object meta-data: Final draft standard IEEE 1484.12.1-2002*. Retrieved January 18, 2007, from ltsc.ieee.org/wg12/files/LOM_1484_12_1_v1_Final_Draft.pdf

IEEE. Learning Technology Standards Committee. (2005). *WG20: Reusable competency definitions*. Retrieved January 18, 2007, from ltsc.ieee.org/wg20/index.html

IMS Global Learning Consortium. (2001). *IMS learning information package specification*. Retrieved January 18, 2007, from www.imsproject.org/profiles

IMS Global Learning Consortium. (2002). *IMS learning resource meta-data specification* (Version 1.3). Retrieved January 18, 2007, from www.imsproject.org/metadata

IMS Global Learning Consortium. (2003a). *IMS learning design specification*. Retrieved January 18, 2007, from www.imsglobal.org/learningdesign

IMS Global Learning Consortium. (2003b). *IMS simple sequencing specification*. Retrieved January 18, 2007, from www.imsproject.org/simplesequencing

IMS Global Learning Consortium. (2006). *IMS question and test interoperability overview*. Retrieved January 18, 2007, from www.imsproject.org/question/qtiv2p1pd2/imsqti_oviewv2p1pd2.html

Kobsa, A. (2002). Personalized hypermedia and international privacy. *Communications of the ACM, 45*(5), 64–67.

Koper, R., & Manderveld, J. (2004). Educational modeling language: Modeling reusable, interoperable, rich and personalized units of learning. *British Journal of Educational Technology, 35*(5), 537–551.

Kuhlthau, C. (2005). Towards collaboration between information seeking and information retrieval. *Information Research, 10*(2), paper 226. Retrieved January 18, 2007, from informationr.net/ir/10-2/paper225.html

Kumar, V., Greer, J., & McCalla, G. (2005). Assisting online helpers. *International Journal of Learning Technology, 1*(3), 293–321.

Laurillard, D. (2002). *Rethinking university teaching: A conversational framework for the effective use of learning technologies* (2nd ed.). London: Routledge Farmer.

Lawless, S., Wade, V., & Conlan, O. (2005). Dynamic contextual e-learning: Dynamic content discovery, capture and learning object generation from open corpus source. *E-Learn 2005, World Conference on E-Learning in Corporate, Government, Healthcare and Higher Education*. Retrieved January 18, 2007, from www.cs.tcd.ie/Owen.Conlan/publications/eLearn_2005_lawless.pdf

Levy, P., Ford, N., Foster, J., Madden, A., Miller, D., Nunes, J. M. B., et al. (2003). Educational informatics: An emerging research agenda. *Journal of Information Science, 29*(4), 298–310.

McCalla, G. (2004). The ecological approach to the design of e-learning environments: Purpose-based capture and use of information about learners. *Journal of Interactive Media in Education, 2004*(7). Retrieved January 18, 2007, from www-jime.open.ac.uk/2004/7

McCalla, G., Greer, J., Vassileva, J., Deters, R., Bull, S., & Kettel, L. (2001). Lessons learned in deploying a multi-agent learning support system: The I-Help experience. In J. Moore, C. Redfield, & W. L. Johnson (Eds.), *Artificial intelligence in education: AI-ED in the wired and wireless future* (410–421). Amsterdam: IOS Press.

McCalla, G., Vassileva, J., Greer, J., & Bull, S. (2000). Active learner modeling. *Proceedings of Intelligent Tutoring Systems*, 53–62.

Melis, E., Goguadze, G., Homik, M., Libbrecht, P., Ullrich, C., & Winterstein, S. (2006). Semantic-aware components and services of ActiveMath. *British Journal of Educational Technology, 37*(3), 405–423.

Merrill, M. D. (2002). First principles of instruction. *Educational Technology Research & Development, 50*(3), 43–59.

Miklos, Z., Neumann, G., Zdun, U., & Sintek, N. (2003). Querying Semantic Web resources using triple views. *Proceedings of the 2nd International Semantic Web Conference,* 517–532.

Miles, A., & Brickley, D. (2005). *SKOS core guide, W3C editor's working draft.* Retrieved January 18, 2007, from www.w3.org/2004/02/skos/core/guide

Mwanza, D., & Engeström, Y. (2005). Managing content in e-learning environments. *British Journal of Educational Technology, 36*(3), 453–463.

Naeve, A. (2005). The human Semantic Web: Shifting from knowledge push to knowledge pull. *International Journal of Semantic Web and Information Systems, 1*(3), 1–30. Retrieved January 18, 2007, from kmr.nada.kth.se/papers/SemanticWeb/HSW.pdf

National Computer Systems. (2004). *NCS: Making IT happen* [presentation on development and outcomes: metadata standard and taxonomy for education content exchange]. Retrieved January 18, 2007, from www.itsc.org.sg/events/metadata04/Details.pdf

Nejdl, W., Wolf, B., Qu, C., Decker, S., Sintek, M., Naeve, A., et al. (2002). EDUTELLA: A P2P networking infrastructure based on RDF. *Proceedings of the 11th World Wide Web Conference.* Retrieved April 2, 2007, from edutella.jxta.org/reports/edutella-whitepaper.pdf

Niu, X., McCalla, G., & Vassileva, J. (2005). Purpose-based user modelling in a multi-agent portfolio management system. *Proceedings of the Workshop on Decentralized, Agent-Based and Social Approaches to User Modeling, held in conjunction with the Tenth International Conference on User Modeling,* 66–69.

O'Keeffe, I., Brady, A., Conlan, O., & Wade, V. (2006). Just-in-time generation of pedagogically sound, context sensitive personalized learning experiences. *International Journal on E-Learning, 5*(1), 113–127.

Paavola, S., Lipponen, L., & Hakkarainen, K. (2002). Epistemological foundations for CSCL: A comparison of three models of innovative knowledge communities. *Proceedings of the Computer-Supported Collaborative Learning Conference,* 24–32.

Papanikolaou, K. A., & Grigoriadou, M. (2006). Building an instructional framework to support learner control in adaptive educational systems. In G. D. Magoulas & S. Y. Chen (Eds.), *Advances in Web-based education: Personalized learning environments* (pp. 127–146). London: Information Science Publishing.

Park, J., & Hunting, S. (2002). *XML topic maps: Creating and using topic maps for the Web.* Boston, MA: Addison-Wesley.

Pask, G. (1976). *Conversation theory: Applications in education and epistemology.* Amsterdam: Elsevier.

Ploetz, P. (2004). Faculty development and learning object technology: Bridging the gap. *Teaching with Technology Today, 10*(4). Retrieved January 18, 2007, from www.uwsa.edu/ttt/articles/ploetz3.htm

Qin, J., & Hernandez, N. (2006). Building interoperable vocabulary and structures for learning objects. *Journal of the American Society for Information Science and Technology, 57*(2), 280–292.

Rothkopf, E. Z. (1970). The concept of mathemagenic activities. *Review of Educational Research, 40,* 325–336.

Sampson, D., & Karampiperis, P. (2006). Towards next generation activity-based learning systems. *International Journal on E-Learning, 5*(1), 129–149.

Scott, B. (2001). Gordon Pask's conversation theory: A domain independent constructivist model of human knowing. *Foundations of Science, 6*(4), 343–360.

Sereno, B., Buckingham Shum, S., & Motta, E. (2005). ClaimSpotter: An environment to support sensemaking with knowledge triples. *Proceedings of the 10th International Conference on Intelligent User Interfaces*, 199–206.

Sfard, A. (1998). On two metaphors for learning and on the danger of choosing just one. *Educational Researcher, 27*(2), 4–13.

Shabajee, P., McBride, B., Steer, D., & Reynolds, D. (2006). A prototype Semantic Web-based digital content exchange for schools in Singapore. *British Journal of Educational Technology, 37*(3), 461–477.

Sheth, A., Ramakrishnan, C., & Thomas, C. (2005). Semantics for the Semantic Web: The implicit, the formal and the powerful. *International Journal on Semantic Web and Information Systems, 1*(1), 1–18.

Sicilia, M. (2006). Semantic learning designs: Recording assumptions and guidelines. *British Journal of Educational Technology, 37*(3), 331–350.

Sicilia, M., & Lytras, M. (2005). On the representation of change according to different ontologies of learning. *International Journal of Learning and Change, 1*(1), 66–79.

Silva, N., & Rocha, J. (2003). Service-oriented ontology mapping system. *Proceedings of the Workshop on Semantic Integration of the International Semantic Web Conference*. Retrieved April 2, 2007, from sunsite.informatik. rwth-aachen.de/Publications/CEUR-WS/Vol-82/SI_demo_06.pdf

Simon, B., Dolog, P., Miklós, Z., Olmedilla, D., & Sintek, M. (2004). Conceptualising smart spaces for learning. *Journal of Interactive Media in Education, 2004*(9). Retrieved January 18, 2007, from www-jime.open. ac.uk/2004/9

Sintek, M., & Decker, S. (2002). Triple: An RDF query, inference, and transformation language. *Proceedings of the International Semantic Web Conference*, 364–378.

Specht, M. (2006). Contextualized learning: Supporting learning in context. In G. D. Magoulas & S. Y. Chen (Eds.), *Advances in Web-based education: Personalized learning environments* (pp. 331–352). London: Information Science Publishing.

Stutt, A., & Motta, E. (2004). Semantic learning Webs. *Journal of Interactive Media in Education, 2004*(10). Retrieved January 18, 2007, from www-jime.open.ac.uk/2004/10

Sun, L., & Fu, Y. (2005). Interoperability for elearning services management and provision. *World Wide Web, 8*(4), 395–412.

Tang, T. Y., & McCalla, G. (2003). Smart recommendation for an evolving e-learning system. *Proceedings of the International Conference on Artificial Intelligence in Education*, 699–710.

Taylor, R. S. (1968). Question-negotiation and information seeking in libraries. *College & Research Libraries, 29*(3), 178-194.

Thornley, C. (2005). *A dialectical model of information retrieval: Exploring a contradiction in terms*. Unpublished doctoral dissertation, University of Strathclyde.

Tramullas, J., & Garrido, P. (2005). Constructing Web subject gateways using Dublin Core, RDF and Topic Maps. *Information Research, 11*(2) paper 248. Retrieved January 18, 2007, from informationr.net/ir/11-2/paper248.html

Uren, V., Buckingham Shum, S., Bachler, M., & Li, G. (2006). Sensemaking tools for understanding research literatures: Design, implementation and user evaluation. *International Journal of Human–Computer Studies, 64*(5), 420–445.

Vargas-Vera, M., & Celjuska, D. (2003). *Ontology-driven event recognition on stories* (KMI Technical Report KMI-TR-135). Milton Keynes, UK: Knowledge Media Institute. Retrieved January 18, 2007, from kmi.open.ac.uk/publications/pdf/kmi-03-11.pdf

Vargas-Vera, M., & Moreale, E. (2003). *A question-answering system using argumentation* (KMI Technical Report KMI-TR-132). Milton Keynes, UK: Knowledge Media Institute.

Vassileva, J., McCalla, G., & Greer, J. (2003). Multi-agent multi-user modeling in I-Help. *Journal of User Modeling and User-Adapted Interaction, 13*, 179–210.

Wiley, D. A., & Edwards, E. K. (2002). Online self-organizing social systems: The decentralized future of online learning. *Quarterly Review of Distance Education, 3*(1), 33–46.

Wilson, T. D. (2006). A re-examination of information seeking behaviour in the context of activity theory. *Information Research, 11*(4). Retrieved January 18, 2007, from InformationR.net/ir/11-4/paper260.html

Yli-Luoma, P. V. J., & Naeve, A. (2006). Towards a semantic e-learning theory by using a modelling approach. *British Journal of Educational Technology, 37*(3), 445–459.

Issues in
Information Science

CHAPTER 12

Information Commons

Nancy Kranich
Consultant

Jorge Reina Schement
Pennsylvania State University

Introduction

This chapter reviews the history and theory of information commons along with the various conceptual approaches used to describe and understand them. It also discusses governance, financing, and participation in these commons. Digital technologies offer unprecedented possibilities for human inventiveness, global communication, innovation, and access to information. These same technologies also provide new opportunities to control—or enclose—intellectual products, thereby threatening to erode political discourse, scientific inquiry, free speech, and the creativity needed for a healthy democracy. Advocates for an open information society face an uphill battle to influence outcomes in the policy arena; yet they are developing *information commons* that advance innovation, stimulate creativity, and promote the sharing of information resources. Designers of these new information resources can learn from those who have studied other commons, such as forests and fisheries. Multidisciplinary research efforts need to go beyond rejecting enclosure to assessing whether alternatives are viable. This requires applying a framework for analysis to determine whether information commons are sustainable as a fundamental information construct for the 21st century.

In this chapter, we conceptualize a phenomenon, a social construction that has become known as the information commons. In a sense, it poses a paradox because while the digital technologies at its core offer vast opportunities for creativity and communication, these same technologies provide opportunities to erode political discourse, scientific inquiry, and free speech; to bar access to intellectual products; to enclose democracy. Our focus is the employment of these technologies for the purpose of organizing information in order for it to be shared by a community of producers or consumers. Generalists and specialists use the term *information commons* loosely, as both metaphor and actual fact, singular and plural, a usage pattern to which we conform. We frame this chapter around the problem of the information commons as an idea with attributes of community, governance, rights, access, openness, patterns of participation, efficiency, equity, distribution, infrastructure, and conflict management. It is our contention that information commons promise a fresh paradigm for advancing innovation, stimulating creativity, and promoting resource sharing. Not only do they offer a response to the challenges posed by enclosure, but they also offer an opportunity to build a fundamental institution for a 21st-century democracy.

Commons in Theory

Americans jointly own, share, and administer a wide range of common assets, including natural resources, public lands, schools, libraries, and scientific knowledge. Yet, supporters often encounter resistance when seeking public funding to sustain these essential resources, especially at a time when the marketplace dominates political priorities, even though neglecting such resources impoverishes culture and endangers democracy. For this reason, "most democracies use a combination of market and nonmarket devices" such as government publications, public libraries, and public broadcasting to assure that citizens get the information they need (Baker, 2002, p. 73).

Historically, the "commons" meant those agricultural fields in England to which certain farmers, called *commoners*, held rights and responsibilities, such as planting crops or grazing animals. Between 1500 and 1800, however, many of those common fields were converted into private property in order to boost agricultural production, redistribute population, advance industrial development, and ultimately bring lands under the control of wealthy aristocrats. Enclosure occurred both piecemeal and by general legislative action, for no single decision or act caused the enclosure of public fields—a story similar to today's enclosure of the commons of the mind. In the end, this "enclosure" movement transformed a traditional, communal method of agriculture into a system in which ownership of property alone determined use rights (Turner, 1984; Yelling 1977).

If the enclosure movement eclipsed the commons, it also launched a debate over rights of access. Lawyers and economists have traditionally considered ownership either within the realm of a marketplace for the exchange of private property or a market failure requiring government management. Resources such as common property have fallen between this private–public ownership dichotomy (Hess & Ostrom, 2003). The 1861 publication of *Ancient Law* by Henry Sumner Maine (1861/1986) fueled this debate about whether landed proprietors have a special role needing legal protection and about the legitimacy of enclosing communally owned properties. In the mid-1950s, H. Scott Gordon (1954) and Anthony Scott (1955) kicked off their own debate about the commons by introducing an economic analysis of fisheries in two articles that outlined a theory of the commons. In 1968 Garrett Hardin wrote his famous article, "The Tragedy of the Commons," which used the example of over-grazing to argue that unlimited access to resources results in excessive demand and, consequently, in overexploitation. His thesis quickly gained acceptance among those proposing personal self-interest as the sole motivator behind the exploitation of shared resources. Unwilling to accept Hardin's argument, scholars from several disciplines countered with studies of common property resources, where group control over the resource need not lead to overuse, but rather to the balancing of benefits and costs (Bromley, 1992; Buck, 1998; Heritier, 2002; National Research Council, 1986; Ostrom, 1990, 2002; Ostrom, Gardner, & Walker, 1994).

Prominent among these counter theorists is Carol M. Rose (1994) who proposes a reverse of the tragedy of the commons where, for certain types of activities, individuals may choose to "underinvest" rather than to overexploit. At a festival or on a dance floor, for example, the more who take part, the greater the benefit to each participant. "Activities of this sort may have value precisely because they reinforce the solidarity and fellow feeling of the community as a whole; thus, the more members of the community who participate, even only as observers, the better for all" (p. 141). Rose (p. 141) refers to this type of behavior as the "comedy of the commons," with the connotation of a happy ending because indefinite numbers and expandability of participation by a defined community enhance rather than diminish value. She elaborates on this idea using the phrase "the more the merrier" and analogizing to economies of scale, where the larger the investment, the higher the rate of return. Rose contends that people need encouragement to join such nonexclusive activities, where their participation produces beneficial externalities for others.

Scholars such as Siegfried Ciriacy-Wantrup and Richard Bishop (1975) distinguished between two types of legal regimes that govern commons: *open-access* (or "no property") *regimes* and *common property regimes*. With open access regimes, nobody has the legal right to exclude anyone else from using the resource, thus the tragedy of the commons may ensue because of overuse or destruction. By contrast, common property regimes, which regulate the use of *common pool resources*, provide members of a clearly defined group with a bundle of legal rights, including the right to exclude nonmembers from using the resource, thereby, promoting the comedy of the commons. Such common-pool resources also resemble what economists call public goods, for example, parks, public transportation, police and fire protection, and national defense. The challenge stems from the difficulties involved when common pool resources management is based on intensity of use and delineation of eligible users; for neither common pool resources nor public goods can easily exclude beneficiaries (Stevenson, 1991).

Others have explored the emergence, efficiency, and stability of common property regimes. Carl Dahlman (1980), Vincent and Elinor Ostrom (1997), and Glenn G. Stevenson (1991) contest the conventional view in economics that communal ownership and collective control are necessarily inefficient.

They maintain that, under certain conditions, economic theory predicts such arrangements are superior to private ownership and individual control. Furthermore, Stevenson has identified seven useful characteristics that distinguish common goods from public and private goods; common goods have (1) well defined boundaries; (2) a well delineated group of users; (3) multiple users of the resource; (4) well understood rules; (5) shared rights to use the resource; (6) competition for the resource; and, (7) a well delineated group of rights holders. His examples include communal forests in Europe that are group-managed for a limited, well defined community, as well as grazing lands available to residents of a particular village during certain predetermined dates for a limited number of animals.

A leader in the field, Elinor Ostrom (1990, 2002) has studied the actual workings of common property resources and observed that common property regimes regulating these resources are distinguished by group, rather than individual control; the group is then responsible for balancing benefits and costs, defining who may participate in resource use and to what degree, as well as designating who will make management decisions. With her colleague Edella Schlager, Ostrom underscores that it is "the difference between exercising a right and participating in the definition of future rights to be exercised ... [that] makes collective-choice rights so powerful" (Schlager & Ostrom, 1992, pp. 250–251).

Further challenging the presumption that all common-pool resources are open access, Ostrom analyzed the exploitation of these resources when they are regulated under common property regimes. Through her work with the National Research Council in the mid-1980s, she outlined the components of governance necessary to sustain common property resources efficiently, focusing initially on natural resources in developing countries (National Research Council, 1986; Ostrom, 1986). Ostrom's (1990) seminal work, *Governing the Commons*, provides a systematic blueprint for understanding the economic and experimental foundations for common property regimes. By studying a variety of common-pool resources, she derives a framework for assessing commons, plus eight design principles that enable people to use these resources over a long period of time. Included in the framework are conditions necessary for self-governance: clearly defined boundaries, the design and enforcement of rules, reciprocity (the equal exchange of goods and knowledge), building trust and social capital, and communication channels (Dietz, Ostrom, & Stern, 2003; Ostrom, Gardner, & Walker, 1994; Ostrom & Ostrom, 1997; Pretty, 2003). Thanks to Ostrom and her colleagues, groups interested in developing and managing common property now have a theory of commons and a useful framework to implement them. Ostrom went on to co-found the International Association for the Study of Common Property (IASCP), which focuses on new topics such as genetic resources, roads, the atmosphere, biodiversity, patents, and the Internet.

Information Commons in History

The emergence of the Internet and the World Wide Web stimulated a growing awareness among scholars of the value of information and intensified the study of information as a common property or shared resource. Although the digital age elevated the notion of information commons for the purpose of scholarly research, the roots of information as a shared resource date back to pre-literate societies—where, from earliest times, people relied on shared stories and songs to pass on their stock of commonly held knowledge. Oral stories, sometimes the purview of bards, belonged to everyone and no one; hence, even today, where lore prevails, the imposition of ownership provokes resistance (Ong, 1982; Goody, 1986). With the advent of writing came the great revolution; people began to fix ideas in texts that gave them portability through space and time. They recorded commercial transactions, religious beliefs, literature, history, and poetry. Hellenistic Greeks collected these texts in great libraries, as in Alexandria, Egypt. Medieval Europeans collected manuscripts in monasteries and palaces, and treated them as sacred objects. Not until the mid-15th century invention of the printing press, and the subsequent emergence of capitalism in Europe, did texts become things—the first commodities to be bought and sold by means of an information market (Schement & Curtis, 1995, p. 6). From the time of the Enlightenment, English speakers began to think of information as a thing, and acted accordingly—by passing laws to enclose information to prevent theft and by constructing systems to deposit or retrieve information.

Three centuries later, the architects of American democracy maintained that a free society must ensure accessible knowledge for all its citizens. Benjamin Franklin, a printer, established the first lending library in America in 1731, well before he helped found the republic; and, at the time, his idea of sharing information resources was a radical one—for, in the rest of the world, libraries were the property of the ruling classes and religious institutions (Zimmerman, 2003). James Madison (1865, p. 276) famously declared that "a popular government without popular information, or means of acquiring it, is but a Prologue to a Farce or a Tragedy, or perhaps both. Knowledge will forever govern ignorance, and a people who mean to be their own Governors must arm themselves with the power which knowledge gives." In Madison's great opus, the U.S. Constitution, two provisions address the need for information that is so crucial to democracy. The Copyright Clause does so both by giving authors "the exclusive right" to profit by their writings "for limited times," and by providing that after the limited term of copyright expires, works enter the public domain, where they are freely available to all (U.S. Constitution, 1789). The First Amendment prohibits government from abridging "the freedom of speech, or of the press, or the right of the people peaceably to assemble."

Franklin and Madison's new society soon became an industrial society, where pioneering information systems and technologies, first developed as management tools, proved critical to controlling the increasingly complex processes of industrial production. Firms, such as those observed by economist Ronald Coase (1937) in the early 20th century, integrated vertically in order to respond to complex and expensive problems of transaction costs. The telegraph and telephone improved the country's capacity to distribute information instantly across long distances and, unlike commodities whose worth increases with scarcity, these emerging communication networks benefited from "network externalities"—that is, they increased in value as the number of participants grew (Beniger, 1986a, 1986b; Schement, 1988; Schement & Curtis, 1995). At the same time, social innovations such as widespread literacy and universal access to public schools and libraries established a popular demand for and interest in information. By the second half of the 19th century, the cumulative value of these externalities led to a dramatic increase in patents and copyrights, thus fueling new technologies as well as demand for information.

In the 20th century, Americans led the way toward articulating a vocabulary speaking of information as if it were a tangible thing to be inserted as a raw material in essential resources. As a result, economic innovations (e.g., new markets for information) and social perspectives derived from this attitude (e.g., judging a newspaper by the "amount" of information contained) became so common that they now constitute the texture of society (Schement & Curtis, 1995). Not surprisingly, the U.S. government also began to recognize that the public had an interest in the deployment of broadcasting and telephone communications. The Communications Act of 1934 (Communications Act, 1934), which created the Federal Communications Commission (FCC), set forth a "public interest, convenience, and necessity" standard[1] for licensing and regulating radio, and later television, broadcasting over the public airwaves, thereby signaling a role for government as a guarantor of public information access. The Act further established the policy of Universal Service, guaranteeing to all the opportunity to subscribe to telephone service at a reasonable cost (McChesney, 1993; Mueller, 1997; Paglin, 1989).

Arriving with the 21st century, a networked society precipitated a shift from hierarchical industrial modes to looser, flexible, cooperative networks as the dominant social organization of the digital age. Manuel Castells (2000) describes networks that offer open, dynamic systems, highly susceptible to nonthreatening innovation. Yochai Benkler (2006) takes that analysis into the marketplace, contending that computer networks shift production into a highly decentralized mode, toward a nonproprietary transactional framework that coexists alongside market-based production. Compared to firms in Coase's day, innovations in the communications environment reduce transaction costs to near zero. Nevertheless, along with the emergence of new enterprises come tensions in traditional power relationships.

The Tensions Between Public and Private

The tensions between information as a public good available to all and information as a private commodity have given rise to a highly contested policy environment. Different goals—equal access to information so that all citizens can meaningfully participate in public discourse, consumer choice among products and services, and protection of the public from government intrusion into the free flow of ideas—have strained the information chain. A longstanding drive to commodify information goods and services often overlooks a central fact about information: It is neither a pure public good nor a pure private good. Information is a good that people do not use up, as they do other commodities. When transmitted, information often exhibits network externalities–that is, its value can escalate with increased use (Benkler, 2003b; Lessig, 2001; Mosco & Wasco, 1988; Stiglitz, 1999). Commodifying information also overlooks its importance as a constitutive force of society as well as its significance to innovation and creativity (Braman, 1989; Reichman & Franklin, 1999).

The tendencies and tensions of the digital age threaten the business models of commercial content producers. In response, content industries have intensified their efforts to strengthen control over the use of their products, and such controls often come at the expense of vital "free expression safety valves" within copyright law. Fair use, the first sale rule, and the public domain balance the public's interest in open access with the property interests of copyright owners (Heins, 2003; Heins & Beckles, 2006; Litman, 2001; National Research Council, 2000; Vaidhyanathan, 2001).

Many content providers respond to the digital age by using new technologies to control access; others seize opportunities presented by the openness of these technologies to enhance access and innovation. From the early days of the Internet, user-friendly software programs empowered consumers to become creators, producers, and distributors of information. Even before the invention of the Web, online conferencing systems such as The Well, search and retrieval agents such as Gopher, online forums such as community freenets, bulletin boards and listservs, and newsgroups organized within the Usenet network allowed those with Internet access to generate, receive, and exchange information readily and easily (Rheingold, 1993a). Between 1995 and 2000, household Internet access grew from 15 percent to 50 percent (National Telecommunications and Information Administration, 2004). In its 1997 Communications Decency Act decision, the Supreme Court recognized the emerging role of the Internet as a vital communication tool:

Through the use of chat rooms, any person with a phone line can become a town crier with a voice that resonates farther than it could from any soapbox. Through the use of Web pages, mail exploders, and newsgroups, the same individual can become a pamphleteer. ... [In short,] "the content on the Internet is as diverse as human thought." (Reno v. American Civil Liberties Union, 1997, p. 870)

In this same case, the Supreme Court expounded four characteristics of transcendent importance to Internet communications:

- Very low barriers to entry;
- Barriers to entry are identical for both speakers and listeners;
- Low barriers ensure the availability of astoundingly diverse content on the Internet; and
- Significant access to all who wish to speak in the medium, creating a parity among speakers (Reno v. ACLU, 1997, p. 877).

The four characteristics delineated by the Court embody the inherent openness of new digital information products and Internet services that offer more accessibility, responsiveness to modification, and sharing. When creators share digitized information, other potential users need not be excluded from access, especially when such non-rivalrous resources create new opportunities for decentralized and collaborative production and distribution. With increased openness come standards and protocols that ease the way for interoperability, allowing information to flow freely over the Internet (Committee for Economic Development. Digital Connections Council, 2006). Indeed, David Bollier and Tim Watts (2002) contend that such standards are essential to open and accessible information commons. Another outcome of openness can be found in the open source movement, where computer programmers design their own versions of software, distribute it freely, and foster worldwide collaboration. With openness, the firm no longer serves as the sole model for organizing production. Rather, new structures emerge that facilitate participation, democratization, and innovation. Many, including Eric von Hippel (2005), consider user-led developments such as the Internet and open source software to be examples of democratizing innovation, part of a broader growing phenomenon of open innovation.

The digitization of content also yields new opportunities as production transforms from a push to a pull economy. According to Bollier (2006b, p. 4), a push economy mass produces goods based on anticipated, predictable consumer demand that mobilizes scarce resources to push products into the marketplace using standardized distribution channels. John Seeley Brown and John Hagel (2005) argue that the highly specified, centralized, and restrictive nature of push systems inhibits innovation. Conversely, a pull economy consolidates highly uncertain user demand to induce sellers to develop customized products for local or specialized needs that are assembled on an open, flexible platform and distributed through networks. A pull environment necessitates collaborative peer production that undermines the central premise of the firm as a hierarchical structure. Pull platforms harness their participants' passion and commitment into niche communities of interest, creating what Chris Anderson (2006) calls the long tail of low volume products available through online aggregators such as Amazon, Netflix, and iTunes. If Anderson's theory is correct, then blockbusters that require huge concentrations of capital may no longer dominate the online retail world. Instead, a pull economy enables niche products to coexist with mass producers, generating such content as blogs, podcasts, and social networking software that is created through a commons-based, peer production model: "Instead of dominant companies using top-down market structures to push and shape consumer demand, the new technologies are enabling the creation of bottom-up, self-organized communities based on fluid and shifting social preferences" (Bollier, 2006a, p. 36). Yet, the shifting balance between creators and users of content also gives rise to policy tensions expressed with force and fervor in the courts and Congress.

Triangulating a Definition

The very idea of an information commons, with its connotation of place, can be something of a puzzle for the uninitiated, especially because the same phrase applies to both the singular and the plural; moreover, such phrases as knowledge commons, digital commons, Internet commons, and electronic commons appear freely interchanged in both popular and technical discourse. With the aforementioned in mind, an *information commons* refers here to information shared by a community of producers and/or consumers. That said, the central fact of an information commons revolves around the question of access to the information available therein; for, much of the debate over the desirability of information commons centers on the degree and management of openness—whether it means free access, no cost access, or unfettered access—all of which come with limitations (Ghosh, 2006; Lessig, 2001). Indeed, a seemingly straightforward commitment to open access carries implications for institutional design and organization. Consequently, scholars who study the functioning of commons emphasize decisions and rules governing the use of information resources, along with the self-governance structures that manage, protect, sustain, and preserve them. In most studies, there follow questions of equity, efficiency, and sustainability (Hess & Ostrom, 2006). Here too, intuitive assumptions do not always follow. Resources such as forests and fisheries deplete, but people may use and share information commons without exhausting them. In fact, their value often increases with greater use. Some people consider the whole Internet, or the public domain,[2] to be types of commons, even though these are essentially open access resources, lacking the clearly defined group governance that is characteristic of common property regimes. Others equate the public sphere with an information commons, although the former refers to an ideal for open debate about the public good (Calhoun, 2004) and the latter focuses on resources. Information commons can be local or global; the term can even refer to a place that academic librarians and computer specialists create and co-manage as collaborative learning spaces for students (Beagle, 1999, 2002, 2006; Bennett, 2003; Brown & Duguid, 1998; Lippincott, 2002, 2006; Lyman, 1999; MacWhinnie, 2003).

Whether called information commons or not, initiatives with characteristics of common property regimes continue to emerge. They share features such as open and free access for designated communities, self-governance, collaboration, free or low cost, and the attempt to achieve sustainability. They offer shared spaces, real and virtual, where communities with common interests and concerns gather. They take advantage of the networked environment to build information communities where escalating participation boosts the value of the resource. Many are interactive, encouraging discourse and exchange among their members. Most charge little, if anything, for access. Their participants contribute new creations and offer strong evidence that they enhance human as well as social capital. They have shared governance structures, with rules and norms defined and accepted by their constituents. They generally espouse self-governance, free expression, and intellectual freedom. Some use the Internet itself as a commons, employing open source software, peer-to-peer file sharing, and collaborative Web sites; others focus more on content creation and dissemination. And, although not every example of an information commons adheres to the form, they all represent alternatives to a purely private or public property-driven approach to information and ideas.

It should come as no surprise that authors employing the term information commons rarely adhere to all of the dimensions of commons elaborated by theorists such as Ostrom and Hess. After all, a concept taking form invites variation. So, in order to understand the conceptualization of information commons across multiple literatures, we examine it within each of four distinct frames: (1) enclosure and control; (2) openness, freedom, and democracy; (3) metaphor; and (4) decentralized information production. Although few confine their narratives to just one of these contexts, it is useful to categorize them in order to grasp how definitions vary and to differentiate them from notions of the public sphere and open access.

Enclosure and Control

In this first frame, much of the discourse surrounding information commons arose after users experienced denial of access to digital information, for example, as a result of privatization, rapidly expanding intellectual property rights, filters, classification, or some other controls.

Initially, few actually referred to information commons when addressing barriers to information access; but, over time, it became clear that the full array of threats affected more than just a few resources. Users experienced a shift from open accessibility to government-imposed or corporate restrictions. Some enclosures were brought about by changes in the physical structure of information, as media changed from print to electronic and analog to digital. Enclosures accelerated during the Cold War when government first computerized information, then privatized it, and more recently further restricted access in the wake of the September 11 attacks. In the private sector, media mergers, telecommunications deregulation, scholarly publishing consolidation, content sharing restrictions, and technological protection measures prevented individuals from accessing information they had previously consumed freely. Some enclosures took place rapidly, others more gradually; some took the form of changes in distribution, others responded to economic exigencies. And, as in medieval times, enclosure occurred both piecemeal and by general legislative action, with no single act proving decisive (Bradley, 2001; Turner, 1984; Yelling, 1977).

The first significant enclosure movement began in the 1960s when the federal government contracted with defense industry companies such as Lockheed to develop databases that could manage defense, educational, and medical data (Borgman, 2000; Summit, 2002). From within the military-industrial complex, the fledgling information industry soon urged government to curtail or eliminate its own publication programs. Paul Zurkowski, the director of the newly formed Information Industry Association (IIA), forecast an Orwellian calamity: "Just as surely as the Berlin Wall stands today, in the absence of a concerted industry-wide effort, user choice in information one day soon will be replaced by 'free information' from one source" (Berry, 1975, p. 795). A decade later, the Reagan Administration eliminated scores of government-produced publications, contracted out then closed federal library and information programs, and placed "maximum feasible reliance" on the private sector to disseminate government information (Office of Management and Budget, 1985, p. 52736).[3] The IIA's privatization strategy succeeded, but not without unflagging public resistance (Hernon & McClure, 1987; McClure, Hernon, & Relyea, 1989; McIntosh, 1990). Government publications in electronic format are now big business, with many no longer produced by the government, included in standard catalogs, distributed through the depository library program, archived, or preserved for permanent public access.

The breakup of the American Telephone & Telegraph Company in 1982, plus subsequent government policies favoring telecommunications deregulation, brought a second wave of enclosures. Telephone companies, previously functioning as common carriers for information produced by others, expanded into production and distribution, even as the cable TV industry moved to provide both connectivity and content (Bolter, 1984; Cole, 1991; Coll, 1986). Thus freed from regulatory constraints, telephone, cable, and newspaper corporations pressed Congress for concessions that would lead to positions of dominance in the technological future. Media consolidation proceeded rapidly over the next two decades (Aufderheide & Barnouw, 1997; Herman & McChesney, 1997; Schiffrin, 2000). At the same time, the computer industry consolidated, resulting in Microsoft's assumption of a dominant market share (Cusumano & Yoffie, 1998; Dvorak, 1994; Ellig, 2001). By the end of the 1990s, a few large corporations oversaw the production and distribution of most of the nation's commercial information.

Amid this ferment, Congress passed the first wholesale revision of communications law since the Communications Act of 1934. The Telecommunications Act of 1996 relaxed earlier limits on how many radio or TV stations a single company could own, as well as eliminating barriers to cross-ownership of local and long distance telephone services, broadcast, cable television, and newspapers, all in the name of market efficiency (Aufderheide, 1999; Hundt, 2000; Telecommunications Act, 1996). Yet, in spite of promises of reduced prices, removed entry barriers, and increased diversity, the 1996 Act resulted in less competition (Baker, 2002; Consumer Federation of America/Consumers Union, 2001; Cooper, 2003; DiCola & Thomson, 2002; McChesney, 1999).[4] The number of corporations controlling most of America's magazines, radio and TV stations, books, movies, and daily mass-circulation newspapers dropped from fifty to ten (Bagdikian, 2000; Zuckerman, 2000). Some observers do argue that the vast resources of the World Wide Web will counteract this trend toward consolidation and top-down control; however, studies at Harvard's Kennedy School of Government suggest that the implementation of the Web's portals and search engines may exacerbate, rather than remedy, the effects of media concentration by making it tougher to find all those independently created resources now available online (Hindman & Cukier, 2003).

A third wave of enclosures came when scholarly societies turned their journal publishing over to private firms in order to contain membership fees and generate income. With ownership transferred to a few conglomerates, expensive licenses, often requiring bundled or aggregated purchase of titles, caused prices of scholarly journals to soar. By the early 1990s, mergers of academic journal publishers allowed a few international conglomerates to charge $20,000 or more for subscriptions to journals such as *Nuclear Physics, Brain Research,* and *Tetrahedron Letters,* while returning profits as high as 40 percent, thereby straining already tight higher education budgets (Turner, 2000; Van Orsdel & Born, 2003). In a study comparing commercial with nonprofit, academic presses, Carl and Theodore Bergstrom (2004) found that the price per page for journals from commercial presses was six times the cost for journals in the same field from nonprofit publishers. Journal costs rose 220 percent between 1986 and 2003 (as compared to an increase in the consumer price index of 64 percent) (Association of College and Research

Libraries, Association of Research Libraries, & Scholarly Publishing and Academic Resources Coalition, 2003) This forced research libraries to cut journal subscriptions and purchase fewer books, particularly titles of limited interest or those published overseas. This, in turn, had an impact on the revenues of university presses that traditionally relied on libraries for primary sales.

Initially, price increases were offset by resource sharing networks that facilitated delivery through interlibrary loan, but restrictive licensing agreements undermined these counterbalancing arrangements. And, once journal prices outpaced library budgets, short-term financial gains for the societies quickly gave way to serious losses in terms of access to research results. In effect, academics found themselves in a quandary: Universities support research from a multitude of sources; researchers must publish that research in approved journals now owned by a few large firms; research is therefore offered freely in exchange for publication; journal publishers sell published research back to university libraries at astronomical prices (Hawkins & Battin, 1998; Information Access Alliance, 2003; Thorin, 2003; Willinsky, 2005). The irony of the situation was not lost on many.

There was more to come. Publishers and information aggregators began requiring restrictive licensing agreements of anyone seeking to acquire or use digital materials—both copyrighted and public domain—compiled in databases such as *LEXIS/NEXIS* and *Science Direct*. Some vendors forced libraries into complex negotiations prior to electronic purchases, and often required libraries to buy bundled suites of items—many of low interest—if they were to receive titles in greater demand. To be sure, such contracts reflect business strategies aimed at protecting investments in database development; however, they also centralize control over the flow of information. Pushed aggressively, they eliminate user protections guaranteed under copyright laws, such as fair-use rights to view, reproduce, and quote limited amounts of copyrighted materials (Okerson, 1999). Licensing contracts may even limit libraries from loaning materials to outsiders or archiving and preserving them for posterity; and, because these licensed databases are leased rather than owned, the library has nothing to offer users if it discontinues its subscription, even after it has paid annual fees for many years (Kahin, 1996). When budget cuts come, "the library has no trace of what it bought: no record, no archive. It's lost entirely" (Vaidhyanathan, 2004, p. 120).

A fourth enclosure tendency follows directly from the aggressive control practices as firms seek legislative endorsement for their strategies. Congress passed the 1998 Digital Millennium Copyright Act (DMCA) imposing criminal penalties for circumventing encryption or even distributing circumvention tools. It then passed the Sonny Bono Copyright Term Extension Act (CTEA), which extends the already lengthy duration of copyright for an additional 20 years, thereby freezing the time boundaries of the public domain.[5] Other Digital Rights Management

(DRM) tools include the broadcast flag, and audio flag, which insert a digital mark that signals conditions allowing or preventing television and audio programs from being copied (Center for Democracy and Technology, 2004; Public Knowledge, n.d.). The courts have followed Congress's lead. In Eldred v. Ashcroft in 2003, the Supreme Court rejected a constitutional challenge to the Sonny Bono law, in a decision that seems to give Congress the power to extend the copyright term at will into the future (Eldred v. Ashcroft, 2003; Heins, 2003). The courts have closed down music file-sharing services such as Napster, Grokster, and KaZaA, which were sued for contributory copyright infringement. The continuing efforts of the recording and movie industries to close down file-sharing services, prosecute individuals for alleged copyright violations, and otherwise lock up or enclose information have resulted in a highly contested policy terrain for information and culture and chilled the exchange of information (A&M Records v. Napster, 2001; Eldred v. Ashcroft, 2003; Heins, 2003). The public interest, civil liberties, library, and academic communities (American Library Association. Office for Information Technology Policy, 2000–2001; Kranich, 2004a, 2004b, 2006) have rallied against enclosure but copyright scholars have led the way in articulating how these enclosures affect information commons. Rose (1986, 1994), Boyle (1996, 2002, 2003a), Benkler (1999), Samuelson (2003), Vaidhyanathan (2001, 2004), Lessig (1999, 2003), and Litman (1990, 2001) have documented how various copyright rules and other techniques such as DRM limit (or enclose) public access rights.

One hotly contested mode of access control merits separate mention—the Internet filter. Initially designed for home use, schools and public libraries are now required to use filters in order to receive federal grant support under the Children's Internet Protection Act (this was upheld by the Supreme Court in June 2003). Filters, however, act more like a cleaver than a scalpel; they block thousands of legal and other resources useful to adults, even as many banned images slip through. And, although Congress mandated filters to shield minors from Internet images deemed harmful, public libraries must install restrictive software on all computers, including those used by adults and staff (National Research Council, 2001; U.S. Children's Online Protection Act Commission, 2000; United States et al. v. American Library Association et al., 2003).

As Congressional debate clouds the future of the Internet, some groups promoting open access to information have also aligned themselves with those calling for network neutrality. Telecommunications giants contend that they cannot deploy broadband technologies or compete without creating separate tiers of service for large content providers willing to pay a premium for high-bandwidth features such as video streaming, online gaming, and voice service. Such a system, where some providers are favored over others, might further disenfranchise public access or non-corporate computer users when navigating a network, thereby limiting their ability to run applications and use services of their choice (Gilroy, 2006; Net Neutrality, 2006; Weitzner, 2006). If access is determined by how much one can pay, small—even not so small—users might find themselves permanently on the slow lane of the Information Superhighway.

A fifth wave of enclosures struck abruptly in the wake of September 11, 2001, when government imposed a series of measures to lock down "sensitive" information. The USA PATRIOT Act, passed just 45 days after the attacks, greatly expands government secrecy at almost every level, and is at odds with the concept of openness in a democracy. For example, the Act requires that confidential library and book store records be made available for law enforcement review (Cole & Dempsey, 2002; Kranich, 2003a, 2003b; Leone & Anrig, 2003). Even before the law passed, Attorney General John Ashcroft sought to restrict access to government information when he sent a memo to government agencies urging them to refuse Freedom of Information Act (FOIA) requests whenever possible, thus reversing previous policy that denied the release of information only if it would result in foreseeable harm (National Security Archive, 2003). As a result, the government released less information under FOIA in 2004 than in 2000, with requests processed by agencies falling by 13 percent and overall use of exemptions to withhold information rising by 22 percent (Coalition of Journalists for Open Government, 2005).

Government also withheld information through the classification process. The U.S. Information Security Oversight Office reported a record 15.6 million documents classified in 2004, an increase of 10 percent over 2003 and 50 percent over 2001. In 2005, classifications dropped back to the 2003 level of 14.2 million actions, but still far ahead of previous decades. Correspondingly, the pace of declassification slowed to a crawl, from a high of 204 million pages in 1997 to just 29.5 million pages in 2005 (McDermott & Feldman, 2006; U.S. Information Security Oversight Office, 2006). Not only do agencies withhold more information because of perceived national security risk, they also label public data as "sensitive but unclassified," further restricting access. In March 2002, White House Chief of Staff Andrew Card (2002) ordered a reexamination of public documents posted on the Internet, resulting in the removal of thousands of items deemed useful to terrorists. Terror-related categories used by the government to "take down" sensitive sites, however, are considered so vague by the American Library Association and others that virtually any type of information conceivably related to terrorism can now be withheld from public scrutiny (American Library Association. Washington Office, 2003). About the same time, President Bush issued Executive Order 13233, which bars public access to presidential records already ordered for release (under the Presidential Records Act of 1987) to a limit of twelve years after he leaves office (American Library Association. Washington Office, n.d.).

The Bush administration also reached into the private research arena. In 2003, editors of peer-reviewed scientific journals agreed to withdraw existing articles and reject future submissions that might compromise national security (Statement on Scientific Publications, 2003). Since then, targeted articles have vanished from electronic versions of scientific journals. This has prompted scholars, civil libertarians, librarians, and even the Chair of the 9/11 Commission to caution that a presumption of secrecy thwarts the openness necessary to accelerate the progress of technical knowledge, which acts against the nation's understanding of potential threats (American Association of University Professors, 2003; National Research Council. Committee on Research Standards and Practices to Prevent the Destructive Application of Biotechnology, 2004; Podesta, 2003; Shane, 2005).

Perhaps inevitably, institutional efforts to control breed their own opposition. One Web site and blog, Beyond the Commons (www.beyond thecommons.com; www.beyondthecommons.com/weblog.html), challenges enclosure by advocating the public domain as the ultimate commons. Indeed, many who take this approach promote the public domain as a counterweight to privatized information. However, within the spectrum of information access models, the public domain represents an open access regime where nobody has the legal right to exclude anyone else from using the resource—ironically, an approach that may itself suffer the tragedy of the commons. According to Hess and Ostrom (2006, p. 12), when new technologies "capture" resources that were "previously unowned, unmanaged, and thus, unprotected," stakeholders are prompted to "renegotiate" their interests, leaving some resources vulnerable to overconsumption and depletion (as described by Hardin, 1968), if not governed, developed, and managed within a framework that can sustain common property resources. In other words, the challenge of information access is not only about enclosure, it is also about managing the resource. Those who view information commons solely through the lens of enclosure may be trading one set of dilemmas for another. The efforts of overzealous governments and aggressive corporations leave a social terrain as uneven as any medieval social hierarchy.

In the first decade of the 21st century, differential access to the Internet and other communications tools excludes many from the benefits of the digital age (Fairlie, 2005). No matter whose data are used to describe the digital divide between rich and poor, between black and white, between urban and rural, between English- and Spanish-speaking, between old and young, between new Americans and Native Americans, the gap between those with high levels of access and those without persists across American communities. Although 73 percent of American adults used the Internet in 2006, with 42 percent of adults using a high speed connection at home, certain groups continue to lag in ownership of computers and online access. In 2005, online access levels stood at 32 percent of Americans age 65 and older, 53 percent of adults living in households with less than $30,000 in annual income, 57 percent of

African-Americans, and 40 percent of those without high school diplomas (Fox, 2005; Madden, 2006). Many cannot identify, evaluate, and apply information and communicate it efficiently, effectively, and responsibly—essential skills if they are to learn, advance knowledge, and flourish in the workplace as well as carry out the day-to-day activities of citizens in a developed, democratic society (Kranich, in press). Even those with access to computers and telecommunications networks often lack the skills necessary to utilize these resources effectively (Hargittai, 2002).

Advocates for the public interest have struggled to protect access to critical resources, balance the rights of users and creators, preserve the public domain, and open public access to all in the digital age; and, although they have fought hard to block enclosure, they face an uphill battle to influence outcomes in a society that emphasizes individual ownership over sharing of resources.

Openness, Freedom, and Democracy

In this second frame, information commons appeal to those attracted to the promises of openness, freedom, and democracy. In contrast to the fear of enclosure, information commons also attract because of their promise of openness, freedom, and democracy. Embraced by several of the same legal scholars who have studied enclosures, for example, Benkler (1998, 2006), Boyle (2006), and Lessig (2001), this view of information commons highlights their potential as promoters of innovation and creativity. For example, in the blog The Innovation Commons (www.innovationcommons.blogspot.com), contributors examine how commons foster interdependent creativity by those who join these shared spaces. Boyle and Lessig advanced the innovation notion by launching the Creative Commons (creativecommons.org) and the Science Commons (sciencecommons.org), both founded to offer a set of flexible copyright licenses for public use. Established in 2001 with support from the Center for the Public Domain, these licenses increase the amount of shared sources available online and also remove unnecessary barriers to collaboration and innovation. Of course, Creative Commons licenses do not create bounded collections, self-governance mechanisms, or sustainability mechanisms. They do, however, foster more robust access to high quality works in a variety of media, as well as promote "an ethos of sharing, public education, and creative interactivity" (Creative Commons, n.d., online) (see also Garlick, 2005).

Like Boyle and Lessig, Benkler emphasizes the importance of the commons for promoting democratic participation. Quoting the Supreme Court's decision in Associated Press v. United States, Benkler (2000, p. 561) argues that a fundamental commitment of American democracy is to ensure "the widest possible dissemination of information from diverse and antagonistic sources" (Associated Press v. United States, 1945). Such a commitment, he contends, requires policies that make access to and use of information resources equally and ubiquitously available to all users of a network. Benkler (2000, p. 568) concludes:

> An open, free, flat, peer-to-peer network best serves the ability of anyone—individual, small group, or large group—to come together to build our information environment. It is through such open and equal participation that we will best secure both robust democratic discourse and individual expressive freedom.

Joining copyright scholars in their quest to promote more open access are Lawrence Grossman (1995), Anthony Wilhelm (2000), Douglas Schuler (1996), Schuler and Peter Day (2004), and Bruce Bimber (2003), who draw attention to the promises and challenges that face access to cyberspace when in search of wider participation for a 21st-century democracy. They consider the commons to be a critical contribution to a community of shared moral values and social purpose that goes far beyond maximizing economic utility. Librarians and other public interest advocates echo these ideas when they describe the commons as a useful tool for reclaiming public space and promoting the public interest in the digital age (Kranich, 2004a, 2004b; Hess, 2000; Lee, 2003). As David Bollier (2001, 2002b, 2003b, 2003c) and his colleague Tim Watts (2002, p. 3) explain it, "a commons analysis gives us a way to speak coherently about another matrix of concerns that are not given sufficient attention: democratic participation, openness, social equity, and diversity."

Similarly, civil society scholars Boyte (1989; Boyte & Evans, 1992), Levine (2001, 2002, 2006), and Friedland and Boyte (2000) underscore the importance of shared information spaces for promoting democracy and the free flow of ideas. Levine (2002) and Friedland and Boyte (2000) further acknowledge the historic role of institutions including newspapers, schools, libraries, and community festivals as foundations for democratic participation and a collective deliberative voice. To promote and sustain newly emerging information commons, they urge continued sponsorship of and collaboration with these traditional institutions.

The Power of Metaphor

Within the third frame, information commons can be understood as a metaphor. Metaphors drive public discourse because they provide a linguistic context in which to articulate and understand the dimensions of an issue. To imagine information as a thing, something concrete leads to the idea of information as property. To imagine information as a commons conveys a sense of giving and receiving. The two metaphors pull in different directions. The language of private property ownership has long dominated economic discourse in the United States. But Carol Rose (1994, p. 6) counters that property regimes and even individual property holdings are "by no means self-evident constructs"; instead, they are social "arrangements that people have quite consciously talked themselves into." For decades, those eager to control access to information have successfully employed the language of property to persuade policymakers and the public of the need to limit access to privately held information. As a result, those standing for greater access face a stiff challenge. If they are to promote the creative potential of digital technologies, they must deploy metaphors that project values central to their agenda—for example, equitable access, free expression, and fair use.

Bollier (2002b) first adopted the language of the commons in response to what he considered unbridled commercialism and privatization of public assets in the 1980s and 1990s. Inspired by the activism of James Love (then with the Nader-founded Taxpayer Assets Project) when he took on West Publishing over its monopoly control of the pagination of court cases, Bollier set out to document what he considered the silent theft of publicly owned assets. The language of information commons gave him a vocabulary to explain how the extraordinary public assets invested in the nation's information infrastructure could provide opportunities for all citizens. Bollier (2001; 2002b; 2003b; 2006a; Bollier & Watts, 2002) saw the commons as a metaphor—a useful framework for promoting the public interest and for helping people recognize what is at stake in the battle to control the flow of information and ideas. He contends that the commons elevates individuals to a role above mere consumers in the marketplace, shifting the focus onto their rights, needs, and responsibilities as citizens. Bollier (2002b, pp. 6, 8) concludes that

> We must begin to develop a new language of the commons. ...
> Developing a discourse of the commons is especially important at a time when our market culture encourages us to believe that we have little in common and can accomplish little when we work together. ... A reckoning of what belongs to the American people is a first step to recovering control of common assets and using them ... to protect them from market exploitation.

But first they must reject the old stories. Whatever story "people have quite consciously talked themselves into," argues Rose (1994, p. 6), can be replaced by "narratives, stories, and rhetorical devices ... essential in persuading people of [the] common good"—thus, the policy value of the information commons as metaphor (Stone, 1997, pp. 148, 156). Those who deploy metaphors to reframe the information access debate take the initiative by embracing the language and values of community, freedom, opportunity, and democracy. When they accept the language and assumptions of the opposition, they find themselves ensnared by a linguistic frame that favors control and enclosure (Lakoff, 2002, 2004).

Beyond serving as a compelling narrative, the information commons metaphor allows those engaged in their own information access struggles to come together under a broader umbrella—to create a movement comparable to environmentalism, a type of "ecosystem for the net" (Boyle, 1997, online; see also Benkler, 2001). In fact, those fighting to counter enclosures of information commons can learn from early environmentalists whose efforts gained strength when they made "intellectual connections among their isolated phenomena" (Bollier, 2006a, p. 30) and then recognized the power of coalitions and partnerships. Bollier (2006a, p. 30) predicts that

> The "information commons" may yet play a similar role in our time. It can help us name and mentally organize a set of novel, seemingly disconnected phenomena that are not yet understood as related to each other or to the health of our democratic polity.

When clearly articulated, the power of information commons rallies opposition to enclosure and implants a vision of a free and open network as intrinsic to the common good.

Decentralized Peer Production

The fourth frame focuses attention on the distribution of information through decentralized peer review production that bypasses the centralized control of traditional publishing. Benkler (2003a, p. 1256) considers peer production "a process by which many individuals, whose actions are coordinated neither by managers nor by price signals in the market, contribute to a joint effort that effectively produces a unit of information of culture." The result is commons-based production of knowledge that, although not challenging individual authorship, fundamentally alters the current system in which commercial producers and passive consumers are the primary players (Benkler, 2000). In effect, peer production allows everyone to be a creator, thereby privileging "more idiosyncratic, unpredictable, and democratic genres of expression" (Bollier, 2003a, p. 98).

Collaborative communities with common interests create and disseminate peer-produced information in a way that embodies many of the characteristics of common property resources. Governance is shared, with rules and norms defined and accepted by constituents. Participants contribute new creations after they gain and benefit from access. In addition, the cost to participate in these communities may be low, thereby enabling equitable, democratic participation that encourages interactive discourse and exchange among members. Accordingly, peer produced digital information commons transform the roles of creators and users of digital information. As creators take control over their intellectual assets, their roles change, in the words of Hess and Ostrom

(2003, pp. 144–145), "from passive *appropriator* of information to active *provider* of information by contributing directly into the common pool," where authors around the world are capable of "not only sustaining the resource (the intellectual public domain), but also building equity of information access and provision, and creating more efficient methods of dissemination through informal, shared protocols, standards, and rules." Ultimately, networked environments provide opportunities to build both real and virtual communities where greater participation increases the value of the resource.

Information Commons in Action

The idea of an information commons is neither intuitive nor self-evident. Individuals have to grasp the metaphors, learn the language, and come to terms with the abstractness inherent in the concept. That such a complex concept has gained traction says much for the resolve of those determined to stem a trend that seems inexorable. Nonetheless, the proof of the idea lies in the practice. The following examples illustrate challenges, opportunities, and proof.

Open Source

The development of open source software illustrates the values of openness, freedom, and democracy, as well as decentralized production. Applications such as GNU/Linux (www.linux.org) (Moody, 2001) can be acquired without the restrictive licensing provisions of commercial software (Benkler, 2002; Weber, 2004). Most open source software, although not in the public domain, is available for little or no cost and distributable without restriction. End users may review, use, and modify the source code without payment of royalties, as long as they share changes with the open source community. The code is protected by a special license so that improvements cannot be distributed without the source code (Boyle, 2003b; Samuelson, 1996). The GNU General Public License (GPL), developed by Richard Stallman in the 1980s (Goetz, 2003; Schweik, 2006), guarantees that users have the freedom to use, distribute, and modify software (www.gnu.org/licenses/licenses.html). His principle of "Copyleft" applies to most of the software distributed by the Free Software Foundation, the organizational sponsor of the GPL Project, and to any other program whose authors commit to using it. When users distribute copies of such programs, the Copyleft license requires that they give all the recipients the same rights and make sure that they receive or can access the source code. Open source, thus, preserves the digital commons and ensures that breaches in licensing terms are subject to rules and an enforcement regime. A prototype for other information commons, open source harnesses the distributive powers of the Internet, parcels the work out to thousands, and uses their contributions to build and improve the software, while allocating entitlements within the scope of copyright law (Stallman, 1999; Van Wendel de Joode, Bruijn, & van Eeten, 2003).

Biologists have applied the principle of open source to build massive databases, such as genetic sequencing, that are essential to lab research (Carlson, 2000; Quackenbush, 2003). The National Aeronautics and Space Administration (NASA) uses the open source approach for its Mars mission, with the help of volunteers who identify craters and map the planet (Goetz, 2003; National Aeronautics and Space Administration. Ames Research Center, n.d.; National Aeronautics and Space Administration. Mars Exploration Rover Mission, n.d.; Szpir, 2002). Prentice Hall publishes a series of open source computer books that readers can modify and redistribute (Shankland, 2003), and Project Gutenberg Distributed Proofreaders (n.d.) uses open source to contribute to a respected online archive of works that are in the public domain.

Democratic Participation

When information communities promote civic engagement among youth, they take up the challenges that come with the promotion of democratic participation in virtual space. Notable examples come from St. Paul, Minnesota (www.stpaulcommons.org) and Prince Georges County, Maryland (www.princegeorges.org). Peter Levine (2002) considers such commons noteworthy because they achieve complex goals without control by bureaucrats, experts, or profit-seeking companies. Moreover, they encourage diverse uses and participation. He also recognizes the vulnerability of such endeavors, especially if they fail to adopt appropriate governance structures, survive challenges from rival alternatives, and avoid anarchy that can result in the tragedy of the commons. What is different about these civic engagement commons is that the very process that creates them builds social capital, strengthens communities, and teaches skills for effective citizenship (Levine, 2006).

Scholarly Commons

Examples of information commons developed to counter enclosure abound in the realm of scholarly communication, where learned communities have created alternative approaches to managing and disseminating their collective knowledge resources. Foremost among these is the Scholarly Publishing and Academic Resources Coalition (SPARC) (www.arl.org/sparc/core/index.asp?page=a0), founded in 1998 as an alliance of research libraries, universities, and organizations. Formed as a constructive response to market dysfunctions (enclosure) in the scholarly communication system, SPARC helps incubate alternatives to high-priced journals and digital aggregated databases, publicize key issues and initiatives, and raise awareness among the scholarly community about new publishing possibilities. Another approach to solving enclosure problems with scholarly publishing is Open Access (OA), which promises to make scholars' ideas more readily available, reduce tolls, and combat the commercialization of online scholarly literature. Peter Suber (2003, 2006, n.d.), editor of SPARC's *Open Access Newsletter*, describes how adopting new standards and structures will not only reduce costs but also overcome barriers to access such as restrictive copyright laws, licenses, and DRM (Association of Research Libraries, n.d.; McKiernan, 2004; Prosser, 2003). Malcolm Getz (2005) predicts that open access will show significant results within five years and become the dominant mode of scholarly communication in ten years. For scholars, the free availability of open access publications over the Internet has dramatically increased the sharing of ideas, with citation count increases of 50 percent to 250 percent, ensuring greater impact and faster scientific progress, particularly beyond the borders of North America and Europe (Lawrence, 2001; OpCit Project, 2006). Among the nearly 2,500 open-access journals now distributed are titles as diverse as *PLoS Biology*, *PLoS Clinical Trials*, *Cell Biology Education*, *Journal of Arabic and Islamic Studies*, and *The New England Journal of Political Science* (Lund University Libraries, n.d.).

Another scholarly commons, the Open Archives Initiative (OAI) (www.openarchives.org), was launched in 1999 to provide low-barrier, free access to digitized research articles through digital repositories. OAI enables universities, disciplines, and individuals to share scholarship, take a more active, collaborative role in modernizing scholarly publishing, and provide an unprecedented alternative to the limited access dictated by ever-more-restrictive copyright legislation, licensing agreements, and technological protection measures employed by many scholarly journals. This effort is boosted by articulation of the characteristics and responsibilities for large-scale, heterogeneous collections, which help digital repositories provide reliable, long-term access to resources (Hess & Ostrom, 2003; Research Libraries Group & OCLC, 2002).

According to Clifford Lynch (2003, online) institutional repositories emerged "as a new strategy that allows universities to apply serious, systematic leverage to accelerate changes taking place in scholarship and scholarly communication." By taking the initiative, universities move "beyond their historic relatively passive role of supporting established publishers" and are able to explore "more transformative new uses of the digital medium" (Lynch, 2003, online; see also Marx, 2003; MIT DSpace [libraries.mit.edu/dspace-mit]; MIT OpenCourseWare [ocw.mit.edu]; Wolpert, 2003).

Academic disciplines have also created a rich array of digital repositories. The first, ArXiv.org, established in 1991 at Los Alamos by Paul Ginsparg, provides low-cost access to scientific research papers in physics and related fields prior to peer review and subsequent publication in journals of record. This open access, electronic archive and distribution server, now maintained by the Cornell University Libraries, receives as many as 300,000 queries per day; it includes more than 350,000 papers (www.arxiv.org; Ginsparg, n.d.). Papers located on the

ArXiv.org e-pre-print service are now cited about twice as often as astrophysics papers that were not part of ArXiv.org (Schwartz, 2003). Following the success of ArXiv.org, numerous other disciplines have created repositories such as EconWPA (econwpa.wustl.edu), the Oxford Text Archive (ota.ahds.ac.uk), the PhilSci Archive (philsci-archive.pitt.edu), the Networked Digital Library of Theses and Dissertations (www.ndltd.org), the Conservation Commons (www.conservation commons.org), and the Digital Library of the Commons (dlc.dlib.indiana.edu).

Individual authors are also distributing their own scholarly papers through personal Web sites or self-archiving. By retaining rights to archival copies of their publications, scholars become part of an international information community that increases access and benefits for everyone. According to Stevan Harnad (2003, n.d.) and researchers at the RoMEO project (SHERPA/RoMEO, 2006) at least 70 percent of journals officially authorize self-archiving and most others will permit it upon request, demonstrating the dedication of many scholarly publications to promote rather than limit the diffusion of research. The more that research is read, used, cited, and applied, the greater its impact (www.lboro.ac.uk/departments/ls/disresearch/romeo; www.eprints.org).

Digital Research Libraries

The decentralized, peer-production features of digital networks have prompted research libraries to develop digital commons by converting works from their retrospective collections to machine-readable form, purchasing and linking to distributed electronic resources, establishing standards and best practices for describing and preserving electronic materials, and teaching the skills users need to utilize these new tools. Only in the last few years have these digital libraries become collaborative, community-based endeavors (Greenstein & Thorin, 2002; New Digital Initiatives, 2003). Authors and publishers have challenged some of these collaborative partnerships, notably Google Print (Carlson & Young, 2004; Markoff & Wyatt, 2004; Vaidhyanathan, 2005), on the basis of copyright infringement. Another model under development by the Open Content Alliance (2005) (www.opencontentalliance.org) involves the provision of universal electronic access to public domain or otherwise open access collections from multiple research institutions. To ensure permanent public access to licensed (leased) subscriptions that reside with publishers, research libraries are experimenting with community-based preservation projects that create trusted third-party agents to store and archive publishers' content (Waters, 2006). Portico has set up an organization to preserve publishers' electronic source files. LOCKSS (lockss.stanford.edu), which stands for Lots Of Copies Keeps Stuff Safe, relies on the collective action of libraries working with publishers to share responsibility for copying and storing journal content, using a common infrastructure for systematic capturing of files.

Private and nonprofit digital library initiatives seek to open research collections to a broader audience. As commons-based digital libraries, they promote a sustainable, equitable, and trustworthy source of knowledge for future generations. Growing from fragmented local experiments to vast global initiatives, these efforts integrate a wealth of trusted interdisciplinary and multi-disciplinary resources managed under common property or open access regimes. As a result, consumption of these resources results in more (not less) production of new ideas, without excluding potential beneficiaries (Coleman, 2006).

Collaborative Reference Tools

Digital reference publications such as Wikipedia (en.wikipedia.org/wiki/Main_Page) offer another example of information commons developed as decentralized, peer-produced commons. An online encyclopedia that enables anyone to contribute and/or edit content, Wikipedia and similar resources are among the most successful collaborative enterprises to emerge through the World Wide Web. Founded by Internet entrepreneur Jimmy Wales and managed by the nonprofit Wikipedia Foundation, the reference work has close to 1.5 million entries in English and versions in 250 different languages. Although highly publicized critics contest the quality and reliability of Wikipedia content (Duguid, 2006), a study published in *Nature* found little difference in its accuracy when compared with articles in the *Encyclopedia Britannica* (Giles, 2005). Benkler (2006) notes that this venture relies on social norms to ensure reliability and objectivity, as well as the trust built among its thousands of contributors and millions of readers. Regardless of whether users trust this resource, the Wikipedia model has diffused to other applications including WikiBooks (en.wikibooks.org/wiki/Main_Page), a collection of free open content books that users can edit; Congresspedia (www.prwatch.org/node/4752), the "citizen's encyclopedia on Congress"; SourceWatch (www.sourcewatch.org/index.php?title=SourceWatch), a reference tool covering public agenda issues; and flu wiki (www.fluwikie.com), a pandemic flu resource. A similar dynamic but more scholarly undertaking, The Stanford Encyclopedia of Philosophy (plato.stanford.edu/about.html), is one of many peer-produced tools maintained and kept up to date by a network of experts, although it is paid for by scholars and libraries following the open access model (Zalta, 2006).

Social Networking Commons

Finally, no discussion of peer-produced information commons should proceed without mentioning participatory, social networking media or "pull" software that is transforming how people interact, news is reported, and virtual communities are formed. Also known as Web 2.0 technologies, these include Web logs, or blogs, that look like Web sites but with journal-style entries displayed and archived in reverse chronological order.

Readers can comment and interact with owners of blogs and create communities of interest around specialized topics. And, in one manifestation of the revolution in news brought about by the Internet, several bloggers have led the news media by breaking stories that would otherwise have been ignored by the mainstream press (Blogs, n.d.). The popularity and importance of this form of social networking is immense; the number of blogs doubles every six months and 75,000 new blogs are launched daily (Burns, 2006).

Part of the reason blogs are so widely used stems from the ease with which readers can follow posts by subscribing to their favorite Web sites through RSS (Really Simple Syndication) feeds that retrieve new items as they are posted. Electronic news aggregators such as Digg and Reddit "pull" posts of interest that readers can readily sort, review, organize, and discard. Collaborative filtering of feeds allows readers to share recommendations with people who have similar interests (Wittenbrink, 2005). Other social networking software, such as MySpace, Facebook, YouTube, Flickr, and podcasting, enables people to contribute their own content, capture and disseminate knowledge, and create their own radio and television broadcasts. Unlike market structures that push demand, these "bottom-up self-organized communities" arise "based on fluid and shifting social preferences" (Bollier, 2006a, p. 36). With social networking tools, intelligence gathering becomes a collective endeavor, innovation comes from the edges, and a clever person with a blog can gain a remarkable level of visibility and exposure. Their very popularity, of course, makes them susceptible to takeover. The question remains, therefore, as to whether these open, egalitarian modes of information production can be sustained as common pool resources, once acquired by multinational corporations such as Rupert Murdoch's News Corporation.

Governance

Democratic control over the creation, dissemination, and preservation of information demands appropriate governance. To this end, Ostrom and Hess (2006; Hess & Ostrom, 2003) offer a useful framework. Self governance requires:

1. Definition of boundaries (which tend to be "fuzzy"),
2. Design and enforcement of rules,
3. Extension of reciprocity,
4. Building of trust and social capital,
5. Delineation of communication channels.

Because information commons resources are necessarily diffused, their dispersal requires stewardship of a kind that transcends space and traditional organizational structures. Stakeholders must negotiate principles *and* procedures, often within the institutional culture giving birth to the commons, whether it be that of libraries, archives, or scholarly societies (Lougee, 2006; Ostrom & Hess, 2006, pp. 50–53). Others, acting independently (e.g., YouTube, Facebook, MySpace, Wikipedia), carve out new structures for control from within their own cultural traditions and experiences. Thus, projects develop rules and structures for governance, whether tacit or explicit; however, if they are to maintain and sustain their activities, they have to convert informality into documentation. Although many open projects have developed rules and structures for governance, their mechanisms still need to be documented and assessed.

Collective action organizations such as open access publishers, digital repositories, and digital libraries face the challenge of developing governance structures that channel motivations toward democratic participation, and away from the exploitation that leads to the tragedy of the commons. They need to raise difficult questions. For example, what are the boundaries of the effort and what are its priorities? What role will contributors play? How will rules be negotiated? Who will determine the scope and effectiveness of activities? What kinds of reciprocity will be required for sustaining these activities? What kinds of channels will maintain communication and facilitate action? And, ultimately, will the venture build trust among its stakeholders?

Collaboration is essential to the successful introduction, development, and widespread utilization of information resources. In the past, authors, publishers, librarians, and readers cooperated, but collaboration today entails something more demanding than these customary relationships. A commonly held mission and goals, new organizational structures, comprehensive planning, additional levels of communication, authority structures with dispersed leadership, and shared and mutual control will be needed for effective governance. If they are to evolve into more open collaborative organizations, information commons will need new organizational frameworks, with serious commitments by administrators and their parent organizations, capable of brokering new relationships, entrepreneurial activities, and communication structures.

Finance

Developing, sustaining, and governing information commons also require significant investment in infrastructure and content, especially if the effort takes place within an institutional setting. Users may gain more free or low cost access but someone must still pay to sustain resources. Moving from an unsustainable subscription-based structure will alter long-standing financial and social relationships. To date, information commons have benefited from support by individuals, foundations, and other grant-making agencies; nonetheless, benefactors such as the Mellon Foundation and the Open Society Institute are unlikely to continue subsidies indefinitely. Originators of commons have demonstrated remarkable ingenuity when it comes to launching their projects, but the course ahead remains to be mapped.

Consider open access publishing, which shifts the burden of production expenses from purchasers to creators. Rather than charge subscriptions, some open access publishers collect author and/or membership fees. Such transitions require start-up capital and streams of revenue for sustainability. BioMed Central (BMC) began by offering electronic journals to libraries on a flat fee basis, but later substituted membership renewal fees based on the estimated number of articles generated by each faculty (Evolution in Open Access, 2004). That is, the more productive a faculty, the higher the membership fee to the institution. Not surprisingly, some participating institutions balked at steep rises in fees. Although many agree that the old financial models do not work, new models based on productivity and membership may fail to solve all the problems they were designed to fix.

For universities especially, financing the transition from a subscription to a production-based business model tests an institution's ability to find additional funding. New publishing ventures on or across campuses that involve libraries, academic presses, technology centers, and scholars require carefully designed business plans. Low-cost journals and digital archives may be welcome, but they arrive at a moment when libraries and universities face serious budget constraints that limit their ability to pay for long-standing commitments, let alone take on new ventures. Universities need to redirect resources if they are to become publishers as well as consumers of their faculty's scholarship. After all, authors need to become aware of the incentives and rewards if they are to migrate toward new publishing ventures that may demand high publication fees. Moreover, professional societies and other publishers need new revenue streams that compensate for the loss of commercial revenues. As the Committee on Institutional Cooperation (2003) has recommended, new efforts to improve scholarly communication should build upon inter-institutional relationships already underway.

Participation

Self-organized commons need strong collective-action and self-governance mechanisms to succeed (Ostrom & Hess, 2006); they demand substantial social capital from their stakeholders. In the sense coined by James Coleman and popularized by Robert Putnam (2000) in *Bowling Alone*, social capital can be thought of as the "values and social networks that enable coordination and cooperation within society ... the relationship between people and organizations, which form the glue that strengthens civil society" (Marschall, 1998, p. 24). For voluntary groups to achieve a shared goal, norms of reciprocity must be embraced by their members; otherwise a small number of activists may dominate proceedings. As the one-to-many broadcast model gives way to the many-to-many common platform, social relations shift from being locally embedded, thick, unmediated, and stable to a more fluid, bridging, weak-tie model. The networked society that fosters peer production and social interaction structures relationships on social norms at a distance and across interests, as well as contexts. The commons endeavor manifests a nonhierarchical and decentralized social structure, bringing together otherwise unconnected people around a similar purpose and common pursuit. In effect, states Benkler (2006, p. 375), "Individuals who are connected to each other in a peer-production community may or may not be bowling alone when they are off-line, but they are certainly playing together online."

Why do people participate in these endeavors? An expansive literature led by Barry Wellman (1999; Wellman, Boase, & Chen, 2002; Wellman & Haythornthwaite, 2002), Howard Rheingold (1993b), Mary Chayko (2002), Mark Smith and Peter Kollock (1998), and Leslie Shade (2002) reveals the many ways in which the Internet decreases, increases, and/or transforms community; but these researchers have less to report on the motivations that prompt participation in this form of gift economy. No doubt, people need incentives to contribute to joint endeavors; and, even as a few popular shared endeavors such as MySpace and YouTube spontaneously foster high levels of participation (or obsession, as some charge), many others, such as digital repositories, experience difficulty generating wide-scale support from potential contributors (Ostrom & Hess, 2006, pp. 54–57). Yuan, Fulk, Shumate, Monge, Alison, and Matsaganis (2006) developed and tested a model to assess motivations to participate in organizational information commons, which found that social influence and technology-specific competence are positively related to use of collective repositories.

Karen Fisher and Joan Durrance (2003; Durrance, 2001) examined how information communities make available their resources in order to unite people around common interests. They described five characteristics that distinguish Internet-based information communities:

1. Information sharing with multiplier effects;
2. Collaboration;
3. Interaction based on needs of participants;
4. Low barriers to entry; and,
5. Connectedness with the larger community.

In online communities that share the production and distribution of information, they found members more likely to experience increased access to and use of information, increased access to people and organizations, and increased dialogue, communication, and collaboration among information providers and constituents. For communities so organized, the Internet functions as a mechanism that facilitates the exchange of ideas, the distribution of works, and interaction with others who have similar interests and needs—in other words, connections and collaborations. As with governance and finance, social ties and competence factors need further investigation. Finally, and most difficult of all, longitudinal studies will determine how these factors evolve over time as technologies, capabilities, and familiarity levels change.

Information Commons as a Research Front

To suggest that new models for creating and distributing digital information appear daily constitutes but a small exaggeration. The simple fact of identifying these models as commons contributes to their development by associating them together within a prevalent framework for analysis. Indeed, this chapter testifies to an extraordinary blossoming of innovations that bring people together as participants in a shared system of information creation, distribution, and consumption. And, as often happens, questions outnumber answers. Most assessments of commons come with underlying assumptions applicable to earlier systems where the distribution of physical resources generates tensions between the market and the state. Only now has a research front begun to materialize as scholars take up the information commons on its own terms (Hess & Ostrom, 2006). The emerging front manifests interdisciplinarity and synthesis. Ostrom and Hess (2006; Hess & Ostrom, 2003), for example, have taken the Institutional Analysis and Development (IAD) framework for commons theory—developed over three decades—and adapted it for multidisciplinary study of knowledge commons. Take the case of digital repositories. Through the IAD, they document attributes of community, rules, rights, incentives for participation, patterns of interaction, efficiency, equity, governance, communication, infrastructure, and conflict management; that is, they attempt to record the full array of factors that influence the behavior of a commons[6] (Ostrom & Hess, 2006; Schweik, 2006; Schweik & Semenov, 2003).

Clearly, the ubiquity of information commons raises a host of research questions:

1. Rights: How should intellectual property be construed? Should communal rights to information have standing?

2. Enclosure: Where are the new enclosures? What are their consequences?

3. Access: Who are the actors? How do they behave as creators, distributors, and consumers? How do they behave toward each other?

4. Governance: Are these commons equitable, efficient, and sustainable? How can their communities avoid the tragedy of the commons? Why do some efforts succeed and others fail? Are there best practices?

5. Metaphor: Can a language of rights and communalism evolve capable of establishing a framework with which to promote commons? Are there metaphors upon which to build and sustain policy?

Conclusion

New technologies, new forms of work, new resources, and new ways of thinking have brought with them the need to organize and share information. Some of these solutions we now call information commons. These commons will replace neither the private nor the public sector components of the information society but they promise to advance learning, enhance civil society, and foster democratic participation. Scholars, practitioners, and activists increasingly embrace the metaphor of the commons as a tool for promoting civic virtue and social purpose in the digital age. In the cause of decentralizing the production of information, they hope to enable openness, freedom, and democracy. As free and open shared resources, however, these dynamic and complex phenomena require resources, governance, and an appropriate discursive framework in order to ensure sustainability. Ultimately, information commons offer the promise of paradox: to share without owning; to own without enclosing; to take by sharing.

Endnotes

1. The "public interest" is not defined in the 1934 law, the Telecommunications Act of 1996, or other federal statutes that use the term. Although the nature of the public interest may be difficult to determine (Barry, 1962, p. 203), one scholar defines a public interest policy as one that, "at least in the long run, affects everyone in an equally beneficial manner, receives public support through a principle of unanimity, and has costs that are widely and equally shared" (Dennis, 1981, online).
2. David Lange (2003) and others assert that the public domain is most usefully seen as a commons, which has been restricted by copyright term extension, privatization, licensing, DRM, and proprietary databases such as Lexis/Nexis (Benkler, 1999). This commons is more like the open-access regimes that are prone to Hardin's tragedy of the commons.
3. When the policy was revised in 1993, it eliminated the phrase "maximum feasible reliance on the private sector."
4. To be fair, this interpretation is not without its critics. For an argument that disputes claims of declining competition, see Compaine (2000, 2004), Brock (1998), Hazlett (2000), and Knee (2003).
5. The public domain consists of works whose copyrights have expired as well as works that, like government resources, were never covered by copyright.
6. Ostrom and Hess (2006) cite numerous other studies that analyze various dilemmas of knowledge commons. These do not apply the IAD framework, however.

References

A failure to communicate? Librarians taken aback by Biomed Central change. (2004, February 17). *Library Journal Academic Newswire*.

A&M Records v. Napster, 239 F.3d 1004 (9th Cir. 2001).

American Association of University Professors. (2003). Report of the AAUP Special Committee on Academic Freedom and National Security in a Time of

Crisis. *Academe, 89*(6). Retrieved October 16, 2006, from www.aaup.org/AAUP/About/committees/committee+repts/crisistime.htm

American Library Association. Office for Information Technology Policy. (2000–2001). The information commons, new technology, and the future of libraries roundtable. Retrieved October 17, 2006, from www.ala.org/ala/washoff/contactwo/oitp/infocommons0204/issue1.htm#info-com

American Library Association. Washington Office. (n.d.) Executive Order 13233, November 1, 2001. Further implementation of the Presidential Records Act. Washington, DC: The Association. Retrieved October 16, 2006, from www.ala.org/ala/washoff/WOissues/governmentinfo/laadmin.htm#exec

American Library Association. Washington Office. (2003). Sensitive homeland security information. Washington, DC: The Association. Retrieved October 16, 2006, from www.ala.org/Template.cfm?Section=governmentinfo&Template=/ContentManagement/ContentDisplay.cfm&ContentID=80795#shsi

Anderson, C. (2006). *The long tail: Why the future of business is selling less of more.* New York: Hyperion.

Associated Press v. United States (1945), 326 U.S. 1, 20.

Association of College and Research Libraries, Association of Research Libraries, & Scholarly Publishing and Academic Resources Coalition. (2003). Create change: New systems of scholarly communication. Washington, DC: Association of Research Libraries. Retrieved October 16, 2006, from www.createchange.org/createchange2003.pdf

Association of Research Libraries. (n.d.) What is open access? Washington, DC: The Association. Retrieved October 21, 2006, from www.arl.org/scomm/open_access/framing.html#openaccess

Aufderheide, P. (1999). *Communications policy and the public interest: The Telecommunications Act of 1996.* New York: Guilford Press.

Aufderheide, P., & Barnouw, E. (1997). *Conglomerates and the media.* New York: New Press.

Bagdikian, B. (2000). *The media monopoly* (6th ed.). Boston: Beacon Press.

Baker, C. E. (2002). *Media, markets, and democracy.* Cambridge, UK: Cambridge University Press.

Barry, B. B. (1962). The use and abuse of "the public interest." In C. J. Friedrich (Ed.), *Nomos v. The Public Interest.* New York: Aldine-Atherton.

Beagle, D. (1999). Conceptualizing an information commons: New service model in academic libraries. *Journal of Academic Librarianship, 25*(2), 82–89.

Beagle, D. (2002). Extending the information commons: From instructional testbed to Internet2. *Journal of Academic Librarianship, 28*(5), 287–296.

Beagle, D. R. (2006). *The information commons handbook.* New York: Neal-Schuman.

Beniger, J. R. (1986a). *The control revolution.* Cambridge, MA: Harvard University Press.

Beniger, J. R. (1986b). Origins of the information society. *Wilson Library Bulletin, 61*(9), 12–19.

Benkler, Y. (1998). Overcoming agoraphobia: Building the commons of the digitally networked environment. *Harvard Journal of Law and Technology, 11*(2), 287–400.

Benkler, Y. (1999). Free as the air to common use: First amendment constraints on enclosure of the public domain. *New York University Law Review, 74,* 354–364.

Benkler, Y. (2000). From consumers to users: Shifting the deeper structures of regulation toward sustainable commons and user access. *Federal Communications Law Journal, 52*(3), 561–579. Retrieved October 21, 2006, from www.law.indiana.edu/fclj/pubs/v52/no3/benkler1.pdf

Benkler, Y. (2001, February). The battle over the institutional ecosystem in the digital environment. *Communications of the ACM, 44*(2), 84–90. Retrieved October 21, 2006, from www.benkler.org/CACM.pdf

Benkler, Y. (2002). Coase's penguin, or, linux and the nature of the firm. *Yale Law Journal, 112* (3), 369–438. Retrieved October 21, 2006, from www.yale.edu/yalelj/112/BenklerWEB.pdf

Benkler, Y. (2003a). Freedom in the commons: Towards a political economy of information. *Duke Law Journal, 55*(6), 1245–1276. Retrieved October 17, 2006, from www.law.duke.edu/shell/cite.pl?52+Duke+L.+J.+1245

Benkler, Y. (2003b, June). The political economy of commons. *Upgrade, 4*(3). Retrieved January 18, 2007, from www.upgrade-cepis.org/issues/2003/3/up4-3Benkler.pdf

Benkler, Y. (2006). *The wealth of networks: How social production transforms markets and freedom.* New Haven, CT: Yale University Press.

Bennett, S. (2003, November). *Libraries designed for learning.* Washington, DC: Council on Library and Information Resources. Retrieved October 21, 2006, from www.clir.org/pubs/reports/pub122/pub122web.pdf

Bergstrom, C. T., & Bergstrom, T. C. (2004). The costs and benefits of library site licenses to academic journals. *Proceedings of the National Academy of Sciences, 101*(3), 897.

Berry III, J. N. (1975, April 15). Free information and the IIA. *Library Journal, 100*(8), 795.

Bimber, B. (2003). *Information and American democracy: Technology in the evolution of political power.* New York: Cambridge University Press.

Blogs. (n.d.) *Wikipedia.* Retrieved October 21, 2006, from en.wikipedia.org/wiki/Blog

Bollier, D. (2001). *Public assets, private profits: Reclaiming the American commons in an age of market enclosure.* Washington, DC: New America Foundation. Retrieved October 17, 2006, from www.newamerica.net/publications/policy/public_assets_private_profits

Bollier, D. (2002a). Ruled by the market?: Reclaiming the commons. *Boston Review, 27*(3–4). Retrieved January 18, 2007, from bostonreview.net/BR27.3/bollier.html

Bollier, D. (2002b). *Silent theft: The private plunder of our common wealth.* New York: Routledge.

Bollier, D. (2003a). *Artists, technology and the ownership of creative content.* Center for the Creative Community. Retrieved October 21, 2006, from www.culturalcommons.org/comment-print.cfm?ID=10

Bollier, D. (2003b, June). The missing language of the digital age: The commons. *The Common Property Resource Digest, 65,* 1–4.

Bollier, D. (2003c, June). The rediscovery of the commons. *UPGRADE, 4*(3), 10–12. Retrieved October 17, 2006, from www.upgrade-cepis.org/issues/2003/3/up4-3Bollier.pdf

Bollier, D. (2006a). The growth of the commons paradigm. In C. Hess & E. Ostrom (Eds.), *Understanding knowledge as a commons: From theory to practice* (pp. 27–40). Cambridge, MA: MIT Press.

Bollier, D. (2006b). *When push comes to pull: The new economy and culture of networking technology.* Washington, DC: Aspen Institute.

Bollier, D., & Watts, T. (2002). *Saving the information commons: A new public interest agenda in digital media.* Washington, DC: New America Foundation and Public Knowledge. Retrieved October 15, 2006, from www.newamerica.net/files/archive/Pub_File_866_1.pdf

Bolter, W. (1984). *Telecommunications policy for the 1980s: The transition to competition.* Englewood Cliffs, NJ: Prentice-Hall.

Borgman, C. (2000). *From Gutenberg to the global information infrastructure: Access to information in the networked world.* Cambridge, MA: MIT Press.

Boyle, J. (1996). *Shaman, software, and spleens: Law and the construction of the information society.* Cambridge, MA: Harvard University Press.

Boyle, J. (1997). A politics of intellectual property: Environmentalism for the Net? *Law in the Information Society.* Retrieved October 21, 2006, from www.law.duke.edu/boylesite/intprop.htm

Boyle, J. (2002, April). Fencing off ideas. *Daedalus, 131*(2), 13–25. Retrieved October 21, 2006, from findarticles.com/p/articles/mi_qa3671/is_200204/ai_n9042086

Boyle, J. (Ed.). (2003a). The public domain. *Law & Contemporary Problems, 66*(1/2). Retrieved October 21, 2006, from www.law.duke.edu/journals/lcp/indexpd.htm

Boyle, J. (2003b). The second enclosure movement and the construction of the public domain. *Law & Contemporary Problems, 66*(1/2), 33–74. Retrieved October 17, 2006, from www.law.duke.edu/shell/cite.pl?66+Law+&+Contemp.+Probs.+33+(WinterSpring+2003)

Boyle, J. (2006). Mertonianism unbound? Imagining free, decentralized access to most cultural and scientific material. In C. Hess & E. Ostrom (Eds.), *Understanding knowledge as a commons: From theory to practice* (pp. 123–143). Cambridge, MA: MIT Press.

Boyte, H. C. (1989). *Commonwealth: A return to citizen politics.* New York: Free Press.

Boyte, H. C., & Evans, S. M. (1992). *Free spaces: The sources of democratic change in America* (Rev. ed.). Chicago: University of Chicago Press.

Bradley, H. (2001). *The enclosures in England: An economic reconstruction.* Kitchener, Ontario: Kitchener Books. (Original work published 1814). Retrieved October 15, 2006, from socserv2.socsci.mcmaster.ca/~econ/ugcm/3ll3/bradley/Enclosure.pdf

Braman, S. (1989). Defining information: An approach for policymakers. In D. M. Lamberton (Ed.), *The economics of communication and information* (pp. 233–242). Brookfield, VT: Edward Elgar.

Brock, G. W. (1998). *Telecommunications policy for the information age: From monopoly to competition.* Cambridge, MA: Harvard University Press.

Bromley, D. (1992). *Making the commons work: Theory, practice, and policy.* San Francisco: Institute for Contemporary Studies.

Brown, J. S., & Duguid, P. (1998). Universities in the digital age. In B. L. Hawkins & P. Battin (Eds.), *The mirage of continuity: Reconfiguring academic information resources for the 21st century* (pp. 39–60). Washington, DC: Council on Library and Information Resources and Association of American Universities.

Brown, J. S., & Hagel III, J. (2005). From push to pull: The next frontier of innovation. *McKinsey Quarterly, 3.* Retrieved October 15, 2006, from www.mckinsey quarterly.com/article_page.aspx?ar=1642&L2=21&L3=37&srid=9&gp=1

Buck, S. (1998). *The global commons: An introduction.* Washington, DC: Island Press.

Burns, E. (2006, April 18). *Blogosphere doubles every six months*. Retrieved October 17, 2006, from www.clickz.com/stats/sectors/traffic_patterns/article. php/3599826

Calhoun, C. (2004). Information technology and the international public sphere. In D. Schuler & P. Day (Eds.), *Shaping the network society: The new role of civil society in cyberspace* (pp. 229–251). Cambridge, MA: MIT Press.

Card, C. (2002, March 21). Memorandum for heads of departments and agencies: Action to safeguard information regarding weapons of mass destruction and other sensitive documents related to homeland security. Washington, DC: U.S. Office of the President. Retrieved October 16, 2006, from www.usdoj.gov/oip/foiapost/2002foiapost10.htm

Carlson, R. (2000, December 10). On the parallels and contrasts (anti-parallels?) between the open-source software movement and open-source biology. *Intentional Biology / Open Source Biology*. Retrieved October 17, 2006, from www.intentionalbiology.org/osb.html

Carlson, S., & Young, J. R. (2004, December 14). Google will digitize and search millions of books from 5 leading research libraries. *Chronicle of Higher Education*. Retrieved January 18, 2007, from chronicle.com/free/2004/ 12/2004121401n.htm

Castells, M. (2000). *The rise of the network society* (2nd ed.). Malden, MA: Blackwell.

Center for Democracy and Technology. (2004). *The broadcast flag: An introduction*. Washington, DC: The Center. Retrieved October 16, 2006, from www.cdt.org/copyright/broadcastflag/introduction.php

Chayko, M. (2002). *Connecting: How we form social bonds and communities in the digital age*. Albany, NY: SUNY Press.

Ciriacy-Wantrup, S. V., & Bishop, R. C. (1975). "Common property" as a concept in natural resource policy. *Natural Resources Journal, 15*, 713–727.

Coalition of Journalists for Open Government. (2005). *When exemptions become the rule*. Washington, DC: The Coalition. Retrieved October 16, 2006, from www.cjog.net/documents/Exemptions_Study.pdf

Coase, R. (1937). The nature of the firm. *Economics, 4*(16), 386–405.

Cole, B. G. (Ed.). (1991). *After the breakup: Assessing the new post-AT&T divestiture era*. New York: Columbia University Press.

Cole, D., & Dempsey, J. (2002). *Terrorism and the constitution*. New York: The New Press.

Coleman, A. (2006). *Commons-based digital libraries*. Retrieved October 17, 2006, from dlist.sir.arizona.edu/1187/01/AscSigSi06.pdf

Coll, S. (1986). *The deal of the century: The breakup of AT&T*. New York: Touchstone.

Committee for Economic Development. Digital Connections Council. (2006, April). *Open standards, open source, and open innovation: Harnessing the benefits of openness*. Washington, DC: The Committee. Retrieved October 15, 2006, from www.ced.org/docs/report/report_ecom_openstandards.pdf#search= %22Open%20standards%20open%20source%20and%20open%20 innovation%22

Committee on Institutional Cooperation. (2003, December 2). *Report of the CIC Summit on Scholarly Communication in the Humanities and Social Sciences*. Chicago: The Committee. Retrieved October 21, 2006, from www.cic.uiuc. edu/groups/CIC/archive/Report/ScholarlyCommSummitReport_Feb04.pdf

Communications Act, 47 U.S.C.A., dd151-614. (1934).

Compaine, B. M. (2000). *Who owns the media: Competition and concentration in the mass communications industry* (3rd ed.). Mahwah, NJ: Erlbaum.

Compaine, B. M. (2004, January). Domination fantasies: Does Rupert Murdoch control the media? Does anyone? *Reason.* Retrieved October 15, 2006, from www.reason.com/0401/fe.bc.domination.shtml

Consumer Federation of America/Consumers Union. (2001, February). *Lessons from the 1996 Telecommunications Act: Deregulation before meaningful competition spells consumer disaster.* Washington, DC: Consumers Union. Retrieved October 15, 2006, from www.consumersunion.org/telecom/lessondc201.htm

Cooper, M. (2003). *Media ownership and democracy in the digital information age: Promoting diversity with First Amendment principles and market structure analysis.* Palo Alto, CA: Center for Internet & Society, Stanford Law School.

Creative commons. (n.d.). *Legal concepts.* Retrieved October 17, 2006, from creativecommons.org

Cusumano, M., &. Yoffie, D. B. (1998). *Competing on Internet time: Lessons from Netscape and its battle with Microsoft.* New York: Free Press.

Dahlman, C. (1980). *The open field system and beyond: A property rights analysis of an economic institution.* New York: Cambridge University Press.

Dennis, W. C. (1981). The public and private interest in wilderness protection. *Cato Journal, 1*(2). Retrieved October 15, 2006, from www.cato.org/pubs/journal/cj1n2-3.html

DiCola, P., & Thomson, K. (2002, November). *Radio deregulation: Has it served citizens and musicians? A report on the effects of radio ownership consolidation following the 1996 Telecommunications Act.* Washington, DC: Future of Music Coalition. Retrieved October 15, 2006, from www.futureofmusic.org/research/radiostudy.cfm

Dietz, T., Ostrom, E., & Stern, P. C. (2003, December 12). The struggle to govern the commons. *Science, 302*(5652), 1907–1912.

Duguid, P. (2006, October). Limits of self-organization: Peer production and "laws of equality." *First Monday, 11*(10). Retrieved January 14, 2007, from firstmonday.org/issues/issue11_10/duguid/index.html

Durrance, J. (2001). The vital role of librarians in creating information communities: Strategies for success. *Library Administration and Management, 15*(3), 161–168.

Dvorak, J. C. (1994). *An insider's look at the computer industry.* Berkeley, CA: Osborne McGraw-Hill.

Eldred v. Ashcroft, 123 S.Ct. 769 (2003). Retrieved October 16, 2006, from www.supremecourtus.gov/opinions/02pdf/01-618.pdf

Ellig, J. (Ed.). (2001). *Dynamic competition and public policy: Technology, innovation, and antitrust issues.* New York: Cambridge University Press.

Evolution in open access: Biomed Central alters its membership model. (2004, February 17). *Library Journal Academic Newswire.*

Fairlie, R. W. (2005, September 20). *Are we really a nation online? Ethnic and racial disparities in access to technology and their consequences.* Washington, DC: Leadership Conference on Civil Rights Education Fund. Retrieved October 16, 2006, from www.civilrights.org/issues/communication/digitaldivide.pdf

Fisher, K., & Durrance, J. (2003). Information communities. In K. Christensen & D. Levinson (Eds.), *Encyclopedia of community* (Vol. 2, pp. 657–660). Thousand Oaks, CA: Sage.

Fox, S. (2005, October 5). *Digital divisions: There are clear differences among those with broadband connections, dial-up connections, and no connections at all to the Internet.* Washington, DC: Pew Internet and American Life Project. Retrieved October 16, 2006, from www.pewinternet.org/pdfs/PIP_Digital_ Divisions_Oct_5_2005.pdf

Friedland, L., & Boyte, H. C. (2000). *The new information commons: Community information partnerships and civic change.* Minneapolis: University of Minnesota Hubert Humphrey Institute, Center for Democracy and Citizenship. Retrieved October 17, 2006, from www.publicwork.org/pdf/workingpapers/ New%20information%20commons.pdf

Fulk, J., Heino, R., Flanagin, A., Monge, P., & Bar, F. (2004). A test of the individual action model for organizational information commons. *Organization Science, 15*(5), 569–585.

Garlick, M. (2005). A review of creative commons and science commons. *EDU-CAUSE Review, 40*(5), 78–79. Retrieved October 17, 2006, from www. educause.edu/apps/er/erm05/erm05510.asp

Getz, M. (2005). *Open scholarship and research universities.* Ithaca, NY: Internet-First University Press. Retrieved October 17, 2006, from dspace.library.cornell.edu/handle/1813/1344

Ghosh, S. (2006). How to build a commons: Is intellectual property constrictive, facilitating, or irrelevant? In C. Hess & E. Ostrom (Eds.), *Understanding knowledge as a commons: From theory to practice* (pp. 209–245). Cambridge, MA: MIT Press.

Giles, J. (2005, December 15). Special report: Internet encyclopedias go head to head. *Nature, 438*(7070), 900–901.

Gilroy, A. (2006, May 16). *Net neutrality: Background and issues.* Washington, DC: Library of Congress, Congressional Research Service. Retrieved October 16, 2006, from www.fas.org/sgp/crs/misc/RS22444.pdf#search=%22angele% 20gilroy%20net%20neutrality%22

Ginsparg, P. (n.d.). Can peer review be better focused? Retrieved October 21, 2006, from arxiv.org/blurb/pg02pr.html

Goetz, T. (2003, November). Open source everywhere: Software is just the beginning ... *Wired, 11*(11). Retrieved October 17, 2006, from www.wired. com/wired/archive/11.11/opensource.html

Goody, J. (1986). *The logic of writing and the organization of society: Literacy, family, culture and the state.* Cambridge, UK: Cambridge University Press.

Gordon, H. S. (1954). The economic theory of a common-property resource: The fishery. *Journal of Political Economy, 62*(2), 124–142.

Greenstein, D., & Thorin, S. E. (2002). *The digital library: A biography.* Washington, DC: Digital Library Federation. Retrieved October 21, 2006, from www.clir.org/pubs/reports/pub109/contents.html

Grossman, L. (1995). *The electronic republic: The transformation of American democracy.* New York: Viking.

Hardin, G. (1968, December). The tragedy of the commons. *Science, 162,* 1243–1248.

Hargittai, E. (2002, April). Second-level digital divide: Differences in people's online skills. *First Monday, 7*(4). Retrieved October 16, 2006, from firstmonday. org/issues/issue7_4/hargittai/index.html

Harnad, S. (2003, December). Self-archive unto others. *University Affairs.* Retrieved October 21, 2006, from www.universityaffairs.ca/issues/2003/ dec/opinion.html

Harnad, S. (n.d.) *Maximizing university research impact through self-archiving.* Montreal, Canada: University of Quebec at Montreal. Retrieved October 21, 2006, from www.ecs.soton.ac.uk/~harnad/Temp/che.htm

Hawkins, B., & Battin, P. (1998). *The mirage of continuity: Reconfiguring academic information resources for the 21st century.* Washington, DC: Council on Library and Information Resources & the Association of American Universities.

Hazlett, T. W. (2000). Economic and political consequences of the 1996 Telecommunications Act. *Regulation, 23*(3), 36–45. Retrieved October 15, 2006, from www.cato.org/pubs/regulation/regv23n3/hazlett.pdf

Heins, M. (2003). *"The progress of science and useful arts": Why copyright today threatens intellectual freedom.* New York: Free Expression Policy Project. Retrieved January 31, 2007, from www.fepproject.org/policyreports/copyright 2d.pdf

Heins, M., & Beckles, T. (2006). *Will fair use survive? Free expression in the age of copyright control.* New York: Brennan Center for Justice.

Heritier, A. (Ed.). (2002). *Common goods: Reinventing European and international governance.* Lanham, MD: Rowman & Littefield.

Herman, E. S., & McChesney, R. (1997). *The global media: The new missionaries of corporate capitalism.* Washington, DC: Cassell.

Hernon, P., & McClure, C. (1987). *Federal information policies in the 1980s: Conflicts and issues.* Norwood, NJ: Ablex.

Hess, C. (2000, May). *Is there anything new under the sun? A discussion and survey of studies on new commons and the Internet.* Paper presented at Constituting the Commons. 8th Biennial Conference of the International Association for the Study of Common Property. Bloomington, IN. Retrieved October 17, 2006, from dlc.dlib.indiana.edu/documents/dir0/00/00/05/12/dlc-00000512-00/iascp2000.pdf

Hess, C., & Ostrom, E. (2003). Ideas, artifacts, and facilities: Information as a common-pool resource. *Law & Contemporary Problems, 66*(1/2), 144–145. Retrieved October 17, 2006, from www.law.duke.edu/shell/cite.pl?66+ Law+&+Contemp.+Probs.+111+(WinterSpring+2003)

Hess C., & Ostrom, E. (Eds.). (2006). *Understanding knowledge as a commons: From theory to practice.* Cambridge, MA: MIT Press.

Hindman, M., & Cukier, K. N. (2003, December). *Measuring media concentration online and offline.* Paper presented at the Ford Foundation Conference on Media Diversity. Retrieved October 16, 2006, from www.cukier.com/writings/ webmedia-jan04.htm

Hundt, R. (2000). *You say you want a revolution: A story of information age politics.* New Haven, CT: Yale University Press.

Information Access Alliance. (2003). *Publisher mergers threaten access to scientific, medical, and research information.* Washington, DC: The Alliance. Retrieved October 16, 2006, from www.arl.org/scomm/mergers/background_ info.pdf

Kahin, B. (1996). Scholarly communication in the networked environment: Issues of principle, policy and practice. In R. P. Peek & G. B. Newby (Eds.), *Scholarly publishing: The electronic frontier* (pp. 277–298). Cambridge, MA: MIT Press.

Knee, J. A. (2003). Should we fear media cross-ownership? *Regulation, 26*(2), 16–20. Retrieved October 15, 2006, from www.cato.org/pubs/regulation/ regv26n2/v26n2-3.pdf

Kranich, N. (2003a, May). *The impact of the USA PATRIOT Act on free expression*. New York: Free Expression Policy Project. Retrieved October 16, 2006, from www.fepproject.org/commentaries/patriotact.html

Kranich, N. (2003b, August). *The impact of the USA PATRIOT Act on free expression: An update*. New York: Free Expression Policy Project. Retrieved October 16, 2006, from www.fepproject.org/commentaries/patriotactupdate.html

Kranich, N. (2004a). *The information commons: A public policy report*. New York: Free Expression Policy Project. Retrieved October 17, 2006, from www.fepproject.org/policyreports/InformationCommons.pdf

Kranich, N. (2004b). Libraries: The information commons of civil society. In D. Schuler & P. Day (Eds.), *Shaping the network society* (pp. 279–299). Cambridge, MA: MIT Press.

Kranich, N. (2006). Countering enclosure: Reclaiming the knowledge commons. In C. Hess & E. Ostrom (Eds.), *Understanding knowledge as a commons: From theory to practice* (pp. 85–122). Cambridge, MA: MIT Press.

Kranich, N. (in press). Literacy in the digital age. In S. Kretchmer (Ed.), *Navigating the network society: The challenges and opportunities of the digital age*. Thousand Oaks, CA: Sage Publications.

Lakoff, G. (2002). *Metaphors we live by* (2nd ed.). Chicago: University of Chicago Press.

Lakoff, G. (2004). *Don't think of an elephant: Know your values and frame the debate*. White River Junction, VT: Chelsea Green.

Lange, D. (2003). Reimagining the public domain. *Law & Contemporary Problems, 66*(1/2), 463–482. Retrieved October 21, 2006, from www.law.duke.edu/shell/cite.pl?66+Law+&+Contemp.+Probs.+463+(Winter Spring+2003)

Lawrence, S. (2001). Online or invisible? *Nature, 411*(6837), 521.

Lee, D. (2003). Constructing the commons: Practical projects to build the information commons. *Knowledge Quest, 31*(4), 13–15.

Leone, R. C., & Anrig, Jr., G. (Eds.). (2003). *The war on our freedoms: Civil liberties in an age of terrorism*. New York: Public Affairs.

Lessig, L. (1999). *Code and other laws of cyberspace*. New York: Basic Books.

Lessig, L. (2001). *The future of ideas: The fate of the commons in a connected world*. New York: Random House.

Lessig, L. (2003). *Free culture: How big media uses technology and the law to lock down culture and control creativity*. New York: Penguin.

Levine, P. (2001). Civic renewal and the commons of cyberspace. *National Civic Review, 90*(3), 205–212. Retrieved October 17, 2006, from www.ncl.org/publications/ncr/90-3/chapter1.pdf

Levine, P. (2002). Building the electronic commons. *The Good Society, 11*(3), 4–9.

Levine, P. (2006). Collective action, civic engagement, and the knowledge commons. In C. Hess & E. Ostrom (Eds.), *Understanding knowledge as a commons: From theory to practice* (pp. 247–276). Cambridge, MA: MIT Press.

Lippincott, J. (2002). Developing collaborative relationships: Librarians, students, and faculty creating learning communities. *College & Research Libraries News, 63*(3), 190–192.

Lippincott, J. (2006). Linking the information commons to learning. In D. G. Oblinger (Ed.), *Learning spaces* (pp. 7.1–7.18). Boulder, CO: Educause. Retrieved October 21, 2006, from www.educause.edu/ir/library/pdf/PUB 7102g.pdf

Litman, J. (1990). The public domain. *Emory Law Journal, 39*, 965–992.

Litman, J. (2001). *Digital copyright*. Amherst, NY: Prometheus Press.

Lougee, W. (2006). Scholarly communication and libraries unbound: The opportunity of the commons. In C. Hess & E. Ostrom (Eds.), *Understanding knowledge as a commons: From theory to practice* (pp. 311–332). Cambridge, MA: MIT Press.

Lund University Libraries. (n.d.) *Directory of open access journals.* Lund, Sweden: The Libraries. Retrieved October 21, 2006, from www.doaj.org

Lyman, P. (1999). Designing libraries to be learning communities: Towards an ecology of places for learning. In S. Criddle, L. Dempsey, & R. Heseltine (Eds.), *Information landscapes for a learning society: Networking and the future of libraries* (pp. 75–87). London: Library Association Publishing.

Lynch, C. A. (2003). Institutional repositories: Essential infrastructure for scholarship in the digital age. *portal: Libraries and the Academy, 3*(2), 327. Retrieved October 21, 2006, from muse.jhu.edu/journals/portal_libraries_and_the_academy/v003/3.2lynch.html

MacWhinnie, L. A. (2003). The information commons: The academic library of the future. *portal: Libraries and the Academy, 3*(2), 241–257.

Madden, M. (2006). *Internet penetration and impact.* Washington, DC: Pew Internet and American Life Project. Retrieved October 16, 2006, from www.pewinternet.org/pdfs/PIP_Internet_Impact.pdf

Madison, J. (1865). *Letter to W. T. Berry, August 4, 1822.* In P. R. Fendall (Ed.), *Letters and other writings of James Madison* (Vol. 3, p. 276). Philadelphia: Lippincott.

Maine, H. S. (1986). *Ancient law: Its connection with the early history of society and its relation to modern idea.* Tucson: University of Arizona Press. (Original work published in 1861).

Markoff, J., & Wyatt, E. (2004, December 14). Google is adding major libraries to its database. *New York Times,* A1.

Marschall, M. (1998). The emergence of civil society and its impact on library associations. In *Twenty-first century information society: The role of library associations* (pp. 22–27). Budapest, Hungary: Open Society Institute.

Marx, V. (2003, August 3). In DSpace, ideas are forever. *The New York Times,* A4, A8.

McChesney, R. (1993). *Telecommunications, mass media, and democracy: The battle for control of U.S. broadcasting, 1928–1935.* New York: Oxford University Press.

McChesney, R. (1999). *Rich media, poor democracy.* Urbana: University of Illinois Press.

McClure, C., Hernon, P., & Reylea, H. (Eds.). (1989). *United States government information policies: Views and perspectives.* Norwood, NJ: Ablex.

McDermott, P., & Feldman, E. (2006). *Secrecy report card 2006: Indicators of secrecy in the federal government.* Washington, DC: OpenTheGovernment.org. Retrieved October 16, 2006, from www.openthegovernment.org/otg/SRC 2006.pdf

McIntosh, T. (1990). *Federal information in the electronic age: Policy issues for the 1990s.* Washington, DC: Bureau of National Affairs.

McKiernan, G. (2004). Open access and retrieval: Liberating the scholarly literature. In D. Fowler (Ed.), *E-serials collection management: Transitions, trends, and technicalities* (pp. 197–220). New York: Haworth Information Press. Retrieved October 21, 2006, from www.public.iastate.edu/~gerrymck/Open.pdf

Moody, G. (2001). *Rebel code: Inside Linux and the open source revolution.* New York: Perseus Publishing.

Mosco, V., & Wasco, J. (Eds.). (1988). *The political economy of information.* Madison: University of Wisconsin Press.

Mueller, M. (1997). *Universal service: Competition, interconnection, and monopoly in the making of the American political system.* Cambridge, MA: MIT Press.

National Aeronautics and Space Administration. Ames Research Center. (n.d.). *Clickworkers project.* Retrieved October 21, 2006, from clickworkers.arc. nasa.gov/top

National Aeronautics and Space Administration. Mars Exploration Rover Mission. (n.d.). *Athena student interns program.* Retrieved October 21, 2006, from marsrovers.jpl.nasa.gov/classroom/students/asip.html

National Research Council. (1986). *Proceedings of the Conference on Common Property Resource Management.* Washington, DC: National Academy Press.

National Research Council. (2000). *The digital dilemma: Intellectual property in the information age.* Washington, DC: National Academy Press.

National Research Council. (2001). *Tools and strategies for protecting kids from pornography and their applicability to other inappropriate Internet content.* Washington, DC: National Research Council. Retrieved October 16, 2006, from books.nap.edu/html/youth_internet

National Research Council. Committee on Research Standards and Practices to Prevent the Destructive Application of Biotechnology. (2004). *Biotechnology research in an age of terrorism.* Washington, DC: National Academies Press.

National Security Archive. (2003). The Ashcroft memo: "Drastic" change or "more thunder than lightning." Washington, DC: National Security Archive. Retrieved October 16, 2006, from www.gwu.edu/%7Ensarchiv/NSAEBB/ NSAEBB84/index.html

National Telecommunications and Information Administration. (2004, September). *A nation online: Entering the broadband age.* Washington, DC: U.S. Department of Commerce. Retrieved January 16, 2007, from www.ntia.doc.gov/reports/anol/NationOnlineBroadband04.pdf

Net neutrality and how it just might change everything. (2006). *American Libraries, 37*(8), 8–9.

New digital initiatives have import for all higher education. (2003, November/December). *CLIRinghouse, 19.* Retrieved October 21, 2006, from www.clir.org/pubs/cliringhouse/house19.html

Office of Management and Budget. (1985, December 24). The management of federal information resources (Circular A-130). *Federal Register, 50,* 52730–52751.

Okerson, A. (1999, September). The LIBLICENSE project and how it grows. *D-lib Magazine, 5*(9). Retrieved January 19, 2007, from www.dlib.org/dlib/ september99/okerson/09okerson.html

Ong, W. (1982). *Orality and literacy: The technologizing of the word.* London: Methuen.

OpCit Project. (2006). *The effect of open access and downloads ("hits") on citation impact: A bibliography of studies.* Retrieved October 23, 2006, from opcit.eprints.org/oacitation-biblio.html

Open Content Alliance. (2005, November 2). *SPARC Open Access Newsletter, 91.* Retrieved October 21, 2006, from www.earlham.edu/~peters/fos/newsletter/ 11-02-05.htm

Ostrom, E. (1986). A method of institutional analysis. In F. X. Kaufmann, G. Majone, & V. Ostrom (Eds.), *Guidance, control, and evaluation in the public sector* (pp. 459–475). New York: Walter de Gruyter.

Ostrom, E. (1990). *Governing the commons: The evolution of institutions for collective action.* New York: Cambridge University Press.

Ostrom, E. (2002). Property-right regimes and common goods: A complex link. In A. Heritier (Ed.), *Common goods: Reinventing European and international governance* (pp. 29–57). Lanham, MD: Rowman & Littlefield.

Ostrom, E., Gardner, R., & Walker, J. (1994). *Rules, games, and common-pool resources.* Ann Arbor: University of Michigan Press.

Ostrom, E., & Hess, C. (2006). A framework for analyzing the knowledge commons. In C. Hess & E. Ostrom (Eds.), *Understanding knowledge as a commons: From theory to practice* (pp. 41–81). Cambridge, MA: MIT Press.

Ostrom, V., & Ostrom, E. (1997). Public goods and public choices. In E. S. Savas (Ed.), *Alternatives for delivering public service: Toward improved performance* (pp. 7–49). Boulder, CO: Westview Press.

Paglin, M. D. (1989). *A legislative history of the Communications Act of 1934.* New York: Oxford University Press.

Podesta, J. (2003). Need to know: Governing in secrecy. In R. C. Leone & G. Anrig, Jr. (Eds.), *The war on our freedoms: Civil liberties in the age of terrorism* (pp. 220–236). New York: Century Foundation.

Pretty, J. (2003, December 12). Social capital and the collective management of resources. *Science, 302*(5652), 1912–1913.

Project Gutenberg Distributed Proofreaders. (n.d.). Retrieved October 17, 2006, from www.pgdp.net/c/default.php

Prosser, D. (2003, April). On the transition of journals to open access. *ARL Bimonthly Report, 227,* 1–3. Retrieved October 21, 2006, from www.arl.org/newsltr/227/openaccess.html

Public Knowledge. (n.d.). *Broadcast flag* [blog]. Retrieved October 16, 2006, from www.publicknowledge.org/articles/51

Putnam, R. (2000). *Bowling alone: The collapse and revival of American community.* New York: Simon and Schuster.

Quackenbush, J. (2003). Open-source software accelerates bioinformatics. *Genome Biology, 4*(9), 336.

Reichman, J. H., & Franklin, J. A. (1999). Privately legislated intellectual property rights: Reconciling freedom of contract with public good uses of information. *University of Pennsylvania Law Review, 147*(4), 875–970.

Reno v. American Civil Liberties Union. (1997). 521 U.S. 842, 870.

Research Libraries Group & OCLC. (2002, May). *Trusted digital repositories: Attributes and responsibilities.* Mountain View, CA: Research Libraries Group. Retrieved October 21, 2006, from www.rlg.org/longterm/repositories.pdf

Rheingold, H. (1993a). *Community, homesteading on the electronic frontier.* Reading, MA: Addison-Wesley. Retrieved October 15, 2006, from www.rheingold.com/vc/book/intro.html

Rheingold, H. (1993b). *The virtual community.* New York: Harper Collins.

Rose, C. (1986). The comedy of the commons: Commerce, custom, and inherently public property. *University of Chicago Law Review, 53,* 711–781.

Rose, C. (2003). Romans, roads, and romantic creators: Traditions of public property in the information age. *Law & Contemporary Problems, 66*(1/2), 89–110. Retrieved October 17, 2006, from www.law.duke.edu/shell/cite.pl?66+Law+&+Contemp.+Probs.+89+(WinterSpring+2003)

Rose, C. M. (1994). *Property and persuasion: Essays on the history, theory, and rhetoric of ownership.* Boulder, CO: Westview Press.

Samuelson, P. (1996, January). The copyright grab. *Wired*, *4*(1). Retrieved October 21, 2006, from www.wired.com/wired/archive/4.01/white.paper_pr.html

Samuelson, P. (2003). Mapping the digital public domain: Threats and opportunities. *Law & Contemporary Problems*, *66*(1/2), 147–172. Retrieved October 17, 2006, from www.law.duke.edu/shell/cite.pl?66+Law+&+Contemp.+Probs.+147+(WinterSpring+2003)

Schement, J. R. (1988). A third vision: Capitalism and the industrial origins of the information society. In J. R. Schement & L. Lievrouw (Eds.), *Competing visions, complex realities: Social aspects of the information society* (pp. 33–45). Norwood, NJ: Ablex.

Schement, J. R., & Curtis, T. (1995). *Tendencies and tensions of the information age*. New Brunswick, NJ: Transaction.

Schiffrin, A. (2000). *The business of books: How international conglomerates took over publishing and changed the way we read*. New York: Verso.

Schlager, E., & Ostrom, E. (1992). Property-rights regimes and natural resources: A conceptual analysis. *Land Economics*, *68*(3), 249–262.

Schuler, D. (1996). *New community networks: Wired for change*. Reading, MA: Addison-Wesley.

Schuler, D., & Day, P. (Eds.). (2004). *Shaping the network society*. Cambridge, MA: MIT Press.

Schwartz, G. (2003, November 13). *Summary of presentation at the November 3–4 meeting of the American Astronomical Society (AAS) Publications Board. PAMnet posting*. Retrieved October 21, 2006, from listserv.nd.edu/cgi-bin/wa?A2=ind0311&L=pamnet&D=1&O=D&P=1632

Schweik, C. (2006). Free/open-source software as a framework for establishing commons in science. In C. Hess & E. Ostrom (Eds.), *Understanding knowledge as a commons: From theory to practice* (pp. 178–309). Cambridge, MA: MIT Press.

Schweik, C., & Semenov, A. (2003). The institutional design of "open source" programming: Implications for addressing complex public policy and management problems. *First Monday*, *8*(1). Retrieved January 15, 2007, from www.firstmonday.org/issues/issue8_1/schweik/index.html

Scott, A. D. (1955). The fishery: The objectives of sole ownership. *Journal of Political Economy*, *63*(2), 116–124.

Shade, L. (2002). *Gender and community in the social construction of the Internet*. New York: Peter Lang.

Shane, S. (2005, July 3). Since 2001, sharp increase in the number of documents classified by the government. *New York Times*, 1, 14.

Shankland, S. (2003, January 16). Book publisher adopts open-source idea. *CNETNews.com*. Retrieved October 17, 2006, from news.com.com/2100-1001-981018.html?tag=cd_mh

SHERPA/RoMEO. (2006, October). *Journal policies: Summary statistics so far*. Retrieved October 23, 2006, from romeo.eprints.org/stats.php

Smith, M., & Kollock, P. (1998). *Communities in cyberspace*. New York: Routledge.

Stallman, R. (1999). The GNU operating system and the free software movement. In C. DiBona, S. Ockman, & M. Stone (Eds.), *Open sources: Voices from the open source revolution* (pp. 53–70). Sebastopol, CA: O'Reilly.

Statement on scientific publication and security, January 2003. (2003, February 21). *Science*, *299*(5610), 1149.

Stevenson, G. G. (1991). *Common property economics: A general theory and land use applications.* New York: Cambridge University Press.

Stiglitz, J. E. (1999). Knowledge as a global public good. In I. Kaul, I. Grunberg, & M. Stern (Eds.), *Global public goods: International cooperation in the 21st century* (pp. 308–325). New York: Oxford University Press for The United Nations Development Program.

Stone, D. (1997). *Policy paradox: The art of political decision making.* New York: Norton.

Suber, P. (2003). Removing the barriers to research: An introduction to open access for librarians. *College & Research Libraries News, 64*(2), 92–94, 113. Retrieved October 17, 2006, from www.earlham.edu/~peters/writing/acrl.htm

Suber, P. (2006). Creating an intellectual commons through open access. In C. Hess & E. Ostrom (Eds.), *Understanding knowledge as a commons: From theory to practice* (pp. 171–208). Cambridge, MA: MIT Press.

Suber, P. (n.d.). *Timeline of the free online scholarship movement.* Retrieved October 21, 2006, from www.earlham.edu/~peters/fos/timeline.htm

Summit, R. (2002, June). Reflections on the beginnings of Dialog: The birth of online information access. *Dialog Corporation history.* Retrieved October 15, 2006, from support.dialog.com/publications/chronolog/200206/1020628.shtml

Szpir, M. (2002). Clickworkers on Mars. *American Scientist Online, 90*(3). Retrieved October 17, 2006, from www.americanscientist.org/template/AssetDetail/assetid/14757

Telecommunications Act. (1996). 110 Stat. 56.

Thorin, S. (2003, August). Global changes in scholarly communication. Paper presented at e-workshops on scholarly communication in the digital era. Feng Chia University, Taichung, Taiwan. Retrieved October 16, 2006, from www.arl.org/scomm/Thorin.pdf

Turner, M. (1984). *Enclosures in Britain 1750–1830.* London: Macmillan.

Turner, S. J. (2000, March 10–16). Library sees red over rising journal prices: Dangling red tags are marking periodicals that have one-year subscription rates of $1,000 or higher. *George Street Journal, 24.* Retrieved October 16, 2006, from www.brown.edu/Administration/George_Street_Journal/vol24/24 GSJ19c.html

U.S. Children's Online Protection Act Commission. (2000, October 20). *Final report of the COPA Commission Presented to Congress.* Washington, DC: Government Printing Office. Retrieved October 16, 2006, from www.copa commission.org/report

U.S. Constitution. (1789). Article I, d8, cl. 8.

U.S. Information Security Oversight Office. (2006). *Report to the President, 2005.* U.S. National Archives and Records Administration, Information Security Oversight Office. Retrieved October 16, 2006, from www.fas.org/sgp/isoo/2005rpt.pdf

United States et al. v. American Library Association, Inc., et al. (2003). Syllabus and opinion of the Court. No. 02–361. Retrieved October 16, 2006, from www.supremecourtus.gov/opinions/02pdf/02-361.pdf

Vaidhyanathan, S. (2001). *Copyrights and copywrongs: The rise of intellectual property and how it threatens creativity.* New York: New York University Press.

Vaidhyanathan, S. (2004). *The anarchist in the library.* New York: Basic Books.

Vaidhyanathan, S. (2005, December 2). A risky gamble with Google. *Chronicle of Higher Education.* Retrieved October 21, 2006, from www.nyu.edu/classes/siva/archives/SivaGoogleChronicle.pdf

Van Orsdel, L., & Born, K. (2003, April 15). Big chill on the big deal? *Library Journal, 128*(7), 51–56.

Van Wendel de Joode, R., Bruijn, J., & van Eeten, M. (2003). *Protecting the virtual commons: Self-organizing open source and free software communities and innovative intellectual property regimes*. The Hague, Netherlands: Asser Press.

von Hippel, E. (2005). *Democratizing innovation*. Cambridge, MA: MIT Press.

Waters, D. (2006). Preserving the Knowledge Commons. In C. Hess & E. Ostrom (Eds.), *Understanding knowledge as a commons: From theory to practice* (pp. 145–167). Cambridge, MA: MIT Press.

Weber, S. (2004). *The success of open source*. Cambridge, MA: Harvard University Press.

Weitzner, D. J. (2006). The neutral Internet: An information architecture for open societies. Cambridge, MA: MIT Computer Science and Artificial Intelligence Laboratory. Retrieved October 16, 2006, from dig.csail.mit.edu/ 2006/06/neutralnet.html

Wellman, B. (1999). *Networks in the global village*. Boulder, CO: Westview Press.

Wellman, B., Boase, J., & Chen, W. (2002, Summer). The networked nature of community: Online and offline. *IT & Society, 1*(1), 151–165. Retrieved October 21, 2006, from www.stanford.edu/group/siqss/itandsociety/v01i01/v01i01 a10.pdf

Wellman, B., & Haythornthwaite, C. (Eds.). (2002). *The Internet in everyday life*. Oxford, UK: Blackwell.

Wilhelm, A. G. (2000). *Democracy in the digital age: Challenges to political life in cyberspace*. New York: Routledge.

Willinsky, J. (2005). *The access principle: The case for open access to research and scholarship*. Cambridge, MA: MIT Press.

Wittenbrink, H. (2005). *RSS and Atom: Understanding and implementing content feeds and syndication*. PACKT Publishing. Retrieved October 17, 2006, from www.packtpub.com/files/RSS_and_Atom_Book_Chapter1_what_are_ newsfeeds.pdf

Wolpert, A. (2003). The role of the research university in strengthening the intellectual commons: The OpenCourseWare and DSpace initiatives at MIT. In National Academy of Sciences, Board on International Scientific Organizations (BISO), *The role of scientific and technical data and information in the public domain: Proceedings of a symposium* (pp. 187–190). Washington, DC: National Academy Press. Retrieved October 21, 2006, from books.nap.edu/books/030908850X/html/187.html#pagetop

Yelling, J. A. (1977). *Common field and enclosure in England 1450–1850*. Hamden, CT: Archon Books.

Yuan, Y., Fulk, J., Shumate, M., Monge, P., Alison, B. J., & Matsaganis, M. (2006). Individual participation in organizational information commons: The impact of team level social influence and technology-specific competence. *Human Communication Research, 31*(2), 212–240.

Zalta, E. (2006). The Stanford encyclopedia of philosophy: A university/library partnership in support of scholarly communication and open access. *C&RL News, 67*(8), 502–504, 507.

Zimmerman, D. (2003). Authorship without ownership: Reconsidering incentives in a digital age. *DePaul Law Review, 52*(4), 1121–1169.

Zuckerman, L. (2000, January 13). Media megadeal: The power: Questions abound as media influence grows for a handful. *New York Times*, C6.

CHAPTER 13

Education for Information Science

Elizabeth M. Mezick and Michael E. D. Koenig
Long Island University

Introduction

The definition of information science (IS) has been stable for nearly forty years. Borko (1968, p. 3) described the discipline as one "that investigates the properties and behavior of information, the forces governing the flow of information, and the means of processing information for optimum accessibility and usability. It is concerned with that body of knowledge relating to the origination, collection, organization, storage, retrieval, interpretation, transmission, transformation, and utilization of information. ... It has both a pure science component, which inquires into the subject without regard to its application, and an applied science component, which develops services and products."

Bates (1999, p. 1043) extended this popular definition to include "the invisible substrate of information science." She emphasized information science's role as a meta-science and as a discipline distinguished by its interest in the subject matter of all conventional disciplines, as well as its unique efforts to organize that subject content in a way that provides value for society. For Bates (p. 1046), the distinguishing characteristic of the information scientist is the ability to "think about a resource in terms of the features that matter to the organization and retrieval of it, rather than in terms of mastering its content."

Education for the field of information science has been a longstanding interest of the *Annual Review of Information Science and Technology* (*ARIST*). Some chapters have discussed the topic broadly (Cooper & Lunin, 1989; Harmon, 1976; Jahoda, 1973; Logan & Hsieh-Yee, 2001) and some have focused on specific topics. The general topic of education has been the most visited (Rothenberg, 1994; Silberman & Filip, 1968; Vinsonhaler & Moon, 1973), followed by education for online systems and retrieval (Caruso, 1981; Wanger, 1979). There have also been two country-specific contributions, one on the U.K. (MacDougall & Brittain, 1993), the other on the Soviet Union (Richards, 1992).

This chapter follows in the tradition of treating the topic of education for information science broadly, with the emphasis on the U.S., Canada, and the U.K. Some attention is given to other regions, although this is limited to material appearing in English language journals. In addition to reviewing the literature, this chapter examines the directions in which information science education is developing.

An Identity for Information Science

The Emergence of the "I" Schools

For most of the last several decades, information science education has to a large degree been coextensive with library science education and referred to by the label Library and Information Science, or LIS. Until comparatively recently, LIS programs were housed in independent schools or colleges within a university, typically reporting to the chief academic officer, and taught primarily at the graduate level.

The last decade, however, has been one of major structural change. As observed by both Hildreth and Koenig (2002) and Koenig and Hildreth (2002), commencing with the incorporation of the LIS program at Rutgers University into the School of Communication, Information, and Library Studies in 1982, and accelerating greatly in the late 1990s, the trend has been for LIS programs to be combined into larger academic units. The modal pattern is for the LIS program to be incorporated either with a School of Communications or Education, the LIS program almost always being the junior partner. Another trend sees LIS programs expanding their base and adding degree programs beyond the master's degree in LIS to become larger and more encompassing academic units. As Hildreth and Koenig point out, the choice for LIS programs is largely between these two options: either narrowly focused on LIS education and a junior partner in a larger enterprise or expanding the scope of interest and adding new programs to become an "I School." Their articles make clear how little overlap there is between the two groups.

This dichotomy seems to be specific to North America. In only one case in the U.S., that of the Palmer School of Long Island University, has the LIS program emerged as the senior partner. No such clear pattern has emerged in the U.K. In at least two cases a formerly independent LIS program has come under the umbrella of a business school. At Robert Gordon University, following several organizational changes, the program is now the Department of Information Management in the Aberdeen Business School (www.rgu.ac.uk/abs). Similarly, at Liverpool's John Moore's University, the LIS school first became the School of Business Information within the Faculty of Law and Business, then became the Information Strategy Group within the Liverpool Business School (www.ljmu.ac.uk/bsn). Meanwhile, Brighton University's Information and Library Studies program is located within the College of Computing, Mathematical and Information Sciences (www.brighton. ac.uk/cmis). Wilson (2002) covers the situation in the U.K. well; however, as reported earlier, there has been considerable churn in recent years.

The "I-School" phenomenon consists of two intertwined threads. One was the informal creation in 1988 of a "gang of four," the University of Pittsburgh, Drexel University, Syracuse University, and Rutgers University. They had the common characteristics of existing undergraduate programs, or at least the intention to start one, and one or more degrees not accredited by the American Library Association (ALA). After a quiescent period, the gang of four re-emerged in 2000 as a gang of five with the addition of the University of Michigan (Carbo, personal communication, August 28, 2006). Over time, the group has added new members and organized semi-formally as the "I-Schools Community." There are now nineteen institutional members. Their first annual conference was held in 2005.

The second thread commenced in 2000, when a number of deans from LIS programs began to attend the information technology (IT) deans group meetings held under the auspices of the Computing Research Association (CRA). The member schools aimed to extend their scope well beyond that of computer science (CS) to include societal aspects of IT. The group was founded by Peter Freeman, then Dean of the College of Computing at Georgia Institute of Technology and longtime member of the CRA Board, as an informal common interest session at the CRA annual conference to engage "emerging and established colleges of computing and interdisciplinary 'IT' schools" (Computing Research Association, 2006, online; see also Cronin, 2002). Freeman recognized that academic programs at the level of schools or colleges faced different challenges than did departments that were part of larger schools. He enlisted the support of several other deans of emerging programs similar to his own, including the University of California, Irvine's Donald Bren School of Information and Computer Sciences, Indiana University's School of Informatics, and the University of Michigan's School of Information. The CRA Board endorsed a plan to host the IT deans and the group rapidly grew to include approximately forty schools from the U.S. and several other countries. The group is organized around schools of computing, schools of information, and/or schools of information technology with heads that report directly to the Provost or Chief Academic Officer of the parent university. Since July 2000, the group has met twice a year to discuss a range of topics and share experiences of creating independent schools and IT units. There is informal talk of merging the two groups into one as a formal subsection of CRA.

The I-Schools movement, as distinguished from the I-Schools Community, has generated real momentum and enthusiasm. Two I-School conferences have been held, the first at Penn State University in 2005, and the second at the University of Michigan in 2006 (iconference. si.umich.edu). The momentum comes with some controversy concerning the perceived elitism of the I-Schools Community. This was manifested at the 2006 I-Schools conference, where considerable hostility surfaced from LIS programs not included within the somewhat restrictive eligibility rules of the I-Schools group (no more than twenty-five members are allowed), and also from I-Schools not within the group.

The Emergence of Informatics

Although use of the term "informatics" or equivalents, such as "informatique," has been common outside the U.S. for some years, only recently have such terms been used in the U.S. as an alternate to "information science." "Informatique" and "informatics" were coined in the same month in 1962—"informatique" by Philippe Dreyfus in France for a software company called "Societé d'Informatique Appliquée" and "informatics" in the U.S. for a software company of that name. In Europe the new word was allowed to become public domain but in the U.S. the name was treated as proprietary. For some years, the Informatics company sent cease and desist letters to anyone attempting to use the term. At one point, the Association for Computing Machinery (ACM) held discussions with the company to determine whether they would consider changing their name to something such as "The Informatics Society" but the response was negative. In 1985, Informatics was taken over by Sterling Software and defense of the name effectively ceased. Gradually during the 1990s the public availability of "informatics" became known (Bauer, 1996).

"Informatics" began to be used in the U.S. to describe an academic domain in similar fashion to that in Europe. The first school of informatics was created in the U.S. at Indiana University in 2000. The school describes informatics as "a bridge connecting IT to a particular field of study such as biology, chemistry, fine arts, telecommunications, geography, business, economics, journalism, etc." (Indiana University School of Informatics, 2006, online). The fledgling school recently absorbed the department of computer science and has articulated links with several other academic units, including the long-established School of Library and Information Science.

The State University of New York at Buffalo created a school of informatics which combined LIS and communications. It was originally intended to include computer science but that idea met with resistance. In 2006, the school was disestablished, split into its original two components, with LIS being merged with the School of Education (Drury, 2006). The Department of Informatics (www.albany.edu/inf) formed within the College of Computing and Information at the State University of New York at Albany continues to operate. In 2004, the Donald Bren School of Information and Computer Sciences at the University of California, Irvine created a degree program in Informatics.

Information Technology as a Discrete Field

Information Science has for some decades been linked with Library and Information Science, and to some extent emerged from LIS; the notion of Information Technology as a field in its own right, however, has more recently begun to emerge from the domain of Computer Science (Abernathy, Gabbert, Treu, Piegari, & Reichgelt, 2005). The Society for Information Technology Education was founded as recently as 2001. Shortly thereafter, the Society successfully petitioned ACM for a Special Interest Group, or SIG, on information technology education (Said, Chaytor, Humpert, Nyland, Schlemmer, Stockman, et al., 2004). Several articles have been published since then that describe new or reconfigured IT programs, almost all at the undergraduate level: Drexel University (Hislop, Kaplan, & Leitner, 2005); Furman University, Virginia Military Institute, and Georgia Southern University (Abernathy et al., 2005); the University of Cincinnati (Said et al., 2004); the University of South Alabama (Owen, 2003); and an inter-institutional online degree developed by Georgia Southern and five other institutions located in the state (Dehoney, Reichgelt, Booth, Rutherfoord, Lau, & Stewart, 2003).

A good discussion of what in principle constitutes IT and IT education is found in Ekstrom and Lunt's (2003) article, "Education at the seams." The title vividly makes a point about the interlinking of IT and Informatics—both are largely about the overlap of information technology with users and applications, what is at the seams. The ACM SIG for Information Technology Education (SIGITE) presents its perception of IT in the set of curriculum guidelines available at the SIG's Web site: www.sigite.org.

Medical and Health Sciences Informatics and Informationists

The literature of medical and health science informatics is large and has been reviewed in *ARIST* by Russell and Brittain (2002), with a section on education and training. This literature goes back decades, to aspects of medical librarianship such as clinical medical librarians. In 2000 the field was galvanized by the publication of "The Informationist, a New Health Profession?" (Davidoff & Florance, 2000) in *The Annals of Internal Medicine*, a medical journal. The term "informationist" is in limited use but has gained some traction (Hersh, 2002). Although still imprecisely defined, it seems to suggest a connection between the traditional meaning of medical informatics, with its emphasis on data analysis and algorithms, and elements of IS and LIS. Detlefson (2002, p. 59) defines it as "a clinical health information professional with added qualifications gained either through education or experience, which enable that individual to work collaboratively and on an equal footing with medical and health professionals to meet information needs that arise during both patient care and medical research." In fact, informationist is used much as informatics is used outside the medical community.

Both Detlefson (2002) and Hersh (2002) provide useful discussions concerning possible tracks for the education and training of informationists. Both accounts make clear that there are many possible paths (and almost as many possible agencies and stakeholders) involved but very little agreement as to what might be optimal or what is likely to emerge as the most practical pedagogic approach.

New Practice Areas

The last decade has seen the emergence of discrete practice areas that fall within the domain of information science education. The most salient are knowledge management, information architecture, and digital libraries.

Knowledge Management

Knowledge Management (KM), bibliometrically at least, is proving to be a popular business fad. In 2002, Ponzi and Koenig, building on previous work by Abrahamson (1996), demonstrated that KM was behaving quite unlike other management fads and was unusually long lasting. Measured by the number of articles in the business literature on the topic, previous management fads showed a consistent pattern of boom and bust over a roughly ten-year cycle, with four or five years of explosive growth followed by an only slightly longer period of almost equally dramatic decline. This was demonstrably the case for Quality Circles, Total Quality Management, and Business Process Reengineering. KM is behaving very differently, with a five-year burst of exponential growth, from 1995 to 1999, followed by continuous but normal growth (Koenig, 2006).

Many articles have been written on KM education. Milne (1999) provides a useful early summary. Garrick and Clegg (2000) do not emphasize technological skills as much as communication, problem solving, and coordination skills. Abell (1998, 2000) also stresses those skills but emphasizes technical skills and contextual knowledge even more. Snowden (1999) acknowledges the importance of tacit or implicit knowledge and the problems of creating the appropriate organizational culture. Authors writing on education for KM consistently note that it is indeed much more than relabeled information management (IM) and requires a completely new perspective (Al-Hawamdeh, 2005; Dunn & Hackney, 2000). A number of KM degree programs have been established; these are described by Southon and Todd (1999), Maes (2003), Srikantaiah (2004), and Al-Hawamdeh (2005). Srikantaiah (2004) provides the broadest coverage; the most detailed report is by Al-Hawamdeh (2005) on the impressive KM program at Nanying Technological University in Singapore. A number of works discuss the curricular areas that need to be covered by KM education. In their book, Koenig and Srikantaiah (2004) devote considerable attention to education for KM. The general theme is the importance of education within KM infinitives (Bennet, 2004; Koenig, 2004; Palmquist, 2004) and the under-recognition of its importance. Srikantaiah (2004) discusses different educational programs for KM in some detail and provides a four-page table of offerings at different institutions, including instructor's names and URLs for course descriptions and syllabi. As this literature has evolved, there appears to be greater emphasis on cultural and contextual aspects and somewhat less on technical matters.

A major theme of the KM education literature is the necessity of an interdisciplinary approach (Chaudhry & Higgins, 2003; Garrick & Clegg, 2000). Breen, Farragher, McQuaid, Callanan, and Burke (2002), in reviewing the competencies required for KM education, conclude that LIS programs are providing the requisite education but that there is still a perceptual disconnect between the marketplace and the LIS community; in other words, "the view of 'the librarian' is impeding entry of LIS graduates into the knowledge management employment sector" (Breen et al., p. 127). However, it is also frequently pointed out that KM is a far broader concept than the norm in LIS education (Broadbent, 1998; Koenig, 2003, 2005). In reviewing the emergence of KM and its relationship to LIS education, Loughridge (2001) notes that more careful attention to the personalities and motivations of career entrants may be required. In a detailed study of the perceptions of deans at some dozen institutions with demonstrated interest in KM education within the U.S., the U.K., and the Asia-Pacific Region, Chaudhry and ur Rehman (2005) conclude that KM's potential is still under-recognized and collaboration is the key in this inter-disciplinary field, but that respondents were surprisingly apprehensive about such collaboration.

Information Architecture

An article by Hyldegaard, Lund, and Seiden (2002) demonstrates the connections between Information Architecture (IA) and KM. Latham (2002a) discusses possible avenues of education for IA, stressing its interdisciplinarity and describing it as a field still in its infancy. He sees five major components to IA education: information organization, graphic design, computer science, usability, and communication. Zhang, Strand, Fisher, Kneip, and Ayoub (2002) review IA offerings in a number of fields and conclude that IA courses and programs cluster into four areas: IA elements, design, implementation technologies, and digital media design.

A number of studies describe IA programs at particular institutions. Eskins and Willson (2003) report on the development of an undergraduate IA degree at Manchester Metropolitan University. Robins (2001/2002) describes the emergence of IA courses within LIS programs, paying particular attention to the interdisciplinary IA and KM degree at Kent State University, which incorporates input from six academic units. Weinberg (2002) elaborates on the development of an IA course at St. John's University that focuses on the information structure aspects, rather than design aspects of IA.

Andrew Dillon wrote an influential column on IA for the *Bulletin of the American Society for Information Science and Technology* for five years. His last piece (Dillon, 2005/2006) nicely summarizes a number of points made and, to a substantial degree, validated over those five years. The first, "No, we never did define it to everyone's satisfaction," and last, "We're still figuring this out, so don't stop trying to shape it," of his ten points are illuminating and provide a good feel for the still emergent nature of this domain (Dillon, 2005/2006, online).

Digital Libraries

The emergence of digital libraries has raised questions regarding professional education for digital library personnel as well as the roles of digital libraries in supporting education. Several authors have examined what is on offer (Bawden, Vilar, & Zabukovec, 2005; Saracevic & Dalbello, 2001; Spink & Cool, 1999). They report that education for digital libraries is taking place at the graduate level and that in most cases, rather than being offered as specific courses about digital libraries, digital library material is incorporated or embedded into existing courses. Furthermore, they report great variation in how the material is handled. Coleman (2002) compares ten core elements outlined by the International Federation of Library Associations and Institutions (IFLA) with fourteen areas of knowledge set out by the Computer Curricula report jointly prepared by the Association for Computing Machinery and the Institute of Electrical and Electronics Engineers (IEEE) in the context of digital libraries. She makes a strong case for the interdisciplinary nature of the domain, reiterating a point made earlier by Saracevic and Dalbello (2001). Tennant (1999) provides a concise and explicit list of skills required for work with digital libraries.

Both Arms (2000) and Roes (2001) make strong arguments for the utility of digital libraries in education, particularly in support of distance education. Reports on the building of digital libraries to support education include Zia's (2001) account of the National Science Foundation (NSF) National Science Mathematics, Engineering, and Technology Digital Library (NSDL) project to support K–12 education, and Kastens, Devaul, Ginger, Mogk, DeFelice, DiLeonardo, et al.'s (2005) report on the Digital Library for Earth System Education (DLESE) component of the NSDL. The latter report is particularly interesting for its illumination of the complexity and number of policy decisions involved in such an undertaking. Their graph of the growth of DLESE collections is intriguing in that it reveals de-accessioning as well as growth. One wishes such instances were explicated. Somewhat less illuminating is Alexander's (2000) report on the development of digital library resources at Edinburgh University.

Curriculum

Any professional education program has content that is relevant to all beginning professionals. Particular courses are designated as the foundation of the discipline because they cover the fundamental theory and principles, as well as the practice and values, of the discipline. These courses are frequently referred to as the "core" of the professional program and all students are required to take them.

Shera (1972) described the core as a search for a unified theory that implies a professional philosophy, which is expressed as a basic course structure required of all students. Shera's discussion of a continuing search for the principles that would fuse the educational program into a cohesive whole is reiterated, and further complicated, by Stieg (1992) when she states that as library schools transform themselves into schools for the information professions, the intellectual difficulty of establishing a core curriculum increases.

In an effort to broaden the appeal of programs, library schools began integrating information science courses and tracks into their curricula in the 1980s. As a result, in discussing information science curricula, it sometimes becomes necessary to discuss the broader LIS curriculum. Issues related to what constitutes the core of library and/or information science education are frequently debated, sometimes heatedly.

The Kellogg foundation funded a major study, known as the Kellogg-ALISE Information Professions and Education Renewal project (KALIPER), that focused on future directions for LIS education (Kaliper Advisory Committee, 2000; Marshall, Wilson, Marshall, & Harris, 2001; Pettigrew & Durrance, 2001). The project analyzed thirty-three LIS schools in 1988 and 1999. Observers and participants hoped that this study would have a major impact on LIS education but references to it in the literature have been comparatively few. A search of Google Scholar reveals 131 hits for the word "KALIPER" with only 49 hits for the "KALIPER project." Some of these are duplicates and the majority are uncited. Most of the references seem to be passing ones. The "h-index" score (i.e., the largest number 'h' for which it can be said that 'h' articles have been cited 'h' times) (Hirsch, 2005) for the corpus of KALIPER hits is five, which is not particularly impressive. Admittedly, this may be the first use of the h-index to consider a project or program rather than the output of an individual researcher, so a comparative benchmark is lacking; nevertheless, the score appears to be rather low compared to those for individual researchers (Cronin & Meho, 2006; Hirsch, 2005). The project revealed that LIS programs are making rapid changes (Pettigrew & Durrance, 2001). However, the KALIPER project seems to have been the result of change, not the cause of it. It can be argued that the project served little purpose other than to report on the changes that were already happening.

Findings by Raju (2003) suggest that, although it is possible to identify certain knowledge and skill components as appropriate for a core curriculum, it is difficult to be precise about what should constitute the core (Grotziner, 1986; Robbins, 1990; Stieg, 1992). The information environment to which education programs respond is itself in a state of flux; the core is therefore continuously evolving. According to Stieg, however, some commonalities can be identified. These include the collection, organization, and dissemination and use of information.

Raju (2003) points out that specifications of the core are couched in generic terminology that embraces the information profession generally, reflecting a trend to prepare students for the wider information market. Ocholla (2001) confirms this trend in Africa. Audunson, Nordlie, and Spangen (2003) describe a redesign of the curriculum at Oslo University College aimed at producing an educational ideal that integrates different knowledge domains of LIS practice.

Societal developments have necessitated a change in the focus of programs from the acquisition of "factual" knowledge to "competence-oriented learning" (Roggema-van Heusden, 2004, p. 98). Roggema-van Heusden discusses the development in the Netherlands of new educational objectives for a curriculum that links professional demands to competencies.

In Raju's (2003) study, employers and students identify materials selection, organization of information and sources, retrieval of information and information sources, and management of libraries and information centers as traditional subject areas they consider to be relevant. Inclusion of subjects pertinent in today's work environment, such as budgeting, human resources management, information and/or knowledge management, and information technology, is suggested. Fieldwork or experiential learning is considered highly relevant.

Ocholla (2001) observes that instruction in cataloging and classification can be considered essential because it provides knowledge of information analysis and synthesis, as well as of the nature and structure of information collections. He also notes a paradigm shift in teaching and learning from traditional rote to student-centered methods, including emphasis on outcome-based methods of assessment; he advocates the use of follow-up studies of program graduates as essential for curriculum development and improvement.

Although effective communication skills are widely sought by employers, few programs seem to address this need systematically. Latham (2002b) argues that the inclusion of technical and professional communication as a central part of the curriculum is vital to the success of information professionals. Most programs offer only a single course in research methods. This raises the question as to whether both qualitative and quantitative methods can be adequately taught. Liebscher (1998) advocates integrated teaching of quantitative and qualitative methods through "between methods" triangulation to ensure that students understand, both conceptually and pragmatically, the major methodological paradigms. He argues that such integration gives students the opportunity to explore research problems from multiple perspectives and to evaluate critically the strengths and weaknesses of each method.

Some programs' curricula provide academic preparation in management principles and practices but there is a limited focus on project management. Winston and Hoffman (2005) argue that—given the growing importance of project management in operations involving IT system migration and implementation, as well as building design, construction, and renovation—programs should offer courses in this area.

Relatively little attention has been focused on the actual process of curriculum development beyond the work done by Zimmerman and Jorgensen (1998). A case study of one Canadian school's curriculum development project offers a process model to guide the design of new curricula, outlines challenges to be addressed, and provides lessons to assist educators in their efforts to create relevant programs that both prepare information professionals and provide continuing education to meet the changing needs of practitioners in the field (Wallace, 2002).

Walster (1995) examines and describes five instructional design theories applicable to LIS education and practice: Gagné-Briggs's prescriptive model, Landa's algo-heuristic theory, Collins and Stevens's cognitive theory of inquiry teaching, Reigeluth's elaboration theory, and Keller's motivational model. She also discusses the impact of critical theory and constructivism on the purpose and role of educators in designing and delivering instruction (see also Day, 2005). Additional investigations of instructional design theories might help to invigorate the delivery of curricula.

Sturges (1999) argues that the agenda for the development of programs should come from established values of LIS education rather than from information disciplines that focus on systems. LIS programs should demonstrate their distinctiveness by emphasizing information content, a niche in which they have very little competition, rather than technologies and systems as the center of their curricula. He notes six areas that provide a bridge between the information profession's previous emphasis on collections and the current emphasis on access to electronic resources: assessing and filtering content, re-intermediation between the user and technology, negotiating ethical and regulatory difficulties, designing user-oriented services, managing knowledge resources, and creating value-added information packages.

Cross-Disciplinary Approaches

The disciplines of business, management, and computing overlap in course content with the field of LIS creating competition. Tyler (2001) notes that information and knowledge management are growing markets in the business world and, therefore, a potential opportunity exists for LIS courses targeted at employees in business who need information skills and related academic qualifications.

Chaudhry and Higgins (2003) highlight the multidisciplinary nature of KM curricula in their study of courses included in the academic disciplines of business, computing, and information. They conclude that, because the term knowledge management is used differently across domains, running KM programs in single departments or schools raises the danger of biasing content in favor of the discipline hosting the program. Their study concludes that a collaborative effort in designing curriculum and conducting the program would provide balance.

A new discourse space is described by Cronin (2002) that brings together deans and directors of computer science, information technology, information systems, and information science programs as their interests progressively converge. In this environment, he sees traditional LIS programs being overshadowed by the wave of informatics and information studies programs being established to meet both labor market and academic administrators' expectations. Cronin believes that arguments concerning resource rationalization, administrative efficiencies, and academic synergies will be invoked by administrators to justify reorganizations. He cites Taylor's (1979) metaphor of a shift from a Ptolemaic to a Copernican information universe to explain how the study of information has become attractive to a wide variety of academic programs.

Virtual Learning Environments

Geographic location once limited students' educational choices; today the Internet provides opportunities for a new population of learners. Tyler (2001) points out three types of academic instruction that are offered via the Internet: self-instruction courses, short credit courses, and full degree programs. Only a few distance learning LIS degree programs are currently offered via the Internet; it is primarily being used as a complementary tool, not as a replacement medium. Oder (2001) notes that it exhibits great potential as a resource for continuing education and lifelong learning.

In discussing Web-supported teaching, Bothma and Snyman (2002) refer to Web-based "telematic" teaching that provides a complex continuum of teaching methodologies and delivery methods. These range from fully Web-based programs, where all materials and interaction are provided solely via the Web, to contact teaching, where the Web is used as a support to facilitate access to study guides and prescribed articles, as well as for communication between lecturers and students. Tyler (2001) notes that LIS is a suitable subject for Internet education. Learning is reinforced because the medium for delivery is also the subject matter: Students utilize the very systems that they will be using in the workplace. Marcella and Baxter (2001) discovered that students found the virtual learning environment stimulating because it allowed them to learn from the environment as well as from the content of the course.

Klobas and Renzi (2000) provide examples of learning methods, their characteristics, and how they may be adapted to the Web environment. Levy (2000) gives examples of the varying forms of distance learning materials and how they can be incorporated into a coherent scheme.

Distance education (DE) programs are often seen as separate from campus-based programs. Levy (2000) shows how the boundaries between distance- and campus-based learning are blurring. Main (1998), however, argues that even campus-based students should take at least one class in a Web-based virtual classroom in order to be prepared to think and work in a virtual networked environment.

Tyler (2001) highlights the issues that must be considered before establishing an online course, including cost of program development and implementation, accreditation and quality assurance, and pressures on existing organizational structures. It is, of course, important that institutions ensure online courses are as rigorous academically as their residential counterparts. Hamilton-Pennell (2002) encourages course developers to make the best use of technology in designing courses that are instructionally sound, allow for individualized learning, involve some level of give-and-take, and incorporate effective assessment and evaluation. Schrum and Benson (2002) note the scarcity of program planning models in the growing body of DE literature. They argue for a remote-student-centered perspective and identify major areas of planning that should be considered prior to establishing successful online courses and programs.

The virtual classroom permits students and instructors living and working in dispersed geographic locations to interact asynchronously, at times most convenient for each. Frey, Alman, Barron, and Steffens (2004) refer to the typical asynchronous learning network (ALN) student as place-bound and part-time. Such a student is typically a mature professional dealing with complex subject material within a social network of career, family, and community that is strongly in place. These students are highly motivated and self-directed. The view of distance learners as independent and autonomous is also supported by Robinson and Bawden (2002).

Buchanan (2004) explores the experiences of students pursuing LIS degrees through a Web-based program. She maintains that DE students are not remote. Their presence is simply different and, therefore, requires different considerations and services. Noting that significant institutional structures, such as registration, advising, library, and technical support, are often overlooked, Buchanan argues that institutions need to maximize students' learning experiences and overall satisfaction with distance education programs to avoid attrition and maximize retention. Among her many recommendations are: creating an office for DE students, which would serve as a link between students and the institution; establishing an online student advisory board to contribute to a true student-centered perspective; and setting up a virtual lounge to provide online students with a space where peer-to-peer information sharing and support could take place.

A recurrent theme in the literature is that remote learning can lead to a decrease in the social presence associated with physical classes (Frey et al., 2004; Hamilton-Pennell, 2002; Marcella & Baxter, 2001;

Oder, 2001). Some students miss the real-life interaction with the instructor and other class participants and feel isolated if there is no interactive or collaborative component to the course. Interestingly, Vrasidas and McIssac (1999) found that moving instruction from the classroom to the online environment increases opportunities for interaction. Hamilton-Pennell (2002) discovered that students using the Internet reported a more engaging, classroom-style learning experience than was possible with earlier, more static forms of distance learning.

In the Marcella and Baxter (2001) study, faculty who taught distance learning classes agreed that the most positive aspect was the standard of communication and interaction with students. Negative comments centered on the time-consuming process of responding to students' individual e-mail inquiries and on technical problems. Apart from the additional time required to correspond with individual students by e-mail, faculty felt that the nature of their interaction with the distance learning students was similar to that with on-campus students.

Hamilton-Pennell (2002) suggests providing instructional design and technology support to instructors who want to teach online. Resources to help instructors may be found on the Internet, including Roblyer and Ekhaml's (2000) useful metric for assessing interaction in distance learning.

Oder (2001) notes variations in school requirements for on-campus components and synchronous chat. A crucial component of the University of Illinois Library Educational Experimental Project (LEEP) is a ten-day "boot camp" where students bond with each other, meet faculty, learn technology, and begin coursework. The MLIS program at the University of Pittsburgh currently requires a five-day visit in the first semester and an intensive weekend on campus each subsequent semester. Students in this program credit the on-campus experiences with enhancing learning relationships (Frey et al., 2004). Florida State University's College of Information requires participation in an online orientation prior to the first term of enrollment. Drexel University's M.S. degree in LIS is offered completely online with optional specialization in either management of digital information or information/library services.

Oder (2001) points out that learning from a distance may make it difficult to access library materials. The Marcella and Baxter (2001) survey highlights the significance of providing student access to library resources immediately upon registering for a course. Access to resources was cited as the most significant DE problem by students.

Searing (2004) discusses three distinguishing features of library services for LIS distance education: an information-intensive curriculum, the enduring importance of the physical library, and the importance of librarians as role models. Caspers (1999) and Hufford (2000) discusses the role of the academic library in supporting distance learners in terms of providing remote access to catalogs and bibliographic and full-text databases; dealing with inter-library loan requests; providing reference services; and conducting literature searches on behalf of distance learners.

One look at the specific challenges and rewards of supporting graduate-level online LIS education is Burnett and Painter's (2001) description of library support for the Florida State University School of Information Studies Web-based curriculum. Kazmer (2002) reported that University of Illinois LEEP students want rich online collections, rapid delivery of printed materials, reference services and technical support during evenings and weekends, training options, and a single point of contact. An overview of the types of library services available to distance learning students who attend ALA-accredited master's programs in library and information studies can be found in the study conducted by Latham and Smith (2003).

Cooper (2000) observes that in the U.S., library services offered by distance programs are minimal. Gibson, Newton, and Dixon (1999) remark that in the U.K., academic libraries have adopted an ad hoc approach, rather than a strategic attitude, to the development of services for distance learners.

Boehm and Horton (1991) suggest that institutions of higher learning that are limited in their ability to expand curricula in a subject can easily enhance their programs by tapping the distributed expertise of individuals whom they could not otherwise engage. Adapting a course for virtual delivery takes time but they believe the investment should be recouped after a course is taught two or three times. Noble (1998) disagrees; he argues that, in reality, online courses are resource intensive—consuming finances, human time, and knowledge—and create new and different pressures on existing organizational structures. Oder (2001) notes that there is growing cooperation among LIS programs, as online DE providers begin forming consortia.

Oder (2001) also observes that, although the stigma of hiring DE graduates is receding, some reluctance still exists. A survey by Wynkoop (2003) gauged the willingness of librarians to hire graduates of LIS distance education programs. Eighty-two percent of respondents would hire someone with a degree earned online; 18 percent would not. Some 43 percent of respondents felt that the degrees were equivalent, 32 percent felt that a traditional course of study was better, and 3 percent preferred the online degree. Twenty-two percent of all respondents felt that they did not know enough about the online course of study to be able to compare it with a traditional one.

Internationalization

According to Davis (1987), the internationalization of library education was taking place as early as 1877 with the organization of an international conference in London. Current economic and cultural globalization; international migration flows; and trans-border mobility of students, academics, and professionals have produced new challenges for LIS education and how LIS schools internationalize their programs. The growing interest in internationalization and cooperation in LIS education in the U.S., Canada, and Europe is motivated by a desire to improve curricula; understand the nature of the LIS profession, teaching, and research; and explore ways in which cooperative schemes can be utilized.

Since its establishment in 1927, the International Federation of Library Associations and Institutions (www.ifla.org) has fostered cooperation between LIS educators and schools throughout the world. The IFLA section on Education and Training has developed guidelines for LIS education programs (International Federation of Library Associations and Institutions, 2000). The organization is currently looking at issues and problems regarding reciprocity of LIS qualifications between different countries.

The European Union (EU) has exerted a major influence on cross-border educational cooperation and schemes for joint recognition of qualifications. Plans for developing a European Higher Education Area are adding new dimensions to collaboration and the networking efforts of LIS schools in Europe. Kajberg (2003) notes that transnational schemes exist but schools have been slow to become involved in cross-country partnerships that go beyond small-scale student mobility. For example, beyond increased communication and networking efforts among European schools through initiatives like SOCRATES (ec.europa.eu/education/programmes/socrates/erasmus/erasmus_en.html) or NORD-PLUS (siu.no/vev.nsf/o/nordplus), visible results in terms of cooperation and coordinated curriculum development are meager (Kajberg, 2002). Courses exhibit great differences in formal structure, curricular content, related qualifications, and diplomas causing comparability and transparency to suffer. In contrast, Juznic and Badovinac (2005) conclude that in spite of a diversity of traditions among countries, there is a surprising degree of homogeneity, spurred by the Bologna Declaration (ec.europa.eu/education/policies/bologna/bologna_en.html). Boekhorst and Owen (2003) review the development of information studies at the University of Amsterdam in light of the Bologna agreement, including an interesting discussion of issues and problems relating to student mobility and the creation of comparable and transferable degrees.

A relationship has developed between the Nordic and Baltic LIS academic communities. Virkus and Harbo (2002) provide a detailed overview of the historical development and present state of cooperation. The authors outline the deliberate process of internationalization of curricula that institutions in the area have implemented. However, even here, there is no defined strategy for the development of cooperation. Decisions to join projects and collaborate have been ad hoc in character. The analysis of IS education programs in the U.K. and the Nordic and Baltic countries by Maceviciute (2002) is particularly informative, not with regard to the types of degrees offered by different institutions in those countries, but in terms of the underlying conceptual views of IS education behind those programs.

BOBCATSS (www.bobcatsss.nu), an acronym composed of the initials of the cities of the nine founding LIS institutions belonging to this network, is a project under the auspices of the European Association for Library and Information Research (EUCLID) (www.jbi.hio.no/bibin/euclid/index.html). BOBCATSS involves a series of annual symposia aimed at practitioners, lecturers, and students. The aim is to enhance communication between students and professionals at an international level.

Internationalization means having a program in which faculty, staff, and students maintain a global view and an appreciation of the importance of the field internationally. Abdullahi and Kajberg (2004) discuss how all library schools should provide an international outlook for students so that they may adapt to the complex and changing world in which national interests are strongly influenced by cross-border relationships. An international climate may be developed through the recruitment of faculty members and students with a variety of national backgrounds and experience. This would be fostered by a core curriculum for cross-border LIS education. They conclude that partnerships that go beyond efforts such as joint study visits, information exchange, or conference contacts are few. Miralpeix and Abadal (2000) found similar conditions in their survey of information science education in Spain.

Research by Dalton and Levinson (2000) looks at educational standards worldwide and the complex issues related to determining the reciprocity of LIS qualifications between different countries. Ur Rehman, Al-Ansari, and Yousef (2002) report on an empirical study designed to present the collective judgment of a select group of academics from North America, Southeast Asia, and the Arabian Gulf region, as well as leading practitioners from the Arabian Gulf, about the content of graduate degree programs in information studies. Tedd (2003) discusses work done by UNESCO's Principal Regional Office for Asia and the Pacific (PROAP) in Bangkok, Thailand, on developing a curriculum for emerging information societies in the Asia-Pacific region (Moore, 1998). A report by Townley, Geng, and Zhang (2003) describes a case study, involving a graduate course on knowledge management in The People's Republic of China and the U.S., that supports the view that DE using current technologies may be employed to overcome operational constraints—such as travel costs, time, and personal commitments—for internationalizing LIS education.

International collaboration is often high on a university's agenda, but does not translate easily into the launch and delivery of successful ventures. Dixon and Tammaro (2003) present the issues involved in developing a course for joint delivery at the University of Parma, Italy, and the University of Northumbria, U.K.

International education has an established body of knowledge and a variety of organizations to serve professionals active in the field. However, there is little indication that LIS educators are using these resources in formal, systematic fashion.

Lifelong Learning

The American Library Association (1988, p. 3) defines continuing professional education as "a learning process which builds on and updates previously acquired knowledge, skills, and attitudes. ... It is usually self-initiated learning in which individuals assume responsibility for their own development and for fulfilling their need to learn." Continuing professional education encompasses informal ongoing learning, such as reading and discussions with colleagues, as well as participation in formal learning opportunities, such as conferences, workshops, and seminars. Professional associations generally claim education as part of their mission.

Learning is no longer something that happens primarily to young people. Instead, it is for everyone at all stages of life, increasingly influenced by practical and vocational needs, and provided in response to the immediate demands of the labor market. Characteristics of adult learners have been enumerated by Rowntree (2000).

Huckle (2000) notes that although core roles remain essentially unchanged—the handling of information, evaluation of quality of information, and education and training of information users—the resources and skills needed to access and disseminate resources are changing. Elkin (1997) believes the shelf life of any qualification is about five years. Therefore, information professionals as individuals need to accept responsibility for their own learning and personal development and must continually adapt to new roles, duties, and work practices. Professional learning requirements change constantly and methods of providing education will inevitably change to keep pace.

Robinson and Bawden (2002, p. 49) argue that it is no longer the function of a "teacher class" to be the sole providers of learning and to determine what is learned and how. Learners, particularly adult learners, dictate what they wish to learn and how they wish to learn it. The important factor is whether and how well learning takes place, not the process or the provider. Teachers thus act as enablers and facilitators of learning. Robinson and Bawden (2002) believe that the increased importance of distance learning has arisen not simply as a result of technical advances, but in the changing context of society and of the place of learning within it.

Rapid developments in technology have required professionals in library and information careers to pursue continuing professional development to keep abreast of changes. Tyler (2001) remarks that there is an increasing need for on-demand, industry-specific, highly focused, short-term learning that satisfies the skills gap in the workplace. She notes evidence suggesting that online courses are often aimed at working professionals, not first-time students. Hamilton-Pennell (2002) argues that Web-based continuing education coursework is a viable way for librarians to pursue professional goals, and Haythornthwaite (1990) looks at the considerable advantages of distance education from an employer's point of view.

Newton (2001) discusses the need for organizations to provide appropriate infrastructure to ensure that staff acquire necessary skills. Staff need time to practice and integrate new skills into their working life. She explains how in Australia various organizations are collaborating to make workplace training and continuing education easier for information professionals through the recognition of accredited workplace training as a legitimate component of LIS graduates. Creth (1996) believes the process of workplace education involves administrators and managers developing a culture in which continuous learning and acceptance of change by staff is the norm.

Accreditation

Mounce (2005) investigates professional perceptions of the impact of current ALA accreditation standards on professional education programs. Survey findings indicate that the standards have more of an overall positive influence, rather than being influential in specific areas such as faculty diversity or access.

Programs in the allied information professions have become closer in substance and intent to those of traditional LIS schools. It seems appropriate to investigate the feasibility of joining with these proximate professions to coordinate program assessment and accreditation. Even as the process seeks to accredit a broader spectrum of programs than ever before, it is critically important to create an accrediting body able to elevate the status of programs for information studies in the 21st century. Perhaps it would be appropriate to consider a revised accreditation process involving an entity other than the ALA that would have the support of the broader information professions (Martin, 2002).

The first Congress on Professional Education was held under the auspices of ALA in 1999. It identified a large number of issues that led to the establishment of four task forces to define direction in the most critical areas, including external accreditation (www.ala.org/ala/hrdr bucket/1stcongressonpro/1stcongresstaskforce.htm). This task force identified weaknesses in the current accrediting system that it felt would be overcome by a federation of library and information-related educational and professional organizations, such as the Association for Library and Information Science Education (ALISE). These could expand the scope of program accreditation both horizontally and vertically. Other issues have delayed further action by the ALA Executive Board but it does plan to restart discussions with the relevant stakeholders.

Established in 1997, the U.K.'s Quality Assurance Agency (QAA) for Higher Education works with institutions to define academic standards, as well as conducting and publishing institutional reviews. Review reports for Librarianship and Information Management programs of individual institutions are accessible at www.qaa.ac.uk/reviews/reports/ SubjReports.asp?subjID=42. There is a convergence of interests between the QAA and the Charted Institute of Library and Information Professionals (CILIP), which was formed in 2002, particularly with respect to subject benchmarking and the expansion of the traditional boundaries of LIS (Enser, 2002).

A thorough and engaging examination of the development of accreditation standards and procedures, specifically focused on professional education programs in Southeast Asia, is presented by Khoo, Majid, and Chaudhry (2003). They considered the accreditation standards of a variety of professional associations, including the Australian Library and Information Association (ALIA), the Charted Institute of Library and Information Professionals in the U.K., and the International Federation of Library Associations and Institutions, in addition to the American Library Association. The organizational model that they propose for accreditation of regional programs under the oversight of the Congress of Southeast Asian Librarians (CONSAL) is based upon this examination. They also discuss the results of a review of four major aspects of an accreditation process—dialogue, self-evaluation, documentation, and external review, as well as a survey conducted in 2002 to obtain views of issues and problems related to accreditation in the region.

Learning Outcomes and Assessment

Prior to the 1950s, assessment meant individual student appraisal with an emphasis on testing. Dick and Carey (1978) discuss the systems view of teaching and learning that appeared in the 1960s, in which a set of components interact to produce learning outcomes. In the systems concept, performance could be improved by feeding it back into the system to provide regulation and refinement. Scriven, Tyler, and Gagne (1967) made functional distinctions between summative and formative evaluation that are still used today. The concepts of instructional systems and formative evaluation are what we now call outcomes assessment. Erwin (1991) recounts the background and purposes of assessment in higher education, provides a summary of the basic references on assessment, and reviews the research.

The 1992 standards issued by the ALA Office for Accreditation call for a continuous planning process as the main criterion of accreditation (American Library Association, 1992). To assist schools in the outcomes assessment process, the ALA Office for Accreditation published the *Outcomes Assessment for Library and Information Studies Resource Manual*, which contains a bibliography of the outcomes assessment literature (American Library Association, 1995). Much of the literature on accreditation and assessment in education consists of reports, working papers, or conference workshops that are not published research in refereed journals.

Perrault, Gregory, and Carey (2002) report on the conceptual phase and outline the strategic planning process of a grant project at the School of Library and Information Science at the University of South Florida in which the goal for teaching is formulated in program objectives for student learning outcomes and in assessment measures for those objectives. Their paper proposes a model for the integration of assessment of student learning outcomes and teaching effectiveness. They suggest that a continuous planning process be operationalized that emphasizes student learning outcomes assessment at the programmatic level. The major focal point of assessment is the cumulative learning of the student—outcomes of the program, rather than outcomes of individual courses. Accountability to the institution and the profession for the effectiveness of the program and to the graduates in their preparation for a professional career are the concerns of the programmatic student learning outcomes goals. Perrault et al. (2002) envision a continuous improvement cycle as more than a statement of mission, goals, and objectives. The system they propose requires that desirable programmatic outcomes be determined, that how well those outcomes are achieved be measured, and that findings be used to improve program delivery. Their data-driven, continuous-improvement process links student learning outcomes with teaching effectiveness. This model integrates assessment of student learning outcomes into a continuous planning process that can be used in annual faculty evaluations, program reviews, and external accreditation reports.

Bothma and Snyman (2002) report that programs within the Department of Information Science at the University of Pretoria, South Africa, are based on outcomes-based education, representing a paradigm shift from content-driven and teacher/trainer-centered education toward a learner-driven model aimed at achieving specific outcomes and lifelong learning. In this model, the teacher/trainer becomes a facilitator by stimulating creativity, self-learning, and critical thinking. They argue that with outcomes-based education and training, learning achievements are more tangible and results can be validated against real world requirements.

A Perception of Crisis

There has been a persistent concern that LIS education is in some sort of crisis. This commonly takes the form of a widening gulf between the academy and the practitioner. Moran (2001) attempts, with some success, to put that genie back in the bottle. The more alarming concern, lurking in the background for some time and rearticulated by Gorman (2004, p. 377) with great fervor, is "that library schools have become hosts to information science and information studies faculty and curricula" and that "these disciplines ... are, at best, peripheral to professional library work and, at worst, inimical to it." Gorman buttresses his argument with a list of nine courses from the curricula of a major LIS program that he believes illustrates his point, but which, with one possible exception, would be instantly recognized as relevant by any corporate librarian. These concerns are rebutted in some detail by both Dillon and Norris (2005) and Stoffle and Leeder (2005). Stoker (2000) provides interesting historical insight on the persistence of various issues in the field.

The corollary concern raised by Gorman (2004) is that the emphasis on information science education has resulted in the loss of an agreed-upon core for LIS education. Marco (1994) flags this concern in his article on the demise of the core curriculum. This is probably still the most lucid and well-thought-out exposition of the concerns of those who feel that there is a crisis in the field. A close study of LIS curricula by Markey (2004), however, indicates that there is actually a consensus as to what constitutes the core of an LIS master's degree program. Gorman should be read after Davenport and Cronin (2000), in which case it emerges as a perfect reaction to, and a predictable result of, the increasing marginalization of LIS education within the larger shift of attention to information as an attractive academic domain, which Davenport and Cronin predict.

Such shifts may be indicative of difficult times ahead for traditionally defined LIS programs, particularly for those that do not possess political capital; have a vocational, rather than a scholastic focus; and are unable to develop creative solutions in a changing environment.

Conclusions

As information science education continues to evolve, the question of what constitutes the core of the professional program will continue to be debated. Educational objectives for curricula need to prepare students for the wider information market and link professional demands to competencies (Ocholla, 2001; Raju, 2003; Roggema-van Heusden, 2004).

The increasing emphasis on outcomes assessment within academe requires measurement of tangible learning achievements and results that can be validated against objectives in a continuous planning process. There is a substantial need for more published research, such as that reported by Perrault, Gregory, and Carey (2002), on this critical area.

As information science continues to overlap with the academic disciplines of business and computing, the necessity of participating in collaborative efforts when designing curricula increases (Chaudhry & Higgins, 2003). At the same time, graduates from information science programs will need to acquire a common set of values and an understanding of the domain that defines the discipline and distinguishes it from others.

Detailed and comprehensive strategies still need to be developed if the full potential of DE is to be realized. The number of distance learning degree programs could be expanded with careful planning and consideration of the unique presence of DE students and the services they require (Buchanan, 2004; Schrum & Benson, 2002; Tyler, 2001). The potential already demonstrated by DE as a resource for continuing education is great (Oder, 2001).

There is little indication that educators are maximizing the potential of internationalization as a means of improving and strengthening curricula or forging cooperative schemes (Kajberg, 2002, 2003). Among the topics related to internationalization are those of curriculum and reciprocity (Dalton & Levinson, 2000; Virkus & Harbo, 2002). Existing international education resources should be exploited to further the process of internationalization.

The field continues to struggle with the problem of identity. Continuing tension between library science and other information-related fields poses serious challenges for educators and practitioners. A focus needs to be maintained on addressing the information needs of individuals and groups that is the main concern of both fields. Programs need to define specializations clearly so as not to compete against each other for students and resources.

What strikes one in reviewing this literature is terminological imprecision, a classic sign of a field in ferment or transition. The Informatics program at the University of California, Irvine, very much an opinion leader in the field (Kay, van der Hoek, & Richardson, 2005), has a great degree of commonality with the IT programs described; on the other hand, the courses added to the computer science program at the Virginia Military Institute to create an IT program—Human Computer Interaction (HCI), and Web Application Development (Abernathy et al., 2005)—come straight out of any LIS curriculum. It is not for nothing that Hislop, Kaplan, and Leitner (2005) speak of a confusing array of majors.

Many challenges face today's information science educators. Core requirements, competition from within and outside the field, and interdisciplinary and international collaboration are just a few of the areas to be addressed. Although some progress has been achieved in confronting the issues facing the profession, its future will require the continuing efforts and creativity of all information professionals.

Information science education appears to be healthy and growing. It exists, however, in an increasingly fragmented environment with multiple stakeholders. What is not clear is whether the "I-Schools movement" will succeed in unifying or standardizing the domain to some degree. At this time, there is a real contradiction between the stated aim of the group—to make the "I School" moniker as well known as phrases like "law school" or "business school"—and the warranted perception of exclusivity. This contradiction needs to be resolved if the movement is to have real success.

Clearly information science education is in great ferment, with many overlapping constituencies and stakeholders—a best of times and a worst of times situation that was foreseen by Van House and Sutton

(1996) in their highly cited "Panda Syndrome" article. An uncertain, but very interesting, future seems guaranteed.

References

Abdullahi, I., & Kajberg, L. (2004). A study of international issues in library and information science education: Survey of LIS schools in Europe, the USA and Canada. *New Library World, 105*(9), 345–356.

Abell, A. (1998). Skills for the 21st century. *Journal of Librarianship and Information Science, 30*, 211–214.

Abell, A. (2000). Skills for knowledge environments. *Information Management Journal, 34*(3), 33–40.

Abernathy, K., Gabbert, P., Treu, K., Piegari, G., & Reichgelt, H. (2005). Impact of the emerging discipline of information technology on computing curricula: Some experiences. *Journal of Computing in Small Colleges, 21*(2), 237–243.

Abrahamson, E. (1996). Managerial fashion. *Academy of Management Review, 21*(1), 254–285.

Alexander, W. (2000). Adaptive developments for learning in the hybrid library. *Ariadne*, (24). Retrieved July 29, 2006, from www.ariadne.ac.uk/issue24/sellic/intro.html

Al-Hawamdeh, S. (2005). Designing an interdisciplinary graduate program in knowledge management. *Journal of the American Society for Information Science & Technology, 56*(11), 1200–1206.

American Library Association. (1988). *Guidelines for quality in continuing education for information, library and media personnel.* Chicago: The Association, Continuing Education Subcommittee of the Standing Committee on Education.

American Library Association. (1992). *Standards for accreditation of master's programs in library and information studies.* Chicago: The Association, Office for Accreditation. Retrieved July 12, 2006, from www.ala.org/ala/accreditation/accredstandards/standardsnumpara.html

American Library Association. (1995). *Outcomes assessment for library and information studies resource manual.* Chicago: The Association, Office for Accreditation.

Arms, W. Y. (2000). Digital libraries for distance education. *D-Lib Magazine, 6*(10). Retrieved July 29, 2006, from www.dlib.org/dlib/october00/10editorial.html

Audunson, R., Nordlie, R., & Spangen, I. C. (2003). The complete librarian – an outdated species? LIS between profession and discipline. *New Library World, 104*(1189), 195–202.

Bates, M. J. (1999). The invisible substrate of information science. *Journal of the American Society for Information Science, 50*(12), 1043–1050.

Bauer, W. F. (1996). Informatics: An early software company. *IEEE Annals of the History of Computing, 18*(2), 70–76.

Bawden, D., Vilar, P., & Zabukovec, V. (2005). Education and training for digital librarians: A Slovenia/UK comparison. *Aslib Proceedings, 57*(1), 85–98.

Bennet, D. H. (2004). Learning and the knowledge worker. In M. E. D. Koenig & T. K. Srikantaiah (Eds.), *Knowledge management, lessons learned: What works and what doesn't* (pp. 511–525). Medford, NJ: Information Today, Inc.

Boehm, E. H., & Horton, F. W. (1991). The ISIM distance-learning methodology and the IRM [information resources management] curriculum. *Journal of Education for Library and Information Science, 32*(1/2), 26–37.

Boekhorst, A. K., & Owen, J. S. M. (2003). Bologna, the Netherlands and information science. *Education for Information, 21*(1), 7–19.

Borko, H. (1968). Information science: What is it? *American Documentation, 19*(1), 3–5.

Bothma, T. J. D., & Snyman, R. (2002). Web-supported teaching in the Department of Information Science at the University of Pretoria. *Journal of Education for Library and Information Science, 43*(4), 249–261.

Breen, C., Farragher, A., McQuaid, M., Callanan, M., & Burke, M. A. (2002). New information management opportunities in a changing world. *Library Review, 51*(3/4), 127–138.

Broadbent, M. A. (1998). The phenomenon of knowledge management: What does it mean to the library profession? *Information Outlook, 2*(5), 23–26.

Buchanan, E. A. (2004). Institutional challenges in Web-based programs: Student challenges and institutional responses. *Journal of Library Administration, 41*(1/2), 65–74.

Burnett, K., & Painter, M. (2001). Learning from experience: Strategies for assuring effective library and information services to Web-based distance learners. *Proceedings of the Tenth National Conference of the Association of College and Research Libraries,* 131–136. Retrieved July 11, 2006, from: www.ala.org/ala/acrl/acrlevents/burnett.pdf

Caruso, E. (1981). Computer aids to learning online retrieval. *Annual Review of Information Science and Technology, 16,* 317–335.

Caspers, J. S. (1999). Outreach to distance learners: When the distance education instructor sends students to the library, where do they go? *The Reference Librarian, 67/68,* 299–311.

Chaudhry, A. S., & Higgins, S. (2003). On the need for a multidisciplinary approach to education for knowledge management. *Library Review, 52*(2), 65–69.

Chaudhry, A., & ur Rehman, S. (2005). KM education in LIS Programs. *Education for Information, 23*(4), 245–258.

Coleman, A. (2002). Interdisciplinarity: The road ahead for education in digital libraries. *D-Lib Magazine, 8*(7/8). Retrieved July 29, 2006, from www.dlib.org/dlib/july02/coleman/07coleman.html

Computing Research Association. (2006). *IT Deans Group.* Retrieved July 27, 2006, from www.cra.org/Activities/itdeans

Cooper, J. L. (2000). A model for library support of distance education in the USA. *Interlending & Document Supply, 28*(3), 123–131.

Cooper, M., & Lunin, L. F. (1989). Education and training of the information professional. *Annual Review of Information Science and Technology, 24,* 295–341.

Creth, S. D. (1996). *The electronic library: Slouching toward the future or creating a new information environment.* Paper presented at the Follett Lecture Series. Retrieved July 12, 2006, from www.ukoln.ac.uk/services/papers/follett/creth/paper.html

Cronin, B. (2002). Holding the center while prospecting at the periphery: Domain identity and coherence in North American information studies education. *Education for Information, 20*(1), 3–10.

Cronin, B., & Meho, L. (2006). Using the *h*-Index to rank influential information scientists. *Journal of the American Society for Information Science and Technology, 57*(9), 1275–1278.

Dalton, P., & Levinson, K. (2000). *An investigation of LIS qualifications throughout the world.* Retrieved June 28, 2006, from www.ifla.org/IV/ifla66/papers/061-61e.htm

Davenport, E., & Cronin, B. (2000). Knowledge management: Semantic drift or conceptual shift? *Journal of Education for Library and Information Science, 41*(4), 294–306.

Davidoff, F., & Florance, V. (2000). The informationist: A new health profession? *Annals of Internal Medicine, 132*(12), 996–998.

Davis, D. G. (1987). The history of library school internationalization. In J. F. Harvey & F. L. Carroll (Eds.), *Internalizing library and information science education: A handbook of politics and procedures in administration and curriculum* (pp. 17–29). New York: Greenwood Press.

Day, R. E. (2005). Poststructuralism and information studies. *Annual Review of Information Science and Technology, 39*, 575–609.

Dehoney, J., Reichgelt, H., Booth, L., Rutherfoord, R. H., Lau, K. F., & Stewart, J. (2003). Many cooks improve the broth: Developing an inter-institutional, online, bachelor of science degree in information technology. *Proceedings of the 4th Conference on Information Technology Curriculum,* 155–159.

Detlefson, E. G. (2002). The education of informationists, from the perspective of a library and information sciences educator. *Journal of the Medical Library Association, 90*(1), 59–67.

Dick, W., & Carey, L. (1978). *The systematic design of instruction.* Glenview, IL: Scott Foresman.

Dillon, A. (2005/2006). The end is nigh. *Bulletin of the American Society for Information Science and Technology, 32*(2), 26–27. Retrieved July 26, 2006, from www.asis.org?Bulletin/Dec-05/dillion.html

Dillon, A., & Norris, A. (2005). Crying wolf: An examination and reconsideration of the perception of crisis in LIS education. *Journal of Education for Library & Information Science, 46*(4), 280–298.

Dixon, P., & Tammaro, A. M. (2003). Strengths and issues in implementing a collaborative inter-university course: The international masters in information studies by distance. *Education for Information, 21*(2/3), 85–96.

Drury, T. (2006, June 23). Changes in informatics program strain UB relationships. *Business First of Buffalo.* Retrieved August 19, 2006, from buffalo.bizjournals.com/buffalo/stories/2006/06/26/story2.html

Dunn, D., & Hackney, R. (2000). Towards a knowledge management model for the information management curricula. *Proceedings of the 15th Annual Conference of the International Academy for Information Management,* 270–275.

Ekstrom, J. J., & Lunt, B. (2003). Education at the seams: Preparing students to stitch systems together; curriculum and issues for 4-year IT programs. *Proceedings of the 4th Conference on Information Technology Curriculum,* 196–200.

Elkin, J. (1997). *Information navigators: Future professionals.* Paper presented at Beyond the Beginning: The Global Digital Library Conference. Retrieved July 12, 2006, from www.cni.org/regconfs/1997/ukoln-content/repor~12.html

Enser, P. (2002). The role of professional body accreditation in library & information science education in the UK. *Libri, 52*(4), 214–219.

Erwin, T. D. (1991). *Assessing student learning and development: A guide to the principles, goals, and methods of determining college outcomes.* San Francisco: Jossey-Bass.

Eskins, R., & Willson, J. (2003). Rebuilding with information architecture. *Library and Information Update, 2*(10), 44–45.

Frey, B. A., Alman, S. W., Barron, D., & Steffens, A. (2004). Student satisfaction with the online MLIS program at the University of Pittsburgh. *Journal of Education for Library and Information Science, 45*(2), 82–97.

Garrick, J., & Clegg, S. (2000). Knowledge work and the new demands of learning. *Journal of Knowledge Management, 4*(4), 279–286.

Gibson, A., Newton, R., & Dixon, D. (1999). Supporting open and distance learners: Practice and policy across further and higher education libraries. *Library Review, 48*(5), 219–231.

Gorman, M. (2004). Whither library education? *New Library World, 105*(1204/1205), 376–380.

Grotzinger, L. A. (1986). Curriculum and teaching styles: Evolution of pedagogical patterns. *Library Trends, 34*(3), 451–468.

Hamilton-Pennell, C. (2002, November 15). Getting ahead by getting online. *Library Journal, 127*(19), 32–35.

Harmon, G. (1976). Information science education and training. *Annual Review of Information Science and Technology, 11*, 347–380.

Haythornthwaite, J. A. (1990). Distance education and the information scientist. *Aslib Proceedings, 42*(1), 31–39.

Hersh, W. (2002). Medical informatics education: An alternative pathway for training informationists. *Journal of the Medical Library Association, 90*(1), 76–79.

Hildreth, C. R., & Koenig, M. (2002). Organizational realignment of LIS programs in academia: From independent standalone units to incorporated programs. *Journal of Education for Library and Information Science, 43*(2), 126–133.

Hirsch, J. E. (2005, September 29). *An index to quantify an individual's scientific research output.* Retrieved July 12, 2006, from arxiv.org/PS_cache/physics/pdf/0508/0508025.pdf

Hislop, G. W., Kaplan, R. M., & Leitner, L. J. (2005). Extending an information systems curriculum to address information technology. *Proceedings of the 6th Conference on Information Technology Education*, 267–270.

Huckle, M. (2000). Lifelong learning and the challenge of change for the information professional: Report of a workshop run for the Education Libraries Group at UmbrelLA 5, 2 July 1999. *Education Libraries Journal, 43*(1), 5–8.

Hufford, J. R. (2000). The university library's role in planning a successful distance learning program. *The Reference Librarian, 69/70*, 193–204.

Hyldegaard, J., Lund, H., & Seiden, P. (2002). LIS meets the EIP. *Library Review, 51*(3/4), 149–156.

Indiana University School of Informatics. (2006, January 24). *What is informatics?* Retrieved August 19, 2006, from www.informatics.indiana.edu/overview/what_is_informatics.asp

International Federation of Library Associations and Institutions. (2000). *Guidelines for professional library/information educational programs.* Retrieved July13, 2006, from www.ifla.org/VII/s23/bulletin/guidelines.htm

Jahoda, G. (1973). Education for information science. *Annual Review of Information Science and Technology, 8*, 321–344.

Juznic, P., & Badovinac, B. (2005). Toward library and information science education in the European Union. *New Library World, 106*(1210/1211), 173–186.

Kajberg, L. (2002). Cross-country partnerships in European library and information science education: Education at the crossroads. *Library Review*, 15(3/4), 164–170.

Kajberg, L. (2003). Cross-country partnerships in international library and information science education. *New Library World*, 104(1189), 218–226.

Kaliper Advisory Committee. (2000, July). *Educating library and information science professionals for a new century: The KALIPER report: Executive summary*. Reston, VA: Association for Library and Information Science Education. Retrieved August 20, 2006, from www.alise.org/publications/kaliper.pdf

Kastens, K., Devaul, H., Ginger, K., Mogk, D., DeFelice, B., DiLeonardo, C., et al. (2005). Questions and challenges arising in building the collection of a digital library for education. *D-Lib Magazine*, 11(11). Retrieved July 29, 2006, from www.dlib.org/dlib/november05/kastens/11kastens.html

Kay, D. G., van der Hoek, A., & Richardson, D. J. (2005). Informatics: A focus on computer science in context. *SIGCSE Bulletin*, 37(1), 23–27.

Kazmer, M. M. (2002). Distance education students speak to the library: Here's how you can help even more. *The Electronic Library*, 20(5), 395–400.

Khoo, C., Majid, S., & Chaudhry, A. S. (2003). Developing an accreditation system for LIS professional education programmes in Southeast Asia: Issues and perspectives. *Malaysian Journal of Library & Information Science*, 8(2), 131–149.

Klobas, J., & Renzi, S. (2000). Selecting software and services for Web-based teaching and learning. In A. Aggarwal (Ed.), *Web-based learning and teaching technologies: Opportunities and challenges* (pp. 43–59). Hershey, PA: Idea Group Publishing.

Koenig, M. E. D. (2003). Knowledge management, user education, and librarianship. *Library Review*, 52(1), 10–17.

Koenig, M. E. D. (2004). Knowledge management and user education: The unrecognized Achilles' heel. In M. E. D. Koenig & T. K. Srikantaiah (Eds.), *Knowledge management, lessons learned: What works and what doesn't* (pp. 487–496). Medford, NJ: Information Today, Inc.

Koenig, M. E. D. (2005). KM moves beyond the organization. *Information Services and Use*, 25(2), 87–93.

Koenig, M. E. D. (2006, April). KM: The forest for all the trees. *KM World*, 15(4), 1, 30.

Koenig, M. E. D., & Hildreth, C. (2002, June 15). The end of the standalone "library school." *Library Journal*, 128(11), 40–41.

Koenig, M. E. D., & Srikantaiah, T. K. (Eds.). (2004). *Knowledge management, lessons learned: What works and what doesn't*. Medford, NJ: Information Today, Inc.

Latham, D. (2002a). Information architecture: Notes toward a new curriculum. *Journal of the American Society for Information Science and Technology*, 53(10), 824–830.

Latham, D. (2002b). The role of technical and professional communication in the LIS curriculum. *Journal of Education for Library and Information Science*, 43(2), 155–163.

Latham, D., & Smith, S. M. (2003). Practicing what we teach: A descriptive analysis of library services for distance learning students in ALA-accredited LIS schools. *Journal of Education for Library and Information Science*, 44(2), 120–133.

Levy, P. (2000). Information specialists supporting learning in the networked environment: A review of trends and issues in higher education. *The New Review of Lifelong Learning, 1,* 35–64.

Liebscher, P. (1998). Quantity with quality? Teaching quantitative and qualitative methods in an LIS master's program. *Library Trends, 46*(4), 668–680.

Logan, E., & Hsieh-Yee, I. (2001). Library and information science education in the nineties. *Annual Review of Information Science and Technology, 35,* 425–477.

Loughridge, B. (2001). Curriculum development in education for librarianship and information work: Factors effecting change at the Department of Information Studies, University of Sheffield, United Kingdom. *Zeitschrift für Bibliothekswesen und Bibliographie, 48*(2), 100–102.

MacDougall, J., & Brittain, J. M. (1993). Library and information science education in the United Kingdom. *Annual Review of Information Science and Technology, 28,* 361–390.

Maceviciute, E. (2002). Information management in the Baltic, Nordic, and UK LIS schools. *Library Review, 51*(3/4), 190–199.

Maes, R. (2003). On the alliance of executive education and research in information management at the University of Amsterdam. *International Journal of Information Management, 23*(3), 249–257.

Main, L. (1998). Web-based virtual classrooms: A model for LIS education. *Education for Information, 16,* 333–340.

Marcella, R., & Baxter, G. (2001). Information and library studies on a virtual campus. *New Library World, 102*(1169), 362–371.

Marco, G. A. (1994). The demise of the American core curriculum. *Libri, 44,* 175–189.

Markey, K. (2004). Current educational trends in the information and library science curriculum. *Journal of Education for Library & Information Science, 45*(4), 317–339.

Marshall, V., Wilson, T., Marshall, J. G., & Harris, R. (2001). Plus ça change, plus c'est différent: A report from the KALIPER Project on six case studies in LIS education. *Journal of Education for Library and Information Science, 42*(3), 206–219.

Martin, S. K. (2002). A new vision for library and information science accreditation. *portal: Libraries and the Academy, 2*(3), 481–483.

Milne, P. (1999). Knowledge management and LIS education. *Education for Library and Information Services: Australia, 16*(3), 31–38.

Miralpeix, C., & Abadal, E. (2000). Education on library and information science in Spain: Development and current tendencies. *Bibliothek. Forschung und Praxis, 24*(1), 44–53.

Moore, N. (1998). *A curriculum for an information society.* Bangkok: Information and Informatics Unit, UNESCO Principal Regional Office for Asia and the Pacific.

Moran, B. B. (2001, November 1). Practitioners vs. LIS educators: Time to reconnect. *Library Journal, 126*(18), 52–55.

Mounce, M. E. (2005, March). The effects of ALA accreditation standards on library education programs. *Libres, 15*(1). Retrieved November 28, 2006, from libres.curtin.edu.au/libres15n1/Mounce%20-%20Final.htm

Newton, S. (2001). Mastering your career: Linking workplace training to tertiary studies. *New Library World, 101*(1160/1161), 34–37.

Noble, D. F. (1998). Digital diploma mills: The automation of higher education. *First Monday*, *3*(1). Retrieved November 28, 2006, from www.firstmonday.org/issues/issue3_1/noble

Ocholla, D. N. (2001). Curriculum response to a changing national and international information environment: Theoretical and methodological paradigms on review and revision. *Education for Information, 19*(2), 143–167.

Oder, N. (2001, October 1). LIS distance ed moves ahead. *Library Journal, 126*(16), 54–56.

Owen, W. (2003). Focus tracks: Specializing in IT education. *Proceedings of the 4th Conference on Information Technology Curriculum*, 135–138.

Palmquist, R. A. (2004). Incentives and techniques for the promotion of knowledge sharing. In M. E. D. Koenig & T. K. Srikantaiah (Eds.), *Knowledge management, lessons learned: What works and what doesn't* (pp. 527–541). Medford, NJ: Information Today, Inc.

Perrault, A. H., Gregory, V. L., & Carey, J. O. (2002). The integration of assessment of student learning outcomes with teaching effectiveness. *Journal of Education for Library and Information Science, 43*(4), 270–282.

Pettigrew, K. E., & Durrance, J. C. (2001). KALIPER: Introduction and overview of results. *Journal of Education for Library & Information Science, 42*(3), 170–180.

Ponzi, L., & Koenig, M. (2002). Knowledge management: Another management fad? *Information Research, 8*(1), paper no. 145. Retrieved July 28, 2006, from InformationR.net/ir/8-1/paper145.html

Raju, J. (2003). The "core" in library and/or information science education and training. *Education for Information, 21*(4), 229–242.

Richards, P. S. (1992). Education and training for information science in the Soviet Union. *Annual Review of Information Science and Technology, 27*, 267–290.

Robbins, J. B. (1990, February 1). Yes Virginia, you can require an accredited master's degree for that job! *Library Journal, 115*(2), 40–44.

Robins, D. (2001/2002). Information architecture in library and information science curricula. *Bulletin of the American Society for Information Science & Technology, 28*(2), 20–22.

Robinson, L., & Bawden, D. (2002). Distance learning and LIS professional development. *Aslib Proceedings, 54*(1), 48–55.

Roblyer, M. D., & Ekhaml, L. (2000). How interactive are your distance courses? A rubric for assessing interaction in distance learning. *Online Journal of Distance Learning Administration, 3*(2). Retrieved July 17, 2006, from www.westga.edu/~distance/roblyer32.html

Roes, H. (2001). Digital libraries and education. *D-Lib Magazine, 7*(7/8). Retrieved July 29, 2006, from www.dlib.org/dlib/july01/roes/07roes05.html

Roggema-van Heusden, M. (2004). The challenge of developing a competence-oriented curriculum: An integrative framework. *Library Review, 53*(2), 98–103.

Rothenberg, D. (1994). Information technology in education. *Annual Review of Information Science and Technology, 29*, 277–302.

Rowntree, D. (2000). *Who are your distance learners?* Open University. Retrieved July 11, 2006, from www-iet.open.ac.uk/pp/d.g.f.rowntree/distance_learners.htm

Russell, M., & Brittain, J. M. (2002). Health informatics. *Annual Review of Information Science and Technology, 36*, 591–628.

Said, H., Chaytor, L., Humpert, D., Nyland, J., Schlemmer, R., Stockman, M., et al. (2004). An implementation of a core curriculum in an information technology degree program. *Proceedings of the 5th Conference on Information Technology Education*, 94–100.

Saracevic, T., & Dalbello, M. (2001). A survey of digital library education. *Proceedings of the 64th Annual Meeting of the American Society for Information Science and Technology*, 209–223.

Schrum, L., & Benson, A. (2002). Establishing successful online distance learning environments: Distinguishing factors that contribute to online courses and programs. In R. Discenza, C. Howard, & K. Schenk (Eds.), *The design and management of effective distance learning programs* (pp. 190–204). Hershey, PA: Idea Group.

Scriven, M., Tyler, R., & Gagne, R. M. (1967). *Perspectives of curriculum evaluation*. Chicago: Rand McNally.

Searing, S. E. (2004). All in the family: Library services for LIS online education. *Journal of Library Administration, 41*(3/4), 391–405.

Shera, J. H. (1972). *The foundations of education for librarianship*. New York: Becker and Hayes.

Silberman, H. F., & Filip, R. T. (1968). Information systems applications in education. *Annual Review of Information Science and Technology, 3*, 357–395.

Snowden, D. (1999). Grappling with knowledge and realizing what you've got—I only know what I know when I need to know it. In *Knowledge Management, The Information Management Event: Conference Papers and Abstracts, Olympia Conference & Exhibition Centre, London, UK, 24–25 March 1999* (pp. 5–10). Oxford, UK: Learned Information Europe.

Southon, G., & Todd, R. (1999). Knowledge management: Education for the knowledge age. *Education for Library and Information Services: Australia, 16*(3), 21–30.

Spink, A., & Cool, C. (1999). Education for digital libraries. *D-Lib Magazine, 5*(5). Retrieved July 29, 2006, from www.dlib.org/dlib/may99/05spink.html

Srikantaiah, T. K. (2004). Training and education in knowledge management. In M. E. D. Koenig & T. K. Srikantaiah (Eds.), *Knowledge management, lessons learned: What works and what doesn't* (pp. 497–510). Medford, NJ: Information Today, Inc.

Stieg, M. F. (1992). *Change and challenge in library and information science education*. Chicago: American Library Association.

Stoker, D. (2000). Persistence and change: Issues for LIS educators in the first decade of the twenty-first century. *Education for Information, 18*(2/3), 115–122.

Stoffle, C. J., & Leeder, K. (2005). Practitioners and library education: A crisis of understanding. *Journal of Education for Library & Information Science, 46*(4), 312–319.

Sturges, P. (1999). The pursuit of content. *Education for Information, 17*(3), 175–185.

Taylor, R. S. (1979, September 15). Reminiscing about the future. Professional education and the information environment. *Library Journal, 104*(16), 1871–1875.

Tedd, L. A. (2003). The what? and how? of education and training for information professionals in a changing world: Some experiences from Wales, Slovakia and the Asia-Pacific region. *Journal of Information Science, 29*(1), 79–86.

Tennant, R. (1999, January 1). Skills for the new millennium. *Library Journal, 124*(1), 39.

Townley, C. T., Geng, Q., & Zhang, J. (2003). Using distance education to internationalize library and information science scholarship. *Libri*, *53*(2), 82–93.

Tyler, A. (2001). A survey of distance learning library and information science courses delivered via the Internet. *Education for Information*, *19*(1), 47–59.

ur Rehman, S., Al-Ansari, H., & Yousef, N. (2002). Coverage of competencies in the curriculum of information studies: An international perspective. *Education for Information*, *20*(3/4), 199–215.

Van House, N., & Sutton, S. A. (1996). The panda syndrome: An ecology of LIS education. *Journal of Education for Library and Information Science*, *37*(2), 131–147.

Vinsonhaler, J. F., & Moon, R. D. (1973). Information systems in education. *Annual Review of Information Science and Technology*, *8*, 277–318.

Virkus, S., & Harbo, O. (2002). The internationalization of Baltic library and information science education with emphasis on the cooperation with Nordic partners. *Education for Information*, *20*(3–4), 217–235.

Vrasidas, C., & McIssac, M. S. (1999). Factors influencing interaction in an online course. *American Journal of Distance Education*, *13*(3), 22–36.

Wallace, D. (2002). Curriculum development in library and information science programs: A design model. *Journal of Education for Library and Information Science*, *43*(4), 283–295.

Walster, D. (1995). Using instructional design theories in library and information science education. *Journal of Education for Library and Information Science*, *36*(3), 239–248.

Wanger, J. (1979). Education and training for online systems. *Annual Review of Information Science and Technology*, *14*, 219–245.

Weinberg, B. H. (2002). New course design: Classification schemes and information architecture. *Bulletin of the American Society for Information Science and Technology*, *28*(5). Retrieved July 29, 2006, from www.asis.org/Bulletin/Jun-02/weinberg.html

Wilson, T. D. (2002). Curriculum and catastrophe: Change in professional education. *Journal of Education for Library and Information Science*, *43*(2), 296–304.

Winston, M. D., & Hoffman, T. (2005). Project management in libraries. *Journal of Library Administration*, *42*(1), 51–61.

Wynkoop, M. (2003). *Hiring preferences in libraries: Perceptions of MLS graduates with online degrees.* Retrieved July 11, 2006, from www.camden.lib.nj.us/survey/default.htm

Zhang, X., Strand, L., Fisher, N., Kneip, J., & Ayoub, O. (2002). Information architecture as reflected in classrooms. *Proceedings of the 65th Annual Meeting of the American Society for Information Science and Technology*, 74–82.

Zia, L. L. (2001). The NSF National Science, Mathematics, Engineering, and Technology Digital Library (NSDL) program. *D-Lib Magazine*, *6*(10). Retrieved July 29, 2006, from www.dlib.org/dlib/october00/zia/10zia.html

Zimmerman, N., & Jorgensen, C. (1998). Seizing the day: A case study of one school's core curriculum revision process. *Journal of Education for Library and Information Science*, *39*(2), 134–147.

Index